ALL-IN-ONE GUIDE

Scotland

AA Publishing

Written by   David Hancock
Introductions by   Nick Channer

Edited and produced by   AA Publishing

Scotland Maps produced by the Cartographic Department of
the Automobile Association.

Typeset by Microset Ltd, Basingstoke, England
Printed and bound by G Canale & C. S.P.A., Torino, Italy
Cover design by Mike Ballard, Twyford, England
Internal design by PPD, Basingstoke, England

Advertisement Sales   Head of Advertisement Sales:
Christopher Heard, ☎ 01256 491544
Advertisement Production:
Karen Weeks, ☎ 01256 491545

A CIP catalogue record for this book is available
from the British Library

ISBN 0-7495-1766-2

AA Ref. 10128

Published by AA Publishing, which is a trading name
of Automobile Association Developments Limited,
whose registered office is Norfolk House, Priestley
Road, Basingstoke, Hampshire RG24 9NY. Registered
number 1878835

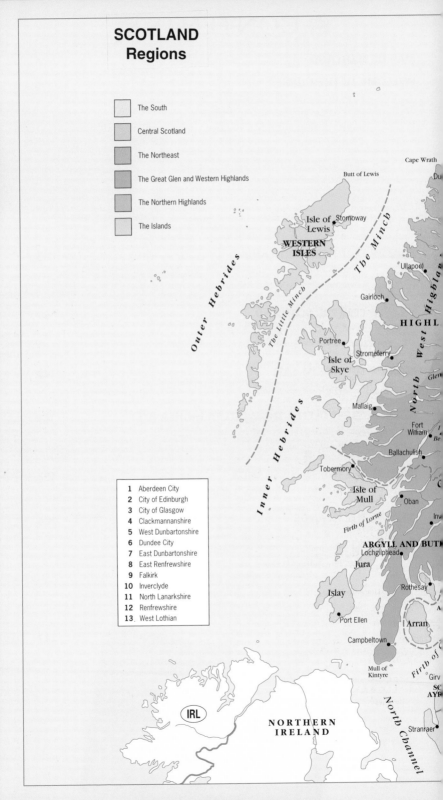

SCOTLAND
Regions

- The South
- Central Scotland
- The Northeast
- The Great Glen and Western Highlands
- The Northern Highlands
- The Islands

1 Aberdeen City
2 City of Edinburgh
3 City of Glasgow
4 Clackmannanshire
5 West Dunbartonshire
6 Dundee City
7 East Dunbartonshire
8 East Renfrewshire
9 Falkirk
10 Inverclyde
11 North Lanarkshire
12 Renfrewshire
13 West Lothian

Cape Wrath

Du

Butt of Lewis

Isle of Lewis · Stornoway

WESTERN ISLES

The Minch

Ullapool ·

Outer Hebrides

The Little Minch

Gairloch ·

HIGHL

North West Highlan

Portree ·

Stromeferry ·

Isle of Skye

Glen

Mallaig ·

Fort William · Be

Ballachulish ·

Inner Hebrides

Tobermory ·

Isle of Mull

Oban ·

Inv

Firth of Lorne

ARGYLL AND BUT

Lochgilphead ·

Jura

Rothesay ·

A

Islay

Arran

Port Ellen ·

Campbeltown ·

Mull of Kintyre

Firth of C

· Girv

SC AYR

North Channel

IRL

NORTHERN IRELAND

Stranraer ·

❀ CONTENTS ❀

MAP OF SCOTLAND   **4**

WELCOME TO THE GUIDE   **6**

How to use the Directory
How to use the Essential Information
Explanation of Hotel Star Ratings,
B&B 'Q' Ratings

How to read the accommodation entries
Notes on accommodation
Campsite Pennant Ratings

How to use the Where to Eat section
Explanation of Rosette Ratings

SOUTHERN SCOTLAND   **13**
Scottish Borders, Dumfries & Galloway, Edinburgh & the Lothians,
Glasgow, the Clyde & Ayrshire

CENTRAL SCOTLAND   **97**
Perth & Kinross, Angus, Dundee, Fife,
Stirling & the Loch Lomond area of Argyll

THE NORTH-EAST   **140**
Aberdeenshire & Moray

GREAT GLEN & THE WESTERN HIGHLANDS   **161**
Fort William, Glencoe, Inverness,
Argyll & Highland South

THE NORTH HIGHLANDS   **193**
Pentland Firth, Sutherland, Caithness, Ross & Cromarty

THE ISLANDS   **206**
Islands of the Clyde (Arran, Bute, Cumbrae)
Inner Hebrides (Coll, Tiree, Colonsay, Gigha
Islay, Jura, Mull, Iona)
Skye & the Small Isles (Rhum, Eigg)
The Western Isles (Outer Hebrides: Lewis, Harris
North Uist, Benbecula, South Uist, Eriska, Barra)

Index   **242**

Orkney Islands

Kirkwall

ORKNEY

Shetland Islands

SHETLAND

Lerwick

Pentland Firth

Thurso

John O'Groats

Wick

Helmsdale

Dornoch

Cromarty

Moray Firth

Nairn

Elgin

Banff

Fraserburgh

MORAY

Inverness

Spey

Strathspey

Huntly

Peterhead

ABERDEENSHIRE

Kingussie

1

Aberdeen

Dee

Ballater

Stonehaven

N O R T H

S E A

Mountains

Pitlochry

ANGUS

Forfar

Montrose

PERTH AND KINROSS

Tay

Dundee

6

Arbroath

Perth

St Andrews

FIFE

R LING

Kinross

Stirling

Forth

4

Kirkcaldy

Culross

Dunfermline

Firth of Forth

EDINBURGH

EAST LOTHIAN

7

9

Falkirk

2

Haddington

St Abbs

3

GLASGOW

13

Livingston

MID LOTHIAN

Eyemouth

11

8

East Kilbride

Clyde

New Lanark

SOUTH LANARKSHIRE

Southern Uplands

Galashiels

Tweed

Kelso

EAST AYRSHIRE

Melrose

SCOTTISH BORDERS

Jedburgh

Cumnock

Hawick

DUMFRIES AND GALLOWAY

Lockerbie

Dumfries

Gretna

Castle Douglas

Kirkcudbright

Solway Firth

E N G L A N D

0   20   40   60   80   100 km

0   20   40   60 miles

WELCOME TO THE GUIDE

Kyleakin and Castle Moil, Isle of Skye

HOW THE GUIDE IS DIVIDED

For the purposes of this guide Scotland has been divided into six areas, each beginning with an area map. There is also a key map of the whole of Scotland and the islands on pages 4 & 5:

Southern Scotland

Central Scotland

The North-East

The Great Glen & the Western Highlands

North Highlands

The Islands

REGIONAL DIVISIONS

Each region starts with a brief introduction and a map. Within the regional directories, information is divided into the following sections:

WHERE TO GO AND WHAT TO DO

Our intention has been to include as many attractions possible to reflect the widest range of interests for the benefit of the reader. To do this entries are necessarily brief, but do include location, a telephone contact number and directions (if applicable and supplied).
The Must See section is generally more informative than the subsequent headings and is intended to give an overall picture of the best tourist attractions at a glance.

Other interests (see below) have been divided into lists for ease of use. Their descriptions may not be so long , but will always incorporate the address and/or directions and a telephone number (if supplied or applicable). For example, if you are on holiday with the children, the Great for Kids section incorporates everything in the area to do. If you prefer exploring the countryside or visiting famous buildings, Big Outdoors or Homes and Gardens may be the sections that appeal to you. On the other hand, there is also a wealth of information about entertainment, theatres, concert halls and cinemas, as well as shopping, markets, sports & leisure, etc.

Where an area has a speciality such as Literary Edinburgh among its places of interest you will find this in the Where to Go, What to Do section.

MUST SEE
ART GALLERIES
MUSEUMS
HISTORIC & ANCIENT SITES
GREAT FOR KIDS
HOMES & GARDENS
BIG OUTDOORS

Must See

Entries include the very best or most interesting places to go in that area. These could include any of the Where to Go and What to Do categories. The entries could range from the most famous tourist attraction - for example, Edinburgh Castle - to something small that captures the essence of the area.

Museums & Art Galleries
Museums of every type and size plus art galleries. The lists may be split where there are sufficient numbers to warrant it.

Historic & Ancient Sites
Scotland has hundreds of famous buildings and ancient landmarks and many are open to the public.

Great for Kids
Many of the big tourist attractions are geared up to children with special exhibitions, audio-visual presentations and the like. The entries in this heading may include some, or none of these, depending on what else is available in the area. Expect to find children's farms, beaches, local activities, leisure centres.

Homes & Gardens
Scotland has many beautiful country houses and stately homes. Many of these have lovely grounds, but there are many other gardens well worth visiting and these are included.

Big Outdoors
Expect to find nature reserves, forest parks, open moorland and places of natural beauty.

ESSENTIAL INFORMATION
Tourist Information
Main tourist information offices have been listed first. Full addresses, telephone and fax numbers are given, where they have been provided.

Access
Main air and sea ports of entry are listed

Transport
Information on buses, trains as applicable, plus car hire, cycle hire

Crafts
Local crafts and where to find them.

Entertainment
Cinemas, theatres and any regional entertainment are included.

Food & drink
Any local specialities to look out for are noted.

Shopping
In larger towns, information on shopping areas and what you will find there.

Sport & Leisure
A wide range of activities is listed and varies from area to area.

WHERE TO STAY

Wide range of accommodation
All AA recommended accommodation from 5-star hotels to small bed & breakfast establishments are include in the area directories.

Quality Assured
When hotels and other guest accommodation apply to join the AA scheme they are visited anonymously by the AA's professional Hotel Inspectorate and are inspected and assessed for facilities and the quality of what they provide. This assessment reflects the quality of the accommodation and services provided by each establishment. Hotels are awarded from one to five stars on a rising scale, and other accommodation is awarded from one to five Qs for its quality.

Only after testing the accommodation and services and having paid their bill do inspectors introduce themselves in order to make a thorough inspection of the entire premises.

PRICE SYMBOLS
The £ symbol has been used as a price guide. The categories below indicate the price of a single room. Prices are per night and are indications only. The information is the most up-to-date available to us at the time of going to press, but prices can and do change without warning during the currency of a guide, so it is essential to check before booking. If the establishment is in the Bed & Breakfast Accommodation section, then the room price will almost certainly include breakfast. Some establishments offer free accommodation to children up to a certain age, provided they share the parents' room. Check for availability of family rooms and terms and conditions.

£	up to £30
££	£31 - £50
£££	£51 - £70
££££	£71 and over

THE RATING SYMBOLS
The Hotel Star-Rating
★ Usually privately owned and run, one-star hotels tend to be small, with a more personal atmosphere than larger ones. Furnishings and services will be good but simple; not all bedrooms may have en suite facilities. Some hotels may not offer all the expected hotel services - e.g. lunch service may be limited.
★★ May include group-owned as well as proprietor-owned hotels. At this star rating they are usually small to medium sized. At least half the bedrooms will have en suite bath/shower rooms and may also have phones and TVs.
★★★ Three-star hotels offer a greater range of facilities and services, including full reception service as well as more formal restaurant and bar arrangements. Bedrooms should all have en suite facilities, mostly with baths.
★★★★ Usually large hotels with spacious accommodation, offering high standards of comfort and food. All bedrooms will have en suite bathrooms with bath and shower and private suites will usually also be available. The range of services should include porterage, room service, formal reception and probably a choice of styles of restaurant.
★★★★★ Five stars denote large, luxury hotels offering the highest international standards of accommodation, facilities, services and cuisine.

RED STAR HOTELS
These awards are made annually to a select number of hotels as a recognition of excellence within their star rating. This is the AA's supreme award for hotels and to earn it, they must consistently provide outstanding levels of hospitality, service, food and comfort.

LODGES (e.g. Travelodge, Travel Inn)
Useful budget accommodation for an overnight stay. They have rooms suitable for family use

which are often charged at a flat rate regardless of number of occupants, and provide a consistent standard of comfortable modern en suite accommodation.

THE GUEST ACCOMMODATION 'Q' (QUALITY)
SYMBOL (Guest Houses, Private Hotels, Inns)
Q Recommended This assessment indicates an establishment with simple accommodation and adequate bathroom facilities.
QQ Recommended This assessment indicates a sound standard of accommodation offering more in terms of decor and comfort and likely to have some bedrooms with en suite bath or shower rooms
QQQ Recommended This assessment indicates well appointed accommodation and a wider range of facilities than a one or two Q establishment. Bedrooms may have en suite bath/shower rooms.
QQQQ Selected This assessment indicates that the accommodation will be comfortable and well appointed, that hospitality and facilities will be of high quality, and that a reasonable proportion of bedrooms will have en suite bath or shower rooms
QQQQQ Premier Selected This is the AA's highest assessment for guest houses, farmhouses or inns. It has been introduced in response to the rapidly growing number of really excellent establishments. It indicates an outstanding level of accommodation and service, with an emphasis on quality, good facilities for guests and an exceptionally friendly and hospitable atmosphere. The majority of bedrooms will have en suite bath or shower rooms.

HOW TO READ ACCOMMODATION ENTRIES
Hotels are listed in each town in alphabetical order within their star rating.
Quality Symbols: all guest accommodation is assessed for quality on a scale of one to five, denoted by the appropriate symbol (see above) and then listed in alphabetical order by 'Q' rating.
Name is followed by the address, and postal code of establishment
Telephone numbers may be changed during the currency of this book in some areas. In case of

difficulty, check with the operator.
Fax numbers are given when supplied.
Opening details – unless otherwise stated, the establishments are open all year, but where dates are shown they are inclusive: e.g. 'Apr-Oct' indicates that the establishment is open from the beginning of April to the end of October.
Some places are open all year, but offer a restricted service off season. The abbreviation **'Res'** indicates this. It may mean either that evening meals are not served or that other facilities listed are not available. If the text does not say what the restricted services are, you should check before booking.

DESCRIPTION OF THE ESTABLISHMENT
Establishments have been described very briefly, but the facilities are shown in italics at the end of each description
Accommodation details
The first figure shows the number of letting bedrooms.
Annexe – shows that bedrooms are available in separate building. The standard is acceptable, but it is advisable to check the nature of the accommodation and tariff before making a reservation.
fmly – indicates family bedrooms.
No smoking – if the establishment is only partly no-smoking, the areas where smoking is not permitted are shown
No children – indicates that children cannot be accommodated. A minimum age may be specified (e.g. No children under 4 yrs = no children under four years old). Although establishments may accept children of all ages they may not necessarily be able to provide special facilities. If you have very young children, check before booking about provisions like cots and high chairs, and any reductions made.
Children's facilities – indicates establishments with special facilities for children, which will include baby-sitting service or baby intercom system, playroom or playground, laundry facilities, drying and ironing facilities, cots, high chairs and special meals.
Additional facilities – such as lifts, leisure activities, conference and/or banqueting facilities.
Leisure activities – could encompass tennis, croquet, cycle hire, fishing, golf, sauna, jacuzzi, spa, horse-riding, swimming pool, snooker.
Parking – denotes on-site car parking.
Credit card symbol -any of the following cards may be accepted, so check when booking: Mastercard, American Express, Visa, Diners, Connect, Delta, Switch

GUESTS WITH DISABILITIES
Guests with any form of disability should notify proprietors, so that arrangements can be made to minimise difficulties, particularly in the event of an emergency.

NOTES ABOUT ACCOMMODATION
Common to all
Whatever the type of establishment, there are certain requirements common to all, including a

well-maintained exterior, clean and hygienic kitchens; good standards of furnishing; friendly and courteous service; access to the premises at reasonable times; the use of a telephone; and a full, cooked breakfast in the Scottish tradition. Bedrooms should be equipped with comfortable beds, a wardrobe, a bedside cabinet, a washbasin (unless there is an en suite or private bath/shower room) with soap, towel, mirror and shaver socket and at least a carpet beside the bed. There should not be an extra charge for the use of baths or lavatories, and heating should not be metered.

CANCELLATION
If you find that you must cancel a booking, let the proprietor know at once, because if the room you booked cannot be re-let, you may be held legally responsible for partial payment. Whether it is a matter of losing your deposit, or of being liable for compensation, you should seriously consider taking out cancellation insurance.

COMPLAINTS
Readers who have any cause to complain are urged to do so on the spot. This should provide an opportunity for the proprietor to correct matters. If a personal approach fails, readers should inform: AA Hotel Services, Fanum House, Basingstoke, Hants, RG21 4EA.

FOOD AND DRINK
If you intend to take dinner at an establishment, note that sometimes the meal must be ordered in advance of the actual meal time. In some cases, this may be at breakfast time, or even on the previous evening. If you have booked on bed, breakfast and evening meal terms, you may find that the tariff includes only the set menu, but, if there is one, you can usually order from the à la carte menu and pay a supplement. **High tea** is a popular meal in Scotland and is served in the early evening instead of dinner; it usually includes a savoury dish, followed by bread and butter, scones, cake, etc.

Payment
Most proprietors will only accept cheques in payment of accounts if notice is given and some form of identification (preferably a cheque card) is produced. If a hotel accepts credit or charge cards, this is shown by a global credit card symbol in its directory entry. Please contact establishments directly to check which are accepted.

Prices
Hotels must display tariffs, either in the bedrooms or at reception. Application of VAT and service charges varies, but all prices quoted must be inclusive of VAT.

FIRE REGULATIONS
For safety, you must read the emergency notices displayed in bedrooms and be sure you understand them.

LICENCE TO SELL ALCOHOL
Unless otherwise stated, all hotels listed are licensed. Hotel residents can obtain alcoholic drinks at all times if the owner or responsible manager is prepared to serve them. Non-residents eating at the hotel restaurant can have drinks with their meals.

CODES OF PRACTICE
The Hotel Industry Voluntary Code of Booking Practice was revised in 1986, and the AA encourages its use in appropriate establishments. Its prime object is to ensure that the customer is clear about the precise services and facilities s/he is buying and what price will have to be paid, before entering into a contractually binding agreement. If the price has not been previously confirmed in writing, the guest should be handed a card at the time of registration, stipulating the total obligatory charge.

Some guest houses offer bed and breakfast only, so guests must go out for the evening meal. It is also wise to check when booking if there are any restrictions to your access to the house, particularly in the late morning and during the afternoon.

However, many guest houses do provide an evening meal. They may only be able to offer a set meal, but many offer an interesting menu and a standard of service that one would expect in a good restaurant. You may have to arrange dinner in advance, so you should ask about the arrangements for evening meals when booking. Many places have a full licence, or at least a table licence and wine list.

BOOKING
Book as early as possible, particularly for the peak holiday period from the beginning of June to the end of September, and this may also include Easter and other public holidays.

Although it is possible for chance callers to find a night's accommodation, it is by no means a certainty, especially at peak holiday times and in popular areas, so it is always advisable to book as far in advance as possible. Some may only accept weekly bookings from Saturday. Some establishments will require a deposit on booking.

Only brief descriptions appear about each establishment, so if you require further information, write to, telephone or fax the establishment itself. Do remember to enclose a stamped addressed envelope, or an international reply-paid coupon if writing from overseas, and please quote this publication in any enquiry. Although we try to publish accurate and up to date information, please remember that any details, and particularly prices, are subject to change without notice and this may happen during the currency of the guide.

CAMPING AND CARAVANNING

Whether you are newcomer to camping and caravanning or an old hand, it is probable that what attracted you in the first place to the

freedom of going where you please. However, in practice, especially during holiday periods, parks in popular parts of Scotland get dreadfully crowded, and if you choose somewhere off the beaten track, you may go for miles without finding anywhere.

Telephone the park before you travel. In the caravan and camping world there may be some restrictions and some categories of visitor e.g. single sex groups, unsupervised groups of young people, and motorcycle clubs are banned altogether.

HOW THE PENNANT RATING WORKS

The AA pennant-rating scheme is based on regular inspections and classification of facilities.

The system emphasises quality as much as quantity, and the higher-rated sites are of a very high all-round standard indeed.

The scheme is designed for touring holidaymakers who travel with their own caravans, motor caravans, or tents. Our officers visit camping and caravanning parks to assess their touring facilities, but do not inspect any static caravans, chalets or ready-erected tents available for hire. All such accommodation is outside the scope of the scheme.

As the pennant rating increases, so the quality and variety of facilities will be greater. The basic requirement of the scheme is that the camping and caravanning parks reserve an acceptable number of pitches for the use of touring caravanners and campers, and that the facilities provided for tourers are well maintained and clean, and comply with our standards of classification. Many parks in the AA scheme display a yellow and black sign showing their pennant rating, but not all parks choose to have one, and some local authorities prohibit the display of signs.

Basic Requirements

All parks must have a local authority site licence (unless specially exempted) and must have satisfied local authority fire regulations. Parks at the higher pennant rating must also comply with the basic requirements, and offer additional facilities according to their classification.

Please note that campsites are legally allowed to use an overflow field which is not normally part of their camping areas for up to 28 days in any one year as an emergency method of coping with additional numbers at busy periods.

When this 28 day rule is being invoked site owners should increase the numbers of sanitary facilities accordingly when the permanent facilities become insufficient to cope with the extra numbers.

Town & Country Pennant Parks

These may offer a simple standard of facilities, and sometimes only drinking water and chemical waste disposal for the really self contained tourer. Do check with individual sites at the time of booking to make sure they satisfy your own personal requirements. All the following should be offered: maximum 30 pitches per campable acre; at least 10 feet between units; urgent telephone numbers signed; whereabouts of an emergency telephone shown; first aid box.

►►► 3-Pennant Family Parks

In addition to the above, these parks guarantee a greater degree of comfort, with modern or modernised toilet blocks offering a minimum of two washbasins and two toilets per 30 pitches per sex. Toilet facilities should include: hot water to wash basins and showers; mirrors, shelves and hooks; shaver/hairdryer points; soap and hand dryer/towels; a reasonable number of modern cubicled showers; all-night internal lighting.
Family parks should also have: evenly surfaced roads and paths; some electric hook-ups; some level ground suitable for motor caravans.

▶▶▶ 4 - Pennant De-Luxe Parks

As well as all of the above, these parks are of a very high standard, with good landscaping, natural screening and attractive park buildings. Toilets are smartly modern and well maintained, plus the following: spacious vanitory-style washbasins; fully-tiled shower cubicles with dry areas, shelves and hooks, at least one per 30 pitches per sex.

Other requirements are: shop on site, or within reasonable distance; warden available 24-hours; reception area open during the day; internal paths, roads and toilet blocks lit at night; electric hook-ups; hardstandings where necessary.

These parks should also ideally offer a late arrivals enclosure, and some fully-serviced toilet cubicles.

▶▶▶▶ 5-Pennant Premier Parks

All parks in this category are of an award-winning standard, and are set in attractive surroundings with superb landscaping. They must offer some fully-serviced pitches or first-class cubicled washing facilities; most pitches should also offer electric hook-ups. Ideally, but not necessarily there may be in addition to the above: heated swimming pool (outdoor, indoor or both); clubhouse with some entertainment; well-equipped shop; café or restaurant and a bar; decent indoor and outdoor leisure facilities for young people; designated dog-walking area if dogs accepted

Electrical Hook-up

This is becoming more generally available at parks with three or more pennants, but if it is important to you, you must check before booking. The voltage is generally 240v AC, 50 cycles, although variations between 200v and 250v may still be found. All parks in the AA scheme which provide electrical hook-ups do so in accordance with International Electrotechnical Commission regulations.

Outlets are coloured blue and take the form of a lidded plug with recessed contacts, making it impossible to touch a live point by accident. They are also waterproof. A similar plug, but with protruding contacts which hook into the recessed plug, is on the end of the cable which connects the caravan to the source of supply, and is dead.

Motor Caravans

At some parks motor caravans are only accepted if they remain static throughout the stay. Also check that there are suitable level pitches at the parks where you intend to stay.

Parking

Some parks insist that cars be put in a parking area separate from the pitches; others will allow more than one car for each caravan or tent.

Park rules

Most parks display a set of rules which you should read on your arrival. Dogs may or may not be accepted on parks, and this is entirely at the owners' or wardens' discretion. We most strongly advise that you check when you book.

Most parks will not accept the following categories of people: single-sex groups, unsupervised youngsters, motorcyclists whether singly or in groups, sometimes even adults travelling on their own are barred. If you are not a family group or a conventional couple, you would be well advised to make sure what rules apply before you book.

Restricted service

This means that full amenities and services are not available during the period stated - e.g. a swimming pool or bar/restaurant may be open only in the summer. Restrictions vary greatly from park to park, so you must check before setting off.

Signposted

This does not refer to AA signs, but indicates that there is an International Direction sign on the nearest main road.

Static van pitches

We give the number of static van pitches available, in order to give a picture of the size and nature of the park. The AA pennant rating system is based on an inspection of the touring pitches and facilities only. AA inspectors do not visit or report on fixed types of accommodation. The AA takes no responsibility for the condition of rented caravans or chalets and can take no action whatsoever about complaints relating to them.

Supervised

This means that the park has someone in attendance 24 hours a day. Other parks may have less comprehensive cover.

CAMPING IN THE ISLANDS

The Shetland Islands

Campers and caravanners are welcome, but there are restrictions on Noss and Fair Isle. Camping is not allowed at all at the Tresta Links in Fetlar. Elsewhere, there are four official campsites, but you can stay in the wild, providing you seek permission from the owner of the land.

Please note that caravans and motor caravans must stick to the public roads. You are strongly advised to check maps and routes carefully so that you don't find yourself in a difficult or dangerous situation.

Böds on a budget Camping böds are a good way of seeing Shetland on a budget, as long as you don't mind a very basic unisex dormitory. Traditionally used by fishermen during the fishing season. Some böds have no electricity, and none has hot water. You need your own sleeping bag and bed roll, camping stove and cooking utensils. You do get a roof over your head and a toilet, table and benches.

The Orkney Islands

There are no restrictions on where you can camp or park your caravan, and there are plenty of beautiful spots to choose from. You can avoid the crowds, but the bird population is never far away. No camping, however, on the tiny Fair Isle and there is no car ferry.

The Western Isles (Outer Hebrides)

Only 13 of the 200 plus islands are inhabited, linked by a network of ferries and causeways. There are official campsites, but you can camp in the wild within reason and with the landowner's prior permission.

Inner Hebrides/Other Scottish Islands:
Rothesay Official camping only; wild camping is discouraged.
Mull, Islay, Coll, Arran Official campsites. Tenters, caravan and motor caravans are all welcome. Offsite camping is allowed, provided the usual permission is obtained.
Iona, Rhum, Eigg All backpackers' paradises.
Colonsay, Cumbrae No camping or caravanning, although organised groups, such as Scouts and Guides, may stay with official permission.
Jura, Gigha No camping or caravanning.
Lismore Caravans are banned. Camping is permitted but there are no official sites and few suitable places in any case.

WHERE TO EAT
There are two distinct sections in this section.
AA Recommended Restaurants
The first lists AA recommended restaurants and hotel restaurants; these are awarded rosettes for the standard of cooking.
Pubs, Inns & Other Places
The second section includes a range of pubs, country inns, village restaurants and quick bite places. Names, addresses and telephone numbers are supplied, plus a short description. These do not have a price guide.

HOW AA ROSETTES ARE AWARDED
The AA makes annual rosette awards on a rising scale of one to five for the quality of food served in restaurants. Every restaurant awarded AA rosettes has had at least one anonymous meal visit from an AA inspector. Many, especially at the higher award levels, have been visited more than once by different inspectors at different times. AA inspection visits are anonymous; no favours are accepted.

All the entries have been written from reports filed by AA inspectors. Although our inspectors are a highly trained and very experienced team of professional men and women, it must be stressed that the opinions expressed are only opinions, based on the experience of one or more particular occasions. Assessments are therefore to some extent necessarily subjective.

AA inspectors are experienced enough to make a balanced judgement, but they are not omniscient.
Vegetarian: almost all restaurants featured will prepare a vegetarian dish or accommodate a special diet if given prior notice
Smoking: establishments that do not allow smoking in the dining room may allow it elsewhere, in a lounge of bar, for instance. If you are a smoker, it is worth checking beforehand.
What the rosettes signify:
❀ One rosette denotes simple, carefully prepared food, based on good quality, fresh ingredients, cooked in such a way as to emphasise honest flavours. Sauces and desserts will be home-made and the cooking will equate to first-class home cooking.
❀❀ Two rosettes denote cooking that displays a high degree of competence on the part of the chef. The menus should include some imaginative dishes, making use of very good raw ingredients, as well as some tried and tested favourites. Flavours should be well balanced and complement or contrast with one another, not over-dominate.
❀❀❀ Only cooking of the highest national standard receives three or more rosettes. Menus will be imaginative; dishes should be accurately cooked, demonstrate well developed technical skills and a high degree of flair in their composition. Ingredients will be first-class, usually from a range of specialist suppliers, including local produce only if its quality is excellent. Most items - breads, pastries, pasta, petits fours - will be made in the kitchens, but if any are bought in, for example, breads, the quality will be excellent.
❀❀❀❀ At this level, cuisine should be innovative, daring, highly accomplished and achieve a noteworthy standard of consistency, accuracy and flair throughout all the elements of the meal. Excitement, vibrancy and superb technical skill will be the keynotes.
❀❀❀❀❀ Five rosettes is the supreme accolade, made to chefs at the very top of their profession. This award recognises superlative standards of cuisine at an international level, evident at every visit in every element of the meal. Creativity, skill and attention to detail will produce dishes cooked to perfection, with intense, exciting flavours in harmonious combinations and faultless presentation. Menus may be innovative or classical, and may use luxury ingredients like lobster, truffles, foie gras, etc., often in unexpected combinations and with secret ingredients that add an extra dimension of taste and interest.
Price Guidelines For AA Recommended Restaurants
ALC is the cost of an à la carte meal for one person, including coffee and service but not wine. **Fixed L** or **Fixed D** shows the approximate price guide for a fixed-price lunch or dinner. The prices quoted are a guide only, and are subject to change without notice.

£	**up to £15**
££	**£16 - £25**
£££	**£30 and upwards**

SOUTH

If you've never been to Scotland before, then this southern half of the country may well be your first taste of one of the last great wildernesses in Europe. Often overlooked by visitors and tourists heading further north to the Highlands or the Western Isles, Southern Scotland is packed with surprises - a veritable treasure trove of hidden riches and unexpected delights. If you look at a map showing the line of the 37-mile Roman Antonine Wall, which runs across the waist of Scotland between the Firths of Forth and Clyde, then all that lies below that frontier makes up this sizeable region, much of it given over to farming.

Southern Scotland is often referred to as the Lowlands, so as to distinguish it from the mountainous grandeur of the North-west Highlands. But don't be fooled by the description. In places, the landscape is anything but flat. In fact, much of it is surprisingly hilly. This is a different Scotland to the rest of the country - different in character and identity, but, in terms of scenery, no less spectacular, and, in many ways, just as fascinating.

Dumfries and Galloway, the Scottish Borders and Dumbartonshire are among the many regions to be found in Southern Scotland - all of them as alluring and individual as they are beautiful and unspoilt. The Ayrshire coast is wonderfully open and breezy, while Edinburgh, Glasgow and the Clyde Valley offer an endless choice of things to do and places to visit, suiting all ages and tastes. At the heart of this beautiful district lie the Southern Uplands, a glorious, scenic tableland of rolling hills and green dales - great for touring and even better for walking.

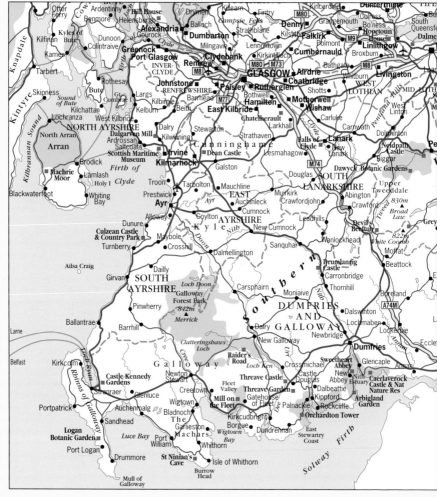

EVENTS & FESTIVALS

March

Country Music Festival, *Selkirk, Borders*
Festival of Music, Arts & Crafts,
Gatehouse of Fleet, Dumfries & Galloway
Scottish Country Dance Festival,
Penicuik, Midlothian

April

Scottish Grand National,
Ayr Racecourse, S Ayrshire
Woodcraft Fair, *Fairlie, N Ayshire*
Folk Festival, *Edinburgh*

May

May Fair, *Coldstream, Borders*
Jazz Festival, *Peebles, Borders*
Vintage Agricultural Rally,
Newtown St Boswells, Borders
Borders Food Fair, *Jedburgh, Borders*

Scottish Beer Festival,
Traquair House, Innerleithen, Borders
Girvan Folk Festival, *S Ayrshire*
Ayr Agricultural Show,
Ayr Racecourse, S Ayrshire
Kelburn Country Fair & Gymkhana,
Kelburn Country Park, Fairlie, N Ayrshire
Garnock Highland Games,
Kilbirnie, N Ayrshire
Festival of Flight,
Kelburn Country Centre, Fairlie, N Ayrshire
New Cumnock Show, *E Ayrshire*
Kirkpatrick MacMillan Cycle Rally,
Dumfries, Dumfries & Galloway
British Gold Panning Championships,
Museum of Lead Mining, Wanlockhead,
Dumfries & Galloway
BMC Car Rally, *Calderglen Country Park,*
East Kilbride, S Lanarkshire
Highland Games, *Gourock, Inverclyde*
Lesmahagow & Shotts South Lanarkshire
Inverclyde Megawatt Festival
Venues throughout Inverclyde

Chiuldren's Festival, *Edinburgh*
Festival Week, *Haddington, E Lothian*

June

Common Riding,
Hawick & Selkirk, Borders
West Linton Whipman Week,
Scottish Borders
Historic Motoring Experience,
Mellerstain House, Gordon, Borders
Seafood Festival, *Eyemouth, Borders*
Melrose Festival, *Scottish Borders*
Midsummer Fair,
Newtown St Boswells, Borders
Beltane Fair, *Peebles, Borders*
Greenlaw Festival Week, *Borders*
Jethart Callant's Festival,
Jedburgh, Borders
Carrick Lowland Gathering,
Victory Park, Girvan, S Ayrshire
RSAC Scottish Rally,
Dumfries, Dumfries & Galloway

August

Traquair Fair, *Innerleithen, Borders*
Kite Festival, *Ayton Castle, Ayton, Borders*
Hawick Summer Festival, *Borders*
Scottish Horse Trials,
Thirlestane Castle, Lauder, Borders
Borders Lifeboat Gala, *Eyemouth, Borders*
Arts Festival *Peebles, Borders*
Culzean Classic Vehicle Show,
Culzean Castle & Country Park, S Ayrshire
Festival of Scottish Music & Dance,
Culzean Castle & Country Park, S Ayrshire
Marymass Festival, *Irvine, N Ayrshire*
Largs Regatta Week, *N Ayrshire*
Largs Viking Festival, *N Ayrshire*
Dumfries & Lockerbie Agricultural Show, *Dumfries, Dumfries & Galloway*
Port William Carnival Week,
Dumfries & Galloway
The Scottish Alternative Games,
Parton, Castle Douglas, Dumfries & Galloway
Sanquhar Riding of the Marches,
Dumfries & Galloway
Creetown Gala Week,
Dumfries & Galloway
The Border Gathering,
Parkgate, Dumfries, Dumfries & Galloway
Langholm & Eskdale Music & Arts Festival, *Dumfries & Galloway*
Calderglen Classic Car Rally,
East Kilbride, S Lanarkshire
Military Tattoo, *Edinburgh Castle*
International Jazz & Blues Festival; Edinburgh Book Festival; Edinburgh Fringe Festival; Edinburgh International Festival; Edinburgh International Film Festival.
Vogrie Festival Day,
Gorebridge, Midlothian
Falkirk Family Show, *Falkirk*

September

Borders Walking Festival,
Lauder, Borders
Highland Games, *Peebles, Borders*
Borders Jazz & Blues Festival,
Hawick, Borders
Vintage, Classic & Veteran Vehicle Show, *Selkirk, Borders*
Jazz Festival, *Girvan, S Ayrshire*
Ayr Gold Cup, *Ayr Racecourse, S Ayrshire*
Scottish Festival,
Museum of Lead Mining, Wanlockhead, Dumfries & Galloway
Creetown Country Music Festival,
Dumfries & Galloway
Victorian Fair, *New Lanark, S Lanarkshire*

October

Border Shepherds Show,
Yetholm, Borders
Sir Walter Scott Literary Weekend,
The Borders
West of Scotland Dairy Show,
Muirhill, Symington, S Ayrshire
Kilmarnock Folk Weekend, *E Ayrshire*
International Scotch Whisky Festival, *Edinburgh*

Kirkconnel & Kelloholm Gala Week,
Kirkconnel, Dumfries & Galloway
Whithorn Medieval Market & Fair,
Dumfries & Galloway
Highland Games, *Airdrie, N Lanarkshire*
Biggar Gala Week, *S Lanarkshire*
Country Fair, *Calderglen Country Park, East Kilbride, S Lanarkshire*
Lanimer Day, *Lanark, S Lanarkshire*
National Gardening Show,
Strathclyde Country Park, Motherwell, North Lanarkshire
Paisley Festival, *Renfrewshire*
Royal Highland Show,
Royal Highland Centre, Ingliston, Edinburgh
Linlithgow Carnival, *W Lothian*
Bo'ness Children's Fair Festival,
Bo-ness, Falkirk

July

Jim Clark Rally, *Kelso/Duns, Borders*
Traditional Music Festival,
Newcastleton, Borders
Duns Summer Festival, *Borders*
Festival of Craft, Fashion & Design,
Mellerstain House, Gordon, Borders

Border Games,
Jedburgh & Innerleithen, Borders
Border Union Show,
Kelso, Borders
Lauder Common Riding, *Borders*
Harbour Festival, *Irvine, N Ayrshire*
New Galloway Gala Week,
Dumfries & Galloway
National Sea Trout Festival,
Lockerbie, Dumfries & Galloway
Kirkcudbright Summer Festivities,
Dumfries & Galloway
Robert Burns - Brow Well Service,
Ruthwell, Dumfries & Galloway
Gatehouse of Fleet Gala Week,
Dumfries & Galloway
Sma' Shot Day, *Paisley, Renfrewshire*
Comet Festival, *Port Glasgow, Inverclyde*
Edinburgh International Strongman & Highland Games,
Honest Toun Festival Week,
Musselburgh, E Lothian
Falkirk Children's Festival, *Falkirk*
Highland Games, *Airth, Falkirk*
Food & Drink Festival, *Falkirk*

EDINBURGH

Edinburgh, with its world-famous castle commanding a truly magnificent setting, is one of Europe's loveliest and most elegant cities. With so much to offer the visitor, you'll be hard-pressed to know where to begin exploring. Dubbed the 'Athens of the North', Edinburgh's atmosphere is unique, and if you tour its splendid maze of medieval streets and Georgian squares, you'll be taking a fascinating journey into the city's past.

August is a very good time to visit Edinburgh – when the city becomes the venue for the annual Edinburgh Festival, offering a breathtaking variety of concerts, ballet, opera and theatre. The military tattoo, which takes place at Edinburgh Castle, is also an integral part of the proceedings. Just outside the city, to the south-west, are the summit ridges of the rolling Pentland Hills, gateway to the Scottish Borders and a haven for anyone who enjoys bracing hikes and exhilarating strolls.

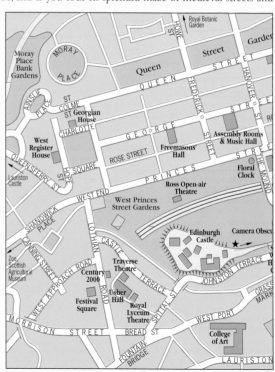

PRINCIPAL TOWNS

HADDINGTON, EAST LOTHIAN

Set on the banks of the Tyne, Haddington is one of the country's most beautifully restored and preserved towns, an outstanding example of Scottish burghal architecture. Pick up one of the 'Historic Walks in Haddington' leaflets and explore its triangular medieval street plan. You will discover a wealth of handsome 18th-century buildings – there are over 200 listed buildings at its heart – especially along the High Street and around the impressive market-place.

LINLITHGOW, WEST LOTHIAN

A former Royal Burgh, containing the impressive ruins of a royal palaceand one of Scotland's finest churches, which enjoys a delightful setting on the banks of the town loch.

NORTH BERWICK, EAST LOTHIAN

Within easy reach of Edinburgh and boasting several golf courses, vast sandy beaches, sailing and sea angling, this ancient burgh, fishing village and fashionable holiday resort is the ideal family destination on the east coast.

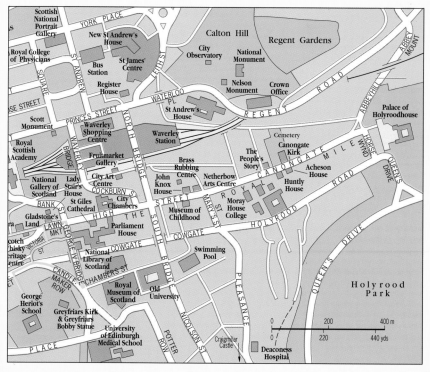

MUST SEE

CALTON HILL,
east of Princes St

If the bustling crowds along Princes St become too much, climb the steep, stepped path from Waterloo Place on to Calton Hill, which, although hardly a dominating height, commands one of the finest panoramic views of the city. It was certainly Robert Louis Stevenson's favourite view of the city. Equally appealing is the extraordinary collection of neo-classical buildings and memorials scattered across its domed top; the numerous columns and temples helped Edinburgh earn its reputation as 'the Athens of the north'.

EDINBURGH CASTLE,
Castlehill ☎ 0131 225 9846

Possibly Scotland's most famous landmark, this magnificent stronghold, perched on the precipitous crag of Castle Rock, dominates the city centre with its silhouette of ramparts and rooftops. Any historic tour of Edinburgh should begin at this impressive castle. An impressive royal court from the 11th century and successively altered, rebuilt and extended until Victorian times, it is a fascinating place to explore. Highlights include the tiny St Margaret's Chapel, the oldest building in Edinburgh, the Royal Apartments, including the bedroom where James VI of Scotland, the first Stuart king of England, was born to Mary, Queen of Scots, and the Crown Room which displays the Scottish crown and other royal regalia, and The Vaults, where you can see gaffiti by 19th-century French prisoners of war. Relax in the restaurant, with its fine views across the city.

HUNTLY HOUSE MUSEUM,
141 Canongate ☎ 0131 529 4143

Browse around a warren of interconnecting rooms in this fine 16th-century building, one of the best preserved in the Old Town, and learn about the history of Edinburgh from the earliest times. Look out for the notable collections of silver, glassware and pottery, as well as artefacts connected with King George's visit, and the original New Town plan signed by the architect, James Craig.

MUSEUM OF CHILDHOOD
Royal Mile ☎ 0131 529 4142

Designed for adults rather than children, this unique museum (the first of its kind in the world) will fascinate 'children' of all ages, especially those of you who have never quite forgotten your old dolls, toys and games. Enthralling exhibits from past centuries include Victorian dolls and German automata, but its the wonderful collection of more recent toys and games that will evoke memories of one's own childhood.

NATIONAL GALLERY OF SCOTLAND,
The Mound ☎ 0131 556 8921

Recognised as one of Europe's best smaller galleries, occupying a handsome neo-classical building designed by William Playfair in 1857, it offers visitors the chance to see some of the best Old Masters in the United Kingdom outside London, as well as exceptional collections of works by Impressionists and, naturally, Scottish artists.

PALACE OF HOLYROODHOUSE,
Canongate ☎ 0131 556 7371

Having evolved from the guesthouse of the adjacent ruined Abbey, the palace, dating from 1530, became the official residence of the Royal Family in Scotland, and remains so today. The Palace is closed to visitors when the Queen is in residence, normally in June and early July. Although much of the present building dates from 1671-80, the earlier tower (King James V's tower) contains the rooms associated with Mary, Queen of Scots, who had her court here from 1561 to 1567. You can see the audience chamber in which she debated with John Knox, and the plaque which marks the spot where her secretary, Rizzio, was murdered. Further highlights of the guided tour are the fine 17th-century state rooms, furnished with tapestries and furniture from the royal collection, and the picture gallery, where 111 portraits of Scottish monarchs hang.

THE ROYAL MILE,

A leisurely stroll down this famous thoroughfare, with its numerous dark courts, alleys, cobbled streets and steps, from the Castle to the Palace of Holyroodhouse is a must for all visitors, as it retains the true flavour of the capital's historic Old Town. In the mid-18th century, 50,000 people inhabited the tall 17th-century houses, or tenements, along the Royal Mile and adjoining narrow streets and courtyards behind. It was here that the poets, Robert Burns and Robert Fergusson, drank with the literati in the taverns and clubs, and where Deacon Brodie, a respectable locksmith by day and a villain by night, lived. Take time to explore some of the courts and alleys, as well as notable landmarks and museums .

ROYAL MUSEUM OF SCOTLAND,
Chambers St ☎ 0131 225 7534

Endless browsing in a spacious and airy environment can be enjoyed at this comprehensive museum, located within a handsome Victorian building, which contains decorative art and archaeology galleries housing local and international exhibits. Visitors will find the natural history section, featuring an excellent exhibition on vertebrae evolution, and, particularly appealing for children, the technological galleries with plenty of working models, most enthralling.

BO'NESS & KINNEIL RAILWAY,
Bo'ness, Falkirk ☎ 01506 822298

Experience the nostalgia and romance of the railway age and travel by steam train between Bo'ness and Birkhill. The 7-mile trip culminates with a conducted tour of the caverns of Birkhill Fireclay Mine. Back in Bo'ness you can trace the history of Scotland's railways at the Scottish Railway Exhibition, and explore the carriages, wagons, locomotives and historic railway buildings on the site. Special events, picnic area, tearoom and souvenir shop.

HOPETOUN HOUSE,
South Queensferry, West Lothian
☎ 0131 331 2451

Scotland's greatest Adam mansion was built in 1699 to a design by William Bruce and later enlarged by William and Robert Adam. Home of the Marquess of Linlithgow, it features magnificent architecture, sumptuous state rooms, fine paintings and furniture, and a collection of china. There is also a museum in the stables, extensive grounds with a deer park and a herd of rare St Kilda sheep, excellent coastal walks, a Ranger Service and a full programme of events throughout the year.

HOUSE OF BINNS,
Linlithgow, West Lothian
☎ 01506 834255

Home of the Dalyell family since 1612, this fine building reflects the transition from fortified stronghold to an attractive spacious mansion. The fascinating collection of portraits, furniture and porcelain reveal the life and interests of one family through the centuries

ROSSLYN CHAPEL,
Roslin, Midlothian ☎ 0131 440 2159

Perched above the wooded Roslin Glen, this Gothic-style 15th-century chapel has the finest example of medieval stone carving in Scotland. The church, still used as a place of worship, is really only the choir of a much larger design which was never completed. Lovely woodland walks.

SCOTTISH MINING MUSEUM,
Lady Victoria Colliery, Newtongrange, Midlothian ☎ 0131 663 7519

Mining comes alive. Entertaining guided tours led by ex-miners. Visit the pit-head, the steam winding engine, and a full-scale replica of a modern underground coalface. Experience the underground working conditions and the life in the mining community through a vivid audio-visual show and life-sized 'talking tableaux'.

TANTALLON CASTLE,
North Berwick, East Lothian
☎ 01620 892727

Formidable 14th-century stronghold of the Douglasses set on the cliff's edge with views of Bass Rock.

ARCHITECTURAL EDINBURGH

Architecturally, the historic and compact heart of the city splits neatly into two distinct areas. The medieval Old Town, dominated by Edinburgh Castle, incorporates the Royal Mile, the Palace of Holyrood. The late 18th century saw a creative period of expansion and the resultant New Town boasts the greatest expanse of Georgian architecture in Britain.

THE OLD TOWN

BRODIE'S CLOSE,
Lawnmarket
Home of William Brodie, town councillor and Deacon of the Wrights, who was an upright citizen by day and burglar by night. He was the inspiration for Stevenson's Dr Jekyll and Mr Hyde.

GLADSTONE'S LAND,
477 Lawnmarket ☎ 0131 226 5856
Built in 1620, this six-storey tenement, once the house of a prosperous Edinburgh merchant, still has its rare arcaded front. It has been fully restored and is furnished as a typical home a 17th-century merchant, complete with a ground-floor shop front.

JOHN KNOX HOUSE,
43-45 High St ☎ 0131 556 9579
This late 15th-century building, built by the goldsmith to Mary, Queen of Scots, with its projecting first-floor gallery is a reminder of what the Royal Mile would once have looked like. It contains a magnificent painted ceiling and an exhibition about his life and times.

PARLIAMENT HOUSE,
Parliament Sq ☎ 0131 225 2595
Hidden behind an 1829 facade, this mid-17th-century building is where the Scottish parliament and courts met until 1707. Visitors can see the Parliament Hall with its fine old hammerbeam roof. Restaurant.

THE NEW TOWN

CHARLOTTE SQUARE,
This square, designed in part by Robert Adam, provides the visitor with some of the finest Georgian architecture in the whole of Europe.

GENERAL REGISTER HOUSE,
Princes St ☎ 0131 535 1314
Splendid Robert Adam building.

THE GEORGIAN HOUSE,
Charlotte Square ☎ 0131 225 2160
The lower floors of this magnificent Georgian-style building have been elegantly restored in the style of around 1800, when the house was new. You will gain a vivid impression of Georgian life, especially in the grand public rooms, and videos provide an insight into life in the house, and the New Town.

MORAY PLACE,
off Queen St
With its cobbled roads and grand buildings, complete with Tuscan porticos, this is regarded by many as being the most impressive of all the New Town streets.

NEW TOWN CONSERVATION CENTRE,
13a Dundas Street ☎ 0131 557 5222
Exhibitions and information on the architecture of the New Town.

THE ROYAL BANK OF SCOTLAND,
St Andrew's Square
Situated on the east side of this grand sqaure, this imposing building was built in 1722 as a splendid town house. It is worth peeping into the main banking hall, added in 1858, to view the ornate ceiling and magnificent dome.

WEST REGISTER HOUSE,
Charlotte Square ☎ 0131 535 1314
Former Church of St George (1811) designed in Greco-Roman style, now housing the exhibition '800 Years of Scottish History' and the modern record branch of the Scottish Record Office.

RELIGIOUS EDINBURGH

CANONGATE KIRK,
Canongate
Built in 1688 for the congregation of the Abbey Church of Holyrood, when King James VII converted the abbey kirk into a chapel of the Knights of the Thistle.

GREYFRIARS KIRKYARD,
George IV Bridge
Occupying the site of an earlier Franciscan monastery, this graveyard is well worth exploring for the marked graves of 56 famous Scots that are buried in it, including Sir Walter Scott.

ST ANDREW'S & ST GEORGE'S CHURCH,
George St
Built in 1784 to an oval design by Major Andrew Foster, it was the first burgh church in the New Town. It features a 168ft steeple and, inside, a superb Adam-style ceiling.

ST GILES' CATHEDRAL,
High St
The High Kirk of Edinburgh was, in fact, only a cathedral during the 17th century. Although heavily restored in 1829, the tower, with its beautiful crown, dates from 1500 and is one of the few remaining examples of 15th-century work to be seen on the High Street today.

LITERARY EDINBURGH

Edinburgh has always had strong literary connections, from famous publishing houses like Batholomeu, Oliver & Boyd and W & R Chambers to famous poets and writers, such as Robert Fergusson, Robert Burns, Sir Walter Scott, Muriel Spark, author of The Prime of Miss Jean Brodie, who was educated in Edinburgh, and the famous Victorian writer Robert Louis Stevenson.

LITERARY PUBS,
Follow in the footsteps of Scotland's literary heroes to famous and infamous pubs frequented by the likes of Burns, Scott and Stevenson. For literary walking tours ☎ 0131 554 0777.

SCOTT MONUMENT,
Princes St Gardens ☎ 0131 529 4068
One of Edinburgh's most famous landmarks, this 200ft (61m) ornate Gothic spire was built between 1840-6 as a monument to Scotland's most enduring writers, Sir Walter Scott. Visitors can climb the 287 steps to the top for superb views.

WRITERS' MUSEUM,
Lady Stair's House, Lady Stair's Close, Lawnmarket ☎ 0131 529 4901
View a fine 17th-century building and various portraits, relics and manuscripts associated with Robert Burns, Sir Walter Scott and Robert Louis Stevenson. Shop.

ART GALLERIES

EDINBURGH

CITY ART GALLERY,
2 Market St ☎ 0131 529 3993
The city's permanent fine art collection.

FRUITMARKET GALLERY,
45 Market St ☎ 0131 225 2383
Exhibitions of contemporary Scottish and international art and design.

THE LEITH GALLERY,
65 The Shore, Leith ☎ 0131 553 5255
Scottish contemporary art.

THE MATTHEW ARCHITECTURE GALLERY,
University of Edinburgh, 20 Chambers Street
☎ 0131 650 2306
Contemporary and historical architecture.

SCOTTISH NATIONAL GALLERY OF MODERN ART,
Belford Rd ☎ 0131 556 8921
Scotland's own collection of 20th-century paintings and graphic art, including works by Matisse, Picasso, Giacometti, Hockney and Hepworth.

SCOTTISH NATIONAL PORTRAIT GALLERY,
1 Queen St ☎ 0131 556 8921
Providing a fascinating visual picture of Scotland from the 16th century to the present day, this striking red Victorian building houses portraits of the people who helped shape it: royals and rebels, poets and philosophers, heroes and villains.

STILLS GALLERY,
23 Cockburn Street ☎ 0131 225 9876
Scotland's premier photographic gallery .

MUSEUMS

EDINBURGH

CAMRA OBSCURA & OUTLOOK TOWER,
Castlehill, Royal Mile ☎ 0131 226 3709
Step inside this magical 1850s 'cinema' for a unique experience of Edinburgh. With the camra's system of revolving lenses and mirrors in operation, you can marvel at the

unfolding panorama of the surrounding city, complete with a guide recounting the city's historic past. Don't miss the view from the Rooftop Terrace.

DALMENY HOUSE,
South Queensferry ☎ 0131 331 1888
Set in beautiful rolling parkland on the shores of the Firth of Forth, this fine Tudor Gothic mansion, houses important collections of 18th century furniture, tapestries, porcelain, and portraits.

THE PEOPLE'S STORY,
Canongate Tolbooth, 163 Canongate
☎ 0131 225 2424 ext 4057
Experience the sights, sounds and smells of bygone Edinburgh, at this vivid audio-visual exhibition that tells the story of the ordinary people of the city from the late 18th century to the present day. Shop.

SCOTCH WHISKY HERITAGE CENTRE,
354 Castlehill ☎ 0131 220 0441
Travel through time at this fascinating attraction and discover the history of Scotland's most famous export - whisky!

SCOTTISH AGRICULTURAL MUSEUM,
Ingliston ☎ 0131 333 2674
Learn about all the aspects of rural life in bygone days, including the old trades associated with farming and the social and home life in the countryside, at Scotland's national farming museum.

FALKIRK & THE LOTHIANS

BIRKHILL CLAY MINE,
Birkhill, Falkirk ☎ 01506 825855
Guided tours of a real clay mine deep in the wooded Avon Gorge. Experience life underground and visit the original mill, clay handling buildings and haulage gear. Picnic area and nature trail.

CANAL MUSEUM,
Manse Rd Basin, Linlithgow, West Lothian
☎ 01506 842125
Discover the history of the Edinburgh & Glasgow Union Canal, which opened in 1822, through photographs and artefacts. Boat trips and tearoom.

JANE WELSH CARLYLE MUSEUM,
Lodge St, Haddington, East Lothian
☎/🖷 01620 823738
Enchanting 18th-century house, the home of Jane Welsh Carlyle, one of the greatest women writers of her time, and the historian Thomas Carlyle.

KINNEIL MUSEUM & ROMAN FORTLET,
Duchess Anne Cottages, Kinneil Estate, Bo'ness, Falkirk ☎ 01506 824318
Explore the remains of a Roman fortlet and 2,000 years of history in the audio-visual theatre, plus the industrial history of Bo'ness and the history and environment of the Kinneil estate. Shop.

MUSEUM OF FLIGHT,
East Fortune, East Lothian ☎ 01620 880308
National collection of aircraft, rockets and aero engines displayed in former RAF wartime hangers. Exhibits include a Spitfire MK16, a Hawker Sea Hawk and a De Haviland Sea Venom.

MYRETON MOTOR MUSEUM,
Aberlady, East Lothian t 01875 870288
Wide-ranging collection of cars and motorcycles from 1896, historic British military vehicles, advertising signs and automobilia. Shop.

PRESTON MILL & PHANTASSIE DOOCOT,
East Linton, East Lothian ☎ 01620 860426
The oldest working water-driven meal mill to survive in Scotland, featuring exhibitions on milling, ducks and geese. A short walk to Phantassie Doocot, built for 500 birds.

SCOTTISH MINING MUSEUM,
Prestonpans, East Lothian ☎ 0131 653 2904
Discover the oldest documented coal-mining site in Britain, with 800 years of history. There is an underground gallery, a coalface and a reconstruction of a colliery workshop.

HISTORIC & ANCIENT SITES

EDINBURGH

CRAIGMILLAR CASTLE,
Craigmillar Castle Road ☎ 0131 661 4445
A fine example of a 14th-century fortified baronial house. Mary, Queen of Scots retreated here after the murder of Rizzio.

THE GRASSMARKET,
directly south of the Castle
One of the oldest parts of the city, where the right to hold regular markets was granted in 1477 by James III.

LAURISTON CASTLE,
Cramond Rd South, Davidson's Mains
☎ 0131 336 2060
Well worth seeking out for an excellent guided tour, this late 16th-century tower house with 19th-century additions is noted for its beautifully preserved Edwardian interior.

NELSON MONUMENT,
Calton Hill ☎ 0131 556 2716
Shaped like an upturned telescope, it was unveiled in 1816 after Nelson's victory at the Battle of Trafalgar in 1806. Climb to the top for wonderful views.

FALKIRK & THE LOTHIANS

ANTONINE WALL,
Falkirk
Built to replace Hadrian's Wall, this was the northernmost frontier of the Roman Empire and much remains to be seen.

BLACKNESS CASTLE,
Linlithgow, West Lothian ☎ 01506 834807
Commanding a dramatic position on the shores of the Firth of Forth, this impressive, 16th-century medieval artillery fortification was one of the most important fortresses in Scotland.

CAIRNPAPPLE HILL,
Torphichen, West Lothian
An ancient temple where prehistoric man worshipped and buried his dead more than 3,000 years ago. You can explore the burial chamber.

CRICHTON CASTLE,
Crichton, Midlothian ☎ 01875 320017
A large and sophisticated castle dating back to the 14th century, with a spectacular facade of Italian stonework on the 16th-century wing.

DIRLETON CASTLE,
Dirleton, East Lothian ☎ 01620 850330
Romantic sandstone castle, dating back in part to the 13th century, features a pit-prison, a dungeon, and, within its grounds, a 16th-century garden.

HAILES CASTLE,
East Linton, East Lothian ☎ 0131 668 8800
Beautifully situated ruins of a fortified manor house featuring a 16th-century chapel.

LINLITHGOW PALACE,
Linlithgow, West Lothian ☎ 01506 842896
Birthplace of Mary, Queen of Scots and James V, and home to all the Stewart kings, this magnificent ruin of a great palace stands above the long high street and overlooks the small loch. The great hall and chapel are particularly fine. The grounds are ideal for a picnic.

ST MICHAEL'S CHURCH,
Linlithgow, West Lothian
Regarded by many to be the finest parish church in Scotland, St Michael's has stood for over 750 years and its rich and royal history has seen the hosting of many events, including the General Assembly of the Church of Scotland c1600.

EDINBURGH PARKS & GARDENS

HOLYROOD PARK,
north side of Holyrood Palace
The largest area of open ground within the city (642 acres/260ha) provides an easy escape into the countryside for both residents and visitors alike. Climb to the top of Arthur's Seat for stunning views across the city.

MALLENY GARDEN,
Balerno ☎ 0131 449 2283
Set around a 17th-century house (not open), these delightful gardens feature shrub roses, the National Bonsai Collection for Scotland and a fine woodland garden.

PRINCES ST GARDENS,
Princes St
Opened in 1876 and containing the world's oldest floral clock (1903), they provide a welcome respite from the hustle and bustle of Edinburgh's busiest shopping street.

ROYAL BOTANIC GARDEN,
Inverleith Row ☎ 0131 552 7171
'Strollable' distance from Princes St, the garden, established here in 1823, offers 70 acres of peace and greenery and is a welcome place to escape to from the bustling city centre. Wander around an arboretum, a woodland garden, magnificent rock gardens and see the largest rhododendron collection in Britain.

GREAT FOR KIDS

EDINBURGH

GORGIE CITY FARM,
51 Gorgie Rd ☎ 0131 337 4202
Meet friendly farm anaimals, explore the wildlife garden and pond and learn about agriculture and country life in the interpretation centre,

ROYAL OBSERVATORY VISITOR CENTRE,
Blackford Hill ☎ 0131 668 8405
Discover the fascinating world of modern astronomy and the work of Scotland's national observatory. Take a tour of 'The Universe' exhibition, where models, 'hands-on' exhibits, videos, computer games and stunning deep-sky photographs explain the solar system. Don't miss the 'Star Chamber', an interactive discovery room.

EDINBURGH ZOO,
Murrayfield *2m/3.2km W on A8*
☎ 0131 334 9171
Explore Scotland's largest and most exciting wildlife attraction, set in 80 acres of leafy hillside parkland. Children will love the famous 'penguin parade' (March-September) through the zoo.

FALKIRK & THE LOTHIANS

ALMOND VALLEY HERITAGE CENTRE,
Millfield, Livingston Village, West Lothian
☎ 01506 414957
Innovative museum which preserves, demonstrates and explains many aspects of West Lothian's varied history. See an oil worker's home, learn about the oil industry; come face to face with fossil life of 340 million years ago; explore Livingston Mill and its array of agricultural vehicles, and meet friendly farm animals at Mill Farm.

DALKEITH COUNTRY PARK,
Dalkeith, Midlothian ☎ 0131 654 1666
Exciting woodland adventure playground, with aerial ropeways, giant slides and a wildwest fort, fields of Highland cows and wild boar and beautiful waymarked walks.

EDINBURGH BUTTERFLY & INSECT WORLD,
Dobbies Garden Centre, Lasswade, Midlothian ☎ 0131 663 4932
Stroll through the wonderful world of an exotic rainforest, with tropical pools and hundreds of richly coloured butterflies flying all around you. Plus live scorpions and tarantulas. Shop, tearoom, adventure playground.

THE LINLITHGOW STORY,
High St, Linlithgow, West Lothian
☎/@ 01506 842498
Learn about the Kings and the Commoners who made Linlithgow's history.

HOMES & GARDENS

FALKIRK & THE LOTHIANS

ARNISTON HOUSE,
Gorebridge, Midlothian ☎ 01875 830238
An 18th-century house designed by Adam and featuring fine furniture and Scottish portraiture. Tearoom.

CALLENDAR HOUSE,
Callendar Park, Falkirk ☎ 01324 503770
Standing in attractive parkland, with a wide range of leisure pursuits, this impressive mansion features an exhibition which illustrates the 900 year history of the building. Costumed interpreters describe early 19th-century life in the restored working kitchen. Period shops, Victorian library, Interpretive areas and interactive displays. Tearoom.

INVERESK LODGE GARDEN,
Inveresk, Musselburgh, East Lothian
☎ 0131 665 1855
Fronting a fine 17th-century house (not open), this charming terraced garden features a fine rose collection.

LENNOXLOVE HOUSE & GARDENS,
Haddington, East Lothian ☎ 01620 823720
Beautiful stately home displaying fine portraits and artefacts relating to Mary, Queen of Scots.

BIG OUTDOORS

EDINBURGH

PENTLAND HILLS,
south-west of the city
Escape the bustling city and head for these rolling grassy hills for breezy, invigorating walks and fine views across the city to the Moorfoot Hills.

FALKIRK & THE LOTHIANS

BASS ROCK,
(island in the Firth of Forth - accessible by boat from North Berwick)
A spectacular setting for nesting pairs of gannets, puffins, guillemots and razorbills.

JOHN MUIR COUNTRY PARK,
Dunbar, East Lothian
70 hectares of excellent coastal habitat, varying from salt marsh to sea buckthorn, around the estuary of the River Tyne. Excellent walks in all seasons.

LINLITHGOW LOCH,
Linlithgow, West Lothian
A rare undrained natural loch. A leaflet illustrates the flora and fauna you may see on a delightful walk around the loch.

MUIRAVONSIDE COUNTRY PARK,
Linlithgow, West Lothian
Woodland walks, relics of former industry and the recreation of a typical 19th-century lowland Scottish farm.

EDINBURGH SHOPPING

Shops are generally open from 9am to 5.30pm, Monday to Saturday, with late night shopping on Thursdays until 8pm. Larger city stores are also open on a Sunday.

ANTIQUES

Head for Bruntsfield Place, St Stephen Street in Stockbridge, Causewayside and the area around Dundas Street.

THE GRASSMARKET,
An area for antiques, arts and crafts shops, designer shops and Mr Wood's Fossil shop.

PRINCES STREET,

Contains most of the larger shops and department stores, including Jenners, the world's oldest independent store.

THE ROYAL MILE,

For souvenir shops and stalls, as well as some select, off-beat stores.

SHOPPING CENTRES,

Waverley Shopping Centre on Princes St has over 80 shops and eateries offering an unusual selection of designer fashion, food and gifts. Pedestrian precincts can also be found at Rose St, in the St James' Centre and the Waverley Market (crafts).

SPECIALIST FASHION & GIFT SHOPS,

Head for the area around William Street and Stafford Street.

ESSENTIAL INFORMATION

TOURIST INFORMATION

EDINBURGH

EDINBURGH & SCOTLAND INFORMATION CENTRE,
Waverley Market, Princes St EH2 2QP
☎ 0131 557 1700 ☎ 0131 557 5118
EDINBURGH AIRPORT TOURIST INFORMATION DESK,
☎ 0131 333 2167

FALKIRK & THE LOTHIANS

BO'NESS *seasonal,*
Car Park, Seaview Place, Bo'ness, Falkirk
☎ 01506 826626
DUNBAR *seasonal,*
High St, Dunbar, East Lothian EH42 1ES
☎ 01368 863353 ☎ 01368 864999
FALKIRK,
2-4 Glebe St, Falkirk ☎ 01324 620244
KINCARDINE BRIDGE *seasonal,*
Pine 'n Oak, Airth, Falkirk ☎ 01324 831422
LINLITHGOW,
Burgh Halls, The Cross, Linlithgow, West Lothian EH49 7AH
☎ 01506 844600 ☎ 01506 671373
OLD CRAIGHALL,
By Musselburgh, East Lothian EH21 8RE
☎ 0131 653 6172 ☎ 0131 653 2805
NORTH BERWICK,
Quality St, North Berwick, East Lothian EH39 4HJ
☎ 01620 892197 ☎ 01620 893667
INFORMATION DESK *seasonal,*
Scottish Mining Museum, Newtongrange, Midlothian EH22 4QN
☎ 0131 663 4262

ACCESS

AIR ACCESS

EDINBURGH INTERNATIONAL AIRPORT
☎ 0131 333 1000
AIRPORT INFORMATION
☎ 0131 344 3136
AIR UK ☎ 0345 666777
BRITISH AIRWAYS ☎ 0345 222111
BRITISH MIDLAND ☎ 0345 554554

CRAFTS

EDINBURGH

The city offers a good range of outlets for Scottish crafts and high quality gifts, as well as pottery, kilts, bagpipes and jewellery made in the city.

BYSANTIUM,
Victoria St
Antiques and crafts market.
CELTIC ART & TRAVEL CENTRE,
Royal Mile ☎ 0131 226 3133
THE GATEHOUSE POTTERY,
Craiglockhart Dr South ☎ 0131 455 7533
GEOFFREY (TAILOR) HIGHLAND CRAFTS,
Royal Mile ☎ 031 557 0256
Highland dress, kilts & tartans,

KILBERRY BAGPIPES,
Gilmore Pl ☎ 0131 221 9925
KINLOCH ANDERSON,
Dock St, Leith ☎ 0131 555 1390
Kilts, tartans from the Royal kiltmakers,
THE ROYAL MILE LIVING CRAFT CENTRE,
12 High St

FALKIRK & THE LOTHIANS

Lookout for pottery and ceramics, fine woollens and tweeds, glassware and small galleries specialising in paintings and crafts by local craftspeople.

BARBARA DAVIDSON POTTERY,
Larbert, Falkirk ☎ 01324 554430

EDINBURGH CRYSTAL VISITOR CENTRE,
Eastfield, Penicuik, Midlothian
☎ 01968 675128
See the various stages in the art of glassmaking during a guided tour

GLENEAGLES OF EDINBURGH,
Broxburn, West Lothian ☎ 01506 852566
Crystal factory shop and gift centre.

KEN LOCHHEAD GALLERY,
East Linton, East Lothian ☎ 01620 860442

SHAPE SCAPE CERAMICS,
The Pottery, Station Hill, North Berwick, East Lothian ☎ 01620 893157

ENTERTAINMENT

EDINBURGH

SCOTTISH EVENINGS

HAIL CALEDONIA SCOTTISH EVENING,
Carlton Highland Hotel ☎ 0131 556 7277
JAMIE'S SCOTTISH EVENING,
King James Thistle Hotel ☎ 0131 556 0111
PRINCE CHARLIE'S SCOTTISH EXTRAVAGANZA,
555 Castlehill, Royal Mile ☎ 0131 226 1555
SPIRIT OF SCOTLAND,
Kingston Mansion House Hotel, Craigend
☎ 0131 664 3363
A TASTE OF SCOTLAND,
Prestonfield House, Priestfield
☎ 0131 668 3346

CINEMAS

ABC FILM CINEMA,
120 Lothian Road ☎ 0131 228 1638
DOMINION CINEMA,
18 Newbattle Terrace ☎ 0131 447 4771
FILMHOUSE,
88 Lothian Road ☎ 0131 228 2688
ODEON CINEMA,
7 Clerk Street ☎ 0131 667 7331

THEATRE

CHURCH HILL THEATRE,
33 Morningside Road ☎ 0131 447 7597
EDINBURGH FESTIVAL THEATRE,
13-29 Nicolson Street ☎ 0131 529 6000
EDINBURGH PLAYHOUSE,
18-22 Greenside Place ☎ 0131 557 2590
KING'S THEATRE,

2 Leven Street ☎ 0131 220 4349
THE QUEEN'S HALL,
Clerk Street ☎ 0131 668 2019
ROSS OPEN AIR THEATRE,
Princes St Gardens ☎ 0131 220 4351
ROYAL LYCEUM THEATRE COMPANY,
Grindlay Street ☎ 0131 229 9697
THOMAS MORTON HALL,
28 Ferry Road ☎ 0131 554 1408
TRAVERSE THEATRE,
Cambridge Street ☎ 0131 228 1404

FALKIRK & THE LOTHIANS

THEATRE

BRUNTON THEATRE,
Musselburgh, East Lothian
☎ 0131 665 2240
HOWDEN PARK CENTRE,
Howden, Livingston, West Lothian
☎ 01506 433634

FOOD & DRINK

EDINBURGH

Edinburgh's many delicatessans offer a wide range of Scottish cheeses, smoked salmon, patés, preserves, shortbread biscuits and oatcakes, among other quality Scottish products. A wide range of regional bread goods and fancies are available in most bakers.

MACSWEEN OF EDINBURGH,
118 Bruntsfield Pl ☎ 0131 229 9141
Haggis and traditional Scottish foods.
ROYAL MILE WHISKIES,
379 High St ☎ 0131 225 3383
Specialist whisky store

FALKIRK & THE LOTHIANS

DUNBAR TROUT FARM & SMOKERY,
South Belton Farm, Dunbar, East Lothian
☎ 01368 863244
Smoked salmon and trout

OATERSON ARRAN LTD,
The Royal Burgh Bakery, Livingston, West Lothian ☎ 01506 431031
Producer of quality shortbread, Scottish mustards, preserves and chutneys.

WHISKY DISTILLERY TOURS

GLENKINCHIE DISTILLERY VISITOR CENTRE,
Pencaitland, East Lothian ☎ 01875 340451

TRANSPORT

BOAT TRIPS & CRUISES

EDINBURGH

EDINBURGH CANAL CENTRE,
Ratho ☎ 0131 333 1320
Canal cruising.
'MAID OF THE FORTH' CRUISES
South Queensferry ☎ 0131 331 4857
Sealife cruises and trips to Inchcolm Island

FALKIRK & THE LOTHIANS

LINLITHGOW UNION CANAL SOCIETY,
Manse Rd Basin, Linlithgow, West Lothian
☎ 01506 671215
Cruise for 2.5 hours to the Avon aqueduct on the Union Canal

BUS/COACH SERVICES

EDINBURGH

LOTHIAN REGIONAL TRANSPORT SERVICE,
27 Hanover Street ☎ 0131 554 4494
Edinburgh's major bus operator.

SCOTTISH CITYLINK COACHES LTD,
☎ 0990 505050

SMT EASTERN SCOTTISH BUSES,
☎ 0131 558 1616
Bus operator, including Citysprinter.

FALKIRK & THE LOTHIANS

LOWLAND BUSES,
Dalkeith, Midlothian ☎ 0131 663 1945

MIDLAND BLUEBIRD,
Larbert, Falkirk ☎ 01324 623901

CAR HIRE

EDINBURGH

ARNOLD CLARK HIRE DRIVE,
☎ 0131 228 4747

CARNIES CAR HIRE ☎ 0131 346 4155

CENTURY SELF DRIVE ☎ 0131 455 7314

CONDOR SELF DRIVE ☎ 0131 229 6333

EDINBURGH AIRPORT
ALAMO ☎ 0131 344 3250

AVIS RENT-A-CAR ☎ 0131 333 1866

FALKIRK & THE LOTHIANS

CONDOR SELF DRIVE,
Dalkeith, Midlothian ☎ 0131 660 1272

HARDIE OF LARBERT,
Larbert, Falkirk ☎ 01324 562799

JAMES MITCHELL,
North Berwick, East Lothian ☎ 01620 892232

PRACTICAL CAR & VAN RENTAL,
Pumpherston, West Lothian
☎ 0131 333 2335

WOODS CAR RENTAL,
Broxburn, West Lothian ☎ 01506 858660

CHAUFFEUR TOURS

CAPITAL EYES PERSONALISED TOURS,
☎ 0131 339 4863

LITTLE'S CHAUFFEUR DRIVE,
☎ 0131 334 2177

W L SLEIGH LTD GUIDED TOURS,
☎ 0131 337 3171

COACH/MINIBUS TOURS

GO BLUE BANANA ☎ 0131 556 2000
Adventurous tours of the Highlands.

GUIDE FRIDAY ☎ 0131 556 2244
Open-top guided bus tours of Edinburgh.

MACBACKPACKERS HOLIDAYS,
☎ 0131 220 1869
Tours of the Highlands.

RABBIE'S TRAIL BURNERS,
☎ 0131 226 3133
Guided minibus tours of the Highlands.

SCOTTISH HISTORIC TOURS,
☎ 0131 226 2202
Day tours of the Highlands.

CYCLE HIRE

EDINBURGH

CENTRAL CYCLE HIRE,
13 Lochrin Place ☎ 0131 228 6633

EDINBURGH CYCLE HIRE,
29 Blackfriars Street ☎ 0131 556 5560

THE NEW BIKE SHOP,
Tollcross ☎ 0131 228 6333

SANDY GILCHRIST CYCLES,
1 Cadzow Place, Abbeyhill ☎ 0131 652 1760

FALKIRK & THE LOTHIANS

CYCLE SERVICES,
3 Hardgate, Haddington, East Lothian
☎ 01620 826989

HELICOPTER TOURS

FORTH HELICOPTERS,
Edinburgh Airport ☎ 0131 554 4261

TRAINS

Frequent trains link Edinburgh with London and a half-hourly service connects Edinburgh with Glasgow. Passenger enquiries ☎ 0345 484950.

SPORT & LEISURE

ACTIVITY CENTRES

MAVIS HALL PARK,
Humbie, East Lothian ☎ 01875 833733

SCOTTISH ARCHERY CENTRE,
North Berwick, East Lothian ☎ 01620 850401

ANGLING

EDINBURGH

Brown and rainbow trout can be fished at many of the reservoirs and lochs located around Edinburgh, with carp, perch, roach and tench in Duddingston Loch (permit required). Fishing is also permitted in the Union Canal and in the Water of Leith. There is sea and shore fishing at South Queensferry, at the mouth of the River Almond, near Cramond, and along the seafront between Seafield and Portobello. For details contact the Tourist Information Centre.

FALKIRK & THE LOTHIANS

For the best fishing head for Gladhouse, Glencorse, Edgelaw and Rosebery Reservoirs, the Union Canal, Beecraigs Loch, near Linlithgow, and many of the coastal harbours for boats and excellent sea angling.

CYCLING

Specially marked cycle lanes exist within the city and cyclists may use the bus lanes. A good network of off-road cycle paths link the city with outlying areas, incorporating old railway lines, riverside paths, through parks, and along the coast. More adventurous mountain bikers will find waymarked routes for all abilities in the Pentland Hills. A map of cycle routes in Edinburgh and across the Lothians, published by Spokes, is available from the Tourist Information Centre.

GOLF COURSES

For a full list of golf courses in Edinburgh, Falkirk & The Lothians, please refer to the AA Guide to Golf Courses, or contact the Tourist Information Centres.

EDINBURGH

LOTHIANBURN ☎ 0131 445 2206
Testing hillside course in the Pentland Hills.

MARRIOTT DALMAHOY HOTEL GOLF & COUNTRY CLUB,
☎ 0131 333 1845
Two outstanding upland courses, meandering around the lake and across picturesque streams.

ROYAL BURGESS ☎ 0131 339 2075
The oldest golfing society in the world, instituted in 1735, with a pleasant and varied parkland course.

FALKIRK & THE LOTHIANS

DUNBAR,
East Lothian ☎ 01368 862317
One of Scotland's oldest links courses. Strong sea breezes can make this a very challenging test.

MUIRFIELD GOLF CLUB,
Gullane, East Lothian ☎ 01620 842123
One of the finest courses, established in 1744.

NORTH BERWICK GOLF CLUB,
East Lothian ☎ 01620 892135
Classic championship links.

HORSE RACING

MUSSELBURGH RACECOURSE,
Musselburgh, East Lothian ☎ 0131 665 7137
Classic flat racing and jumping throughout the year at this popular racecourse overlooking the Firth of Forth.

ICE RINK

MURRAYFIELD ICE RINK,
Riversdale Crescent ☎ 0131 337 6933

LEISURE CENTRES

EDINBURGH

AINSLIE PARK,
Pilton Drive ☎ 0131 551 2400

CRAIGLOCKHART SPORTS CENTRE,
Colinton Road ☎ 0131 443 0101

GRACEMOUNT LEISURE CENTRE,
Gracemount Drive ☎ 0131 658 1940

JACK KANE CENTRE,
Niddrie Mains Road ☎ 0131 669 0404

MEADOWBANK SPORTS CENTRE,
139 London Road ☎ 0131 661 5351

PORTOBELLO LEISURE CENTRE,
West Bank St, Portobello ☎ 0131 669 0878

FALKIRK & THE LOTHIANS

AUBIGNY SPORTS CENTRE,
Haddington, East Lothian
☎ 01620 826806

BATHGATE SPORTS CENTRE,
West Lothian ☎ 01506 634561

BONNYRIGG LEISURE CENTRE,
Midlothian ☎ 0131 663 7579

BUBBLES LEISURE CENTRE,
Livingston, West Lothian ☎ 01506 461886

DRUMYAT LEISURE CENTRE,
Menstrie, Falkirk ☎ 01259 769439

DUNBAR LEISURE CENTRE,
East Lothian ☎ 01368 865456

GRANGEMOUTH SPORTS COMPLEX,
Falkirk ☎ 01324 504560

KIRKLISTON LEISURE CENTRE,
West Lothian ☎ 0131 333 4700

LINLITHGOW LEISURE CENTRE,
West Lothian ☎ 01506 846358

LOANHEAD LEISURE CENTRE,
Midlothian ☎ 0131 440 4516

MEADOWMILL SPORTS CENTRE,
Tranent, East Lothian ☎ 01875 614900

MUSSELBURGH SPORTS CENTRE,
East Lothian ☎ 0131 653 6367

NORTH BERWICK LEISURE CENTRE,
East Lothian ☎ 01620 893454

RIDING

EDINBURGH

TOWER FARM RIDING STABLES,
85 Liberton Drive ☎ 0131 664 3375

FALKIRK & THE LOTHIANS

APPIN EQUESTRIAN CENTRE,
Drem, North Berwick, East Lothian
☎ 01620 880366

EDINBURGH & LASSWADE RIDING CENTRE,
Lasswade, Midlothian ☎ 0131 663 7676

FALKIRK RIDING CENTRE,
Woodend Farm, Falkirk ☎ 01324 625626

GRANGE RIDING CENTRE,
West Calder, West Lothian ☎ 01506 871219

HOUSTON FARM RIDING SCHOOL,
Broxburn, West Lothian ☎ 01506 811351

PENTLAND HILLS ICELANDICS,
Carlops, Midlothian ☎ 01968 661095

WESTMUIR RIDING CENTRE LTD,
By Winchburgh, West Lothian
☎ 0131 331 2990

RUGBY

MURRAYFIELD SCOTTISH RUGBY UNION GROUND,
Roseburn Street, Edinburgh
☎ 0131 346 5000

SAILING

PORT EDGAR SAILING SCHOOL,
South Queensferry, Edinburgh
☎ 0131 331 3330
Cramond and Portobello are also popular places for boating and sailing.

SKIING *Dry ski slopes*

MEADOWMILL SPORTS CENTRE,
Tranent, East Lothian ☎ 01875 614900

MIDLOTHIAN SKI CENTRE,
Hillend, Midlothian ☎ 0131 445 4433

POLMONTHILL SKI CENTRE,
Polmont, Falkirk ☎ 01324 503835

SWIMMING

EDINBURGH

see also Leisure Centres

DALRY SWIM CENTRE,
Caledonian Crescent ☎ 0131 313 3964

GLENOGLE SWIM CENTRE,
Glenogle Road ☎ 0131 343 6376

LEITH WATERWORLD,
Easter Rd, Leith ☎ 0131 555 6000

ROYAL COMMONWEALTH POOL,
Dalkeith Road ☎ 0131 667 7211

FALKIRK & THE LOTHIANS

BEACHES
Fine sandy beaches stretch from Edinburgh to Dunbar, notably at Gullane, Belhaven Bay, North Berwick and Dunbar, offering safe bathing in shallow waters.

ARMADALE SWIMMING POOL,
West Lothian ☎ 01501 730465

BATHGATE SWIMMING POOL,
West Lothian ☎ 01506 652783

BROXBURN SWIMMING POOL,
West Lothian ☎ 01506 854723

NEWBATTLE SWIMMING POOL,
Newtongrange, Midlothian
☎ 0131 663 4485

WHITBURN SWIMMING POOL,
West Lothian ☎ 01501 743496

TOURS

By coach:

CLAYMORE TRAVEL,
Stenhousemuir, Falkirk ☎ 01324 551919

WILLIAM HUNTER,
Loanhead, Midlothian ☎ 0131 440 0704

WILSON OF BONNYRIGG,
Newtongrange, Midlothian
☎ 0131 663 8005

Other:

ROUTES TO ROOTS,
Livingston, West Lothian ☎ 01506 416854
Tours/transfers in executive cars.

TRAPRAIN TRAILS,
Gullane, East Lothian ☎ 01620 842113
Tours in East Lothian and the Borders.

WALKING

From breezy coastal walks, pleasant woodland rambles and level canalside strolls to energetic rough moorland hikes in the Lammermuir and Pentland Hills, the region has a variety of terrains to satisfy walkers of all levels of experience.

EDINBURGH WALKING TOURS

AULD ALLIANCE TOURS,
44 Cluny Gardens ☎ 0131 447 3810

Historical town walks.

AULD REEKIE TOURS,
29 Niddry Street ☎ 0131 557 4700
Edinbugh's grisly past and ghostly present.

THE CADIES - WITCHERY TOURS,
352 Castlehill ☎ 0131 225 6745

EDINBURGH FESTIVAL VOLUNTARY GUIDES,
Clovenstone Park ☎ 0131 453 4878

MERCAT GHOST & HISTORY WALKS,
47 Willowbrae ☎/℅ 0131 661 4541

ROBIN'S GHOST & HISTORY TOURS,
66 Willowbrae Road ☎ 0131 661 0125

WATERSPORTS

MUSSELBURGH WATER SKI CLUB,
East Lothian ☎ 0131 665 6482

WINDSURFING
Conditions are ideal at Longniddry and Gullane.

THE LOTHIANS

If you want to escape the bustle and hectic pace of Edinburgh for a few hours, then Lothian, with its fine blend of castles and coastal scenery, is just the place to explore and relax. Midlothian offers the chance to step back a few centuries by visiting various ancient churches and defensive strongholds.

East Lothian includes some impressive houses and gardens, miles of fertile countryside and a stretch of scenic coastline.

To the west of Edinburgh lies the Forth Road Bridge and beyond is West Lothian and Falkirk, where the many attractions of Linlithgow are an essential part of any tour in this corner of Scotland.

WHERE TO STAY

5-STAR HOTELS

AA RECOMMENDED

EDINBURGH

BALMORAL ❀
1 Princes St EH2 2EQ
☎ 0131 556 2414 ℻ 0131 557 8740
Elegant Edwardian building. Comfortable
and well equipped bedrooms and
excellent suites. Popular Brasserie, elegant
Palm Court , and Lobby bar. Formal, yet
intimate, restaurant.
*£££ 186 bedrooms No smoking in 43
bedrooms Lift Night porter Air conditioning
Indoor swimming pool (heated) Sauna
Solarium Gym Beauty salon Aromatheraphy
massage Hairdressers No smoking area in
restaurant* 🐦

CALEDONIAN ❀❀
Princes St EH1 2AB
☎ 0131 459 9988 ℻ 0131 225 6632
Popular hotel. Tastefully furnished
bedrooms some with Castle views.
Extensive lounge and bar areas, and
elegant Pompadour Restaurant.
*£££ 236 bedrooms No smoking in 58
bedrooms No dogs (ex guide dogs) Lift Night
porter Indoor swimming pool (heated) Sauna
Solarium Gym Jacuzzi/spa Weekly live
entertainment No smoking area in
restaurant* 🐦

SHERATON GRAND ❀❀❀
1 Festival Square EH3 9SR
☎ 0131 229 9131 ℻ 0131 228 4510
A professional, discreet level of service at
this imposing hotel. Smartly appointed, air
conditioned bedrooms. Boutique shops.
Popular Lobby Bar. Classical, innovative
menus in restaurant.
*£££ 261 bedrooms (23 fmly) No
smoking in 75 bedrooms No dogs (ex guide
dogs) Lift Night porter Air conditioning
Indoor swimming pool (heated) Sauna
Solarium Gym Jacuzzi/spa Weekly live
entertainment* 🐦

4-STAR HOTELS

AA RECOMMENDED

CARLTON HIGHLAND ❀
North Bridge EH1 1SD
*(on North Bridge which links Princes St to the
Royal Mile, opposite `The Scotsman' offices)*
☎ 0131 556 7277 ℻ 0131 556 2691
Popular hotel close to the Royal Mile.
Bedrooms range from suites and executive
rooms, to standard rooms. Rendezvous in
lounge , Carlyles Patisserie, Quills or
Eureka restaurants.
*£££ 197 bedrooms (20 fmly) No
smoking in 56 bedrooms Lift Night porter
Indoor swimming pool (heated) Squash
Snooker Sauna Solarium Gym Pool table
Jacuzzi/spa Table tennis Dance studio
Creche Weekly live entertainment ch fac No
smoking area in restaurant* 🐦

GEORGE INTER-CONTINENTAL ❀❀
19-21 George St EH2 2PB (City centre, East
side parallel to Princess Street)
☎ 0131 225 1251 ℻ 0131 226 5644
Long established hotel, at the city's heart.
Popular, clubby bar, ornate 18th-century
Carvers Restaurant, the rosette awarded
Chambertin Restaurant. Comfortably
appointed bedrooms vary in size.
*£££ 195 bedrooms No smoking in 57
bedrooms No dogs (ex guide dogs) Lift Night
porter No smoking area in restaurant* 🐦

MARRIOTT DALMAHOY ❀❀
Kirknewton EH27 8EB
(7m W of Edinburgh on the A71)
☎ 0131 333 1845 ℻ 0131 333 1433
 Original Adam house retaining original
character.Traditional and modern
bedrooms. Imaginative menus in the
stylish Pentland Restaurant. *£££ 43
bedrooms 108 annexe bedrooms (3 fmly) No
smoking in 67 bedrooms No dogs (ex guide
dogs) Lift Night porter Indoor swimming
pool (heated) Golf 18 Tennis (hard) Sauna
Solarium Gym Putting green Jacuzzi/spa
Health & beauty treatments Steam room,
Dance Studio No smoking in restaurant* 🐦

ROYAL TERRACE
18 Royal Ter EH7 5AQ
*(from A1 - follow sign into city centre, turn left
at the end of London Road into Bleinheim
Place continuing onto Royal Terrace)*
☎ 0131 557 3222 ℻ 0131 557 5334
In attractive cobbled street, fine Georgian
mid-terrace building offering attractive,well
equipped bedrooms with whirlpool baths.
*£££ 94 bedrooms (19 fmly) No dogs (ex
guide dogs) Lift Night porter Indoor
swimming pool (heated) Sauna Solarium
Gym Jacuzzi/spa Beauty salon Giant
Chess No smoking area in restaurant* 🐦

SWALLOW ROYAL SCOT
111 Glasgow Rd EH12 8NF
(on A8 on western outskirts of city)
☎ 0131 334 9191 ℻ 0131 316 4507
This purpose-built hotel attracts an
international clientele. Smart bedrooms -
spacious executive rooms and smaller
standard rooms. Bar and restaurant offer
carvery and carte meals.
*£££ 259 bedrooms (17 fmly) No
smoking in 160 bedrooms Lift Night porter
Indoor swimming pool (heated) Sauna
Solarium Gym Jacuzzi/spa Steam room* 🐦

3-STAR HOTELS

AA RECOMMENDED

Braid Hills

APEX INTERNATIONAL
31/35 Grassmarket EH1 2HS
☎ 0131 300 3456 📠 0131 220 5345
Modern hotel in city's Old Town. Bedrooms
are spacious and well equipped.
Restaurant with spectacular views.
*£ 99 bedrooms No smoking in 78 bedrooms
No dogs Lift Night porter* 🍽

BARNTON THISTLE
Queensferry Rd, Barnton EH4 6AS
☎ 0131 339 1144 📠 0131 339 5521
Distinctive hotel near city, airport and
Forth Road Bridge. Bedrooms are well
equipped, though some are compact.
Plentiful free parking. *££££ 50 bedrooms
(9 fmly) Lift Night porter Sauna Weekly live
entertainment* 🍽

BRAID HILLS
134 Braid Rd, Braid Hills EH10 6JD
(2.5m S A702, opposite Braid Burn Park)
☎ 0131 447 8888 📠 0131 452 8477
Welcoming, popular business hotel.
Comfortable foyer lounge, cocktail bar and
restaurant. All day food in Buckstone Bistro.
*£££ 68 bedrooms (2 fmly) No smoking in
8 bedrooms Night porter No smoking in
restaurant* 🍽

BRUNTSFIELD
69/74 Bruntsfield Place EH10 4HH
(on A702, S of city centre)
☎ 0131 229 1393 📠 0131 229 5634
Uninterrupted views over Bruntsfield Links,
this hotel is in a quiet location, near city
centre. Attentive staff, with a genuine
interest in the guests. Several bars and
restaurant.
*£££ 50 bedrooms (2 fmly) No smoking in
22 bedrooms Lift Night porter No smoking
in restaurant* 🍽

CHANNINGS ❀
South Learmonth Gardens EH4 1EZ
*(approach Edinburgh on the A90 from Forth
Road Bridge, follow signs for city centre)*
☎ 0131 315 2226 📠 0131 332 9631
Historic charm remains at this Edwardian
townhouse hotel with club-like

atmosphere. Smart, individual interior
designed bedrooms. Popular brasserie and
bar .
*££££ 48 bedrooms (1 fmly) No smoking
in 16 bedrooms No dogs (ex guide dogs) Lift
Night porter No smoking in restaurant
Closed 24–26 Dec* 🍽

EDINBURGH CAPITAL MOAT HOUSE
187 Clermiston Rd EH12 6UG
*(take A90 over the Forth Road Bridge, along
Queensbury Rd, hotel at top on the right)*
☎ 0131 535 9988 📠 0131 334 9712
Modern hotel near airport and city centre.
Bedrooms are bright and well equipped.
Meals in room, or in Monty's Restaurant.
*££ 111 bedrooms (10 fmly) No smoking in
6 bedrooms Lift Night porter Indoor
swimming pool (heated) Sauna Solarium
Gym Pool table Jacuzzi/spa Leisure Club
Steam room Weekly live entertainment No
smoking in restaurant* 🍽

GREENS HOTEL
24 Eglinton Crescent EH12 5BY
☎ 0131 337 1565 📠 0131 346 2990
Sound value for money at this friendly
hotel. Bedrooms include superior and
standard rooms. Bar, choice of restaurants,
and quiet lounge. *££ 57 bedrooms (3 fmly)
Lift Night porter No smoking area in
restaurant* 🍽

HOLIDAY INN GARDEN COURT
107 Queensferry Rd EH4 3HL
(on the A90 approx 1m from city centre)
☎ 0131 332 2442 📠 0131 332 3408
Centrally situated modern hotel with
panoramic city views. Spacious public
areas and ample parking.
*119 bedrooms (53 fmly) No smoking in 59
bedrooms Lift Night porter Gym No
smoking in restaurant* 🍽

KING JAMES THISTLE
107 Leith St EH1 3SW
☎ 0131 556 0111 📠 0131 557 5333
Just off Princess Street, this modern hotel
offers smart bedrooms, a choice of bars
and dining options.
*£££ 143 bedrooms (4 fmly) No smoking in
48 bedrooms No dogs (ex guide dogs) Lift
Night porter Weekly live entertainment* 🍽

KINGS MANOR
100 Milton Rd East EH15 2NP
*(follow A720 east until Old Craighall
Junction then head left into the city until
turning right at the A1/A199 intersection,
hotel 200m on right)*
☎ 0131 669 0444 📠 0131 669 6650
Former Laird's home converted to create
this popular hotel. Executive to standard
modern rooms. Foyer lounge, a choice of
bars and restaurant.
££ 69 bedrooms (8 fmly) Lift Night porter
🍽

MALMAISON ❀
1 Tower Place, Leith EH6 7DB
*(A900 from city centre towards Leith, at
bottom of Leith walk go straight over lights
through 2 more sets of lights, left into Tower St-
hotel on right)*
☎ 0131 555 6868 📠 0131 555 6999
Originally a Seaman's Mission, now a most
individual and stylish hotel. Bedrooms,
understated in decor, offer mini bar, video
and stereo system. Bar and brasserie.
*££ 60 bedrooms (6 fmly) Lift Night porter
Gym* 🍽

Bruntsfield

Channings

NORTON HOUSE ◉◉

Ingliston EH28 8LX

(off A8, 5m W of city centre)

☎ 0131 333 1275 ⓕ 0131 333 5305

In fifty acre park, close to airport and motorway network. Smart, thoughtfully equipped accommodation. Comfortable lounge areas, Oak bar and Conservatory restaurant.

££££ 47 bedrooms (2 fmly) No smoking in 15 bedrooms Night porter Archery Laser clay pigeon shooting ch fac ◥

OLD WAVERLEY

43 Princes St EH2 2BY

(in the centre of city, opposite the Scott Monument)

☎ 0131 556 4648 ⓕ 0131 557 6316

Very conveniently positioned hotel (dating back to 1883) provides bright, well equipped bedrooms. Restaurant offers a carvery, carte menu and excellent views.

££££ 66 bedrooms (6 fmly) No smoking in 8 bedrooms Lift Night porter No smoking in restaurant ◥

PRESTONFIELD HOUSE

Priestfield Rd EH6 5UT

☎ 0131 668 3346

Set in 13 acres of parkland, one of Scotland's finest historic mansions. Convenient for city centre. Spacious, smartly appointed bedrooms. Small team of friendly staff.

31 bedrooms

QUALITY COMMODORE

Marine Dr, Cramond Foreshore EH4 5EP

☎ 0131 336 1700 ⓕ 0131 336 4934

This hotel enjoys marvellous views over the Firth of Forth, especially from the restauant. Well equipped bedrooms vary in size and style.

£££ 86 bedrooms (6 fmly) No smoking in 30 bedrooms Lift Night porter P Indoor swimming pool (heated) Sauna Solarium Gym Jacuzzi/spa No smoking area in restaurant ◥

ROXBURGHE

38 Charlotte Square EH2 4HG

☎ 0131 225 3921 ⓕ 0131 220 2518

Well established hotel providing high quality service by smartly presented staff. Informal Melrose Bistro ideal for lunches, plus an elegant restaurant.

£££ 75 bedrooms (1 fmly) Lift Night porter No smoking in restaurant ◥

Malmaison

2-STAR HOTELS

AA RECOMMENDED

Allison House

ALLISON HOUSE

15/17 Mayfield Gardens EH9 2AX

(1m S of city centre on A701)

☎ 0131 667 8049 ⓕ 0131 667 5001

Genuine hospitality and personal service at this comfortable family run hotel. Bedrooms with attractive fabrics vary in size and style.

££ 23 bedrooms (5 fmly) ch fac No smoking in restaurant ◥

HARP TOBY

St John's Rd, Corstorphine EH12 8AX *(3.5m W)*

☎ 0131 334 4750 ⓕ 0131 334 6941

Successful hotel with convenient access to central amenities and airport. Choice of bars and ever popular Toby Carving Room offering excellent value fare.

24 bedrooms (2 fmly) No smoking in 9 bedrooms No dogs (ex guide dogs) Night porter ◥

THE HOWARD ◉◉

Great King St EH3 6QH

(turn off Princes St into Frederick St for 0.5m and turn right into Great King St. Go past traffic lights, hotel on left)

☎ 0131 557 3500 ⓕ 0131 557 6515

Very individual classical hotel with beautifully furnished rooms including three mini suites. Elegant breakfast room, and modern bar/restaurant for innovative menus.

££££ 15 bedrooms No dogs (ex guide dogs) Lift Night porter No smoking in restaurant Closed 4–8 Dec ◥

Call the AA Hotel Booking Service on
0990 050505 to book at AA recognised
hotels and B&Bs in the UK,
or through our internet site:
http://www.theaa.co.uk/hotels

Thrums Private Hotel

IONA
Strathearn Place EH9 2AL

(from Morningside Rd (main access into Edinburgh) turn left at lights into Chamberlain Rd, turn right at the end of the road, at junction turn left)

☎ 0131 447 6264 & 0131 447 5050
🖷 0131 452 8574

In a leafy residential area offering good value accommodation. Bedrooms are bright and well maintained. The bar has a loyal local following.

£ 17 bedrooms (3 fmly) ⬛

MURRAYFIELD
18 Corstorphine Rd EH12 6HN

☎ 0131 337 1844 🖷 0131 346 8159

Close to the national rugby stadium. Spacious bar is a popular rendezvous while the smart restaurant offers extensive eating options.

23 bedrooms 10 annexe bedrooms (1 fmly) Night porter Closed 2 days Xmas & 2 days New Year ⬛

ORWELL LODGE
29 Polwarth Terrace EH11 1NH

(From A702 turn into Gilmore Place (opposite King's Theatre) hotel 1m on the left)

☎ 0131 229 1044 🖷 0131 228 9492

Sympathetically converted Victorian house, now a friendly hotel. Bedrooms are nicely presented. No lounge but the bar is spacious.

££ 10 bedrooms No smoking in all bedrooms or restaurant No dogs (ex guide dogs) Weekly live entertainment Closed 25 Dec ⬛

ROTHESAY
8 Rothesay Place EH3 7SL

(follow M8 into Edinburgh to the Haymarket Station, turn left at traffic lights into Palmerston Place, Rothesay Place is second on right)

☎ 0131 225 4125 🖷 0131 220 4350

Victorian terrace with modern main house bedrooms and ten luxurious bedrooms in adjacent town house. Foyer lounge, bar and smart restaurant.

£ 46 bedrooms (3 fmly) Lift Night porter No smoking in restaurant ⬛

Orwell Lodge

ROYAL ETTRICK
13 Ettrick Rd EH10 5BJ

(from W end of Princes Street follow Lothian Road, turn right onto Gilmour Place for 0.75m, hotel on right behind Bowling Green)

☎ 0131 228 6413 🖷 0131 229 7330

Set in a residential suburb this hotel offers well equipped bedrooms, a bar renowned for real ales and a two-tier conservatory serving good-value meals.

££ 12 bedrooms (2 fmly) No smoking area in restaurant ⬛

THRUMS PRIVATE HOTEL
14 Minto St EH9 1RQ

☎ 0131 667 5545 & 0131 667 8545
🖷 0131 667 8707

Two adjacent Victorian houses comprise this homely and relaxing hotel. Cosy bar, residents' lounge and conservatory dining room.

££ 6 bedrooms 8 annexe bedrooms (5 fmly) Closed Xmas ⬛

FORTE POSTHOUSE EDINBURGH
Corstorphine Rd EH12 6UA

(adjacent to Edinburgh Zoo)

☎ 0131 334 0390 🖷 0131 334 9237

Bright hotel offers modern, well equipped bedrooms and an informal bar and dining area.

204 bedrooms

HILTON NATIONAL EDINBURGH
69 Belford Rd EH4 3DG

☎ 0131 332 2545 🖷 0131 332 3805

Bright hotel offers modern, well equipped bedrooms and an informal bar and dining area.

££££ 144 bedrooms

TRAVEL INN
288 Willowbrae Rd EH8 7NG

(2m from City east)

☎ 0131 661 3396 🖷 0131 652 2789

This modern building offers smart, spacious and well equipped bedrooms, suitable for family use.

££ (fmly room) 39 bedrooms

TRAVEL INN
Carberry Rd, Inveresk EH21 8PT

☎ 0131 665 3005

Modern building offers smart, spacious and well equipped bedrooms, suitable for family use. Refreshments at the nearby family restaurant.

££ (fmly room) 40 bedrooms

TRAVEL INN (CITY CENTRE)
1 Morrison St EH3 8DN

☎ 01582 414341 🖷 01582 400024

Modern building offers smart, spacious and well equipped bedrooms, suitable for family use. Refreshments at the nearby family restaurant.

££ (fmly room) 128 bedrooms

Iona

BED & BREAKFAST ACCOMMODATION

AA RECOMMENDED

DRUMMOND HOUSE ◨◨◨◨◨
17 Drummond Place EH3 6PL
(NW corner of Drummond Place at E end of Great King St)
☎ 0131 557 9189 ⊕ 0131 557 9189
Lovingly restored Georgian house provides accommodation furnished with artefacts from around the world. Breakfast served at one table in dining room.
£££ 4 bedrooms No smoking No dogs No children under 12yrs Closed Xmas ⊛

ELMVIEW ◨◨◨◨◨
15 Glengyle Ter EH3 9LN
(take A702 S up Lothian Road, turn first left past Kings Theatre into Valley Field Street one way system leading to Glengyle Terrace)
☎ 0131 228 1973 ⊕ 0131 622 3271
Luxurious guesthouse offering a very high standard of accommodation. Bedrooms have many extras including ironing boards.
£££ 3 bedrooms No smoking No dogs No children under 15yrs ⊛

SIBBET HOUSE ◨◨◨◨◨
26 Northumberland St EH3 6LS
☎ 0131 556 1078 ⊕ 0131 557 9445
Imposing town house affording the visitor every comfort. Antique furniture throughout but modern facilities in all bedrooms.
£££ 5 bedrooms (2 fmly) No smoking No dogs ⊛

ACORN LODGE ◨◨◨◨
26 Pilrig St EH6 5AJ
☎ 0131 555 1557 ⊕ 0131 555 4475
Tastefully appointed, centrally situated Georgian terraced home. Bright airy bedrooms with attractive antique pine decor and fabrics. *£ 7 bedrooms (2 fmly) No smoking No dogs (ex guide dogs)* ⊛

ADAM HOTEL ◨◨◨◨
19 Lansdowne Crescent EH12 5EH
(from Airport follow signs City Centre and on reaching Haymarket Terrace turn left oppr Station car park and follow road which bears right)
☎ 0131 337 1148 ⊕ 0131 337 1729
Part of a Georgian crescent, retaining many original features, facing a park.

Bedrooms are attractively furnished, with smartly tiled bathrooms.
££ 13 bedrooms (3 fmly) No smoking No dogs (ex guide dogs) Licensed ⊛

ASHGROVE HOUSE ◨◨◨◨
12 Osborne Ter EH12 5HG
(on A8 between Murrayfield & Haymarket opposite Donaldson's College for Deaf, under 1 mile to Princes Street)
☎ 0131 337 5014 ⊕ 0131 337 5043
Welcoming atmosphere prevails at this family-run guest house with attractive modern-style bedrooms, elegant dining room and sun lounge.
£ 7 bedrooms (2 fmly) No smoking (ex sun lounge) No dogs (ex guide dogs) ⊛

BONNINGTON ◨◨◨◨
202 Ferry Rd EH6 4NW
☎ 0131 554 7610
Semi-detached, immaculate Georgian house with stylish colour schemes and furnishings. Lounge, with grand piano books and board games.
£ 6 bedrooms (3 fmly) No smoking in bedrooms or in dining room

BRUNSWICK HOTEL ◨◨◨◨
7 Brunswick St EH7 5JB
☎ 0131 556 1238 ⊕ 0131 557 1404
Elegant Georgian terraced house near city centre. Spacious lounge with plush, deep seating. Well equipped bedrooms include two on the ground floor.
£ 11 bedrooms (1 fmly) No smoking No dogs No children under 2yrs Closed Xmas ⊛

DORSTAN PRIVATE HOTEL ◨◨◨◨
7 Priestfield Rd EH16 5HJ
(turn off A68 at Priestfield Road, just before Commonwealth Swimming Pool)
☎ 0131 667 6721 & 667 5138
⊕ 0131 668 4644
Personal attention at this tastefully appointed Victorian house, set in a desirable residential area. Bedrooms furnished and decorated to a high standard.
££ 14 bedrooms (2 fmly) No smoking No dogs (ex guide dogs) ⊛

Brunswick Hotel

ELLESMERE HOUSE ◨◨◨◨
11 Glengyle Ter EH3 9LN
(central Edinburgh off the A702)
☎ 0131 229 4823 ⊕ 0131 229 5285
Guests return time and time again here. Individually decorated modern bedrooms offer all the expected facilities.
£ 6 bedrooms (2 fmly) No smoking in dining room No dogs (ex guide dogs) No children under 10yrs

GROSVENOR GARDENS HOTEL ◨◨◨◨
1 Grosvenor Gardens EH12 5JU
☎ 0131 313 3415 ⊕ 0131 346 8732
Ground and lower ground floors of a Victorian Town House. Well proportioned bedrooms decorated to a high standard. Drawing room with deep cushioned sofas.
££ 8 bedrooms 3 fmly) No smoking in dining room or lounges No dogs (ex guide dogs) No children under 5yrs ⊛

A HAVEN ◨◨◨◨
180 Ferry Rd EH6 4NS
☎ 0131 554 6559 ⊕ 0131 554 5252
Welcoming town house tastefully decorated. Open plan lounge/dining room for enjoyable home cooked Scottish fare.
££ 12 bedrooms (2 fmly) No smoking in bedrooms or in dining room No dogs (ex guide dogs) Licensed ⊛

INTERNATIONAL ◨◨◨◨
37 Mayfield Gardens EH9 2BX
(1.5m S of Princes Street on A701, 4m from the Straiton Junction on Edinburgh City by-pass)
☎ 0131 667 2511 ⊕ 0131 667 1112
Bedrooms, though variable in size, are attractively decorated and comfortably furnished in mixed modern styles. Combined lounge/dining room.
9 bedrooms (3 fmly) No smoking in 4 bedrooms No smoking in dining room or lounges No dogs (ex guide dogs) ⊛

Elmview

Crion

KEW ▨▨▨▨
1 Kew Ter, Murrayfield EH12 5JE *(situated on the main A8 Glasgow Road, 1m west of city centre, continue approx 2.75m to large rdbt straight on, located 6 buildings on right) (The Independents)*

☎ 0131 313 0700 ☏ 0131 313 0747

Immaculately maintained house. Smart contemporary bedrooms are very well equipped with many extras. Dinners are not served but light snacks are available.

££ 6 bedrooms (2 fmly) No smoking 🛏

KILDONAN LODGE HOTEL ▨▨▨▨
27 Craigmillar Park EH16 5PE
(from city by pass (A720), exit A701 city centre, continue approx 2.75m to large rdbt straight on, located 6 buildings on right) (The Independents)

☎ 0131 667 2793 ☏ 0131 667 9777

The owner's personal pride in maintaining high standards shows here. One bedroom with huge four poster for those looking for something special. Home cooked dinners now available.

£ 13 bedrooms (4 fmly) No smoking in bedrooms or in dining room No dogs (ex guide dogs) Licensed 🛏

KILMAURS ▨▨▨▨
9 Kilmaurs Rd EH16 5DA
(Lies parallel to A7 close to Commonwealth Swimming Pool)

☎ 0131 667 8315 ☏ 0131 662 6949

Bright decor and smart pine furnishings in this welcoming family run guest house. Comfortable lounge and dining room.

£ 4 bedrooms (2 fmly) No smoking No dogs (ex guide dogs) 🛏

THE LODGE HOTEL ▨▨▨▨
6 Hampton Ter, West Coates EH12 5JD
(on A8, 1m W of city centre)

☎ 0131 337 3682 ☏ 0131 313 1700

Georgian home where fresh fruit and a welcoming glass of sherry await new arrivals. Snug bar, cosy lounge and attractive breakfast room.

££ 10 bedrooms No smoking in bedrooms or in dining room No dogs Licensed 🛏

MAITLAND HOTEL ▨▨▨▨
25-33 Shandwick Place EH2 4RG
(west end of Princes Street)

☎ 0131 229 1467 ☏ 0131 229 7549

Value for money, combined with quality. Ten executive rooms with CD players. Breakfast buffet in extended dining room.

£££ 65 bedrooms (1 fmly) No smoking in 10 bedrooms No smoking in dining room No dogs (ex guide dogs) Licensed Lift Closed 20-29 Dec 🛏

PRIORY LODGE ▨▨▨▨
The Loan EH30 9NS

☎ 0131 331 4345 ☏ 0131 331 4345

Delightful purpose built guest house with antique pine furniture in bedrooms and the use of kitchen facilities. Hearty Scottish breakfasts served at individual tables.

££ 5 bedrooms (3 fmly) No smoking 🛏

ROSELEA ▨▨▨▨
11 Mayfield Rd EH9 2NG
(on A701, 1m N of the Royal Observatory)

☎ 0131 667 6115 ☏ 0131 667 3556

A genuine welcome awaits at this charming Victorian terraced house. Attractive furnishings are used to dramatic effect throughout.

£ 7 bedrooms (1 fmly) No smoking in dining room or lounges No dogs (ex guide dogs) Closed 1 week Xmas 🛏

STUART HOUSE ▨▨▨▨
12 East Claremont St EH7 4JP
(east along Princes Street, turn onto Leith Street, left down Broughton Street, located bottom of Broughton Street 2nd road on right)

☎ 0131 557 9030 ☏ 0131 557 0563

Georgian-style town house within easy reach of central amenities. All bedrooms offer a wide range of amenities together with useful extras.

££ 7 bedrooms (1 fmly) No smoking No dogs No children under 2yrs Closed 18-27 Dec 🛏

THE TOWN HOUSE ▨▨▨▨
65 Gilmore Place EH3 9NU
(city centre, access from A1, A8, A702, entrance to Gilmore Place opp Kings Theatre)

☎ 0131 229 1985

A former manse with many original features carefully preserved. The attractive bedrooms are decorated to a high standard.

£ 5 bedrooms (1 fmly) No smoking No dogs (ex guide dogs) No children under 8yrs

ABCORN ▨▨▨
4 Mayfield Gardens EH9 2BU
(1.5m S from city centre)

☎ 0131 667 6548 ☏ 0131 667 9969

Friendly, family-run guest house offering

---

good value accommodation. Spacious bedrooms are smartly decorated in pine. Hearty Scottish breakfasts.

£ 7 bedrooms (1 fmly) No smoking in dining room or lounges No dogs (ex guide dogs)

ABERCORN ▨▨▨
33 Abercorn Ter, Joppa, Portobello EH15 2DF
(directly off A1)

☎ 0131 669 6139

Set back in its own gardens, a homely feel prevails. Well proportioned bedrooms. Hearty Scottish breakfasts served.

£ 4 bedrooms (2 fmly) No smoking in 1 bedroom No smoking in dining room or lounges

AMARYLLIS ▨▨▨
21 Upper Gilmore Place EH3 9NL
(directly opp King's Theatre)

☎ 0131 229 3293 ☏ 0131 229 3293

Friendly family-run guest house within easy reach of various cinemas and theatres. Comfortable bedrooms are spacious. No lounge.

£ 5 bedrooms (3 fmly) No smoking in dining room No dogs (ex guide dogs) 🛏

AN FUARAN ▨▨▨
35 Seaview Ter, Joppa EH15 2HE

☎ 0131 669 8119

Overlooking the Firth of Forth, this family run guest house offers good value accommodation. Brightly decorated bedrooms.

£ 4 bedrooms (2 fmly) No smoking No dogs Closed 24-26 Dec

ARDEN ▨▨▨
126 Old Dalkeith Rd EH16 4SD
(on A7)

☎ 0131 664 3985 ☏ 0131 621 0866

Extended detached house provides good value accommodation. The attractive bedroomsare all on the ground floor. No lounge.

£ 3 bedrooms No smoking in 2 bedrooms No smoking in dining room or lounges No dogs 🛏

ARDEN HOUSE ▨▨▨
26 Linkfield Rd, Musselburgh EH21 7LL
(follow signs to Musselburgh/Racecourse)

☎ 0131 665 0663 ☏ 0131 665 0663

Substantial turreted end terrace house. Guests may use of rear garden and separate conservatory beside the patio.

£ 4 bedrooms (2 fmly) No smoking 🛏

ASHDENE HOUSE ▨▨▨
23 Fountainhall Rd EH9 2LN
(A701 northbound from A720, turn left at Mayfield Church)

☎ 0131 667 6026

In quiet conservation area. Attractive decor in comfortable variable-sized bedrooms. Substantial breakfasts served in attractive conservatory dining room.

5 bedrooms (2 fmly) No smoking No dogs Closed 2 wks in winter

AULD REEKIE ▩▩▩
16 Mayfield Gardens EH9 2BZ
(follow A701, exit at Straiton Jnct follow signs for city centre, approx 2.5km)
☎ 0131 667 6177 ⓕ 0131 662 0033
Welcoming atmosphere prevails at this Victorian terraced house. Both Scottish and vegetarian breakfasts served.
£ 7 bedrooms (2 fmly) No smoking in dining room or lounges

BEVERLEY HOTEL ▩▩▩
40 Murrayfield Ave EH12 6AY
(near Murrayfield Rugby Ground on A8)
☎ 0131 337 1128 ⓕ 0131 445 1994
Welcoming hotel with bright and airy bedrooms. First floor lounge with beverage making facilities. Wide range of breakfast choices.
£ 7 bedrooms (3 fmly) Licensed Closed 20–27 Dec

BUCHAN HOTEL ▩▩▩
3 Coates Gardens EH12 5LG *(W along A8)*
☎ 0131 337 1045 ⓕ 0131 538 7055
Good value accommodation at this friendly family run establishment. Varied breakfast menu is offered in the attractive dining room.
£ 12 bedrooms (5 fmly) No smoking in dining room ⬤

CLASSIC HOUSE ▩▩▩
50 Mayfield Rd EH9 2NH *(turn off onto A701, 0.5 mile on left just after Kings Building)*
☎ 0131 667 5847 ⓕ 0131 662 1016
Comfortable personally-run house with tastefully decorated and well-equipped, cleverly designed accommodation. Conservatory dining room.
£ 4 bedrooms No smoking No dogs ⬤

CORSTORPHINE ▩▩▩
188 St Johns Rd, Corstorphine EH12 8SG
(from M8 take city bypass north towards city centre for 1m on A8, guest house on left)
☎ 0131 539 4237 & 0131 334 7365
ⓕ 0131 539 4945
Immaculately maintained home, convenient for airport and central amenities. Traditional, continental, or vegetarian menus at breakfast.
£ 4 bedrooms (2 fmly) No smoking No dogs (ex guide dogs) ch fac ⬤

CRION ▩▩▩
33 Minto St EH9 2BT
(from south A701 & A7)
☎ 0131 667 2708 ⓕ 0131 662 1946
Semi-detached Georgian house with colourful window boxes. Tastefully decorated bedrooms with mixed modern appointments.
6 bedrooms (1 fmly) No smoking in dining room or lounges No dogs (ex guide dogs)

DUNSTANE HOUSE ▩▩▩
4 West Coates EH12 5JQ
☎ 0131 337 6169 5320 ⓕ 0131 337 6169
Well proportioned Victorian house in gardens that offers comfortable bedrooms in a variety of sizes. Relaxing lounge with bar.
£ 15 bedrooms (5 fmly) No smoking in dining room Licensed ⬤

ECOSSE INTERNATIONAL ▩▩▩
15 McDonald Rd EH7 4LX
(E end Princes St exit to Leith St. Past rndbt,(Playhouse Theatre on R). L at service station, McDonald Rd on R)
☎ 0131 556 4967 ⓕ 0131 556 7394
Immaculately maintained guest house, ideal for exploring the city. Dining room and lounge with bar on lower ground.
5 bedrooms (3 fmly) No smoking in bedrooms or in dining room No dogs (ex guide dogs) ⬤

ELDER YORK ▩▩▩
38 Elder St EH1 3DX
☎ 0131 556 1926
Occupying the fourth and fifth floors of a Victorian building close to city centre, this friendly guest house offers good value accommodation.
£ 13 bedrooms (2 fmly) No smoking in dining room or lounges No dogs (ex guide dogs) ⬤

FINLAY ▩▩▩
4 Hartington Place, Bruntsfield EH10 4LE
☎ 0131 229 1620 ⓕ 0131 229 1548
Sympathetically converted terraced home with bedrooms decorated in antique pine, one room with four-poster bed. Hearty breakfasts are served at individual tables.
£ 6 bedrooms (1 fmly) No smoking in 2 bedrooms No smoking in area of dining room No dogs (ex guide dogs) ⬤

GALLOWAY ▩▩▩
22 Dean Park Crescent EH4 1PH
☎ 0131 332 3672
Residential area, terraced house close to shops and bistros in the Stockbridge area. Modern style bedrooms with en suite bathrooms.
£ 10 bedrooms (6 fmly)

GLENALMOND ▩▩▩
25 Mayfield Gdns EH9 2BX *(on A701)*
☎ 0131 668 2392 ⓕ 0131 668 2392
Welcoming, family-run guest house within ten minutes of the city centre. Smartly decorated bedrooms with pine furnishings.
10 bedrooms (4 fmly) No smoking in 3 bedrooms No smoking in dining room or in 1 lounge No dogs (ex guide dogs)

GREENSIDE HOTEL ▩▩▩
9 Royal Ter EH7 5AB *(follow A1 into London Road, at the end turn L at rdbt)*
☎ 0131 557 0022 & 557 0121
ⓕ 0131 557 0022
Comfortable private hotel, which is part of an elegant Georgian terrace. Dining room with small residents' bar.
£ 14 bedrooms (5 fmly) No smoking in dining room No dogs (ex guide dogs) Licensed ch fac Arrangement with 4 star hotel to use facilities ⬤

HOUSE O'HILL ▩▩▩
7 House O'Hill Ter, Queensferry Rd EH4 2AA
☎ 0131 332 3674 ⓕ 0131 343 3446
Convenient for the city this cosy guest house is immaculately kept. Bedrooms, with en suite showers, are quietly located at the rear.
4 bedrooms (2 fmly) No smoking in bedrooms or in dining room or lounges ⬤

INVERESK HOUSE ▩▩▩
3 Inveresk Village, Musselburgh EH21 7UA
☎ 0131 6655855 ⓕ 0131 6650578
Historic mansion house in extensive grounds. Pleasant first-floor sitting room with extensive views. Bedrooms on ground and first floors.
£ 3 bedrooms (1 fmly) No smoking No dogs (ex guide dogs) ⬤

IVY HOUSE ▩▩▩
7 Mayfield Gardens EH9 2AX
(on A701 1.5m S of Princes Street)
☎ 0131 667 3411
Victorian terraced guest house with large bedrooms all with modern en suite or private bathrooms. No lounge.
£ 8 bedrooms (4 fmly) No smoking in dining room

JOPPA ROCKS ▩▩▩
99 Joppa Rd EH15 2HB *(from city centre follow signsf or Portobello & Musselburgh A1)*
☎ 0131 669 8695 & 0831 362080
ⓕ 0131 669 8695
Good value accommodation is offered at family-run guest house, part of a terraced row and close to Portobello beach.
£ 4 bedrooms (1 fmly) No smoking in dining room ⬤

THE LAIRG ▩▩▩
11 Coates Gardens EH12 5LG
(from A8, pass under rail bridge, 150yds on there is a stately home on left. Coates Gardens is two streets further on left)
☎ 0131 337 1050 ⓕ 0131 346 2167
A warm welcome awaits from enthusiastic owners. Smart bedrooms offer high standards of accommodation.
10 bedrooms (4 fmly) No smoking Licensed ⬤

LEAMINGTON ▩▩▩
57 Leamington Ter EH10 4JS *(off Bruntsfield Place - 1m from W end of Princes Street)*
☎ 0131 228 3879 ⓕ 0131 221 1022
After ambitious improvements this welcoming and comfortably appointed guest house offers tastefully decorated bedrooms, one with four-poster.
£ 8 bedrooms (3 fmly) No smoking

MARDALE ▩▩▩
11 Hartington Place EH10 4LF *(city centre)*
☎ 0131 229 2693 ⓕ 0131 229 2693
Friendly family run guest house offering good value accommodation. Attractive fabrics adorn the comfortable bedrooms. Freshly prepared breakfasts served in attractive first floor dining room.
£ 6 bedrooms (2 fmly) No smoking in dining room or lounges ⬤

MEADOWS ▩▩▩
17 Glengyle Ter EH3 9LN *(E of A702, between Kings Theatre & Bruntsfield Links)*
☎ 0131 229 9559 ⓕ 0131 229 2226
Overlooking Bruntsfield Links, Meadows offers comfortable accommodation within its generously proportioned rooms. Breakfast is served in the bright dining room at two communal tables.
£ 5 bedrooms (2 fmly) No smoking in dining room Closed 18-28 Dec ⬤

MURRAYFIELD PARK ◙◙◙
89 Corstorphine Rd EH12 5QE
☎ 0131 337 5370 ☎ 0131 337 3772
Within sight of Murrayfield stadium this comfortable home has ground floor and lower level bedrooms. Comfortable lounge and breakfasts in the rear dining room.
£ 6 bedrooms No smoking in dining room or lounges No dogs (ex guide dogs) Closed Xmas & New Year

THE NEWINGTON ◙◙◙
18 Newington Rd EH9 1QS
(between A7 and A68)
☎ 0131 667 3356 ☎ 0131 667 8307
Traditional values and comforts are all part of the appeal of this welcoming guest house. Bedrooms, some with lovely antique furnishings, offer a wide range of amenities.
£ 8 bedrooms (1 fmly) No smoking Licensed

PARKLANDS ◙◙◙
20 Mayfield Gardens EH9 2BZ
(1.5m S of Princes Street on A7/A701)
☎ 0131 667 7184 ☎ 0131 667 2011
Long established comfortable terraced home. Bedrooms are tastefully decorated while freshly prepared breakfasts are served in the attractive dining room.
£ 6 bedrooms (1 fmly) No smoking in 1 bedrooms No smoking in dining room or lounges No dogs (ex guide dogs)

RAVENSDOWN ◙◙◙
248 Ferry Rd EH5 3AN
(A1-A199 Leith & Granton, near Royal Botanic Gardens, N side of Princess Street)
☎ 0131 552 5438 ☎ 0131 552 7559
Comfortable home enjoying wonderful views over Edinburgh. Bedrooms, some en suite, are bright and airy. Guests may use music centre and piano in the lounge.
£ 7 bedrooms (4 fmly) No smoking No dogs Licensed

RAVENSNUEK ◙◙◙
11 Blacket Av EH9 1RR
(0.5m N on A7 from Cameron Toll rdbt. 1.5m S of Princes St on North Bridge)
☎ 0131 667 5347 ☎ 0131 6675347
Pretty fabrics have been used to good effect in the comfortable bedrooms. which offer all the expected amenities. Attractive combined lounge/dining room.
7 bedrooms No smoking No dogs

ROWAN ◙◙◙
13 Glenorchy Ter EH9 2DQ
☎ 0131 667 2463 ☎ 0131 667 2463
Situated in a desirable south side residential area, this friendly family run guest house offers good value accommodation.
£ 9 bedrooms (2 fmly) No smoking in dining room or lounges P

ST MARGARET'S ◙◙◙
18 Craigmillar Park EH16 5PS
(from the city bypass A720, exit at Straiton jnctn on A701)
☎ 0131 667 2202 ☎ 0131 667 2202
Warm welcome extended to guests old and new at this comfortable terraced

home. Immaculately kept bedrooms vary in size.
££ 8 bedrooms (3 fmly) No smoking in bedrooms or in dining room No dogs

SALISBURY HOTEL ◙◙◙
45 Salisbury Rd EH16 5AA
(L off A7 - opp Royal Commonwealth Pool)
☎ 0131 667 1264 ☎ 0131 667 1264
An attractive Georgian house conveniently situated. Bedrooms, with all the expected amenities, are mostly spacious.
12 bedrooms (3 fmly) No smoking No dogs (ex guide dogs) Licensed Closed Xmas-New Year

SALISBURY VIEW HOTEL ◙◙◙
64 Dalkeith Rd EH16 5AE
(on A7/A68, adjacent to Holyrood Park)
☎ 0131 667 1133 ☎ 0131 667 1133
Large detached sandstone house provides comfortable accommodation. Comfortable lounge with small dispense bar.
£ 8 bedrooms (1 fmly) No smoking in dining room Licensed

SANDILANDS HOUSE ◙◙◙
25 Queensferry Rd EH4 3HB
(on A90 NW from Princes Street in direction of Forth Road Bridge)
☎ 0131 332 2057 ☎ 0131 332 2057
1930s detached private house on the road to the Forth Road Bridge and the north. It displays many interesting items of art deco.
£ 3 bedrooms (2 fmly) No smoking No dogs

SHERWOOD ◙◙◙
42 Minto St EH9 2BR
(1m up North Bridge from Princes St)
☎ 0131 667 1200
Enthusiastic owner constantly strives to improve standards at her comfortable and welcoming guest house. Bedrooms, 5 en suite, have smart pine furnishings.
£ 6 bedrooms (2 fmly) No smoking No dogs Closed 20-29 Dec

SIX MARY'S PLACE ◙◙◙
6 Mary's Place, Raeburn Place, Stockbridge EH4 1JD
☎ 0131 332 8965 ☎ 0131 624 7060
Terraced Georgian house with spacious first floor lounge, conservatory dining for breakfasts and vegetarian evening meals.
8 bedrooms No smoking No dogs (ex guide dogs)

SONAS ◙◙◙
3 East Mayfield EH9 1SD
(from A720 exit Edinburgh/Peebles sign towards city centre through 4 lights, 1 rdbt, turn R at next lights)
☎ 0131 667 2781 ☎ 0131 667 0454
Bright and cheerful in both atmosphere and appearance. Bedrooms with hair dryers, tissues and other extras.
£ 7 bedrooms (3 fmly) No smoking in dining room No dogs (ex guide dogs) Closed 21-26 Dec

STRATHMOHR ◙◙◙
23 Mayfield Gardens EH9 2BX
(from E end of Princes St, turn R into North

Bridge (A7), after 1.4m establishment on L)
☎ 0131 667 8475
Huge comfortable bedrooms are hallmarks of this well proportioned detached period house. Small lounge area in dining room.
£ 7 bedrooms (5 fmly) No smoking No dogs (ex guide dogs)

STRA'VEN ◙◙◙
3 Brunstane Rd North, Joppa EH15 2DL
☎ 0131 669 5580 ☎ 0131 657 2517
Family-run guest house, a semi-detached villa situated close to Portobello beach. Bedrooms are all en suite.
£ 7 bedrooms (3 fmly) No smoking No dogs (ex guide dogs)

TERRACE HOTEL ◙◙◙
37 Royal Ter EH7 5AH
(E from Waverley Station/Princes St along Regent Road turn L into Regent Terrace, then Royal Terrace)
☎ 0131 556 3423 ☎ 0131 556 2520
Part of an impressive Georgian terrace with fine views across the city. Bedrooms furnished with quality pieces.
14 bedrooms (7 fmly) No smoking in dining room No dogs

YELLOW ROSE (BUIDHE RÙS) ◙◙◙
9 Hawkshead Crescent EH16 6LR
(turn off A720 onto A701 city centre, Crescent on L, 1.75m)
☎ 0131 621 7111 ☎ 0131 621 7111
Comfortable semi-detached home. Excellent value bed and breakfast accommodation. Street parking readily available.
£ 3 bedrooms (2 fmly) No smoking No dogs Jun-Sep

THE ADRIA HOTEL ◙◙
11-12 Royal Ter EH7 5AB
☎ 0131 556 7875 ☎ 0131 558 7782
Good value accommodation at this personally run hotel, part of an elegant Georgian terrace beside Calton Hill. Most of the bedrooms are spacious.
24 bedrooms (8 fmly) No smoking in dining room No dogs (ex guide dogs) Closed Nov-Dec

ANVILLA ◙◙
1a Granville Ter EH10 4PG
(w end of Princes St, up Lothian Rd to Kings Theatre, located in road opposite(Gilmore Place), Granville Terrace is a continuation)
☎ 0131 228 3381
Comfortable detached Victorian house. Cheerful bedrooms furnished in period and modern styles. First floor lounge.
£ 6 bedrooms (2 fmly) No smoking in dining room or lounges

BEN DORAN ◙◙
11 Mayfield Gardens EH9 2AX
(from east side of Princes Street, take A701, on L, about 1.5 miles)
☎ 0131 667 8488 ☎ 0131 667 0076
Bedrooms, all with CTV, are variable in size and offer mixed practical appointments. Beverage making facilities on each landing.
£ 10 bedrooms (5 fmly) No smoking

BOISDALE HOTEL ◨◨
9 Coates Gardens EH12 5LG
☎ 0131 337 1134 ☏ 0131 313 0048
Situated close to Haymarket Station, this friendly, personally-run guest house offers good value for money. Hearty breakfasts served in basement dining room.
11 bedrooms (6 fmly) Licensed

BUCHANAN ◨◨
97 Joppa Rd EH15 2HB
(Exit A1 onto A199. At lights turn L to B6415. 1m on left)
☎ 0131 657 4117
Friendly guest house close to the sea and Firth of Forth views from upper floor front bedrooms. Hearty breakfasts served in combined lounge/dining room.
4 bedrooms (1 fmly) No dogs 🍽

CHALUMNA ◨◨
5 Granville Ter EH10 4PQ
☎ 0131 229 2086 ☏ 0131 221 0880
Good value accommodation at this guest house.Top floor bedrooms have been tastefully refurbished while first floor rooms are more practical in style.
9 bedrooms (2 fmly) No smoking in dining room 🍽

CLIFTON PRIVATE HOTEL ◨◨
1 Clifton Ter, Haymarket EH12 5DR
(opposite Haymarket Rail Station on Glasgow Road nr city centre)
☎ 0131 337 1002 ☏ 0131 337 1002
Friendly hotel within easy reach of the Station and Conference Centre. Bright bedrooms. Comfortable first floor lounge.
11 bedrooms No smoking in dining room 🍽

GLENISLA HOTEL◨◨
12 Lygon Rd EH16 5QB
(off A7 towards city 1st exit on R after rdbt at Lady Road Jnctn)
☎ 0131 667 4877 ☏ 0131 667 4098
Warm welcome is assured at this guest house. Bedrooms offer a good range of amenities. First floor lounge.
8 bedrooms (1 fmly) No smoking in dining room Licensed 🍽

GLENORCHY HOTEL◨◨
22 Glenorchy Ter EH9 2DH
☎ 0131 667 5708 ☏ 0131 667 1201
Good value accommodation at this

friendly, family-run guest house. Smart bedrooms offer modern and traditional furnishings.
£ 8 bedrooms (2 fmly) No smoking No dogs 🍽

HARVEST ◨◨
33 Straiton Place, Portobello EH15 2BH
☎ 0131 657 3160 ☏ 0131 468 7028
Overlooking the beach, a family run guest house offers good value accommodation. Bedrooms are mostly compact.
£ 7 bedrooms (2 fmly) No smoking No dogs 🍽

HERIOTT PARK ◨◨
256 Ferry Rd, Goldenacre EH5 3AN
☎ 0131 552 6628 ☏ 0131 552 6628
Benifiting from lovely views of the city good value accommodation is offered here. Breakfasts served in dining room cum lounge.
6 bedrooms (4 fmly) No smoking

HOPETOUN ◨◨
15 Mayfield Rd EH9 2NG
(nr University Kings Buildings Campus, nr Mayfield church)
☎ 0131 667 7691
Near the University this small, strictly no smoking guest house has good sized bedrooms.
£ 3 bedrooms (2 fmly) No smoking No dogs Closed Xmas 🍽

KARIBA ◨◨
10 Granville Ter EH10 4PQ
☎ 0131 229 3773
Welcoming terraced guest house with variable sized bedrooms offering mixed modern furnishings. Comfortable lounge adjacent to dining room.
£ 9 bedrooms (3 fmly) No smoking in dining room or lounges

KINGSLEY ◨◨
30 Craigmillar Park, Newington EH16 5PS
(S on A701)
☎ 0131 667 8439 ☏ 0131 667 8439
Offering good value accommodation, including family rooms. Spacious lounge and bright dining room where full breakfast is served.
£ 6 bedrooms (3 fmly) No smoking in bedrooms or dining room No dogs No children under 6yrs 🍽

KIRKLEA ◨◨
11 Harrison Rd EH11 1EG
(exit city bypass at Baberton Mains Jnctn, follow city centre signs, turn R after Hearts FC, Kirklea on L after lights)
☎ 0131 337 1129 ☏ 0131 337 1129
Warm welcome assured to new or old guests. Hearty breakfasts served at individual tables in attractive dining room.
£ 6 bedrooms (1 fmly) No smoking in dining room or lounges 🍽

LINDSAY ◨◨
108 Polwarth Ter EH11 1NN
(exit A720 at Colinton/Redford link to 2nd rdbt, at end turn L past Napier University. L at mini rdbt at bottom of hill)
☎ 0131 337 1580 ☏ 0131 337 9174
Well maintained, substantial semi-detached villa in pleasant residential area. Modern and traditionally furnished rooms.
£ 8 bedrooms (2 fmly) No smoking in dining room or lounges 🍽

MARCHHALL HOTEL ◨◨
14-16 Marchhall Crescent EH16 5HL *(off A720 onto A7, over Cameron toll rdbt, after 0.5m at lights turn into Priestfield Road, 1st right)*
☎ 0131 667 2743 ☏ 0131 662 0777
Personally run small hotel with lounge bar to relax in and enjoy a drink or meal. Small carte available in dining room.
£ 14 bedrooms (4 fmly) No smoking in 4 bedrooms No smoking in dining room or lounges No dogs (ex guide dogs) Licensed 🍽

SYLVERN ◨◨
22 West Mayfield EH9 1TQ
☎ 0131 667 1241
Long established, family-run detached villa, near good public transport links to city centre. Hearty breakfasts. Car park.
6 bedrooms (4 fmly) No smoking in dining room or lounges No dogs Closed 22-29 Dec

TIREE ◨◨
26 Craigmillar Park EH16 5PS
(on A701 near Cameron Toll shopping centre)
☎ 0131 667 7477 ☏ 0131 662 1608
Terraced family-run guest house close to Cameron Toll shopping centre. Bedrooms vary in size and appointment.
£ 7 bedrooms (2 fmly) No smoking in dining room or lounges

VILLA NINA ◨◨
39 Leamington Ter EH10 4JS
☎ 0131 229 2644
Good value at this friendly family run guest hous. Bedrooms some with shower cabinets. Hearty breakfasts.
£ 4 bedrooms (1 fmly) No dogs No children under 12yrs Closed Xmas & New Year

AVERON ◨
44 Gilmore Place EH3 9NQ
(turn left at the west end of Princes Street and follow A702 and turn right at Kings Theatre)
☎ 0131 229 9932 ☏ 0131 228 9265
Terraced guest house close to Kings Theatre offering good value. Bedrooms vary in size. Shared breakfasts.
£ 10 bedrooms (3 fmly) No smoking in dining room No dogs 🍽

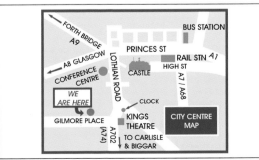

Averon

HALCYON HOTEL ☒
8 Royal Ter EH7 5AB

☎ 0131 556 1033 & 0131 556 1032

Part of an elegant Georgian terrace, the upper bedrooms enjoy views of the Firth of Forth. Spacious first floor lounge.

16 bedrooms (6 fmly) Tennis (hard)

MENZIES ☒
33 Leamington Ter EH10 4JS *(from Princes Street, left up Lothian Road, right into Home Street (Toll Cross) straight onto Brunstfield Hotel, on right and turn right)*

☎ 0131 229 4629 ☎ 0131 229 4629

Terraced guest house offering good value accommodation. Bedrooms are variable in size. Breakfast at shared tables.

£ 6 bedrooms (3 fmly) No smoking in dining room or lounges No dogs ☒

FORTH BRIDGES ★★★
1 Ferrymuir Gate, Forth Bridge EH30 9SF

(adjacent to Forth Road Bridge, follow signs - M90 then A8000, hotel on left)

☎ 0131 469 9955 ☎ 0131 319 1733

The Firth of Forth is the breathtaking backdrop for this modern hotel. Spacious bedrooms. Choice of dining venues.

££ 108 bedrooms (15 fmly) No smoking in 43 bedrooms Lift Night porter Indoor swimming pool (heated) Squash Sauna Solarium Gym Jacuzzi/spa Dance studio No smoking in restaurant ☒

PRIORY LODGE ☒☒☒☒
The Loan EH30 9NS

☎ 0131 331 4345 ☎ 0131 331 4345

Delightful purpose built guest house. Attractive bedrooms are maintained to a high standard and kitchen facilities available.

££ 5 bedrooms (3 fmly) No smoking ☒

Call the AA Hotel Booking Service on 0990 050505 to book at AA recognised hotels and B&Bs in the UK, or through our internet site: http://www.theaa.co.uk/hotels

CAMPING & CARAVANNING

MORTONHALL CARAVAN PARK
38 Mortonhall Gate EH16 6TJ

(Take the new city bypass to junction with A702 and follow signs to Mortonhall.)

☎ 0131 664 1533

De-Luxe Park

Within 20 minutes' car ride of the city centre. Part of a 200-acre estate around the Mortonhall mansion. 22 acres with 250 touring pitches and 18 statics.

Open 28 Mar–Oct Booking advisable Jul–Aug Last arrival 22.00hrs Last departure noon

RESTAURANTS
AA RECOMMENDED

Duck's at Le Marché Noir

ATRIUM ※ ※ ※
Cambridge Street, Lothian EH1 2ED

☎ 0131 2288882 ☎ 0131 2288808

Sharp-featured restaurant with a kitchen to match. Pan–fried monkfish on buttered vegetables with a sun–dried tomato butter sauce; steak and kidney in a rich refined sauce with perfectly seasoned creamed potato with chopped spring onion.

ALC ££ ☒

L'AUBERGE RESTAURANT ※ ※
56 St Mary's Street EH1 1SX

☎ 0131 5565888 ☎ 0131 5562588

True to its name, L'Auberge creates the mood of a modest eating place somewhere in France. A choice of menus provides a wide range of dishes with some interesting ideas and unexpected touches.

Fixed L £ ALC £££ ☒

CALEDONIAN HOTEL ※ ※
Princes Street EH1 2AB

☎ 0131 4599988 ☎ 0131 2256632

The 'Cally' is an Edinburgh institution, and dinner in the magnificent Pompadour dining-room is a special occasion. Classically-based French cooking brings caramelised squab pigeon with spiced pear tartlet, and loin of lamb with a cassoulet of smoked bacon and boudin noir.

ALC £££ ☒

CARLTON HIGHLAND HOTEL ※
North Bridge, EH1 1SD

☎ 0131 556 7277 ☎ 0131 556 2691

Quills restaurant, with its library theme, oak panelling and wooden beams, provides elegant surroundings for some serious eating at the Carlton Highland. Flambé options and vegetarian dishes are offered.

Fixed L £ ALC ££ ☒

CHANNINGS ※
South Learmonth Grdns, Midlothian EH4 1EZ

☎ 0131 3152226 ☎ 0131 3329631

Channings Brasserie offers the likes of Parmesan tart topped with roasted plum tomatoes, basil and 'Paris browns', and glazed peppered duck with pak choy and crispy polenta cake.

Fixed D ££ ☒

DUCK'S AT LE MARCHÉ NOIR ※ ※ ※
2/4 Eyre Place EH3 5EP

☎ 0131 5581608 ☎ 01314677230

An unpretentious little French restaurant in the New Town. Haggis gets the French provincial treatment in a baked filo parcel on a bed of sweet potato purée with a thyme scented sauce.

Fixed L ££ ☒

Kelly's

GEORGE INTER-CONTINENTAL ⊛
19-21 George Street EH2 2PB
☎ 0131 225 1251 ☏ 0131 226 5644
Le Chambertin sports high ceilings, huge
chandeliers, and an intimate atmosphere.
The highlight of a meal in March was roast
monkfish tarte Tatin, served on a compote
of red onion.
Fixed L/D £££ ALC ££ 🖥

IGGS ⊛⊛
15 Jeffrey Street, EH1 1DR
☎ 0131 557 8184 ☏ 0131 441 7111
Ignacio "Igg" Campos offers a blend of
Spanish and Scottish dishes, including a
lively selection of tapas. Full menus may
offer artichoke mousseline with blue
cheese and coriander sauce, or roast
guinea fowl with smoked bacon, judion
beans, and spring cabbage.
Fixed L £ ALC ££ 🖥

JACKSONS ⊛
209 High Street EH1 1PZ
☎ 0131 225 1793 ☏ 0131 220 0620
This popular, stone-walled cellar restaurant
offers a relaxed atmosphere and sound,
modern Scottish cooking. Dishes may
include haggis with a creamy whisky
sauce, or chargrilled sea bass.
Fixed L £ ALC £££ 🖥

KELLY'S ⊛⊛
46 West Richmond Street EH8
☎ 0131 6683847
Kelly's offers an understated menu that
mixes classical and modern dishes. Main
courses may include rack of lamb with
roast ratatouille on polenta, and
chargrilled steak with superb rösti.

MALMAISON ⊛
1 Tower Place Leith EH6 7DB
☎ 0131 5556868 ☏ 0131 5556999
There's a good choice of simple Med-style
food at this modishly designed brasserie
and hotel. Fettucine with tomatoes, basil
and roast garlic and huge bowls of moules
marinière may be on the menu.
Fixed L/D £ ALC ££ 🖥

MARRIOTT DALMAHOY ⊛⊛
Kirknewton, Midlothian EH27 8EB,
☎ 0131 3331845 ☏ 0131 3331343
The Pentland restaurant offers a varied
menu, and some really interesting and
successful flavour combinations.
Fixed L £ ALC ££ 🖥

MARTIN'S RESTAURANT ⊛⊛⊛
70 Rose Street North Lane EH2 3DX
☎ 0131 2253106
Martin and Gay Irons have long
championed the cause of organic produce
and wild foods so the quality of the raw
materials is beyond reproach. Fish
dominates, closely followed by game and
lamb, while beef is generally noticeable by
its absence
Fixed L £ ALC £££ 🖥

NORTON HOUSE ⊛⊛
Ingliston EH28 8LX
☎ 0131 3331275 ☏ 0131 3335305
Formal meals are served in the
Conservatory restaurant and may feature
venison with celeriac purée served on a
sloe berry sauce tinged with vanilla, or
seared loin of lamb with broccoli mousse
and rosemary juice.
Fixed D ££ ALC £££ 🖥

SHERATON GRAND HOTEL ⊛⊛⊛
1 Festival Square Midlothian EH3 9SR
☎ 0131 2299131 ☏ 0131 2296254
Classical French cooking is the influence
here, and specialities include mosaic of
pot-au-feu with crudités, and fillet of
Dover sole with fondant potatoes and
braised fennel.
Fixed L ££ ALC £££ 🖥

36 AT THE HOWARD ⊛⊛
36 Great King Street EH3 6QH
☎ 0131 5563636 ☏ 0131 5563663
Stylish modern menu featuring very rare
seared tuna served with salad niçoise, and
a terrine of duck confit with plum chutney.
Main courses include monkfish, or lamb
wrapped in cabbage stuffed with a ginger
pesto.
ALC ££ 🖥

THE VINTNERS ROOM ⊛⊛
87 Giles Street, Leith Midlothian EH6 6BZ
☎ 0131 5546767 ☏ 0131 4677130
Lively restaurant/wine bar set above 800-
year-old wine vaults. Menu may feature
pan-fried scallops with risotto nero and
squid ink sauce followed by chargrilled
halibut with contrasting sauces.
Fixed L £ ALC ££ 🖥

THE WITCHERY BY THE CASTLE ⊛⊛
Castle Hill EH2 1NE
☎ 0131 2255613 ☏ 0131 2204392
The Witchery is two rooms, each with its
own individual look. The same menu is
offered in both: tartare of tuna with
cucumber spaghetti, tomato and avocado
salsa; escalope of salmon cooked in goose
fat with roast chicory and celeriac purée.

Iggs

PUBS, INNS & OTHER PLACES TO EAT

The Bridge Inn

EDINBURGH

ALP RESTAURANT
167 Rose Street
☎ 0131 225 4787
Swiss restaurant where specialities include Fondues, Veal Zurichoise, Rosti plus Swiss wines.

CREELERS SEAFOOD BAR
3 Hunter Square, Royal Mile
☎ 0131 220 4447
Carte and bistro menus offer exciting cuisine whether Scottish fare, vegetarian or game.

DRAGON WAY
74/78 South Clerk Street
☎ 0131 668 1328
Cantonese, Peking and Szechuen cuisine served in authentic Chinese surroundings. A la carte and pre-theatre menus.

DUBH PRAIS RESTAURANT
123b High Street
Small cosy cellar restaurant siuated on the historic Royal Mile serving high quality Scottish cuisine.

GIULIANO'S
18/19 Union Place
☎ 0131 556 6590
Very friendly, family-run Italian restaurant with a lively atmosphere. Children welcome.

GRAINSTORE
1st Floor, 30 Victoria Street
☎ 0131 225 7635
Fresh ideas with fresh food in a relaxed informal atmosphere. All tastes catered for.

HARRY RAMSDEN'S
Pier Place, Newhaven Harbour
☎ 0131 551 5566
World famous for their fish and chips and just ten minutes from Princes Street. Ample parking.

HELIOS FOUNTAIN
7 Grassmarket
☎ 0131 229 7884
Friendly coffee house serving wholesome vegatarian food.

LE SEPT RESTAURANT
7 Old Fishmarket Close
☎ 0131 225 5428
Informal and busy ,well established restaurant offering excellent value for rmoney meals in a friendly atmosphere.

PANCHO VILLAS RESTAURANT
240 Canongate, Royal Mile
☎ 0131 557 4416
Quality Mexican dishes at affordables prices. Lively informal atmosphere.

SURUCHI RESTAURANT
14A Nicolson Street
☎ 0131 556 6583
Innovative cuisine from different regions of India including vegetarian.

THE TATTLER
23 Commercial St EH6 6JA
(5 mins from city centre in Port of Leith)
☎ 0131 554 9999
A comfortable Victorian pub in the Port of Leith. Local fish is a speciality of the modern Scottish menu, including fresh mussels and seared salmon suprlme.

RATHO

THE BRIDGE INN
27 Baird Rd City of Edinburgh EH28 8RA
(From Newbridge roundabout A89/A8 follow signs for Ratho)
☎ 0131 3331320/ 3331251
At the Bridge Inn, dating from 1750, a meal may include Ratho haggis fillet steak, venison casserole, roast duckling, or Newhaven haddock fillet.

SOUTH QUEENSFERRY

HAWES INN
Newmalls Rd City of Edinburgh EH30 9TA
(A90 from Edinburgh)
☎ 0131 3311990
R L Stevenson stayed here while writing Kidnapped. Eat haggis, neaps and tatties, Man of Glen mussels, steaks and fish dishes. Live blues and jazz on Mondays.

Call the AA Hotel Booking Service on 0990 050505 to book at AA recognised hotels and B&Bs in the UK, or through our internet site: http://www.theaa.co.uk/hotels

WHERE TO STAY
FALKIRK & THE LOTHIANS

ABERLADY

East Lothian

KILSPINDIE HOUSE ★★
Main St EH32 0RE
(from Edinburgh take A1,then A198 signed to N Berwick. Centre of village)
☎ **01875 870682** 🖶 **01875 870504**
Long established hotel particularly welcoming golfers. Staff are friendly and willing to please.
££ 26 bedrooms No smoking in restaurant

BO'NESS

Falkirk

KINGLASS ◙◙◙
Borrowstoun Rd EH51 9RW
(from M9 J3, turn R, 1st left for 1.5m, farm on R)
☎ **01506 822861 & 824185**
🖶 **01506 824433**
Welcoming farmhouse with tastefully decorated. Enjoyable . farmhouse fare.
£ 6 bedrooms (1 fmly) Licensed 750 acres arable

BONNYRIGG

Midlothian

DALHOUSIE CASTLE HOTEL ★★★
EH19 3JB
(take A7 S from Edinburgh, R at Shell Garage onto B704, hotel 0.5m)
☎ **01875 820153** 🖶 **01875 821936**
Imposing 13th-century castle by the River Esk, with delightful outlook across fields, is a peaceful retreat.
££££ 29 bedrooms (5 fmly) No smoking in 2 bedrooms Night porter Fishing ch fac No smoking in restaurant Closed 4–23 Jan 🍴

Kinglass

DALKEITH

Midlothian

ESKBANK MOTOR ★★
29 Dalhousie Rd EH22 3AT
(on B6392)
☎ **0131 663 3234** 🖶 **0131 660 4347**
Relaxed friendly atmosphere at this privately run hotel. Within easy reach of the city bypass.
££ 16 bedrooms (3 fmly) Night porter Golf parties catered for / Le Boulle rink Wkly live entertainment 🍴

DENNY

Falkirk

THE TOPPS ◙◙◙
Fintry Rd FK6 5JF
(just off B818, 4m W)
☎ **01324 822471** 🖶 **01324 823099**
'Feels like the top of the world'. Panoramic views from its elevated position. Renowned for dinners and hearty breakfasts.
£ 8 bedrooms (1 fmly) No smoking Licensed Fishing 300 acres cashmere goats sheep 🍴

DIRLETON

East Lothian

THE OPEN ARMS ★★★ ✿ ✿
EH39 5EG
(from A1 follow signs for North Berwick)
☎ **01620 850241** 🖶 **01620 850570**
Long established traditional country hotel in a picturesque village. Innovative menus in Bistro.
££££ 10 bedrooms P No smoking in restaurant 🍴

CASTLE ◙
EH39 5EP *(off A198)*
☎ **01620 850221**
19th-century coaching inn overlooking the 13th-century Dirleton Castle. Popular base for golfers.
4 bedrooms 4 annexe bedrooms Pool table Closed 21 Dec–5 Jan Res Nov–Apr 🍴

DUNBAR

East Lothian

REDHEUGH ★★
Bayswell Park EH42 1AE
(L at N end of High St, facing Sphinx, follow rd closest the sea for 250mtrs)
☎ **01368 862793** 🖶 **01368 865599**
Near the beach this small family run hotel offers a welcoming atmosphere. Enjoyable home cooking.
10 bedrooms (2 fmly) No children under 8yrs 🍴

BAYSWELL ★★
Bayswell Park EH42 1AE
☎ **01368 862225** 🖶 **01368 862225**
Popular hotel on the cliff top enjoys panoramic views over the Firth of Forth.
££ 13 bedrooms (4 fmly) Petanque Wkly live entertainment 🍴

Dalhousie Castle Hotel

Ashcroft Farmhouse

OVERCLIFFE ◨◨◨
11 Bayswell Park EH42 1AE
(off A1, opposite Lauderdale Park)
☎ 01368 864004
Attractive semi-detached villa within easy reach of the town centre and seafront.
£ 6 bedrooms (3 fmly) No smoking in dining room Licensed

SPRINGFIELD ◨◨◨
Edinburgh Rd EH42 1NH
(turn off A1 onto Dunbar Loop. Springfield on main rd W side of Dunbar nr Belhven Church)
☎ 01368 862502
Detached Victorian house that has special appeal for family visitors and golfers. Enjoyable home cooking.
£ 5 bedrooms (2 fmly) Licensed Feb-Nov ⬛

ST BEYS ◨◨
2 Bayswell Rd EH42 1AB
☎01368 863571
Friendly and informal guest house with sea views. Hearty breakfasts.
6 bedrooms (3 fmly) Feb-Dec ⬛

EAST CALDER

West Lothian

ASHCROFT FARMHOUSE ◨◨◨◨
EH53 0ET
(on B7015, off A71)
☎ 01506 881810 ☏ 01506 884327
Many guests return to this modern home. Bedrooms all on the ground floor.
£ 6 bedrooms (2 fmly) No smoking No dogs (ex guide dogs) 5 acres cattle sheep ⬛

OVERSHIEL FARM ◨◨◨
EH53 0HT
(from Edinburgh A71, onto B7015, 2nd R, 0.5m on R)
☎ 01506 880469 ☏ 01506 883006
Good value accommodation at this welcoming Victorian farmhouse in sheltered gardens. Hearty breakfasts.
£ 1 bedrooms 2 annexe bedrooms (1 fmly) No smoking No dogs (ex guide dogs) Children's playground 340 acres mixed

Call the AA Hotel Booking Service on
0990 050505 to book at AA recognised hotels and B&Bs in the UK,
or through our internet site:
http://www.theaa.co.uk/hotels

FALKIRK

Falkirk

COMFORT FRIENDLY INN ★★
Manor St FK1 1NT
☎ 01324 624066 ☏ 01324 611785
Tourist and commercial hotel in town centre offering competitively priced accommodation.
£ 33 bedrooms (5 fmly) No smoking in 16 bedrooms Lift Night porter Air conditioning Gym No smoking area in restaurant ⬛

GIFFORD

East Lothian

TWEEDDALE ARMS ★★
EH41 4QU
☎ 01620 810240 ☏ 01620 810488
Georgian coaching inn overlooking the village green, that retains much original character.
16 bedrooms (2 fmly) ⬛

GRANGEMOUTH

Falkirk

GRANGE MANOR ★★★❀
Glensburgh FK3 8XJ
(from W exit M9 J6. Hotel 200m to R/from E exit M9 J5, A905 for 2m)
☎ 01324 474836 ☏ 01324 665861
Comfortable family run hotel with easy access to M9. Restaurant and alternative bar and food option.
£££ 7 bedrooms (2 fmly) No dogs (ex guide dogs) No smoking area in restaurant ⬛

GULLANE

East Lothian

GREYWALLS ★★★❀❀
Muirfield EH31 2EG
(A198, hotel is signposted at E end of village)
☎ 01620 842144 ☏ 01620 842241
Warmly welcoming atmosphere in this wonderful Lutyens house in Gertrude Jekyll designed gardens. Views of the Firth of Forth.
££££ 17 bedrooms 5 annexe bedrooms Night porter Tennis (hard) Croquet lawn Putting green No smoking in restaurant Closed Nov-Mar ⬛

FAUSSETTHILL HOUSE ◨◨◨◨
20 Main St EH31 2DR *(on A198)*
☎ 01620 842396 ☏ 01620 842396
Elegant detached Edwardian home in well tended garden beside the main road. A warm welcome assured.
£ 3 bedrooms No smoking No dogs No children under 10yrs Mar-Dec ⬛

HUMBIE

East Lothian

JOHNSTOUNBURN HOUSE ★★★
EH36 5PL *(A68, B6368, 1.5m S of Humbie)*
☎ 01875 833696 ☏ 01875 833626
Surrounded by acres of gardens and rolling farmland this 17th-century country house is a haven of peace.
££££ 11 bedrooms 9 annexe bedrooms (5 fmly) Fishing Croquet lawn Clay pigeon shooting All terrain vehicle Off road driving Golf practise driving range No smoking in restaurant ⬛

LINLITHGOW

West Lothian

BELSYDE HOUSE ◨◨◨
Lanark Rd EH49 6QE
(1.5m SW on A706, 1st L after crossing Union Canal)
☎ 01506 842098 ☏ 01506 842098
Large traditional farmhouse, peacefully set in 100 acres, with a welcoming atmosphere.
£ 4 bedrooms (1 fmly) No smoking No dogs (ex guide dogs) 106 acres sheep Closed Xmas ⬛

Belsyde House

West Lothian

HILTON NATIONAL LIVINGSTON
Almondview EH54 6QB
📞 01506 431222 📠 01506 434666
This bright hotel broadly in line with four
stars, offers modern accommodation.
120 bedrooms

TRAVEL INN
Deer Park Av Knightsbridge EH54 8AD
📞 01506 439202 📠 01506 438912
Modern building offering smart, spacious
and well equipped bedrooms, suitable for
family use. Nearby family restaurant.
££ (fmly room) 40 bedrooms

WHITCROFT ◻◻◻◻
7 Raw Holdings, East Calder EH53 0ET
(A71 onto B7015, establishment on R)
📞 01506 882494 📠 01506 884327
Genuine welcome at this comfortable
modern detached bungalow. Hearty
breakfasts.
*££ 3 bedrooms No smoking No dogs (ex
guide dogs)* ⬛

Midlothian

AARON GLEN ◻◻◻
7 Nivensknowe Rd EH20 9AU
(on A768-just off A701 1m from city bypass)
📞 0131 440 1293 📠 0131 440 2155
Welcoming family run guest house with
well equipped bedrooms. Ground floor
room suitable for disabled guests.
£ 5 bedrooms (3 fmly) No smoking Licensed
⬛

East Lothian

THE MARINE ★★★
Cromwell Rd EH39 4LZ
*(from A198 into Hamilton Rd at lights, then
take 2nd R)*
📞 01620 892406 📠 01620 894480
Long-established hotel with stunning
views over the golf course and the Firth of
Forth. Restaurant and '9th Hole' bar.
*83 bedrooms No smoking in 20 bedrooms
Lift Night porter Outdoor swimming pool
(heated) Tennis (hard) Squash Snooker
Sauna Solarium Putting green Childrens
playground ch fac No smoking in restaurant*
⬛

NETHER ABBEY ★★
20 Dirleton Av EH39 4BQ
(on A198)
📞 01620 892802 📠 01620 895298
Relaxed informal atmosphere at this
popular golfing and tourist hotel. Bar and
bistro.
£ 16 bedrooms (5 fmly) ⬛

Whitecroft

CRAIGVIEW ◻◻
5 Beach Rd EH39 4AB
(A198 to North Berwick off A1. Town centre)
📞 01620 892257
1920 house, overlooking the beach, where
the cheery and enthusiastic hostess
provides vegetarian and healthy options
breakfasts.
£ 3 bedrooms No smoking No dogs

Falkirk

INCHYRA GRANGE ★★★★❀
Grange Rd FK2 0YB
(just beyond BP Social Club)
📞 01324 711911 📠 01324 716134
This former manor house provides smart,
spacious and thoughtfully equipped
accommodation. Dining options.
*£££ 109 bedrooms (5 fmly) No smoking in
57 bedrooms Lift Night porter Indoor
swimming pool (heated) Tennis (hard) Sauna
Solarium Gym-Jacuzzi/spa Steam room
Beauty therapy room Aerobics studio
Aromatherapist No smoking in restaurant*

Midlothian

ROSLIN GLEN ★★
2 Penicuik Rd EH25 9LH
(1m from A701, 2m S of Edinburgh)
📞 0131 440 2029 📠 0131 440 2229
Relaxed welcoming atmosphere at this
family-run hotel in the centre of a
conservation village. Eating options.
7 bedrooms (2 fmly) Night porter ⬛

OLDE ORIGINAL ROSSLYN ◻◻◻
4 Main St EH25 9LD
📞 0131 440 2384 📠 0131 4402514
Welcoming family run inn offering a choice
of bars and restaurant. Some bedrooms
with four-poster beds.
6 bedrooms ⬛

West Lothian

HOUSTOUN HOUSE ★★★★❀❀
EH52 6JS
*(from M8 J3 follow signs for Broxburn. Over
rdbt then at mini rdbt turn R for Uphall, hotel
on R)*
📞 01506 853831 📠 01506 854220
Dating back to the 16th century this
historic building is set in 20 acres of
woodland gardens. Gabled tower with
vaulted bar and three dining rooms.
*££££ 27 bedrooms 47 annexe bedrooms (8
fmly) No smoking in 63 bedrooms No dogs
(ex guide dogs) Night porter Sauna
Solarium Gym Steam room Gymnasium
No smoking in restaurant* ⬛

West Lothian

THE HILCROFT ★★★
East Main St EH47 0JU
(off M8 J4 to Whitburn. Hotel 0.5m on L)
📞 01501 740818 📠 01501 744013
Family run, welcoming business hotel.
Varying sized bedrooms. Informal Bistro
with good value menu.
*£££ 31 bedrooms (7 fmly) No dogs (ex
guide dogs) Night porter No smoking area
in restaurant* ⬛

WHERE TO EAT

RESTAURANTS

AA RECOMMENDED

Champany Inn

East Lothian

OPEN ARMS HOTEL ❀ ❀
EH39 5EG
☎ 01620 850241 📠 01620 850570
Good classic Scottish cooking comes through in such dishes as roulade of smoked salmon and cream cheese, collops of Aberdeen Angus fillet beef on a fried dumpling with a whisky and bramble sauce, and bread and butter pudding flavoured with peaches, nutmeg and sultanas.
Fixed D ££ 🗺

East Lothian

BONARS RESTAURANT ❀ ❀
Main Street EH41 4QH
☎ 01620 810264
The modern Scottish carte is excellent value and although dishes sound a little fussy, each ingredient has its place. Starters might include timbale of trout mousseline with steamed mussels; a main courses of breast of chicken stuffed with three cheeses, and the desserts,well worth leaving space for, a brandied date pudding with hot caramel sauce.
Fixed L £ 🗺

Falkirk

GRANGE MANOR HOTEL ❀
Glensburgh Road FK3 8XJ
☎ 01324 474836 📠 01324 665861
Visitors to the smart restaurant enjoy the excellent Scottish produce that forms the base of the kitchen's modern cooking. Pan-fried breast of chicken with noodles and pesto cream sauce, or medallion of venison loin with apricot and apple chutney, show the range.
Fixed L £ ALC ££ 🗺

East Lothian

GREYWALLS HOTEL ❀ ❀
Muirfield, EH31 2EG
☎ 01620 842144 📠 01620 842241
Modern British dishes which take full advantage of Scotland's larder. A typical spring meal might start with lightly pan-fried scallops in white wine, lime spiked sauce, and continue with mignons of beef with a red wine sauce. To finish, perhaps a light vanilla soufflé with a strong blackcurrant sauce.
Fixed L £ 🗺

LA POTINIERE ❀ ❀ ❀
Main Street, EH31 2AA ☎/📠 01620 843214
Starting with pea, lettuce and mint soup, then a warm mousse of Arbroath smokie, next a finely sliced maize-fed chicken on a bed of shredded cabbage with a aigre-doux sauce. Then comes a bowl of salad before concluding with a rich flavoured, light textured chocolate sponge
Fixed L ££

West Lothian

CHAMPANY INN ❀ ❀ ❀
EH49 7LU
☎ 01506 834532 📠 01506 834302
This restaurant will produce a meal, in winter for example, of chargrilled North Sea prawns with home-made pasta and a light butter sauce, roast breast of Gressingham duckling, and a bread-and-butter pudding, vanilla ice cream and crème anglaise to finish.
Fixed L ££ ALC £££ 🗺

LIVINGSTON'S RESTAURANT ❀
52 High Street, EH49 7AE
☎ 01506 846565
Tucked away down a courtyard this restaurant provides an intimate old world atmosphere. A lunch menu could feature celery soup, sea bass encased in a crêpe, and a delicious crème brûlée with roast banana.
Fixed L £ ALC £ 🗺

East Lothian

THE GRANGE ❀ ❀
35 The High Street, EH39 4HH
☎/📠 01620 895894
Inventive fish dishes are a particular strength - lightly seared salmon fillet with sliced avocado and a delicate tarragon dressing, for example. A main course is breast of chicken filled with herb mousseline on a bed of seaweed.
Fixed L £ 🗺

West Lothian

HOUSTON HOUSE HOTEL ❀ ❀ ❀
Broxburn EH52 6JS
☎ 01506 853831 📠 01506 854220
Boudin of west coast fish with a light lemon and vegetable broth, and an individual venison and black pudding Wellington are but two typical dishes.
Fixed L ££ ALC £££ 🗺

SCOTTISH BORDERS

One of Britain's most bitterly contested borders was for so long the frontier that separated England from Scotland. The Border Line - all 110 miles (176km) of it - still evokes images of the long and violent struggle for political supremacy, though the scene here today is very different, a far cry from the years of lawlessness, battle and bloodshed. Approximately 1800 square miles of dense forest, softly swelling hills and broad sweeps of open heather moorland, the Scottish Borders region - once the hunting ground of kings - includes some of the wildest and most spectacular scenery anywhere in Britain and is a walkers' paradise.

A good base for exploring the region is Hawick, the largest of all the Border towns. From here it is an easy journey to some of Scotland's most historic sites. Among them are Traquair House, near Peebles, Floors Castle, near Kelso, and Thirlstane Castle at Lauder. However, no tour of the Scottish Borders is complete without a visit to Hermitage Castle, a grim 13th-century fortress overlooked by wild and lonely hills. With its settled spells of weather and range of outdoor pursuits, the region is perfect for either a touring holiday or a short break. And there is always a wonderful sense of calm and tranquility, belying its colourful past and the part it played in more than 1,000 years of history.

PRINCIPAL TOWNS

MELROSE

Melrose, a cosy and tweedy little town, nestles between the River Tweed and the beautiful Eildon Hills in the heart of Sir Walter Scott country. If you're on your way to Abbotsford House, Scott's former home, just outside Melrose, a visit to the town, however brief, will not disappoint.

PEEBLES

Excellent salmon fishing, walking and golf, quality antique and craft shops, and some of the prettiest Tweeddale countryside, attract both visitors and day-trippers from Edinburgh to this respectable little woollen town. Former home of Robert Louis Stevenson and Mungo Park, whose exploration helped to open up Africa, it features some impressive municipal buildings. With numerous historic houses and castles, notably imposing Neidpath Castle - a short walk away along the banks of the Tweed, and beautiful gardens nearby, you'll find Peebles an excellent base from which to tour from.

SELKIRK

Famous for its tweed manufacturing, its associations with Sir Walter Scott, who presided as sheriff here for 33 years, and the Common Ridings, a tradition linked to a banner captured at the nearby Battle of Flodden in 1513, the ancient burgh of Selkirk is a good centre for exploring the lovely Yarrow and Ettrick Valleys.

MUST SEE

ABBOTSFORD HOUSE,
Melrose ☎ 01896 752043
Formerly the home of Sir Walter Scott, this romantic turreted mansion is in a wonderful setting. Still lived in by his descendants, it contains Scott's extraordinary collection of antiquities, armour and many other curious mementoes and relics of his remarkable life, including a lock of Bonnie Prince Charlie's hair. Charming tea room in a greenhouse designed by Scott.

BOWHILL HOUSE & COUNTRY PARK,
Selkirk ☎ 01750 22204
Dating from the early 19th century, this splendid Georgian mansion contains a world renowned art collection, and many 17th- and 18th-century clocks. Extensive grounds with a visitor centre, woodland walks, and a theatre.

DRYBURGH ABBEY,
Dryburgh ☎ 01835 822381
Standing in a lovely setting on the Tweed, this romantic, well-preserved ruined abbey was one of the Border monasteries founded by David I. Both Sir Walter Scott and Earl Haig are buried here.

FLOORS CASTLE,
Kelso ☎ 01573 223333
Scotland's largest inhabited castle was designed by William Adam in 1721, with wings added in the 19th century. Superb collections of furniture, porcelain, tapestries and paintings. Walled garden, adventure play area, picnic area and woodland walks.

JEDBURGH ABBEY,
Jedburgh ☎ 01835 863925
Often described as 'the most perfect and beautiful example of the Saxon and early Gothic in Scotland', this striking and remarkably complete ruined abbey, founded as a priory in the 12th century by David I, dominates the skyline of this small Border town. Informative visitor centre.

MELROSE ABBEY & ABBEY MUSEUM,
Melrose ☎ 01896 822562
Thought to be the final resting place of Robert the Bruce's heart, this romantic, ruined Cistercian Abbey, arguably Scotland's finest example of ecclesiastical architecture, dates from 1136 and is strongly associated with Sir Walter Scott. The fascinating museum is housed in the 16th-century Commendator's House.

ROBERT SMAIL'S PRINTING WORKS,
High St, Innerleithen ☎ 01896 830206
Step back in time at this completely restored printing works and see how printing was done at the beginning of the century. The Victorian office, paper store, composing room and machine room all survived as a unique time capsule. 'Hands-on' experience of typesetting.

ST ABB'S HEAD,
2m/3.2km north of Coldstream off A1107
☎ 01890 771443
Favoured by 10,000 guillemots alone, this is a birdwatcher's paradise, especially during the breeding season. Stand on top of sheer cliffs and watch the countless numbers of birds wheeling and diving below. Reached from the car park at Northfield Farm, where there is an exhibition and tea room.

TRAQUAIR HOUSE,
Traquair, Innerleithen ☎ 01896 830323
Experience the unique atmosphere of Scotland's oldest inhabited and most romantic castle. Dating back to the 12th century, this grand fortified mansion has played host to 27 Scottish monarchs, including Bonnie Prince Charlie, and has rich associations with Mary, Queen of Scots and the Jacobite risings. Very much a family home, the Stuarts or Maxwell-Stuarts have lived here since 1491. Unique 18th-century brewhouse still brewing strong Ale. Woodland walks, a splendid maze, craft workshops, art gallery, shop, restaurant and regular events.

Jedburgh Abbey

ART GALLERIES

BROUGHTON GALLERY,
Broughton ☎ 01899 830234
Paintings and crafts by living artists housed in a tower house.

HAWICK MUSEUM & SCOTT ART GALLERY,
Hawick ☎ 01450 373457
Excellent museum on the history, trades and wildlife of the Borders. Fine collection 19th & 20th-century Scottish art.

KELSO MUSEUM & THE TURRET GALLERY,
Abbey Court, Kelso ☎ 01573 225470
Museum displays reflect the life and times of the lively market town and abbey. Also local artists and crafts.

TWEEDDALE MUSEUM & PICTURE GALLERY,
High St, Peebles ☎ 01721 720123
Lively local history displays and contemporary art exhibitions.

MUSEUMS

AIKWOOD TOWER,
By Selkirk ☎ 01750 52253
An exhibition of the life and work of James Hogg, the Ettrick Shepherd, and art exhibitions in a 16th-century tower house.

HALLIWELLS HOUSE MUSEUM,
Market Place, Selkirk ☎ 01750 20096
Selkirk's oldest surviving dwelling, formerly an ironmonger's, recreated as an enterprising museum illustrating the town's development.

JIM CLARK ROOM,
44 Newtown St, Duns ☎ 01361 883960
Commemorates the life and career of Jim Clark, twice world motor racing champion in the 1960s, who lived in Duns.

JOHN BUCHAN CENTRE,
Broughton ☎ 01899 221050
Memorial display to John Buchan, the acclaimed novelist, historian and politician, who spent much of his childhood here and who used the area as background in many of his books.

MARY QUEEN OF SCOTS HOUSE,
Queen St, Jedburgh ☎ 01835 863331
Beautiful 16th-century fortified dwelling housing a museum devoted to the memory of Mary, Queen of Scots, who visited the town in 1566. Thought-provoking interpretation of her tragic life.

SIR WALTER SCOTT'S COURTROOM,
Market Place, Selkirk ☎ 01750 20096
Displays and audio-visual presentations relating to the life and writings of novelist Sir Walter Scott, especially his time as Sheriff of Selkirk.

TRIMONTIUM EXHIBITION,
The Square, Melrose ☎ 01896 822463
Learn about life in a Roman fort at this fascinating modern exhibition situated close to Trimontium, a fort/town amphitheatre which was the centre of Roman Scotland.

HISTORIC & ANCIENT SITES

EDIN'S HALL BROCH,
Abbey St, Bathans, Duns
One of the few Iron Age Brochs in lowland Scotland and unusually large.

HERMITAGE CASTLE,
Hermitage ☎ 01387 376222
Vast, eerie ruin of the 14th and 15th centuries, associated with Mary, Queen of Scots and extensively restored.

KELSO ABBEY,
Kelso ☎ 0131 668 8800
Founded by David I in 1128 and probably the greatest of the four famous Border abbeys, Kelso served as a fortress in 1545 but only fragments of the once-imposing abbey church survive.

SMAILHOLM TOWER,
Smailholm ☎ 01573 460365
Well restored example of a classic Border tower-house, erected on a rocky outcrop in the 15th century. Standing 57ft high, it houses an exhibition of dolls and a display based on Sir Walter Scott's book 'Minstrels of the Border'.

GREAT FOR KIDS

CRUMSTANE FARM PARK,
Duns ☎ 01361 883268
Over 60 varieties of animals and poultry, including many rare breeds, to view at close quarters. Picnic area.

DRUMLANRIG TOWER,
Tower Knowle, Hawick ☎ 01450 373457
Using the latest audio-visual technology, this exciting museum, housed in a beautifully restored fortified tower house, interprets Hawick's turbulent history from medieval times.

THE HIRSEL,
Coldstream ☎/🄵 01890 882834
Woodland nature trails, a wildfowl sanctuary and the Homestead Museum.

JEDFOREST DEER & FARM PARK,
Camptown, Jedburgh ☎ 01835 840364
Working farm with rare breeds, a deer park, waymarked walks, an adventure playground. Pets corners.

JEDBURGH CASTLE JAIL & MUSEUM,
Castlegate, Jedburgh ☎ 01835 863254
Models dressed in contemporary costume and audio-visual period artifacts in reconstructed rooms, illustrate prison life.

TEDDY MELROSE TEDDY BEAR MUSEUM,
The Wynd, Melrose ☎ 01896 822464
Timeless enjoyment to children of all ages. Tea room.

HOMES & GARDENS

AYTON CASTLE,
Ayton, Eyemouth ☎ 018907 81212
Beautifully restored red sandstone building. Fine Victorian decoration and furniture. Splendid painted ceilings.

DAWYCK BOTANIC GARDEN,
Stobo ☎ 01721 760254
An impressive collection of mature specimen trees, flowering trees, shrubs and herbaceous plants. Woodland walks and tearoom.

KAILZIE GARDENS,
Peebles ☎ 01721 720007
Extensive grounds with fine old trees and a burnside walk flanked by rhododendrons and azaleas. Walled garden, greenhouses and rose gardens.

MANDERSTON,
Duns ☎ 01361 883450
This grandest of grand houses gives an fascinating picture of Edwardian life, with superb state rooms, and the world's only silver staircase. Fine gardens..

MELLERSTAIN HOUSE,
Gordon ☎ 01573 410225
Scotland's finest Adam mansion with beautiful plasterwork, colourful ceilings, period furniture and paintings. Terraced gardens. Tea room and shop.

MONTEVIOT HOUSE GARDENS,
Monteviot, Jedburgh ☎ 01835 830380
Extensive rose gardens and water gardens with views over the River Tweed.

NEIDPATH CASTLE,
Peebles ☎/🄵 01721 720333
Spectacular position. Well-preserved 14th-century stronghold with a pit prison, museum and a tartan display. Good walks and fine views. Picnic area.

PAXTON HOUSE,
Paxton, Berwick-upon-Tweed
☎ 01289 386291
Splendid country house designed by the Adam family and furnished by Chippendale and Trotter. An outpost of the National Galleries of Scotland. Gardens and walks.

THIRLESTANE CASTLE,
Lauder ☎ 01578 722430
Fairy-tale Border fortress, home of the Earls of Lauderdale since the 12th century. Collection of antique toys and doll. Border Country Life Museum. Woodland walks, picnic area & tearoom.

BIG OUTDOORS

DUNS CASTLE NATURE RESERVE
(on B6365)
Bird-lovers should follow the nature trail through wildlife-rich woodland to the 'Hen Poo', a stretch of water favoured by wildfowl.

ST MARY'S LOCH *(west of Selkirk on A708)*
Surrounded by glorious upland scenery on the Southern Upland Way. The area inspired such writers as Sir Walter Scott and James Hogg.

SCOTT'S VIEW
(on B6356 north of St Boswells)
Sir Walter Scott's favourite viewpoint in the Eildon Hills.

SIR WALTER SCOTT
Sir Walter Scott was so moved by the grandeur and remoteness of the Scottish Borders that he wrote ' To my eye, these grey hills and all this wild border country have beauties peculiar to themselves. I like the very nakedness of the land; it has something bold and stern and solitary about it. If I did not see the heather at least once a year I think I should die.' Scott devoted much of his time to the preservation of what little remained of the region's beautifu; but battle-scarred abbeys, so keeping alive the spirit and character of the Borders. His country home, Abbotsford, near Melrose, is open to the public.

ESSENTIAL INFORMATION

TOURIST INFORMATION

COLDSTREAM *seasonal*,
Town Hall, High St, Coldstream TD12 4DH
☎ 01890 882607

EYEMOUTH *seasonal*.
Auld Kirk, Market Place, Eyemouth TD14 5HE
☎ 01890 750678

GALASHIELS *seasonal*,
3 St John's St, Galashiels TD1 3JX
☎ 01896 755551

HAWICK *seasonal*,
Drumlanrig's Tower, Tower Knowe, Hawick
TD9 9EN
☎ 01450 372547 🖷 01450 373993

JEDBURGH,
Murray's Green, Jedburgh TD8 6BE
☎ 01835 863435 & 863688
🖷 01835 864099

KELSO *seasonal*,
Town House, The Square, Kelso TD5 7HF
☎ 01573 223464

MELROSE *seasonal*
Abbey House, Abbey St, Melrose TD6 9LG
☎ 01896 822555

PEEBLES,
High St, Peebles EH45 8AG
☎ 01721 720138 🖷 01721 724401

SELKIRK *seasonal*,
Halliwell's House, Selkirk TD7 4BL
☎ 01750 20054

ACCESS

AIR ACCESS

EDINBURGH AIRPORT ☎ 0131 333 1000
BRITISH AIRWAYS ☎ 0345 222111
BRITISH MIDLAND ☎ 0345 554554

CRAFTS

The area is renowned for its woollen mills and the weaving of tweeds, tartans, rugs, tapestries and fine quality knitwear. Also lookout for local artists and craftsmen demonstrating woodturning, glassblowing, jewellery making, pottery and furniture making.

BRADEN CRAFTS,
Coldstream ☎ 01890 882445
Hand-crafted wooden items.

THE HIRSEL,
Coldstream ☎ 01890 882834
Crafts centre with glass, jewellery,
leatherwork, pottery and weaving.

HORN & COUNTRY CRAFTS,
Hermitage, Hawick ☎ 01387 376215

KELSO POTTERY,
The Knowes, Kelso ☎ 01573 224027

KINSMAN - BLAKE CERAMICS,
Smailholm, Kelso ☎ 01573 460666

LINDEAN MILL GLASS,
Lindean Mill, Galashiels ☎ 01750 20173

PEEBLES CRAFT CENTRE,
9 Newby Court, Peebles
Studio porcelain, woodworks, hand-
painted silk and pine furniture making.

SELKIRK GLASS,
Selkirk ☎ 01750 20954

TRAQUAIR HOUSE,
Traquair, Innerleithen
☎ 01896 830323 & 830785
Craft workshops including leathermaking,
pottery, wood-painting and printmaking

WOOLLEN MILLS.

ANDREW ELLIOT LTD,
Forest Mill, Selkirk ☎ 01750 20412

LOCHCARRON CASHMERE & WOOL CENTRE,
Waverley Mill, Galashiels ☎ 01896 752091

PETER SCOTT & CO LTD,
11 Buccleuch St, Hawick ☎ 01450 372311

ENTERTAINMENT

CINEMAS

PAVILION,
Market St, Galashiels ☎ 01896 752767

THEATRES

LITTLE THEATRE,
Bowhill House, Selkirk ☎ 01899 830234
Theatre in the grounds of a mansion.

WYND THEATRE,
Melrose ☎ 01450 372555

FOOD & DRINK

Delicious specialities abound within the
region, from unusual home-baked
shortbreads, buns (Selkirk Bannock) and
tarts (Eyemouth Tart), award-winning
chesses, notably the camembert-like
Bonchester and the hard cheddar-like
Stichill), smoked locally-caught salmon
(Teviot Game Fare Smokery at Eckford),
champion haggis-makers (David Palmer
Butchers of Jedburgh and Selkirk, Lindsay
Grieve Butchers of Hawick) and mouth-
watering confectionery (Jethart Snails,
Hawick Balls, Soor Plooms & Berwick
Cockles) for the sweet-toothed. St Ronan's
Spring Water is produced at Innerleithen
and a superb strong real ale is brewed at
Traquair House, the only private house in
Britain to hold a licence to brew beer.

TRANSPORT

BOAT TRIPS & CRUISES

ST ABBS BOAT CHARTER,
Murrayfield, St Abbs ☎ 01890 771681

CAR HIRE

D.S. DALGLEISH & SON,
Weensland Rd, Hawick ☎ 01450 376028

DAVID HARRISON LTD,
Edinburgh Rd, Peebles ☎ 01721 721350

CYCLE HIRE

BIKESPORT,
Peebles Rd, Innerleithen
☎/🖷 01896 830000

HAWICK CYCLE CENTRE,
Mart St, Hawick

SCOTTISH BORDER TRAILS,
Venlaw High Rd, Peebles ☎ 01721 720336
Hire and on and off-rd tours.

GUIDED TOURS

AULD REEKIE TOURS,
☎/🖷 0131 557 4700
Tours of the Border towns, castles and
abbeys in a stretch limousine.

TRAINS

The east coast line from London to
Edinburgh stops at Berwick-upon-Tweed.
Passenger Enquiries ☎ 0345 484950.

SPORT & LEISURE

ACTIVITY & LEISURE CENTRES

BACKCOUNTRY ADVENTURE,
Glen Estate, Innerleithen ☎ 01896 830647

BRAIDWOOD SPORTING CLAYS,
Midlem, Selkirk ☎ 01835 870280

DUNS SPORTS COMPLEX,
Duns ☎ 01361 883397

EYEMOUTH LEISURE CENTRE,
North St, Eyemouth ☎ 01890 750557

GYTES LEISURE CENTRE,
Walkershaugh, Peebles ☎ 01721 723688

JEDBURGH SPORTS CENTRE,
Pleasance, Jedburgh ☎ 01835 862 566

SCOTTISH ACADEMY OF FALCONRY,
Hawick ☎ 01450 860666

SCOTTISH BORDER TRAILS,
Venlaw High Rd, Peebles ☎ 01721 720336

TEVIOTDALE LEISURE CENTRE,
Mansfield Rd, Hawick ☎ 01450 374440

ANGLING

Whether you want to cast for salmon in
the famous River Tweed, seek sea trout on
its tributaries, notably the Till and
Whiteadder, fish on lochs and streams for
brown and rainbow trout, or take a boat
from Eyemouth, Burnmouth or St Abbs for
some excellent sea fishing, the Scottish
Borders has everything for the keen angler.
Enquire at Information Centres for the free
Scottish Borders Angling Guide.

CYCLING

The Scottish Borders is prime cycling
country, offering an endless choice of on
and off-road routes for the novice and
experienced cyclist. From an extensive
network of relatively quiet country
roads, many following gently undulating
river valleys, and miles of waymarked
routes through unspoilt Border Forests to
energetic mountain biking on open

moorland trails in the hilly areas to the south and west, the region is a cyclists paradise. Leaflets are available from Information Centres.

TWEED CYCLEWAY
Discover this 90 miles/144km signposted route through the beautiful Tweed Valley from Biggar to Berwick-on-Tweed.

FOUR ABBEYS CYCLE ROUTE,
A gentle signposted tour linking the famous abbey towns of Melrose, Dryburgh, Kelso and Jedburgh.

GOLF COURSES

ROXBURGHE,
Kelso ☎ 01573 450331
Undulating course is set in 200 acres of mature parkland and features deep challenging bunkers and dramatic water hazards.

Also:

DUNS ☎ 01361 882717
EYEMOUTH ☎ 01890 750551
GALASHIELS ☎ 01896 753724
HAWICK ☎ 01450 372293
HIRSEL ☎ 01890 882678
INNERLEITHEN ☎ 01896 830951
JEDBURGH ☎ 01835 863587
KELSO ☎ 01573 223009
LAUDER ☎ 01578 722526
MELROSE ☎ 01896 822855
MINTO ☎ 01450 870220
NEWCASTLETON ☎ 01387 375257
PEEBLES ☎ 01721 720197
ST BOSWELLS ☎ 01835 823527
SELKIRK ☎ 01750 20621
TORWOODLEE, Galashiels
☎ 01896 752260
WEST LINTON ☎ 01968 660256

HORSE RACING

KELSO RACECOURSE,
Wooler, Northumberland ☎ 01668 281611
National Hunt racing at most picturesque course.

HORSE RIDING

BUCCLEUCH COUNTRY RIDE,
A 57-mile, 3-4 day route for the independant rider on bridleways, tracks and quiet country roads. Accommodation and stabling available.

THE BORDER COUNTRY ROUTE,
An exhilarating 100-mile circular route through Kielder Forest and the Cheviot Hills on the Borders/Northumberland border. Details from Tourist Information Centres.

BAILEY MILL TREKKING CENTRE,
Bailey, Newcastleton ☎ 01697 748617

COWDENKNOWES EQUICENTRE,
Earlston ☎ 01896 848020

FERNIEHIRST MILL LODGE,
Jedburgh ☎ 01835 863279

HAZELDEAN RIDING CENTRE,
Hassendeanburn, Hawick ☎ 01450 870373

NENTHORN RIDING STABLES,
Nenthorn, Kelso ☎ 01573 24073

PEEBLES HYDRO STABLES,
Innerleithen Rd, Peebles ☎ 01721 721325

SAILING

The stunning scenery around St Mary's Loch, situated west of Selkirk on the A708, provides a magnificent setting for sailing enthusiasts. Coastal sailing can be enjoyed from Eyemouth and St Abbs.

SCENIC DRIVES

Rewarding drives that reveal the best of the Scottish Borders countryside include a leisurely drive through the Tweed Valley, a trip along the spectacular coastline, taking in quaint fishing villages and the dramatic cliffs at St Abb's Head, a journey along the Yarrow and Ettrick Valleys for the beautiful views of the Border Hills, and a circular route through the heart of the region, incorporating the abbey towns and unspoilt Border scenery.

SWIMMING
BEACHES

Sandy beaches exist near the mouth of the River Eye at Eyemouth and in small coves along the dramatic coastline between St Abbs and Cove.

See also Leisure Centres
GALASHIELS SWIMMING POOL,
Livingstone Pl, Galashiels ☎ 01896 752154

KELSO SWIMMING POOL,
Inch Rd, Kelso ☎ 01573 224944

PEEBLES SWIMMING POOL,
Port Brae, Peebles ☎ 01721 720779

SELKIRK SWIMMING POOL,
Victoria Rd, Selkirk ☎ 01750 20897

WATERSIDE FITNESS CENTRE,
Oxnam Rd, Jedburgh ☎ 01835 863430

WALKING

From gentle, well waymarked walks through the woodlands in the Tweed Valley (Glentress Woodland Park) and upland forests in the Cheviot Hills to wild, open moorland rambles and invigorating cliff walks, the Borders offers excellent year-round walking for all abilities on a varied network of paths and tracks.

SOUTHERN UPLAND WAY,
The longest trail, 212 miles/340km, crossing Southern Scotland from Portpatrick on the west coast to Cocksburnpath on the east coast. Some 82 miles/130km of its route traverses the Scottish Borders, passing through large tracts of unspoilt country from St Mary's Loch, via Traquair, Melrose and the Lammermuir Hills, to the coast. Only experienced and well-equipped backpackers should tackle the whole route.

ST CUTHBERT'S WAY,
Marked with the symbol of St Cuthbert's cross, this 62 mile/100km walking route links Melrose Abbey with Lindisfarne on the Northumberland coast.

WALKING TOURS & HOLIDAYS

SCOTTISH BORDER TRAILS,
Venlaw High Rd, Peebles ☎ 01721 720336
SCOTWALK LTD,
TInnerleithen ☎/🖷 01896 830515
STOORIFIT LTD,
40 Damside, Innerleithen ☎ 01721 724068

A WALKER'S PARADISE

Without question the Borders is a walker's paradise. Two long-distance trails, the Southern Upland Way and St Cuthbert's Way, explore the heart of the region but there are also plenty of other routes to tempt those who enjoy short strolls amd lengthy hikes. The Scottish Borders Countryside Ranger Service operates a full Guided Walks programme from spring to autumn each year, as well as a choice of winter walks. Even in the huge Border forests, provision has been made for the visitor in search of peaceful recreation.

With numerous woodland paths, mountain bike trails, ancient monuments and wildlife conservation, these sprawling woodland areas offer excellent opportunities for fresh air and exercise. The Scottish Borders is also the northern terminus for the Pennine Way; you can join the route at Kirk Yetholm near Kelso and follow it south for a total of 250 miles (402km) to the Derbyshire Peak District. However, some stretches of the trail are pretty tough and should not be attempted by the inexperienced.

WHERE TO STAY

AA RECOMMENDED

ANCRUM

ANCRUM CRAIG ◙◙◙◙
TD8 6UN *(B6400, just before Ancrum take 1st fork L toward Denholm continue for 1.75m turn R toward Lilliesleaf, uphill 0.75m turn L)*
☎ 01835 830280 ☐ 01835 830259
Imposing mansion in peaceful setting amidst farmland with views across the Teviot valley. Hearty and tasty Scottish breakfast.

£ *3 bedrooms No smoking in dining room Mar-Oct*

BURNMOUTH

GREYSTONELEES ◙◙◙
Greystonelees TD14 5SZ
☎ 01890 781709
Although no longer a working farm its still an animal lover's paradise. A warm welcome assured.

3 bedrooms No smoking No children under 5yrs 140 acres mixed 🛇

CHIRNSIDE

CHIRNSIDE HALL COUNTRY HOUSE HOTEL ★★ ֎֎
TD11 3LD *(on A6105)*
☎ 01890 818219 ☐ 01890 818231
Friendly country house hotel, overlooking the magnificent Borders countryside with a luxurious atmosphere throughout.

££ *10 bedrooms (2 fmly) No smoking in 4 bedrooms Snooker Putting green No smoking in restaurant* 🛇

COLDINGHAM BAY

DUNLAVEROCK HOUSE ◙◙◙◙◙
TD14 5PA
☎ 018907 71450 ☐ 018907 71450
Commands a spectacular cliff-top setting with magnificent views. Contemporary decor alongside antique furnishings. Excellent dining.

6 bedrooms (1 fmly) No smoking in 3 bedrooms No smoking in dining room Licensed No children under 12yrs Closed 1 Dec-31 Jan 🛇

GALASHIELS

KINGSKNOWES ★★★
Selkirk Rd TD1 3HY
(off A7 at Galashiels/Selkirk rdbt)
☎ 01896 758375 ☐ 01896 750377
Friendly and informal atmosphere at this family-run hotel close to the River Tweed. Eating options.

££ *11 bedrooms (3 fmly) Tennis (hard) Children's facilities* 🛇

WOODLANDS HOUSE HOTEL & RESTAURANTS ★★★
Windyknowe Rd TD1 1RG
(A7 into Galashiels, A72 towards Peebles, 1st L into Hall St, then 2nd rd on R)
☎ 01896 754722 ☐ 01896 754722

Fine Victorian mansion in large grounds with the relaxed atmosphere of a country house. Restaurant and steak house.

££ *9 bedrooms (3 fmly)* 🛇

ABBOTSFORD ARMS ★★
63 Stirling St TD1 1BY *(turn off A7 down Ladhope Vale, turn L opp bus station)*
☎ 01896 752517 ☐ 01896 750744
Friendly commercial hotel is near the town centre. Food served all day in the bar and restaurant.

£ *14 bedrooms (2 fmly) No dogs (ex guide dogs) Night porter Closed 24-25 & 31 Dec & 1 Jan* 🛇

KING'S ★★
56 Market St TD1 3AJ
(adjacent to southbound A7 in town centre)
☎ 01896 755497 ☐ 01896 755497
Family-run hotel near the town centre with a friendly and relaxing atmosphere. Good value meals.

££ *7 bedrooms (1 fmly) No dogs (ex guide dogs) Closed 1-3 Jan* 🛇

MAPLEHURST ◙◙◙◙◙
42 Abbotsford Rd TD1 3HP *(on A7)*
☎ 01896 754700 ☐ 01896 754700
Large, detached house, built in 1907, still retains many original features. Home cooking is well worth sampling.

£ *3 bedrooms (1 fmly) No smoking No dogs (ex guide dogs) Closed Xmas & New Year* 🛇

BINNIEMYRE ◙◙◙◙
Abbotsford Rd TD1 3JB
☎ 01896 757137 ☐ 01896 757137
Fine period house sympathetically restored to become a charming guest house. Welcoming lounge with stove for cooler weather.

5 bedrooms (3 fmly) No smoking in bedrooms No smoking in dining room No smoking in 1 lounge Snooker 🛇

ASHLYN ◙◙◙
7 Abbotsford Rd TD1 3DP
☎ 01896 752416 ☐ 01896 752416
Substantial period house offering attractive bedrooms with modern en suite shower rooms.

£ *3 bedrooms No smoking*

ISLAND HOUSE ◙◙◙
65 Island St TD1 1PA *(opposite B & Q store)*
☎ 01896 752649
Attractively decorated and spotlessly clean town house with bright bedrooms, one on the ground floor.

3 bedrooms No smoking in bedrooms No smoking in dining room **HAWICK**

ELM HOUSE ★★
17 North Bridge St TD9 9BD
(on A7 in centre of Hawick)
☎ 01450 372866 ☐ 01450 374715
Family-run hotel offering good value

accommodation and food. Inexpensive meals in the lounge bar or restaurant.

£ *7 bedrooms 8 annexe bedrooms (3 fmly) No smoking in restaurant* 🛇

KIRKLANDS ★★
West Stewart Place TD9 8BH *(0.5m N from Hawick High St, 200yds W of A7)*
☎ 01450 372263 ☐ 01450 370404
Fine Victorian house and long-established hotel with extremely well equipped bedrooms.

££ *5 bedrooms 4 annexe bedrooms Snooker Pool table Children's facilities No smoking area in restaurant* 🛇

HOUNDWOOD

WESTWOOD HOUSE ◙◙◙◙
TD14 5TP
(just off A1. Turn off 2m S of Grantshouse)
☎ 01361 850232 ☐ 01361 850333
Former 18th-century coaching inn has been tastefully renovated. Bright cheery bedrooms. Praiseworthy home-cooked meals.

£ *6 bedrooms (2 fmly) No smoking No dogs Children's facilities*

INNERLEITHEN

TRAQUAIR ARMS HOTEL ◙◙◙
Traquair Rd EH44 6PD *(from A72 take B709 for St Mary's Loch & Traquair)*
☎ 01896 830229 ☐ 01896 830260
This small hotel enjoys a reputation for its good-value meals. Two-bedroom family suite on the top floor.

££ *10 bedrooms (2 fmly) No smoking in dining room Direct dial from bedrooms Children's facilities Fishing* 🛇

JEDBURGH

THE SPINNEY ◙◙◙◙◙
Langlee TD8 6PB *(2m S on A68)*
☎ 01835 863525 ☐ 01835 864883
Two roadside cottages extended to become an attractive modern home. Spacious bedrooms. Hearty breakfasts.

£ *3 bedrooms No smoking in bedrooms No smoking in dining room No dogs (ex guide dogs) Closed mid Nov-Feb*

FROYLEHURST ◙◙◙◙
Friars TD8 6BN *(from town centre Market Place leave by Exchange St then 1st R into Friars for 3rd turn on L)*
☎ 01835 862477 ☐ 01835 862477
Imposing Victorian house in secluded gardens with fine views. Well proportioned bedrooms.

£ *5 bedrooms (3 fmly) No smoking in bedrooms No smoking in dining room No dogs No children under 5yrs Mar-Nov*

Cringletie House

KENMORE BANK HOTEL ◙◙◙
Oxnam Rd TD8 6JJ *(off A68. Into Jedburgh from S, take 1st R by church)*
☎ 01835 862369
Enjoys fine views of the abbey from its elevated position. Cosy and relaxing atmosphere.
£ 6 bedrooms (2 fmly) No smoking in dining room Licensed Fishing ➻

MEADHON HOUSE ◙◙◙
48 Castle Gate TD8 6BB
(A68 into Jedburgh, up to Abbey turn L into Castle Gate, 1st B&B on L)
☎ 01835 862504 ☎01835 862504
17th-century building now a modern guesthouse conveniently situated. Attractively decorated it sparkles throughout.
5 bedrooms (3 fmly) No smoking

WILLOW COURT ◙◙◙
The Friars TD8 6BN *(from Market Sq take Exchange St, Friars 50yds on R. 1st house on L)*
☎ 01835 863702 ☎ 01835 864601
Modern house in two acres of gardens in an elevated position off the town centre. Three ground floor bedrooms.
£ 4 bedrooms (1 fmly) No smoking in bedrooms No smoking in dining room No smoking in 1 lounge Licensed Children's facilities

FERNIEHIRST MILL LODGE ◙◙
TD8 6PQ *(2.5m S on A68, at the end of a private track off A68)*
☎ 01835 863279
Modern chalet-style lodge in secluded riverside setting. Part of a riding centre (experienced adult riders only).
£ 9 bedrooms No smoking in dining room Direct dial from bedrooms Licensed Fishing Riding ➻

SUNLAWS HOUSE HOTEL & GOLF COURSE ★★★ ❀❀
Heiton TD5 8JZ *(3m S on A698)*
☎ 01573 450331 ☎ 01573 450611
Built in 1885 this wonderfully positioned hotel offers individually decorated and thoughtfully equipped bedrooms.
££££ 16 bedrooms 6 annexe bedrooms (2 fmly) Night porter Golf 18 Tennis (hard) Fishing Croquet lawn Putting green Shooting Health & Beauty Saloon No smoking in restaurant ➻

CROSS KEYS ★★★
36-37 The Square TD5 7HL
☎ 01573 223303 ☎ 01573 225792
Originally a coaching inn this family-run hotel overlooks Kelso's fine cobbled square. Restaurant and bar/bistro.
££ 24 bedrooms (4 fmly) No dogs (ex guide dogs) Lift Night porter Air conditioning Snooker ➻

EDNAM HOUSE ★★★
Bridge St TD5 7HT
☎ 01573 224168 ☎01573 226319
Mansion overlooking the River Tweed, so making it popular with salmon fishers. Old-fashioned style and traditional standards.
£££ 32 bedrooms (2 fmly) Night porter Croquet lawn Closed 25 Dec-10 Jan ➻

LAUDERDALE ★★
1 Edinburgh Rd TD2 6TW
(on A68 from S, centre of Lauder, hotel on R)
☎ 01578 722231 ☎ 01578 718642
An ideal stop-over for those travelling north and south of the border. Good value meals.
££ 9 bedrooms ➻

THE GRANGE ◙◙
6 Edinburgh Rd TD2 6TW *(on A68, between war memorial and petrol station)*
☎ 01578 722649
A welcoming cuppa greets guests on arrival at this substantial detached house in sheltered gardens.
3 bedrooms (2 fmly) No smoking No dogs (ex guide dogs) Closed 24-26 Dec

BURT'S ★★★ ❀❀
The Square TD6 9PN
(A6091)
☎ 01896 822285 ☎ 01896 822870
Once a coaching inn, this long established family-run hotel is a haven for good food.
££ 20 bedrooms No smoking in all bedrooms Shooting Salmon Fishing No smoking in restaurant Closed 24-26 Dec ➻

BON ACCORD ★★
Market Square TD6 9PQ
☎ 01896 822645 ☎01896 823474
Friendly hotel is attractively decorated throughout and offers bright well furnished bedrooms.
££ 10 bedrooms (1 fmly) No dogs (ex guide dogs) No children under 12yrs Closed 25 Dec ➻

GEORGE & ABBOTSFORD ★★
High St TD6 9PD
(from A68 or A7 take A6091 to Melrose)
☎ 01896 822308 ☎ 01896 822308
Substantial 18th-century former coaching inn serving food throughout the day, including bar meals.
££ 30 bedrooms (3 fmly) Fishing No smoking area in restaurant ➻

DUNFERMLINE HOUSE ◙◙◙
Buccleuch St TD6 9LB
(opposite Abbey car park)
☎ 01896 822148 ☎ 01896 822148
Charming Victorian house close to the abbey. Spotlessly clean and very well maintained.
£ 5 bedrooms No smoking No dogs

CRINGLETIE HOUSE ★★★ ❀
EH45 8PL *(2.5m N on A703)*
☎ 01721 730233 ☎ 01721 730244
Imposing turreted baronial mansion in 28 acres of grounds. Lovely walled garden. Immaculately maintained throughout.
£££ 13 bedrooms (2 fmly) Lift Tennis (hard) Croquet lawn Putting green No smoking in restaurant Closed 2 Jan-8 Mar ➻

Dryburgh Abbey

Castle Venlaw Hotel

PARK ★★★
Innerleithen Rd EH45 8BA
☎ 01721 720451 📠 01721 723510
The little sister to the Hydro, with its own
individual style. Guests can use the
Hydro's extensive leisure facilities.
*£££ 24 bedrooms Night porter Putting
green* 🍴

PEEBLES HYDRO ★★★
EH45 8LX
(on A702, 0.3m out of town)
☎ 01721 720602 📠 01721 722999
Well established hotel nestling into the
hillside with fine views. Friendly welcome
from attentive and caring staff.
*££££ 137 bedrooms (25 fmly) No dogs (ex
guide dogs) Lift Night porter Indoor
swimming pool (heated) Tennis (hard)
Squash Riding Snooker Sauna Solarium
Gym Pool table Croquet lawn Putting green
Jacuzzi/spa Badminton Beautician
Hairdressing Weekly live entertainment
Children's facilities* 🍴

CASTLE VENLAW HOTEL ★★
Edinburgh Rd EH45 8QG
(off A703)
☎ 01721 720384
Turreted mansion surrounded by woods -
this is a peaceful and impressive place to
stay. High standards of hospitality and
service.
*££ 12 bedrooms (4 fmly) No smoking in
restaurant* 🍴

KINGSMUIR ★★
Springhill Rd EH45 9EP
*(from High St cross Tweed Bridge, straight
ahead up Springhill Rd, hotel 300 yds on R)*
☎ 01721 720151 📠 01721 721795
South of the River Tweed, near the town
centre this friendly hotel offers smart bar,
restaurant and comfortable lounge.
*10 bedrooms (2 fmly) No smoking in 5
bedrooms No smoking in restaurant* 🍴

VENLAW FARM ◨◨◨◨◨
EH45 8QG
(turn off A703 opp David Harrisons garage)
☎ 01721 722040
Modern bungalow on a hillside amidst
peaceful and secluded farmland.
*£ 3 bedrooms (1 fmly) No smoking No dogs
100 acres beef sheep Apr-Oct*

WINKSTON◨◨◨
Edinburgh Rd EH45 8PH
(0.5m from Peebles on the A703 on R)
☎ 01721 721264
Fine Georgian farmhouse in attractive
gardens. Bright and cheery bedrooms and
comfortable lounge. Home baking.
*£ 3 bedrooms No smoking No dogs (ex
guide dogs) 40 acres sheep Etr-Oct*

WHITESTONE HOUSE ◨◨
Innerleithen Rd EH45 8BD
(on A72, 100yds W of junct with A703)
☎ 01721 720337
Former manse with fine views across the
park to distant hills. Carefully maintained
and traditionally furnished.
*£ 3 bedrooms (1 fmly) No smoking in
dining room No dogs (ex guide dogs)*

DRYBURGH ABBEY ★★★
TD6 0RQ
(off B6356)
☎ 01835 822261 📠 01835 823945
Impressive red sandstone mansion,
sympathetically upgraded, beside
Dryburgh Abbey ruins and the River
Tweed.
*£££ 25 bedrooms 1 annexe bedrooms (3
fmly) Lift Night porter Indoor swimming
pool (heated) Fishing Putting green No
smoking in restaurant* 🍴

Buccleuch Arms

BUCCLEUCH ARMS ★★
The Green TD6 0EW
(on A68, 8m N of Jedburgh)
☎ 01835 822243 📠 01835 823965
Former coaching inn opposite the village
green. Well equipped bedrooms. Good
range of meals.
*££ 18 bedrooms (1 fmly) No smoking area
in restaurant* 🍴

TIBBIE SHIELS ◨◨◨
TD7 5NE
(just off A708 between Moffat/Selkirk)
☎ 01750 42231
Historic drovers inn on the shores of the
loch is a haven for walkers. Cosy bar and
snug, residents' lounge.
*£ 5 bedrooms (2 fmly) No smoking in area
of dining room No smoking in 1 lounge No
dogs (ex guide dogs) Fishing RS Mon & Tue
Nov-Feb* 🍴

HILLHOLM ◨◨◨◨
36 Hillside Ter TD7 4ND
*(on A7. On the S side near tennis courts &
golf course)*
☎ 01750 21293
Immaculate maintained semi-detached
Victorian house with comfortable
accommodation.
*£ 3 bedrooms No smoking in bedrooms No
smoking in dining room No dogs No
children under 10yrs Mar-Nov*

WHEATSHEAF HOTEL ◨◨◨
TD11 3JJ
(6m N of Duns on A6112)
☎ 01890 860257 📠 01890 860688
Overlooking the village green this country
inn could be considered a restaurant with
rooms.
*£ 5 bedrooms (1 fmly) No smoking in
bedrooms No smoking in dining room
Children's facilities Closed last week Oct &
last 2 wks Feb rs Mon* 🍴

TWEED VALLEY HOTEL
& RESTAURANT ★★
Galashiels Rd EH43 6AA *(on A72)*
☎ 01896 870636 📠 01896 870639
Friendly and informal, this family-run
Edwardian country hotel sits on high
ground with views over Tweed Valley.
*££ 16 bedrooms (3 fmly) Fishing Sauna
Solarium No smoking in restaurant* 🍴

WHERE TO EAT

RESTAURANTS

AA RECOMMENDED

CHIRNSIDE

CHIRNSIDE HALL ☺☺
TD11 3LD
☎ 01890 818219 📠 01890 818231
Fresh local produce inspires interesting combinations, note a superb courgette soup with blue Dunsyre cheese, main course crisp-edged duckling with a honey and soy sauce. and a dessert of nougatine parfait.
Fixed D ££ ALC ££ 🦐

KELSO

SUNLAWS HOUSE HOTEL ☺☺
Heiton, TD5 8JZ
☎ 01573 450331 📠 01573 450611
Of one thing guests can be certain, the cooking at Sunlaws is well worth a detour. Using the best local ingredients, the kitchen produces sound modern Scottish dishes such as Loch Fyne oysters with shallot dressing and roast rack of Borders lamb with mint-scented red wine jus.
Fixed L £ Fixed D £££ 🦐

MELROSE

BURTS HOTEL ☺☺
The Square TD6 9PN
☎ 01896 822285 📠 01896 822870
The kitchen handles Scottish ingredients effectively for a modern menu that pulls together many strands and influences. Chicken and haggis sausage is sliced around quenelles of clapshot with a whisky jus, and lasagne of salmon and halibut is served with ratatouille.
Fixed L ££ ALC £££ 🦐

PEEBLES

CRINGLETIE HOUSE ☺
EH45 8PL
☎ 01721 730233 📠 01721 730244
The impressive first-floor dining room offers a short fixed-price menu, with dishes such as smoked salmon, sautéed suprême of guinea fowl with Drambuie cream, and Jamaican banana torte with coffee and rum.
Fixed D £££ ALC ££ 🦐

SWINTON

WHEATSHEAF HOTEL ☺
Main Street, TD11 3JJ
☎/📠 01890 860257
This hotel has a well-deserved reputation for food with seasonal produce taking centre stage. Smoked haddock and Mull cheddar soup, and roast beef fillet with malt whisky and wild mushroom sauce, show the range.
ALC ££ 🦐

Call the AA Hotel Booking Service on
0990 050505 to book at AA recognised hotels and B&Bs in the UK,
or through our internet site:
http://www.theaa.co.uk/hotels

DUMFRIES &
GALLOWAY
& AYRSHIRE

Dumfries & Galloway is one of those wonderfully undiscovered corners of Scotland – a romantic land of wooded glens, high hills and exposed moorland, haunted by its colourful past and the ghosts of those who fell in fierce and bloody battles. Its close proximity to the English border makes it very accessible and, once over the border, you are ideally placed to discover the delights of this beautiful region. Heading west from Gretna Green you soon reach Dumfries, where Robert Burns spent his final years. Away to the north lies a vast and endless landscape; mile upon mile of open moorland and afforested slopes stretching towards the Ayrshire coast. On the long haul to Stranraer, you'll want to make regular stops and visit places like Gatehouse of Fleet, a delightful 18th-century planned town, and Creetown, a planned village on the estuary of the River Cree. Perfect for walking and fishing, Dumfries and Galloway seems gloriously untouched by 20th-century progress.

A mixture of wide sandy beaches, cliffs and rocky coves, the Ayrshire coastline looks out towards the Isles of Arran and Bute and enjoys a fine, mild climate fanned by the warm currents of the Gulf stream. Like so many parts of Scotland, Ayrshire is excellent for walking and the area is renowned for its superb championship golf courses, as well as boasting a wealth of historic landmarks to seek out, including lots of castles and ancient strongholds. Robert Burns, one of Scotland's most famous sons, was born at Alloway, near Ayr, in 1759, and if you're familiar with his work, why not follow in his footsteps by visiting the many towns and villages featured in his lyrics.

PRINCIPAL TOWNS

DUMFRIES

Long regarded as the 'Queen of the South' by the Scots, historic Dumfries, with its old bridges, a fascinating local museum and Camra Obscura, and a wealth of attractions associated with the national bard Robert Burns, who wrote some of his most famous songs while living in the town, has much to offer visitors. Straddling the River Nith and just 8 miles (12.9km) from the sea and glorious stretches of unspoilt coastline, it is a pleasant town with handsome Georgian and Victorian buildings lining neat streets, including pedestrianised Friars Vennel, one of Scotland's oldest streets. Those of you at the end of the Burns' Trail (he died here in 1796), will find it a most rewarding place to end your pilgrimage, while, for others, it makes a most convenient base for exploring the host of attractions in the surrounding area.

AYR

A favoured holiday resort on the Clyde coast, with its 2.5 miles (4km) of seafront espanade, splendid sandy beaches, spacious gardens and parks, and famous golf courses, Ayr, a Royal Burgh dating back to 1202, is also home to Scotland's premier race course, where the Scottish Grand National is run, and, more importantly to fans of Robert Burns, the literary heart of the Burns' Heritage Trail. With its modern facilities, good shopping and wealth of family outdoor recreation, it makes an excellent centre for exploring Burns country.

MUST SEE

DUMFRIES MUSEUM & CAMERA OBSCURA,
The Observatory, Church St, Dumfries
☎ 01387 253374
Trace the history of south-west Scotland through fascinating geology, natural history and archaeology exhibitions, housed within and around an 18th-century windmill tower. Don't miss the Camra Obscura: on the table-top screen you can see a panoramic view of Dumfries.

CAERLAVEROCK CASTLE,
Glencaple, Caerlaverock ☎ 01387 770244
Ruins of a massive and menacing 13th-century castle, formerly the ancient seat of the Maxwell family, that are well worth closer inspection for its unique triangular moated design and its peaceful position beside the Solway Firth. Adventure park, nature trail and tea room. Shop.

CAERLAVEROCK NATIONAL NATURE RESERVE,
Eastpark Farm, Caerlaverock
☎/🖶 01387 770200
Combine a castle visit with de-luxe birdwatching on the marshes. Enjoy the sights and sounds of the most spectacular wildlife in Britain, including the entire Svalbard population of barnacle geese which spends the winter on the Solway Firth, making this site one of the most important for wintering wildfowl in the UK, and, indeed, an internationally important wetland. Nature trails, hides and heated observatory, plus closed-circuit television to view barn owls. Picnic area.

Drumlanrig Castle

CASTLE KENNEDY GARDENS,
Stair Estates, Stranraer
(5m/8km E on A75)
☎ 01776 702024
Best visited in May or early June for the swathes of shrubs in full bloom. Superb vistas down the monkey puzzle avenue, beautiful woodland walks and a fine walled garden, they are well worth the excursion to the extreme west of Galloway.

DRUMLANRIG CASTLE,
Thornhill
(4m/6.4km N off A76)
☎ 01848 331682
Enjoy a full family day out at this enormous, 17th-century palace set within extensive grounds and country park. Erected on the site of earlier Douglas strongholds, it contains a celebrated art collection and relics of Bonnie Prince Charlie. Adventure woodland play area, woodland walks, bird of prey centre, cycle museum, craft centre, shop & tearoom.

LOGAN BOTANIC GARDEN,
Port Logan ☎ 01776 860231
Plant enthusiasts should not miss this magnificent exotic garden. Established over 100 years ago as a walled garden, it is virtually surrounded by the sea and influenced by the mild conditions attributed to the Gulf Stream. Unusual flowering shrubs, climbers and herbaceous plants. Shop, garden centre & restaurant.

ART GALLERIES

CASTLE DOUGLAS ART GALLERY,
Castle Douglas ☎ 01557 331643
Exhibitions featuring local artists.

GRACEFIELD ARTS CENTRE,
Dumfries ☎ 01387 262084
Gallery with over 400 Scottish paintings and exhibitions of contemporary art.

TOLBOOTH ARTS CENTRE,
High St, Kirkcudbright ☎ 01557 331556
The story of the Kirkcudbright artists colony from 1880 and displays of paintings.

WATERLOO GALLERY,
Stranraer ☎ 01776 702888

MUSEUMS

BURNS HOUSE,
Burns St, Dumfries ☎ 01387 255297
Ordinary backstreet 18th-century house where Robert Burns spent the last three years of his life. Enthusiasts making the pilgrimage here will see many evocative items connected with the poet.

CREETOWN GEM ROCK MUSEUM,
Chain Rd, Creetown ☎ 01671 820357
Three large exhibition halls displaying gemstones and minerals from around the world, plus replicas of the world's largest diamonds. Polishing demonstrations. Restaurant.

CRICHTON ROYAL MUSEUM,
Dumfries ☎ 01387 255301
Collection of hospital related artefacts, stained glass and patients' art therapy from 1839.

DUMFRIES & GALLOWAY AVIATION MUSEUM,
Dumfries ☎ 01387 259546
Various aircraft and memorabilia housed in a World War II airfield control tower.

GLENLUCE MOTOR MUSEUM,
Glenluce ☎ 01581 300534
Vintage and classic cars, and motor cycle memorabilia. Shop and tearoom.

JOHN PAUL JONES BIRTHPLACE MUSEUM,
Kirkbean ☎ 01387 880613
Exhibition on the life of John Paul Jones, the 'Father of the American Navy', set within the cottage in which he was born in 1747.

MILL ON THE FLEET,
Gatehouse of Fleet ☎ 01557 814099
Former 18th-century bobbin mill with high-tech audio-visual displays of cotton spinning. Shop, craft centre & tearoom.

OLD BRIDGE HOUSE MUSEUM,
Mill Rd, Dumfries ☎ 01387 256904
Museum of everyday life housed within Dumfries's oldest house. Includes an early 20th-century dentist's surgery and a Victorian nursery.

JAMES PATERSON MUSEUM,
Moniavie ☎ 01848 200583
Memorablilia and photographic exhibition relating to the life and work of the artist.

ROBERT BURNS CENTRE,
Mill Rd, Dumfries ☎ 01387 264808
An award-winning centre concentrating on the connections between the poet Robert Burns and Dumfries. Shop & tearoom.

SANQUHAR POST OFFICE,
High St, Sanquhar ☎ 01659 250201
Museum featuring period rooms with interactive displays, a collection of historic postal artefacts, and audio-visual displays.

SANQUHAR TOLBOOTH MUSEUM,
High St, Sanquhar ☎ 01659 250186
Housed in fine 18th-century tolbooth, this interesting museum focuses on the history of Upper Nithsdale.

SAVINGS BANK MUSEUM,
Ruthwell ☎ 01387 870640
Trace the growth and development of the Savings Bank from 1810 to the present day within the building in which the bank first began.

SHAMBELLIE HOUSE MUSEUM OF COSTUME,
New Abbey ☎ 01387 850375
Step back in time and view Victorian and Edwardian clothes and furniture in appropriate room settings at this striking house set in attractive wooded grounds. Shop, tearoom & picnic area.

THE STEWARTRY MUSEUM,
Saint Mary St, Kirkcudbright
☎ 01557 331643
A large collection of archaeological, social history and natural history exhibits relating to the Stewartry district.

STRANRAER MUSEUM,
Stranraer ☎ 01776 705088
Displays on Wigtownshire farming, folk life and archaeology.

WHITHORN - CRADLE OF CHRISTIANITY,
George St, Whithorn ☎/❻ 01988 500508
Learn about the discoveries of the Whithorn Dig - the site of the first Christian settlement in Scotland - by way of an audio-visual show, exhibitions, murals, models and displays of finds.

HISTORIC & ANCIENT SITES

BURNS MAUSOLEUM,
St Michael's Churchyard, Dumfries
☎ 01387 255297
Resembling a Greek temple, it contains the tombs of Robert Burns, his wife Jean Armour and their five sons.

CARDONESS CASTLE,
Gatehouse of Fleet ☎ 01557 814427
Austere 15th-century tower house overlooking the Water of Fleet, displaying quality architectural details, including some fine fireplaces.

CASTLE OF ST JOHN,
Stranraer ☎ 01776 705088
Visitor centre within a late medieval tower house. A prison in Victorian times, it now houses displays on life in both.

COMLONGON CASTLE,
Clarencefield ☎ 01387 870283
Well-preserved 15th-century Border Castle. Set in gardens and woodland with peaceful walks, it displays many original features, including dungeons, the great hall and bed chambers with 'privies'.

DUNDRENNAN ABBEY,
Dundrennan ☎ 01557 500262
Mary, Queen of Scots is thought to have spent her last night in Scotland in May 1568 at this Cistercian Abbey founded by David I in the 12th century.

GLENLUCE ABBEY,
Glenluce *(2m/3.2km N)*
☎ 01581 300541
Founded in 1192 by Roland, Earl of

Galloway, the ruins of this fine Cistercian Abbey, including a vaulted chapter house, stand in a beautiful setting.

KING ROBERT THE BRUCE'S CAVE,
Kirkpatrick Fleming ☎ 01461 800285
The secret cave where Sir William Irving hid the King for three months.

LOCHMABEN CASTLE,
Lochmaben *(1m/1.6km S by Castle Loch)*
Ruined 14th- to 16th-century castle, once the seat of King Robert the Bruce's family, situated on a promontory in Castle Loch

MOTTE OF URR
(2.5m/4km N of Dalbeattie, off B794)
The most extensive earthwork castle in Scotland dating back to the 12th century.

ORCHARDTON TOWER,
Palnackie ☎ 0131668 8800
Rare example of a circular 15th-century tower house.

RUTHWELL CROSS,
Ruthwell ☎ 0131 668 8800
Dating from the 7th or 8th centuries, this carved cross shows scenes from the Life of Christ, scroll work and parts of an ancient poem in Runic characters. Now housed in the parish church.

ST NINIAN'S CAVE.
(3m/4.8km south of Whithorn)
Reached via an attractive walk from a farmhouse, this cave displays an 8th-century carving, and is reputed to have been used as a retreat by St Ninian.

SWEETHEART ABBEY,
New Abbey ☎ 01387 850397
One of Scotland's most beautiful ruins. Late 13th and early 14th-century Cistercian abbey.

THREAVE CASTLE,
Castle Douglas ☎ 01831 618512
A gaunt 14th-century tower, built by Archibald the Grim, rising out of the watery scenery on an island in the River Dee. Accessible by boat.

WHITHORN PRIORY & MUSEUM,
Whithorn ☎ 01988 500508
St Ninian founded the first Christian church in Scotland here in 397, but the present ruins date from the 12th century. Archaeological excavations and a fine collection of early Christian stones.

GREAT FOR KIDS

BARHOLM MAINS OPEN FARM,
Creetown ☎ 01671 820346
Help feed the animals, including rare breeds, at this working farm on the edge of the village.

CLATTERINGSHAWS FOREST WILDLIFE CENTRE,
(6m/10km W of New Galloway)
☎ 01644 420285
Excellent walks and forest drives. Informative displays of forest wildlife in its natural setting in the Wildlife Centre.

CLATTERINGSHAWS RED DEER RANGE AND WILD GOAT PARK,
(on A712 SW of New Galloway)
☎ 01556 503626
Ranger Service and guided tours to see red deer and goats at close quarters.

KELTON MAINS OPEN FARM,
Castle Douglas ☎ 01556 502120
Working farm with conducted educational tours. You can touch many of the animals, including rare breeds.

MONREITH ANIMAL WORLD, SHORE CENTRE & MUSEUM,
Low Knock Farm ☎ 01988 700217
Learn about the seashore, otters and the life of Gavin Maxwell.

MUSEUM OF LEAD MINING,
Wanlockhead ☎ 01659 74387
Explore the underground world of Lochnell Lead Mine by taking a guided tour along a 1.5m/2.4km walkway to the 18th-century mine, smelt mill and miners' cottages. 'Hands-on' displays, an open-air visitor trail, a multi-media interactive presentation, and a gold panning centre.

SOPHIES PUPPENSTUBE & DOLLS HOUSE MUSEUM,
Newton Stewart ☎ 01671 403344
Exhibition of dolls houses depicting life throughout the ages. Displays of over 200 beautifully dressed dolls.

TROPIC HOUSE,
Newton Stewart *(2m/3.2km S, off A714)*
☎ 01671 402485
Enjoy free flying, exotic butterflies in a natural setting of tropical plants and ponds. Plant, gift and craft sales.

WILDLIFE PARK,
Kirkcudbright ☎ 01557 331645
See the animals and learn about conservation at a premier zoological park and wild animal conservation centre, with species from all around the world.

HOMES & GARDENS

ARBIGLAND GARDENS,
Kirkbean ☎ 01387 880283
Extensive woodland, formal and water gardens around a delightful sandy bay. Ideal for children.

ARDWELL HOUSE GARDENS,
Ardwell *(10m/16km S of Stranraer, on A716)*
☎ 01776 860227
Country house gardens and grounds with woodland walks. Shop & tearoom.

BROUGHTON HOUSE & GARDEN,
High St, Kirkcudbright ☎ 01557 330437
The 18th-century house in which Edward A Hornel, the artist of 'Glasgow Boys' fame lived and worked from 1901-1933. Collection of his work and the Japanese-style garden he created.

MAXWELTON HOUSE,
Moniaive ☎ 01848 200385
Historic 15th- to 17th-century house that was the birthplace in 1682 of Annie Laurie of the famous Scottish ballad.

THREAVE GARDEN & ESTATE,
Castle Douglas ☎ 01556 502575
Visit these fine gardens in spring to see a dazzling display of some 200 varieties of daffodil. Later, the highlight is the peat garden, while all year interest can be found in the Victorian hot house and in the walled garden. Shop, exhibition, restaurant & disabled facilities.

BIG OUTDOORS

GALLOWAY FOREST PARK,
Created in 1943 and covering 620sq km, a third of it open land, this Forestry Commision property offers unlimited access to the public and is a major recreation area, offering waymarked walks, cycle trails, scenic drives and picnic sites.

GLEN TROOL,
Large tracts of forest and open moorland characterise this magnificent glen. Robert the Bruce won an early victory here. Drive to the head of the glen for Loch Trool and unrivalled views. Stop off at the visitor centre at Bargrennan ☎ 01671 840302.

GREY MARE'S TAIL,
(10m/16km N of Moffat, off A708)
☎ 01721 722502
Spectacular 200ft waterfall that pours over the lip of a hanging valley below White Coomb (2,696ft/822m), one of the highest hills in the Southern Uplands.

KEN-DEE MARSHES NATURE RESERVE,
Lauriston, Castle Douglas ☎ 01671 402861
Woodland and marshes along Loch Ken and River Dee . RSPB reserve with nature trails, hides, wintering wildfowl and summer migrants.

MERSEHEAD NATURE RESERVE,
Southwick ☎ 01387 780298
Situated on the north shore of the Solway Firth, this area of marsh and wetland is a favoured wintering ground for wildfowl.

WOOD OF CREE NATURE RESERVE,
(4m/6.4km N of Newton Stewart)
☎ 01671 402861
RSPB reserve of some 212 hectares, featuring the largest oak wood left in the south west, dippers and several summer warblers.

Call the AA Hotel Booking Service on 0990 050505 to book at AA recognised hotels and B&Bs in the UK, or through our internet site: http://www.theaa.co.uk/hotels

ESSENTIAL INFORMATION

TOURIST INFORMATION

CASTLE DOUGLAS *seasonal,*
Markethill, CastleDouglas ☎ 01556 502611
DALBEATTIE *seasonal,*
Town Hall, Dalbeattie ☎ 01556 610117
DUMFRIES,
64 Whitesands, Dumfries DG1 2RS
☎ 01387 253862
GATEHOUSE OF FLEET *seasonal,*
Car Park, Gatehouse of Fleet
☎ 01557 814212
GRETNA GATEWAY TO SCOTLAND
M74 Service Area
☎ 01461 338500 ☎ 01461 338700
GRETNA GREEN *seasonal,*
Headless Cross, Gretna Green
☎ 01461 337834
KIRKCUDBRIGHT *seasonal,*
Harbour Sq, Kirkcudbright ☎ 01557 330494
LANGHOLM *seasonal,*
Kilngreen, Langholm ☎ 013873 80976
MOFFAT *seasonal,*
Churchgate, Moffat ☎ 01683 220620
NEWTON STEWART *seasonal,*
Dashwood Sq, Newton Stewart
☎ 01671 402431
SANQUHAR *seasonal,*
High St, Sanquhar ☎ 01659 50185
STRANRAER,
Harbour St, Stranraer ☎ 01776 702595

ACCESS

AIR ACCESS

PRESTWICK AIRPORT ☎ 01292 479822
GLASGOW AIRPORT ☎ 0141 887 1111

SEA ACCESS

P & O EUROPEAN SERVICES,
Cairnryan ☎ 0990 980 666
Ferry and Jetliner servives to Larne, Northern Ireland

SEACAT,
West Pier, Stranraer ☎ 0345 523523
Catamaran service to Belfast.

STENA LINE LTD,
Port Rodie, Stranraer ☎ 01776 802102
Catamaran service to Belfast.

CRAFTS

Craft workshops and studios include glassblowing, jewellery making, wood carving, pottery and ceramics, knitwear and exhibitions of watercolours by local artists.

G.C.G. CRAFTS,
76 King St, Castle Douglas
The showcase of the Galloway Craft Guild (60 local craftworkers)

KATHRYN ADE JEWELLERY,
Carsluith, Newton Stewart ☎ 01557 840249
THE CLOG & SHOE WORKSHOP,
Balmaclellan, Castle Douglas
☎ 01644 420465
CORSOCK CRAFTS,
Corsock, Castle Douglas ☎ 01644 440259
CREEBRIDGE MOHAIR & WOOLLENS,
Newton Stewart ☎ 01671 402868
CREETOWN GOLD & SILVERSMITHING WORKSHOP,
St John St, Creetown ☎ 01671 820396
DEUGH STUDIO,
Carsphairn ☎ 01644 460654
ISLE CRAFTS,
Isle of Whithorn ☎ 01988 500426
MICHAEL GILL JEWELLERY,
High St, Kirkcudbright
ANN HUGHES POTTERY,
Auchreoch, Balmaclellan ☎ 01644 420205
ALAN LEES - WOODCARVER,
Kirkmichael ☎ 01655 750386
WILSON LOCHHEAD POTTERY,
Kirkcudbright ☎ 01557 330468
MAINSRIDDLE POTTERY,
Mainsriddle, Kirkbean ☎ 01387 780633

MOFFAT POTTERY,
High St, Moffat ☎ 01683 220235
SCOTKIN SCOTTISH COUNTRY WORKSHOP,
Star St, Moffat ☎ 01683 220075
ALEXANDRA WOLFFE STUDIO GALLERY,
Gatehouse of Fleet ☎ 01557 814300

ENTERTAINMENT

CINEMAS

ROBERT BURNS FILM CENTRE,
Dumfries ☎ 01387 264808

THEATRES

RYAN CENTRE THEATRE,
Fairhurst Rd, Stranraer
THEATRE ROYAL,
Dumfries ☎ 01387 254209

FOOD & DRINK

CHEESES

Among the excellent traditional cheeses are Loch Arthur, a farmhouse organic cheddar, and Dunlop, a soft textured cheese that resembles Scottish cheddar (also made at the major creameries in Stranraer and Lockerbie).

SMOKED SALMON

SOLWAY SALMON,
Balmaghie, Castle Douglas ☎ 01556 670278
WIGTOWN BAY SALMON COMPANY LTD,
Creeside, Newton Stewart ☎ 01671 403458

ICE CREAM

DRUMMUIR FARM ICE CREAM,
Collin, Dumfries ☎ 01387 750599
CREAM O'GALLOWAY DAIRY COMPANY,
Gatehouse of Fleet ☎ 01557 814040
Delicious farm ice cream, plus nature trails, playground and viewing gallery.

WHISKY DISTILLERY TOURS

BLADNOCH DISTILLERY VISITOR CENTRE,
Bladnoch Wigtown ☎ 01988 402605

TRANSPORT

BUS SERVICES

STAGECOACH WESTERN BUSES
☎ 01292 613700

COACH TOURS

DUMFRIES OPEN TOPPED BUS TOUR,
Whitesands, Dumfries ☎ 0345 090510
GIBSONS COACHES,
16 Church St, Moffat ☎ 01683 220200
WILD GOOSE MINIBUS TOURS,
Cairnryan ☎ 01581 200361

CYCLE HIRE

ACE CYCLES,
Castle St, Castle Douglas ☎ 01556 504542
GRIERSON & GRAHAM,
Academy St, Dumfries ☎ 01387 259483
RIKS BIKE SHED,
Mabie Forest, Dumfries ☎ 01387 750360

TRAINS

There are mainline stations at Annan,
Dumfries, Gretna Green, Lockerbie,
Sanquhar, Kirkconnel and Stranraer
☎ 0345 484950.

SPORT & LEISURE

ACTIVITY & LEISURE CENTRES

BEECHGROVE SPORTS CENTRE,
Moffat ☎ 01683 220697
BRIDGEND SPORTING AGENCY,
Bridgend, Stranraer ☎ 01776 705529
DUMFRIES & GALLOWAY ACTIVITY LINE,
☎ 01659 66200
GALLOWAY COUNTRY SPORTS,
Bladnoch, Wigtown ☎ 01988 402346
HILLVIEW LEISURE CENTRE,
Kelloholm, Kirkconnel ☎ 01659 60000
LOCHMABEN CENTRE,
Stanedyke Crescent ☎ 01387 810599
MARTHROWN OF MABIE
EDUCATION CENTRE,
Mabie Forest, Dumfries ☎ 01387 247727
THE RYAN LEISURE CENTRE,
Fairhurst Rd, Stranraer ☎ 01776 703535

ANGLING

Exceptional spate rivers in the region for
both salmon and sea trout are the Nith
and its tributaries, notably Cairn Water, the
Annan, and the Border Esk. You will find
numerous fish farms across the region,
offering good brown and rainbow trout
fishing, plus Newton Loch, near Gatehouse
of Fleet is a popular coarse fishing lake.
Sea angling is available from most of the
lfishing villages and ports along the coast.

CYCLING

Upland forests, especially the Galloway
Forest Park, offer plenty of easy and
challenging off-road trails for mountain
bikers. Contact Forest Enterprise
☎ 01671 402420 for details. Dumfries &
Galloway also has miles of uncrowded,
unspoilt and beautiful country roads for
the touring cyclist to explore. Tourist
Information Offices have several guides
that suggest routes across the region

GOLF COURSES

POWFOOT GOLF CLUB,
Cummertrees ☎ 01461 700276
Views across the Solway Firth to the
Cumbrian Hills this compact semi-links
seaside course a scenic treat.

NEW GALLOWAY GOLF CLUB,
High St, New Galloway ☎ 01644 420737
Set on the edge of the Galloway Hills and
overlooking Loch Ken, the course has
excellent tees and first class greens.

Also:

CASTLE DOUGLAS ☎ 01556 502180
COLVEND ☎ 01556 630398
DUMFRIES & COUNTY ☎ 01387 253585
DUMFRIES & GALLOWAY ☎ 01387 263848
GATEHOUSE OF FLEET ☎ 01644 450263
GRETNA ☎ 01461 338464
KIRKCUDBRIGHT ☎ 01557 330314
LANGHOLM ☎ 013873 80673
LOCHMABEN ☎ 01387 810552
LOCKERBIE ☎ 01576 202462
MOFFAT ☎ 01683 220020
NEWTON STEWART ☎ 01671 402172
PORTPATRICK ☎ 01776 810273
SANQUHAR ☎ 01659 50577
SOUTHERNESS ☎ 01387 880677
STRANRAER ☎ 01776 870245
THORNHILL ☎ 01848 330546
WIGTOWN & BLADNOCH
☎ 01988 403354
WIGTOWNSHIRE COUNTY, Glenluce
☎ 01581 300420

ICE RINK

DUMFRIES ICE BOWL,
King St, Dumfries ☎ 01387 251300

RIDING

BAREND RIDING CENTRE,
Dandyhills, Dalbeattie ☎ 01387 780663
DEEPWATER EQUITATION CENTRE,
Dalskairth, Dumfries ☎ 01387 268311
ETTRICK VALLEY STABLES,
Closeburn, Thornhill ☎ 01848 31346

LOCHNAW CASTLE EQUESTRIAN CENTRE,
Leswalt, Stranraer ☎ 01776 87227
WEST DRUMRAE FARM,
Whithorn ☎ 01988 700518

SCENIC DRIVES

The scenic road up Glen Trool and the
beautiful forest drive (10m/16km) beside
Clatteringshaw Loch, are very popular.
Roads throughout the Southern Uplands,
especially in the Galloway Forest Park,
traverse some magnificent and unspoilt
tracts of countryside. The 190 mile route
along the Solway Coast, from Annan in the
east to the Mull of Galloway, is particularly
scenic.

SWIMMING

ANNAN SWIMMING POOL,
St John's Rd ☎ 01461 204773
CASTLE DOUGLAS SWIMMING POOL,
Market St ☎ 01556 502745
DUMFRIES SWIMMING POOL,
Greensands ☎ 01387 252908

WALKING

Miles of open moorland and large tracts of
forest, especially in the Galloway Forest
Park, offer a wealth of walking
opportunities for both experienced
ramblers and climbers, and families
seeking gentle woodland strolls. Forest
Enterprise ☎ 01671 402420 **(Newton Stewart),**

THE PILGRIM WAY,
A modern pilgrim path that follows
historic routes across The Machars
between Whithorn Priory and Glenluce
Abbey. For details ☎ 01988 402633

SOUTHERN UPLAND WAY,
Scotland's longest trail traverses Dumfries
and Galloway from Portpatrick on the west
coast to Moffat, via the Galloway Hills and
Glen Trool Forest Park, to Cocksburn on
the east coast in the Scottish Borders. The
official guide and map is available at
Tourist Information Centres.

WATERSPORTS

GALLOWAY SAILING CENTRE,
Parton, Loch Ken, ☎ 01644 420626
KIRKCUDBRIGHT MARINA,
Kirkcudbright ☎ 01557 331135
WIG BAY SAILING SCHOOL,
Kirkcolm, Stranraer ☎ 01776 703535

Newton Stewart Golf Course

WHERE TO STAY

HOTELS

AA RECOMMEND

Hetland Hall

ANNAN

QUEENSBERRY ARMS ★★
DG12 6AD *(in town square, 1.5m from A75)*
☎ 01461 202024 📠 01461 205998
18th-century coaching inn with black and white façade, in town centre. Steak house.
££ 24 bedrooms (3 fmly) Night porter Darts Weekly live entertainment No smoking area in restaurant 🐾

WARMANBIE HOTEL & RESTAURANT ★★
DG12 5LL *(1.5m E off B722)*
☎ 01461 204015 📠 01461 204015
Refined personal touches are standard at this elegant Georgian house in 45 acres of woodland. Taste of Scotland menu.
££ 8 bedrooms (1 fmly) Fishing Clay pigeon shooting No smoking in restaurant 🐾

AUCHENCAIRN

BALCARY BAY ★★★
DG7 1QZ *(on coast 2m from village)*
☎ 01556 640217 & 640311
📠 01556 640272
Lovely, historical country house with fine views, in large gardens beside Balcary Bay.
£££ 17 bedrooms (1 fmly) Snooker Closed Dec–Feb 🐾

BEATTOCK

AUCHEN CASTLE ★★★
DG10 9SH *(1m N of Beattock, village access sign posted from A74)*
☎ 01683 300407 📠 01683 300667
Stay in luxury in this hotel with gorgeous gardens. Splendidly appointed main house bedrooms.
££ 15 bedrooms 10 annexe bedrooms (1 fmly) Night porter Fishing Clay pigeon shooting Conference room Parking Closed 3 wks Xmas–New Year 🐾

BEATTOCK HOUSE ★★
DG10 9QB *(off A74)*
☎ 01683 300403 📠 01683 300403
Fine Victorian house remains appealingly old fashioned with an aura of yesteryear.
7 bedrooms (2 fmly) Fishing 🐾

CARRUTHERSTOWN

HETLAND HALL ★★★
DG1 4JX
(midway between Annan & Dumfries on A75)
☎ 01387 840201 📠 01387 840211
This Georgian mansion, in parkland, is run with enthusiasm, and informal yet attentive service.
£££ 27 bedrooms (3 fmly) No smoking in 3 bedrooms Night porter Indoor swimming pool (heated) Fishing Snooker Sauna Solarium Gym Putting green Indoor badminton Children's facilities No smoking in restaurant 🐾

CASTLE DOUGLAS

DOUGLAS ARMS ★★
King St DG7 1DB *(in centre of town)*
☎ 01556 502231 📠 01556 504000
Friendly service by cheerful staff in this former coaching inn. Good-value meals.
££ 24 bedrooms (1 fmly) No smoking in 8 bedrooms No smoking area in restaurant 🐾

IMPERIAL ★★
King St DG7 1AA
(leave A75 at sign for Castle Douglas. In main street opp library)
☎ 01556 502086 📠 01556 503009
Former coaching inn, popular with golfers, offers good value meals.
££ 12 bedrooms (1 fmly) No smoking in 6 bedrooms Weekly live entertainment No smoking in restaurant 🐾

KING'S ARMS ★★
St Andrew's St DG7 1EL
(through main street, L at town clock, hotel on corner site)
☎ 01556 502626 📠 01556 502097
Former 17th-century coaching in a quiet setting. Bars and dining room overlook the courtyard.
££ 10 bedrooms (2 fmly) No smoking in 2 bedrooms No smoking in restaurant Closed 25–26 Dec & 1–2 Jan 🐾

URR VALLEY COUNTRY HOUSE ★★
Ernespie Rd DG7 3JG
(off A75 towards Castle Douglas)
☎ 01556 502188 📠 01556 504055
Friendly country house hotel in mature woodland. Roaring log fires set the scene. Wonderful views.
£ 20 bedrooms (5 fmly) No smoking in 2 bedrooms Fishing No smoking in r estaurant 🐾

COLVEND

CLONYARD HOUSE ★★
DG5 4QW
(through Dalbeattie & L onto A710 for approx 4m)
☎ 01556 630372 📠 01556 630422
Family run hotel in large grounds with children's play area.
££ 15 bedrooms (2 fmly) Children's facilities 🐾

King's Arms

Murray Arms

CROCKETFORD

LOCHVIEW MOTEL ★
Crocketford Rd DG2 8RF
(on A75, 10 m W of Dumfries)
☎ 01556 690281 🖷 01556 690277
On the shores of Auchenreoch Loch, this is a good-value, no-frills, operation. Modest chalet bedrooms.
£ 7 bedrooms Fishing Closed 26 Dec & 5 Jan 🍽

DUMFRIES

CAIRNDALE HOTEL & LEISURE CLUB ★★★
English St DG1 2DF *(from S exit M6 onto A75 to Dumfries, L at 1st rdbt, cross rail bridge, on to lights, hotel 1st on L)*
☎ 01387 254111 🖷 01387 250555
Accommodation in the main house and a small cottage which includes an apartment.
£££ 76 bedrooms (9 fmly) No smoking in 16 bedrooms Lift Night porter Indoor swimming pool (heated) Sauna Solarium Gym Jacuzzi/spa Steam room Toning tables Weekly live entertainment No smoking area in restaurant 🍽

STATION ★★★
49 Lovers Walk DG1 1LT
(from A35 towards Dumfries centre, hotel opp rail station)
☎ 01387 254316 🖷 01387 250388
Conveniently situated this Victorian hotel retains much original character. Bistro and restaurant.
££ 32 bedrooms (2 fmly) Lift Night porter Children's facilities No smoking area in restaurant 🍽

TRAVELODGE
Annan Rd, Collin DG1 3SE *(on A75)*
☎ 01387 750658 🖷 01387 750658
Modern building offering smart, spacious and well equipped bedrooms, suitable for family use. Nearby family restaurant.
££ (fmly room) 40 bedrooms

GATEHOUSE OF FLEET

CALLY PALACE ★★★★
DG7 2DL *(1m from Gatehouse)*
☎ 01557 814341 🖷 01557 814522
In 500 acres of forest and parkland, this imposing 18th-century country mansion is a grand resort. Elegant, spacious, and luxurious.
££ (inc dinner) 56 bedrooms (7 fmly) No dogs (ex guide dogs) Lift Night porter Indoor swimming pool (heated) Golf 18 Tennis (hard) Fishing Sauna Solarium Croquet lawn Putting green Jacuzzi/spa Table tennis Practice fairway Weekly live entertainment No smoking in restaurant Closed 3 Jan–Feb 🍽

MURRAY ARMS ★★★
DG7 2HY
(off A75, at edge of town, nr clock tower)
☎ 01557 814207 🖷 01557 814370
Friendly and informal, former coaching inn. All day good value meals.
££ 12 bedrooms 1 annexe bedrooms (3 fmly) Night porter Croquet lawn 🍽

GRETNA (WITH GRETNA GREEN)

GARDEN HOUSE ★★★
Sarkfoot Rd CA6 5EP
☎ 01461 337621 🖷 01461 337692
Modern hotel near famous Blacksmith's Shop. Spacious bedrooms. Several honeymoon suites.
21 bedrooms (2 fmly) No dogs (ex guide dogs) 🍽

GRETNA CHASE ★★
DG16 5JB *(off A74 onto B7076, L at top of slip road, hotel 400 yards on R)*
☎ 01461 337517 🖷 01461 337766
Seemingly in no man's land between the 'Scotland' and 'England' signs! Four-poster bedrooms.
££ 9 bedrooms (4 fmly) No smoking in 3 bedrooms No dogs (ex guide dogs) Jacuzzi/spa 🍽

SOLWAY LODGE ★★
Annan Rd DG16 5DN *(A74(M), take Gretna/Longtown exit, turn L at top past Welcome to Scotland sign, BP petrol stn turn L for town centre, 250 yds on right)*
☎ 01461 338266 🖷 01461 337791
Friendly hotel near Blacksmith's Shop offers varied accommodation. Two honeymoon suites with four posters.
££ 3 bedrooms 7 annexe bedrooms No smoking in restaurant Closed 25 & 26 Dec Res 10 Oct–Mar 🍽

WELCOME BREAK
CA6 5HQ *(on A74, northbound)*
☎ 01461 337566
££ (fmly room) 64 bedrooms

KIRKCUDBRIGHT

ROYAL ★★
St Cuthbert St DG6 4DY *(turn off A75 onto A711, town centre, on corner at crossroads)*
☎ 01557 331213 🖷 01557 331513
In the town centre this pleasant hotel offers reasonably priced accommodation and good value meals.
17 bedrooms (7 fmly) Weekly live entertainment 🍽

SELKIRK ARMS ★★ ✿
Old High St DG6 4JG *(turn off A75 5m W of Castle Douglas onto A711 for 5m)*
☎ 01557 330402 🖷 01557 331639
Town centre 18th-century inn that Robert Burns once frequented. Friendly restaurant and lounge bar.
££ 15 bedrooms 1 annexe bedrooms (2 fmly) No smoking in 3 bedrooms No smoking in restaurant 🍽

LANGHOLM

ESKDALE ★★
Market Place DG13 0JH
(A7 to Langholm, hotel in town centre)
☎ 013873 80357 & 81178 🖷 013873 80357
Offers good value accommodation in a relaxed atmosphere. Tempting range of dishes.
££ 15 bedrooms (3 fmly) No smoking in 3 bedrooms 🍽

Station

LOCKERBIE

DRYFESDALE ★★★⊛

DG11 2SF *(from A74 take 'Lockerbie North' junct, 3rd L at 1st rdbt, 1st L at 2nd rdbt, hotel 200yds on L)*

☎ 01576 202427 ⊕ 01576 204187

Bedrooms in the 18th-century main house and in modern wing. Some rooms suitable for the less able. Excellent food.

£££ 15 bedrooms (1 fmly) No smoking in restaurant 🛌

KINGS ARMS HOTEL ★★

High St DG11 2JL *(A74 0.5m into town centre, hotel opp town square)*

☎ 01576 202410

Said to have hosted Bonnie Prince Charlie and Sir Walter Scott, this hotel attracts a busy custom.

£ 13 bedrooms (2 fmly) Night porter No smoking in restaurant 🛌

SOMERTON HOUSE ★★

Carlisle Rd DG11 2DR *(off A74)*

☎ 01576 202583 ⊕ 01576 204218

Proprietors provide warm welcome and comfortable accommodation. Well preserved Victorian decor.

7 bedrooms (2 fmly) No smoking in 2 bedrooms or restaurant 🛌

RAVENSHILL HOUSE ★

12 Dumfries Rd DG11 2EF *(on A709, 400yds from A74 slip road)*

☎ 01576 202882 ⊕ 01576 202882

Enjoy true hospitality at this traditional hotel, set in pleasant gardens. Interesting menus.

££ 7 bedrooms (1 fmly) No smoking in restaurant 🛌

MOFFAT

MOFFAT HOUSE ★★★

High St DG10 9HL *(from M74 at Beattock take A70. Hotel in 1m)*

☎ 01683 220039 ⊕ 01683 221288

Imposing Adam style mansion with extensive gardens. Some bedrooms in converted coach house.

££ 20 bedrooms (2 fmly) No smoking in 6 bedrooms or restaurant 🛌

ANNANDALE ARMS HOTEL ★★

High St DG10 9HF *(1mile off A74 on A701. Hotel in town centre)*

☎ 01683 220013 ⊕ 01683 221395

Prominent position with cosy bar offering tasty bar meals, plus a restaurant. Spacious chalet-style bedrooms.

£ 23 bedrooms (11 bth) (2 fmly) 🛌

BEECHWOOD COUNTRY HOUSE ★★⊛

Harthope Place DG10 9RS

(N end of town. Turn R at St Marys Church into Harthope Place follow 'Hotel' sign)

☎ 01683 220210 ⊕ 01683 220889

Country house with beechwood backdrop and views across the valley. Relaxed and convivial atmosphere. Assured Scottish cuisine.

£££ 7 bedrooms (1 fmly) No smoking in restaurant Closed 2 Jan-14 Feb 🛌

THE STAR ★★

44 High St DG10 9EF

☎ 01683 220156 ⊕ 01683 221524

Heralded as the narrowest hotel in the world (just 20ft wide), with eight stylish, comfortable bedrooms.

££ 8 bedrooms (1 fmly) No smoking in restaurant 🛌

Knockinaam Lodge

WELL VIEW ★⊛⊛⊛

Ballplay Rd DG10 9JU

(on A708 from Moffat, past fire station & 1st L)

☎ 01683 220184 ⊕ 01683 220088

This family hotel is "Small is beautiful". Spotlessly maintained throughout. Dinner is to be savoured and not rushed.

£ 6 bedrooms No smoking in bedrooms or restaurant Closed week in Jan & week in Nov 🛌

NEWTON STEWART

BRUCE ★★★

88 Queen St DG8 6JL

☎ 01671 402294 ⊕ 01671 402294

Good value hotel. Popular bar meals are available as an alternative to the restaurant.

20 bedrooms (2 fmly) 🛌

KIRROUGHTREE HOUSE ★★★⊛⊛⊛

Minnigaff DG8 6AN

(from A75 take A712 for hotel on L)

☎ 01671 402141 ⊕ 01671 402425

In an elevated position this impressive mansion is surrounded by landscaped gardens and forestry. Friendly staff present impeccable service.

£££ 17 bedrooms Tennis (grass) Croquet lawn Pitch and putt No children under 10yrs No smoking in restaurant Closed 4 Jan-13 Feb 🛌

CREEBRIDGE HOUSE ★★

DG8 6NP *(off A75)*

☎ 01671 402121 ⊕ 01671 403258

Secluded, former shooting lodge in its own grounds. Restaurant and bar/bistro offer interesting dishes.

££ 19 bedrooms (3 fmly) Fishing Croquet lawn Putting green No smoking in restaurant Res Nov-Mar 🛌

FERNHILL ★★★

DG8 8TD *(R off A77 at War Memorial)*

☎ 01776 810220 ⊕ 01776 810596

Set high above the village, this friendly hotel offers spectacular views of the harbour towards Ireland.

£££ 15 bedrooms 4 annexe bedrooms (1 fmly) No smoking area in restaurant Closed Xmas 🛌

KNOCKINAAM LODGE ★★★⊛⊛⊛

DG9 9AD

(from A77 or A75 follow Portpatrick signs. 2m W of Lochans - hotel sign on R, next L & follow signs)

☎ 01776 810471 ⊕ 01776 810435

Small hotel with a reputation for hospitality and fine cuisine, beautifully located on the edge of the Irish Sea.

££££ 10 bedrooms (6 fmly) Croquet lawn Children's facilities No smoking in restaurant 🛌

PORTPATRICK ★★★

DG9 8TQ

(A77, R at War Memorial, hotel 0.5m on R)

☎ 01776 810333 ⊕ 01776 810457

Perched high on the cliff with fine sea views. Popular, large hotel offering spacious and comfortable accommodation.

57 bedrooms (5 fmly) No smoking in 12 bedrooms Lift Night porter Outdoor swimming pool (heated) Tennis (grass) Snooker 9 Hole par 3 golf Games room Weekly live entertainment Children's facilities Closed mid Nov-early Mar (ex Xmas/New Year) 🛌

PORT WILLIAM

CORSEMALZIE HOUSE ★★★

DG8 9RL

(from Newton Stewart take A714, R after Bladnoch onto B7005 for Culmazie)

☎ 01988 860254 ⊕ 01988 860213

Unspoilt country mansion in large woodland grounds offers good levels of comfort throughout.

££ 14 bedrooms (1 fmly) Fishing Croquet lawn Putting green Game shooting No smoking in restaurant Closed 21 Jan-5 Mar 🛌

POWFOOT

GOLF ★★
Links Av DG12 5PN
(leave A74 at Gretna onto A75, hotel sign 2m. Turn L for Powfoot)
☎ 01461 700254 ☏ 01461 700288
Next to the sea with panoramic views of the Solway Firth and Cumbrian Mountains. Popular retreat for golfers.
££ 19 bedrooms (2 fmly) No smoking in 2 bedrooms No dogs (ex guide dogs) Air conditioning Golf 18 Fishing No smoking area in restaurant

SANQUHAR

BLACKADDIE HOUSE ★★
Blackaddie Rd DG4 6JJ
(leave A76 just N of Sanquhar at Burnside Service Station. Private road to hotel 300mtrs on R)
☎ 01659 50270 ☏ 01659 50270
Former rectory in colourful gardens. Popular hotel with friendly, relaxing atmosphere.
££ 9 bedrooms (2 fmly) No dogs (ex guide dogs) Fishing Riding Game shooting Gold panning Bike hire Children's facilities No smoking in restaurant

Trigony House

STRANRAER

NORTH WEST CASTLE ★★★★
DG9 8EH
(on seafront, close to Stena ferry terminal)
☎ 01776 704413 ☏ 01776 702646
Imposing 19th-century house with hospitality and traditional service that are hard to beat.
££ 70 bedrooms 3 annexe bedrooms (22 fmly) No dogs (ex guide dogs) Lift Night porter Indoor swimming pool (heated) Snooker Sauna Solarium Gym Jacuzzi/spa Curling (Oct–Apr) Games room

THORNHILL

TRIGONY HOUSE ★★
Closeburn DG3 5EZ *(1m S off A76)*
☎ 01848 331211 ☏ 01848 331303
Former Edwardian hunting lodge that retains intimate, relaxed and convivial atmosphere. Comfortable throughout.
££ 8 bedrooms No dogs (ex guide dogs) No children under 8yrs No smoking in restaurant

BED & BREAKFAST ACCOMMODATION

BEATTOCK

COGRIE'S⬛⬛⬛
DG10 9PP*(3m S off A74)*
☎ 01576 470320 Mr & Mrs Bell Mar-Oct
Every effort made to make you feel at home on this farm. Huge farmhouse breakfasts.
£ 4 bedrooms (3 fmly) No dogs 275 acres dairy mixed

CASTLE DOUGLAS

BARRINGTON HOUSE ⬛⬛⬛
39 St Andrew St DG7 1EN
(turn off A75 (Gretna/Stranraer rd) to 1st rdbt at edge of town, 2nd L-Queen St & 3rd L-St Andrew St)
☎ 01556 502601
Delightful period house with spacious and comfortable accommodation in a traditional environment.
£ 4 bedrooms No smoking No children under 12yrs

ROSE COTTAGE ⬛⬛⬛
Gelston DG7 1SH
(beside B727, 2m from Castle Douglas)
☎ 01556 502513
Cosy little cottage bordered by a stream and fields. Ground floor bedrooms. Chalet-style rooms ideal for families.
£ 3 bedrooms 2 annexe bedrooms (1 fmly) No smoking in dining room Feb–Oct

DALBEATTIE

AUCHENSKEOCH LODGE⬛⬛⬛⬛⬛
DG5 4PG*(5m SE off B793)*
☎ 01387 780277 ☏ 01387 780277
Peace and quiet at this fine Victorian shooting lodge, in large grounds. Small fishing loch and maze.
££ 3 bedrooms No smoking in dining room Licensed No children under 12yrs Fishing Snooker Croquet lawn Closed Dec and Jan

ANCHOR HOTEL ⬛⬛⬛
Kippford DG5 4LN
(off A710)
☎ 01556 620205 ☏ 01556 620205
Inn enjoying views over the Solway coast and yachting marina. Bright and cheerful bedrooms.
£ 7 bedrooms (2 fmly) No smoking in area of dining room No smoking in 1 lounge No dogs Golf 12 Children's games room

PHEASANT HOTEL⬛⬛
1 Maxwell St DG5 4AH
☎ 01556 610345 ☏ 01557 331513
Lively inn with great value buffet lunch and friendly service. Real ale.
7 bedrooms (3 fmly) Discounts on Golf courses

DUMFRIES

ORCHARD HOUSE ⬛⬛⬛
298 Annan Rd DG1 3JE
☎ 01387 255099
Expect to be looked after with care and enthusiasm. Bright, cheery ground floor bedrooms in old stable block.
£ 3 annexe bedrooms (1 fmly) No smoking No dogs

GATEHOUSE OF FLEET

BOBBIN ⬛⬛
36 High St DG7 2HP
(signposted from A75, near clocktower)
☎ 01557 814229
Part B & B, part tea shop, with lovely home baking. Popular family attic suite.
6 bedrooms (3 fmly) No smoking in dining room or lounges Golf 9 Tennis (hard)

GRETNA (WITH GRETNA GREEN)

THE BEECHES ⬛⬛⬛
Loanwath Rd, Off Sarkfoot Rd DG16 5EP
(turn L off B7076 at Crossways Garage, down Sarkfoot Road for 0.25m)
☎ 01461 337448
Former farmhouse overlooking countryside towards the Solway Firth and distant Lakeland Hills.
£ 2 bedrooms (1 fmly) No smoking No dogs No children under 10yrs Closed Dec-Jan

SURRONE HOUSE ◨◨◨
Annan Rd DG16 5DL
(exit M74 onto B721, then B7076, town centre, 500yds on R)
☎ 01461 338341 ☏ 01461 338341
Former farmhouse, in own grounds, well back from the main street. Honeymoon suite available.
7 bedrooms (4 fmly) No dogs (ex guide dogs) Licensed ⬛

GREENLAW ◨◨
DG16 5DU *(off A74)*
☎ 01461 338361
Large house near the Old Smithy. The largest bedroom has four-poster.
10 bedrooms (1 fmly) No smoking in dining room

THE MILL ◨◨
Grahams Hill, Kirkpatrick Fleming DG11 3BQ
☎ 01461 800344 ☏ 01461 800255
Evolved from former farm buildings. Lodge style accommodation offered in single storey chalet.
££ 24 annexe bedrooms (7 fmly) Function suite Licensed Closed Jan ⬛

KIRKBEAN

CAVENS HOUSE ◨◨◨◨
DG2 8AA *(on A710)*
☎ 01387 880234 ☏ 01387 880234
Peaceful large country mansion in mature grounds. Home-cooked dinners and hearty breakfasts.
6 bedrooms (1 fmly) No smoking in dining room Licensed ⬛

KIRKCUDBRIGHT

BAYTREE HOUSE ◨◨◨◨
110 High St DG6 4JQ
(from A75 take A711 into town and turn R 200yds past St Cuthberts into High St. House at junction of Castle St and High St)
☎ 01557 330824
Sympathetically restored 18th-century town house. A glass of sherry on arrival. Impressive standard of cuisine.
££ 3 bedrooms No smoking anywhere No dogs (ex guide dogs) ⬛

GLADSTONE HOUSE ◨◨◨◨
48 High St DG6 4JX
(5 minutes walk from harbour)
☎ 01557 331734 ☏ 01557 331734
Charming Georgian terraced house is a little gem, where everything sparkles. Memorable breakfasts.
£ 3 bedrooms No smoking No dogs No children under 14yrs ⬛

LANGHOLM

REIVERS REST ◨◨
81 High St DG13 0DJ
(adjacent to town hall)
☎ 01387 381343 ☏ 013873 81343
Contemporary inn offers attractive modern accommodation. Meals to suit all tastes.
£ 4 bedrooms (1 fmly) No smoking in bedrooms or dining room Licensed Golf 9 Tennis (hard) ⬛

LOCKERBIE

ROSEHILL ◨◨◨
Carlisle Rd DG11 2DR *(south end of town)*
☎ 01576 202378
A warm welcome at this splendid, long established hotel. Elegant lounge. Spacious bedrooms.
£ 5 bedrooms (2 fmly)

MOFFAT

BOLESKINE ◨◨◨◨
4 Well Rd DG10 9AS
(exit M74 at junct for Moffat, in town turn into Well St, at end turn R into Well Rd, Boleskine on R)
☎ 01683 220601
Lovingly restored Victorian house. Exceptionally well appointed bedrooms. Top class breakfast menu.
£ 4 bedrooms No smoking in dining room or lounges

GILBERT HOUSE ◨◨◨◨
Beechgrove DG10 9RS
(from A74, through town & R after school, 3rd house on L)
☎ 01683 220050
Large Victorian house with modern bedrooms. Home-cooked meals and decent wine list.
£ 6 bedrooms (2 fmly) No smoking Licensed ⬛

HARTFELL HOUSE ◨◨◨◨
Hartfell Crescent DG10 9AL
(exit A74 at A701 to town centre. At clock tower turn R up Well St. cross into Old Well Rd, then 1st R)
☎ 01683 220153
High above the town enjoying superb views, this large Victorian house offers gracious accommodation.
£ 9 bedrooms (2 fmly) No smoking in dining room Licensed Children's facilities Closed 24 Dec-2 Jan Res 1-23 Dec 2 Jan-29 Feb

BARNHILL SPRINGS ◨◨
Country DG10 9QS
(0.5m E of A74 - access at Moffat junction)
☎ 01683 220580
Peaceful Victorian country house with fine views. Bedrooms are well proportioned.
£ 5 bedrooms (1 fmly) No smoking in dining room Licensed

ST OLAF ◨◨
Eastgate, Off Dickson St DG10 9AE
(from A74, 2m to town centre. R at War Memorial & into Well St. L at Semple & Ferguson. 50yds on L)
☎ 01683 220001
Typical Scottish hospitality at this quiet guest house. Bedrooms have beverage making facilities and radio-clocks.
£ 7 bedrooms (1 fmly) No smoking in dining room or lounges Apr-Oct

NEWTON STEWART

OAKBANK ◨◨◨◨
Corsbie Rd DG8 6JB
(from A75 rdbt, L then R at square, pass church & bowling green, then L into Corsbie Rd, last house on R)
☎ 01671 402822 ☏ 01671 403050
Spacious Victorian house in large gardens near the town centre. Cosy accommodation. Hearty Scottish breakfasts.
£ 3 bedrooms No smoking No children under 2yrs Croquet Mar-Nov

PORTPATRICK

BLINKBONNIE ◨◨◨
School Brae DG9 8LG
☎ 01776 810282
Elevated, detached villa overlooking the town and harbour. Extremely well maintained. Ground floor accommodation.
6 bedrooms No smoking No dogs Closed Dec

STRANRAER

WINDYRIDGE VILLA ◨◨◨◨
5 Royal Crescent DG9 8HB
(from A75, follow ferry terminal signs to bottom of Stair Dr. L & L again into Royal Cres)
☎ 01776 889900
Immaculately-kept overlooking the seafront, with views across the Irish Sea.
£ 3 bedrooms (1 fmly) No smoking in bedrooms or dining room

TWYNHOLM

FRESH FIELDS ◨◨◨◨
DG6 4PB
(turn off A75 into Twynholm, past church, R into Arden Rd - then 0.5m on L)
☎ 01557 860221 ☏ 01557 860221
Three-gabled white house in gardens and meadows. Many guests return to this peaceful home from home.
££ 5 bedrooms No smoking in 2 bedrooms No smoking in dining room or lounges Licensed No children Mar-Oct

WIGTOWN

JACOBS LADDER ◨◨◨
Whauphill DG8 9BD
(leave Wigtown on A714, through Bladnoch onto B7005 for 3m, L onto B7052 & in 0.5m take unclassed rd, farm on R)
☎ 01988 860227
A very warm welcome awaits at this cosy, comfortable guest house with modern accommodation.
3 bedrooms (1 fmly) No smoking in dining room 8 acres beef & sheep

CAMPING & CARAVANNING

ANNAN

GALABANK CARAVAN PARK
North St DG12 5BQ

(Follow B721 into town centre, turn rt at traffic lights into Lady St and site 500yds on left.) Signposted

☎ 01461 203311 ext 67257

Town & Country Pennant Park

Well-maintained grassy site close to centre of town with pleasant rural views, skirted by River Annan. 1 acre with 30 touring pitches.

Open Easter–Sep

AUCHENMALG

COCK INN CARAVAN PARK
DG8 0JT *Signposted Nearby town: Stranraer*

☎ 01581 500227

Family Park

A grassy site in meadowland, close to sea, beach and main road. Overlooks Luce Bay. 2 acres with 40 touring pitches and 80 statics.

Open Mar–Oct Booking advisable bank hols & Jul–Aug Last arrival 22.00hrs Last departure 11.00hrs

BALMINNOCH

THREE LOCHS HOLIDAY PARK
DG8 0EP *(N off A75 Signed off B7027 on an unclass road in Glenluce direction) Nearby town: Newton Stewart*

☎ 01671 830304

De-Luxe Park

A spacious, well-maintained site in moorland close to lochs. 15 acres with 45 touring pitches and 90 statics.

Open Easter–mid Oct Booking advisable bank hols & Jul–Aug Last arrival 22.00hrs Last departure 11.00hrs Games room & snooker.

BEATTOCK

BEATTOCK HOUSE HOTEL CARAVAN PARK
DG10 9QB

(adjacent to A74) Nearby town: Moffat

☎ 01683 300403 & 300402

Town & Country Pennant Park

Pleasant, well-maintained level touring site set amongst trees in the grounds of a country house, adjacent to A74. 2 acres with 35 touring pitches.

Open Mar–Oct (rs winter parking limited) Booking advisable Fishing.

BEESWING

BEESWING CARAVAN PARK
Kirkgunzeon DG2 8JL *(Midway between Dumfries and Dalbeattie on A711, 0.5m S of Beeswing.) Nearby town: Dumfries*

☎ 01387 760242

Family Park

A delightful park in open countryside, with lovely rural views in a peaceful setting. A 6 acres with 25 touring pitches and 3 statics.

Open Mar–Oct Booking advisable

BRIGHOUSE BAY

BRIGHOUSE BAY HOLIDAY PARK
DG6 4TS

(Turn left off B727 4 miles S of Kircudbright at signpost to Brighouse Bay on unclass rd.) Signposted Nearby town: Kirkcudbright

☎ 01557 870267

Premier Park

Grassy site in marvellous coastal setting adjacent to the beach with superb sea views. Winner of the 1997/8 Campsite of the Year Award, and Best Campsite for Scotland. 30 acres with 190 touring pitches and 120 statics.

Open all year Booking advisable Easter, Spring bank hol & Jul–Aug Last arrival 21.30hrs Last departure 11.30hrs Mini golf, riding, fishing, watersports, 9 hole golf.

CAIRNRYAN

CAIRNRYAN CARAVAN & CHALET PARK
DG9 8QX

Signposted Nearby town: Stranraer

☎ 01581 200231

Family Park

Mainly static site immediately opposite ferry terminal for N Ireland (Larne). Ideal stopover site with good views of Loch Ryan. 7 acres with 15 touring pitches and 83 statics.

Open Easter/Mar–Oct (rs Apr–21 May restricted pub hours) Booking advisable Jul–Aug Last arrival 23.00hrs Last departure noon

CASTLE DOUGLAS

LOCHSIDE CARAVAN & CAMPING SITE
Lochside Park DG7 1EZ

(Situated off B736 Auchencairn road) Signposted

☎ 01556 502949 & 01556 502521

Family Park

Municipal touring site incorporating park with recreational facilities, on southern edge of town in attractive setting adjacent to Carlingwark Loch. 5 acres with 161 touring pitches.

Open Easter–mid Oct Last departure noon Putting, rowing boats (wknds & high season)

CREETOWN

CASTLE CARY HOLIDAY PARK
DG8 7DQ *Signposted*

☎ 01671 820264

Premier Park

Attractive site in the grounds of Cassencarie House. Winner of the 1996 Campsite of the Year Award for Scotland. A 6 acres with 50 touring pitches and 26 statics.

Open all year (rs Oct–Mar reception/shop, no heated outdoor pool) Booking advisable Bank hols & Jul–Aug Last arrival anytime Last departure noon Mountain bike hire, crazy golf, snooker & fishing.

CREETOWN CARAVAN PARK
Silver St DG8 7HU *(Off A75 into village of Creetown, turn between clock tower and hotel, then turn left along Silver Street) Signposted*

☎ 01671 820377

Family Park

Neat and well-maintained park set in village centre with views across the estuary. 2 acres with 15 touring pitches and 50 statics.

Open Mar–Oct Booking advisable Jul & Aug Last arrival 22.30hrs Last departure 14.00hrs

CROCKETFORD

PARK OF BRANDEDLEYS
DG2 8RG *Signposted Nearby town: Dumfries*

☎ 01556 690250

Premier Park

A well-maintained site in an elevated position off the A75, with fine views of Auchenreoch Loch and beyond. Excellent on-site amenities. 9 acres with 80 touring pitches and 27 statics.

Open Easter–Oct (rs Mar–Easter some facilities restricted) Booking advisable public hols & Jul–Aug Last arrival 22.00hrs Last departure noon Putting, badminton court & outdoor draughts. ⬛

DALBEATTIE

ISLECROFT CARAVAN & CAMPING SITE
Colliston Park, Mill St DG5 4HE *Signposted*

☎ 01556 610012 & 502521

Town & Country Pennant Park

A neat site in two sections tucked away to rear of town, close to local park. Access is via Mill Street. 3 acres with 74 touring pitches.

Open Easter–Sep Last departure noon

ECCLEFECHAN

HODDOM CASTLE CARAVAN PARK
Hoddom DG11 1AS *(2m SW of Hoddom Bridge which carries B725 over River Annan) Signposted Nearby town: Lockerbie*

☎ 01576 300251

Premier Park

A beautiful site within the grounds of Hoddom Castle, with amenities housed in the keep and outhouses. Winner of the Best Campsite for Scotland Award 1996/7. 12 acres with 170 touring pitches and 29 statics.

Open Easter or Apr–Oct (rs early season cafeteria closed) Booking advisable bank hols & Jul–Aug Last arrival 21.00hrs Last departure 15.30hrs Nature trails, visitor centre & 9 hole golf course. ⬛

CRESSFIELD CARAVAN PARK
DG11 3DR

(Take loop service road from A74(M) to Ecclefechan, and site is at S end of town.) Signposted Nearby town: Lockerbie

☎ 01576 300702

De-Luxe Park

An open, spacious park with views to the hills, ideal as a stopover or for touring the

DUMFRIES & GALLOWAY & AYRSHIRE

area. 12 acres with 65 touring pitches and 48 statics.
Open all year Booking advisable Last arrival 23.00hrs Last departure 13.00hrs Sports enclosure, golf nets,petanque,giant chess.

GATEHOUSE OF FLEET

AUCHENLARIE HOLIDAY FARM
DG7 2EX *(Direct access off A75, 5m W of Gatehouse-of-Fleet.)*
☎ 01557 840251
De-Luxe Park
A well-organised family park with good facilities, set on cliffs overlooking Wigtown Bay towards the Isle of Whithorn, and with its own sandy beach. 5 acres with 35 touring pitches and 202 statics.
Open Mar-Oct Booking advisable all year

ANWOTH CARAVAN SITE
DG7 2JU *Signposted*
☎ 01557 814333 & 840251
Family Park
A sheltered touring site close to the town centre, signed from town centre, on right towards Stranraer direction. 2 acres with 28 touring pitches and 38 statics.
Open Mar-Oct Booking advisable Jul-Aug Last arrival 22.00hrs Last departure noon

MOSSYARD CARAVAN & CAMPING PARK
DG7 2ET
(Located 0.75m off A75 on private tarmaced farm road, 4.5m W of Gatehouse-of-Fleet.)
☎ 01557 840226
Family Park
A grassy park with its own beach, located on a working farm, and offering an air of peace and tranquility. 6 acres with 35 touring pitches and 15 statics.
Open Easter/Apr-Oct Booking advisable

GLENLUCE

GLENLUCE CARAVAN & CAMPING PARK
DG8 0QR
(Off A75 Stranraer road. Concealed entrance at telephone kiosk in centre of main street.) Signposted Nearby town: Stranraer
☎ 01581 300412
Family Park
A neat, well-maintained site situated beside a small river close to the village centre. 5 acres with 30 touring pitches and 30 statics.
Open Mar-Oct Booking advisable Jul-Aug Last arrival 22.00hrs Last departure noon

WHITECAIRN FARM CARAVAN PARK
DG8 0NZ
(1.5m N of Glenluce village on Glenluce-Glassnock Bridge Rd.) Signposted Nearby town: Stranraer
☎ 01581 300267
Family Park
A well-maintained farmland site, in open countryside with extensive views. 3 acres with 10 touring pitches and 40 statics.
Open Mar-Oct Booking advisable all times Last arrival 22.00hrs Last departure 11.00hrs

GLEN TROOL

CALDONS CAMPSITE
DG8 6SU *(13m N of Newton Stewart.)*
☎ 01671 402420
Family Park
Secluded Forestry Commission site amidst fine hill, loch and woodland scenery in Galloway Forest Park. 25 acres with 160 touring pitches.
Open Easter-Sep Booking advisable Easter, Spring bank hol & Jul-Aug

GLEN TROOL HOLIDAY PARK
DG8 6RN
(9m N of Newton Stewart.) Signposted
☎ 01671 840280
Family Park
A small compact site close to the village of Glen Trool and bordered by the Galloway National Park. 1 acre with 14 touring pitches and 26 statics.
Open Mar-Oct Booking advisable Jul-Aug Last arrival 21.00hrs Last departure noon Trout pond for fly fishing, bikes for hire.

GRETNA

BRAIDS CARAVAN PARK
Annan Rd DG16 5DQ*(Situated on B721 .5m from village on right, towards Annan.) Signposted*
☎ 01461 337409
Family Park
A well-maintained grassy site in centre of the village just inside Scotland. 4 acres with 70 touring pitches and 8 statics.
Open all year Booking advisable Jul-Sep Last arrival 24.00hrs Last departure noon

IRONGRAY

BARNSOUL FARM
DG2 9SQ *(Leave A75 between Dumfries and Crocketford at brown site sign onto unclass rd signed Shawhead at T-junc. Turn right and immed left signed Dunscore, and site 1m on left.)*
☎ 01387 730249
Town & Country Pennant Park
A scenic farm site set in 250 acres of woodland, parkland and ponds. 4 acres with 50 touring pitches and 6 statics.
Open Apr-Oct Booking advisable Jul & Aug

ISLE OF WHITHORN

BURROWHEAD HOLIDAY VILLAGE
DG8 8JB *Leave A75 at Newton Stewart on A714, take A746 to Whithorn, then road to Isle of Whithorn.*
☎ 01988 500252
Family Park
Large holiday park in 100 acres on coast of Solway Firth. 100 acres with 100 touring pitches and 400 statics.
Open Mar-Oct Booking advisable

KIPPFORD

KIPPFORD CARAVAN PARK
Kippford Caravan Park DG5 4LF *(On A710.) Signposted Nearby town: Dalbeattie*
☎ 01556 620636
Family Park
Part-level, part-sloping grass site surrounded by trees and bushes, set in

hilly country adjacent to Urr Water estuary and stony beach. 18 acres with 45 touring pitches and 119 statics.
Open Mar-Oct Booking advisable Last arrival 21.00hrs Last departure 11.00hrs Childrens adventure playground.

KIRKCUDBRIGHT

SEAWARD CARAVAN PARK
Dhoon Bay DG6 4TJ
(2m SW off B727 Borgue Road) Signposted
☎ 01557 870267 & 331079
De-Luxe Park
Elevated site with outstanding views of the Dee estuary. Facilities are well organised and neatly kept. 8 acres with 26 touring pitches and 30 statics.
Open Mar-Oct (rs Mar-mid May & mid Sep-Oct swimming pool closed) Booking advisable Spring bank hols & Jul-Aug Last arrival 21.30hrs Last departure 11.30hrs TV aerial hook-up, mini golf. Dishwashing.

SILVERCRAIGS CARAVAN & CAMPING SITE
Silvercraigs Rd DG6 4BT *Signposted*
☎ 01557 330123 & 01556 502521
Town & Country Pennant Park
A well-maintained municipal site overlooking town and harbour, just a short stroll to the town centre. 6 acres with 50 touring pitches.
Open Easter-mid Oct Last departure noon

LOCHMABEN

HALLEATHS CARAVAN SITE
DG11 1NA
(From Lockerbie on A74 (M) take A709 to Lochmaben - .5m on right after crossing River Annan.) Signposted Nearby town: Lockerbie
☎ 01387 810630
Family Park
Level, grassy site in a sheltered position with a wood on one side and a high hedge on the other. 8 acres with 70 touring pitches and 12 statics.
Open Mar-Nov Booking advisable bank hols & Jul-Aug Last arrival 22.00hrs Last departure noon Fishing (charged).

KIRKLOCH BRAE CARAVAN SITE
Signposted
☎ 01461 203311
Town & Country Pennant Park
A grassy lochside site with superb views and well-maintained facilities. Signed from centre of town. 1 acre with 30 touring pitches.
Open Easter-Oct

LOCHNAW

DRUMLOCHART CARAVAN PARK
DG9 0RN *(5m NW of Stranraer on B7043.) Signposted Nearby town: Stranraer*
☎ 01776 870232
De-Luxe Park
A peaceful rural site in hilly woodland, adjacent to Loch Ryan and Luce Bay, offering coarse fishing. 9 acres with 30 touring pitches and 96 statics.
Open Mar-Oct Booking advisable bank hols & Jul-Aug Last arrival 22.00hrs Last departure noon Fly-fishing on stocked trout loch.

LOCKERBIE

See **ECCLEFECHAN**

MOFFAT

CAMPING & CARAVANNING CLUB SITE
Hammerlands Farm DG10 9QL

(Leave A74 onto A701 to Moffat centre, take A708 and site is signed.)

☎ 01683 220436 (in season)
& 01203 694995

Family Park

Well-maintained level grass touring site. 14 acres with 200 touring pitches.

Open end Mar–early Nov Booking advisable Spring bank hol & peak periods Last arrival 21.00hrs Last departure noon ⬛

MONIAIVE

WOODLEA HOTEL
DG3 4EN *(Situated 1.5m W of Moniaive on A702.) Nearby town: Dumfries*

☎ 01848 200209

Town & Country Pennant Park

A small site in hotel grounds with bays amongst shrubs and trees. 1 acre with 8 touring pitches.

Open Apr–Oct Booking advisable anytime Last arrival 23.00hrs Last departure noon Badminton, bowls, croquet, putting, sauna & solarium.

NEWTON STEWART

CREEBRIDGE CARAVAN PARK
Minnigaff DG8 6AJ

(.25m E of Newton Stewart at Minnigaff on the bypass, signed off A75.)

☎ 01671 402324 & 402432

Family Park

A level urban site a short walk from the amenities of town. 4 acres with 36 touring pitches and 50 statics.

Open Apr–Oct (rs Mar only one toilet block open) Booking advisable Jul–Aug Last arrival 20.00hrs Last departure noon Security street lighting.

TALNOTRY CAMPSITE
Queens Way, New Galloway Rd DG8 7BL

(7m NE off A712) Signposted

☎ 01671 402420 & 402170

Town & Country Pennant Park

An attractive open grassy site set amidst Galloway Forest Park close to A712 and the picturesque Queens Way. 15 acres with 60 touring pitches.

Open Apr–Sep Booking advisable Etr ⬛

PALNACKIE

BARLOCHAN CARAVAN PARK
DG7 1PF *(On A711.) Signposted Nearby town: Dalbeattie*

☎ 01556 600256 & 01557 870267

Family Park

An attractive terraced site in a sheltered position but with fine, open views. A 9 acres with 20 touring pitches and 40 statics.

Open Apr–Oct (rs Apr–mid May & mid Sep–end Oct swimming pool) Booking advisable Spring bank hol & Jul–Aug Last arrival 21.30hrs Last departure 11.30hrs Fishing, pitch & putt. Dishwashing facilities.

PARTON

LOCH KEN HOLIDAY PARK
DG7 3NE *(on A713) Signposted Nearby town: Castle Douglas*

☎ 01644 470282

Family Park

An attractive touring site on eastern shores of Loch Ken, with superb views. 7 acres with 52 touring pitches and 33 statics.

Open mid Mar–mid Nov (rs Mar/Apr (ex Easter) & late Sep–Nov restricted shop hours) Booking advisable Easter, Spring bank hol & Jun–Aug Last arrival 20.00hrs Last departure noon Bike, boat & canoe hire, fishing on loch.

PENPONT

PENPONT CARAVAN AND CAMPING PARK
DG3 4BH *(From Thornhill on the A702, site on left 0.5 miles before Penpont village.) Signposted*

☎ 01848 330470

Town & Country Pennant Park

Peaceful, grassy, slightly sloping site in a rural area, excellently situated for touring. 1 acre with 20 touring pitches and 20 statics.

Open Easter or Apr–Oct Booking advisable Jul–Aug Last arrival 23.00hrs Last departure 14.00hrs

PORTPATRICK

GALLOWAY POINT HOLIDAY PARK
Portree Farm DG9 9AA *(1m S of town.) Signposted Nearby town: Stranraer*

☎ 01776 810561

Family Park

Looks out on the North Channel. 18 acres with 100 touring pitches and 60 statics.

Open Easter–Oct Booking advisable Mar, & May–Oct Last arrival 23.00hrs Last departure 14.00hrs

SUNNYMEADE CARAVAN PARK
DG9 8LN

(Approach on A77, then 1st unclassified road on left after entering village. First caravan park on left at top of hill.) Nearby town: Stranraer

☎ 01776 810293

Town & Country Pennant Park

A mainly static park with mostly grass touring pitches, and views of the coast and Irish Sea. 2 acres with 15 touring pitches and 75 statics.

Open mid Mar–Oct Booking advisable

POWFOOT

QUEENSBERRY BAY CARAVAN PARK
DG12 5PU *(Follow sign to Powfoot off B724 and drive through village past golf club on single track road on shore edge to site in .75m.) Signposted Nearby town: Annan*

☎ 01461 700205

Family Park

A flat, mainly grassy site on the shores of the Solway Firth with views across the estuary to Cumbrian hills. 5 acres with 100 touring pitches and 60 statics.

Open Easter–Oct Booking advisable Jul–Aug Last arrival 20.00hrs Last departure noon

ROCKCLIFFE

CASTLE POINT CARAVAN PARK
DG5 4QL *(Leave A710 onto unclass rd to Rockcliffe, site signed on left before descent into village.) Signposted Nearby town: Dalbeattie*

☎ 01556 630248

Family Park

A level, grassy site with superb views across the estuary and surrounding hilly countryside. 3 acres with 29 touring pitches and 8 statics.

Open Easter–Sep (rs Mar–Easter & 1–30 Oct limited supervision) Booking advisable Whit wk & Jul–Aug Last arrival 23.00hrs Last departure 11.00hrs

SANDHEAD

SANDS OF LUCE CARAVAN PARK
D69 9JR *(Turn left off A75 onto B7084 2m from Glenluce, signed Sandhead and Drummore, and site signed on left in 5m.) Signposted Nearby town: Stranraer*

☎ 01776 830456

De-Luxe Park

A friendly site on a beautiful sandy beach, with lovely views across Luce Bay. 5 acres with 36 touring pitches and 34 statics.

Open mid Mar–Oct Booking advisable Jul–Aug Last arrival 22.00hrs Last departure noon Boat launching, dishwashing sinks.

SANDYHILLS

SANDYHILLS BAY LEISURE PARK
DG5 4NY *(7m from Dalbeattie, 6.5m from Kirkbean. Site on A710 coast road.) Signposted Nearby town: Dalbeattie*

☎ 01557 870267 & 01387 780257

Family Park

A flat, grassy site adjacent and with access to Sandyhills Bay and beach. 6 acres with 26 touring pitches and 34 statics.

Open Apr–Oct Booking advisable Spring bank hol & Jun–Aug Last arrival 21.30hrs Last departure 11.30hrs Dishwashing sinks.

SOUTHERNESS

SOUTHERNESS HOLIDAY VILLAGE
DG2 8AZ *Signposted Nearby town: Dumfries*

☎ 01387 880256 & 880281

De-Luxe Park

A large family campsite with plenty of on-site entertainment situated close to sandy beach. Near centre of Southerness. 8 acres with 200 touring pitches and 350 statics.

Open Mar–Oct Booking advisable Last departure 16.00hrs Amusement centre, disco, videos. ⬛

STRANRAER

AIRD DONALD CARAVAN PARK
London Rd DG9 8RN *Signposted*

☎ 01776 702025

De-Luxe Park

A spacious touring site, mainly grass but with tarmac hard-standing area. 12 acres with 100 touring pitches.

Open all year Booking advisable Last departure 16.00hrs

WHERE TO EAT

RESTAURANTS

AA RECOMMENDED

KIRKCUDBRIGHT

SELKIRK ARMS ❀
Old High Street, DG6 4JG
☎ 01557 330402 📠 01557 331639
The bright and attractive restaurant signals its ambitions with dishes such as savoury smoked salmon and trout cheesecake, pan-fried saddle of venison with green lentils, and crème brûlée with compote of summer berries.
Fixed D ££

LOCKERBIE

DRYFESDALE HOTEL ❀
DG11 2SF
☎ 01576 202427 📠 01576 204187
Imaginative cooking in the restaurant with its sweeping views. Highly recommended are double-baked cheese soufflé, sole and prawn raviolis with deep-fried vegetables and whisky sauce, and profiteroles with chocolate sauce.
Fixed L £ Fixed D ££ 🍽

MOFFAT

BEECHWOOD COUNTRY HOUSE HOTEL ❀
Harthorpe Place, DG10 9RS
☎ 01683 220210 📠 01683 220889
Traditional country house style epitomises the dining room, and the short menu might offer smoked eel pâté, roast duck with a plum tartlet, and hot chocolate muffins with chocolate sauce.
Fixed L £ 🍽

WELL VIEW HOTEL ❀❀
Ballplay Road, DG10 9JU
☎ 01683 220184 📠 01683 220088
Dinner is a leisurely occasion of six courses. The style is contemporary, with the emphasis on flavours rather than fussy gestures. Highlights on one occasion were a light chicken mousseline with fine herbs, roasted cod and a treacle and orange steamed pudding.
Fixed L £ Fixed D £££ 🍽

NEWTON STEWART

KIRROUGHTREE HOUSE ❀❀❀
Minnigaff, DG8 6AN
☎ 01671 402141 📠 01671 402425
There is an air of opulence throughout, and the cooking is precise. Start maybe with a terrine of Ayrshire bacon and chicken followed 'superb' rump of (their own) venison with braised red cabbage, and finish with a raspberry soufflé.
Fixed L £ ALC ££ 🍽

PORTPATRICK

KNOCKINAAM LODGE ❀❀❀
Stranraer , DG9 9AD
☎ 01776 810471 📠 01776 810435
Guests are greeted with a warmth almost as great as that of the roaring fires. Fine, local produce is used in, for example, ravioli of smoked salmon or fillet of poached west coast turbot. Desserts include chocolate pudding tart.
Fixed D £££ 🍽

PUBS, INNS & OTHER PLACES

CASTLE DOUGLAS

GLEN ISLE INN
Palnackie
☎ 01556 600284
Small bar and restaurant offering fine wines, beers and spirits. Lunches and dinners, and high teas served on Sundays.Vegetarian menu. Children welcome.

DUMFRIES

BENVENUTO PIZZERIA TRATTORIA
42 Eastfield Road
☎ 01387 259890
Italian Trattoria specialising in seafood, steaks, pizzas and pasta. Popular with families. Happy hour from 5-7pm

DOONHAMER RESTAURANT
17 Church Crescent
☎ 01387 253832
Friendly, family-run licensed restaurant serving freshly made meals and snacks all day. Breakfast, 3-course lunch and fish teas. Take-away service also available.

GLOBE INN
56 High Street
☎ 01387 252335
Established in 1610, this was the favourite haunt of Robert Burns. Food is freshly prepared and reflects a taste of the Burns Country.

GATEHOUSE-OF-FLEET

MURRAY ARMS HOTEL
Ann Street
☎ 01557 814207
White-washed coaching inn established over 300 years ago. Now has two bars and the Lunky Hole Restaurant serving snacks and meals.

ISLE OF WHITHORN

THE STEAM PACKET INN
Harbour Row Dumfries & Galloway DG8 8HZ
(From Newton Stewart take A714, then A746 to Whithorn, then Isle of Whithorn)
☎ 01988 500334
A busy hotel with a relaxed atmosphere and nautical flavour. Dishes range from haggis and chips to fresh lobster or chicken with Cinzano beurre blanc.
Free House Accommodation £

KIRKCUDBRIGHT

THE ROYAL HOTEL
St Cuthbert St Dumfries & Galloway DG6 4DY
(Off A75 into Kirkcudbright on A711)
☎ 01557 331213
The Pheasant Carvery & Grill offers a varied menu including world-wide dishes such as Cajun mushrooms, hot mozzarella melt, Galloway sauce steak, and deep-fried ice cream.
Free House Accommodation £

MINNIGAFF

CREEBRIDGE HOUSE HOTEL
Dumfries & Galloway DG8 6NP
(From A75 into Newton Stewart, turn right over river bridge, hotel 200yds on left)
☎ 01671 402121
The 18th-century former home of the Earls of Galloway offers a choice between Scottish bistro cooking in the brasserie, or Scottish/French cuisine in the Garden Restaurant.
Free House Accommodation ££

MOFFAT

BLACK BULL INN
Churchgate Dumfries & Galloway DG10 9EG
☎ 01683 220206
Scottish bard Robert Burns was a frequent visitor circa 1790. A varied menu includes Moffat ram pie, Devilis beef tub pie, Rabbieis roast and haggis.
Free House Accommodation £

NEW ABBEY

CRIFFEL INN
2 The Square Dumfries & Galloway DG2 8BX
☎ 01387 850305
A small 19th-century country inn. Scottish home might include lamb gigot in tomato and red pepper sauce or cottage pie.
Free House Accommodation £

MUST SEE

Culzean Castle & Country Park

BURNS HERITAGE PARK,
Murdoch's Lone, Alloway, South Ayrshire
☎ 01292 443700
Mecca for literary fans and incurable romantics in search of the life and times of poet Robert Burns, Scotland's national baird. The trail starts here with the thatched cottage in which he was born in 1759, now housing an audio-visual presentation depicting his life, with the adjacent museum featuring many artefacts and original manuscripts relating to the great man. Nearby is the Burn's Monument, built in 1823 and decorated with sculptures of characters in Burns' poems. A short walk away is the Tam O'Shanter Experience, an exciting multi-media dramatisation of the poem and the life of Burns. Shop and tearoom.

ART GALLERIES

DICK INSTITUTE,
Elmbank Avenue, Kilmarnock, East Ayrshire
☎ 01563 26401
Paintings and exhibitions of prints, photography and crafts. Also a local history museum.

MACLAURIN ART GALLERY & ROZELLE HOUSE,
Rozelle Park, Monument Rd, Ayr, South Ayrshire ☎ 01292 445447
Displays of local history, notably the area's military history, and exhibitions of work by British and International artists.

MUSEUMS

BACHELORS' CLUB,
Sandgate St, Tarbolton, South Ayrshire
☎ 01292 541940
Follow in the footsteps of Robert Burns when you visit the 17th-century thatched house where he and his friends formed a debating club in 1780.

BURNS HOUSE MUSEUM,
Castle St, Mauchline, South Ayrshire
☎ 01290 550526
Burns's first home with Jean Armour; one room has been converted to house various memorabilia of his days here. In the nearby kirkyard are the graves of four of his children.

CULZEAN CASTLE & COUNTRY PARK,
Culzean Castle, South Ayrshire
4m/6.4km west of Maybole off A77
☎ 01655 760274
Perched on a clifftop with stunning views to Arran and Ailsa Craig, this magnificent, battlemented 18th-century castle, arguably the finest Adam designed building in the country, and its beautiful surrounding parkland, make the perfect destination for a great day out on the Ayrshire coast. Inside the elegant sandstone building, completed in 1792, you can see ornate plasterwork, the Eisenhower Room, which explores the general's link with Culzean, and an oval staircase that rises through three tiers of columns to the splendid first-floor salon. With 563 acres (225ha) of grounds, complete with shoreline, a deer

BURNS MEMORIAL TOWER,
Mauchline, South Ayrshire ☎ 01563 526401
Apart from an interpretation centre on two floors, visitors can enjoy panoramic views .

GLASGOW VENNEL MUSEUM & BURNS HECKLING SHOP,
10 Glasgow Vennel, Irvine, North Ayrshire
☎ 01294 275059
Behind the museum and gallery (noted for its exciting exhibitions), situated on the historic, cobbled street where Robert Burns once lodged, visitors can view the thatched Heckling Shop, where Burns spent learnt the trade of flax dressing.

HUNTERSTON POWER STATION,
Hunterston, North Ayrshire
☎ 0800 838557
Learn how nuclear power is generated, through fascinating exhibits, interactive models, videos and a guided tour.

NORTH AYRSHIRE MUSEUM,
Manse St, Kirkgate, Saltcoats, North Ayrshire
☎ 01294 464174
Trace life in the area down the centuries at this fascinating museum housed within an old 18th-century church.

SCOTTISH MARITIME MUSEUM,
Harbour St, Irvine, North Ayrshire
☎ 01294 278283
Climb aboard the world's oldest clipper ship, the Carrick, as well as Clyde 'puffers'

park, woodland walks, walled and terraced gardens, an adventure playground, and an interpretation centre, there's plenty to fill the day at Ayrshire's most famous castle.

KELBURN COUNTRY CENTRE,
Fairlie, Largs, North Ayrshire
☎ 01475 568685
Set around a beautiful castle, the historic home of the Earls of Glasgow, the estate and Kelburn Glen is a magical world for children. Here they can explore the Secret Forest on a maze of winding paths to reach a gingerbread house, a Chinese pagoda and crocodile swamp, join a Ranger for a guided country walk, expend some energy in the adventure play areas, and enjoy the Kelburn Story Cartoon Exhibition in the converted farm buildings. There is also a pets' corner, a nature centre, museum and tea room.

VIKINGAR!,
Greenock Rd, Largs, North Ayrshire
☎ 01475 689777
Vikingar! is the amazing multi-media experience that takes you from the first Viking raids in Scotland to their defeat at the Battle of Largs. This exciting and award-winning all-weather attraction brings the time of the Vikings alive with fascinating interactive exhibits, live action and dramatic special effects. The attraction also boasts a swimming pool, a theatre/cinema, a children's Viking themed soft play area, and a restaurant.

and tugs, and explore a restored shipyard worker's house to discover Irvine's long history as a seaport and all aspects of Scotland's maritime history.

SOUTER JOHNNIE'S COTTAGE,
Main Rd, Kirkoswald, South Ayrshire
☎ 01655 760603
Restored to its 18th century condition and housing a Burns museum, this thatched cottage was the home of John Davidson, a 'souter' or cobbler, who was the inspiration for the character Souter Johnnie is Burns's ballad Tam O'Shanter.

HISTORIC & ANCIENT SITES

ARDROSSAN CASTLE,
Ardrossan, North Ayrshire
Remains of Ayrshire's oldest castle, built over 800 years ago.

CROSSRAGUEL ABBEY,
Maybole, South Ayrshire ☎ 01655 883113
Impressive remains of a 13th-century abbey, one of the very few Cluniac monasteries in Scotland.

EGLINTON CASTLE & COUNTRY PARK.
Kilwinning, North Ayrshire ☎ 01294 552448
Ruins of an 18th-century castle with an unusual pencil-shaped tower, surrounded by a beautiful country park.

GREENAN CASTLE,
Ayr, South Ayrshire
Romantic 15th-century cliff-top ruins
thought to be the setting for Camelot, the
legendary castle of King Arthur.

KILWINNING ABBEY,
Kilwinning, North Ayrshire
Ruins of a 12th-century abbey destroyed
during the Reformation in 1561.

SKELMORLIE AISLE,
Largs, North Ayrshire
Remains of the 17th-century church, a
Renaissance gem with an elaborately
painted wooden roof and fine carvings.

GREAT FOR KIDS

BLACKSHAWE FARM PARK,
West Kilbride, North Ayrshire
☎ 01563 534257
As well as participating in the day to day
activities on this working farm, children
can enjoy tractor and trailer rides, the
indoor adventure fort, pony rides and four-
wheeled all-terrain bikes. Coffee shop.

DUNASKIN HERITAGE CENTRE,
Dalmellington Rd, Waterside, Patna, South
Ayrshire ☎ 01292 531144
Step back in time and explore 100 acres
of industrial heritage at Scotland's largest
developing open-air museum. Discover
the the simulated coal face display at the
Craigton Pit Experience.

HEADS OF AYR FARM PARK,
Dunure Rd, Ayr, South Ayrshire
☎ 01292 441210
Pet and make friends with pigmy goats,
wallabies, goats, peacocks and Johnny the
lama, then enjoy buggy or pony rides, or
a trip down the aerial runway.

LOUDON CASTLE THEME PARK,
Galston, East Ayrshire ☎ 01563 822296
Take a ride on Britain's biggest Carousel, a
55ft-high helter-skelter, a roller coaster
and many other amusement rides at
Scotland's largest theme park..

SCOTTISH INDUSTRIAL RAILWAY CENTRE,
Minnivey, Dalmellington, East Ayrshire
Railway buffs and fascinated youngsters
will enthuse at the fine range of
locomotives and rolling stock that span a
period of eighty years housed here.
WONDERWEST WORLD,
Dunure Rd, Ayr, South Ayrshire
☎ 01292 265141
Splendid family entertainment at
Scotland's largest theme park, featuring
'Wondersplash' sub tropical Waterworld
and over 22 funfair rides.

HOMES & GARDENS

DEAN CASTLE,
Kilmarnock, East Ayrshire ☎ 01563 522702
Set in a beautiful wooded country park,
this fine castle, complete with a 14th-
century fortified keep and 15th-century
palace, displays an eclectic collection of
medieval arms and armour, early musical
instruments and Burns' manuscripts.
Nature trails and adventure playground.

SORN CASTLE,
Mauchline, East Ayrshire ☎ 01505 612124
An extensively refurbished 14th-century
castle with 18th and 19th century
additions standing on a cliff above the
River Ayr. Charming riverside grounds.

BIG OUTDOORS

AISLA CRAIG,
island off coast at Girvan
Huge dome of granite rising to 1,114ft out
of the sea off the coast at Girvan.
Enthusiastic ornithologists should take the
boat trip to view the vast gannet colony.

CARRICK FOREST,
Excellent walking and off-road cycling
oppotunities within the huge Galloway
Forest Park that straddles the Ayrshire and
Dumfries & Galloway border. Forest drives,
picnic sites and loch fishing.
Forest Enterprise ☎ 01556 503626.

CROY BRAE,
9m/14.4km south of Ayr
More familiarly kown as the Electric Brae,
this unique attraction, literally on the coast
road, is the site of an inexplicable and
effective optical illusion. The road gives
the impression of going downhill when it
is actually going up, so lookout for
bemused motorists trying to freewheel
'uphill'.

LOCH DOON,
off A713 south of Dalmellington
A beautiful lake that forms the border with
Dumfries & Galloway. At nearly 6.5
miles/10.8km in length, it offers peaceful
picnic areas beside the road on its
western shore and delightful walks in the
surrounding forests and upland areas.

ESSENTIAL INFORMATION

TOURIST INFORMATION
INFORMATION CENTRES

AYRSHIRE & ARRAN TOURIST BOARD,
Burns House, Burns Statue Square, Ayr,
South Ayrshire
☎ 01292 262555 ☻ 01292 269555
AYR,
Burns House, Burns Statue Square, Ayr,
South Ayrshire
☎ 01292 288688 ☻ 01292 288686
GIRVAN *seasonal,*
Bridge St, Girvan, South Ayrshire
☎ 01465 714950
KILMARNOCK,
62 Bank St, Kilmarnock, East Ayrshire
☎ 01563 539090 ☻ 01563 572409
IRVINE,
New St, Irvine, North Ayrshire
☎ 01294 313886 ☻ 313339
LARGS,
The Promenade, Largs, North Ayrshire
☎ 01475 673765 ☻ 01475 676297
TROON *seasonal,*
South Beach, Troon, South Ayrshire
☎ 01292 317696

ACCESS
AIR ACCESS

PRESTWICK AIRPORT ☎ 01292 479822

SEA ACCESS

CALEDONIAN MACBRAYNE,
☎ 01475 650313
Daily services from Wemyss Bay to
Rothesay (Isle of Bute), Largs to Millport
(Isle of Cumbrae) and Ardrossan to
Brodick (Isle of Arran).

CRAFTS

*Lookout for knitwear, embroidery and,
in particular, fine Ayrshire lace,
stained glass, pottery, small galleries
selling paintings and crafts, and
regular craft fairs.*

ALOFT - LARGS YACHT HAVEN GALLERY,
Largs - North Ayrshre ☎ 01475 689677
BALMORAL MILL SHOP,
Galston, East Ayrshire ☎ 01563 820213
FLEMINGS LACES,
Kilmarnock, East Ayrshire ☎ 01563 525203

MOONWEAVE MILL SHOP,
Newmilns, East Ayrshire ☎ 01560 321216
Traditional lace.
THE POTTERY,
Girvan, South Ayrshire ☎ 01465 841662

ENTERTAINMENT
CINEMAS

ABC
Kilmarnock, East Ayrshire ☎ 01563 525234
MAGUM LEISURE CENTRE,
Irvine, North Ayrshire ☎ 01294 278381
ODEON,
Ayr, South Ayrshire ☎ 01292 284244

THEATRES

BARRFIELDS PAVILION,
Largs, North Ayrshire ☎ 01475 689777
BORDERLINE THEATRE
Ayr, South Ayrshire ☎ 01292 611222
PALACE THEATRE,
Kilmarnock, East Ayrshire ☎ 01563 523590

FOOD & DRINK

CHEESES

Specialities to lookout for are Bonnet, a mild, pressed goatsmilk cheese, Dunlop, a soft textured cheese resembling Scottish cheddar, and Swinzie, a vignotte style, white moulded unpasteurised cheese.

TRANSPORT

BOAT TRIPS & CRUISES

AYR SEA ANGLING CENTRE,
Ayr, South Ayrshire ☎ 01292 285297
A.S.W. FISHING CHARTERS,
Dalry, North Ayrshire ☎ 01294 833724
FLAMINGO YACHT CHARTER,
Largs, North Ayrshire ☎ 01475 568526
'FLYING EAGLE' CHARTERS,
Saltcoats, North Ayrshire ☎ 01294 469294
Angling, diving and pleasure trips.

'VERONICA' CHARTERS,
Ardrossan, North Ayrshire ☎ 0589 706819
Cruises on 1935 Weatherheads MFV.

CAR HIRE

ARNOLD CLARK LTD,
Prestwick, South Ayrshire ☎ 01292 470545
COMPASS SELF DRIVE,
Kilmarnock, East Ayrshire ☎ 01563 537799
MELVILLE'S SELF DRIVE,
Irvine, North Ayrshire ☎ 01294 277550

COACH/MINI-BUS TOURS

CAMPBELL'S EXECUTIVE TRAVEL,
Maybole, South Ayrshire ☎ 01655 882666
CLYDE COAST COACHES LTD,
Ardrossan, North Ayrshire ☎ 01294 605454
KEENAN OF AYR COACH TRAVEL,
Ayr, South Ayrshire ☎ 01292 591252
LIDDELL'S COACHES,
Auchinleck, East Ayrshire ☎ 01290 424300
MARBILL COACH SERVICES,
Beith, North Ayrshire ☎ 01505 503367

CYCLE HIRE

CARRICK CYCLES,
Girvan, South Ayrshire ☎ 01465 714189
A M G CYCLES LTD,
Ayr, South Ayrshire ☎ ☎ 01292 287580
D. CROZIER SALES & SERVICES.
Maybole, South Ayrshire ☎ 01655 882619

TRAINS

Frequent rail services throughout Ayrshire link major towns with Glasgow and mainline services to London
☎ 0141 332 7133

SPORT & LEISURE

ACTIVITY CENTRES

COWANS LAW SHOOTING SCHOOL,
Moscow, East Ayrshire ☎/☎ 01560 700666
DALVENNAN COUNTRY SPORTS GROUND,
Kirkmichael, South Ayrshire ☎ 01292 531134

ANGLING

With over 20 lochs and reservoirs and over 100 miles of coastline, Ayrshire has plenty to offer the keenest of anglers. The Girvan, Ayr and Stinchar rivers and their tributaries are popular watercourses for salmon, sea and brown trout. Those fishermen after conger eel, mackerel and cod will find the rich waters of the Firth of Clyde well worth the cost of chartering a boat.

CYCLING

Easy and challenging off-road forest and moorland trails can be explored in the Galloway Forest Park, which straddles the borderlands with Dumfries & Galloway Forest Enterprise ☎ 01556 503626. Country Parks have easy family cycling trails, while the excellent network of quiet, gently undulating country roads make exploring the coast and inland sights a real pleasure on two wheels.

GOLF COURSES

For a full list of golf courses in Ayrshire, contact the Tourist Information Offices or refer to the AA Guide to Golf Courses.

GLASGOW,
Irvine, North Ayrshire ☎ 0141 942 2011
A lovely seaside links with glorious greens and fairways providing tireless play

KILMARNOCK ☎/☎ 01292 313920
Magnificent seaside links.

ROYAL TROON ☎ 01292 311555

Created in 1878, Royal Troon is one of the finest links courses in the world, revered by the game's greatest golfers.

TURNBERRY HOTEL
South Ayrshire ☎ 01655 331000
Set around a sumptuous hotel, the great Ailsa and Arran links are, like nearby Troon, regarded as magical courses within the world of golf. Unfortunately, you must be a resident at the hotel to play a round.

ICE RINKS

AYR ICE RINK,
☎ 01292 263024
Also at the Galleon Centre, Kilmarnock and Magnum Leisure Centre, Irvine.

LEISURE CENTRES

CITADEL LEISURE CENTRE,
Ayr, South Ayrshire ☎ 01292 269793
GALLEON CENTRE,
Kilmarnock, East Ayrshire ☎ 01563 524014
HARVIES LEISURE CENTRE,
Stevenston, North Ayrshire ☎ 01294 605126
MAGNUM LEISURE CENTRE,
Irvine, North Ayrshire ☎ 01294 278381
WONDERWEST WORLD,
Ayr, South Ayrshire ☎ 01292 265141

RACECOURSE

AYR RACECOURSE,
☎ 01292 264179
Scotland's premier racecourse, attracting select fields for the Scottish Grand National in April and the Gold Cup at the popular Great West Meeting in September.

RIDING

AYRSHIRE EQUITATION CENTRE,
South Ayrshire ☎ 01292 266267
BROOM FARM RIDING SCHOOL,
Stevenston, North Ayrshire ☎ 01294 465437
DEAN CASTLE COUNTRY PARK RIDING CENTRE,
Kilmarnock, East Ayrshire ☎ 01563 541123
LIONSGATE STABLES,
Ayr, South Ayrshire ☎ 01292 261556
MUIRDYKE STUD FARM,
Cumnock, East Ayrshire ☎ 01290 423021
SHANTER RIDING CENTRE,
Girvan, South Ayrshire ☎ 01655 31636

SAILING

With picturesque harbours and purpose-built marinas along the length of the Ayrshire coast, combined with the sheltered waters of the Firth of Clyde, the region is a popular destination for sailing enthusiasts from around the world. Good mooring facilties can be found at Ardrossan, Ballintrae, Girvan and, in particular, at Troon and Largs.

SCENIC DRIVES

The moorland and forested areas around Loch Doon in the Galloway Forest Park on the edge of the Southern Uplands are particularly picturesque areas for leisurely day drives. Car-bound visitors will also find the network of country roads along the extensive coastline, dotted with secluded sandy bays and romaNtic castle ruins, well worth exploring.

SWIMMING

See Leisure Centres

BEACHES

The South Ayrshire coastline is blessed with sheltered coves and miles of sandy beaches, especially at Ayr, Prestwick and Troon.

WALKING

From gentle riverside strolls and woodland nature trails within Country Parks and interesting heritage town trails, to breezy clifftop and shoreline walks along miles of unspoilt coastline, well waymarked paths through upland forests and more adventurous open moor walks in the Galloway Forest Park, Ayrshire enjoys a rich and varied landscape to satisfy both the novice and experienced rambler.

WATERSPORTS

Keen windsurfers will find the safe and well-equipped beaches at Prestwick and the inland lochs (Loch Doon) in South Ayrshire perfect venues. In North Ayrshire, Kilbirnie Loch has facilities for a range of watersports, including canoeing and waterskiing. Countless wrecks lie off the coast attracting experienced divers
☎ 01294 833724 for the best sites.

WHERE TO STAY

South Ayrshire
See also Dunure

FAIRFIELD HOUSE ★★★★ ✿✿
12 Fairfield Rd KA7 2AR
(from A77 head for Ayr South (A30). Follow signs to town centre, down Miller Road and turn L then R into Fairfield Road)
☎ 01292 267461 📠 01292 261456
Fine Victorian mansion in quiet location near town centre. Fine views of the Firth of Clyde. Conservatory dining and formal Fleur de Lys Restaurant.
24 bedrooms 9 annexe bedrooms(4 fmly) Night porter Indoor swimming pool (heated) Sauna Solarium Gym Jacuzzi/spa Children's facilities

SAVOY PARK ★★★
16 Racecourse Rd KA7 2UT *(from A77 take A70 for 2 m, through Parkhouse St and turn L into Beresford Terrace, 1st R into Bellevue Rd)*
☎ 01292 266112 📠 01292 611488
Built in 1890 this long-established, friendly hotel stands in its own grounds near town centre. Bedrooms vary in size.
15 bedrooms (3 fmly) Night porter Children's facilities No smoking in restaurant 🐾

QUALITY FRIENDLY HOTEL ★★★
Burns Statue Square KA7 3AT
☎ 01292 263268 📠 01292 262293
Victorian railway hotel near centre of town. Bedrooms offer the benefits of their original design, with high ceilings and large windows.
70 bedrooms (3 fmly) No smoking in 26 bedrooms Lift Night porter Sauna Solarium Gym 🐾

GRANGE ★★
37 Carrick Rd KA7 2RD
(0.5m from rail station & city centre, turn off A77 at A713 into Ayr, straight through rdbt 0.25m to Chalmers Rd, at the end turn right hotel 100yds)
☎ 01292 265679 📠 01292 285061
Small hotel near town centre and seafront. Bedrooms, all en suite, decorated to a pleasing standard. Popular lounge where seafood is a regular feature.
8 bedrooms (2 fmly) 🐾

CARRICK LODGE ★★
46 Carrick Rd KA7 2RE *(from A77, take A79 to T-junct, then R, hotel on L)*
☎ 01292 262846 📠 01292 611101
Friendly family run hotel not far from the shopping areas. Bar ideal for good value meals, also formal dining room. Satellite TV available.
8 bedrooms (3 fmly) No dogs Night porter No smoking in restaurant 🐾

ELMS COURT ★★
Miller Rd KA7 2AX
(from A77 onto A719 past racecourse, L at lights past rail station. Turn R & take town centre lane, L at 2nd lights)
☎ 01292 264191 & 282332
📠 01292 610254
Family run hotel located near town centre and sea front. Bright and comfortable the hotel is popular for its food.
20 bedrooms (3 fmly) Night porter Free entry to local Fitness Centre No smoking in restaurant 🐾

TRAVEL INN
Kilmarnock Rd, Monkton KA9 2RJ *(on A77/A78 roundabout by Prestwick Airport)*
☎ 01292 678262 📠 01292 678248
Modern building offers smart, spacious and well equipped bedrooms, suitable for family use. Refreshments may be taken at the nearby family restaurant.
40 bedrooms

BRENALDER LODGE ◫◫◫◫
39 Dunure, Doonfoot KA7 4HR
(2m S on A719)
☎ 01292 443939
Modern house in quiet location. Attractively decorated bedrooms may be compact but they have pretty fabrics and modern furnishings.
3 bedrooms (1 fmly) No smoking in bedrooms or dining room No children under 7yrs Res During props holiday

THE CRESCENT ◫◫◫◫
26 Bellevue Crescent KA7 2DR
(enter Ayr on Ayr South A70, continue to double rdbt, take town centre, 1st lights turn L then 1st R Bellevue St, 1st L Bellevue Cr)
☎ 01292 287329 📠 01292 286779
Terraced Victorian property in quiet area close to town centre. Bedrooms individually decorated and comfortably furnished.
4 bedrooms No smoking No dogs Closed Dec 🐾

GLENMORE ◫◫◫◫
35 Bellevue Crescent KA7 2DP
(into Ayr on A77 from S or A71 from North. Take town centre turn, L at Tourist info, L at lights, first R then L into Bellevue Cres)
☎ 01292 269830 📠 01292 269830
In a quiet tree-lined terrace south of the town centre. Bedrooms are stylishly decorated some with period furniture.
5 bedrooms (2 fmly) No smoking in dining room or lounges No dogs

CRAGGALLAN ◫◫◫
8 Queens Ter KA7 1DU
☎ 01292 264998
A true Scottish welcome at this pristine guest house located in a street just off the seafront. Bright bedrooms with modern amenities.
4 bedrooms (1 fmly) No smoking in 2 bedrooms or dining room

DARGILL ◫◫◫
7 Queens Ter KA7 1DU *(situated on the seafront)*
☎ 01292 261955
Friendly, terraced guest house backing onto the promenade. Fine views from many rooms of the Firth of Clyde and Arran.
4 bedrooms (2 fmly) No smoking in lounges No children under 3yrs

WINDSOR HOTEL ◫◫
6 Alloway Place KA7 2AA *(from Ayr, take A19 through Wellington Sq and hotel 1st on right)*
☎ 01292 264689
Friendly private hotel, near seafront and town centre. Bright and modern bedrooms; some on ground floor. Fresh home cooking.
10 bedrooms (4 fmly) No smoking in dining room Closed Xmas & New Year 🐾

South Ayrshire

COSSES COUNTRY HOUSE ◫◫◫◫◫
Cosses KA26 0LR *(from A77 cross river, 1st left, continue approx 2m)*
☎ 01465 831363 📠 01465 831598
In 12 acres of woodland and gardens, this welcoming country house offers comfortable ground floor accommodation.
££ 3 bedrooms (2 fmly) No smoking in bedrooms or dining room Licensed Games room Table tennis Snooker Darts Dogs welcome Closed 24 Dec–5 Jan 🐾

BALKISSOCK LODGE ◫◫◫
KA26 0LP *(from A77 first left turn S of river to T-junct. Turn right, Lodge signed 1m ahead, last white house on right)*
☎ 01465 831537 📠 01465 831537
Georgian styled home set amidst rolling countryside. Guest facilities are mostly on ground floor.
3 bedrooms (1 fmly) No smoking No dogs (ex guide dogs) 🐾

THE HAVEN ◫◫◫
75 Main St KA26 0NA *(on A77)*
☎ 01465 831306
Attractive bungalow with views to the Irish Sea in pretty coastal village. Pleasant bedrooms offering good standards each with its own adjacent bath or shower room.
£ 2 bedrooms (1 fmly) No smoking No dogs Res Xmas & 1 Jan

North Ayrshire

GARNOCK LODGE ◫◫◫◫
Boydstone Rd, Lochwinnoch PA12 4JT
(1m N, just off A737)
☎ 01505 503680 📠 01505 503680
A welcoming atmosphere at this comfortable bungalow that offers a high standard of accommodation.
£ 4 bedrooms No smoking in bedrooms or dining room 🐾

SHOTTS FARM◙◙◙
KA15 1LB
☎ 01505 502273
Relaxed atmosphere at this modernised farmhouse in rolling countryside. Bedrooms offer comfortable modern appointments. Communal breakfasts.
£ 3 bedrooms (1 fmly) No dogs 200 acres dairy

CUMNOCK

East Ayrshire

ROYAL ★★
1 Glaisnock St KA18 1BP
(opposite church in main square)
☎ 01290 420822 ☑ 01290 425988
In town centre, this mainly commercial hotel offers pleasant accommodation and value for money prices.
11 bedrooms (1 fmly) Night porter 🔳

DARVEL

East Ayrshire

SCORETULLOCH HOUSE ◙◙◙◙
KA17 0LR *(turn off the A71 just east of Darvel and follow signs for 1m)*
☎ 01560 323331 ☑ 01560 323441
Restored into a dream house resembling a Scottish shooting lodge, high on a hillside, with fine views across the valley. Very personal service and relaxed atmosphere.
£££ 4 bedrooms No smoking Licensed No children under 12yrs Pheasant & clay pigeon shooting 🔳

DUNLOP

East Ayrshire

STRUTHER FARMHOUSE ◙◙◙
Newmill Rd KA3 4BA *(within village approx 200yds from railway station)*
☎ 01560 484946
Welcoming atmosphere and good food are part of the attraction here. Spacious bedrooms. Good range of Taste of Scotland dishes.
£ 4 bedrooms (2 fmly) Children's facilities Closed 2wks spring & autumn Res Sun & Mon

DUNURE

South Ayrshire

DUNDUFF ◙◙◙◙
Dunure KA7 4LH
(on A719, 400yds past village school on left)
☎ 01292 500225 ☑ 01292 500222
Old farmhouse occupies a wonderful elevated position with lovely views towards Arran. Genuine Scottish hospitality.
£ 3 bedrooms (2 fmly) No smoking No dogs (ex guide dogs) Fishing 600 acres beef sheep – working Closed Nov – Feb 🔳

FENWICK

East Ayrshire

FENWICK ★★★◉
KA3 6AU ☎ 01560 6478
Conveniently situated, the hospitality and refreshingly good cooking really make this hotel worth seeking out. Friendly staff provide a high level of customer care.
££ 10 bedrooms

GALSTON

East Ayrshire

AUCHENCLOIGH◙◙◙
KA4 8NP *(5m S on B7037-Sorn Road)*
☎ 01563 820567 ☑ 01563 820567
Surrounded by gentle rolling countryside, this spacious 18th-century farmhouse enjoys views towards Arran and the Firth of Clyde. Friendly and personal service provided.
£ 3 bedrooms No smoking No dogs Sauna 240 acres beef mixed sheep-working farm Closed Xmas and New Year

IRVINE

North Ayrshire

HOSPITALITY INN ★★★★
46 Annick Rd KA11 4LD
(follow signs to Irvine/Irvine central, at end dual carriageway take 2nd exit down to rdbt, 2nd exit follow rd to rdbt turn R hotel on L)
☎ 01294 274272 ☑ 01294 277287
Modern business hotel offers executive rooms plus standard rooms. Two eating options, well equipped meeting rooms and a swimming pool.
££££ 127 bedrooms (44 fmly) No

smoking in 16 bedrooms Night porter Indoor swimming pool (heated) Golf 9 Pool table Putting green Jacuzzi/spa Weekly live entertainment No smoking area in restaurant* 🔳

KILMARNOCK

East Ayrshire

TRAVEL INN
The Moorfield, Moorfield Roundabout KA1
☎ 01582 414341
Modern building offering smart, spacious and well equipped bedrooms, suitable for family use. Refreshments may be taken at the nearby family restaurant.
40 bedrooms

TRAVELODGE
Kilmarnock By Pass KA1 5LQ (A71)
☎ 01563 573810 ☑ 01563 573810
Modern building offering smart, spacious bedrooms, suitable for family use. Refreshments available at nearby family restaurant.
40 bedrooms

BURNSIDE HOTEL ◙◙◙◙
18 London Rd KA3 7AQ
(on main road opposite Dick Institute, Library and Museum)
☎ 01563 522952 ☑ 01563 573381
Small hotel in a conservation area. Inviting lounge and a separate dining room for good home cooking and hearty breakfasts.
££ 10 bedrooms (4 fmly) No smoking in dining room 🔳

ERISKAY ◙◙
2 Dean Ter KA3 1RJ *(from town centre follow one-way system and right at railway station and follow Glasgow signs)*
☎ 01563 532061
Friendly family-run guest house offering good value accommodation. Bedrooms offer mixed modern appointments together with all expected amenities.
£ 7 bedrooms (3 fmly) No smoking in dining room Children's facilities

AULTON FARM ◙◙◙
Kilmaurs KA3 2PQ *(Irvine to Stewerton road A769. First turn right past Cunningham Head crossroads, first farm on the left)*
☎ 01563 538208/0378 530564
Comfortable farmhouse set amid peaceful countryside offering good value accommodation. Two bedrooms on the ground floor.
4 bedrooms (1 fmly) No smoking No dogs Children's facilities Riding 22 acres beef

KILWINNING

North Ayrshire

MONTGREENAN MANSION HOUSE★★★◉

Montgreenan Estate KA13 7QZ
(4m N of Irvine on A736)
☎ 01294 557733 ☑ 01294 850397
Attentive service at this imposing 19th-century mansion in 50 acres of peaceful

Burnside Hotel

parkland. Gracious day rooms and elegant restaurant.

£££ 21 bedrooms Lift Night porter Golf 5 Tennis (hard) Snooker Croquet lawn Clay pigeon shooting

LARGS

North Ayrshire

PRIORY HOUSE ★★★

John St, Broomfields KA30 8DR
(on A78 midway between Greenock and Irvine, hotel on seafront)
☎ 01475 686460 🖷 01475 689070
Waterfront position with fine views. Bedrooms range from well proportioned superior rooms to more modest standard rooms.

££ 21 bedrooms (2 fmly) No smoking in 5 bedrooms Night porter Jacuzzi/spa No smoking area in restaurant

BRISBANE HOUSE ★★★❀

14 Greenock Rd, Esplanade KA30 8NF
☎ 01475 687200 🖷 01475 676295
Centrally situated Georgian house by the promenade. Bedrooms mostly spacious and tastefully appointed.

£££ 23 bedrooms (2 fmly) No smoking in 5 bedrooms No dogs (ex guide dogs) Night porter Jacuzzi/spa Weekly live entertainment No smoking area in restaurant

MANOR PARK ★★★

PA17 5HE *(2m N of Largs, 200 yds off A78)*
☎ 01475 520832 🖷 01475 520832
Victorian house that enjoys superb views of the Firth of Clyde. Main house bedrooms are traditional whilst those in the former stable block are more modern.

10 bedrooms 13 annexe bedrooms Putting green Children's facilities

WILLOWBANK ★★

96 Greenock Rd KA30 8PG *(on A77)*
☎ 01475 672311 🖷 01475 672311
Relaxed friendly atmosphere prevails at this well maintained hotel. Well decorated bedrooms tend to be spacious.

££ 30 bedrooms (4 fmly) Weekly live entertainment

SPRINGFIELD ★★

Greenock Rd KA30 8QL
(situated on esplanade next to Vikingar, 400yds from town centre)
☎ 01475 673119 🖷 01475 673119
On the seafront with views over the Firth of Clyde. Bedrooms, varing in size, have mixed modern appointments.

££ 58 bedrooms (4 fmly) Lift Putting green Weekly live entertainment No smoking in restaurant

LEA-MAR ◙◙◙◙

20 Douglas St KA30 8PS *(A78, on reaching town turn left at sign for Brisbane Glen/Inverclyde Sports Centre. Lea-Mar 100yds on right)*
☎ 01475 672447 🖷 01475 672447

Quiet, detached house near the seafront. Attractively decorated bedrooms are designed to maximise available space.

£ 4 bedrooms No smoking No dogs (ex guide dogs) No children under 12yrs

TIGH-NA-LIGH ◙◙◙◙

104 Brisbane Rd KA30 8NN
(from promenade on A78, turn up Brisbane St between Sringfield & Queens Hotel, travel to top turn L, establishment opposite bowling green)
☎ 01475 673975
Extended red sandstone bungalow with nice views of surrounding countryside. Spacious bedrooms with expected facilities.

£ 5 bedrooms (1 fmly) No smoking No children under 2yrs

WHIN PARK ◙◙◙◙

16 Douglas St KA30 8PS
(off A78 at Brisbane Glen sign)
☎ 01475 673437
Comfortable bungalow near seafront. Relaxed and informal atmosphere.

£ 4 bedrooms (1 fmly) No smoking in bedrooms or dining room No dogs (ex guide dogs) Closed Feb

SOUTH WHITTLIEBURN ◙◙◙◙

Brisbane Glen KA30 8SN *(2m NE of Largs, off the road signed Brisbane Glen)*
☎ 01475 675881 🖷 01475 675881
Welcoming farmhouse surrounded by gently rolling countryside. Contempory styled bedrooms are bright and cheerful.

£ 3 bedrooms (1 fmly) No smoking in bedrooms or dining room No dogs (ex guide dogs) Children's facilities 155 acres sheep Res Xmas & New Year

---

PRESTWICK

South Ayrshire

CARLTON TOBY ★★

187 Ayr Rd KA9 1TP
(on A79 2m from Prestwick International Airport, just past Centrum Ice Arena)
☎ 01292 476811 🖷 01292 474845
Modern hotel offering well appointed and equipped bedrooms. Split level conservatory restaurant.

££ 34 bedrooms (2 fmly) No smoking in 9 bedrooms Night porter Weekly live entertainment No smoking in restaurant

Tigh-na-Ligh

PARKSTONE ★★

Esplanade KA9 1QN
(from Prestwick Main St (A79) turn west to seafront - hotel 600 yards)
☎ 01292 477286 🖷 01292 477671
Quiet sea front hotel caters for business visitors as well as golfers. Lounge bar and restaurant menus plus high teas.

££ 22 bedrooms (2 fmly) No dogs Night porter

ST NICHOLAS ★★

41 Ayr Rd KA9 1SY
☎ 01292 479568 🖷 01292 475793
Two houses have been linked to create this popular hotel. Bedrooms vary in size with a mix of modern appointments.

17 bedrooms (2 fmly) No smoking in 5 bedrooms TV in 4 bedrooms No dogs (ex guide dogs) P

FAIRWAYS HOTEL ◙◙◙◙

19 Links Rd KA9 1QG
(turn west off A79 at Prestwick Cross, after 800yds, the hotel on left)
☎ 01292 470396 🖷 01292 470396
Attractive semi-detached Victorian house with modern, bright bedrooms. First-floor lounge has lovely views over the golf course.

£ 5 bedrooms No smoking in bedrooms or dining room No dogs (ex guide dogs) Licensed

GOLF VIEW HOTEL ◙◙◙◙

17 Links Rd KA9 1QG *(take A77 to Prestwick Airport, turn at Prestwick Cross, opposite Prestwick Golf Course)*
☎ 01292 671234 🖷 01292 671244
Friendly hospitality at this hotel opposite the golf course and just 200 yards from the beach, with fine views over the Firth of Clyde to Arran.

£ 6 bedrooms (1 fmly) No smoking in bedrooms or dining room Licensed

FERNBANK ◙◙◙

213 Main St KA9 1LH
(from airport to Prestwick house is on left beyond St Nicholas church (large tower) at 4th set of lights)
☎ 01292 475027 🖷 01292 475027
Well maintained house near town centre and airport.

£ 7 bedrooms (1 fmly) No smoking No dogs (ex guide dogs) No children under 2yrs

Malin Court

KINCRAIG PRIVATE HOTEL ◙◙
39 Ayr Rd KA9 1SY *(follow A72 onto A79 and continue for 1m past Prestwick Airport)*
☎ 01292 479480
Substantial sandstone property offering sound modern accommodation, both in the house and in a small cottage.
6 bedrooms (1 fmly) No smoking in bedrooms or dining room Licensed No children under 3yrs

STEWARTON

East Ayrshire
See Dunlop

CHAPELTOUN HOUSE ★★★❀❀
KA3 3ED *(off B796, 2m SW of town)*
☎ 01560 482696 ☏ 01560 485100
Fine country house, quietly located in 20 acres, continues to provide high standards of comfort and a high standard of skilfully prepared innovative cuisine.
£££ 8 bedrooms Fishing No children under 12yrs No smoking in restaurant ◄

TROON

South Ayrshire

MARINE HIGHLAND ★★★★❀
KA10 6HE *(turn off A77 onto B749, hotel on left about 2m past municipal golf course)*
☎ 01292 314444 ☏ 01292 316922
Smart hotel overlooking the 18th fairway of Royal Troon Golf Course. A range of standard, executive rooms and suites available and several eating options.

£££ 72 bedrooms (7 fmly) No smoking in 12 bedrooms Lift Night porter Indoor swimming pool (heated) Tennis (hard) Squash Sauna Solarium Gym Putting green Jacuzzi/spa Aerobics Beautician Steam room Weekly live entertainment ◄

LOCHGREEN HOUSE ★★★❀❀
Monktonhill Rd, Southwood KA10 7EN *(off Ayr-Prestwick road)*
☎ 01292 313343 ☏ 01292 318661
Splendid mansion with views across the golf links to the sea. Bedrooms are spacious with luxurious bathrooms.
££££ 7 bedrooms 7 annexe bedrooms No dogs Night porter Tennis (hard) No smoking in restaurant ◄

HIGHGROVE HOUSE ★★★❀❀
Old Loans Rd KA10 7HL
☎ 01292 312511 ☏ 01292 318228
Standing on a hillside above town, this hotel enjoys a spectacular outlook. Split-level restaurant provides innovative modern cooking.
£££ 9 bedrooms (2 fmly) No dogs (ex guide dogs) Night porter ◄

PIERSLAND HOUSE ★★★❀
Craigend Rd KA10 6HD *(just off A77 on the B749 beside Royal Troon Golf Club)*
☎ 01292 314747 ☏ 01292 315613
Close to the golf course, this fine hotel has elegantly furnished bedrooms.
£££ 15 bedrooms 13 annexe bedrooms (2 fmly) Night porter Croquet lawn Putting green ◄

CRAIGLEA ★★
South Beach KA10 6EG
(turn off A79 onto B749, follow rd to seafront past Royal Troon golf club, 3rd building on left)
☎ 01292 311366 ☏ 01292 311366
Full family involvement coupled with solid homely comforts. Fine sea views, ample lounges and a good range of food.
20 bedrooms (2 fmly) No smoking in restaurant ◄

TURNBERRY

South Ayrshire

TURNBERRY HOTEL, GOLF COURSES & SPA ★★★★★❀❀
KA26 9LT *(off A77)*
☎ 01655 331000 ☏ 01655 331706
Situated in over 800 acres of stunning countryside with spectacular views of the Firth of Clyde, this world-famous hotel offers a first class range of facilities. The staff are noted for their friendliness, charm and professional service.
££££ 132 bedrooms Lift Night porter Indoor swimming pool (heated) Golf 18 Tennis (hard) Squash Riding Snooker Sauna Solarium Gym Putting green Jacuzzi/spa Health spa Weekly live entertainment ◄

MALIN COURT ★★★❀
KA26 9PB *(on A719)*
☎ 01655 331457 ☏ 01655 331072
On the coast, this comfortable hotel enjoys lovely views towards the Isle of Arran. Standard and executive bedrooms.
£££ 17 bedrooms (9 fmly) Lift Night porter Tennis (grass) Croquet lawn Putting green Pitch & putt Childrens play area Netball No smoking in restaurant RS 25 Dec ◄

BLAWEARIE HOUSE ◙◙◙
Kirkoswald Rd KA26 9NJ *(exit A77 on S side of Kirkoswald onto Kirkoswald Road. Follow signpost for Maidens, house 1m on R before hairpin bend)*
☎ 01655 889602
Large detached country house looking toward the golf course and Arran. Comfortable, simply furnished bedrooms.
6 bedrooms No smoking No dogs No children under 10yrs Golf 18

WHERE TO EAT
RESTAURANTS
AA RECOMMENDED

AYR

South Ayrshire

FAIRFIELD HOUSE HOTEL ❀❀
12 Fairfield Road, KA7 2AR
☎ 01292 267461 ☏ 01292 261456
An imaginative fixed-price menu is offered in the Fleur de Lys restaurant, and a carte

of no less creative dishes in the informal Conservatory. Dinner opened with slivers of salmon and scallops marinated in a mango vinaigrette and served with a crab salad. Roast tomato soup, then the centrepiece, fillet of lamb with a ragout of garlic and shallots with a hint of rosemary and a red wine sauce.
Fixed L £ Fixed D ££ ◄

FOUTERS BISTRO ❀❀
2A Academy Street, KA7 1HS
☎ 01292 261391 ☏ 01292 619323
There's plenty of character in dishes such as roast saddle of Carrick venison with gin and juniper sauce, or breast of guinea fowl with a plum and chicken stuffing. Local hake fillet may be pan-seared and served with parsley flavoured mash and

roast red pepper coulis, and a large bowl of steamed Loch Fyne mussels arrives aromatic with wine, garlic, parsley and lemon.
Fixed D ££

Fouters Bistro

DALRY

North Ayrshire

BRAIDWOODS ❀❀
Drumastle Mill Cottage, KA2 44LN
☎ 01294 833544
Fixed–price menus change regularly, although some dishes such as roast loin of red deer with caramelised shallots are fixtures. Vegetables are individually tailored to each dish and they look good – a tower of creamy leaf spinach, or a tube of thinly sliced courgette containing carrot, for example. Puddings include dark chocolate soufflé containing chocolate sauce and Grand Marnier ice cream.
Fixed D £££

DARVEL

East Ayrshire

SCORETULLOCH HOUSE ❀
KA17 0LR
☎ 01560 323331 ☏ 01560 323441
Beef black velvet' braised and marinated in Guinness gravy, and Annie's 'famous bread-and-butter pudding', may make up a meal at this
Fixed D ££ ALC ££

GIRVAN

South Ayrshire

WILDINGS ❀❀
Montgomerie Street, KA26 9HE
☎ 01465 713481
Family-run restaurant with fish specialities being a popular choice. Both fresh prawns in garlic butter and butterfly prawns with spicy sauce are good choices. Meat dishes include peppered steak and rack of lamb with potato pancake and cabbage. Crêpes filled with caramelised pears with toffee ice cream, and iced caramel soufflé with a raspberry and a mango coulis feature amongst the desserts.

KILWINNING

North Ayrshire

MONTGREENAN MANSION HOUSE ❀
Montgreenan Estate, KA13 7QZ
☎ 01294 557733 ☏ 01294 850397
West coast seafood hors d'oeuvre, seared Tay salmon with a prawn and mussel broth and cannon of Ayrshire lamb with a duo of mint and rosemary sauce, are amongst local ingredients given an upmarket treatment.
Fixed L £ ALC ££

LARGS

North Ayrshire

BRISBANE HOUSE ❀
14 Greenock Road, KA30 8NF
☎ 01475 687200 ☏ 01475 676295
A typical meal could be chef's home-made pâté, Dover sole served with a lobster sauce with prawns, and a milk chocolate torte.
Fixed D ££ ALC £££

STEWARTON

East Ayrshire

CHAPELTOUN HOUSE ❀❀
KA3 3ED
☎ 01560 482696 ☏ 01560 485100
A Chapeltoun House meal may open with canapés of stir-fry of vegetables in filo pastry, followed by smoked haddock encased in smoked salmon, then neatly grilled tuna with a Japanese sea vegetable cake. Dessert was a creative idea: Belgian milk chocolate mousse sandwiched between sesame wafers.
Fixed L ££

TROON

South Ayrshire

HIGHGROVE HOUSE ❀❀❀
Old Loans Road, KA10 7HL
☎ 01292 312511 ☏ 01292 318228
Good value lunches might include breast of chicken with creamy curried sauce and rice with raisins, plus two sorts of potato, courgettes, and cauliflower with cheese. After the bread-and-butter pudding, save a little space for the light shortbread served with good filter coffee.
Fixed L £ ALC ££

LOCHGREEN HOUSE ❀❀❀
Monktenhill Road, Southwood, KA10 7EN
☎ 01292 313343 ☏ 01292 318661
There is plenty of variety here from a port wine and orange preserve and mousseline of fish with white wine sauce and mussels to main courses such as slices of duck breast with onion marmalade. The wide choice continues at the dessert stage, ranging from lemon posset with petticoat tails and vanilla parfait, to rich chocolate torte with Cointreau sauce.
Fixed L ££ Fixed D £££

MARINE HIGHLAND HOTEL ❀
KA10 6HE
☎ 01292 314444, ☏ 01292 316922
There's a choice of restaurants at this hotel, which overlooks the 18th fairway of the Royal Troon Golf Course. Rizzios, which offers a full Italian menu, and Fairways with views of the course.
Fixed L £ ALC ££

PIERSLAND HOUSE HOTEL ❀
Craigend Road, KA10 6HD
☎ 01292 314747, ☏ 01292 315613
The four-course menu might include prawns with salmon in a seafood mayonnaise. Chicken Piersland flambé is a house speciality.
Fixed L £ Fixed D ££

TURNBERRY

South Ayrshire

MALIN COURT ❀
KA26 9PB
☎ 01655 331457 ☏ 01655 331072
Smoked mackerel pâté with horseradish dressing might be followed by Ayrshire lamb rolled in a garlic crust on ratatouille. And to finish, perhaps lemon tart with basil ice cream.
Fixed L £ Fixed D ££

TURNBERRY HOTEL ❀❀❀
KA26 9LT
☎ 01655 331000 ☏ 01655 331706
Lobster Thermidor, foie gras terrine with black truffle, and Loch Fyne oysters for starters, then maybe carpaccio of Aberdeen Angus beef, veal cutlet sautéed with morel mushrooms and Marsala essence, and seared confit of magret duck with mandarins and rosemary scented haricot beans.
Fixed D £££ ALC £££

AA Hotel Booking Service

AA

The AA Hotel Booking Service - Now AA Members have a free, simple way to find a place to stay for a week, weekend, or a one-night stopover.

Are you looking for somewhere in the Lake District that will take pets; a city-centre hotel in Glasgow with parking facilities, or do you need a B & B near Dover which is handy for the Eurotunnel? The AA Booking Service can

not only take the hassle out of finding the right place for you, but could even get you a discount on a leisure break or business booking.

And if you are touring round the UK or Ireland, simply give the AA Hotel Booking Service your list of overnight stops, and from one phone call all your accommodation can be booked for you.

Telephone 0990 050505

to make a booking.
Office hours 8.30am - 7.30pm
Monday - Saturday.

Full listings of the 7,920 hotels and B & Bs available through the Hotel Booking Service can be found and booked at the AA's Internet Site:

http://www.theaa.co.uk/hotels

GLASGOW AND THE CLYDE VALLEY

If you're flying to Scotland or travelling there by train, Glasgow is often your first port of call, so why not begin a tour of the country by having a look at its largest city and cultural capital. Characterised by the famous Victorian architecture of its many streets and squares and packed with museums and art galleries, Glasgow is exciting, sophisticated and vibrant; it's certainly come a long way since its key role in the Industrial Revolution. Thanks to its position on the mighty Clyde, Glasgow grew during the 19th century as a centre for shipbuilding and heavy engineering. But things are changing. The slums have been pulled down, the grime of the factories has gone and now the city's image is much cleaner and greener. When you've seen enough of Glasgow, it's only a matter of minutes before you're out in the countryside and a world away from the noise and bustle of the city.

Greater Glasgow and the Clyde Valley offer a host of attractions. As well as a good road and rail network, including more than 100 local stations, there are various sightseeing tours which illustrate the character and heritage of the district. One of the most popular tourist routes in the Clyde Valley begins at Abington in the south and follows the meandering Clyde to Hamilton, just outside Glasgow. The river rises miles away to the south, high in the Lowther Hills of the Southern Uplands, and close to its source, the fledgling Clyde runs through a remote, rural landscape of scattered communities.

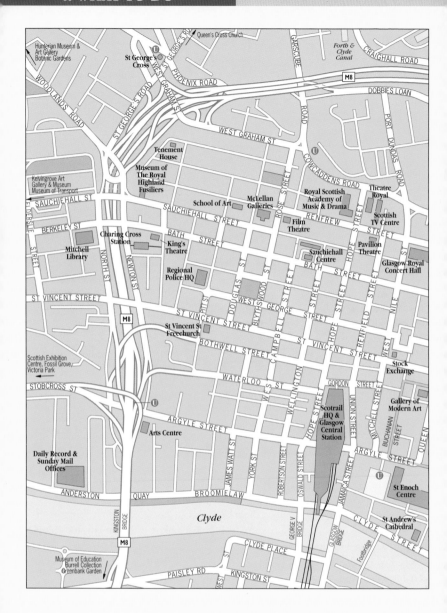

On the north bank of the Clyde, nestling between Glasgow and the Trossachs, Dumbartonshire boasts a fascinating and unusual past. But there is much more to this region than its colourful history and Clydeside setting. Get out and explore it for yourself; following the path of the Antonine Wall, or taking a stroll along the banks of the Forth and Clyde Canal. If you're feeling particularly adventurous, why not tackle a stretch of the West Highland Way, following a section of disused railway track beneath the jagged scarp of the Campsie Fells, a rolling patchwork of green volcanic hills and picturesque villages, renowned for their dazzling floral displays.

Situated at the northern end of the Firth of Clyde, Inverclyde may be small but this lesser-known corner of Scotland is packed with interest, from outdoor pursuits to historic houses, gardens and country parks.

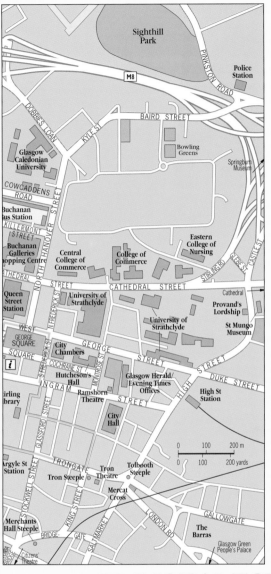

EVENTS & FESTIVALS

May
Mayfest
West End Festival

June
International Jazz Festival
Lord Provost's Procession

July
Folk Festival

August
International Early Music Festival
Great Scottish Run
World Pipe Band Championships

October
Fotfeis (Festival of photography & associated arts)

PRINCIPAL TOWNS

LANARK, SOUTH LANARKSHIRE

Historic Lanark, a Royal Burgh since 1140 and later home to William 'Braveheart' Wallace, is a busy market centre perched on a hillside above the River Clyde. Most visitors descend into the beautiful Clyde Gorge to visit to the adjoining, preserved 18th-century model mill village of New Lanark, Scotland's important memorial to the Industrial Revolution.

PAISLEY, RENFREWSHIRE

Despite its suburbs merging with those of mighty Glasgow, industrial Paisley is one of Scotland's most historic towns, famed for its 12th- century Abbey, its Paisley Shawls and thread production. Don't miss the Abbey, with its towering Gothic nave, the town's museum and art gallery and its priceless collection of 500 different shawls.

MUST SEE

People's Palace

BURRELL COLLECTION,
Pollok Country Park *2m/3.2km S*
☎ 0141 649 7151

An extraordinary art collection amassed over some 80 years by Sir William Burrell, a wealthy Glasgow shipping magnate, and generously bequeathed to the city in 1944. With strict instructions to house the 8,000-odd items in a rural and pollution-free setting, it was some years before this suitable site, a beautiful, specially designed, glass-walled building in the heart of the Pollok estate, was opened in 1983. Exhibits range from Chinese ceramics and Japanese prints to every kind and period of European art, including medieval tapestries, ivories, stained glass and bronzes, Venetian table glass, plus silver, furniture and paintings by Manet, Whistler, Monticelli and Cézanne. With so much to see, allow a day to leisurely explore this vast and beautiful collection.

GALLERY OF MODERN ART,
Royal Exchange Sq ☎ 0141 229 1996

Housed on four floors of an elegant neo-classical building, formerly the Royal Exchange and Stirling Library, in one of the city's most graceful squares, this gallery is one of Scotland's major contemporary art venues. Here, visitors can view Glasgow's collection of post-war art and design, themed to reflect the natural elements of Fire, Earth, Water and Air, in particular, exhibits by world-renowned innovators and distinguished Scottish artists.

GLASGOW ART GALLERY & MUSEUM,
Argyle St, Kelvingrove ☎ 0141 287 2699

Designed in French Renaissance style in 1901, this striking building probably houses the finest municipal collection of British and Continental paintings in Britain, so is well worth setting time aside for. The gallery's extraordinary wealth of pictures, many bequeathed by Glasgow's richest industrial giants over the years, includes works by Giorgione, Rembrandt, French Impressionists and Scottish artists from the 17th century to the present day. Archaeology, natural history and displays of porcelain feature in the museum.

GLASGOW CATHEDRAL,
Castle St ☎ 0141 552 6891

Founded in the 6th century by St Kentigern (St Mungo), this is the most complete medieval cathedral surviving on the Scottish mainland, dating from the 13th century. It is the best relic of the medieval city and well worth the walk from the Merchant City to view the fascinating interior, notably the choir and nave, separated by a rare 15th-century screen, and the ancient stone and woodwork, the carvings and memorialst.

HUNTERIAN MUSEUM & ART GALLERY,
82 Hillhead St ☎ 0141 330 5431

High on the 'must see' list of most visitors is the fascinating art gallery, the core of its collection being a group of paintings bequeathed in the 18th century by Sir William Hunter, a famous physician. Added to over the years, it now displays important works by James McNeill Whistler, the best outside Washington, and an ever-growing collection of 19th- and 20th-century French and Scottish paintings. Fans of Charles Rennie Mackintosh will find furniture and fittings from the architect's home displayed in a reconstruction of the principal rooms of his house.

MUSEUM OF TRANSPORT,
Kelvin Hall, 1 Burnhouse Rd
☎ 0141 287 2628

A real treat for all ages, this gleaming and comprehensive collection of historic vehicles offers a feast of nostalgia for older Glaswegians and a fascinating look at the past for younger visitors. Here, a memorable few hours can be enjoyed viewing huge steam locomotives, fire-engines, horse-drawn vehicles, cycles, and a display of around 25 historic motorcycles. Walk along a reconstructed Glasgow side street from 1938, watch a newsreel of the last tram journey in the city on 1962, and look for the notable collection of scale model ships, many of the full-size versions of which were Clyde-built.

PEOPLE'S PALACE,
Glasgow Green ☎ 0141 554 0223

Backed by a splendid glass conservatory called the Winter Gardens, filled with exotic tropical plants, this idiosyncratic museum explores, as its name implies, the work and leisure of the ordinary people of Glasgow. Visitors will find a real treasure house of all kinds of items connected with city, from a 2nd-century Roman bowl and mementoes of the Jacobite risings to football games, one of Billy Connolly's stage costumes and displays of products from the city's potteries, textile mills and foundaries. After your visit, relax over tea in the Winter Gardens.

THE TENEMENT HOUSE,
145 Buccleuch St, Garnethill
☎ 0141 333 0183

Take a nostalgic trip back in time by visiting this typical Victorian tenement flat, a remarkable 'time capsule' of Glasgow life in the early 20th century. Built in 1892 and home to Miss Agnes Toward between 1911 and 1965, this first-floor flat, comprising a parlour, bedroom, kitchen and bathroom, is furnished as it might have been during her lifetime. You will see the old black kitchen range, gas-lighting, the mangle and washboard by the sink, box beds, masses of letters, bills and newspaper cuttings collected from 1911, and the parlour table set for tea.

The Tenement House,

ARCHITECTURAL GLASGOW

Glasgow's great expansion period began around the 1800s and lasted for nearly 100 years, thanks to wealthy merchants, whose fortunes, made from the tobacco, textiles, engineering and shipbuilding industries, helped construct the grand buildings in what is now the city centre.

CITY CHAMBERS,
George Sq
Designed in Italian Renaissance style by William Young and completed in 1880.

GLASGOW SCHOOL OF ART,
167 Renfrew St ☎ 0141 353 4526
Designed by Mackintosh when he was only 28 and built in two stages between 1897 and 1909, this famous building houses collections of the designers furniture and paintings.

HOUSE FOR AN ART LOVER,
Bellahouston Park ☎ 0141 353 4770
Built from an unrealised Mackintosh design and completed in 1996, it houses a permanent exhibition room, café and design shop.

HUTCHESONS' HALL,
158 Ingram St ☎ 0141 552 8391
An elegant early 19th-century building, designed by David Hamilton, incorporating on its frontage the statues of an earlier building of 1641. Visitor centre and shop.

MERCHANTS' HOUSE,
George Sq
Built in 1877, it is a lavish memorial to Glasgow's trade.

QUEENS CROSS CHURCH,
Queens Cross, 870 Garscube Rd
☎ 0141 946 6600
The only church designed by Mackintosh that was built (1897-1899), housing a small exhibition, specialist shop and the HQ of the Mackintosh Society.

STOCK EXCHANGE,
Nelson Mandela Place
One of the most exuberant (Venetian Gothic) buildings in the city centre.

TEMPLETON'S CARPET FACTORY,
Glasgow Green
Modelled on the Doges' Palace in Venice, this striking building, built in 1889, is one of the city's architectural highlights.

TRADES HALL,
Glassford St
A Robert Adam building of 1794 which continues to house Glasgow's 14 guilds.

WILLOW TEA ROOMS,
217 Sauchiehall St
Restored to its original decor, this famous (and very popular) tearoom was designed by Mackintosh and opened in 1903. A must for all on the Mackintosh trail.

RELIGIOUS GLASGOW

GOVEN OLD PARISH CHURCH,
The Pearce Institute, 840 Govan Rd
Built between 1884 and 1888 on an early Christian site, it houses 30 early Christian sculptured stones.

ST MARY'S CATHEDRAL,
300 Great Western Rd G4 9JB
Featuring outstanding murals by Gwyneth Leech, this fine Gothic Revival church was designed by Sir George Gilbert Scott.

ST GEORGE'S TRON CHURCH,
Buchanan St
Distinctive early 19th-century church noted for·its classical-baroque steeple.

WELLINGTON CHURCH OF SCOTLAND,
University Av, 77 Southpark Av
One of the few surviving classical revival churches in Glasgow with a temple-like frontage.

ART GALLERIES

THE ANNAN GALLERY,
164 Woodlands Rd ☎ 0141 332 0028
CENTRE FOR CONTEMPORARY ARTS,
350 Sauchiehall St ☎ 0141 332 7521
COMPASS GALLERY,
178 West Regent St ☎ 0141 221 6370
CYRIL GERBER FINE ART,
148 West Regent St ☎ 0141 221 3095
MCLELLAN GALLERIES,
270 Sauchiehall St ☎ 0141 331 1854
Victorian gallery designed to bring to Glasgow major touring exhibtions.

POLLOK HOUSE,
2060 Pollockshaws Rd ☎ 0141 632 0274
18th-century house containing the remarkable Stirling Maxwell collection of Spanish paintings. Tearoom and shop.

MUSEUMS

MITCHELL LIBRARY,
North St ☎ 0141 287 29999
A striking building housing Europe's largest reference library, founded in 1874. It contains over one million volumes, including the world's largest collection of work by Robert Burns.

MUSEUM OF THE 602 SQUADRON,
Queen Elizabeth Av, Hillington
☎ 0141 810 6204
Various collections of uniforms, medals, maps and memorabilia illustrate the history of this famous Air Squadron from 1925 to 1957.

POLICE MUSEUM,
173 Pitt St ☎ 0141 532 2000
Learn about the history of policing in the west of Scotland from the early 1800's.

PROVAND'S LORDSHIP,
3 Castle St ☎ 0141 552 8819
Explore the oldest domestic building in Glasgow. Built in 1471 and carefully restored, it displays a fine collection of 17th-century Scottish furniture.

PROVAN HALL,
Auchinlea Rd ☎ 0141 771 6372
Standing in Auchinlea Park, this fine 15th-century mansion house has remained virtually unchanged since before the Reformation - a remarkable survivor in a built-up part of Glasgow.

THE ROYAL HIGHLAND FUSILIERS MUSEUM,
518 Sauchiehall St ☎ 0141 332 0961
Memorabilia vividly bring to life the fascinating 300 year history of the regiment.

ST MUNGO MUSEUM OF RELIGIOUS LIFE & ART,
2 Castle St ☎ 0141 553 2557
Explore the universal themes of life and death and the hereafter through beautiful and evocative art objects associated with different religious faiths at this unique museum.

HISTORIC & ANCIENT SITES

CROOKSTON CASTLE,
Pollok ☎ 0131 668 8600
A ruined 15th-century tower house standing on a wooded hilltop

NEOCROPOLIS,
Castle St
Glasgow's largest cemetery provides a fascinating and macabre insight into the Victorian attitude to the dead, and includes many grand tombstones of wealthy merchants.

TOLBOOTH STEEPLE,
Glasgow Cross
Built in 1626, this seven storey tower with its distinctive crown marked the centre of Glasgow until Victorian times.

GREAT FOR KIDS

GLASGOW TOURIST INFORMATION ORIENTATION CENTRE,
11 George Sq ☎ 0141 204 4400
Discover Glasgow's attractions through fun multi-media touch screens and explore the rich heritage of the city through displays and films in this informative centre.

HAGGS CASTLE MUSEUM,
St Andrew's Drive, Dumbreck
As children will find out from worksheets and quizzes, this tower house was built in the 16th century and, out of all the museums in the city, this one is devoted to children, with hands-on exhibits and a pretty Victorian children's room.

SHARMANKA KINETIC GALLERY & THEATRE,
14 King St ☎/📠 0141 552 7080
The amazing theatre of Eduard Berudsky's mechanical sculptures constructed from wooden carved figures and bits of old junk.

PARKS & GARDENS

With over 70 public parks and gardens, Glasgow certainly lives up to its Gaelic name 'Glas ghu' which means 'Dear Green Place' .

BELLAHOUSTON PARK,
Dumbreck Rd
Featuring lawns which sweep up to a wooded viewpoint ridge, this park was the site of the great Empire Exhibition of 1938.

BOTANIC GARDENS,
Queen Margaret Dr ☎ 0141 334 2422
The highlight of this outstanding plant collection, established in 1817 and moved to this site in 1842, is the 23,000 sq ft Kibble Palace, one of the finest glasshouses in the country, with a unique collection of Australasian plants.

GLASGOW GREEN,
Greendyke St
Scotland's oldest park (1662) situated on the banks of the Clyde.

KELVINGROVE PARK,
Octago St
Laid out on the banks of the River Kelvin in the 1850s, it features riverside and woodland walks.

POLLOK COUNTRY PARK,
2060 Pollokshaws Rd ☎ 0141 632 9299
Home to two major museums, the Burrell Collection and Pollok House, this leafy 361-acre park offers a wealth of outdoor attractions, waterside and woodland trails and beautiful gardens. Tearoom.

QUEENS PARK,
520 Langside Rd
Woodlands, tree-lined avenues and grassy picnic areas on a sweeping hillside that affords impressive views of Glasgow.

TOLLCROSS PARK,
Tollcross Rd
Noted for its splendid international rose trial beds, nature walks and children's play area and zoo.

VICTORIA PARK & FOSSIL GROVE,
Whiteinch
Fossil remains, some 230 million years old, are housed in the Fossil Grove building.Tree-lined walks and an arboretum.

SHOPPING

You'll find the main shopping streets between Argyle St and Sauchiehall St, taking in the pedestrianised Buchanan St and neighbouring bustling streets.

SHOPPING MALLS

Scotland's premier centre is Princes Sq, off Buchanan St, a modern, upmarket mall featuring fashion, interior design and quality gift shops, and a food court. The less sophisticated St Enoch Centre has four major stores, 80 shops and good parking facilities. The Italian Centre, just of Ingram St, is the place to buy top designer clothes. For fine antique jewellery head for the Argyle Arcade, a remarkable Victorian arcade of iron and glass with a unique atmosphere.

THE BARRAS MARKET,

The Barras Centre, Unit 1, 54 Calton Entry, *off London Rd*
Glasgow's famous outdoor and indoor flea market is open at weekends only. Exploring the hundred's of stalls provides great entertainment - you may even come away with a bargain!

ESSENTIAL INFORMATION

TOURIST INFORMATION

INFORMATION CENTRE

GREATER GLASGOW & CLYDE VALLEY TOURIST BOARD,
11 George Sq, G2 1DY
☎ 0141 204 4400

ACCESS

AIR ACCESS

GLASGOW INTERNATIONAL AIRPORT,
☎ 0141 887 1111

CRAFTS

For high-quality Scottish wares and crafts, including knitwear, kilts and tweeds, Glasgow has some fine outfitters and craft centres.

GEOFFREY (TAILOR) HIGHLAND CRAFTS,
309 Sauchiehall St ☎ 0141 332 0397
Scottish knitwear and tweeds.

HECTOR RUSSELL KILTMAKERS
110 Buchanan St ☎ 0141 221 0217

NATIONAL TRUST FOR SCOTLAND,
Hutcheson's Hall, 158 Ingram St
☎ 0141 552 8391

SCOTCH ON THE ROCKS,
Unit 72, 1st Floor, St Enoch Centre
☎ 0141 248 1502

THE SCOTTISH CRAFT CENTRE,
The Courtyard, Princes Sq, G1 3JN
☎ 0141 248 2885

ENTERTAINMENT

CINEMAS

GLASGOW FILM THEATRE,
12 Rose St ☎ 0141 332 8128

ODEAN CINEMA,
56 Renfield St ☎ 0141 332 3413

THEATRES

CITIZEN'S THEATRE,
119 Gorbals St ☎ 0141 429 5561

CITY HALLS,
Candleriggs ☎ 0141 287 5511

CRAWFORD THEATRE,
76 Southbrae Dr ☎ 0141 950 3438

KING'S THEATRE,
287 Bath St ☎ 0141 287 5511

MITCHELL THEATRE,
Granville St ☎ 0141 287 5511

OLD FRUITMARKET,
Albion St ☎ 0141 287 5511

ROYAL CONCERT HALL,
2 Sauchiehall St ☎ 0141 332 6633

ROYAL SCOTTISH ACADEMY OF MUSIC & DRAMA,
100 Renfrew St ☎ 0141 332 5057

SCOTTISH EXHIBITION & CONFERENCE CENTRE,
Finnieston St ☎ 0141 248 3000

SCOTTISH MASK & PUPPET CENTRE,
8-10 Balcarres Av, Kelvindale
☎ 0141 339 6185

THEATRE ROYAL,
Hope St ☎ 0141 332 9000

TRAMWAY,
25 Albert Dr ☎ 0141 287 3900

TRON THEATRE,
63 Trongate ☎ 0141 552 4267

HENRY WOOD HALL,
73 Claremont St ☎ 0141 204 4540

TRANSPORT

BOAT TRIPS & CRUISES

WAVERLEY EXCURSIONS LTD,
Anderston Quay, ☎ 0141 221 8152
Sailings on the Firth of Clyde on board the world's last sea-going paddle steamer.

BUS/COACH SERVICES

CITYLINK COACHES LTD (SCOTTISH) & NATIONAL EXPRESS,
Buchanan Bus Station, Killermont St
☎ 0141 332 9644

THE TRAVEL CENTRE,
St Enoch Sq ☎ 0141 226 4826
Sells zonecard tickets for local services; tickets for coach tours, excursions and long distance services.

CAR HIRE

ALEX M RITCHIE ☎ 0141 423 2961

AVIS RENT-A-CAR ☎ 0141 221 2827

BUDGET RENT-A-CAR ☎ 0141 226 4141

FORD RENT-A-CAR ☎ 0141 954 1500

HERTZ UK LTD ☎ 0141 248 7736

MCDONALD MOTORS LTD,
☎ 0141 422 1616

UNIVERSAL GARAGE CAR HIRE,
☎ 0141 554 5174

COACH TOURS

CAMERON TOURS ☎/☎ 0141 647 7283

DISCOVERING SCOTLAND TOURS
☎ 0141 204 04HALDANES OFCATHCART
☎ 0141 637 2234

STRATHCLYDE BUSES
☎ 0141 636 3190

GUIDED TOURS

DISCOVERING GLASGOW TOURS
☎ 0141 204 0444
Guided bus tours of Glasgow.

GUIDE FRIDAY,
☎ 0131 556 2244
Guided bus tours of Glasgow.

MERCAT TOURS,
☎ 0141 772 0022
History and ghost walking tours.

**SCOTTISH TOURIST GUIDES
ASSOCIATION,**
☎ 0131 453 1297
Guided walks in Glasgow city centre.

**THE SPIRIT OF GLASGOW
TOUR COMPANY,**
☎ 0141 248 3400
Walking tours of Glasgow - ghosts, historic pubs, murder tours.

TRAINS

Regular and efficient services to Glasgow from all over the UK are run by Scotrail, Virgin Trains and Greater North Eastern Railway. Passenger Enquiries
☎ 0345 484 950

UNDERGROUND TRAINS

STRATHCLYDE PASSENGER TRANSPORT
☎ 0141 333 3159
Frequent trains connect the city centre with the west end via two circular underground lines.

SPORT & LEISURE

CYCLING

CLYDE COAST CYCLE ROUTES,
A route from Bells Bridge passes through Glasgow parks and the old PaisleY & Ardrossan Canal to Paisley, where traffic-free routes extend to Greenock (Inverclyde) and Irvine (Ayrshire).

GLASGOW - LOCH LOMOND CYCLEWAY,
Follows canal towpaths and disused railway lines out of the city, and a mix of forest trails and peaceful minor roads, to Killin in the Highlands.

For more details on cycle paths & routes
☎ 0141 572 0234 (Scottish Sustrans).

GOLF COURSES

COW GLEN ☎ 0141 632 0556
Undulating and challenging park and course.

HAGGS CASTLE ☎ 0141 427 1157
A quite difficult wooded, parkland course.

ALEXANDRA ☎ 0141 556 1294

KIRKHILL ☎ 0141 641 8499

KINGS PARK ☎ 0141 630 1597

KNIGHTSWOOD ☎ 0141 959 6358

LETHAMHILL ☎ 0141 770 6220

LINN PARK ☎ 0141 637 5871

POLLOK ☎ 0141 632 4351

RUCHILL ☎ 0141 946 8793

WILLIAMWOOD ☎ 0141 637 4311

ICE RINK

CROSSMYLOOF ICE RINK,
Titwood Rd ☎ 0141 423 3093

LEISURE CENTRES

ALL SAINTS LEISURE CENTRE,
Scotsburn Rd, Barmulloch ☎ 0141 558 8627

BELLAHOUSTON LEISURE CENTRE,
31 Bellahouston Dr ☎ 0141 427 5454

CASTLEMILK SPORTS CENTRE,
Dougrie Rd ☎ 0141 634 8187

EASTERHOUSE SPORTS CENTRE,
Auchinlea Rd ☎ 0141 771 1963

KELVIN HALL SPORTS ARENA,
Kelvin Hall, Argyle St ☎ 0141 357 2525

NORTH WOODSIDE LEISURE CENTRE,
Braid Sq, St George's Cross
☎ 0141 332 8102

POLLOCKSHAWS SPORT CENTRE,
Ashtree Rd, G43
☎ 0141 632 2200

SCOTSTOUN LEISURE CENTRE,
Danes Dr, Scotstoun ☎ 0141 959 4000

SPRINGBURN LEISURE CENTRE,
Kay St, Springburn
☎ 0141 557 5878

TOLLCROSS PARK LEISURE CENTRE,
Tollcross Park, Wellshot Rd
☎ 0141 763 2345

RIDING

DUMBRECK RIDING SCHOOL,
82 Dumbreck Rd ☎ 0141 427 0660

SWIMMING

see also Leisure Centres

CASTLEMILK SWIMMING POOL,
Castlemilk Drive ☎ 0141 634 8254

DRUMCHAPEL POOL,
199 Drumry Rd East ☎ 0141 944 5812

EASTERHOUSE SWIMMING POOL,
Bogbain Rd ☎ 0141 771 7978

GOVAN FUN POOL,
1 Harehill St ☎ 0141 445 1899

GOVANHILL SWIMMING POOL,
Calder St ☎ 0141 423 0233

POLLOK LEISURE POOL,
27 Cowglen Rd ☎ 0141 881 3313

WHITEHILL SWIMMING POOL,
Dennistoun ☎ 0141 551 9969

WALKING

CLYDE WALKWAY,
A delightful path beside the River Clyde stretching from the Exhibition & Conference Centre to Cambuslang.

FORTH & CLYDE CANAL,
Towpath walks along the canal. 'Walk-cards' available from British Waterways
☎ 0141 332 6936

GLASGOW TO EDINBURGH TRAIL,
Incorporating the Clyde Walkway, Airdrie to Bathgate Railway Path, Livingston Paths Network and the Lothian Cycle Routes, this routes links Glasgow & Edinburgh.

KELVIN WALKWAY,
Follows the River Kelvin through Kelvingrove Park to the city's west end.

MERCHANT CITY TRAIL,
Explores the 'old' town, originally home to 18th-century tobacco lords.

WALKING TOURS

SCOT-TREK,
9 Lawrence St ☎/☎ 0141 334 9232

WHERE TO STAY

5-STAR HOTELS

AA RECOMMENDED

GLASGOW

GLASGOW HILTON ✿✿
1 Williams St G3 8HT
(M8 J18, through 3 sets of lights, hotel on left)
☎ 0141 204 5555 ✆ 0141 204 5004
Magnificent polished granite and mirrored glass building, the Glasgow Hilton has become a landmark in the city centre.
££££ 319 bedrooms (4 fmly) No smoking in 126 bedrooms No dogs (ex guide dogs) Lift Night porter Air conditioning Indoor swimming pool (heated) Sauna Solarium Gym Jacuzzi/spa Leisure centre No smoking area in restaurant ⬛

4-STAR HOTELS

GLASGOW MOAT HOUSE ✿✿
Congress Rd G3 8QT
(M8 J19, follow signs for SEC, hotel adjacent)
☎ 0141 306 9988 ✆ 0141 221 2022
Ultra modern and one of the tallest buildings in Scotland this impressive hotel on the River Clyde offers smart accommodation.
££££ 284 bedrooms (45 fmly) No smoking in 120 bedrooms Lift Night porter Air conditioning Indoor swimming pool (heated) Sauna Solarium Gym Jacuzzi/spa Weekly live entertainment No smoking area in restaurant ⬛

BEARDMORE ✿✿
Beardmore St G81 4HX
☎ 0141 951 6000 ✆ 0141 951 6018
Beside the River Clyde this impressive purpose-built modern hotel is an ideal base for the business traveller. Staff throughout are friendly and willing to please.
££ 168 bedrooms No smoking in 112 bedrooms Lift Night porter Air conditioning Indoor swimming pool (heated) Sauna Solarium Gym Jacuzzi/spa ⬛

GLASGOW MARRIOTT ✿✿
500 Argyle St, Anderston G3 8RR
(off M8 J19)
☎ 0141 226 5577 ✆ 0141 221 7676
Modern purpose-built hotel in the shadow of the Kingston Bridge with two different eating options both with the emphasis on informality.
££££ 300 bedrooms (89 fmly) No smoking in 185 bedrooms Lift Night porter Air conditioning Indoor swimming pool (heated) Squash Sauna Solarium Gym Jacuzzi/spa Heated whirlpool Hairdresser Weekly live entertainment No smoking area in restaurant ⬛

GLASGOW THISTLE ✿
36 Cambridge St G2 3HN
(behind Sauchiehall St, opp rear entrance to Marks & Spencer and Boots)
☎ 0141 332 3311 ✆ 0141 332 4050
Busy hotel, with an underground car park, near Sauchiehall Street. Formal and informal dining.
££££ 302 bedrooms (69 fmly) No smoking in 120 bedrooms Lift Night porter ⬛

THE COPTHORNE GLASGOW
George Square G2 1DS
(from M8 J15 follow signs City Centre/George Sq, along Cathedral St past Strathclyde University, turn L into Hanover St)
☎ 0141 332 6711 ✆ 0141 332 4264
Imposing Victorian hotel centrally situated. Bedrooms vary in size, but all are well equipped. Guests have the choice of eating options.
££££ 141 bedrooms (4 fmly) No smoking in 45 bedrooms No dogs (ex guide dogs) Lift Night porter No smoking area in restaurant ⬛

3-STAR HOTELS

ONE DEVONSHIRE GARDENS ✿✿✿
1 Devonshire Gardens G12 0UX
(M8 J17, follow signs for A82, after 1.5 miles L into Hyndland Rd, 1st R. R at mini rdb. R at end & continue to end)
☎ 0141 339 2001 ✆ 0141 337 1663
Very individual hotel comprising three adjoining town houses, each with bedrooms notable for their bold, striking decor and sumptuous appointments.
££££ 27 bedrooms (3 fmly) Night porter No smoking in restaurant ⬛

The Devonshire Hotel of Glasgow

THE DEVONSHIRE HOTEL OF GLASGOW
5 Devonshire Gardens G12 0UX

☎ 0141 339 7878 🖷 0141 339 3980

Remains one of the most stylish hotels in the city offering the charm, elegance and comfort one would expect of such a grand house. *14 bedrooms (3 fmly) Night porter P*

MALMAISON ☁
278 West George St G2 4LL

(from South/East-M8 J18 (Charing Cross), from West/North-M8 City Centre Glasgow)

☎ 0141 221 6400 🖷 0141 221 6411

Smart hotel with bedrooms striking in design with a plethora of thoughtful features such as CD players, mini-bars and ISDN telephone lines.

££££ 73 bedrooms (4 fmly) No smoking in 8 bedrooms Lift Night porter Gym small fitness room ☁

KINGS PARK
Mill St G73 2LX

(on A730 East Kilbride road)

☎ 0141 647 5491 🖷 0141 613 3022

Close to Rutherglen this modern hotel is appointed to a high standard throughout. Staff give caring and courteous service.

££ 26 bedrooms Night porter Pool table Jacuzzi/spa Weekly live entertainment Conference suites Function rooms ☁

EWINGTON
Balmoral Ter, 132 Queens Dr, Queens Park G42 8QW

(M8 J20 onto A77, through 8 sets of lights, after crossroads hotel is 2nd left)

☎ 0141 423 1152 🖷 0141 422 2030

Stylish town house hotel offering a relaxing retreat from the hustle and bustle. Service throughout is unobtrusively attentive.

££££ 44 bedrooms (1 fmly) No smoking in 6 bedrooms Lift Night porter Computer games No smoking area in restaurant ☁

Holiday Inn

SWALLOW
517 Paisley Rd West G51 1RW

(off junc 23 of M8)

☎ 0141 427 3146 🖷 0141 427 4059

Just five minutes from the Burrell Collection, and ten from the city centre this purpose-built hotel has rooms offering high levels of comfort.

££££ 117 bedrooms (1 fmly) No smoking in 56 bedrooms or restaurant Lift Night porter Indoor swimming pool (heated) Sauna Solarium Gym Jacuzzi/spa Steam room ☁

JURYS GLASGOW
Great Western Rd G12 0XP *(W of city, off A82)*

☎ 0141 334 8161 🖷 0141 334 3846

On a main approach to the city this hotel is popular with both the business and leisure guest. Neatly uniformed staff provide attentive service.

£££ 133 bedrooms (12 fmly) No smoking in 55 bedrooms Lift Night porter Indoor swimming pool (heated) Sauna Solarium Gym Jacuzzi/spa Whirlpool Children's facilities No smoking area in restaurant ☁

QUALITY CENTRAL HOTEL
99 Gordon St G1 3SF *(exit M8 J19 L into Argyle St and L into Hope St)*

☎ 0141 221 9680 🖷 0141 226 3948

Former Victorian railway hotel, an integral part of the Central Station, retains the charming hallmarks of that era.

£££ 222 bedrooms (8 fmly) No smoking in 70 bedrooms Lift Night porter Indoor swimming pool (heated) Sauna Solarium Gym Jacuzzi/spa Hair & beauty salon Steamroom No smoking area in restaurant ☁

HOLIDAY INN
161 West Nile St G1 2RL *(M8 J16, follow signs for Royal Concert Hall, hotel is opposite)*

☎ 0141 332 0110 🖷 0141 332 7447

This contemporary hotel features a trendy café style French restaurant, bar area and conservatory. Staff are friendly and attentive.

££ 80 bedrooms (4 fmly) No smoking in 60 bedrooms No dogs (ex guide dogs) Lift No smoking area in restaurant ☁

TINTO FIRS THISTLE
470 Kilmarnock Rd G43 2BB

(4m S of Glasgow City Centre on A77)

☎ 0141 637 2353 🖷 0141 633 1340

This modern purpose-built hotel is just 4 miles from the city centre. Bedrooms are mostly cosy studio singles, attractively appointed.

££££ 28 bedrooms (4 fmly) No smoking in 4 bedrooms Night porter No smoking area in restaurant ☁

KELVIN PARK LORNE
923 Sauchiehall St G3 7TE

☎ 0141 314 9955 🖷 0141 337 1659

Popular city centre hotel, just five minutes walk from the SEC offers well equipped accommodation. Several eating options.

98 bedrooms (7 fmly) No smoking in 20 bedrooms No dogs (ex guide dogs) Lift Night porter Weekly live entertainment ☁

CARRICK
377 Argyle St G2 8LL

(from M8 J19 bear L into Argyle St, hotel opp Cadogan Sq)

☎ 0141 248 2355 🖷 0141 221 1014

Modern hotel, centrally situated with compact, but well equipped bedrooms and a popular first floor restaurant and lounge bar.

£££ 121 bedrooms No smoking in 79 bedrooms Lift Night porter No smoking area in restaurant ☁

Malmaison

2-STAR HOTELS

Glynhill Hotel & Leisure Club

THE BELHAVEN
15 Belhaven Ter, Dowanhill G12 0TG
(W from M8 J17 on A82 after approx 1.5m (before sign for Dowanhill) Hotel is on L)
☎ 0141 339 3222 🖷 0141 339 2212
Fine terraced property, off Great Western Road and close to the Botanic Gardens, offers both spacious and standard accommodation.
££ 17 bedrooms (3 fmly) No dogs Night porter 🔔

FORTE POSTHOUSE GLASGOW CITY
Bothwell St G2 7EN
☎ 0141 248 2656 🖷 0141 221 8986
Bright hotel offering modern accommodation, well equipped en suite bedrooms, informal bar and dining area.
247 bedrooms

TRAVEL INN
Glasgow Zoo, Hamilton Rd G71 7SA
☎ 0141 773 1133 🖷 0141 771 8354
Modern building offering smart, spacious and well equipped bedrooms, suitable for family use. Nearby family restaurant.
££ (fmly room) 40 bedrooms

TRAVELODGE
Paisley Rd G3
☎ 0800 850950 🖷 01384 78578
Modern building offering smart, spacious and well equipped bedrooms, suitable for family use. Nearby family restaurant.
££ (fmly room) 43 bedrooms

DEAUVILLES ◙ ◙ ◙ ◙ ◙
62 St Andrews Dr, Pollockshields G41 5EX
☎ 0141 427 1106 🖷 0141 427 1106
Imposing Victorian house tastefully furnished and stylishly decorated. Bedrooms include trouser press, hair dryer and radio.
6 bedrooms (1 fmly) Licensed 🔔

ANGUS HOTEL ◙ ◙ ◙
970 Sauchiehall St G3 7TH
☎ 0141 357 5155 🖷 0141 339 9469
Occupying a corner position this pleasant guest house has good modern standards of accommodation, with all the expected facilities.
££ 18 bedrooms (7 fmly) No smoking in bedrooms No smoking in dining room No dogs (ex guide dogs) 🔔

BOTANIC HOTEL ◙ ◙ ◙
1 Alfred Ter, Great Western Rd G12 8RF
(off M8 J17, R in 1m hotel on left, directly above A625)
☎ 0141 339 6955 🖷 0141 339 6955
Victorian property occupying an elevated corner position. Rooms, on three floors, are generally well appointed and spacious.
£ 17 bedrooms (4 fmly) No smoking in dining room 🔔

HOTEL ENTERPRISE ◙ ◙ ◙
144 Renfrew St G3 6RF
☎ 0141 332 8095 🖷 0141 332 8095
City centre hotel in an attractive Victorian terrace. Bedrooms include telephone and TV, and hearty breakfasts are served.
££ 6 bedrooms (2 fmly) No smoking in 1 bedrooms or dining room Licensed 🔔

BELGRAVE ◙ ◙
2 Belgrave Ter, Hillhead G12 8JD
(diagonally opposite Kelvinbridge Post Office)
☎ 0141 337 1850 & 337 1741
🖷 0141 429 8608
In a Victorian terrace beside Great Western Road this guest house has smartly decorated, mostly compact bedrooms.
£ 11 bedrooms (2 fmly) No smoking in 5 bedrooms or dining room No dogs (ex guide dogs) 🔔

CHARING CROSS ◙ ◙
310 Renfrew St, Charing Cross G3 6UW
(off M8 into Sauchiehall St up Scott St to Buccleugh St, turn L & into Renfrew St)
☎ 0141 332 2503 🖷 0141 353 3047
Convenient for city centre attractions this Victorian property offers a good standard of facilities in its mostly compact bedrooms.
£ 24 bedrooms (8 fmly) No dogs (ex guide dogs) 🔔

KELVIN PRIVATE HOTEL ◙ ◙
15 Buckingham Ter, Great Western Rd, Hillhead G12 8EB *(leave M8 J17 onto A82 Kelvinside/Dumbarton. 1m on R before Botanic Gardens)*
☎ 0141 339 7143 🖷 0141 339 5215
Two Grade A Victorian linked terraced houses create this friendly private hotel. Various sized bedrooms on offer.
£ 21 bedrooms (5 fmly) 🔔

LOMOND HOTEL ◙ ◙
6 Buckingham Ter, Great Western Rd, Hillhead G12 8EB
(on A82, on R before Botanic Gardens)
☎ 0141 339 2339 🖷 0141 339 5215
Good value is offered at this friendly hotel, which stands in a tree-lined Victorian terrace. Bedrooms offer mixed modern appointments. *£ 17 bedrooms (6 fmly)* 🔔

MCLAYS ◙ ◙
264/276 Renfrew St, Charing Cross G3 6TT
(from M8 head for Charing Cross)
☎ 0141 332 4796 🖷 0141 353 0422
Close to the Art School this large budget hotel has spacious family rooms, compact doubles and single rooms;.Three breakfast rooms.
£ 62 bedrooms (14 fmly) No smoking in area of dining room No smoking in 1 lounge No dogs (ex guide dogs) Lift 🔔

GLASGOW AIRPORT

Renfrewshire
See also Howwood

DALMENY PARK COUNTRY HOUSE
Lochlibo Rd G78 1LG
(on A736 towards Irvine)
☎ 0141 881 9211 🖷 0141 881 9214
Guests at this fine 19th-century mansion in pleasant gardens will receive caring, friendly and professional attention from the staff.
££ 20 bedrooms (2 fmly) No smoking in 2 bedrooms Night porter Jacuzzi/spa Children's facilities No smoking area in restaurant 🔔

GLYNHILL HOTEL & LEISURE CLUB
Paisley Rd PA4 8XB
(from M8 J27 take A741 towards Renfrew. 300 yards, over small rndbt- Hotel on R)
☎ 0141 886 5555 & 885 1111
🖷 0141 885 2838
Much extended hotel, offering a range of accommodation from standard to spacious executive rooms. All have excellent facilities.
££££ 125 bedrooms (25 fmly) No smoking in 51 bedrooms Night porter Indoor swimming pool (heated) Snooker Sauna Solarium Gym Jacuzzi/spa Solaria & impulse showers Weekly live entertainment No smoking area in restaurant 🔔

LYNNHURST
Park Rd PA5 8LS
☎ 01505 324331 🖷 01505 324219
Two detached yet linked Victorian houses with bright, tastefully modern bedrooms, bar, conservatory lounge and panelled dining room.
21 bedrooms (2 fmly) No dogs (ex guide dogs) Arrangement with local leisure centre No smoking area in restaurant Closed 1-3 Jan 🔔

DEAN PARK
91 Glasgow Rd PA4 8YB *(exit at M8 J26 onto A8 for Renfrew, 200yds, hotel on L)*
☎ 0141 304 9955 ⓕ 0141 885 0681
Modern purpose built hotel, provides courtesy transport to the airport and there's complimentary use of the David Lloyd Sports and Leisure Centre nearby.
££ 118 bedrooms (6 fmly) No smoking in 6 bedrooms Night porter Snooker Beautician No smoking in restaurant

FORTE POSTHOUSE GLASGOW AIRPORT
Abbotsinch PA3 2TR
(from E M8 J 28 follow signs for Hotel; from W M8 J29 follow airport slip road to Hotel)
☎ 0141 887 1212 ⓕ 0141 887 3738
Suitable for both the business and leisure traveller, this bright hotel offers modern accommodation, and well equipped en suite bedrooms.
297 bedrooms

FORTE POSTHOUSE GLASGOW/ERSKINE
North Barr PA8 6AN *(off A726)*
☎ 0141 812 0123 ⓕ 0141 812 7642
Suitable for both the business and leisure traveller, this bright hotel offers modern accommodation, well equipped en suite bedrooms.
166 bedrooms

TRAVEL INN
Whitecart Rd PA3 2TH
(close to airport terminal follow signs)
☎ 0141 842 1563 ⓕ 0141 842 1570
Modern building offering smart, spacious and well equipped bedrooms, suitable for family use. Nearby family restaurant.
££ (fmly room) 81 bedrooms

BED & BREAKFAST ACCOMMODATION

MYFARRCLAN ◍◍◍◍◍
146 Corsebar Rd PA2 9NA
(with Royal Alexandra Hospital on L house 0.5m up hill on R with tall evergreen hedge)
☎ 0141 884 8285 ⓕ 0141 884 8285

Nicely located in a leafy suburb this nicely decorated bungalow offers comfortable bedrooms and warm hospitality.
££ 3 bedrooms No smoking No dogs

WHERE TO EAT

RESTAURANTS

AA RECOMMENDED

BUTTERY RESTAURANT ❀❀
652 Argyle Street G3 8U
☎ 0141 2218188 ⓕ 0141 2044639
Lunch is excellent value for curried egg on a warm croissant, lamb's liver and onions with grain mustard sauce, and warm banana crêpe with chocolate sauce. Evening brings more Scottish ideas such as mignons of Highland venison layered with redcurrants and apple chutney, or fillet of beef with skirlie and a dark malted sauce. There's also a full menu for vegetarians.
Fixed L £ ALC £££

DEVONSHIRE HOTEL ❀
5 Devonshire Gardens, G12 0UX
☎ 0141 339 7878 ⓕ 0141 339 3980
Imaginative Scottish dishes are served in the intimate four–table restaurant, where the menu might include loin of Border lamb with redcurrant and basil glaze and braised fillet of sea bass on a 'tricolour of vegetables'.
ALC £££

GLASGOW HILTON ❀❀
1 William Street G3 8HT
☎ 0141 2045555 ⓕ 0141 2045004
East coast smoked salmon, salmon cured in Glayva and whisky, Loch Fyne oysters, Oban scallops, Ayrshire pork, Black Angus beef. Confit of Barbary duck on bitter leaves with a Puy lentil dressing, pan-fried turbot with a confit of new potatoes and baby tomatoes, and a chocolate cup of Ovaltine ice cream and pecan cookies served with a mango and vanilla sauce, formed the components of one well-reported meal.
Fixed L ££ ALC £££

GLASGOW MOAT HOUSE ❀❀
Congress Road G3 8QT
☎ 0141 3069988 ⓕ 0141 2212022
Cooking is classically upmarket - sausage of brill is flanked by quenelles of pike, saffron and chive cream, and a tartlet of foie gras, beetroot and red wine vinaigrette accompanies breast of duck. Game is frequently on the menu, as in terrine of rabbit and smoked bacon, and venison and pigeon on a bed of braised Savoy cabbage.
Fixed L ££ ALC £££

HOLIDAY INN GARDEN COURT ❀
161 West Nile Street G1 2RL
☎ 0141 332 0110 ⓕ 0141 332 7447
French inspired menu includes dishes such as pan-fried duck supreme with salsa verde and cheese quiche with a herb sauce, and roasted breast of chicken with Chardonnay and mushroom cream.
Fixed L £ ALC ££

KILLERMONT POLO CLUB ❀
2002 Maryhill Road, Maryhill Park G20 0AB
☎ 0141 946 5412
Ultra–smart Indian whose menu includes lamb korma and rogan josh and more innovative dishes such as hariali (chicken cooked with three types of spinach); garlic nan and gulab jamun which have also been recommended. Lunch is particularly good value.
Fixed L £ ALC £

MALMAISON HOTEL ❀
278 West George Street G2 4LL
☎ 0141 2216400 ⓕ 0141 2216411
This restaurant, in the old crypt of a remodelled church, with the original vaulted ceiling, is modelled on a French-style brasserie. The cooking is good, and the highlight of a recent meal was the salmon fishcakes served with parsley sauce.

> **Call the AA Hotel Booking Service on 0990 050505 to book at AA recognised hotels and B&Bs in the UK, or through our internet site: http://www.theaa.co.uk/hotels**

ONE DEVONSHIRE GARDENS ❀ ❀ ❀
1 Devonshire Gardens G12 0UX
☎ 0141 3392001 ☏ 0141 3371663
Dinner here may open with a glazed onion tart with bacon, walnuts, Roquefort and creamed onion sauce, followed by a mushroom consommé bolstered by tarragon and chervil, then seared fillet of salmon on a bed of buttered spinach with root vegetables in a herb broth. Lemon mousse with pink grapefruit sorbet and spiced port wine sauce showed an ability to achieve perfect balance with textural contrasts.
Signature dishes: Roast stuffed saddle of spring lamb with aubergine and garlic purée and grilled Mediterranean vegetables; home-smoked lobster with warm herb butter sauce; warm salad of roasted teal with ceps.
Fixed L ££ Fixed D £££ 🍷

PAPINGO RESTAURANT ❀
104 Bath Street G2 2EN
☎ 0141 3326678 ☏ 0141 3326549
An excellent value modern menu takes in the likes of a fresh tasting mussel, leek and crab soup, aromatic breast of duck with port and orange, and ratatouille tartlet with Parmesan cream.
Fixed D ££ 🍷

Papingo Restaurant

ROGANO ❀ ❀
11 Exchange Place, G1 3AN
☎ 0141 2484055 ☏ 0141 2482608
Rogano is the oldest surviving restaurant in the city. Fish and seafood have always been the thing here, and the carte offers a wide choice from poached mussels marinière, and their famous fish soup, to grilled halibut with cracked peppercorns and Cognac cream, and steamed scallops with Mornay sauce on spinach. Lobster comes either with lemon mayonnaise, grilled or thermidor, and there are chilled oysters on the half shell. There are also a couple of meat and vegetarian choices. The basement Café Rogano offers a cheaper, faster alternative and there is also an excellent choice of bar food.
Fixed L ££ ALC ££ 🍷

STRAVAIGIN ❀ ❀
30 Gibson Street G12
☎ 0141 3342665 ☏ 0141 3344099
Roast breast of Galloway pheasant, onion tatties and Muscatel gravy may be on Stravaigin's menu. Global influences abound - Hanoi duck soup, for example, is an aromatic broth of marinated roast duck, shiitake mushrooms, egg noodles and fresh herbs, and curanto is a traditional Chilean dish made with mixed shellfish, roasted meats, and potatoes.
Fixed L £ ALC ££ 🍷

UBIQUITOUS CHIP ❀
12 Ashton Lane G12 8SJ
☎ 0141 334 5007 ☏ 0141 337 1302
Simple city suburb diner with stone floors, lots of greenery and a lively, informal atmosphere. A bistro menu offers meaty pan-fried scallops and tender wood pigeon with wild mushroom sauce. Good selection of Scottish cheeses.

YES ❀ ❀
22 West Nile Street G1 2PW
☎ 0141 2218044 ☏ 0141 2489159
Eclectic and original cooking in a similar environment, enthusiastically drawing on influences from near and far. Local pride is satisfied with a cream of Finnan haddock soup with lentils and crisp bacon, gâteau of haggis, and neeps and tatties with a whisky sauce. More wide-ranging is best end of lamb with ratatouille and minted couscous, and roast chicken breast with buttered spinach and gratin of macaroni, Parmesan and Parma ham. The Brasserie also serves a good choice of dishes.
Fixed L ££ ALC £££ 🍷

Call the AA Hotel Booking Service on 0990 050505 to book at AA recognised hotels and B&Bs in the UK, or through our internet site: http://www.theaa.co.uk/hotels

Stravaigin

LA PARMIGIANA ❀ ❀
447 Great Western Road Strathclyde
☎ 0141 3340686 ☏ 0141 332 3533
Fixed–price lunches include tuna with borlotti beans, earthy rabbit alla cacciatore, and crostata di frutta. The carte features fresh pasta in plenty of guises, plus crespelle, carpaccio and pollo alla diavola, fillet of beef served on a crouton with stewed artichoke hearts and escalope of veal alla Parmigiana. Fish specials vary with the market. Home–made ice creams, zabaglione and cantuccini (almond biscuits for dunking into vin santo) are typical finales.
Fixed L £ ALC £ 🍷

Yes

PUBS, INNS & OTHER PLACES

GLASGOW

L'ARIOSTO RISTORANTE
92-94 Mitchell Street, G1 3NQ *(City centre)*
☎ 0141 2210971/8543 📠 0141226 5718
One of Glasgow's longest established, privately owned Italian restaurants. Authentic cuisine, live music and hospitality.

BOURBON STREET
108 George Street G1 1RF
☎ 0141 552 0141 📠 0141 552 8860
Jazz oriented New Orleans style bar and restaurant with live music and dancing. Extensive a la carte menu.

BRADFORDS
245 Sauchiehall Street, G2
☎ 0141 332 1008 📠 0141 353 2671
Popular rendezvous. Traditional style tearoom serving light meals and tempting handmade chocolates.

THE BUTTERY
652 Argyle St City of Glasgow G3 8UF
(Town centre)
☎ 0141 221 8188
Victorian pub which offers a varied menu. From Buttery Scottish steak sandwich with wild mushrooms, to aubergine and tomato gateau.

CAFÉ GANDOLFI
64 Albion Street G1 1NY *(City centre)*
☎ 0141 552 6813
A blend of a traditional Glasgow tearoom and a European café restaurant which is uniquely Scottish. Cuisine is international and varied, including vegetarian.

CANTINA DEL REY
10 King's Court (off King Street)G1 5RB
(City centre)
☎/📠 0141 552 4044
'A great taste of Mexico' with fajitas, mega margaritas and great service. Children can eat free.

CAIRNS
5/15 Miller Street G1 1EA *(City centre)*
☎ 0141 248 5007
A centrally located pub that is an ideal venue to relax in and enjoy good food.

THE CASK & STILL
154 Hope Street G2 2TH *(City centre)*
☎ 0141 333 0980
One of Scotland's finest collections of malt whisky is complemented by a wide range of real ales and traditional food.

CUL DE SAC WESTEND
44 Ashton Lane G12 8SJ
☎ 0141 334 4749
Popular west end establishment with internatioanl cuisine at modest prices. Between 5 and 7pm there's a third off pastas, crepes and burgers everyday.

DI MAGGIO'S PIZZERIA
21 Royal Exchange Square G1 3AJ
☎ 0141 248 2111 📠 0141 221 6101
61 Ruthven Lane off Byres Street G12
☎ 0141 334 8560

1038 Pollokshaws Road Shawlands G41
☎ 0141 632 8888 *(City centre)*
Atmospheric Italian-American restaurants where families and large parties are welcome. Menus are based on traditional recipes with the accent on value for money.

HARRY RAMSDENS
251 Paisley Road G5 8RA
☎ 0141 429 3700 📠 0141 429 1088
'The world's most famous fish and chips'. Restaurant, take-away, café, children's fun park and ample parking.

IL PAVONE ITALIAN RESTAURANT
Unit 13-14 Courtyard Princes Square 48 Buchanan Street G1 3JN *(City centre)*
☎ 0141 221 0543 📠 0141 221 6647
In the elegant surroundings of Princes Square this establishment specialises in seafood, pasta and pizzas, and continental breakfasts. Patisserie, coffee shop and sandwich bar.

JOCK TAMSON'S
70 Renfield Street G2 *(City centre)*
☎ 0141 332 1842
Traditional Scottish bar with food always available. Wide selection of malt whiskies. Live music Friday and Saturday evenings.

JOCK TAMSON'S
256 Byres Street G12
☎ 0141 334 1284
Scottish pub offering Scottish beer, food, music, films, humour and 'patter'. Live music Thursday to Sunday.

D'ARCYS WINE BAR AND RESTAURANT
The Basement Courtyard Princes Square Buchanan Street G1 3JN *(City centre)*
☎ 0141 226 4309 📠 0141 248 5639
Restauarant hidden behind a continental style bar with al fresco tables in the courtyard. No-smoking room.

THE FIRE STATION RESTAURANT
33 Ingram Street G1 1HA *(City centre)*
☎ 0141 552 2929
Listed Victorian fire stataion with many of the original features. Friendly service and children are made very welcome. Half-price pasta from 5-7pm.

FROGGIES RESTAURANT & NEW ORLEANS BAR
53 West Regent Street G2 2AE *(City centre)*
☎ 0141 572 0007/1118 📠 0141 572 1117
The restaurant, with a relaxed atmosphere, and the adjacent and more lively New Orleans theme bar, are both places to enjoy a wide variety of foods. French, cajun and creole, traditional and vegetarian choices.

THE GRANARY
10 Kilmarnock Road G41 3NH
☎ 0141 632 8487 📠 0141 649 3724
An established eating place where there's a wide range of food on offer.

THE JENNY
18-20 Royal Exchange Square G1 3AB
(City centre)
☎ 0141 204 4988
Bistro waitress service for breakfast, coffee, teas, cakes, pastries, lunch, sandwiches, and afternoon teas plus beers, wines and spirits.

JUNKANOO TAPAS BAR/CAFÉ
111 Hope Street G2 6LL *(City centre)*
☎/📠 0141 248 7102
Glasgow's only Spanish tapas bar and gallery offering a wide selection of inexpensive appertisers and specialities.

KINCAID HOUSE HOTEL
Birdston Road Milton of Campsie G65 8BZ
☎ 0141 776 2226
The seat of the Kincaid clan and a Grade A listed house dating back to 1690 there is a restaurant, conservatory and stable bar serving food all day.

KOH I NOOR RESTAURANT
235 North Street G3 7DL *(City centre)*
☎ 0141 221 1555/204 1444
📠 0141 221 1444
Oldest Indian restaurant in Glasgow with buffet nights on Mon-Sat and buffet brunches on Sundays and a pre-theatre menu available.

MOLLY MALONES
224 Hope Street G2 2UG *(City centre)*
☎ 0141 332 2757
Traditional Irish Bar with wholesome food and so much more. Live music every night from 10.30pm.

MUNGO JERRI'S
25 Parnie Street G1 5RJ *(City centre)*
☎ 0141 552 7999
A non-smoking café specialising in original and classic American made-to-order sandwiches 'to go' or 'sit in'. Wide range of vegetarian choices.

RAB HA'S
53 Hutchieson St City of Glasgow G1 1SH
(City centre) ☎ 0141 5531545
Named after a renowned Glaswegian glutton, this friendly establishment comprises a bar and cellar restaurant.

78 ST VINCENT
78 St Vincent Street G2 5UB *(City centre)*
☎ 0141 221 7710 📠 0141248 7878
Turn of the century Parisian style restaurant specialising in good, value-for-money fixed priced menus, utilising fresh local produce.

UBIQUITOUS CHIP
12 Ashton Ln, Off Byres Rd City of Glasgow G12 8SJ
☎ 0141 3345007
'Genuine heavy drinking Scottish pub', the eating is done 'Upstairs at the Chip', There's vegetarian haggis with neeps and tatties, silverside beef with rich gravy, roasted chicken leg stuffed with skirlie, and baked salmon marinated in honey, tamari and ginger.

MUST SEE

BOTHWELL CASTLE,
Bothwell, S. Lanarkshire ☎ 01698 816894
Finest suriving 13th-century castle in Scotland. Beseiged, captured and partly demolished several times during the Scottish-English wars, it was once a stronghold of the Douglasses. Visitor centre and shop.

CHATELHERAULT,
Ferniegair, Hamilton, S. Lanarkshire
☎ 01698 426213
Built in the 1730's as a hunting lodge, historic Chatelherault is set in a magnificent 500 acre country park, with 10 miles of footpaths along a gorge. Café, shop, adventure playgrounds, deer park, and a visitor centre which tells the history of the Hamiltons and the estate.

FALLS OF CLYDE,
New Lanark, S. Lanarkshire
Well worth the short walk upstream from New Lanark, these spectacular waterfalls - Bonnington Linn, Dundaff Linn and the impressive Corra Linn - set in 100 acres of woodland, plunge through A rocky gorge and are best seen when the Clyde is in spate, or when the flow of water is fully restored from the nearby power station. Discover the 'Wild Woods' exhibition, an interactive exhibit on the story of the woods, in the visitor centre, then explore the Scottish Wildlife Trust's reserve on excellent footpaths. Ranger-led walks, badger watches and tearoom.

NEW LANARK VISITOR CENTRE,
New Lanark Mills, By Lanark, S. Lanarkshire
☎ 01555 661345
Discover this award-winning conservation village, a beautifully restored example of an 18th-century planned village, nestling in the wooded Clyde Valley. A World Heritage Site, it holds a unique place in social history, for this is where Robert Owen, mill owner and social pioneer, operated the most successful spinning complex in Britain supporting 2,000 people. Here, he abolished child labour, provided schools and good living and working conditions. Soak up the atmosphere among the various restored mill buildings, including a millworker's house, Robert Owen's house, a period village store, then learn about what life was like in the 1800s, through the high-tech effects in 'The Anne McLeod Experience', a dark ride in the company of the spirit of a 10 year old mill girl as guide, in the fascinating visitor centre. Tearoom, shops and picnic areas.

PAISLEY ABBEY,
Abbey Close, Paisley, Renfrewshire
☎ 0141 889 7654
Founded in 1163 as a Cluniac establishment and later elevated to abbey in 1245, the monastery bacame one of the richest and most powerful, before being almost completely destroyed by Edward I's troops in 1307. Rebuilt after Bannockburn in the 15th century, this magnificent abbey lies at the heart of the town and is noted for its fine wood carvings, stonework, memorials to King Robert III, fine choir stalls and its beautiful stained glass windows. Abbey tearoom and shop.

SUMMERLEE HERITAGE TRUST,
West Canal St, Coatbridge, N. Lanarkshire
☎ 01236 431261
Scotland's 'noisiest' museum makes a great family day out. Occupying a 20-acre site, centring on the remains of the Summerlee Ironworks which were uncovered in the 1980s, it is a fascinating museum of social and industrial history, that preserves and interprets the history of the local iron, steel and engineering industries and the communities that depended upon them for a living. Take a ride on Scotland's only working electric tramway, go underground and explore a reconstructed 19th-century coalmine and see how miners of that time worked, and visit refurbished miner's cottages that outline the changes in living conditions from the mid-19th century to the 1970s. View Scotland's largest collection of 19th- and 20th-century working machinery and various themed displays in the vast exhibition hall, and watch ancient steam rollers and lorries in operation around the site. There is also a shop, picnic and play areas, and a tearoom.

ART GALLERIES

MCLEAN MUSEUM & ART GALLERY,
15 Kelly St, Greenock, Inverclyde
☎ 01475 723741
Scottish and European paintings, and local and natural history displays.

PAISLEY MUSEUM & ART GALLERIES,
High St, Paisley, Renfrewshire
☎ 0141 889 3151
Pride of place here is given to a world-famous collection of Paisley shawls. The art gallery features 19th-century Scottish artists and an important studio ceramics collection.

MUSEUMS

BIGGAR GASWORKS MUSEUM,
Gasworks Rd, Biggar, S. Lanarkshire
☎ 01899 221070
Learn how coal was heated to produce gas at Scotland's only remaining gasworks, dating from 1839.

COATS OBSERVATORY,
49 Oakshaw St West, Paisley, Renfrewshire
☎ 0141 889 2013
Astronomy, meteorology and space flight, along with the history of the building, are the subjects of displays on show in this observatory built in 1883.

McLean Museum & Art Gallery

GLADSTONE COURT MUSEUM,
North Back Rd, Biggar, S. Lanarkshire
☎ 01899 221573
A fascinating reproduction of an old-fashioned village street, with shops, a bank, library, schoolroom and many other nostalgia-inducing artefacts.

GREENHILL COVENANTERS' HOUSE,
Burn Braes, Biggar, S. Lanarkshire
☎ 01899 221572
A 17th-century farmhouse relocated stone by stone and housing relics of the turbulent 'Conventanting' period.

GREENOCK CUSTOM HOUSE MUSEUM,
Greenock, Inverclyde ☎ 01475 726331
Illustrates the Customs & Excise Service with enlightening displays on former employees, including Robert Burns.

HUNTER HOUSE,
Maxwelton Rd, East Kilbride, S. Lanarkshire
☎ 01355 261261
Talking exhibits and interactive displays give an insight into the early medical discoveries of the pioneering medical brothers John and William Hunter.

LANARK MUSEUM,
8 Westport, Lanark, S. Lanarkshire
☎ 01555 666680
Discover the heritage of one of Scotland's oldest burghs at this fascinating local museum. Special exhibitions, shop.

LOW PARKS,
129 Muir St, Hamilton, S. Lanarkshire
☎ 01698 283981
Learn about Hamilton and its palace, the Clyde Valley and the Cameronians Scottish Rifle Regiment.

MOAT PARK HERITAGE CENTRE,
Kirkstyle, Biggar, S. Lanarkshire
☎ 01899 221050
See how the Clyde and Tweed Valleys were formed, rub shoulders with an Iron Age family and encounter figures from the past, including a Roman soldier.

MOTHERWELL HERITAGE CENTRE,
High Rd, Motherwell, N. Lanarkshire
☎ 01698 251000
The social history and heritage of
Motherwell from the 19th-century are
illustrated through an interesting multi-
media exhibition.

QUARRIERS VILLAGE,
Bridge of Weir, Renfrewshire
☎ 01505 612224
Conservation village of stone-built villas,
founded by William Quarrier as the orphan
home of Scotland.

SHOTTS HERITAGE CENTRE,
Benhar Rd, Shotts, N. Lanarkshire
☎ 01501 821556
Join a Covenanters meeting and listen to a
sermon, visit the Co-op shop and listen to
a local miner describe his experiences
down the pit, at this centre which
illustrates the history of Shotts.

SMA' SHOT COTTAGES,
George Pl, Paisley, Renfrewshire
☎ 0141 889 1708
Fully restored and furnished 18th-century
weaver's cottages. Tearoom.

WEAVERS' COTTAGES MUSEUM,
Wellwynd, Airdrie, N. Lanarkshire
☎ 01236 747712
A reconstruction of a weaver's house
dating from 1800-1850, with exhibitions
and regular craft demonstrations.

WEAVER'S COTTAGE,
The Cross, Kilbarchan, Renfrewshire
☎ 01505 705588
Together with a fascinating display of
weaving equipment and early domestic
utensils, occasional demonstrations of the
craft are given within an 18th-century
weaver's cottage.

HISTORIC & ANCIENT SITES

CRAIGNETHAN CASTLE,
by Crossford, Lanark, S. Lanarkshire
☎ 01555 860364
Occupying a promontory overlooking the
Nethan Gorge, the castle, built between
1530 and 1540, is a splendid example of
military fortification.

HAMILTON MAUSOLEUM,
Hamilton, S. Lanarkshire
☎ 01698 283981
An extraordinary Victorian mausoleum,
complete with mosaic floor and soaring
dome, built by the 10th Duke of Hamilton
as an extravagant setting to house his
remains.

HAMILTON OLD PARISH CHURCH,
Leechlee Rd, Hamilton, S. Lanarkshire
☎ 01698 459950
Containing the pre-Norman Netherton
Cross, this is the only church to have been
designed by William Adam, dating from 1734.

NEWARK CASTLE,
Port Glasgow, Inverclyde ☎ 01475 741858
The one-time home of the Maxwells,
dating from the 15th and 17th centuries.

TINTO HILL, *5m/8km west of Biggar*
The highest in the Clyde Valley
(2,320ft/711m), topped by one of
Scotland's largest Bronze Age cairns.

GREAT FOR KIDS

BIGGAR PUPPET THEATRE,
Broughton Rd, Biggar, S. Lanarkshire
☎ 01899 220631
A beautiful Victorian style 100 seat theatre
showing large scale puppet shows for all
the family. .

CALDERGLEN COUNTRY PARK,
Strathaven Rd, East Kilbride, S. Lanarkshire
☎ 01355 236644
A fun day out for all the family can be had
at this exciting country park, which
spreads for three miles along the beautiful
valley of the Rotten Calder River. 'Hidden
World's' wildlife experience, nature trails,
children's zoo, and adventure play areas.

CLYDE VALLEY HAWKS,
Crossford, S. Lanarkshire
☎ 01555 860227
Enjoy the unique opportunity of seeing
some of the world's most beautiful birds
of prey at very close quarters.

**DISCOVER CARMICHAEL VISITOR
CENTRE,**
Carmichael, S. Lanarkshire
☎ 01899 308169
View the famous Edinburgh wax model
collection of famous Scots figures, and
learn about the history of clans, and the
agricultural and environmental heritage of
this ancient country estate, through
innovative displays in the visitor centre.
Outdoors, visit the deer farm park and
baby animal farm.

DRUMPELLIER COUNTRY PARK,
Townhead Rd, Coatbridge, N. Lanarkshire
☎ 01236 440702
An ideal family venue for a great day out.
Facilities include a butterfly house, pets'
corner, road train, and nature trail.

EASTWOOD BUTTERFLY KINGDOM,
Rouken Glen Park, Giffnock, E. Renfrewshire
☎ 0141 620 2084
Tropical butterfly house with free-flying
butterflies, and an insect area with many
different species.

GLASGOW ZOOPARK,
Calderpark, Uddingston, S. Lanarkshire
☎ 0141 771 1185
Spacious enclosures and buildings at this
open-plan zoo, Scotland's second largest,
houses birds, mammals and reptiles,
including cats, bears and wolves.

DAVID LIVINGSTONE CENTRE,
165 Station Rd, Blantyre, S. Lanarkshire
☎ 01698 823140
Share the adventurous life of Scotland's
greatest explorer, from his childhood in
the Blantyre Mills to his explorations in the
heart of Africa, all dramatically illustrated
in the tenement where he was born.

M & D'S THEME PARK,
Strathclyde Country Park, Motherwell, N.
Lanarkshire ☎ 01698 333999
Experience the thrill and excitement of
over 30 rides and attractions, and a family
entertainment centre packed with games,
rides, restaurants and a huge soft play
area.

OLD MCDONALD'S FARM PARK,
Dalserf, Garrion Bridge, South Lanarkshire
☎ 01698 889389
A fun farm where children can see and
feed their favourite animals. See or
participate in a circus show and expend
some energy in the indoor and outdoor
adventure areas.

PALACERIGG COUNTRY PARK,
Cumbernauld, N. Lanarkshire
☎ 01236 720047
A 700-acre park with a Scottish and
European wildlife collection, exhibition
centre, play area and nature trails.

THE TIME CAPSULE,
Buchanan St, Coatbridge, N. Lanarkshire
☎ 01236 449572
Swim through dinosaur infested waters,
ride over river rapids and skate in
snowstorms across a frozen loch at this
themed water, ice and adventure centre.

HOMES & GARDENS

COLZIUM HOUSE & ESTATE,
Kilsyth, N. Lanarkshire ☎/☎ 01236 823281
At the heart of the estate is the old castle,
while at Colzium House (open by
appointment), you will find a small
museum and a beautifully designed small
walled garden. Peaceful walks.

FINLAYSTONE COUNTRY ESTATE,
Langbank, Renfrewshire ☎ 01475 540285
Set in beautiful gardens, historic
Finlaystone House, with its charming
exhibition of Victoriana, overlooks the
River Clyde. Delightful woodland walks,
formal gardens, adventure playgrounds,
and visitor centre.

GREENBANK HOUSE & GARDENS,
Flenders Rd, Clarkston, Renfrewshire
☎ 0141 639 3281
An elegant Georgian mansion surrounded
by a 13 acre walled garden.

BIG OUTDOORS

BLACKHILL
*on the B7018 between Kirkfieldbank and
Lesmahagow, S. Lanarkshire*
A viewpoint at 951ft affording views to
Arran and Ben Lomond, complete with a
Bronze Age cairn and the remains of the
largest Iron Age fort in Lanarkshire.

DALZELL COUNTRY PARK,
Motherwell, N. Lanarkshire
☎ 0141 304 1800
Eighteenth-century parkland dipping down
to the Clyde, offering walks, Japanese
gardens and a magnificent arboretum

JAMES HAMILTON HERITAGE PARK,
Stewartfield, East Kilbride, S. Lanarkshire
☏ 01355 276611
With the picturesque Mains Castle as a backdrop, the park features a 16 acre loch, offering a wealth of watersport activities, a bird sanctuary and children's play area.

LOCHWINNOCH RSPB NATURE RESERVE,
Largs Rd, Lochwinnoch, Renfrewshire
☏ 01505 842663
From a first-floor viewing gallery in an attractive Norwegian timber building, and from ground-level hides, visitors can view the whole reserve and observe numerous species of duck and wildfowl.

STRATHCLYDE COUNTRY PARK,
Hamilton Rd, Motherwell, N. Lanarkshire
☏ 01698 266155
One of the leading Scottish centres for outdoor recreation offering a wide range of activities, from sailing, fishing and sunbathing to birdwatching, horse riding and bicycling within 1100 acres of countryside.

ESSENTIAL INFORMATION

TOURIST INFORMATION

INFORMATION CENTRES

ABINGTON,
Service Area Junction 13 M74, Abington, S. Lanarkshire ML12 6RG
☏ 01864 502436

BIGGAR *seasonal,*
155 High St, Biggar, S. Lanarkshire ML12 6DL
☏ 01899 221066

COATBRIDGE *seasonal,*
The Time Capsule, Buchanan St, Coatbridge, N. Lanarkshire ML5 1DL
☏ 01236 431133

GLASGOW AIRPORT,
Paisley, Renfrewshire, PA3 2ST
☏ 0141 848 4440

GREENOCK,
Clyde Square, Greenock, Inverclyde
☏ 01475 722007

HAMILTON,
Service Area M74 Northbound, Hamilton, S. Lanarkshire ML3 6JW
☏ 01698 285590

LANARK,
Horsemarket, Ladyacre Rd, Lanark, S. Lanarkshire ML11 7LQ
☏ 01555 661661

PAISLEY *seasonal,*
The Lagoon Leisure Centre, Mill St, Paisley, Renfrewshire PA1 1LZ
☏ 0141 889 0711

ACCESS

AIR ACCESS

GLASGOW INTERNATIONAL AIRPORT,
☏ 0141 887 1111

SEA ACCESS

CALEDONIAN MACBRAYNE FERRIES,
☏ 01475 650100
Sailings to 23 Scottish islands.

CLYDE MARINE MOTORING COMPANY,
☏ 01475 721281
Passenger ferry service from Gourock to Kilcreggan (all year) and Helensburgh across the Clyde (summer only).

RENFREW FERRY ☏ 0141 226 4826
Passenger ferry across the Clyde.

CRAFTS

CALEDONIAN CRAFTS MARKETING LTD,
Anchor Mills, Paisley, Renfrewshire
☏ 0141 887 4430
Specialist needlecraft manufacturer

LOCHNAGAR CRAFT SHOP,
Bridge of Weir, Renfrewshire
☏ 01505 613410

MACKINNON MILLS,
Coatbridge, N. Lanarkshire
☏ 01236 440702
Knitwear.

ENTERTAINMENT

THEATRE

AIRDRIE ARTS CENTRE,
N. Lanarkshire ☏ 01236 755436

BELLSHILL CULTURAL CENTRE,
N. Lanarkshire ☏ 01698 841831

COATBRIDGE COLLEGE THEATRE,
N. Lanarkshire ☏ 01236 440213

CORN EXCHANGE THEATRE,
Biggar, S. Lanarkshire ☏ 01899 220486

CUMBERNAULD THEATRE,
N. Lanarkshire ☏ 01236 737235

EAST KILBRIDE ARTS CENTRE,
S. Lanarkshire ☏ 01355 261000

EAST KILBRIDE VILLAGE THEATRE,
S. Lanarkshire ☏ 01355 248669

GREENOCK ARTS GUILD THEATRE,
Inverclyde ☏ 01475 723038

MOTHERWELL CONCERT HALL & THEATRE,
N. Lanarkshire ☏ 01698 267515

PAISLEY ARTS CENTRE,
Renfrewshire ☏ 0141 887 1010

FOOD & DRINK

CHEESE

Lanark Blue - an unpasteurised ewes milk blue-veined cheese in the style of Roquefort.

TRANSPORT

BOAT TRIPS & CRUISES

CLYDE MARINE MOTORING CRUISES,
Greenock, Inverclyde ☏ 01475 721281
Day cruises to the scenic Clyde lochs.

BUS/COACH SERVICES

SCOTTISH CITYLINK,
☏ 0990 505050

CAR HIRE

AVIS,
East Kilbride, S Lanarkshire ☏ 01355 233111

EURODOLLAR,
Hamilton, S. Lanarkshire ☏ 01698 828281

EUROPCAR,
Motherwell, N. Lanarkshire ☏ 01698 266534

EUROPEAN CAR RENTAL,
Renfrew, Renfrewshire ☏ 0141 886 1072

PRACTICAL CAR & VAN HIRE,
Johnstone, Renfrewshire ☏ 01505 331155

ROSS'S GARAGE,
Lanark, S. Lanarkshire ☏ 01555 665025

COACH TOURS

ALLANDER TRAVEL,
Milngavie, E. Dunbartonshire
☏ 0141 956 3636

MCGOVERN COACHES & EXECUTIVE HIRE,
Newton Mearns, E. Renfrewshire
☏/☏ 0141 639 5976

PARKS,
Hamilton, S. Lanarkshire ☏ 01698 281222

SOUTHERN COACHES,
Barrhead, E. Renfrewshire ☏ 0141 881 1147

CYCLE HIRE

MGB RALTON CYCLES,
Hamilton, S. Lanarkshire ☏ 01698 284926

WILLIAM WITHERS,
Lanark, S. Lanarkshire ☏ 01555 665878

GUIDED TOURS

FERNIE GUIDED TOURS OF PAISLEY,
☏ 0141 561 8078
Historical walking tour of Paisley.

NORTHERN PROSPECTS,
☏/☏ 01505 615774
Day tours from Glasgow to explore Lanarkshire, Lomond and the Cowal peninsula.

PERSONALISED TOURS,
☏ 0500 011412
Landrover tours from Glasgow.

TRAVEL-LITE,
☏ 0141 956 7890
Collects and drops your rucksack at convenient locations along the West Highland Way.

TRAINS

Scotrail, Virgin Trains and Greater North Eastern Railways all run fast and efficient services into the Clyde Valley and Glasgow. Passenger Enquiries ☎ 0345 484 950.

SPORT & LEISURE

ACTIVITY CENTRES

CENTRAL SCOTLAND SHOOTING SCHOOL
Cumbernauld, N. Lanarkshire
☎ 01324 851672

CLYDE VALLEY FARM PARK,
Garrion Bridge, S. Lanarkshire
☎ 01698 889389

STRATHCLYDE COUNTRY PARK,
Motherwell, N. Lanarkshire
☎ 01698 266155

ANGLING

Excellent trout, and, possibly, salmon and sea trout fishing is to had on the River Clyde, especially for trout on its upper reaches in the Lowther Hills around Crawford, Hazelbank and Crossford in S. Lanarkshire. Loch Thom, near Greenock in Inverclyde, offers good trout fishing, as do the numerous reservoirs and small lochs - Hillend Reservoir, Banton Loch, Strathclyde Park Loch - around Glasgow. The Forth & Clyde Canal provides good coarse fishing.

CYCLING

Short traffic-free routes exist around Glasgow; one follows the old Strathblane to Kirkintilloch railway line and the Forth & Clyde Canal towpath to Cadder (E. Dunbartonshire), beneath the Campsie Fells. S. Lanarkshire, especially in the Lowther Hills and close to the Clyde Valley, has a good network of quiet lanes to explore by bike.

GLASGOW - LOCH LOMOND CYCLEWAY,
A flat, waymarked route from Glasgow city centre to Loch Lomond using old railway lines, riverside paths and quiet streets.

PAISLEY - GREENOCK CYCLE ROUTE,
Linking up with a designated route from Glasgow, incorporating the Paisley & Ardrossan Canal and Glasgow Parks, this trail follows an old railway line from Paisley to Octavia Park in Greenock, via Elderslie, Kilbarchan, Bridge of Weir and Port Glasgow on the Clyde coast.

For further details of cycle routes contact Sustrans Scotland ☎ 0141 572 01234.

GOLF COURSES

BONNYTON GOLF CLUB,
Eaglesham, E. Renfrewshire
☎ 01355 302781
Dramatic moorland course offering spectacular views across beautiful countryside, as far as snow-capped Ben Lomond.

**WESTERWOOD HOTEL
GOLF & COUNTRY CLUB,**
Cumbernauld, N. Lanarkshire
☎ 01236 457171
Undulating parkland/woodland course designed by Dave Thomas and Seve Ballesteros.

There are over 60 golf courses in the Clyde Valley counties of South & North Lanarkshire, Renfrewshire, East Renfrewshire and East Dunbartonshire. For a complete list please refer to the AA Guide to Golf Courses, or contact the Tourist Information Offices.

ICE RINKS

EAST KILBRIDE ICE RINK,
S. Lanarkshire ☎ 01355 244065
WATERFRONT LEISURE COMPLEX,
Greenock, Inverclyde ☎ 01475 742386

LEISURE CENTRES

BLANTYRE SPORTS CENTRE,
S Lanarkshire ☎ 01698 821767
SIR MATT BUSBY SPORTS COMPLEX,
Bellshill, N. Lanarkshire ☎ 01698 747466
LARKHALL LEISURE CENTRE,
S. Lanarkshire ☎ 01698 881742
LINWOOD SPORTS CENTRE,
Renfrewshire ☎ 01505 331233
NEILSTON LEISURE CENTRE,
E. Renfrewshire ☎ 0141 881 9416
TRYST SPORTS CENTRE,
Cumbernauld, N. Lanarkshire
☎ 01236 728138
WATERFRONT, LEISURE COMPLEX,
Greenock, Inverclyde ☎ 01475 742386
WISHAW SPORTS CENTRE,
N. Lanarkshire ☎ 01698 355821

RACECOURSE

HAMILTON PARK RACECOURSE,
S. Lanarkshire ☎ 01698 283806
Enjoying a beautiful parkland setting, this popular flat racing course offers day and evening meeting from April to September, with the famous Saints and Sinners charity meeting being held in June.

RIDING

BANKELL FARM STABLES,
Milngavie, E. Dunbartonshire
☎ 0141 9425889
BANKFOOT RIDING SCHOOL,
Inverkip, Inverclyde ☎ 01475 521390
FORDBANK RIDING & LIVERY STABLES,
Johnstone, Renfrewshire ☎ 01505 705829
GLEDDOCH RIDING SCHOOL,
Langbank, Renfrewshire ☎ 01475 540350
HAZELDEN SADDLERY,
Newton Mearns, E. Renfrewshire
☎ 0141 639 3191
HILLHEAD, EQUESTRIAN CENTRE,
Carluke, S. Lanarkshire ☎ 01555 772151
LANARKSHIRE RIDING CENTRE,
Lanark, S. Lanarkshire ☎ 01555 661853
MID DRUMLOCH FARM RIDING & LIVERY,
Hamilton, S. Lanarkshire ☎ 01357 300273
ROUNDKNOWE FARM,
Uddingston, S. Lanarkshire ☎ 01698 813690

SAILING

Inverkip, Greenock and Port Glasgow on the Inverclyde coast have safe marinas and offer opportunities to sail in the Firth of Clyde.

SCENIC DRIVES

For the best views and scenery in the region, follow the waymarked Clyde Valley Tourist Route from the heart of the Lowther Hills to Hamilton, a short distance from the River Clyde.

SWIMMING

see also Leisure Centres
THE AQUATEC,
Motherwell, N. Lanarkshire
☎ 01698 276464
DOLLAN AQUA CENTRE,
East Kilbride, S. Lanarkshire
☎ 01355 260000
ERSKINE SWIMMING POOL,
Renfrewshire ☎ 0141 812 0044
GOUROCK POOL,
Inverclyde ☎ 01475 631561
HAMILTON WATER PALACE,
S. Lanarkshire ☎ 01698 459950
JOHN SMITH SWIMMING POOL,
Airdrie, N. Lanarkshire ☎ 01236 750130
KILSYTH SWIMMING POOL,
N. Lanarkshire ☎ 01236 822334
LANARK SWIMMING POOL,
S. Lanarkshire ☎ 01555 666800
RENFREW SWIMMING POOL,
Renfrewshire ☎ 0141 886 2088

WALKING

Challenging rambles can be had in the Campsie Fells in East Dunbartonshire, or in the remote upland areas in the Lowther Hills, close to the upper reaches of the River Clyde. Easy woodland and riverside walks and strolls can be enjoyed beside the Clyde, along the towpath beside the Forth & Clyde Canal, along the course of the Antonine Wall, and within the numerous country parks dotted around the region. More adventurous ramblers can undertake the West Highland Way, which begins at Milngavie, East Dunbartonshire, en route to Fort William in the Highlands.

WATERSPORTS

CASTLE SEMPLE COUNTRY PARK,
Lochwinnoch, Renfrewshire
☎ 01505 842882
JAMES HAMILTON HERITAGE PARK,
East Kilbride, S. Lanarkshire
☎ 01355 276611
STRATHCLYDE COUNTRY PARK,
Motherwell, N. Lanarkshire
☎ 01698 266155

Call the AA Hotel Booking Service on 0990 050505 to book at AA recognised hotels and B&Bs in the UK, or through our internet site: http://www.theaa.co.uk/hotels

WHERE TO STAY
THE CLYDE VALLEY
HOTELS
AA RECOMMENDED

ABINGTON

South Lanarkshire

WELCOME LODGE
Welcome Break Service Area ML12 6RE
(off junct 13 of M74) ☎ **01864 502782**
££ (fmly room) 56 bedrooms

BARRHEAD

East Renfrewshire

DALMENY PARK COUNTRY HOUSE★★★
Lochlibo Rd G78 1LG *(on A736 towards Irvine)*
☎ **0141 881 9211** 📠 **0141 881 9214**
Fine 19th-century mansion where caring and professional staff makes the hotel a delight to stay at.
£££ 20 bedrooms (2 fmly) No smoking in 2 bedrooms or part of restaurant Night porter Jacuzzi/spa Children's facilities 📞

BEARSDEN

East Lanarkshire

BURNBRAE ★★
Milngavie Rd G61 3TA
(take A81 & Milngavie Rd is off main rdbt towards Milngavie, from Bearsden follow A809 & take A806 towards the centre)
☎ **0141 942 5951** 📠 **0141 943 0742**
Conveniently situated with the central highlands almost on the doorstep. Popular restaurant and comfortable lounge bar.
££ 18 bedrooms (1 fmly) No dogs (ex guide dogs) Night porter area in restaurant 📞

BIGGAR

South Lanarkshire

SHIELDHILL ★★★◉◉◉
Quothquan ML12 6NA *(from A702 onto B7016. In middle of Biggar, after 2m turn L into Shieldhill Rd, hotel 1.5m on R)*
☎ **01899 220035** 📠 **01899 221092**
In extensive grounds amidst rolling hills and farmland, this fortified mansion has country house distinction.
££££ 12 bedrooms No smoking in bedrooms or restaurant Croquet lawn Cycling Clay shoot Hot air ballooning 📞

TINTO ★★★
Symington ML12 6PQ *(SW on A72)*
☎ **01899 308454** 📠 **01899 308520**
This hotel suits both business people and tourists. Good range of dishes satisfies the heartiest of appetites.
££ 29 bedrooms (2 fmly) Night porter Children's facilities No smoking in restaurant 📞

BOTHWELL

South Lanarkshire

BOTHWELL BRIDGE ★★★
89 Main St G71 8EU *(turn off M74 J5 & follow signs to Uddingston, turn R at mini-rndbt. Hotel just past shops on L)*
☎ **01698 852246** 📠 **01698 854686**
Mansion house now a popular business and conference centre. Conservatory bar and restaurant for meals.
££ 90 bedrooms (14 fmly) No smoking in 14 bedrooms No dogs (ex guide dogs) Lift Night porter Weekly live entertainment 📞

SILVERTREES ★★
Silverwells Crescent G71 8DP
(M74 J5 follow signs for Hamilton, 1st R at mini rndbt. Hotel 0.25m on L)
☎ **01698 852311** 📠 **01698 852311 ext200**
Well established hotel in large grounds. Dining room offers fixed price and carte menus.
£££ 7 bedrooms 19 annexe bedrooms (1 fmly) Children's facilities 📞

CLYDEBANK

West Dunbartonshire

BEARDMORE ★★★★◉◉
Beardmore St G81 4HX
☎ **0141 951 6000** 📠 **0141 951 6018**
Modern hotel beside the River Clyde ideal for the business traveller. Spacious bedrooms.
££ 168 bedrooms No smoking in 112 bedrooms Lift Night porter Air conditioning Indoor swimming pool (heated) Sauna Solarium Gym Jacuzzi/spa 📞

PATIO ★★★
1 South Av, Clydebank Business Park G81 2RW
☎ **0141 951 1133** 📠 **0141 952 3713**
In the local business park, this modern hotel is ideal the business traveller. Contemporary bar, restaurant and small lounge.
£££ 80 bedrooms No smoking in 16 bedrooms Lift Night porter 📞

CUMBERNAULD

North Lanarkshire

WESTERWOOD HOTEL GOLF & COUNTRY CLUB ★★★★◉
1 St Andrews Dr, Westerwood G68 0EW
☎ **01236 457171** 📠 **01236 738478**
Modern purpose built business hotel set on a hillside. Suites, executive and standard rooms.
49 bedrooms (20 fmly) No smoking in 4

---

bedrooms No dogs (ex guide dogs) Lift Night porter Air conditioning Indoor swimming pool (heated) Golf 18 Tennis (hard) Snooker Solarium Gym Putting green Jacuzzi/spa Steam room Bowling green Driving range 📞

TRAVEL INN
4 South Muirhead Rd G67 1AX
(from A80 take A8011 follow signs to Cumbernauld & then town centre)
☎ **01236 725339** 📠 **01236 736380**
Modern building offering smart, spacious and well equipped bedrooms, suitable for family use. Nearby family restaurant.
££ (fmly room) 37 bedrooms

EAGLESHAM

East Renfrewshire

EGLINTON ★★
Gilmour St G76 0LG
☎ **01355 302631** 📠 **01355 302955**
This hotel retains its old world atmosphere in spite of the provision of all modern facilities. Busy, vibrant local trade in bars.
14 bedrooms Night porter Shooting Children's facilities 📞

EAST KILBRIDE

South Lanarkshire

BRUCE HOTEL ★★★
Cornwall St G74 1AF
☎ **013552 29771** 📠 **013552 42216**
Part of the main shopping centre, this purpose-built hotel offers various grades of rooms. Friendly and attentive staff.
££££ 78 bedrooms No smoking in 23 bedrooms or restaurant Lift Night porter 📞

STUART ★★★
2 Cornwall Way G74 1JR *(6m from M74 J5, follow town centre signs, hotel on roundabout)*
☎ **013552 21161** 📠 **013552 64410**
Purpose built business hotel conveniently positioned beside the central shopping area. Various eating options.
£££ 39 bedrooms (2 fmly) No dogs (ex guide dogs) Lift Night porter Weekly live entertainment No smoking area in restaurant Res Christmas & New Year's Day 📞

TRAVEL INN
Brunel Way, The Murray G75 0JY
(follow signs for Paisley A726, left at Murray roundabout & left into Brunel Way)
☎ **01355 222809** 📠 **01355 230517**
Modern building offering smart, spacious and well equipped bedrooms, suitable for family use. Family restaurant nearby.
££ (fmly room) 40 bedrooms

ERSKINE

Renfrewshire

FORTE POSTHOUSE GLASGOW/ERSKINE
North Barr PA8 6AN *(off A726)*
☎ 0141 812 0123 📠 0141 812 7642
Bright hotel with modern accommodation,
informal bar and dining area.
166 bedrooms

GIFFNOCK

East Renfrewshire

MACDONALD THISTLE ★★★
Eastwood Toll G46 6RA *(on A77 at Eastwood
Toll, Giffnock - take 1st exit onto A726 East
Kilbride, then 1st R to hotel)*
☎ 0141 638 2225 📠 0141 638 6231
Mainly a business hotel, conveniently for
city centre and airport. Choice of bars.
Modern Scottish cuisine.
*££££ 56 bedrooms (4 fmly) No smoking
in 4 bedrooms or part of restaurant Night
porter Sauna Solarium Weekly live
entertainment* 🐾

THE REDHURST ★★
Eastwoodmains Rd G46 6QE
*(on A726 , from city centre take M74/M8
follow signs for A77/A726 to East Kilbride)*
☎ 0141 638 6465 📠 0141 620 0419
Popular business hotel with easy access to
city. Menus to suit all tastes and pockets.
*££ 19 bedrooms (2 fmly) No dogs (ex guide
dogs) Night porter No smoking area in
restaurant* 🐾

HAMILTON

South Lanarkshire
See also Bothwell

HOLIDAY INN EXPRESS
Strathclyde Country Park ML1 3RB *(M74 J5
follow signs for Strathclyde Country Park)*
☎ 01698 858585 📠 01698 852375
Modern building offering smart, spacious
and well equipped bedrooms, suitable for
families. Informal restaurant.
£ 80 bedrooms

HAMILTON MOTORWAY SERVICE AREA

South Lanarkshire

ROADCHEF MOTORWAY LODGE
M74 Northbound ML3 6JW *(1m N of M74 J6)*
☎ 01698 891904 📠 01698 891682
Modern building offering smart, spacious

and well equipped bedrooms, suitable for
family use. Nearby family restaurant.
£ 36 bedrooms

HOWWOOD

Renfrewshire

**BOWFIELD HOTEL & COUNTRY CLUB
★★★**
Lands of Bowfield PA9 1DB *(M8, A737 for
6m, L onto B787, R after 2m, 1m to hotel)*
☎ 01505 705225 📠 01505 705230
Close to airport, in open countryside this
popular hotel is a converted textile mill.
Bedrooms in separate wing.
*££ 23 bedrooms (3 fmly) No dogs (ex guide
dogs) Indoor swimming pool (heated) Squash
Snooker Sauna Solarium Gym Jacuzzi/spa
Health & beauty treatment rooms Weekly live
entertainment No smoking in restaurant* 🐾

LANARK

South Lanarkshire
See also Biggar

CARTLAND BRIDGE ★★★
Glasgow Rd ML11 9UF
☎ 01555 664426 📠 01555 663773
Well established hotel in grounds, with
many species of mature trees. Bedrooms
have attractive suites and furnishings.
*18 bedrooms (2 fmly) No smoking in 9
bedrooms or restaurant Night porter
Children's facilities* 🐾

LANGBANK

Renfrewshire

GLEDDOCH HOUSE ★★★★ ⊕ ⊕
PA14 6YE *(signposted from B789)*
☎ 01475 540711 📠 01475 540200
Set in extensive grounds high above the
River Clyde and with spectacular views to
distant mountains, this historic mansion
combines the character of a country house
with many sporting amenities.
*£££ 39 bedrooms (4 fmly) No smoking in
6 bedrooms Night porter Golf 18 Squash
Riding Snooker Sauna Clay pigeon shooting*
🐾

MILNGAVIE

East Dunbartonshire

BLACK BULL THISTLE ★★★
Main St G62 6BH *(leave M8 J15 onto A879)*
☎ 0141 956 2291 📠 0141 956 1896

Once a village inn, this hotel retains much
original character. First-floor restaurant,
cocktail bar and lounge.
*££££ 27 bedrooms (2 fmly) No smoking
in 8 bedrooms Night porter Res 25-26 Dec
& 1-2 Jan* 🐾

MOTHERWELL

North Lanarkshire

TRAVEL INN
Glasgow Rd, Newhouse ML1 5SY
*(leave M74 J5 onto A725 then A8 to M8
rndnt. Turn R onto A73 then 1st L)*
☎ 01698 860277 📠 01698 861353
Modern building offers smart, spacious
and well equipped bedrooms, suitable for
family use. Nearby family restaurant.
££ (fmly room) 40 bedrooms

ROSEBANK

South Lanarkshire

POPINJAY ★★★
Lanark Rd ML8 5QB
(on A72 between Hamilton & Lanark)
☎ 01555 860441 📠 01555 860204
Well established Tudor style hotel beside
the River Clyde. Roaring fires in colder
weather welcome guests.
*42 bedrooms 5 annexe bedrooms (2 fmly)
Night porter Fishing Children's facilities* 🐾

STRATHAVEN

South Lanarkshire

STRATHAVEN ★★★
Hamilton Rd ML10 6SZ
☎ 01357 521778 📠 01357 520789
Robert Adam designed mansion house
with modern and traditional bedrooms
equipped to a high specification.
*£££ 22 bedrooms No dogs (ex guide dogs)
Night porter No smoking in restaurant* 🐾

UDDINGSTON

South Lanarkshire

REDSTONES ★★
8-10 Glasgow Rd G71 7AS *(1m along A721)*
☎ 01698 813774 & 814843 📠 01698 815319
Two linked Victorian villas form this
friendly hotel. Several eating options.
*£££ 18 bedrooms No dogs (ex guide dogs)
Night porter No smoking area in restaurant
Closed 1-2 Jan* 🐾

BED & BREAKFAST ACCOMMODATION

AIRDRIE

North Lanarkshire

ROSSLEE 🖿 🖿
107 Forrest St ML6 7AR *(1m E on A89)*
☎ 01236 765865 📠 01236 748535
Family-run licensed guesthouse offering good value accommodation with modern bedrooms.
£ 6 bedrooms (2 fmly) No smoking in dining room Licensed

BRIDGE OF WEIR

Renfrewshire

GARTH HOUSE 🖿 🖿 🖿
Bank End Rd PA11 3EU
☎ 01505 614414 📠 01505 614414
Victorian house, with fine views, in attractive garden just 15 minutes from the airport.
4 bedrooms (2 fmly) No smoking in bedrooms, dining room or 1 lounge 🖥

COATBRIDGE

North Lanarkshire

AUCHENLEA 🖿 🖿 🖿
153 Langmuir Rd, Bargeddie, Baillieston G69 7RS *(A8 onto A752, 0.5m on R before A89)*
☎ 0141 771 6870
Welcoming atmosphere at this comfortable semi-detached cottage-style house, backed by farmland.
3 bedrooms (1 fmly) No smoking No dogs (ex guide dogs)

CRAWFORD

South Lanarkshire

FIELD END 🖿 🖿
ML12 6TN
☎ 01864 502276
Large house overlooking countryside reached by a steep, narrow drive. Cosy lounge with books, TV and video.
£ 3 bedrooms (1 fmly) No smoking No dogs (ex guide dogs) Closed Xmas & New Year 🖥

EAGLESHAM

NEW BORLAND 🖿 🖿 🖿
Glasgow Rd G76 0DN *(9 miles S of Glasgow centre at junct of B764 & B767)*
☎ 01355 302051 📠 01355 302051
Quietly situated converted barn with the aura of a family home. Smart bedrooms, 2 en suite.
£ 4 bedrooms No smoking No dogs (ex guide dogs) No Children under 12yrs

GLENMAVIS

North Lanarkshire

BRAIDENHILL 🖿
ML6 0PJ *(on B803 on outskirts of Airdrie/Coatbridge)*
☎ 01236 872319 Mrs M Dunbar
Good value accommodation on a working farm in semi-rural area. Friendly and honest service.
£ 3 bedrooms (1 fmly) No smoking in bedrooms or dining room No dogs 50 acres arable mixed

KILBARCHAN

Renfrewshire

ASHBURN 🖿 🖿
Milliken Park Rd PA10 2DB *(follow signs for Johnstone onto B787, turn R opp bus garage)*
☎ 01505 705477 📠 01505 705477
Family-run guest house, near the airport, remains a popular stop-over.
6 bedrooms (3 fmly) Licensed 🖥

KIRKMUIRHILL

South Lanarkshire

DYKECROFT 🖿 🖿
ML11 0JQ *(from S-exit M74 J10, take B7078 for 2m, then B7086 to Strathaven for 1.5m, past Boghead, 1st bungalow on L)*
☎ 01555 892226 Mrs I H McInally
Friendly modern farmhouse continues to offer good value accommodation.
£ 3 bedrooms No smoking in bedrooms or dining room 60 acres sheep

LOCHWINNOCH

Renfrewshire

EAST LOCHHEAD 🖿 🖿 🖿 🖿 🖿
Largs Rd PA12 4DX
☎ 01505 842610 📠 01505 842610
Relaxed country house atmosphere in attractive 100 year old former farmhouse. One ground floor bedroom.
£ 2 bedrooms (1 fmly) No smoking Cycle track 🖥

WOODLANDS

WOODLANDS 🖿 🖿 🖿 🖿
Newton-of-Barr PA12 4AP *(from airport follow signs for Lochwinnoch/A737. 'Woodlands' on L past indoor bowling alley)*
☎ 01505 843237 📠 01505 843237
Guests can stroll in the 16 acres of wooded grounds. Both ground floor bedrooms are very individual with a host of extras.
£ 2 bedrooms (1 fmly) No smoking No dogs Sauna Solarium Gymnasium

HIGH BELLTREES 🖿 🖿
PA12 4JN *(1m off A737 Glasgow-Largs rd)*
☎ 01505 842376
Welcoming traditional farmhouse that overlooks surrounding countryside towards the loch.
4 bedrooms (2 fmly) No smoking in bedrooms or area of dining room No dogs (ex guide dogs) 220 acres dairy mixed sheep + poultry

NEWBIGGING

South Lanarkshire

NESTLERS 🖿 🖿 🖿
ML11 8NA *(on A721, 2m S of Carnwath)*
☎ 01555 840680
Emphasis on food and the friendly atmosphere at this cosy family-run village inn. Good home cooked meals.
£ 3 bedrooms (1 fmly) No smoking in dining room or lounges Golf 🖥

STRATHAVEN

South Lanarkshire

AVONLEA 🖿 🖿
46 Millar St, Glassford ML10 6TD
(Strathaven - Commercial Rd, then 2m. 3rd terraced house on L)
☎ 01357 521748 & 521369
Warm welcome awaits at this comfortable home in a pretty conservation village. Hearty breakfasts.
£ 2 bedrooms No smoking in bedrooms No dogs No Children under 7yrs Closed Dec

SPRINGVALE HOTEL 🖿 🖿
18 Letham Rd ML10 6AD
☎ 01357 521131 📠 01357 521131
Overlooking playing fields, this family-run guest house has a friendly relaxed atmosphere.
£ 14 bedrooms (2 fmly) Licensed Closed 26-27 Dec & 1-3 Jan

CAMPING & CARAVANNING

BALLOCH

TULLICHEWAN CARAVAN PARK
Old Luss Rd G83 8QP *(Close to the A82.)*
☎ 01389 759475
Family Park
A popular, well-equipped site at S end of Loch Lomond, surrounded by woodland and hills. 9 acres with 120 touring pitches and 35 statics.
Open all year Booking advisable bank hols & Jul-Aug Last arrival 22.00hrs Last departure noon Leisure suite - sauna,spa bath, sunbeds. Bike hire. 🖥

KIRKFIELDBANK

CLYDE VALLEY CARAVAN PARK
ML11 9TS *(From Glasgow on A72, cross river bridge at Kirkfieldbank and site is on left. From Lanark on A72, turn right at bottom of very steep hill before going over bridge.) Signposted*
☎ 01555 663951
Town & Country Pennant Park
Level, grass site with trees and bushes set in hilly country with access to river. 5 acres with 50 touring pitches and 115 statics.
Open Apr-Oct Booking advisable anytime Last arrival 23.00hrs Last departure noon

LANARK

NEWHOUSE CARAVAN & CAMPING PARK
Ravenstruther ML11 8NP
(Situated on A70 Ayr–Edinburgh road, 3m E of Lanark.)
☎ **01555 870228**
Family Park
Pleasant level grass and gravel site, with young trees and bushes. 5 acres with 45 touring pitches and 3 statics.
Open mid Mar–mid Oct Booking advisable Jul–Aug Last arrival 22.00hrs Last departure noon Caravan storage compound.

MOTHERWELL

STRATHCLYDE COUNTRY PARK CARAVAN SITE
366 Hamilton Rd ML1 3ED
(Direct access to park from junc 5 of M74.)
Signposted Nearby town: Hamilton
☎ **01698 266155**
Family Park
A level grass site situated in a country park amidst woodland and meadowland with lots of attractions. 250 touring pitches.
Open Apr–Oct Booking advisable Jun–Aug Last arrival 10.30hrs Last departure noon

WHERE TO EAT

RESTAURANTS

AA RECOMMENDED

BALLOCH

West Dunbartonshire

CAMERON HOUSE HOTEL ❀ ❀ ❀
Alexandria, G83 8QZ
☎ **01389 755565** 🆽 **01389 759522**
A selection from the menu includes pan-fried foie gras with crisp rounds of celeriac and oniony spinach, fillet of Aberdeen Angus beef with an oxtail galette and braised vegetables and walnut and apple tart topped with cinnamon ice cream.
Fixed L ££ ALC £££

BIGGAR

South Lanarkshire

SHIELDHILL HOTEL ❀ ❀
Quothquan, ML12 6NA
☎ **01899 220035** 🆽 **01899 221092**
Drawing much nspiration from the Scottish larder there might be confiture of duck leg on stewed Puy lentils, cream of snow pea soup, saddle of local venison and crème vanilla with autumn berries. *Fixed D £££* 🍴

CLYDEBANK

West Dunbartonshire

BEARDMORE HOTEL ❀ ❀ ❀
Beardmore Street, G81 4SA
☎ **0141 9516000** 🆽 **0141 9516018**
A dinner menu, in winter, featured a risotto of queen scallops with spaghetti of leeks, then vichyssoise of oak-smoked haddock, followed by collops of guinea fowl breast, and finally apple strudel.
Fixed L/D £ ALC 🍴

Cameron House Hotel

CUMBERNAULD

North Lanarkshire

WESTERWOOD HOTEL ❀
1 St Andrews Drive, Westerwood, G68 0EW
☎ **01236 457171** 🆽 **01236 738478**
The kitchen adopts a modern approach, using the best quality ingredients. Game terrine with poacher's chutney and winter salad, for instance, followed by baked fillet of Atlantic cod with seasoned cabbage, crisp pancetta and red wine jus.
Fixed L £ ALC ££ 🍴

LANGBANK

Renfrewshire

GLEDDOCH HOUSE HOTEL ❀ ❀
PA14 6YE
☎ **01475 540711** 🆽 **01475 540201**
There's an ambitious modern carte offering the likes of oven–baked gâteau of aubergine, a seafood risotto with Parmesan 'scrolls', pot–roast guinea fowl stuffed with apricot and pine kernels and a tangy orange and passion fruit tart.
Fixed L ££ ALC ££ 🍴

STRATHAVEN

South Lanarkshire

STRATHAVEN HOTEL ❀
Hamilton Road, ML10 6SZ
☎ **01357 521778** 🆽 **01357 520789**
Interesting blends of flavours feature in such carefully prepared dishes as venison, duck and rabbit pâté with berry compote and noisettes of lamb with roasted vegetables and redcurrant and rosemary essence.
Fixed L £ ALC ££ 🍴

AA Hotel Booking Service

The AA Hotel Booking Service - Now AA Members have a free, simple way to find a place to stay for a week, weekend, or a one-night stopover.

Are you looking for somewhere in the Lake District that will take pets; a city-centre hotel in Glasgow with parking facilities, or do you need a B & B near Dover which is handy for the Eurotunnel? The AA Booking Service can

not only take the hassle out of finding the right place for you, but could even get you a discount on a leisure break or business booking.

And if you are touring round the UK or Ireland, simply give the AA Hotel Booking Service your list of overnight stops, and from one phone call all your accommodation can be booked for you.

Telephone 0990 050505

to make a booking.
Office hours 8.30am - 7.30pm
Monday - Saturday.

Full listings of the 7,920 hotels and B & Bs available through the Hotel Booking Service can be found and booked at the AA's Internet Site:

http://www.theaa.co.uk/hotels

CENTRAL

North of Edinburgh and Glasgow, sandwiched between the lush lowlands and the breathtaking landscapes of Northern Scotland, lies some of the country's most picturesque scenery. Central Scotland may not have the obvious appeal and timeless beauty of the Highlands or the Western Isles, but it does offer a rich variety of natural attractions, as well as a wide assortment of things to do and places to visit.

Here, you can devise your own grand tour, enjoying a fine mixture of tranquil lochs, ancient strongholds, fishing rivers, wooded glens and tracts of open moorland. Unquestionably, Central Scotland represents some excellent walking country. In fact, there is great potential for all kinds of outdoor recreation. Alternatively, if you enjoy clifftop strolls and stiff breezes, bringing with them the faint tang of the sea,. then head for the region's coast, where a host of delights awaits you.

You may want to spend some time touring the Fair City of Perth, once the capital of Scotland, before visiting Dundee, its near neighbour. Once you've explored two of the country's most historic cities, try out several excursions in the region – including a tour of the Sidlaw Hills and Glen Almond. Wherever you venture in Central Scotland however, make sure the superb scenery of the Trossachs, Loch Lomond and Stirling – often described as 'the Highlands in miniature' – is on your itinerary.

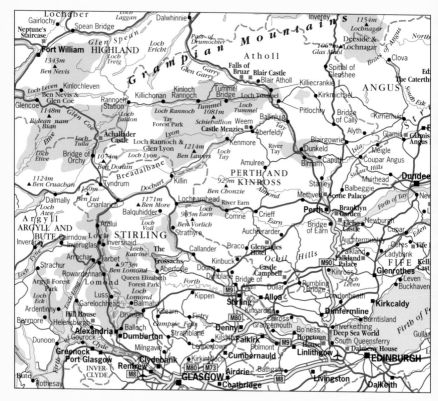

EVENTS & FESTIVALS

April

Festival of Women in Art,
St Andrews, Fife

Kirkcaldy Links Market (Street Fair)
Kirkcaldy, Fife

City of Dundee Spring Flower Show,
Dick McTaggart Centre, Dundee

Kate Kennedy Procession - historic university pageant
St Andrews, Fife

Food Festival
Perth, Perthshire

May

Country Music Festival,
Arbroath, Angus

Antique and Collectors Fair,
St Andrews, Fife

Craigtoun Country Fair,
Craigtoun Park, St Andrews, Fife

Festival of Arts,
Perth Theatre, Perth, Perthshire

Pitlochry Festival Theatre Season (May-October)
Pitlochry, Perthshire

Highland Gathering,
Blair Atholl, Perthshire

Fife Show,
Balcormo Mains, by Leven, Fife

Highland Games,
Blackford, Perthshire

Open Carriage Driving Championships & Festival of Country Sports
St Fort, Newport-on-Tay, Fife

May Festival,
Clackmannanshire

Doune & Dunblane Fling
Stirling

Agricultural Show,
Drymen, Stirling

June

City of Dundee Dog Show,
Dundee

Highland Games,
Arbroath & Forfar, Angus
Markinch & Strathmiglo, Fife

Lowland Games,
Monifieth, Angus

Gala Week,
Aberfeldy, Perthshire

Scone Palace Coronation Pageant,
Scone Palace, Perthshire

Jazz Festival,
City of Dundee

Folk Festival,
City of Dundee

Dunkeld & Birnam Arts Festival,
Dunkeld, Perthshire

Provincial Mod (Gaelic Festival)
Aberfeldy, Perthshire

Veteran & Vintage Car Rally,
Leven Promenade, Leven, Fife

Vintage Agricultural Machinery Club's Rally,
Praytis Farm Park, by Leven, Fife

Historic Vehicle Club's Rally & Motoring Cavalcade,
Pittencrieff Park, Dunfermline, Fife

National Coal Carrying Championships,
Kelty, Fife

Cove Regatta,
Argyll

Stirling Agricultural Show,
Stirling

Traditional Music & Dance Festival,
Killin, Stirling

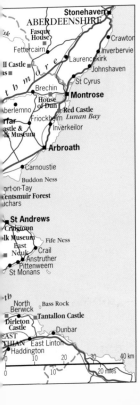

Doune & Dunblane Agricultural Show,
Stirling

Loch Lomond World Invitational Golf Tournament,
Luss, Argyll

July

Gala Week,
Carnoustie, Angus

Dundee Water Festival,
Dundee

East Neuk Fish Festival,
Pittenweem Harbour, Fife

Highland Games & Classic Car Rally,
Memorial Park, Thornton, Fife

Gala Week,
Broughty Ferry, City of Dundee

Glamis Extravaganza,
Glamis, Angus

Highland Games,
Alva, Clackmannanshire
Balloch, West Dunbartonshire
Rosneath & Clynder, Argyll
Luss, Argyll
Balquhidder, Callander, Stirling, Strathyre & Lochearnhead, Stirling

Ceres, Newburgh, Cupar, Burntisland & St Andrews, Fife
Kenmore, Perthshire

Victorian Market,
Letham, Angus

Vintage Car Rally,
Craigtoun Park, St Andrews, Fife

Scottish Food Festival,
Upper Largo, Fife

Trossachs Highland Festival,

Loch Lomond & Clyde Festival,

Elie Fair Day,
Elie Harbour, Fife

East Coast Sailing Week,
River Tay, City of Dundee

Crail Festival,
Crail & immediate area, Fife

Comrie Festival,
Comrie, Perthshire

European Boat and Line Championships,
Pittenweem, Fife

Atholl Festival,
Pitlochry, Perthshire

Aberdour Festival,
Aberdour, Fife

August

Aberfeldy Show & Highland Games,
Aberfeldy, Perthshire

Auchtermuchty Festival,
Auchtermuchty, Fife

Highland Games,
Montrose & Glenisla, Angus
Bridge of Allan & Killin, Stirling
Crieff, Birnam, Perth, Strathardle & Blairgowrie, Perthshire
Ballast Bank, Inverkeithing, Fife

Vintage Vehicle Rally,
Camperdown Park, City of Dundee

Angus Fair (National Trust For Scotland),
House of Dun, By Montrose, Angus

Perth Agricultural Show,
Perthshire

Strathearn Music Festival,
Perthshire

Killin Agricultural Show,
Stirling

Kinross Show,
Perthshire

Scottish Wildlife & Countryside Fair,
Vane Farm, Kinross, Perthshire

Lifeboat Gala Day,
Anstruther, Fife

Scottish Orienteering Championships,
Aberfeldy, Perthshire

Arbroath Sea Fest,
Angus

Pittenweem Festival,
Fife

Vintage Vehicle Owners Rally,
Falkland, Fife

Medieval Fair,
Village Green, Culross, Fife

Lammas Fair (street fair),
St Andrews, Fife

International 3-day Event Horse Trials,
Blair Castle, Blair Atholl, Perthshire

Rannoch Gathering,
Kinloch Rannoch, Perthshire

Pipe Band & Highland Dancing Competition,
Pittencrieff Park, Dunfermline, Fife

Summer Flower Show,
Town Hall, St Andrews, Fife

September

Dundee Flower Show,
Camperdown Park, City of Dundee

Jazz & Blues Festival,
Dunfermline, Fife

Dunfermline & West Fife Arts Festival
Fife

Highland Games,
Pitlochry, Perthshire

Battle of Britain Airshow,
RAF Leuchars, Fife

Folk Festival,
Culross, Fife

October

October Festival,
Clackmannanshire

November

Scottish Music Festival,
Caird Hall, City of Dundee

Dundee Mountain Film Festival,
Bonar Hall, City of Dundee

December

Flambeaux Festival,
Comrie, Perthshire

ANGUS, DUNDEE & FIFE

The Angus coast is the jewel in the region's crown, and the beaches here are some of the best on the East Coast. From the seaside town of Arbroath you can enjoy a stunning walk along Seaton Cliffs, with an amazing wall of red sandstone keeping you company as you stroll beside the North Sea. Carnoustie, between Dundee and Arbroath, is a popular seaside base, as well as a famous golfing centre. But there is much more to Angus than its spectacular coastline. The lush Vale of Strathmore lies at the heart of Angus and is the setting for Glamis Castle, where Queen Elizabeth the Queen Mother spent her childhood. Travelling further west, you will soon find yourself entering a tranquil, unspoilt world of hills, glens, mountains, far away from bustling centres of Dundee, Arbroath, Forfar and Montrose.

Fife, 20-mile wide peninsula between the Firth of Forth and the Firth of Tay, is an ancient Kingdom, once the home of Scotland's kings and saints. Despite its modern bridges it still seems curiously detached from the rest of the country. Fife, widely acknowledged as the proud home of golf, includes some of the grandest coastline in Britain. By taking a leisurely drive along it you can discover the region's fascinating legacy of caves, castles, and ancient fishing ports. A great way to blend coast and countryside is by following stretches of the Fife Coastal Path. Away from the coast, if you're feeling particularly adventurous, you might like to blow away the cobwebs with an exhilarating trek in the Fife Regional Park.

PRINCIPAL TOWNS

DUNDEE

Covering some 20 square miles of hillside above the north bank of the Firth of Tay, this port and industrial city, Scotland's fourth largest city, traditionally prospered on the three J's – jute, jam and journalism, with the help of whaling and, more recently, high-tech industries. In contrast to other major Scottish city's, you will find Dundee very modern in appearance, with its open roadways and malls but, despite its lack of historic charm, you can experience some new, innovative attractions, as well as some excellent shopping and a lively nightlife.

ST ANDREWS

St Andrews has a unique place in Scotland's rich heritage. According to legend, the city was founded by St Regulus (or St Rule) in the 4th century, who was carrying relics of St Andrew, the patron saint of Scotland, when his ship was wrecked off the coast. Thereafter, the town grew as an important religious centre, eventually possessing the largest church in Scotland, now an attractive ruin, with the powerful bishops wielding great influence over church and state. Today, St Andrews is famous for its university, the oldest in Scotland, having been founded in 1414, and as world golfing Mecca. The Old Course at the Royal and Ancient Golf Club claims to have 15th century origins, and to play a round on these hallowed links is still the dream of many golfers, both young and old. Best explored leisurely on foot, the self-guided town trails (available in the tourist information centre) identify all the points of interest and provide informative notes to aid your exploration and understanding of the town's history.

MUST SEE

ANGUS GLENS,
north of Kirrimuir

Explore the unspoilt and wild hill country and the picturesque Glens of Clova, Esk, Isla, Lethnot and Prosen in the north of the county, one of Scotland's best kept secrets. Each has its own character and all over the opportunity for climbing, walking, mountain biking and birdwatching.

DISCOVERY POINT,
Discovery Quay, Riverside Dr, Dundee
☎ 01382 201245
Home of RRS Discovery, Captain Scott's famous Antarctic ship. Spectacular lighting, graphics and special effects in an innovative exhibition complex re-create key moments in the Discovery story.

EDZELL CASTLE,
Edzell ☎ 01356 648631
An impressive, early 16th-century red-stoned tower, incorporated into a large courtyard mansion of 1580, with a remarkable walled garden created by Sir David Lindsay in 1604. Flower-filled recesses in the walls are alternated with heraldic and symbolic sculptures.

GLAMIS CASTLE,
Glamis ☎ 01307 840393
Turreted Glamis Castle is the epitome of a Scottish castle. Built between 1675 and 1687 on the site of an earlier building, amid a deer park and tree-lined avenues, it is the family home of the Earls of Strathmore, and was the childhood home of HM The Queen Mother. The fictional links with Shakespeare's Macbeth (Thane of Glamis) make this vast, architecturally pleasing castle a popular place to visit. Most noteworthy rooms are the chapel with its painted panels, the vaulted drawing room and the magnificent 17th-century reception rooms.

HOUSE OF DUN,
Montrose ☎ 01674 810264
A beautiful Georgian house, overlooking Montrose Basin, built in 1730 to designs by William Adam, and particularly noted for its exuberant plasterwork. The interior contains fine collections of family portraits,

Glamis Castle,

furniture and porcelain. There is also a handloom weaving workshop, a walled garden, woodland walks and a restaurant.

VERDANT WORKS,
West Henderson's Wynd, Dundee
☎ 01382 225282
Scotland's premier Industrial Heritage Centre housed in an old Jute Mill dating from 1830. Restored as a living museum of Dundee and Tayside's textile history, covering 50,000 square feet around a cobbled courtyard, it features working machinery, and displays and interactive computers illustrating the uses of jute and its effects on Dundee's social history.

CULROSS - PALACE, TOWN HOUSE & THE STUDY,
Culross ☎ 01383 880359
Unique Royal Burgh that has remained virtually unchanged for 200 years, when it prospered in the coal and salt trades developed by Sir George Bruce. Sixteenth- and 17th-century buildings and cobbled streets create a time-warp for visitors as they explore the old town. The refurbished Palace dates from 1597 and has fine terraced gardens. The Town House features an exhibition outlining the burgh's 400 years of history.

DEEP-SEA WORLD,
North Queensferry ☎ 01383 411411
Scotland's revolutionary aquarium that presents a diver's view of a spectacular underwater universe. A moving walkway travels along the largest underwater transparent viewing tunnel where large sharks and giant rays swim by. There are also rock pools for children to explore.

FALKLAND PALACE & GARDEN,
Falkland ☎ 01337 857397
Former country residence and hunting lodge of Stewart Kings and Queens set in the heart of a unique medieval village beneath the Lomond Hills. Built between 1502 and 1541 it is a prime example of Renaissance architecture. Of particular note are the beautiful interiors of the Chapel Royal and the King's Bedchamber, the Royal Tennis Court of 1539, reputedly the oldest in the world, and the gardens.

HILL OF TARVIT MANSIONHOUSE & GARDEN,
Cupar ☎ 01334 653127
A fine Edwardian mansion, rebuilt and designed by Sir Robert Lorimer in 1906, renowned for its notable collections of French Chippendale and venacular furniture, Dutch paintings and fine pictures by Raeburn and Ramsay, Flemish tapestries and Chinese porcelain. Beautiful gardens and grounds and hilltop walks.

KELLIE CASTLE & GARDEN,
Pittenweem ☎ 01333 720271
Dating in part from about 1360, Kellie Castle is a superb example of 16th-and 17th-century domestic lowland Scottish architecture. Interesting features include magnificent painted ceilings and plasterwork, furniture designed by Sir Robert Lorimer, a Victorian playroom and a fine late Victorian walled garden.

ST ANDREWS CASTLE & VISITOR CENTRE,
St Andrews ☎ 01334 477196
Teetering on the sea's brink, this 13th-century stronghold was the setting for the murder of Cardinal Beaton in 1546. Not to be missed are the impressive bottle dungeon, the Secret Passage that was

Discovery Point,

tunnelled under the castle during a 16th-century seige, and the exciting multi-media exhibition describing the history of the castle and nearby cathedral in the adjacent visitor centre.

SCOTTISH FISHERIES MUSEUM,
Anstruther ☎ 01333 310628
A cobbled courtyard lined with 16th-to 19th-century buildings at the harbour is the setting for the displays on Scotland's fishing history. Award-winning attractions include the boats (real historic vessels and models), and the fisherman's cottage.

Verdant Works,

ART GALLERIES

ANGUS & DUNDEE

EDUARDO ALESSANDRO STUDIOS,
30 Gray St, Broughty Ferry, City of Dundee
☎ 01382 737011
MCMANUS GALLERIES,
Albert Square, Dundee ☎ 01382 432020
Important collections of Scottish and Victorian art, as well as Dundee's main museum.

MEFFAN GALLERY & MUSEUM,
West High St, Forfar ☎ 01307 464123
Houses the 'Forfar Story' and monthly exhibitions.

FIFE

THE COURTYARD GALLERY,
Marketgate, Crail ☎ 01333 450797
CRAWFORD ARTS CENTRE,
North St, St Andrews ☎ 01334 474610
Scottish and international art exhibitions.

MUSEUMS

ANGUS & DUNDEE

ANGUS FOLK MUSEUM,
Glamis ☎ 01307 840288
An attractive row of 19th-century cottages houses this splendid collection of domestic equipment and cottage furniture.

ARBROATH SIGNAL TOWER MUSEUM,
Ladyloan, Arbroath ☎ 01242 875598
Local history museum housed in the 1813 shore station of Stevenson's Bell Rock Lighthouse.

BARRACK STREET NATURAL HISTORY MUSEUM,
Barrack St, Dundee ☎ 0182 432004
Displays on Scottish wildlife of the Lowlands and Highlands.

BARRIE'S BIRTHPLACE,
9 Brechin Rd, Kirriemuir ☎ 01575 572646
The novelist and playwright J M Barrie, creator of Peter Pan, was born in this two-storeyed house in 1860. No 11 houses an exhibition about his literary and theatrical works.

BARRY MILL,
Barry ☎ 01241 856761
A restored 18th-century working mill. Displays trace the history of milling on the site.

BROUGHTY CASTLE MUSEUM,
Broughty Ferry, City of Dundee
☎ 01382 776121
A 15th-century castle housing displays on Dundee's whaling history.

MILLS OBSERVATORY,
Balgay Park, Glamis Rd, Dundee
☎ 01382 667138
Opened in 1935, this is Britain's only full time public observatory. The 10-inch telescope can be used on clear winter's evenings. Display galleries.

MONTROSE MUSEUM & ART GALLERY,
Panmure Place ☎ 01674 673232
Extensive local collections cover the history of Montrose, the natural history of Angus, and local art.

THE RETREAT, FOLK MUSEUM,
Glenesk, By Brechin ☎ 01356 670254
Displays showing everday life in Glenesk from the 18th-century to the present day

ST VIGEANS MUSEUM,
St Vigeans ☎ 01241 872433
Small cottage containing over 40 Pictish, Celtic, and early Christian carved stones.

FIFE

ANDREW CARNEGIE BIRTHPLACE MUSEUM,
Moodie St, Dunfermline ☎ 01383 724302
The 'rags to riches' tale of Andrew Carnegie, self-made industrialist and benefactor, in the 18th-century weaver's cottage where he was born.

BRITISH GOLF MUSEUM,
St Andrews ☎ 01334 478880
Themed galleries and interactive displays explore the history of the major championships and trace the development of golfing equipment and costume since the game's origins 500 years ago.

CRAIL MUSEUM & HERITAGE CENTRE,
Marketgate, Crail ☎ 01333 450869
Provides an insight into the past life of this Royal Burgh, its Kirk and fishing tradition.

DUNFERMLINE HERITAGE TRUST,
Maygate, Dunfermline ☎ 01383 733266
Journey through the 1000-year history of Scotland's ancient capital.

FIFE FOLK MUSEUM,
High St, Ceres ☎ 01334 828683
A fascinating collection illustrating the social, economic and cultural history of Fife, housed in historic buildings.

KIRKCALDY MUSEUM & ART GALLERY,
War Memorial Gardens, ☎ 01592 260732
Set in lovely grounds it features a superb collection of 19th-and 20th-century Scottish paintings and a local history exhibition. Gallery shop & café.

LAING MUSEUM,
High St, Newburgh ☎ 01337 840223
Good collections of antiquities and geological specimens from the area, and a display of Victorian Scotland.

PITTENCRIEFF HOUSE MUSEUM,
Dunfermline KY12 8QH
☎ 01383 722935
A fine 17th-century mansion housing galleries with displays on the history of the house, park and costume.

ST ANDREWS MUSEUM,
Doubledykes Park ☎ 01334 412690
The story of St Andrews.

ST ANDREWS PRESERVATION TRUST MUSEUM,
12 North St ☎ 01334 477629
Displays include 19th-century grocer's and chemist's shops, paintings, photographs and furniture.

SCOTTISH VINTAGE BUS MUSEUM,
By Dunfermline ☎ 01383 623380
Over 100 buses from the 1920s.

HISTORIC & ANCIENT SITES

ANGUS & DUNDEE

ABERLEMNO SCULPTURED STONES,
Aberlemno, By Brechin
Pictish standing stones decorated with symbols lie in the churchyard.

ARBROATH ABBEY,
Arbroath ☎ 01241 878756
Well preserved abbot's house and interesting church remians..

ARDESTIE & CARLUNGIE EARTH-HOUSES,
off A92 3m N of Carnoustie
Roofless earth-houses; Ardestie dates from the Iron Age and has an 80ft curved underground gallery; Carlungie comprises a 150ft long passage.

BRECHIN CATHEDRAL & ROUND TOWER,
Brechin
One of two remaining round towers attached to the cathedral of the Irish type in mainland Scotland dating back to the 11th century.

THE CATERTHUNS
By Brechin *5m/8km NW of Brechin*
Well preserved remains of two large Iron Age hill forts.

FOWLIS CHURCH,
Fowlis, Easter by Liff
Splendid small medieval church with fine rood screen and medieval paintings.

RED CASTLE,
Lunan Bay
15th-century red stone tower situated on a steep mound overlooking Lunan Bay.

RESTENNETH PRIORY,
2m NE of Forfar on B9113
A priory church of Augustinian canons probably founded by David I. Of note is the tall tower with its brooch spire.

FIFE

ABERDOUR CASTLE,
Aberdour ☎ 01383 860519
Extensive remains of a splendid castle overlooking the harbour, the earliest surviving part being the 14th-century keep.

BALERMINO ABBEY,
Balermino
Peaceful ruins of a Cistercian Abbey, founded in 1227 and destroyed in 1559.

DUNFERMLINE ABBEY,
Pittencrieff Park ☎ 01383 739026
Known as the 'Westminster of the North', this powerful Benedictine house was founded in the 11th century by Queen Margaret and is the burial place of King Robert the Bruce.

INCHHOLM ISLAND & ABBEY,
reached by boat from North Queensferry
☎ 0131 331 4857
Twelfth-century abbey with octagonal chapter house, cloisters, living quarters and hermit cell on a small island noted for its seal and sea bird colonies.

MACDUFF CASTLE,
East Wemyss
Castle ruins thought to be the home of 'Macduff' of Shakespeare's 'Macbeth'.

ST ANDREWS CATHEDRAL & MUSEUM,
☎ 01334 472563
Extensive 12th-and 13th-century ruins of a once magnificent structure, formerly the largest cathedral in Scotland. Fascinating museum.

SCOTSTARVIT TOWER,
Ceres *keys at Hill of Tarvit Mansionhouse*
16th-century fortified tower house.

GREAT FOR KIDS
ANGUS & DUNDEE

CAMPERDOWN COUNTRY PARK,
Coupar Angus Rd, Dundee
☎ 01382 434296
A 400-acre park containing rare trees, a wildlife centre with a big collection of native and domestic animals, an adventure play area and forest trails.

HM FRIGATE UNICORN,
Victoria Dock, Dundee ☎ 01382 200900
The oldest British warship afloat. The wooden vessel makes an apt setting for a fascinating museum of life in the Navy.

KERRS MINIATURE RAILWAY,
West Links Park, Arbroath ☎ 01241 879249
Fifth size railway established in 1935 along 400yds of seafront. Steam and diesel locomotives and miniature platforms.

MONTROSE BASIN WILDLIFE CENTRE,
Rossie Braes, Montrose ☎ 01674 676336
Wildlife Visitor Centre and Reserve. Superb viewing facility, bird hide, exhibits and hands-on activities for all the family.

SHAWS DUNDEE SWEET FACTORY,
34 Mains Loan, Dundee ☎ 01382 461435
Children can watch sweets being made from traditional recipes by period machinery.

FIFE

OSTRICH KINGDOM VISITOR CENTRE,
Collessie ☎ 01337 831830
View and handle many exotic and domestic animals and birds.

ST ANDREWS SEA LIFE CENTRE,
The Scores ☎ 01334 474786
Exhibition of hundreds of different species of marine life all native to the British coast in displays designed to recreate their natural habitat.

SCOTLAND'S SECRET BUNKER,
Crown Buildings, St Andrews
☎ 01333 310301
Discover the twilight world of the government Cold War at the now not so secret nuclear command bunker, built on two levels 100ft below ground.

SCOTTISH DEER CENTRE,
Bow-of-Fife, By Cupar ☎ 01337 810391
Guided tours allow visitors to meet and stroke deer and children can help feed young fawns.

HOMES & GARDENS
ANGUS & DUNDEE

PITMUIES GARDENS,
Guthrie By Forfar ☎/☎ 01241 828245
An outstanding garden set around an 18th-century house.

UNIVERSITY BOTANIC GARDEN,
Riverside Dr, Dundee ☎ 01382 566939
Tropical and temperate planthouses, 21 acres of trees, plants and shrubs from around the world, and a visitor centre.

FIFE

BALCASKIE HOUSE,
near Pittenweem
An imposing 17th-century mansion noted for its splendid Italianate terraces of its formal garden, the earliest in Scotland.

CAMBO GARDENS,
Kingsbarns, St Andrews ☎ 01333 450054
Two acres of charming Victorian walled garden sweeping down to a bubbling burn spanned by picturesque little bridges.

EARLSHALL CASTLE & GARDENS,
Leuchars ☎ 01334 839205
A well-restored tower house built by Sir William Bruce in 1546, featuring an outstanding painted ceiling and beautiful topiary gardens.

ST ANDREWS BOTANIC GARDEN,
Canongate, St Andrews ☎ 01334 477178
Impressive 18-acres of landscaped gardens with sheltered paths and interpretation boards.

BIG OUTDOORS
ANGUS & DUNDEE

ARBROATH CLIFF NATURE TRAIL,
Kings Dr, Arbroath
Unusual rock formations and bird life are among the attractions along this sandstone cliff trail to Carlinheugh Bay

MONIKIE COUNTRY PARK,
Broughty Ferry, City of Dundee
☎ 01382 370202
Reservoirs, woodland and parkland with wildlife trails, watersports, play areas and Ranger service.

REEKIE LINN FALLS,
Wooded gorge with a spectacular waterfall where the River Isla drops 80ft.

RSPB LOCH OF KINNORDY RESERVE,
1m west of Kirriemuir on B951
☎ 01575 574553
Lookout for ospreys and otters at this mecca for wetland birds.

ST CYRUS NATURE RESERVE,
off A92 north of Montrose
Fascinating reserve and visitor centre housing displays of natural history, local history and salmon fishing.

FIFE

CRAIGTOUN COUNTRY PARK,
St Andrews ☎ 01334 473666
Surrounding Mount Melville House (hospital), this 50-acre parkland has an Italianate garden, a Dutch village, miniature railway and nature walks.

ISLE OF MAY,
off the coast at Anstruther
☎ 01333 310103 *boat information*
An hour's boat trip from Anstruther, the island was created a nature reserve in 1956 and is an important breeding ground for sea birds, including puffins and eider duck, as well as grey seals.

LOMOND HILLS
north-west of Glenrothes
East Lomond has the highest hillfort in Fife; both enjoy magnificent views and 20 miles of footpaths.

TENTSMUIR POINT & FOREST,
Leuchars *2m/3.2km north-east*
The oldest and largest forestry plantation in lowland Scotland. Both the beach and woodland provide an interesting habitat for a diverse range of wildlife, including deer and seals.

ESSENTIAL INFORMATION

TOURIST INFORMATION

ANGUS & DUNDEE

ANGUS & DUNDEE TOURIST BOARD,
4 City Square, Dundee DD1 3BA
☎ 01382 434664 ✆ 01382 434665
ARBROATH,
Market Place, Arbroath
☎ 01242 872609 ✆ 01241 878550
BRECHIN
St Ninian's Place, Brechin t 01356 623050
CARNOUSTIE *seasonal,*
High St, Carnoustie ☎ 01241 852258
FORFAR *seasonal,*
40 East High St, Forfar ☎ 01307 467876
KIRRIEMUIR *seasonal,*
Cumberland Close, Kirriemuir
☎ 01575 574097
MONTROSE *seasonal,*
Bridge St, Montrose ☎ 01674 672000

FIFE

FIFE TOURIST BOARD,
7 Hanover Court, Glenrothes KY7 5SB
☎ 01592 750066
ANSTRUTHER *seasonal,*
Scottish Fisheries Museum, St Ayles, Harbour
Head, Anstruther KY10 3AB
☎ 01333 311073
CRAIL *seasonal,*
Crail ☎ 01333 450869
DUNFERMLINE *seasonal,*
Abbot House ☎ 01383 720999
FORTH ROAD BRIDGE,
Inverkeithing ☎ 01383 417759
KIRKCALDY ,
The Esplanade, Kirkcaldy ☎ 01592 267775
ST ANDREWS ,
70 Market St, St Andrews ☎ 01334 472021

ACCESS

AIR ACCESS

Dundee Airport ☎ 01382 643242

CRAFTS

ANGUS & DUNDEE

Lookout for pottery, paintings, semi-precious jewellery, knitwear and stoneware

EDZELL TWEED WAREHOUSE
1 Dunlappie Rd, Edzell ☎ 01356 648348
MEARNS CRAFT,
Kirriemuir ☎ 01575 575950
Kiltmakers.

PEEL FARM CRAFTS,
Lintrathen By Kirriemuir ☎ 01575 560205
TIKI-BU POTTERY,
Kingoldrum ☎ 01575 574725

FIFE

Fife boasts a wealth of craft galleries and workshops; lookout for pottery, ceramics, paintings, woodcraft, jewellery making and basketmaking.

BALBIRNIE CRAFT CENTRE,
Markinch ☎ 01592 756016
BUTTERCHURN CRAFT CENTRE,
Kelty ☎ 01383 830169
CRAIL POTTERY,
75 Nethergate, Crail ☎ 01333 450413
GRISELDA HILL POTTERY,
Kirkbrae, Ceres ☎ 01334 828273

ENTERTAINMENT

CINEMAS

ABC CINEMA,
Dundee ☎ 01382 226865
THE STEPS FILM THEATRE,
Dundee ☎ 01382 434037

THEATRES

ANGUS & DUNDEE

ABBEY THEATRE,
Arbroath ☎ 01241 876420
DUNDEE REP THEATRE,
☎ 01382 223530
THE LITTLE THEATRE,
Dundee ☎ 01382 225835
WEBSTER THEATRE,
Arbroath ☎ 01241 874637
WHITEHALL THEATRE LTD
Dundee ☎ 01382 322684

FIFE

ADAM SMITH THEATRE,
Bennochy Rd, Kirkcaldy ☎ 01592 412929
BUCKHAVEN THEATRE,
Lawrence St ☎ 01592 715577
BYRE THEATRE,
Abbey St, St Andrews ☎ 01334 476288
CARNEGIE HALL,
Dunfermline ☎ 01383 314127
CRAWFORD ARTS CENTRE,
North St, St Andrews ☎ 01334 474610
ROTHES HALLS,
Glenrothes ☎ 01592 611101

FOOD & DRINK

ANGUS & DUNDEE

ARBROATH SMOKIES

Smoked haddock.

FORFAR BRIDIES

A horseshoe-shaped, meat-filled pastry
originating in 19th-century Forfar bakeries.

CAKES

Puggy or Scotch Buns (slashed ginger
bread dough surrounds bun), Dundee
Cake (a rich fruit cake topped with
almonds), Sair Heads (iced sponge
biscuits wrapped in a paper band), and
Paving Stones (gingerbread biscuits with a
boiled sugar coating), among many others
to be found in local bakeries.

Shaw's Sweet Factory (see Great For Kids)
still makes boiled sweets and fudge in the
traditional way. The original 'Star Rock'

and other sweets are made at the Star
Rock Shop in Kirriemuir ☎ 01575 572579.

WHISKY DISTILLERY TOURS

FETTERCAIRN DISTILLERY,
near Edzell ☎ 01561 340244

FIFE

REEDIEHILL DEER FARM,
Auchtermuchty ☎ 01337 828369
Britain's first deer farm specialising in
tours and tastings.
SCOTLAND'S LARDER.
Upper Largo ☎ 01333 360414
Exhibition on Scottish food -
demonstrations, shop and restaurant.

TRANSPORT

BOAT TRIPS & CRUISES

FIFE

ANSTRUTHER PLEASURE TRIPS,
☎ 01333 310103
Daily sailings to the Isle of May
EASTERN DAWN BOAT CHARTER,
Methilhill ☎ 01592 712606
Fishing/diving trips, sightseeing tours .
MAID OF THE FORTH,
North Queensferry ☎ 0131 331 4857
Ferries to Incholm Island, sea life cruises.

CAR HIRE

ANGUS & DUNDEE

ABERCROMBY PEUGEOT,
Dundee ☎ 01328 202781
ARNOLD CLARK HIRE DRIVE,
Dundee ☎ 01382 225382
AVIS RENT A CAR,
Dundee ☎ 01382 832264
BUDGET RENT A CAR,
Dundee ☎ 01382 644664
KERR'S SELF DRIVE, Arbroath
☎ 01241 877990
RITCHIES SELF DRIVE,
Brechin ☎ 01356 622343 & 623558

COACH TOURS

ANGUS & DUNDEE

FISHERS TOURS,
Dundee ☎ 01382 227290
RIDDLER'S COACHES,
Arbroath ☎ 01241 873464
SIDLAW EXECUTIVE TRAVEL,
Auchterhouse ☎ 01382 320280
TRAVEL GREYHOUND,
Dundee ☎ 01382 202655

TOURS

FIFE

ST ANDREWS OPEN TOP BUS,
☎ 01334 474238
CAPERCAILLIE LUXURY TOURS,
Coaltown of Wemyss ☎ 01592 653678

TRAINS

The main line through Angus & Dundee and Fife follows the coast, en route from Edinburgh to Aberdeen. Scotrail
☎ 0345 484950

SPORT & LEISURE

ACTIVITY CENTRES

ANGUS & DUNDEE

ANCRUM CENTRE FOR THE ENVIRONMENT,
☎ 01382 435911

AUCHTERHOUSE COUNTRY SPORTS,
☎ 01382 320476

HIGHLAND ADVENTURE OUTDOOR PURSUITS CENTRE,
Glenisla by Alyth ☎ 01575 582238

FIFE

EAST NEUK OUTDOORS,
Anstruther ☎ 01333 311929

COLZIE HILL RECREATION,
Auchtermuchty ☎ 01337 827075

GLENTARKIE OFF-RD,
Strathmiglo ☎ 01337 860528

LOCHORE MEADOWS COUNTRY PARK,
By Lochgelly ☎ 01592 414300

LOMOND CENTRE,
Glenrothes ☎ 01592 415678

NEWTON HILL COUNTRY SPORTS,
Wormit, St Andrews ☎ 01382 542513

ANGLING

ANGUS & DUNDEE

For sea trout and salmon look to the spate rivers North Esk and South Esk which tumble off the Grampians through two of the Angus glens, Rainbow and brown trout can be fished at various fisheries near Dundee, and some of the best sea angling along east coast can be enjoyed from Arbroath and Montrose.

FIFE

Brown trout, boat, bank and sea angling are all available throughout Fife. Contact the Tourist Information Offices for details.

CYCLING

SCOTTISH CYCLING HOLIDAYS,
☎ 01250 876100
Explore the unspoilt Angus glens or Dundee's circular cycle route.

GLIDING

ANGUS GLIDING CLUB,
Roundyhill, Forfar, Angus ☎ 01241 871400

GOLF

ANGUS & DUNDEE

CARNOUSTIE ☎ 01241 853789
One of the finest links courses in Britain, offering a marvellous test of golf.

EDZELL ☎ 01356 647283
A delightful course situated in the foothills of the Scottish Highlands.

LETHAM GRANGE RESORT,
Colliston, Arbroath ☎ 01241 890373
Often referred to as the 'Augusta of Scotland', the Old Course provides championship standards in spectacular surroundings.

PANMURE,
Barry ☎ 01241 855120
A nerve-testing, adventurous course set amongst sandhills.

ARBROATH ☎ 01241 872069
BRECHIN ☎ 01356 622383
CAIRD PARK,
Dundee ☎ 01382 453606
CAMPERDOWN,
Dundee ☎ 01382 623368
FORFAR ☎ 01307 463773
KIRRIEMUIR ☎ 01575 573317
MONIFIETH ☎ 01382 532767
MONTROSE ☎ 01674 672932

FIFE

ST ANDREWS ☎ 01334 475757
The Old Course, one of six courses around the town, is the most famous and challenging links in the world. You too can wander out with your clubs to conquer some holes, maybe, and to be brought to a humbling halt by others.

BALCOMIE ☎ 01333 450686
Picturesque and sporting course perched on the edge of the North Sea.

ELIE ☎ 01333 330301
One of Scotland's most delightful holiday courses with panoramic views.
ABERDOUR ☎ 01383 860080
ANSTRUTHER ☎ 01333 310956
BALBIRNIE PARK,
Markinch ☎ 01592 612095
CANMORE,
Dunfermline ☎ 01383 724969
CHARELTON,
Colinsburgh ☎ 01333 340505
COWDENBEATH ☎ 01383 511918
CUPAR ☎ ☎ 01334 653549
DUNFERMLINE ☎ 01383 723534
DUNNIKIER PARK,
Kirkcaldy ☎ 01592 261599
FALKLAND ☎ 01337 857404
GLENROTHES ☎ 01592 754561
KINGHORN ☎ 01592 890345
KIRKCALDY ☎ 01592 205240
LADYBANK ☎ 01337 830814
LESLIE ☎ 01592 620040
LEVEN LINKS ☎/☎ 01333 428859
LOCHGELLY ☎ 01592 780174
LUNDIN ☎ 01333 320202
ST MICHAEL'S,
Leuchars ☎ 01334 839365
SALINE ☎ 01383 852591
SCOTSCRAIG,
Tayport ☎ 01382 552515
THORNTON ☎ 01592 771111
TULLIALLAN,
Kincardine ☎ 01259 730396

ICE SKATING

ICE WORLD ICE RINK,
Forfar, Angus ☎/☎ 01307 468668
KIRKCALDY ICE RINK,
☎/☎ 01592 595100

LEISURE CENTRES

ANGUS & DUNDEE

ARBROATH SPORTS CENTRE,
Keptie Rd ☎ 01241 872999
LOCHEE SWIMMING & LEISURE CENTRE,
St Mary's Lane, Dundee ☎ 01382 432690
OLYMPIA LEISURE CENTRE,
Earl Grey Pl, Dundee ☎ 01382 434888
WEBSTER SPORTS CENTRE,
Glamis Rd, Kirriemuir ☎ 01575 574849

FIFE

BEACON LEISURE CENTRE,
Burntisland ☎ 01592 872211
CARNEGIE LEISURE CENTRE,
☎/☎ 01383 314200
COWDENBEATH LEISURE CENTRE,
☎ 01383 514520
CUPAR SPORTS CENTRE,
Elmwood Carslogie Rd ☎ 01334 412290
EAST SANDS LEISURE CENTRE,
St Andrews ☎ 01334 476506
EDEN PARK LEISURE CENTRE,
Cupar ☎ 01334 654968

RIDING

ANGUS & DUNDEE

BALHALL RIDING STABLES,
Menmuir, By Brechin ☎ 01356 660284

Letham Grange Resort,

CAMPERDOWN STABLES,
Dundee ☎ 01382 623879
DENMILL STABLES,
Denmill, Kirriemuir ☎ 01575 572757
Kirkton of Glenisla, ☎/☏ 01575 582223
GLENTAIRIE RIDING CENTRE,
Glen Prosen ☎ 01575 540253
MUIRHEAD RIDING SCHOOL & STABLES,
☎ 01382 580246
ROWANLEA RIDING SCHOOL LTD,
Barry, Carnoustie ☎ 01382 532536

FIFE

BARBARAFIELD RIDING SCHOOL,
Craigrothie, Cupar ☎ 01334 828223
DUNVEGAN EQUESTRIAN TRAINING,
Newburgh ☎ 01337 840205
EDENSIDE RIDING STABLES,
Garbridge ☎ 01334 839353
GLENROTHES RIDING CENTRE,
☎ 01592 742428
INCHARVIE EQUESTRIAN CENTRE,
Leven ☎ 01333 340640
KINSHALDY RIDING STABLES,
Leuchars ☎ 01334 838527
LOCHORE MEADOWS RIDING CENTRE,
By Lochgelly ☎ 01592 861596
SHIELDBANK RIDING CENTRE LTD,
North Rd, Saline ☎ 01383 852874

SCENIC DRIVES

The best drives are to found through the Angus Glens in the north of the county. Memorable drives from St Andrews, Fife,

include a tour of the East Neuk, Fife's scenic coastline, which is graced by some of Scotland's most appealing fishing villages and some enchanting properties and gardens. A leisurely tour of rich agricultural heart of the Fife peninsula should incorporate the Royal Burgh of Falkland and the equally interesting Fife Folk Museum at Ceres.

SKIING

GLENSHEE SKI CENTRE,
Glenshee, Angus ☎ 01339 741320

SWIMMING

ANGUS & DUNDEE

See also Leisure Centres

BEACHES
Splendid sandy beaches can be found at Broughty Ferry, Monifieth, Montrose and Lunan Bay.

FORFAR SWIMMING POOL,
The Vennel ☎ 01575 574849

MONTROSE SWIMMING POOL,
The Mall ☎ 01674 672026

FIFE

BEACHES
In Fife, seek out the sandy beaches at Kingsbarns, Silver Sands at Aberdour, Elie and Kinshaldy Beach at Tentsmuir Point.

BOWHILL SWIMMING POOL,
Cardenden ☎ 01592 414860
KIRKCALDY SWIMMING POOL,
☎ 01592 412655
LEVENMOUTH SWIMMING POOL,
Leven ☎ 01333 592500

WALKING

Walking enthusiasts have a rich variety of landscapes to explore, from unspoilt coastal paths, forest trails and riverside walks to more adventurous rambles through the beautiful valleys and wild hill country of the Glens of Angus.

WALKING HOLIDAYS/TOURS

TAYSIDE TOURS
☎ 01307 462045
Guided walks through the Angus glens.

WATERSPORTS

CLATTO COUNTRY PARK,
Dundee ☎ 01382 436505
MONIKIE COUNTRY PARK,
Broughty Ferry, Dundee ☎ 01382 370300
BURNTISLAND WATERSPORTS CENTRE,
☎/☏ 01592 874380
ELIE WATERSPORTS,
☎/☏ 01333 330962
SCOTTISH NATIONAL WATERSKI CENTRE,
By Dunfermline, Fife ☎ 01383 620123

WHERE TO STAY
ANGUS & DUNDEE
AA RECOMMENDED

The Shaftesbury

LETHAM GRANGE ★★★★
Colliston DD11 4RL
(A92 onto A933 to Brechin. Hotel signposted at Colliston)
☎ 01241 890373 🖷 01241 890414
Impressive mansion house, sympathetically restored, is the centrepiece of a sporting complex.
19 bedrooms (22 annexe) (1 fmly) No smoking in 2 bedrooms Night porter Golf Snooker Croquet Putting Curling rink 🗲

HOTEL SEAFORTH ★★
Dundee Rd DD11 1QF
(on southern outskirts, on A92)
☎ 01241 872232 🖷 01241 877473
Good value accommodation at this friendly hotel overlooking the sea. Competitively priced meals.
££ 20 bedrooms (2 fmly) Indoor swimming pool Snooker Solarium Jacuzzi/spa 🗲

KINGSLEY ◪◪
29 Market Gate DD11 1AU
(from A92 follow sign for harbour. 1st rd on L (100 metres from harbour))
☎ 01241 873933 🖷 01241 873933
Comfortable family-run guest house near the harbour and central amenities.
£ 16 bedrooms (3 fmly) No smoking in dining room Licensed Childrens play ground 🗲

FARMHOUSE KITCHEN ◪◪◪◪◪
Grange of Conon DD11 3SD
(6m N, signposted from A933 just beyond Colliston)
☎ 01241 860202 🖷 01241 860424
Delightful family farmhouse set in peaceful countryside. Hearty farmhouse breakfasts.
3 bedrooms No smoking in bedrooms or dining room No dogs (ex guide dogs) No children under 3yrs Fishing Snooker Solarium Games room 560 acres arable

OLD MANSION HOUSE ★★★
DD3 0QN
(A923 from Dundee to Muirhead then B954 for 2m. Hotel on L)
☎ 01382 320366 🖷 01382 320340
Baronial mansion, set in attractive grounds. Eat in distinctive restaurant or Courtyard Bistro.
££££ 6 bedrooms (1 fmly) No dogs (ex guide dogs) Outdoor swimming pool Tennis (grass) Squash Croquet No smoking in restaurant Closed 26 Dec-10 Jan 🗲

NORTHERN ★★
2/4 Clerk St DD9 6AE
☎ 01356 625505 🖷 01356 622714
Traditional country town hotel offering honest unassuming standards. Good value home-cooked meals.
£ 20 bedrooms (1 fmly) No smoking in 5 bedrooms No smoking in restaurant 🗲

DONIFORD ◪◪◪◪
26 Arlie St DD9 6JX
(A90 onto A935, turn into Airlie St)
☎ 01356 622361
Lovely Victorian house, close to central amenities. Attractive en suite, spacious bedrooms.
£ 3 bedrooms No smoking No dogs (ex guide dogs) No children Closed Xmas

CARLOGIE HOUSE ★★
Carlogie Rd DD7 6LD
(take A92. At crossroads onto A930. Hotel 1km on R)
☎ 01241 853185 🖷 01241 856528
Friendly hotel in its own grounds. Four rooms suitable for the disabled. Extensive range of food.
£ 12 bedrooms 4 annexe bedrooms (2 fmly) No dogs (ex guide dogs) No smoking area in restaurant Closed 1-3 Jan 🗲

GLENCOE ★★
Links Pde DD7 7JF
(off A92, adjoining golf course)
☎ 01241 853273 🖷 01241 853319
Relaxed and friendly, small hotel overlooking the 18th green of the Championship golf course.
££ 7 bedrooms (4 fmly) No smoking in restaurant 🗲

PARK HOUSE ◪◪◪◪
12 Park Av DD7 7JA
(A92 onto the Muirdrum rd(A930). L at 2nd mini rdbt, bottom of avenue on R)
☎ 01241 852101
Centrally situated hotel near the Championship golf course. Tastefully decorated bedrooms. Substantial breakfasts.
£ 3 bedrooms No smoking No dogs (ex guide dogs) Large lawn, BBQ area, 🗲

Swallow

DUNDEE

STAKIS DUNDEE EARL GREY ★ ★ ★ ★ ✿
Earl Grey Place DD1 4DE

☎ 01382 229271 📠 01382 200072

Well equipped, stylish accommodation at hotel on the old quay. Bar and restaurant. Lunch Carvery buffet.

£ 104 bedrooms (4 fmly) No smoking in 41 bedrooms No dogs (ex guide dogs) Lift Night porter Indoor swimming pool Sauna Solarium Gym Jacuzzi/spa ent Weekly live entertainment No smoking area in restaurant Business centre 🍴

SWALLOW ★ ★ ★
Kingsway West Invergowrie DD2 5JT

(from A90/A929 rdbt follow sign for Denhead of Gray, hotel on L)

☎ 01382 641122 📠 01382 568340

Fine Victorian mansion in carefully tended gardens. Suites, executive and standard rooms. Friendly, helpful staff.

£££ 107 bedrooms (11 fmly) No smoking in 60 bedrooms Night porter Indoor swimming pool Sauna Solarium Gym Putting Jacuzzi/spa Trim trail Mountain bike hire Weekly live entertainment No smoking in restaurant 🍴

Links Hotel

INVERCARSE ★ ★ ★
371 Perth Rd DD2 1PG

(from A90 take A85 (Taybridge). Follow signs to University on B911)

☎ 01382 669231 📠 01382 644112

Fine period house now a smart modern hotel. Split level bar, comfortable lounge and restaurant.

£££ 32 bedrooms No smoking in 17 bedrooms Night porter Closed 24-26 Dec & 31 Dec-2 Jan 🍴

QUEENS ★ ★ ★
160 Nethergate DD1 4DU

☎ 01382 322515 📠 01382 202668

Imposing and spacious popular Victorian hotel. Some bedrooms with Tay Estuary views. Eating options.

£££ 47 bedrooms (4 fmly) Lift Night porter Weekly live entertainment 🍴

THE SHAFTESBURY ★ ★
1 Hyndford St DD2 1HQ

(from Perth follow signs to airport. 1st L at circle then R, follow Perth rd & turn R)

☎ 01382 669216 📠 01382 641598

Former jute baron's mansion, with much original character, now a friendly family-run hotel near the university.

££ 12 bedrooms (2 fmly) No smoking in restaurant 🍴

TRAVEL INN
Kingsway West, Invergowrie DD2 5JU

(on A972 between Invergowrie & Dundee)

☎ 01382 561115 📠 01382 568431

Modern building offering smart, spacious and well equipped bedrooms, suitable for family use. Nearby family restaurant.

££(fmly room) 40 bedrooms

TRAVEL INN
Discovery Quay, Riverside Dr DD1 4XA

☎ 01382 203240 📠 01382 203237

Modern building offering smart, spacious and well equipped bedrooms, suitable for family use. Nearby family restaurant.

££(fmly room) 40 bedrooms

BEACH HOUSE HOTEL ◙ ◙ ◙ ◙
22 Esplanade, Broughty Ferry DD5 2EN

☎ 01382 775537 & 776614

📠 01382 480241

Traditional-style, seafront guesthouse in pretty village. Good value evening meals served.

££ 5 bedrooms (1 fmly) No smoking in 2 bedrooms No smoking in dining room No dogs Licensed 🍴

ERROL BANK ◙ ◙ ◙
9 Dalgleish Rd DD4 7JN

(off Broughty Ferry/Arbroath rd - opposite gates of cemetery - going E from Dundee centre)

☎ 01382 462118 📠 01382 462118

Immaculately maintained detached villa with bright airy bedrooms. Hearty breakfasts.

£ 6 bedrooms (1 fmly) No smoking in dining room 🍴

INVERMARK HOTEL ◙ ◙ ◙
23 Monifeith Rd Broughty Ferry DD5 2RN

(3m E A930)

☎ 01382 739430

Large detached house in its own grounds near The Esplanade. Hearty breakfasts.

£ 8 bedrooms No smoking No dogs (ex guide dogs) Licensed

DUNKELD

KINNAIRD ★ ★ ★ ✿ ✿ ✿
Kinnaird Estate PH8 0LB

(A9 from Perth towards Inverness. At Dunkeld North take B898)

☎ 01796 482440 📠 01796 482289

Charming hotel on extensive estate overlooking the Tay Valley. Well proportioned bedrooms offer unashamed luxury.

£££ 9 bedrooms No dogs Lift Tennis (hard) Fishing Snooker Croquet Shooting No children under 12yrs No smoking in restaurant RS 6 Jan-16 Mar 🍴

ATHOLL ARMS ★ ★ ✿
Bridgehead PH8 0AQ

(12m N of Perth, turn off A9 into Dunkeld. Hotel on R overlooking bridge & RTay)

☎ 01350 727219 & 727759

📠 01350 727219

Popular and welcoming former coaching inn overlooking the River Enjoyable home-style cooking.

£ 16 bedrooms (1 fmly) No smoking in 5 bedrooms No smoking area in restaurant 🍴

EDZELL

GLENESK ★ ★ ★
High St DD9 7TF

(off A90 just after Brechin Bypass)

☎ 01356 648319 📠 01356 647333

Warm welcome at this family run hotel beside the golf course. Fully equipped leisure centre.

25 bedrooms (5 fmly) Indoor swimming pool Snooker Sauna Solarium Gym Croquet Jacuzzi/spa 🍴

FORFAR

IDVIES HOUSE ★ ★ ★
Letham DD8 2QJ

(B9128 from Forfar towards Carnoustie. L after 2m at fork Letham & Arbroath. 1m to T junct, turn L signed Arbroath. 0.5m hotel on L)

☎ 01307 818787 📠 01307 818933

Charming and tranquil Victorian country house hotel in wooded grounds. Extensive dinner menu.

££ 11 bedrooms (1 fmly) Squash Snooker Croquet ch fac Closed 28 Dec-2 Jan 🍴

FINAVON FARMHOUSE ◙ ◙ ◙ ◙ ◙
Finavon DD8 3PX

(turn off A90 at Milton of Finavon exit, approx 5m N of Forfar)

☎ 01307 850269 📠 01307 850269

Modern house in large garden with a summer house. Hearty breakfasts and, by arrangement, a set dinner.

£ 3 bedrooms Badminton Putting 9 hole Pitch & putt Closed Dec & Jan

GLAMIS

CASTLETON HOUSE ★★★❀
DD8 1SJ *(on A94 between Forfar/Cupar Angus. 3mW of Glamis)*

☎ 01307 840340 📠 01307 840506

Distinctive country house hotel in own grounds. Quiet lounge, cosy bar and conservatory. Eating options.

£££ 6 bedrooms No dogs Putting

MONTROSE

LINKS HOTEL ★★★
Mid Links DD10 8RL

☎ 01674 72288

Fine period house with extensions. Main house and annexe bedrooms available. Staff are very friendly and helpful.

21 rms

PARK ★★★
61 John St DD10 8RJ *(off High St)*

☎ 01674 673415 📠 01674 677091

Long established family run hotel within easy reach of central and leisure amenities. Staff are friendly and willing to please.

££ 59 bedrooms (4 fmly) No smoking in 6 bedrooms Night porter No smoking in restaurant

MURRAY LODGE❑❑❑
2-8 Murray St DD10 8LB

(on main A92 situated opposite swimming pool towards the north end of Montrose Town Centre)

☎ 01674 678880 📠 01674 678877

18th-century linen mill converted to create a small, comfortable, popular hotel. All-day tea shop.

£ 12 bedrooms No smoking in 9 bedrooms No smoking in dining room No dogs (ex guide dogs) Licensed

OAKLANDS ❑❑❑
10 Rossie Island Rd DD10 9NN

(on A92 - south end of town)

☎ 01674 672018 📠 01674 672018

Comfortable family-run guest house with friendly atmosphere.

£ 7 bedrooms (1 fmly) No smoking in dining room Childrens facilities

WHERE TO EAT
ANGUS & DUNDEE

RESTAURANTS
AA RECOMMENDED

CARNOUSTIE

11 PARK AVENUE ❀
11 Park Avenue, DD7 7JA

☎/📠 01241 853336

Visitors to this unpretentious restaurant tucked away down a side street can enjoy the likes of fresh west coast mussels cooked in white wine, and lightly grilled fillet of salmon served with a spring onion and Vermouth sauce.

Fixed D ££ ALC £££

GLAMIS

CASTLETON HOUSE HOTEL ❀
Forfar DD8 1SJ

☎ 01307 840340

A distinctive country house hotel where the kitchen offers a daily changing fixed-price menu and an imaginative carte built around Scotland's larder of game, lamb, beef and fish.

INVERKEILOR

GORDON'S RESTAURANT ❀
Homewood House Main Street DD11 5RN

☎ 01241 830364

Traditional menu reflecting classical French influences, backed up by prime Scottish produce, at this cottage-style hotel. Expect dishes such as fishmarket soup, king scallops with white wine sauce and mushrooms, and suprême of chicken stuffed with haggis and served with Drambuie sauce.

Fixed D ££ ALC £

PUBS, INNS & OTHER PLACES

ARBROATH

COLLISTON INN
by Arbroath

☎ 01241 890232

Newly enlarged restaurant with something for everyone.

MEADOWBANK INN
Montrose Road

☎ 01241 875755

Classically refined, with open fire, food prepared from Angus and Scottish ingredients.

THE OLD BREW HOUSE
1 High Street

☎ 01241 879945

Water's edge setting, serene in summer, wild in winter. Enjoy lobster, steak, fish and chips or steak pie.

AUCHMITHIE

BUT'N BEN
Nr Arbroath

☎ 01241 877223

Licensed restaurant serving traditional Scottish cooking using fresh local ingredients, specialising in fish and shellfish dishes.

CARNOUSTIE

THE BELMONTE FISH AND CHIP SHOP
81-83 Dundee Street

☎ 01241 417171

Traditional suppers, pizzas and pasta.

11 PARK AVENUE
11 Park Avenue

☎ 01241 853336

A personally run restaurant offering the best of fresh Scottish produce at reasonable prices.

EDZELL

THE COFFEE SHOP
1 Dunlappie Road

☎ 01356 648348

A wide range of wholesome snacks, coffees and teas, soups and sandwiches.

GLENISLA

THE GLENISLA HOTEL
PH11 8PH *(On B951)*

☎ 01575 582223

17th-century coaching inn where the choices include casserole of Glenisla pheasant cooked in cider, Perthshire ham with parsley sauce, casseroled venison with fruits of the forest, and grilled duck with ginger wine sauce.

Accommodation

WHERE TO STAY
FIFE

Balgeddie House

ABERDOUR

WOODSIDE ★★
High St KY3 0SW
(E of Forth Rd Bridge, across rbt into town, hotel on L after garage)
☎ 01383 860328 📠 01383 860920
Welcoming family-run hotel with well equipped bedrooms. Scottish and Oriental cuisine.
££ 20 bedrooms (1 fmly) Night porter Free golf at local course arranged when booking room(s) No smoking area in restaurant 🗏

ANSTRUTHER

SMUGGLERS INN ★★
High St KY10 3DQ
(A917, or on B9131 from St.Andrews or A917 from Kirkcaldy)
☎ 01333 310506 📠 01333 312706
With harbour views this welcoming inn, steeped in Jacobite history, offers genuine hospitality.
££ 8 bedrooms 🗏

BURNTISLAND

INCHVIEW HOTEL ★★
69 Kinghorn Rd KY3 9EB
(from A921 towards town centre, hotel overlooks the links)
☎ 01592 872239 📠 01592 874866
Relaxed and welcoming atmosphere at this Georgian terrace hotel overlooking the links.
££ 12 bedrooms (1 fmly) 🗏

CRAIL

BALCOMIE LINKS ★★
Balcomie Rd KY10 3TN
(A917 towards Crail follow rd for golf course, hotel last on L)
☎ 01333 450237 📠 01333 450540
Close to the golf course, this friendly family run hotel offers good value.
11 bedrooms (1 fmly) Snooker Games room 🗏

CROMA ★
Nethergate KY10 3TU *(take A917 to Crail)*
☎ 01333 450239
Quietly situated traditional-style hotel, with neat bedrooms maintained to a high standard.
£ 8 bedrooms (6 fmly) No smoking in restaurant Closed Dec-Mar

CUPAR

EDEN HOUSE ★★❀
2 Pitscottie Rd KY15 4HF
(overlooking Haigh Park on A91, 8m W of St Andrews)
☎ 01334 652510 📠 01334 652277
Comfortable small hotel sympathetically furnished in keeping with the house's Victorian character.
££ 9 bedrooms 2 annexe bedrooms (3 fmly) No dogs (ex guide dogs) Weekly live entertainment 🗏

DUNFERMLINE

ELGIN ★★★
Charlestown KY11 3EE
(3m W of M90 J1, on loop road off A985, signposted Limekilns & Charlestown)
☎ 01383 872257 📠 01383 873044
Welcoming, family-run hotel overlooking the Firth of Forth. Play areas a big hit with children.
££ 12 bedrooms (3 fmly) No dogs (ex guide dogs) Children's facilities No smoking in restaurant 🗏

KEAVIL HOUSE ★★★❀❀
Crossford KY12 8QW
(2m W of Dunfermline on A994)
☎ 01383 736258 📠 01383 621600
Has popular, broad appeal. Choice of bars, smart lounge, and conservatory restaurant.
£££ 33 bedrooms (2 fmly) Night porter Indoor swimming pool (heated) Sauna Solarium Gym Jacuzzi/spa Aerobics studio Steam room Children's facilities No smoking in restaurant 🗏

KING MALCOLM THISTLE ★★★
Queensferry Rd, Wester Pitcorthie KY11 5DS
(on A823, S of town)
☎ 01383 722611 📠 01383 730865
Popular modern hotel near M90 access. Compact, well equipped bedrooms. Several eating options.
48 bedrooms (2 fmly) No smoking in 12 bedrooms Night porter Weekly live entertainment 🗏

PITBAUCHLIE HOUSE ★★★
Aberdour Rd KY11 4PB
(1m S of town centre on B916)
☎ 01383 722282 📠 01383 620738
Welcoming family run hotel in wooded grounds. Spacious executive to standard bedrooms.
££ 40 bedrooms (2 fmly) Night porter Gym No smoking in restaurant 🗏

PITFIRRANE ARMS ★★★
Main St, Crossford KY12 8NJ
(from Kincardine-follow A985, at large rdbt take A994 to Dunfermline, Crossford is 2nd village from rdbt, hotel on R)
☎ 01383 736132 📠 01383 621760
Good value accommodation and meals are the hallmarks of this popular hotel.
££ 39 bedrooms (1 fmly) Night porter No smoking in restaurant 🗏

FREUCHIE

LOMOND HILLS ★★
Parliament Square KY15 7EY
☎ 01337 857329 & 857498
📠 01337 858180
Extended former coaching inn offers well equipped leisure centre.
££ 25 bedrooms (3 fmly) No smoking in 3 bedrooms Indoor swimming pool (heated) Sauna Solarium Gym Jacuzzi/spa No smoking area in restaurant 🗏

GLENROTHES

BALGEDDIE HOUSE ★★★
Balgeddie Way KY6 3ET
(from M90 J3 take A92. Over 2 rdbts & 1st L after garage for Cadham Rd. At 2nd rbt into Fortmanthills Rd then 3rd L)
☎ 01592 742511 📠 01592 621702
In own landscaped grounds, this comfortable hotel is popular with business visitors.
££ 20 bedrooms (3 fmly) No smoking in 3 bedrooms No dogs (ex guide dogs) Night porter Riding Croquet lawn Weekly live entertainment Children's facilities 🗏

RESCOBIE ★ ★ ☸

Valley Dr, Leslie KY6 3BQ

(at end of village turn W at sharp bend, 50 yards turn L)

☎ 01592 742143 ☏ 01592 620231

Genuine hospitality at this delightful small hotel, a converted Edwardian house. Tempting Taste of Scotland fare.

££ 10 bedrooms (1 fmly) No dogs (ex guide dogs) Putting green Children's facilities ☜

TRAVEL INN

Beaufort Dr, Bankhead Roundabout KY7 4UJ

(from M90 J3 take A92 to Glenrothes. 1st rdbt is Bankhead)

☎ 01592 773473 ☏ 01592 773453

Modern building offering smart, spacious and well equipped bedrooms, suitable for family use. Nearby family restaurant.

££ (fmly room) 40 bedrooms

INVERKEITHING

QUEENSFERRY LODGE ★ ★ ★

St Margaret's Head, North Queensferry KY11 1HP

☎ 01383 410000 ☏ 01383 419708

Russell Hotel

20 minutes from Edinburgh. Hotel overlooks the famous bridges. Choice of restaurants.

££££ 32 bedrooms No smoking in 16 bedrooms Lift Night porter No smoking area in restaurant ☜

KIRKCALDY

DEAN PARK ★ ★ ★

Chapel Level KY2 6QW

(signposted from A92, Kirkcaldy West junc)

☎ 01592 261635 ☏ 01592 261371

Popular business hotel, with main house and annexe rooms.

20 en suite bedrooms 12 annexe bedrooms (1 fmly) No dogs (ex guide dogs) Night porter ☜

THE BELVEDERE ★ ★

Coxstool, West Wemyss KY1 4SL

(A92 from Perth, at Kirkcaldy East take A915, 1m NE turn R to Coaltown, at Tjunct turn R then L, 1st building in village)

☎ 01592 654167 ☏ 01592 655279

Wonderful views from this comfortable small hotel. Bedrooms in a cluster of houses in the grounds.

££ 4 bedrooms 16 annexe bedrooms (2 fmly) ☜

LETHAM

FERNIE CASTLE HOTEL ★ ★ ★ ☸

KY15 7RU *(on A914 1.25m N of Melville Lodges rdbt intersection of A91)*

☎ 01337 810381 ☏ 01337 810422

Dating back to the 12th century, this historic castle has been a hotel for many years. Restaurant and vaulted keep bar.

££ 15 bedrooms (2 fmly) No smoking in 3 bedrooms Croquet lawn Putting green ☜

LEVEN

CALEDONIAN ★ ★ ★

81 High St KY8 4NG

(follow A912 to Letham Glen rdbt then R, turn R 0.5m into Mitchell St)

☎ 01333 424101 ☏ 01333 421241

Modern hotel, a popular base for the visiting businessman. Small restaurant. Contrasting bars.

££ 24 bedrooms (1 fmly) Night porter Weekly live entertainment ☜

LUNDIN LINKS

OLD MANOR ★ ★ ★ ☸

Leven Rd KY8 6AJ

(1m E of Leven on A915)

☎ 01333 320368 ☏ 01333 320911

Country house hotel with nice views over Largo Bay. Attentive and courteous service.

£££ 24 bedrooms (3 fmly) No smoking in 4 bedrooms No smoking in restaurant ☜

MARKINCH

BALBIRNIE HOUSE ★ ★ ★ ★ ☸ ☸

Balbirnie Park KY7 6NE

(A92 onto B9130, entrance 0.5 miles on L)

☎ 01592 610066 ☏ 01592 610529

Luxury Georgian mansion hotel in country park providing exemplary standards of personal attention and genuine hospitality.

££££(inc dinner) 30 bedrooms (9 fmly) Night porter Golf 18 Croquet lawn Putting green No smoking in restaurant ☜

PEAT INN

PEAT INN ★ ★ ☸ ☸

KY15 5LH *(6 m SW of St Andrews at junct B940/B941)*

☎ 01334 840206 ☏ 01334 840530

Originally a coaching inn, now with adjacent house having luxury suites. Attention to detail is considerable.

££££ 8 bedrooms No smoking in restaurant Closed Sun, Mon, Xmas day & New Year's day ☜

Rescobie

Peat Inn

Old Manor

GLADYER INN ★★
Heath Rd, off Ridley Dr KY11 2BT
(from M90 J1 along Admiralty Rd, past rdbt then 1st on L)
☎ 01383 419977 🖨 01383 411728
Friendly commercial hotel ideal for the those visiting the dockyard and Naval Base.
££ 21 bedrooms (3 fmly) Night porter Weekly live entertainment ⬛

THE OLD COURSE HOTEL ★★★★★🏵🏵
KY16 9SP
(close to A91 on the outskirts of the city)
☎ 01334 474371 🖨 01334 477668
Internationally renowned hotel. A range of stylish suites some with balconies overlooking the golf course. Several eating options available.
££££ 125 bedrooms (6 fmly) Lift Night porter Indoor swimming pool (heated) Golf 18 Sauna Solarium Gym Jacuzzi/spa Health spa Steam room No smoking in restaurant Closed 24-28 Dec ⬛

RUSACKS ★★★★🏵
Pilmour Links KY16 9JQ
☎ 01334 474321 🖨 01334 477896
Imposing Victorian hotel with fine views of the first tee and the 18th green, offering well appointed and equipped accommodation. A choice of dining is offered by Champs bistro or the restaurant.
50 bedrooms No smoking in 5 bedrooms Lift Night porter Sauna Solarium No smoking in restaurant ⬛

RUFFLETS COUNTRY HOUSE ★★★🏵🏵
Strathkinness Low Rd KY16 9TX
(1.5m W on B939)
☎ 01334 472594 🖨 01334 478703
One of Scotland's oldest country house hotels. Individually styled bedrooms with many thoughtful extras.
£££ 22 bedrooms 3 annexe bedrooms (8 fmly) No smoking in 13 bedrooms No dogs (ex guide dogs) Night porter Putting green Golf driving net No smoking in restaurant ⬛

Rusacks

ST ANDREWS GOLF ★★★🏵
40 The Scores KY16 9AS
(follow signs 'Golf Course' into Golf Place, 200yds turn R)
☎ 01334 472611 🖨 01334 472188
Long established hotel by the sea with views of the bay and famous Old Course. Bedrooms decorated to a high standard.
££££ 22 bedrooms (9 fmly) Lift Night porter No smoking in restaurant ⬛

SCORES ★★★
76 The Scores KY16 9BB
(on entering St Andrews follow signs to West Sands and Sea Life Centre. Hotel diagonally opp the Royal & Ancient Clubhouse)
☎ 01334 472451 🖨 01334 473947
Near the Old Course this hotel is popular with golfers from all over the world.
£££ 30 bedrooms (1 fmly) No dogs (ex guide dogs) Lift Night porter No smoking in restaurant Closed 24-29 Dec ⬛

ARDGOWAN ★★
2 Playfair Ter KY16 9HX
☎ 01334 472970 🖨 01334 478380
Family-run hotel particularly popular for meals in lounge bar and Playfair's Restaurant.
£ 12 bedrooms (2 fmly) Closed 18 Dec-17 Jan Res Nov-17 Dec & 16 Jan-Mar ⬛

PARKLANDS HOTEL & RESTAURANT ★★🏵
Kinburn Castle, Double Dykes Rd KY16 9DS
(opposite Kinburn Park and Museum)
☎ 01334 473620 🖨 01334 473620
Friendly, family run hotel that appeals to golfers, tourists, and business guests.
££ 15 bedrooms (2 fmly) No dogs (ex guide dogs) No smoking in restaurant Closed Xmas/New Year ⬛

RUSSELL HOTEL ★★
26 The Scores KY16 9AS
(A91-St Andrews. R at 2nd rdbt into Golf Place, 200 yards turn R, hotel 300yds on L)
☎ 01334 473447 🖨 01334 478279
Small family run hotel enjoying lovely sea views and near the Old Course.
10 bedrooms (3 fmly) No dogs Night porter No smoking in restaurant ⬛

Ardgowan

BED & BREAKFAST ACCOMMODATION

ABERDOUR

HAWKCRAIG HOUSE ▨▨▨▨▨
Hawkcraig Point KY3 0TZ
☎ 01383 860335
Glorious views across the Firth of Forth
from this converted ferryman's house on
the shore.
*££ 2 bedrooms No smoking No dogs ex
guide dogs) No children under 10yrs mid
Mar-27 Oct*

THE ABERDOUR HOTEL ▨▨▨
38 High St KY3 0SW *(on A921)*
☎ 01383 860325 ⊕ 01383 860808
This friendly family-run inn has
comfortable bedrooms with satellite TV
and telephone.
16 bedrooms (1 fmly) 🗲

ANNSTRUTHER

HERMITAGE ▨▨▨▨▨
Ladywalk KY10 3EX
*(from Shore St turn L at Ship Inn, L along
lane, Hermitage on L)*
☎ 01333 310909
Lovely sea views from this charming
Georgian house with the elegance of a
former era.
*£ 4 bedrooms (2 fmly) No smoking No dogs
(ex guide dogs) Licensed* 🗲

BEAUMONT LODGE ▨▨▨▨
43 Pittenweem Rd KY10 3DT
*(B9131 from St Andrews to Anstruther. R at
crossroads, Lodge on L past the hotel)*
☎ 01333 310315 ⊕ 01333 310315
Many guests return to this comfortable
home in a pretty fishing village. Bedrooms
are bright and airy.
*£ 4 bedrooms (1 fmly) No smoking No dogs
(ex guide dogs)* 🗲

THE SPINDRIFT ▨▨▨▨
Pittenweem Rd KY10 3DT
(from W 1st building on L/from E last on R)
☎ 01333 310573 ⊕ 01333 310573
Welcoming atmosphere and good value
accommodation at this comfortable
Victorian house.
*£ 8 bedrooms (3 fmly) No smoking No dogs
Licensed Closed17 Nov-10 Dec & Xmas* 🗲

AUCHTERMUCHTY

ARDCHOILLE ▨▨▨▨▨
Dunshalt KY14 7EY *(on B936)*
☎ 01337 828414 ⊕ 01337 828414
Guests regularly return here for the unique
blend of humour and style provided. Taste
of Scotland dishes.
*3 bedrooms (1 fmly) No smoking No dogs
(ex guide dogs) 2 acres* 🗲

FOREST HILLS HOTEL ▨▨▨
23 High St, The Cross KY15 7AP
☎ 01337 828318 ⊕ 01337 828318
Popular, informal inn. Restaurant featuring
Flemish murals, small bistro and bar.
10 bedrooms No smoking in 2 bedrooms 🗲

COWDENBEATH

STRUAN BANK HOTEL ▨▨▨
74 Perth Rd KY4 9BG
*(from M90 J3 E to Cowdenbeath, through
town centre & up hill)*
☎ 01383 511057 ⊕ 01383 511057
Welcoming and personally run small hotel
offering good value for money.
*£ 9 bedrooms (2 fmly) No smoking in
dining room Licensed* 🗲

CRAIL

GOLF HOTEL ▨▨▨
4 High St KY10 3TB
☎ 01333 450206 & 450500
⊕ 01333 450795
Many visitors, especially golfers, return to
this welcoming historic inn. Atmospheric
bars and restaurant.
5 bedrooms (1 fmly) rs 26 Dec & 1 Jan 🗲

SELCRAIG HOUSE ▨▨▨
47 Nethergate KY10 3TX
(opposite the Marine Hotel)
☎ 01333 450697 ⊕ 01333 451113
Dating back to the 1700's with original
features preserved. Bedrooms vary in style.
£ 6 bedrooms (1 fmly) No smoking

CAIPLIE ▨▨
53 High St KY10 3RA
☎ 01333 450564 ⊕ 01333 450564
Good value accommodation and
enjoyable home cooking. Bright and airy
bedrooms.
*£ 7 bedrooms (1 fmly) No smoking in
dining room Licensed Closed Dec-Feb*

CUPAR

TODHALL HOUSE ▨▨▨▨▨
Dairsie KY15 4RQ
*(2m E of Cupar, off A91 - look for tall beech
tree on L, sign for Todhall by tree)*
☎ 01334 656344 ⊕ 01334 656344
Lovingly restored country home with
countryside views. Warm welcome
assured.
*£ 3 bedrooms No smoking No dogs No
children under 10yrs Outdoor swimming
pool Golf net Closed Nov-Mid Mar* 🗲

RATHCLUAN ▨▨▨
Carslogie Rd KY15 4HY
(on A91, adjacent to police station)
☎ 01334 657856/7 ⊕ 01334 657856/7
Substantial building in its own gardens
offering spacious if practical
accommodation.
*£ 10 bedrooms (2 fmly) No smoking in
bedrooms or dining room Licensed Tennis
(grass)* 🗲

DUNFIRMLINE

CLARKE COTTAGE ▨▨▨▨
139 Halbeath Rd KY11 4LA
*(exit M90 J3, towards Dunfermline, pass
Halbeath Retail Park, Clarke Cottage on L
after 2nd lights)*
☎ 01383 735935
Lovely detached Victorian home offering
attractive pine decorated bedrooms.
Conservatory dining room.
*£ 9 bedrooms No smoking No dogs
(ex guide dogs) Licensed*

HOPETOUN LODGE ▨▨▨▨
141 Halbeath Rd KY11 4LA
*(exit M90 J3 ,1.5m through Halbeath, past
Retail Park on R, over rdbt and two sets of
lights. On L after Kwik-Fit)*
☎ 01383 620906 & 624252
Guests old and new are warmly welcomed
to this comfortable home with spacious
accommodation.
*3 bedrooms (1 fmly) No smoking No dogs
(ex guide dogs)*

PITREAVIE ▨▨▨
3 Aberdour Rd KY11 4PB
☎ 01383 724244
Comfortable and well maintained guest
house. Bright, airy en suite bedrooms.
Hearty breakfasts.
6 bedrooms

INVERKEITHING

THE ROODS ▨▨▨▨
16 Bannerman Av KY11 1NG
(off A90/M90 onto B981)
☎ 01383 415049 ⊕ 01383 415049
In secluded gardens, a charming house
with ground floor bedrooms appointed to
a high standard.
*£ 2 bedrooms No smoking No dogs (ex
guide dogs)*

FORTH CRAIG PRIVATE HOTEL ▨▨▨
90 Hope St KY11 1LL
*(exit A90 at 1st exit after Forth Bridge, hotel
0.5m on R next to church)*
☎ 01383 418440
Views over the Firth of Forth from this
welcoming family run private hotel.
*£ 5 bedrooms No smoking in bedrooms or
dining room Licensed* 🗲

LEUCHARS

HILLPARK HOUSE ▨▨▨▨
96 Main St KY16 0HF
(on A919 Dundee-St Andrews road)
☎ 01334 839280 ⊕ 01334 839280
Fine Edwardian house, adorned with many
personal touches, surrounded by open
farmland. Tranquil atmosphere.
*£ 3 bedrooms (1 fmly) No smoking in
bedrooms or dining room*

MARKINCH

TOWN HOUSE HOTEL ▨▨▨
1 High St KY7 6DQ

(opposite railway station in Markinch)

☎ 01592 758459 ⓕ 01592 755039

Welcoming atmosphere together with hearty wholesome fare at this personally hotel.

4 bedrooms (1 fmly) No smoking in area of dining room No smoking in 1 lounge 🛏

ST ANDREWS

BELL CRAIG ▨▨▨▨
8 Murray Park KY16 9AW

☎ 01334 472962 ⓕ 01334 472962

Conveniently situated between the central amenities and the sea front. Hearty breakfasts.

5 bedrooms (3 fmly) No smoking in dining room 🛏

CRAIGMORE ▨▨▨▨
3 Murray Park KY16 9AW

(on a91 from Cupar over 2 mini-rdbts, 1st L down Golf Place, 1st R then 1st R again to top of street)

☎ 01334 472142 ⓕ 01334 477963

Great pride is taken to provide the highest standards and a warm welcome.

£ 6 bedrooms (4 fmly) No smoking No dogs 🛏

EDENSIDE HOUSE ▨▨▨▨
Edenside KY16 9SQ

(visible from A91, 2m W of St Andrews on estuary shore)

☎ 01334 838108 ⓕ 01334 838493

A modernised 18th-century house enjoying fine views of Eden Estuary and nature reserve.

£ 3 bedrooms 6 annexe bedrooms No smoking No children under 10yrs Located on bird sanctuary Stables adjacent Closed Nov-Mar 🛏

FOSSIL HOUSE ▨▨▨▨
12-14 Main St, Strathkinness KY16 9RU

(Fossil House at top end of village near pub)

☎ 01334 850639 ⓕ 01334 850639

A charming home in picturesque village. Carefully designed bedrooms in cottage and main house.

£ 2 bedrooms 2 annexe bedrooms (1 fmly) No smoking No dogs (ex guide dogs) Children's facilities Croquet lawn Bar-B-Q patio 🛏

GLENDERRAN ▨▨▨▨
9 Murray Park KY16 9AW

☎ 01334 477951 ⓕ 01334 477908

Welcoming and stylish terraced guest house offering well maintained, bright, airy, en suite bedrooms.

£ 5 bedrooms No smoking No dogs No children under 12yrs 🛏

LORIMER HOUSE▨▨▨▨
19 Murray Park KY16 9AW

(A91 to St Andrews, L into Golf Place, R into The Scores, R into Murray Park)

☎ 01334 476599 ⓕ 01334 476599

High standards are uppermost at this attractive, conveniently situated terraced house.

£ 6 bedrooms (2 fmly) No smoking No children under 15yrs 🛏

SPINKSTOWN FARMHOUSE ▨▨▨▨
KY16 8PN

(2m E of St Andrews on A917 to Crail, 3rd farmhouse on R)

☎ 01334 473475 ⓕ 01334 473475

Guests are warmly welcomed to this modern and spacious farmhouse amid the gentle rolling Fife countryside.

£ 3 bedrooms No smoking No dogs 250 acres arable cattle

AMBERSIDE ▨▨▨
4 Murray Pk KY16 9AW

☎ 01334 474644

In a terraced row close to the sea with comfortable, fresh and inviting bedrooms.

£ 6 bedrooms (2 fmly) No smoking No dogs (ex guide dogs) 🛏

HAZLEBANK PRIVATE HOTEL ▨▨▨
28 The Scores KY16 9AS

☎ 01334 472466 ⓕ 01334 472466

In a terraced row near the Old Course, this hotel has modern, comfortable bedrooms; several with bay views.

££ 10 bedrooms (6 fmly) No smoking in dining room No dogs (ex guide dogs) Licensed Closed 16 Dec-31 Jan 🛏

WEST PARK HOUSE ▨▨▨
5 St Mary's Place KY16 9UY

(to the W end of Market St, just beyond Hope Park Church)

☎ 01334 475933

Attractive Georgian house offering good value accommodation. Two ground floor bedrooms.

£ 4 bedrooms (1 fmly) No smoking No dogs (ex guide dogs) Closed Jan 🛏

YORKSTON HOUSE ▨▨▨
68 & 70 Argyle St KY16 9BU

(400 yards from petrol station and West Port)

☎ 01334 472019 ⓕ 01334 472019

Long established family run guest house with mostly spacious, tastefully decorated bedrooms.

£ 10 bedrooms (2 fmly) No smoking in 1 bedrooms, dining room or lounges No dogs Licensed Closed Xmas & New Year

ARRAN HOUSE ▨▨
5 Murray Park KY16 9AW

☎ 01334 474724 ⓕ 01334 474724

Comfortable guest house in a terrace offers bedrooms of various sizes. Carefully prepared breakfasts.

£ 5 bedrooms (2 fmly) No smoking No dogs 🛏

BEACHWAY HOUSE ▨▨
6 Murray Park KY16 9AW

☎ 01334 473319

In a terraced row, near the sea and central amenities, this personally run guest house offers good value.

6 bedrooms (2 fmly) Closed Jan

BURNESS HOUSE ▨▨
Murray Park KY16 9AW

☎ 01334 474314 ⓕ 01334 474314

Genial hospitality and personal attention at this terraced, centrally situated home.

£ 6 bedrooms (2 fmly) No smoking in 3 bedrooms, dining room or lounges No dogs (ex guide dogs)

CLEVEDEN HOUSE ▨▨
3 Murray Place KY16 9AP

(A91 into St.Andrews, over 2 rdbts into North St. L into Murray Place after lights)

☎ 01334 474212 ⓕ 01344 474212

Good value accommodation is offered at this friendly terraced establishment.

£ 6 bedrooms (1 fmly) No smoking in bedrooms or dining room No dogs (ex guide dogs)

STRATHMIGLO

WESTER CASH FARMHOUSE ▨▨▨
Wester Cash Farm KY14 7RG

(exit M90 J8 onto A91, through Burnside & Gateside, take 2nd sign for Strathmiglo (& Falkland) A912, 2nd R, farm on hill)

☎ 01337 860215 ⓕ 01337 860215

Overlooking the Lomond Hills with comfortably traditional lounge. Enjoyable home cooked farmhouse fare.

£ 3 bedrooms (1 fmly) No dogs Parking 400 acres arable

CAMPING & CARAVANNING

ELIE

SHELL BAY CARAVAN PARK
KY9 1HB
(1.5m NW of Elie off A917, signed off unclass road.) Signposted Nearby town: Leven
☎ 01333 330283
Family Park
Large, mainly static holiday site utilizing natural coastal area of a secluded bay, with direct access to beach. 5 acres with 120 touring pitches and 250 statics.
Open 21 Mar–Oct Booking advisable Jul–Aug Last arrival 20.00hrs Last departure noon 🛏

KIRKCALDY

DUNNIKIER CARAVAN PARK
Dunnikier Way KY1 3ND
(From A92 (signed Kirkcaldy) travel S, at 1st rndbt turn W onto B891, and site on right in 500 yds after Asda store.) Signposted
☎ 01592 267563 & 266701
De-Luxe Park
A level site set in mature parkland adjacent to the B981 but screened by trees. 8 acres with 60 touring pitches.
Open Mar–Jan Booking advisable peak periods Last arrival 19.00hrs Last departure noon

LUNDIN LINKS

WOODLAND GARDENS CARAVAN & CAMPING SITE
Blindwell Rd KY8 5QG
(turn off A915 at E end of town, signposted on A915) Nearby town: Leven
☎ 01333 360319
Family Park
A secluded and sheltered site off the A917 coast road at Largo. Approach along narrow, well signed road. 1-acre with 20 touring pitches and 5 statics.
Open Mar–Oct Booking advisable Jul–Aug Last arrival 22.00hrs Last departure 10.00hrs

ST ANDREWS

CRAIGTOUN MEADOWS HOLIDAY PARK
Mount Melville KY16 8PQ *(2m from St Andrews on the Craigtoun road.) Signposted*
☎ 01334 475959
Premier Park
An attractive site set unobtrusively in mature woodlands with large pitches in hedged paddocks, 2m from sea and sandy beaches. 10 acres with 98 touring pitches and 143 statics.
Open Mar–Oct Booking advisable bank hols & Jun–Aug Last arrival 21.00hrs Last departure 13.00hrs Adult mini-gymnasium. 🛏

KINKELL BRAES CARAVAN SITE
KY16 8PX
(On A917 1m S of St Andrews.)
☎ 01334 474250
Family Park
A mainly static site with touring area giving views across St Andrews and the Eden estuary. 4 acres with 100 touring pitches and 392 statics.
Open 21 Mar–Oct Booking advisable Jun–Aug Last departure noon 🛏

ST MONANS

ST MONANS CARAVAN PARK
KY10 2DN
(On A917, 100yds E of St Monans.) Signposted Nearby town: St Andrews
☎ 01333 730778 & 310185
Family Park
Mainly static site on fringe of coastal village adjacent to main road and public park. 1 acre with 18 touring pitches and 112 statics.
Open 21 Mar–Oct Booking advisable Jul–Aug Last arrival 22.00hrs Last departure noon

WHERE TO EAT
FIFE
RESTAURANTS
AA RECOMMENDED

ANSTRUTHER

CELLAR RESTAURANT ❀ ❀ ❀
24 East Green KY10 3AA
☎ 01333 310378
Seafood is the main theme. A signature dish of roasted monkfish and scallops with herb, garlic and spiced butter and courgette and pepper stew is typical. Other delights are marinated herring, crayfish bisque, pan-seared scallops served simply with chopped mushrooms.
Fixed D £££ ALC ££ 🛏

CUPAR

EDEN HOUSE HOTEL ❀
2 Pitscottie Road KY15 4HF
☎ 01334 652510 📠 01334 652277
Good use of local ingredients results in honest dishes such as salmon terrine with dill mayonnaise, and grilled fillet of halibut with tangy citrus butter, followed perhaps by spicy apple strudel.
Fixed D ££ ALC ££ 🛏

Cellar Restaurant

OSTLERS CLOSE RESTAURANT ❀ ❀ ❀
Bonnygate, KY15 4BU
☎ 01334 655574 📠 01334 654036
Signature dishes include new season's lamb saddle with caramelised shallots and coriander; seared scallops on a bed of samphire and the Gamekeeper's Bag - a roast selection of local game. Desserts are equally delicious - home-made honey, Drambuie and oatmeal ice-cream for instance.
ALC £££ 🛏

Ostlers Close Restaurant

restaurant in rural Fife might start with pan-fried venison liver and kidney with rhubarb in a rich red wine sauce, followed by delicious whole lobster poached in a vegetable and herb broth, and to finish caramelised banana with white chocolate mousse.

Fixed D £££ 🍷

DUNFERMLINE

KEAVIL HOUSE HOTEL ❀
Crossford, KY12 8QW
📞 01383 736258 📠 01383 621600
Keeping faith with Scottish produce dishes such as Shetland salmon with malt whisky cream and braised topside of Perthshire beef with a red wine and shallot demi-glace will appear on the menu.

Fixed L £ ALC ££ 🍷

GLENROTHES

RESCOBIE HOTEL ❀
Valley Drive Leslie KY6 3BQ
📞 01592 742143 📠 01592 620231
Food is a high priority at this hotel and menus might feature crab bisque with white wine, monkfish wrapped in bacon and a 'simply wicked' chocolate pot.

Fixed D ££ 🍷

KINCARDINE-ON-FORTH

UNICORN INN ❀❀
15 Excise Street, FK10 4LN
📞 01259 730704 📠 01259 731567
A rustic bistro producing an eclectic range of dishes with a forthright Mediterranean bias. For instance whole roasted vine tomatoes with samphire and roasted duck with melted onions and Marsala. Lime mousse topped with fresh strawberries makes a good finale.

Fixed L £ ALC ££ 🍷

LETHAM

FERNIE CASTLE HOTEL ❀
Cupar, KY7 7RU
📞 01337 810381 📠 01337 810422,
Up-to-date dishes along the lines of salad of seared red mullet with ratatouille and cherry tomato coulis, and honey roasted duck breast with sweet potato rösti and wild cherry sauce.

ALC ££ 🍷

LUNDIN LINKS

OLD MANOR HOTEL ❀❀
Leven Road, KY8 6AJ
📞 01333 320368 📠 01333 320911
Look out for the house speciality, 'Symphony of Seafood', a combination of local fish and shellfish lightly steamed on a saffron sauce. Main courses feature roasted loin of smoked lamb and the grilled Aberdeen Angus steaks.

Fixed L £ ALC £££ 🍷

MARKINCH

BALBIRNIE HOUSE ❀❀
Balbirnie Park, KY7 6NE
📞 01592 610066 📠 01592 610529
Traditional Scottish produce influences the menus as in Glen Moray smoked salmon, roast rack of lamb with pesto crust, seared halibut and prime Scottish steaks.

Fixed D £££ 🍷

PEAT INN

THE PEAT INN ❀❀❀
KY15 5LH
📞 01334 840206 📠 01334 840530
A typical dinner at this charming

ST ANDREWS

THE OLD COURSE HOTEL ❀❀
KY16 9SP
📞 01334 474371 📠 01334 477668
Moodern and international dishes include seared loin of venison with arugula, and egg plant, and for those more classic combinations there is braised veal shin with mustard sauce, carrots and garlic potatoes and seared halibut with grilled fennel and Provençale vinaigrette.

Fixed L ££ ALC £££ 🍷

PARKLAND HOTEL ❀
Kinburn Castle Double Dykes Road KY16 9DS
📞/📠 01334 473620
Sound skills are evident in dishes such as breast of pheasant with wild mushrooms and rich game sauce, collops of Angus fillet steak with a mustard grain and whisky cream sauce, and crème caramel with summer berries.

Fixed L £ 🍷

RUFFLETS ❀❀❀
Strathkinness KY16 9TX
📞 01334 472594 📠 01334 478703
In the civilised setting of The Garden Restaurant the menu might include a warm salad of king scallops seared with ginger, spring onion and lime juice, fillet of lamb baked with minted pine kernel crust, and iced cranachan parfait with a compote of local berries.

Fixed L ££ 🍷

ST ANDREWS GOLF HOTEL ❀
40 The Scores, KY16 9AS
📞 01334 472611 📠 01334 472188
The kitchen delivers an ambitious menu of lasagne of Tay salmon and asparagus, breast of Kildrummy pheasant, the thigh boned and filled with smoked ham forcemeat, and baked chocolate tart.

Fixed L £ ALC £££ 🍷

PUBS, INNS & OTHER PLACES

ANSTRUTHER

THE DREEL TAVERN
16 High St Fife KY10 3DL
📞 01333 310727
16th-century coaching inn with oak beams and coal fire. The menu offers ploughman's, fish or steak pie, burgers, baked potatoes and fried chicken, with daily specials.

ELIE

THE SHIP INN
Fife KY9 1DT *(Follow A915 & A917 to Elie. Follow signs from High St to Watersport Centre to the Toft)*
📞 01333 330246
Traveller's hostelry since 1838, only feet away from the beach of Elie Bay. On offer is a wide ranging menu.

Accommodation £

FALKLAND

KIND KYTTOCK'S KITCHEN
Cross Wynd Fife KY15 7BE
(A92 N from Glenrothes and take A912)
📞 01337 857477
Country tea room in a listed building. Lunchtime offerings include Scotch broth with home-made wholemeal bread, pizzas, salads and sandwiches.

STIRLING & LOCH LOMOND, PERTH & KINROSS

STIRLING & LOCH LOMOND area is one of Scotland's hauntingly beautiful places – particularly the treasured mountain landscape of the Trossachs, once the domain of the famous 18th-century hero/outlaw, Rob Roy MacGregor.

From Callander, the gateway to the Highlands, you can easily reach Loch Lomond, the largest and one of the most romantic lochs in Scotland, famed in song.
If you've seen the film Braveheart then you'll want to visit Stirling, with its imposing castle perched on a rock. At Bannockburn Robert the Bruce famously routed the English.

PERTH & KINROSS district, sheltered by the Grampian Mountains, is often regarded as the Heart of Scotland, and its mountains, lochs and glens yearn to be explored.

Just outside the ancient city of Perth is Scone, home of the mystical Stone of Destiny, on which 42 Scottish Kings were crowned. Not far south-west lies the world-famous Gleneagles Hotel, with its fine golf courses and wealth of sports and leisure facilities.

The Tay Valley is one of the region's most scenic features, with its popular holiday resorts of Pitlochry and Blair Atholl, while Rannoch Moor is a magnificent wilderness that represents one of Scotland's great walking experiences.

PRINCIPAL TOWNS

STIRLING

Dominated by one of Scotland's grandest castles, perched high on a rocky crag, Stirling, is, undoubtedly, Scotland's heritage capital and should be top of everyone's 'must see' list. Visit Stirling Visitor Centre, for a fascinating audio-visual tour through 1,000 years of history.

CALLANDER

Set against a craggy Highland backdrop, Callander is a bustling, colourful holiday town, on the edge of The Trossachs in the heart of Rob Roy country.

PERTH

Once Scotland's capital, this commercial centre with its port on the Tay estuary and fine Georgian buildings, maintains the atmosphere of a country town and is now a favoured base from which to explore Central Scotland.

PITLOCHRY

With its setting on the wooded banks of the Tummel, this Victorian town is one of Scotland's premier resorts, and has a famous summer drama festival. Nearby are Blair Castle, the Pass of Killiecrankie and the beauty spot known as The Queen's View.

MUST SEE

BANNOCKBURN HERITAGE CENTRE,
Bannockburn, Stirling ☎ 01786 812664
The Heritage Centre stands close to the Borestone site, which by tradition was King Robert the Bruce's command post before the Battle of Bannockburn, June 1324, at which the Scots trounced the English. Displays of Scottish life and historical characters, audio-visual display of the battle and a bronze equestrian statue of Bruce.

BLAIR DRUMMOND SAFARI & LEISURE PARK,
Blair Drummond, Stirling ☎ 01786 841456
Drive through the wild animal reserves and see at close range the monkeys, zebras, North American bison, antelope, tigers and camels. Other attractions include a pet farm, sea lion show, a boat safari through the waterfowl sanctuary, an adventure playground, giant astraglide and pedal boats.

CASTLE CAMPBELL,
Dollar, Stirling ☎ 01259 742408
Traditionally known as the 'Castle of Gloom', this impressive 15th-to 17th-century tower is accessible by car or a dramatic walk through the magnificent Dollar Glen. Once owned by the 1st Earl of Argyll, Chancellor of Scotland to King James IV, it stands high in the Ochil Hills above a wooded glen and commands wonderful views from its ramparts.

DOUNE CASTLE,
Doune, Stirling ☎ 01786 841742
Built in the 14th century on the banks of the River Teith by Robert Stewart, Duke of Albany, it is regarded as the finest surviving medieval stronghold in Scotland. A formidable range of buildings, including a striking tower, gatehouse and hall, surround an inner courtyard.

ART GALLERIES

ALLOA GALLERY & MUSEUM,
29 Primrose St, Alloa, Clackmannanshire
☎ 01259 213131
History and arts exhibitions.

THE GREEN GALLERY,
Aberfoyle, Stirling ☎ 01877 382873
Paintings, ceramics and unusual crafts.

INVERBEG GALLERIES,
Inverbeg, Argyll & Bute ☎ 01436 860277
Oil and watercolour paintings.

SMITH ART GALLERY & MUSEUM,
Dumbarton Rd, Stirling ☎ 01786 471917
Lively, award-winning museum and gallery.

MUSEUMS

BREADALBANE FOLKLORE CENTRE,
Killin, Stirling ☎ 01567 820254
Discover the fascinating tales and legends of Breadalbane, from ancient prophesies to mythical giants.

Queen Elizabeth Forest Park, Visitor Centre

HILL HOUSE,
Helensburgh, Argyll & Bute
☎ 01436 673900
An exquisite building, built in 1904 as the family home of the Glasgow publisher Walter Blackie, complete with original furnishings, is renowned as the finest domestic masterpiece of the Scottish architect, Charles Rennie Mackintosh

NATIONAL WALLACE MONUMENT,
Causewayhead, Stirling ☎ 01786 472140
This 220ft tower was built in 1869 and recalls Scotland's first freedom fighter William Wallace; his two-handed sword is preserved inside. Displays include a Hall of Heroes, and a audio-visual show on the life of Wallace, the Forth Panorama. Seven battlefields and a fine view towards the Highlands can be seen from the top.

QUEEN ELIZABETH FOREST PARK,
☎ 01877 382258
Vast upland forest stretching from Loch Lomond into the heart of the Trossachs. 100km of woodland trails, forest drives and cycle routes. Information, exhibitions and audio-visual displays about the Forest Park at the Visitor Centre, Aberfoyle.

BYGONES MUSEUM & BALQUIHIDDER VISITOR CENTRE,
Balquihidder, Lochearnhead, Stirling
☎ 01877 384688
Collection of everyday items, curios and toys of the past displayed in a typical Laird's mansion overlooking Loch Voil. Tearoom & shop.

THE CATHEDRAL MUSEUM,
Dunblane, Stirling ☎ 01786 823440
Houses an array of ancient religious relics and fragments of choir stalls, one of only two sets surviving from the middle ages.

DOUNE MOTOR MUSEUM,
Doune, Stirling ☎ 01786 841203
See the second oldest surviving Rolls Royce at this private collection of over 50 historic vehicles.

MENSTRIE CASTLE,
Menstrie, Clackmannanshire
☎ 01259 213131
Restored 16th-century tower house

ROB ROY & TROSSACHS VISITOR CENTRE,
Callendar, Stirling ☎ 01877 330342
The fascinating history of Scotland's most famous outlaw, Rob Roy MacGregor, is vividly portrayed through an exciting multi-media theatre and explained in the carefully researched 'Life & Times' exhibition. There is also a spectacular cinematic introduction to the Trossachs.

STIRLING CASTLE,
Upper Castle Hill, Stirling ☎ 01786 450000
Set on a high rocky outdrop with a breathtaking panorama, this former royal court is considered by many to be the grandest of Scotland's castles. Much of the castle that remains today dates from the 15th and 16th centuries. Among its finest features are the splendid Renaissance palace built by James V, and the Chapel Royal, rebuilt by James VI.

> Call the AA Hotel Booking Service on
> **0990 050505 to book at AA recognised
> hotels and B&Bs in the UK,
> or through our internet site:
> http://www.theaa.co.uk/hotels**

containing a small exhibition on the adventures of Sir William Alexander, poet and founder of Nova Scotia, who was born here.

MUSEUM OF THE ARGYLL & SUTHERLAND HIGHLANDERS,
The Castle, Stirling ☎ 01786 475165
Learn about the history of the regiment from 1794 to the present day, through displays of uniforms, silver, paintings and a fine medal collection.

ROYAL BURGH OF STIRLING VISITOR CENTRE,
Castle Esplanade, Stirling ☎ 01786 462517
Dicover the story of Royal Stirling from the Wars of Independence through life in the medieval burgh to the present day.

SCOTTISH MARITIME MUSEUM,
Castle St, Dumbarton, West Dumbartonshire
☎ 01389 763444
Step back in time to the days of the Victorian ship designer. See the Denny

Experiment Tank, the world's first commercial experimental tank for shipbuilders' scale models, built in 1882 and used for over 100 years.

HISTORIC & ANCIENT SITES

ALLOA TOWER,
Alloa, Clackmannanshire ☎ 01259 211701
A traditional, beautifully restored 14th-century tower house.

CAMBUSKENNETH ABBEY,
Stirling
The remains of a once great abbey, founded in about 1147 by Augustinian Canons, including an attractive, free-standing 13th-century belfry. It was the scene of Robert Bruce's Parliament in 1326 and the burial place of James III and his Queen.

DUMBARTON CASTLE,
Dumbarton, West Dunbartonshire
☎ 01389 732167
Remains of a fortress built on the natural defensive site of Dunbarton Rock. Mary Queen of Scots stayed here before her departure for France in 1548.

DUNBLANE CATHEDRAL,
Dunblane, Stirlingshire ☎ 01786 823388
The seat of the Bishop of the Diocese of Dunblane since the 13th century. Predominantly Gothic, with the lower parts of the tower being Romanesque, and several 19th and 20th century restorations, including a new roof in 1893 after being roofless for 300 years. Well worth exploring for its many treasures.

INCHMAHOME PRIORY,
Port of Monteith, Stirling ☎ 01877 385284
Ruins of an Augustinian house, built on an island in the Lake of Monteith in 1328 and famous as the retreat of the infant Mary, Queen of Scots in 1543.

MARS WARK,
Broad St, Stirling ☎ 0131 668 8800
Now partly ruined, this ornate Renaissance-style mansion, built in 1570, features a gatehouse enriched with sculptures.

ROB ROY'S GRAVE,
Balquihidder, Stirling
The final resting place of the notorious outlaw Rob Roy, along with his wife and their four sons.

GREAT FOR KIDS

COVE CONSERVATION PARK.
Cove, Helensburgh, Argyll & Bute
☎ 01436 850123
Set in 50 acres of unspoilt countryside, it features an entertaining 'hands-on' approach to rare breeds and sustainable energy resources. Tearoom.

HAMILTON TOY COLLECTION,
Main St, Callendar, Stirling ☎ 01877 330004
Interesting family collection of toys dating from 1880 to 1980. Collectors shop.

LOCH LOMOND PARK CENTRE,
The Old Station, Balloch Rd, Balloch, West Dunbartonshire ☎ 01389 758216
Offers a fascinating insight into one of Scotland's most famous stretches of inland water.

OLD TOWN JAIL,
St John St, Stirling ☎ 01786 450050
Learn about the daily life of the prisoners through this living history performance set within the old prison, built in 1874 and an outstanding example of Victorian architecture.

SCOTTISH WOOL CENTRE,
Aberfoyle, Stirling ☎ 01877 382850
Discover the history of sheep in Scotland and the story of wool from sheep to the shops, through films, working sheepdogs and hands-on demonstrations of spinning and weaving. Children's farm.

HOMES & GARDENS

THE LINN GARDENS,
Cove, Helensburgh, Argyll & Bute
☎ 01436 842242
Extensive water garden, formal ponds, herbaceous borders, glen with waterfall and cliff garden, all set around an Italianate villa.

BIG OUTDOORS

BRACKLINN FALLS,
Bracklinn Rd, Callendar, Stirling
Impressive wooded gorge with a series of dramatic falls on the Keltie Water. Accessed via a pleasant woodland walk.

CALLENDAR CRAGS,
Callendar, Stirling
Steep crags overlooking a dense bowl of woodland above the town. Good woodland walks.

CULCREUCH CASTLE & COUNTRY PARK,
Fintry, Stirling ☎ 01360 860555
Scotland's oldest inhabited castle surrounded by magnificent parkland.

FALLS OF LENY,
Callendar, Stirling
Foaming waterfall at the narrow Pass of Leny.

OCHIL HILLS WOODLAND PARK,
Alva, Clackmannanshire ☎ 01259 213131
Scenic woodland walks, informative visitor centre, craft shop and café. Nearby Alva and Hillfoot Glens are worth exploring.

THE TROSSACHS
A beautiful combination of hills, burns, woods and lochs, the Trossachs stretch from Callendar to the shores of Loch Lomond and offers some of Scotland's most spectacular views. A paradise for outdoor enthusiasts, vistors have the opportunity to enjoy walking, climbing, cycling, fishing, birdwatching and a wide range of watersports.

ESSENTIAL INFORMATION

TOURIST INFORMATION

ARGYLL, THE ISLES, LOCH LOMOND, STIRLING & TROSSACHS TOURIST BOARD,
Old Town Jail, St John St, Stirling FK8 1EA
☎ 01786 445222 ☎ 01786 471301
ABERFOYLE *seasonal,*
Main St, Aberfoyle, Stirlingshire
☎ 01877 382352
ALVA,
Mill Trial Visitor Centre, West Stirling St, Clackmannanshire ☎ 01259 769696
BALLOCH *seasonal,*
Balloch Rd, Balloch, West Dunbartonshire
☎ 01389 753533
CALLANDER *seasonal,*
Rob Roy & Trossachs Visitor Centre, Ancaster Sq, Callander, Stirlingshire
☎ 01877 330342

DRYMEN *seasonal,*
The Square, Drymen, Stirlingshire
☎ 01360 660068
DUMBARTON,
Milton, Dumbarton, West Dunbartonshire (A82 northbound) ☎ 01389 742306
DUNBLANE *seasonal,*
Stirling Rd, Dunblane, Stirlingshire
☎ 01786 824428
HELENSBURGH *seasonal*
Clock Tower, The Pier, Helensburgh, Argyll & Bute ☎ 01436 672642
KILLIN *seasonal,*
Breadalbane Folk Centre, Falls of Dochart, Killin, Stirlingshire ☎ 01567 820254
STIRLING,
41 Dumbarton Rd, Stirlingt
Royal Burgh of Stirling Visitor Centre, Castle Esplanade, Stirling ☎ 01786 479901

TARBET *seasonal,*
Tarbet, Loch Lomond, Argyll & Bute
☎ 01301 702260

ACCESS

AIR ACCESS

GLASGOW AIRPORT ☎ 0141 887 1111

CRAFTS

Lookout for hand-made ceramics, pottery and porcelain, batik work, spinning and weaving, knitwear, bagpipe making, jewellery and glass-making.

BUCHLYVIE POTTERY SHOP,
Buchlyvie, Stirling ☎ 01360 850405

GRAHAM STEWART GOLD & SILVERSMITH
High St, Dunblane, Stirling ☎ 01786 825244
HANDLOOM WEAVERS,
Tarbet, Argyll & Bute ☎ 01301 702685
HERONCRAFT SCOTLAND,
Taigh Na Corra, Ghriothaich, Strathyre,
Stirling ☎ 01877 384618
Hand-made Highland dresswear.

MADDY MOSS LTD,
Glentana Mill, West Stirling St, Alva,
Clackmannanshire ☎ 01259 762756
Traditional Scottish woollens.

OCHIL CRAFT ASSOCIATION,
Alva, Clackmannanshire ☎ 01259 715363
ROB ROY TRYST CRAFT CENTRE,
Balquhidder, Stirling ☎ 01877 384646.
THISTLE BAGPIPE WORKS,
Luss, Argyll & Bute ☎ 01436 860250
VILLAGE GLASS,
Bridge of Allan, Stirling ☎ 01786 832137

ENTERTAINMENT
THEATRES

MACROBERT ARTS CENTRE,
Stirling ☎ 01786 461081

FOOD & DRINK
WHISKY DISTILLERY TOURS

GLENGOYNE DISTILLERY,
Dumgoyne, Killearn, Stirling
☎ 01360 550254
Scotland's most scenic distillery.

TRANSPORT
BOAT TRIPS & CRUISES

CLYDE MARINE CRUISES,
Helensburgh, Argyll & Bute ☎ 01475 721281

CRUISE LOCH LOMOND LTD,
Tarbet, Argyll & Bute ☎ 01301 702356

MACFARLANE & SON,
Balmaha, Stirling ☎ 01360 870214
Cruises, boat hire on Loch Lomond.

MULLENS CRUISES,
Balloch North Marina, Riverside, Balloch,
West Dunbartonshire ☎ 01389 751481
Daily cruises on Loch Lomond.

SINBAD CHARTERS,
Aidenkyle House, Kilcreggan, Helensburgh,
Argyll & Bute ☎ 01436 842247
Sailing the scenic Firth of Forth.

SS SIR WALTER SCOTT,
Trossachs Pier Complex, Loch Katrine,
Callander, Stirling ☎ 01877 376316
Historic steamship cruises on Loch Katrine.

CAR HIRE

EUROPCAR INTER RENT,
Drip Rd, Stirling FK8 1RB
☎ 01786 472164
HARDIE OF STIRLING,
Kerse Rd, Stirling FK7 7RT
☎ 01786 451616

COACH/MINI-BUS TOURS

CLAYMORE TRAVEL,
☎/⊞ 01324 551919
Guided mini-bus tours.

THE HIGHLAND ROVER,
84 Cardross Rd, Dumbarton, West
Dunbartonshire ☎/⊞ 01389 761265
'Classic Car' personalised tours with
chauffeur guide.

MIDLAND BLUEBIRD LTD,
☎ 01324 613777
Bus and coach charter; day tours and
excursions.

**STAGS (STIRLING TOURS & GUIDING
SERVICES)**
☎ 01786 446044
Open-top bus tours of Stirling.

CYCLE HIRE

HELENSBURGH CYCLES,
39 East Clyde St, Helensburgh, Argyll & Bute
☎ 01436 675239
KILLIN OUTDOOR CENTRE,
Killin, Stirling ☎ 01576 820652
LOCHSIDE MOUNTAIN BIKE HIRE,
Arrochar, Argyll & Bute ☎ 01301 702467
LOMOND ACTIVITIES,
64 Main St, Drymen, Loch Lomond, Stirling
☎ 01360 660066
TROSSACHS CYCLE HIRE,
Trossachs Holiday Park, Aberfoyle, Stirling
☎ 01877 382614
WHEELS CYCLE HIRE,
Callendar, Stirlingshire ☎ 01877 331100
WILDCAT CYCLES,
Bridge of Allan, Stirling ☎/⊞ 01786 832321

TRAINS

Main lines from Glasgow and Edinburgh
pass through Stirling, en route to Perth
and Dundee. Scotrail ☎ 0345 550033

SPORT & LEISURE
ACTIVITY & LEISURE CENTRES

ALLOA LEISURE BOWL,
Park Way, Alloa, Clackmannanshire
☎ 01259 723527
JOHN COCKBURN OFF ROAD,
Cambusbarron, Stirling ☎ 01786 448356
FINTRY SPORTS & RECREATION CENTRE,
Fintry, Stirling ☎ 01360 860205
HOWIE IRVINE LOCH LOMOND,
Arden, Argyll & Bute ☎ 01389 850660
MEADOW SPORTS CENTRE,
Dumbarton, West Dunbartonshire
☎ 01389 734094
RAINBOW SLIDES LEISURE CENTRE,
Goosecroft Rd, Stirling ☎
SHANDON COUNTRY PURSUITS LTD,
Shandon, Helensburgh, Argyll & Bute
☎ 01436 820838
☎ 01786 462521

ANGLING

Tumbling streams and burns and lochs are
the habitat of wild brown trout, sea trout
and the mighty salmon. Loch Tay at Killin
and the Rivers Teith, Devon, Allan and

Forth and Loch Lomond are best for
salmon and sea trout. Pike and perch can
be fished in Loch Lomond, and excellent,
inexpensive trout fishing can be enjoyed in
the Trossachs on Lochs Ard and Vennachar
and the Lake of Menteith, as well as at
Gartmorn Dam in Clackmannanshire. The
sheltered waters around Helensburgh on
the Firth of Clyde provide pier fishing
locations and boat hire.

CYCLING

From scenic country lanes and level
lochside roads to well waymarked off-rd
trails through forests, notably the Queen
Elizabeth Forest Park, Loch Lomond,
Stirling and The Trossachs offer a wealth of
opportunities for cyclists of all abilities.
The private road beside magnificent Loch
Katrine in Rob Roy Country offers excellent
traffic-free cycling for families.

CYCLING HOLIDAYS

WILDCAT CYCLE TOURS,
15a Henderson St, Bridge of Allan, Stirling
☎ 01786 832321

GOLF COURSES

ABERFOYLE,
Stirling ☎ 01877 382493
ALLOA,
Clackmannanshire ☎ 01259 722745
ALVA,
Clackmannanshire ☎ 01259 760431
BRIDGE OF ALLAN,
Stirling ☎ 01786 832332
BUCHANAN CASTLE,
Drymen, Stirling ☎ 01360 660307
CALLANDER,
Stirling ☎ 01877 330090 & 330975
CARDROSS,
Argyll & Bute ☎/⊞ 01389 841754
DOLLAR,
Clackmannanshire ☎ 01259 742400
DUMBARTON,
West Dunbartonshire ☎ 01389 732830
DUNBLANE,
Stirling ☎ 01786 823711
HELENSBURGH,
Argyll & Bute ☎ 01436 674173
KILLIN,
Stirling ☎ 01567 820312
LOCH LOMOND,
Luss, Argyll & Bute ☎ 01436 860223
MUCKHART,
Clackmannanshire ☎ 01259 781423
STIRLING ☎ 01786 464098
TILLICOULTRY,
Clackmannanshire ☎ 01259 750124

GREYHOUND RACING

CORBIEWOOD STADIUM LTD,
Bannockburn, Stirling

ICE SKATING

STIRLING ICE RINK,
Williamfield, Stirling ☎ 01786 450389

RIDING

CLAISH FARM PONY TREKKING,
Callendar, Stirlingshire ☎ 01877 330647

COLGRAIN EQUESTRIAN CENTRE,
Cardross, West Dunbartonshire
☎ 01389 842022
DEVON RIVER RIDING CENTRE,
Howe Town, Fishcross, Alloa,
Clackmannanshire ☎ 01259 216992
DUNCRYNE TREKKING CENTRE,
Gartocharn, Loch Lomond, West
Dunbartonshire ☎ 01389 830425
EASTERHILL FARM TREKKING CENTRE,
Gartmore, Aberfoyle, Stirling
☎ 01877 382875
LOMONDSIDE EQUESTRIAN CENTRE,
Drymen, Stirling ☎ 01360 660481
MAPLE LEAF QUARTER HORSES,
Clynder, Argyll & Bute ☎ 01436 831214
MYOTHILL HOUSE EQUESTRIAN CENTRE,
Denny, Stirling ☎ 01324 823420

SCENIC DRIVES

In the Trossachs take the meandering
Duke's Pass from Aberfoyle for spectacular
views of lochs and forests, then escape
the crowds and enjoy seven miles of
peaceful forest rd beside Lochs Drunkie
and Achray.

SKIING

FIRPARK SKI CENTRE,
Tillicoultry, Clackmannanshire
☎ 01259 213131
Dry ski slope.

SWIMMING

See also Leisure Centres

HELENSBURGH SWIMMING POOL,
West Clyde St, Argyll & Bute

VALE OF LEVEN SWIMMING POOL,
Argyll Park, Alexandria, West Dunbartonshire
☎ 01389 756931

WALKING

Forest walks and strolls abound within the
Queen Elizabeth Forest Park on well
waymarked trails (leaflets/routes available
at information centres). More adventurous
hikers can enjoy walking the open
hillsides of the Trossach hills, notably
massive Ben Lawers, and the peaks
around Loch Lomond. Gentler walking
terrain can be found in the Ochil Hills and
across the Campsie Fells.

WEST HIGHLAND WAY

A 95mile (153km) long-distance walk
linking Milngavie, near Glasgow in the
Lowlands, to Fort William in the heart of
the Highlands. Best walked from the
south, it follows close to the eastern shore
of Loch Lomond, and beneath the lower
slopes of Ben Lomond, before ascending
old drove roads into the Highlands to
reach Glencoe and Ben Nevis.

WALKING HOLIDAYS/TOURS

ABOUT ARGYLL WALKING HOLIDAYS,
☎/☎ 01369 860274

C-N-DO SCOTLAND LTD
☎ 01786 445703
Guided walks, rock climbing and
navigation instruction.

LOMOND WALKING HOLIDAYS,
☎ 01786 447752
Guided day and week-long walks in the
Trossachs, Ochil Hills, Loch Lomond and
Arrochar areas.

WILD COUNTRY EXPEDITIONS,
☎ 01389 731875
Wildlife walking holidays.

WATERSPORTS

ARDULI HOTEL,
MARINA & HOLIDAY PARK,
Loch Lomond, Argyll & Bute
☎ 01301 704242

LOCHEARNHEAD WATERSPORTS LTD,
Lochearnhead, Stirling ☎ 01567 830330

LOCH LOMOND WATER SKI CLUB,
☎ 01389 753000

Sir Walter Scott

WHERE TO STAY

AA RECOMMENDED

Roman Camp Country House

ALLOA

GEAN HOUSE ★★★ ֎֎
Gean Park, Tullibody Rd FK10 2HS
(W of town centre off B9096)
☎ 01259 219275 ⓕ 01259 213827
Small country house hotel of distinction,
peacefully set amid wooded parkland.
Imaginative modern cuisine.
*£££ 7 bedrooms No dogs No smoking in
restaurant* ➤

BALLOCH

CAMERON HOUSE HOTEL ★★★★ ֎֎֎
G83 8QZ
☎01389 755565 ⓕ 01389 759522
*(from Glasgow Airport M8, Erskine Toll
Bridge A82 follow signs Loch
Lomond/Crianlarich, at Balloch rdbt follow
signs for Luss for 1m, first R)*
Beautifully situated luxurious hotel where
you are made to feel cosseted and
important by professional and courteous
staff. Superb cuisine.
*96 bedrooms (9 fmly) (no smoking in some)
No dogs (ex guide dogs) Lift Night porter
Indoor swimming pool Golf Tennis Fishing
Squash Snooker Sauna Solarium Gym Pool
Croquet Jacuzzi/spa Laserclays Archery
Quad bikes Hovercrafts Childrens facilities*
➤

ARBOR LODGE ◙◙◙
Old Luss Rd G83 8QW
(400yds from Glasgow to Loch Lomond road)
☎ 01389 756334 ⓕ 01389 78988
Friendly guest house with attractive
bedrooms. Hearty breakfasts. Convenient
touring base.
*4 bedrooms No smoking No dogs
(ex guide dogs)* ➤

BALMAHA

MONIACK ◙◙◙◙
Moniack G63 0TQ
☎ 01360 870388 & 870357
ⓕ 01360 870350
Detached house in gardens. Thoughtful
extras include a foot spa - popular with
walkers. Owner's restaurant opposite.
*3 bedrooms (1 fmly) No smoking in
bedrooms or dining room No dogs Fishing*

BALQUHIDDER

MONACHYLE MHOR ★★ ֎֎
FK19 8PQ
☎ 01877 384622 ⓕ 01877 384305
*(11m N of Callander on A84, turn R at
Kingshouse Hotel this road takes you under
the A84 towards Balquhidder, the hotel is 6m
on the R)*
Haven of peace and quiet and the place to
enjoy complete relaxation, good food, and
genuine warmth of welcome.
*££ 5 bedrooms (5 annexe) No dogs (ex
guide dogs) Fishing Croquet No children
under 10yrs No smoking in restaurant
Closed part Jan* ➤

STRONVAR HOUSE ◙◙◙◙
FK19 8PB
☎ 01877 384688 ⓕ 01877 384230
*(turn off A84 2m N of Strathyre, signposted
"Rob Roy's Grave", 200yds past church turn
L and follow signs)*
Victorian mansion full of character. Also a
tea room, gift shop, and Bygones Museum.
Two rooms have four-poster beds.
*££ 4 bedrooms No smoking in dining room
Licensed Mar–Oct* ➤

ROYAL ★★★
Henderson St FK9 4HG
☎ 01786 832284 ⓕ 01786 834377
*(at the end of the M9 turn R at roundabout
for Bridge of Allan. Hotel is in centre on L)*
Comfortable Victorian hotel with oak
panelled lounge and attractive restaurant.
*£££ 32 bedrooms (2 fmly) Lift Night
porter Childrens facilities No smoking area
in restaurant* ➤

**ROMAN CAMP COUNTRY HOUSE
★★★֎֎**
FK17 8BG
☎ 01877 330003 ⓕ 01877 331533
*(heading north on the A84 turn L at the east
end of Callander High street, down a 300
yard driveway into the hotel grounds)*
Charming country house hotel in idyllic
parkland. Individual bedrooms and lovely
day rooms. Innovative menu.
*£££ 14 bedrooms (3 fmly) Fishing No
smoking in restaurant* ➤

BRIDGEND HOUSE ★★
Bridgend FK17 8AH
☎ 01877 330130 ⓕ 01877 331512
*(down Callander main st, turn onto A81
(Aberfoyle) over bridge, hotel on R)*
Welcoming personally-run hotel beside
river near town centre. Characterful rooms,
pleasant gardens.
*£ 6 bedrooms (1 fmly) Pool Weekly live
entertainment Childrens facilities* ➤

DALGAIR HOUSE ★★
113 Main St FK17 8BQ
☎ 01877 330283 ⓕ 01877 331114
*(300 metres beyond access road to golf course
on main street)*
Friendly, informal family-run hotel with
pleasant open-plan public areas.
Comfortable bedrooms.
£ 8 bedrooms (1 fmly) ➤

Monachyle Mho

LUBNAIG ★★
Leny Feus FK17 8AS

(travelling W on A84 thro Callander main street to W outskirts, turn R into Leny Feus)

☎ 01877 330376 📠 01877 330376

The friendly atmosphere and enthusiastic commitment of the owners ensure that this is somewhere special. Home-cooked dinners & hearty breakfasts.

£ 6 bedrooms 4 annexe) No dogs No children under 7yrs No smoking in restaurant Closed Nov-Easter 🗲

ARRAN LODGE ⬛⬛⬛⬛⬛
Leny Rd FK17 8AJ *(on W outskirts on the A84)*

☎ 01877 330976

The owner's eye for things theatrical adds style and humour to the house. Imaginative cooking. Lovely gardens leading down to river.

£££ 4 bedrooms (1 fmly) No smoking No dogs No children under 12yrs Fishing mid Mar-Oct

ARDEN HOUSE ⬛⬛⬛⬛
Bracklinn Rd FK17 8EQ

☎ 01877 330235 📠 330235

(from A84 in Callander turn N, opposite Roman Camp. Hotel also signposted golf course and Bracklinn Falls)

Charming Victorian home with wonderful views. Excellent bedrooms Enjoyable home cooking.

£ 6 bedrooms (2 fmly) No smoking Childrens facilities Putting green Mar-Oct

BROOK LINN COUNTRY HOUSE ⬛⬛⬛⬛
Leny Feus FK17 8AU

☎ 01877 330103 📠 01877 330103

(take A84 thro Callander from Stirling, turn R at Pinewood Nursing Home into Leny Feus. R again & uphill at sign)

Sympathetically restored, elegant Victorian home with bright, airy bedrooms. Home-cooked fare. Large gardens.

£ 7 bedrooms (2 fmly) No smoking Licensed Easter-Oct

ABBOTSFORD LODGE ⬛⬛⬛
Stirling Rd FK17 8DA

☎ 01877 330066

(off A84 eastern approach to town)

Welcoming Victorian house in its own grounds offers good value accommodation. Pleasant bedrooms and lounges.

£ 18 bedrooms (7 fmly) No smoking in dining room Licensed

ALMARDON ⬛⬛⬛
Leny Rd FK17 8AJ

☎ 01877 331597

(W of town next to Meadows Park on A84)

Attractive detached bungalow offering good value and a warm welcome. Hearty breakfasts.

£ 3 bedrooms No smoking in bedrooms or dining room No dogs No children under 12yrs

Almardon

ANNFIELD ⬛⬛⬛
18 North Church St FK17 8EG

☎ 01877 330204

Good value, comfortable Victorian house. Inviting lounge featuring a foreign doll collection. Good breakfasts.

£ 7 bedrooms (1 fmly) No smoking in bedrooms or dining room No children under 10yrs Closed 20 Dec-5 Jan

HIGHLAND HOUSE ⬛⬛⬛
South Church St FK17 8BN

☎ 01877 30269

Comfortable bedrooms, genuine hospitality and good home cooking.

9 bedrooms (2 fmly) No smoking in bedrooms or dining room Licensed Closed Dec-Jan 🗲

Call the AA Hotel Booking Service on 0990 050505 to book at AA recognised hotels and B&Bs in the UK, or through our internet site: http://www.theaa.co.uk/hotels

BENMORE LODGE
FK20 8QS

☎ 01838 300210 📠 01838 300218

(300 yds out of town towards Stirling on A85)

Small lodge complex with timbered chalets. Convenient touring stop-off. Adjacent restaurant/bar.

11 annexe bedrooms (2 fmly) Fishing Canoeing Skiing Res Nov-19 Mar 🗲

THE LODGE HOUSE ⬛⬛⬛
FK20 8RU ☎ 01838 300276

(on A82, 1m NW of Crianlanich)

Welcoming house with comfortable accommodation. Nearby Scandinavian-style chalet ideal for families. Good value 5-course dinners.

£ 5 bedrooms No smoking in bedrooms or dining room Licensed Fishing Mar-Oct 🗲

GLENARDRAN GUEST HOUSE ⬛⬛
FK20 8QS ☎ 01838 300236

(beside A85 on eastern approach to village)

Good value, family-run guest house. Comfortable lounge and smart dining room.

6 bedrooms (1 fmly) No smoking Licensed 🗲

BUCHANAN ARMS ★★★
G63 0BQ

☎ 01360 660588 📠 01360 660943

(travelling N from Glasgow on A81 take A811, hotel is at the S end of Main Street)

Original coaching inn, near Loch Lomond and not far from both Glasgow and Stirling. Oak beamed bar and a very popular restaurant.

££££ 52 bedrooms (3 fmly) No smoking in 6 bedrooms Night porter Indoor swimming pool Squash Sauna Solarium Gym Jacuzzi/spa No smoking in restaurant 🗲

WINNOCK ★★
The Square G63 0BL

☎ 01360 660245 📠 660267

Welcoming 17th-century inn by village green with much original character. Popular rendezvous. Good value Scottish fare.

£££ 49 bedrooms (12 fmly) No smoking in 17 bedrooms or restaurant No dogs (ex guide dogs) Petanque Weekly live entertainment Childrens facilities 🗲

CROFTBURN COTTAGE ⬛⬛⬛
Croftamie G63 0HA

☎ 01360 660796

(2m S of Drymen on A809 next to Dlanair House)

Comfortable, former keeper's cottage in spacious gardens with good views. Friendly, relaxed atmosphere. Home-cooked fare.

£ 3 bedrooms (1 fmly) No smoking in bedrooms or area of dining room Croquet Putting

Winnock

Cromlix House

DUMBARTON

DUMBUCK ★★
Glasgow Rd G82 1EG
☎ 01389 734336 🖷 01389 742270
(from S follow M8 for Glasgow and exit junct 30, follow A82 for 4 miles, at traffic lights follow A814 and hotel is 1/2 mile on R)
Family-owned hotel with many modern-style bedrooms. Attractive restaurant with extensive menu.
££ 22 bedrooms (2 fmly) Night porter Pool

TRAVELODGE
Milton G82 2TY *(1m E, on A82 westbound)*
☎ 01389 765202 🖷 01389 765202
Modern building with smart, spacious and well equipped bedrooms, suitable for family use. Nearby family restaurant.
££ 32 bedrooms (all family)

DUNBLANE

CROMLIX HOUSE ★★★@@
Kinbuck FK15 9JT *(3 m NE B8033)*
☎ 01786 822125 🖷 01786 825450
Style without stuffiness is the affectionate description of this country house hotel set in extensive grounds. Five-course dinner menu.
££££ 14 bedrooms Tennis Fishing Croquet Clay pigeon shooting No smoking in restaurant Private chapel Closed 2-29 Jan Res Oct-Apr

STIRLING ARMS ★★
Stirling Rd FK15 9EP *(on B8033)*
☎ 01786 822156 🖷 01786 825300
Former 17th-century coaching inn by Allan Water near station and Cathedral. Attractive panelled restaurant with extensive menu.
7 bedrooms (1 fmly)

WESTWOOD ◻◻◻◻
Doune Rd FK15 9ND
☎ 01786 822579 🖷 822579
(leave A9 on A820, turn towards Doune 0.5m on L)
Comfortable modern house with a welcoming atmosphere with tasteful bedrooms, one on ground floor.
£ 3 bedrooms No smoking No dogs (ex guide dogs) No children Closed Nov-Feb

GARTOCHARN

ARDOCH COTTAGE ◻◻◻◻
Main St G83 8NE
(on A811 between Ballock & Drymen)
☎ 01389 830452 🖷 01389 830452
Lovingly restored cottage overlooking rolling countryside. Pretty bedrooms & relaxing sun lounge. Enjoyable home cooking.
£ 3 bedrooms No smoking

MARDELLA ◻◻◻◻
Old School Rd G83 8SD
☎ 01389 830428 🖷 01389 830428
(off A811 into Old School Road, 200m 2nd house on R)
Excellent, welcoming house, set amid spectacular scenery. Collection of peacocks, geese, ducks and sheep outside are a hit with children.
£ 3 bedrooms (2 fmly) No smoking Childrens facilities 9 acres sheep poultry

HELENSBURGH

COMMODORE TOBY ★★
112 West Clyde St G84 8ES *(on A814 seafront, 400m W of Pier)*
☎ 01436 676924 🖷 01436 676233
Attractive hotel with splendid views and a warm and relaxing atmosphere. Popular restaurant.
£££ 45 bedrooms (3 fmly) No smoking in 11 bedrooms No dogs (ex guide dogs) Lift Night porter No smoking in restaurant Res 27-30 Dec

KILLEARN

BLACK BULL ★★★@ @
The Square G63 9NG
☎ 01360 550215 🖷 01360 550143
(N from Glasgow on A81, thro Blanefield, just past Distillery, take A875 to Killearn)
Village inn with lovely views, convenient for the Trossachs. Try the popular brasserie or the excellent restaurant.
£££ 11 bedrooms (2 fmly) No smoking in 5 bedrooms or restaurant Night porter Fishing Childrens facilities

KILLIN

DALL LODGE COUNTRY HOUSE ★★★
Main St FK21 8TN
☎ 01567 820217 🖷 01567 820726
(3m beyond Lochearnhead turn R onto A827 to Killin)
Welcoming small family-run hotel with high levels of personal attention. Comfortable bedrooms.
££ 10 bedrooms (2 fmly) Tennis No smoking in restaurant Closed Nov-Feb

LOCHEARNHEAD

LOCHEARNHEAD ★
Lochside FK19 8PU
(turn R at T-junct, hotel is 500metres ahead)
☎ 01567 830229 🖷 01567 830364
Comfortable, small hotel with lovely loch views and a relaxed and friendly atmosphere. Good dining options.
£ 12 bedrooms Fishing Water skiing Windsurfing Sailing Childrens facilities Apr-mid Nov

MANSEWOOD COUNTRY HOUSE ◻◻◻◻
FK19 8NS *(first building on the L)*
☎ 01567 830213
Delightful home in lovely gardens. Cleverly designed, comfortable accommodation. Enjoyable home-cooked food.
£ 6 bedrooms No smoking No dogs (ex guide dogs) Licensed No children under 15yrs

Westwood

LUSS

THE LODGE ON LOCH LOMOND ★★★⊛
G83 8PA
(turn off A82 at Luss, hotel to N of car park)
☎ 01436 860201 📠 01436 860203
Modern hotel with panoramic views of loch. Pine clad throughout, the bedrooms have their own sauna.
££ *29 bedrooms (20 fmly) Night porter No smoking in restaurant* 🌙

INVERBEG INN ★★
Inverbeg G83 8PD
(from Glasgow follow the signs for Erskine Bridge, from the bridge take the L hand fork sign posted Loch Lomond and the A82)
☎ 01436 860678 📠 860686
Busy roadside inn with a popular bar. Some of the lovely rooms have fine views.
££ *12 bedrooms (8 annexe) (1 fmly) No smoking in 8 bedrooms or restaurant Fishing water skiing windsurfing Weekly live entertainment* 🌙

PORT OF MENTEITH

LAKE ★★⊛⊛
FK8 3RA *(on B8034 to Arnproir)*
☎ 01877 385258 📠 01877 385671
Charming hotel with a most relaxed and civilised atmosphere by lakeshore with gorgeous views. Superb food.
£££ *15 bedrooms No children under 12yrs No smoking in restaurant Res 1 Nov–28 Feb* 🌙

RHU

ROSSLEA HALL COUNTRY HOUSE ★★★
G84 8NF *(on A814, past post office)*
☎ 01436 439955 📠 01436 820897
Victorian mansion set in grounds near Gareloch with wonderful views. Comfortable bar provides informal eating to the main restaurant.
36 bedrooms (9 annexe) (2 fmly) No smoking in 5 bedrooms Night porter 🌙

STIRLING

STIRLING HIGHLAND ★★★★⊛
Spittal St FK8 1DU
☎ 01786 475444 📠 01786 462929
(follow signs to Castle until the Albert Hall. Turn L and L again, follow signs to Castle)
Imaginative conversion of the old High School with superb views over the city. Good eating options. Hospitality is a strength here.
££££ *78 bedrooms (23 fmly) No smoking in 42 bedrooms or bedrooms Lift Night porter Indoor swimming pool Squash Snooker Sauna Solarium Gym Jacuzzi/spa Weekly live entertainment* 🌙

TERRACES ★★
4 Melville Ter FK8 2ND *(off A872)*
☎ 01786 472268 📠 01786 450314
Large modern city centre hotel with all-day food. Separate carvery in the evening. Pleasant bedrooms come in two sizes.
£££ *18 bedrooms (4 fmly) Night porter Weekly live entertainment* 🌙

TRAVEL INN
Whins of Milton, Glasgow Rd FK7 8EX
☎ 01786 811256
Modern building with smart, spacious and well equipped bedrooms, suitable for family use. Nearby family restaurant.
££ *(fmly room) 40 bedrooms*

TRAVELODGE
Pirnhall Roundabout, Snabhead FK7 8EU
(junct M9/M80)
Central Res ☎ 8000 555300
📠 01525 878450
Modern buildingwith smart, spacious and well equipped bedrooms, suitable for family use. Nearby family restaurant.
££ *(fmly room) 37 bedrooms*

LYNEDOCH ◨◨◨◨
100 Causewayhead Rd FK9 5HJ
☎ 01786 473877
(leave M9 junc 10 toward Stirling via Drip Road, L at Clocktower roundabout over river, past traffic lights onto Causeway road 300m on L)
Welcoming, comfortable home with excellent bedrooms and breakfasts.
£ *2 bedrooms No smoking No children*

CASTLECROFT ◨◨◨
Ballengeich Rd FK8 1TN
(leave M9 junc 10 toward Stirling, turn first R into Raploch Road. Drive to fire station, turn L at Back'O'Hill then immediately R)
☎ 01786 474933 📠 01786 466716
Glorious views over surrounding countryside from welcoming modern house near the castle walls. Hearty breakfasts are served at shared tables.
6 bedrooms (1 fmly) No smoking in bedrooms or dining room Lift Closed Xmas & New Year 🌙

WHITE GABLES ◨◨◨◨
112 Causewayhead Rd FK9 5HT
☎ 01786 479838 📠 01786 479838
Colourful window boxes adorn this comfortable Tudor-style house. Pleasant bedrooms. Landscaped garden.
£ *5 bedrooms (2 fmly) No smoking in dining room No dogs (ex guide dogs)* 🌙

CARSEVIEW ◨◨
16 Ladysneuk Rd, Cambuskenneth FK9 5NF
☎ 01786 462235
Homely, welcoming atmosphere at comfortable home set in pretty gardens. Pre-book dinner.
£ *3 bedrooms No smoking*

STRATHBLANE

KIRKHOUSE INN ★★★
G63 9AA
☎ 01360 770621 📠 01360 770896
Comfortable hotel in village centre. Best rooms are those at the front. Popular good value bar foodand attractive restaurant.
£ *15 bedrooms (2 fmly) Night porter Pool Beauty therapyWeekly live entertainment* 🌙

Creagan House

STRATHYRE

CREAGAN HOUSE ★⊛
FK18 8ND *(0.25m N of Strathyre on A84)*
☎ 01877 384638 📠 01877 384319
Charming 17th-century farmhouse, now a hotel of some distinction. The pretty bedrooms have antiques. Impressive baronial-style restaurant.
5 bedrooms (1 fmly) No smoking in bedrooms or restaurant Closed 2-28 Feb 🌙

TILLICOULTRY

HARVIESTOUN COUNTRY INN ★★
Dollar Rd FK13 6PQ
☎ 01259 752522 📠 01259 752523
This popular small hotel has been created by the sympathetic renovation of a former farmstead and stable block. There is a bar brasserie and a more formal dining room across the courtyard.
££ *10 bedrooms (2 fmly) No smoking in bedrooms or area in restaurant Tennis Fishing Riding Putting green Weekly live entertainment Childrens facilities Closed 1-2 Jan* 🌙

WHERE TO EAT

RESTAURANTS

AA RECOMMENDED

ABERFOYLE

BRAEVAL ⊛⊛⊛
Braeval, FK8 3UY
☎ 01877 382711 ⓕ 01877 382400
The format is simple - dinner and Sunday lunch are a four course affair with no choice until dessert (weekday lunches are three courses). Try perhaps a lightly seared, fully flavoured fillet of fresh salmon on saffron risotto and finished with a green-coloured herb oil.
Fixed L ££ Fixed D £££ ◤

BALQUHIDDER

MONACHYLE MHOR ⊛⊛
Lochearnhead, FK19 8PQ ☎ 01877 384622
Super little family-run restaurant with an unpretentious, individual style all its own. Quality raw ingredients are treated with due respect in the two daily-changing fixed-price cartes. Local game often stars in mouthwatering dishes, and bread is baked fresh daily.
Fixed L/D ££ ◤

CALLANDER

LUBNAIG HOTEL ⊛
Leny Feus, FK17 8AS ☎/ⓕ 01877 330376
Dinner might consist of honest, straightforward dishes like pea pod soup, roast duck with Morello cherry sauce, and casseroled pork with apples and red wine.
Fixed D ££ ◤

ROMAN CAMP HOTEL ⊛⊛
FK17 8BG
☎ 01877 330003 ⓕ 01877 331533
A five–course 'taster' menu offers a chance to sample some of the chef's specialities, such as parsnip consommé with a curried dumpling and tournedos of Aberdeen Angus beef with a thyme rösti and caramelised onions.
Fixed L ££ ALC £££ ◤

DUNBLANE

CROMLIX HOUSE HOTEL ⊛⊛
Kinbuck By Dunblane FK15 9JT
☎ 01786 822125
Dinner menu runs to five courses and the kitchen deals appropriately with well–sourced raw materials. Perhaps marinated saddle of venison carved over carrot rösti with woodland mushrooms and sherry jus may be on the menu, or hot caramelised lemon tart with Cassis coulis.
Fixed L ££ Fixed D £££ ◤

KILLEARN

BLACK BULL ⊛⊛
The Square, G63 9WG ☎ 01360 550215
A two or three course fixed-price dinner is served in The Conservatory, with a choice of four dishes at each course. There's a New Mexico look to the Brasserie, where you can enjoy dishes such as cod fishcakes and parsley sauce or grilled Cumberland sausages.
Fixed D ££ ALC ££ ◤

PORT OF MENTEITH

LAKE HOTEL ⊛⊛
FK8 3RA ☎ 01877 385258
Art Deco-style Restaurant with short, well-priced menu which includes dishes such as warm duck liver salad with raspberry vinaigrette and garlic croutons, breast of guinea fowl with oyster mushrooms and port and redcurrant sauce.
Fixed L £ Fixed D ££ ◤

STIRLING

STIRLING HIGHLAND HOTEL ⊛
Spittal Street, FK8 1DU ☎ 01786 475444
Attractive restaurant with a 'Scottish Larder' menu and a 'Chef's Signature' selection, both offering the best of Scottish seafood, meat and game.
Fixed L £ ALC £££ ◤

STRATHYRE

CREAGAN HOUSE ⊛
Callander, FK18 8ND ☎ 01877 384638
Meals are taken in the dining room of this former farmhouse. The cooking is innovative, with dishes such as 'Smokie in a Pokie' and 'Fig 'n' Lamb with roast aubergine and vodka peppered sauce'.
Fixed D ££ ALC ££ ◤

Call the AA Hotel Booking Service on 0990 050505 to book at AA recognised hotels and B&Bs in the UK, or through our internet site: http://www.theaa.co.uk/hotels

MUST SEE

BLAIR CASTLE,
Blair Atholl ☎ 01798 481207
White, turreted baronial castle, the traditional home of the Dukes of Atholl dating back to the 13th century, enclosed within a park-like garden amid the beautiful Atholl Hills. Within the 32 rooms open to the public are exceptional collections of antiquities, notably 17th-century furniture, paintings, Jacobite relics, arms and porcelain. Deer park, nature trails and an 18th-century restored walled garden.

EDRADOUR DISTILLERY,
Pitlochry ☎ 01796 472095
Founded in 1825, Edradour is Scotland's smallest distillery and remains virtually unchanged since Victorian times. Sample a dram while watching an audio-visual show.

KILLIECRANKIE,
Pitlochry *2m/3.2km N off B8079*
☎ 01796 473233
A dramatic battlesite set within a beautiful wooded gorge. It was here in 1689 that the Jacobite army, led by 'Bonnie Dundee' overcame King William's troops. On the edge of the glen is the National Trust for Scotland Visitor Centre which features 'hands-on' natural history exhibits, models and maps of the battle and woodland management displays. Guilded walks.

QUEEN'S VIEW VISITOR CENTRE,
Queen's View, Pitlochry
7m/11.2km W on B8019
☎ 01350 727284
One of the finest and most photographed views in Scotland, a beautiful vista up Loch Tummel and much admired by Queen Victoria who visited here in 1866. Delightful forest walks lead visitors to the viewpoints, an excavated ring fort and a reconstructed 18th-century farm village. Informative visitor centre with an exhibition about the history of the area.

SCONE PALACE,
Scone, Perth *on A93*
☎ 01738 552300
One of Scotland's grandest stately homes, built in Gothic style in 1803 on the site of 16th century and earlier buildings. Scottish monarchs were traditionally crowned at Scone until 1651, and the famous Stone of Scone was taken from here to Westminster Abbey by Edward I in 1296. The magnificent castellated mansion contains fine English and French furnishings, porcelain and 16th-century needlework. Splendid pinetum and woodland gardens.

Killiecrankie

ART GALLERIES

FERGUSSON GALLERY,
Marshall Pl, Perth ☎ 01738 441944
Converted former waterworks of 1832 housing the work of J D Fergusson (1874-1961), one of Scotland's finest artists.

STRATHEARN GALLERY & POTTERY,
West High St, Crieff ☎ 01764 656100

MUSEUMS

ABERFELDY WATER MILL,
Mill St, Aberfeldy ☎ 01887 820330
A restored working oatmeal water mill.

ATHOLL COUNTRY COLLECTION,
The Old School, Blair Atholl
☎ 01796 481232
Artefacts and photographs illustrate local life and trades from 1850 onwards. Displays include a crofter's kitchen, post office and a school.

BLACK WATCH REGIMENTAL MUSEUM,
Balhousie Castle, Perth ☎ 01738 621281
Learn about the story of the 42nd/73rd Highland Regiment from 1739 to the present day.

CLAN DONNACHAIDH (ROBERTSON) MUSEUM,
Bruar *4m/6.4km north of Blair Atholl on B8079*
☎ 01796 483264
Clan centre for Robertsons, Duncans, Reids and other associated names.

Displays feature the history of the clan and its people, exhibits include Jacobite relics.

LOWER CITY MILLS,
West Mill St, Perth ☎ 01738 627958
Restored water-powered corn mill with Scotland's largest working water wheel and an exhibition on the Perth Mills.

PERTH MUSEUM & ART GALLERY,
78 George St, Perth ☎ 01738 632488
Houses collections of fine and applied art, social and local history, natural history and archaeology.

SCOTTISH CRANNOG CENTRE,
Kenmore, Loch Tay ☎ 01887 830583
Crannogs are a type of ancient loch dwelling, built out into the water as defensive homesteads. Visit a reconstructed timbered and thatched dwelling and learn about the crannog people and their way of life in the shore-based exhibition centre.

HISTORIC & ANCIENT SITES

BURLEIGH CASTLE,
Milnathort, Kinross
A 16th-century tower-house with an enclosed courtyard and roofed angle tower.

DUNKELD CATHEDRAL,
Dunkeld
Ruined 14th-century cathedral idyllically set amidst lawns close to the River Tay.

ELCHO CASTLE,
Perth *3m/4.8km SE*
Splendid and complete ruin of a fortified mansion overlooking the River Tay.

LOCH LEVEN CASTLE,
Castle Island, Kinross
Mary, Queen of Scots was imprisoned here in this five-storey castle in 1567 - she escaped 11 months later and gave the its special place in history.

MEIKLEOUR BEECH HEDGE,
Meikleour *south on A93*
Planted in 1746, the hedge is now 600yards long and up to 100ft high - the highest beech hedge of its kind in the world.

TULLIBARDINE CHAPEL,
Auchterarder *3m/4.8km NW off A823*
This attractive red sandstone church, founded in 1446 and enlarged in the 16th century, is one of the few medieval rural churches in Scotland to be completed and has survived unaltered ever since.

GREAT FOR KIDS

AUCHINGARRICH WILDLIFE CENTRE,
Comrie ☎ 01764 679469
Award-winning collection of rare and ornamental birds and animals set high in the Perthshire hills. Unique wild bird hatchery, Highland cattle, play areas, rural life museum, bird handling area and woodland walks.

GLENGOULANDIE DEER PARK,
Aberfeldy *8m/12.8km NW on B846*
☎/❻ 01887 830261
See Highland cattle, red deer, rare breeds of sheep and other native birds and animals in their natural environment.

HYDRO-ELECTRIC VISITOR CENTRE, DAM & FISH PASS,
Pitlochry **☎ 01796 473152**
Exhibition showing how electricity is brought from the power station to the customer, and access to the turbine viewing gallery. The salmon ladder offers views of fish jumping or swimming past the viewing chamber.

THE 'MACBETH' EXPERIENCE,
Bankfoot, Perth **☎ 01738 787696**
A multi-media display and exhibition using the latest technology that explains the historical facts about Macbeth and his achievements as they really happened. Crafts and restaurant.

RSPB NATURE RESERVE VANE FARM,
By Loch Leven, Kinross **☎ 01577 862355**
Popular visitor centre and reserve noted for its pink-footed geese, whooper swans and long-eared owls. Nature trail and hide overlooking Loch Leven.

HOMES & GARDENS

BRANKLYN GARDEN,
116 Dundee Rd, Perth **☎ 01738 625535**
Once described as the finest garden of its size in Britain, Branklyn covers little more than two acres and is noted for its spring colour from azaleas and blue poppies.

CASTLE MENZIES,
Weem, Aberfeldy **☎ 01887 820982**
A fine example of a 16th-century Z-plan fortified tower house housing a small clan museum.

CLUNY HOUSE,
Aberfeldy **☎ 01887 820795**
Fine woodland garden with many rare Himalayan species.

DRUMMOND CASTLE GARDENS,
Muthill **☎ 01764 681257**
Established in 1630 by John Drummond and Italianised in 1830, the formal terraced gardens are said to be among the finest in Europe.

HUNTINGTOWER CASTLE,
Perth **☎ 01738 627231**
A 15th-century castellated mansion featuring some splendid painted ceilings.

BIG OUTDOORS

FASKALLY,
Pitlochry **☎ 01350 727284**
Mature mixed woodland on the shores of Loch Faskally. Forest walks and nature trail.

THE HERMITAGE,
Dunkeld *2m/3.2km W off A9*
A woodland trail beside the River Braan leads to a 1758 folly called the Hermitage or Ossian's Hall, a famous 18th-century beauty spot overlooking the Falls of Braan.

FALLS OF BRUAR,
Blair Atholl *3m N*
A short walk from the old A9 leads to these beautiful falls, where the River Bruar cascades through rocky chasms.

KINNOULL HILL WOODLAND PARK,
Perth
Five hills make up this Woodland Park, the craggy cliffs of Kinnoull Hill at 222m commanding extensive views across the Tay valley.

LOCH OF THE LOWES NATURE RESERVE,
Dunkeld **☎ 01350 727337 (Visitor Centre)**
This 242 acres Scottish Wildlife Trust reserve covers the freshwater of the loch and surrounding woodland. Beautiful Highland-edge scenery, nesting ospreys, which can be viewed from a hide, and a visitor centre.

RUMBLING BRIDGE GORGE,
Kinross *SE off A977*
An attractive rocky gorge where the River Devon tumbles beneath an unusual double bridge.

ESSENTIAL INFORMATION

TOURIST INFORMATION

PERTHSHIRE TOURIST BOARD,
West Mill St, Perth PH1 5QP
☎ 01738 627958 ❻ 01738 630416
ABERFELDY,
The Square, Aberfeldy PH15 2DD
☎ 01887 820276 ❻ 01887 829495
AUCHTERARDER,
90 High St, Auchterarder PH3 1BJ
☎ 01764 663550 ❻ 01764 664235
BLAIRGOWRIE ,
26 Wellmeadow, Blairgowrie PH10 6AS
☎ 01250 872960 ❻ 01250 873701
CRIEFF,
Town Hall, High St, Crieff PH7 3HU
☎ 01764 652578 ❻ 01764 655422
DUNKELD,
The Cross, Dunkeld PH8 0AN
☎/❻ 01350 727688
KINROSS,
Turfhills Junction 6 M90, Kinross KY13 7NQ
☎ 01577 863680 ❻ 01577 863370
PERTH,
45 High St, Perth PH1 5TJ
☎ 01738 638353 ❻ 01738 444863
PERTH,
Caithness Glass, Inveralmond PH1 3TZ
☎ 01738 638481

PITLOCHRY ,
22 Atholl Rd, Pitlochry PH16 5BX
☎ 01796 472215 ❻ 01796 474046

ACCESS

DUNDEE AIRPORT ☎ 01382 643242

CRAFTS

Lookout for lace making, knitwear, pottery and glassware, oatmeal milling, paperweight making, jewellery, metalwork sculpture and woodturning.

BENNYBEG CRAFT CENTRE,
Muthill Rd, Crieff **☎ 01764 655401**
CAITHNESS GLASS VISITOR CENTRE,
Inveralmond, Perth **☎ 01738 673373**
Watch skilled glassmakers making paperweights from the viewing gallery.
CRIEFF VISITOR CENTRE,
Muthill Rd, Crieff **☎ 01764 654014**
Tours of the Thistle Pottery, Scotland's oldest working pottery.
JUNE DUNN JEWELLERY,
Netherlea, Scone **☎ 01738 52107**
MARI DONALD KNITWEAR,
Pudding Lane, Comrie **☎ 01764 670150**

OLD SMIDDY,
Blair Atholl **☎ 01796 481488**
Hand-crafted metalwork.
POTS OF PITLOCHRY,
Mill Lane, Pitlochry **☎ 01796 474367**
STUART CRYSTAL,
Muthill Rd, Crieff **☎ 01764 654004**

ENTERTAINMENT

PERTH THEATRE,
High St, Perth **☎ 01738 621031**
PITLOCHRY FESTIVAL THEATRE,
Port-na-Craig, Pitlochry **☎ 01796 472680**

FOOD & DRINK

Perthshire specialities include freshly ground oatmeal, best from one of the few restored watermills, quality raspberries and other soft fruits grown on the fertile, south-facing slopes around Blairgowrie, wild salmon from the River Tay, pure spring water (Highland Spring) from deep below the Ochil Hills, and fine whisky.

GORDON & DURWARD,
18 West High St, Crieff
Traditional confectionary manufacturer.

DUNKELD SMOKHOUSE
Brae St, Dunkeld
Tay salmon smoked in the traditional way.

WHISKY DISTILLERY TOURS

ABERFELDY DISTILLERY,
Aberfeldy ☎ 01887 820330
BLAIR ATHOL DISTILLERY,
Pitlochry ☎ 01796 472234
Producer of Bell's whisky, Scotland's most popular dram.
GLENTURRET DISTILLERY,
Crieff ☎ 01764 656565
Scotland's oldest distillery.

TRANSPORT

CAR HIRE

ABERFELDY MOTOR SERVICES,
☎ 01887 820433
ARNOLD CLARK HIRE DRIVE,
Perth ☎ 01738 638511
AUCHTERARDER MOTORS,
☎ 01764 662136
BURNSIDE SELF-DRIVE HIRE,
Pitlochry ☎ 0796 472080
STRUAN RENTAL,
102 Scott St, Perth PH1 2NP
☎ 01738 633441

COACH/BUS TOURS

GUIDE FRIDAY BUS TOURS
☎ 0131 556 2244
Open-top bus tours of Perth.
STAGECOACH,
Ruthvenfield Rd, Perth ☎ 01738 629339

CYCLE HIRE

ABERFELDY MOUNTAIN BIKES,
Taybridge Dr, Aberfeldy ☎ 01887 820298
ATHOLL MOUNTAIN BIKES,
Old School Park, Blair Atholl
☎ 01796 473553
DUNKELD MOUNTAIN BIKES,
Tay Terrace, Dunkeld ☎ 01350 728744
ESCAPE ROUTE,
West Moulin Rd, Pitlochry ☎ 01796 473859
R. S. FINNIE,
Leadenflower Rd, Crieff ☎ 01764 654091
MOUNTAINS & GLENS,
Railway Rd, Blairgowrie ☎ 01250 874206
PERTHSHIRE MOUNTAIN BIKES,
Pier Rd, Kenmore ☎ 01887 830291

TRAINS

Main line stations are at Auchterarder, Birnam (Dunkeld), Perth and Pitlochry. Information enquiries ☎ 0345 484950.

SPORT & LEISURE

ACTIVITY/LEISURE CENTRES

ABERFELDY RECREATION CENTRE,
Crieff Rd ☎ 01887 820922
BLAIRGOWRIE RECREATION CENTRE,
Beeches Rd t 01250 873724
LOCH LEVEN LEISURE,
Lathro, Kinross ☎ 01557 863368
PERTH LEISURE POOL,
Glasgow Rd ☎ 01738 630535

PERTHSHIRE ACTIVITY LINE
☎ 01738 444144
Activity days out and weekend breaks.

ANGLING

Perthshire is famous for its salmon fishing, notably on the River Tay, Loch Tay, River Earn and Loch Earn. Brown and rainbow trout fishing is very popular on Loch Leven. Small mountain lakes, huge lochs, fast flowing rivers and numerous fisheries abound within the county, making it an angler's paradise. Tourist Information Centres produce fishing factsheets.

CYCLING

From mountain biking in Highland forests and glens to gentle pedalling along lochside roads and gently undulating country lanes, Perthshire offers a varied terrain for all cycling abilities.

SCOTTISH CYCLING HOLIDAYS,
☎ 01250 886201
Cycle hire, maps and routes.

GLIDING

SCOTTISH GLIDING UNION,
Portmoak Airfield, Kinross ☎ 01592 840543

GOLF COURSES

GLENEAGLES HOTEL,
Auchterarder ☎ 01764 662231
Situated in the lee of the Ochil Hills and beside the famous Gleneagles Hotel, the splendid King's and Queen's courses represent the best in beautiful, undulating moorland golf, complete with magnificent panoramas.. To play this 5-star course you must be a resident at the hotel.

ABERFELDY ☎ 01887 820535
ALYTH ☎ 01828 632268
AUCHTERARDER ☎ 01764 662804
BLAIR ATHOLL ☎ 01796 481407
BLAIRGOWRIE ☎ 01250 872622
COMRIE ☎ 01764 760055
CRAIGIE HILL,
Perth ☎ 01738 620829
CRIEFF ☎ 01764 652909
DUNKELD & BIRNAM,
Dunkeld ☎ 01350 727524
DUNNING ☎ 01764 684747
KENMORE ☎ 01887 830226
KILLIN ☎ 01567 820312
KING JAMES VI,
Perth ☎/☎ 01738 445132
MILNATHORT ☎ 01577 864069
MUCKHART ☎ 01259 781423
MUTHILL ☎ 01764 681523
PITLOCHRY ☎ 01796 474792
ST FILLANS ☎ 01764 685312
STRATHTAY ☎ 01350 727797
TAYMOUTH CASTLE,
Kenmore ☎ 01887 830228

ICE RINKS

ATHOLL CURLING RINK,
Pitlochry ☎ 01796 473337
DEWARS RINKS,
Glover St, Perth ☎ 01738 624188

RACING

PERTH HUNT RACECOURSE
Scone, Perth ☎ 01738 551597
Hidden away among the picturesque woodland of Scone Park, this intimate racecourse features some exciting National Hunt racing. The highlight is the three-day Perth Festival in late April.

RIDING

ARMOURY TREKKING CENTRE,
Armoury Rd, Pitlochry ☎ 01796 2102
BALNAKILLY RIDING CENTRE,
Kirkmichael ☎/☎ 01250 81305
BLAIR CASTLE RIDING CENTRE,
Blair Atholl, Pitlochry ☎ 01796 481263
BORELAND RIDING CENTRE,
Fearnan, By Aberfeldy ☎ 01887 830212
CALEDONIAN EQUESTRIAN CENTRE,
Balbeggie, Perth ☎ 01821 640426
CULLODEN RIDING SCHOOL,
Station Rd, Stanley ☎ 01738 827094
THE GLENEAGLES MARK PHILLIPS EQUESTRIAN CENTRE,
Auchterarder ☎ 01764 663507
GLENMARKIE FARM RIDING CENTRE,
Glenisla, Blairgowrie ☎/☎ 01575 582341
LOCH TAY HIGHLAND EQUESTRIAN CENTRE,
Milton Morenish, By Killin ☎ 01567 820323
SCOTTISH EQUITATION CENTRE,
Greenloaning, Dunblane ☎ 01786 88278

SCENIC DRIVES

Particularly enjoyable routes are along Glen Lyon, Scotland's longest glen at 42 miles in length, through the Ochil Hills by way of lovely Glen Devon, and the appealing glens to the north of Blairgowrie, notably the dramatic landscapes of Glen Shee, which incorporates Britain's highest main road pass at 2182ft (665m).

SKIING

GLENSHEE CHAIRLIFT & SKI CENTRE
☎ 01339 741320

WALKING

Perthshire provides plenty of scope for all levels of walkers, from short woodland trails and riverside rambles to spectacular hill and moorland long-distance walks. Leaflets on local walks are available from Information Centres.

WALKING HOLIDAYS/TOURS

AVALON TREKKING SCOTLAND,
☎/☎ 01738 624194

WATERSPORTS

CROFT-NA-CABER WATERSPORTS CENTRE,
Kenmore ☎ 01887 830588
LOCH TAY BOATING CENTRE,
Pier Rd, Kenmore ☎ 01887 830291
LOCHEARNHEAD WATERSPORTS CENTRE,
Lochearnhead ☎ 01567 830330

WHERE TO STAY

The Weem

ABERFELDY

THE WEEM ★★
Weem PH15 2LD *(1m NW B846)*
☎ 01887 820381 ☏ 01887 820187
Wonderfully relaxed and informal atmosphere at this historic roadside inn.
£ 12 bedrooms (4 fmly) No smoking in 4 bedrooms Shooting No smoking in restaurant 🍴

GUINACH HOUSE ★🏵🏵
"By The Birks", Urlar Rd PH15 2ET
(access off A826 Crieff road)
☎ 01887 820251 ☏ 01887 829607
(Rosettes awarded for dinner only)
The dedicated owners look forward to welcoming you to their delightfully peaceful small hotel in three acre gardens.
££ 7 bedrooms No smoking in restaurant Closed 4 days Xmas 🍴

FERNBANK HOUSE 🟦🟦🟦🟦🟦
Kenmore St PH15 2BL*(on exiting town on A827 to Kenmore and Killin)*
☎ 01887 820345
Large Victorian house with attractive, traditional accommodation.
£ 7 bedrooms (2 fmly) No smoking No dogs

ALYTH

DRUMNACREE 🟦🟦🟦🟦🟦🏵🏵
St Ninians Rd, Alyth by Blairgowrie PH11 8AP
(turn off A926 towards Alyth, 1st turn L after Clydesdale Bank, 300yds on R)
☎ 01828 632194 ☏ 01828 632194
Lovely detached house below Glenisla.
Scottish and Cajun menus.
££ 6 bedrooms (3 fmly) No smoking in bedrooms No smoking in dining room Licensed Apr-20 Dec 🍴

LOSSET 🟦🟦
Losset Rd PH11 8BT
(A926 into Alyth, A952 Losset Inn 1m into town on road to the "Glens")
☎ 01828 632393
Original character carefully maintained at this popular, welcoming 300 year old village inn.
3 bedrooms No smoking in area of dining room

AUCHTERARDER

THE GLENEAGLES HOTEL
★★★★★🏵🏵🏵
PH3 1NF *(on A823)*
☎ 01764 662231 ☏ 01764 662134
Renowned world-wide as a mecca for golfers and as a top class international resort hotel in beautiful countryside.
££££ 234 bedrooms No smoking in 60 bedrooms Lift Night porter Indoor swimming pool (heated) Golf 18 Tennis (hard & grass) Fishing Squash Riding Snooker Sauna Solarium Gym Pool table Croquet lawn Putting green Jacuzzi/spa Bowls Shooting Falconry Equestrian Off-Road Driving Weekly live entertainment Children's facilities No smoking area in restaurant 🍴

AUCHTERARDER HOUSE ★★★🏵🏵
PH3 1DZ *(NW off B8062)*
☎ 01764 663646 ☏ 01764 662939
Rather splendid Victorian mansion house in peaceful landscaped grounds offering splendid views of the countryside.
££££ 15 bedrooms (3 fmly) Croquet lawn Putting green No children under 12yrs No smoking in restaurant 🍴

CAIRN LODGE ★★🏵
Orchil Rd PH3 1LX
(from A9 take A824 into Auchterarder then A823 signposted Crieff & Gleneagles. In approx 200yds hotel on Y junct)

☎ 01764 662634 & 662431
☏ 01764 664866
Attractive turreted house near Gleneagles.
Innovative carte using quality ingredients.
££ 7 bedrooms (2 fmly) No smoking in 2 bedrooms No dogs (ex guide dogs) Putting green No smoking in restaurant 🍴

MORVEN HOTEL 🟦🟦🟦
196 High St PH3 1AF
☎ 01764 662578 ☏ 01764 664710
Relaxed informal atmosphere at this small hotel enjoying much local support.
9 bedrooms (3 fmly) Direct dial from bedrooms Pool table 🍴

BIRNAM

BIRNAM HOUSE ★★★
Birnam PH8 0BQ *(off A9)*
☎ 01350 727462 ☏ 01350 728979
Baronial style village hotel offering a warm welcome. Good value carte menu.
££ 28 bedrooms (6 fmly) Lift No smoking in restaurant 🍴

BLACKFORD

YARROW HOUSE 🟦🟦
Moray St PH4 1PY
(turn off A9 & continue through village to church on L. House opposite)
☎ 01764 682358
Colourful floral baskets adorn the front of this welcoming guest house. Hearty breakfasts.
£ 3 bedrooms (1 fmly) No smoking in bedrooms No smoking in dining room

BLAIR ATHOLL

ATHOLL ARMS ★★
PH18 5SG
(off A9 to B8079, 1m into Blair Atholl, hotel in village past the Post Office)
☎ 01796 481205 ☏ 01796 481550
Traditional values at this long established hotel. Tempting range of Scottish fare.
££ 30 bedrooms (3 fmly) Fishing Pool table Rough shooting No smoking in restaurant 🍴

Kinloch House

TILT ★★
Bridge of Tilt PH18 5SU *(1m off A9 in Blair Atholl, 0.50m from Blair Castle)*
☎ 01796 481333 📠 01796 481335
Welcoming hotel close Blair Castle. Bedrooms, are bright, airy and modern.
28 bedrooms (8 fmly) Fishing Games room Closed Jan-Etr 🍴

DALGREINE 🏠🏠🏠🏠
Bridge of Tilt PH18 5SX *(turn off A9 at Blair Atholl sign. Dalgreine is between garage & butcher's shop, 1 row back from main road)*
☎ 01796 481276
Welcoming atmosphere at this comfortable detached home a short walk from Blair Castle.
£ 6 bedrooms (1 fmly) No smoking No dogs (ex guide dogs) Small snooker table

KINLOCH HOUSE ★★★🌼🌼🌼
PH10 6SG *(3m W on A923)*
☎ 01250 884237 📠 01250 884333
High levels of hospitality, service and fine cuisine at this charming country house in 25 acres.
£££££ 2 bedrooms (1 fmly) Indoor swimming pool(heated) Fishing Sauna Gym Croquet lawn Jacuzzi/spa No children under 7yrs No smoking in restaurant Closed 20-29 Dec 🍴

ANGUS ★★
46 Wellmeadow PH10 6NQ
☎ 01250 872455 📠 01250 875615
Long established hotel overlooking town square gardens. Good value fixed price menu.
££ 81 bedrooms (4 fmly) Lift Night porter Indoor swimming pool (heated) Sauna Solarium Jacuzzi/spa Wkly live entertainment No smoking in restaurant 🍴

DALMORE HOUSE HOTEL 🏠🏠🏠
Rosemount PH10 6QB *(on A93)*
☎ 01250 872150
Relaxed and friendly atmosphere at this comfortable small hotel, close to the golf course.
£ 5 bedrooms (1 fmly) No smoking in bedrooms No smoking in dining room No dogs Pool table Mini golf Feb-Nov

DUNCRAGGAN 🏠🏠🏠
Perth Rd PH10 6EJ *(on A93 from Perth pass Shell station on L, 2 bungalows, Duncraggon on corner of Essendy &Perth Rd)*
☎ 01250 872082 📠 01250 872098
Lovely detached house offering hearty breakfasts, light suppers and more substantial dinners.
£ 4 bedrooms No smoking No dogs (ex guide dogs) 9 hole putting and table tennis

GILMORE HOUSE 🏠🏠🏠
Perth Rd PH10 6EJ *(on A93 from Perth at the beginning of Blairgowrie)*
☎ 01250 872791
Guests will certainly receive a warm welcome at this comfortable detached home to the south of town.
£ 3 bedrooms (1 fmly) No smoking

HEATHPARK LODGE 🏠🏠🏠
Coupar Angus Rd PH10 6JT
(on A923 at Rosemount)
☎ 01250 874929 📠 01250 874929
Inviting lodge style home with sun lounge. Breakfasts include fish dishes.
£ 2 bedrooms No smoking in bedrooms No smoking in dining room No dogs (ex guide dogs) No children under 3yrs

THE LAURELS 🏠🏠🏠
Golf Course Rd, Rosemount PH10 6LH
(S on A93)
☎ 01250 874920
Close to golf course, this welcoming guest house offers sound value accommodation.
6 bedrooms No smoking No dogs Licensed No children under 12yrs Closed Dec 🍴

NORWOOD HOUSE 🏠🏠🏠
Park Dr PH10 6PA
☎ 01250 874146 📠 01250 874146
Detached Victorian house with spacious bedrooms, inviting lounge and small dining room.
£ 4 bedrooms No smoking No children Mar-Oct

The Gleneagles Hotel

BRIDGE OF CALLY ★
PH10 7JJ
(beside bridge over River Ardle (A93), 6m N of Blairgowrie)
☎ 01250 886231 📠 01250 886231
Relaxed atmosphere at this small hotel with grounds stretching down to the river. Excellent value bar meals.
££ 9 bedrooms Fishing Closed 25-26 Dec RS mid Oct-mid Dec 🍴

NIVINGSTON HOUSE ★★★
Cleish Hills KY13 7LS *(2m W of M90 J5)*
☎ 01577 850216 📠 01577 850238
Very civilised and peaceful country house where friendly staff are dedicated to their guests' well being.
17 bedrooms (1 fmly) Snooker Croquet lawn Putting green Golf driving range Closed 4-20 Jan 🍴

**Call the AA Hotel Booking Service on 0990 050505 to book at AA recognised hotels and B&Bs in the UK, or through our internet site:
http://www.theaa.co.uk/hotels**

ROYAL ★★★
Melville Square PH6 2DW
(on main square in Comrie)
☎ 01764 679200 📠 01764 679219
Town centre hotel combining the best of traditional and modern styles. Bistro and more formal dining room.
£££ 11 bedrooms No dogs (ex guide dogs) Fishing Pool table Croquet lawn No children under 5yrs 🍴

MOSSGIEL 🏠🏠🏠
Burrell St PH6 2JP
(on A85 opposite Parish Church)
☎ 01764 670567 📠 01764 670567
Popular with golfers. Bright and airy bedrooms. Enjoyable Scottish fare. Satellite TV.
£ 4 bedrooms No smoking in bedrooms No smoking in dining room No dogs Licensed No children under 5yrs Golf packages Physical therapy clinic 🍴

MOORFIELD HOUSE ★★★🌼🌼
Myreriggs Rd PH13 9HS
(from Perth A94 to Coupar Angus. A923 towards Blairgowrie, in 2.5m hotel on R)
☎ 01828 627303 📠 01828 627339
(Rosettes awarded for dinner only)
Country hotel exuding an air of quality and comfort. Innovative modern cooking.
££ 12 bedrooms No smoking in 5 bedrooms 🍴

CRIEFF HYDRO ★★★
Ferntower Rd PH7 3LQ *(from Perth 1st R into Connaught Terrace, 1st R again)*
☎ 01764 655555 📠 01764 653087
Above the town, this hotel has a range of leisure and sporting facilities beyond compare.
££ 210 bedrooms 15 annexe bedrooms (34 fmly) No dogs (ex guide dogs) Lift Night porter Indoor swimming pool (heated) Golf 9 Tennis (hard) Fishing Squash Riding Snooker Sauna Solarium Gym Pool table Croquet lawn Putting green Jacuzzi/spa Bowling Off-road Football pitch Adventure playground Water ski-ing Cinema Wkly live entertainment Childrens facilities 🍴

Killiecrankie

CRIEFF ★★

47-49 East High St PH7 3JA

(A9 to Dunblane, exit at Braco & follow A82 to A822 into Crieff. Through town centre to East High St, hotel on R)

☎ 01764 652632 & 653854
📠 01764 655019

A relaxed friendly atmosphere at this family hotel in the town centre.

£ 12 bedrooms (1 fmly) Sauna Solarium Gym Pool table Hair & beauty salon No smoking area in restaurant 🍷

CULTOQUHEY HOUSE ★★

Gilmerton by Crieff PH7 3NE

(A85 from Perth to Gilmerton, hotel on L in village)

☎ 01764 653253 📠 01764 654535

Relaxed and quite Mediterranean in style, this country house features Italian specialities strongly on the menus.

£££ 20 bedrooms (9 fmly) No dogs Fishing Snooker Shooting No smoking area in restaurant Closed Feb 🍷

THE DRUMMOND ARMS ★★

James Square PH7 3HX

☎ 01764 652151 📠 01764 655222

Town centre, long established family run hotel popular with visiting tour groups.

29 bedrooms 7 annexe bedrooms (3 fmly) Lift Pool table 🍷

MURRAYPARK ★★

Connaught Ter PH7 3DJ

(off A85 to Perth, near Crieff Golf Club)

☎ 01764 653731 📠 01764 655311

Staff are friendly and willing to please at this hotel. Choice of lounges, bar and restaurant.

20 bedrooms (1 fmly) Shooting Stalking No smoking in restaurant 🍷

LOCKE'S ACRE ★

7 Comrie Rd PH7 4BP

(in Crieff take A85 Comrie/Lochearnhead rd, hotel on R just outside Crieff)

☎ 01764 652526 📠 01764 652526

Comfortable small hotel with views of the surrounding hills. Enjoyable home cooking.

7 bedrooms (1 fmly) No dogs (ex guide dogs) No smoking in restaurant 🍷

COMELEY BANK ◼◼◼◼

32 Burrell St PH7 4DT *(on A822)*

☎ 01764 653409

Terraced house close to town centre.

Ground floor bedroom suitable for disabled guests.

£ 5 bedrooms (2 fmly) No smoking in bedrooms No smoking in dining room Licensed

GWYDYR HOUSE HOTEL ◼◼◼

Comrie Rd PH7 4BP

(on A85, 0.25m from town centre, on R opp Macrosty Park entrance)

☎ 01764 653277 📠 01764 653277

Good value at this welcoming hotel, with views to the hills beyond.

£ 8 bedrooms (2 fmly) No smoking in dining room Licensed Closed 20-28 Dec 🍷

FORGANDENNY

CRAIGHALL◼◼◼

PH2 9DF

(0.5m W off B935 Bridge of Earn-Forteviot Rd)

☎ 01738 812415 📠 01738 812415

Comfortable modern home amid gentle countryside adjacent to the main farm complex.

3 bedrooms (1 fmly) No dogs Fishing 1000 acres beef mixed sheep

FORTINGALL

FORTINGALL ★★

PH15 2NQ

(take B846 out of Aberfeldy for 6m, then turn left (Fortingall) for 3m, hotel is in centre of village)

☎ 01887 830367 & 830368
📠 01887 830367

Tourist and anglers' hotel that is the focal point of this picturesque conservation village.

££ 10 bedrooms (3 fmly) Fishing Sailing Pony trekking Closed Nov-Feb 🍷

GLENFARG

GLENFARG ★★

Main St PH2 9NU

(M90 southbound exit J9 turn L, hotel 5m/M90 northbound exit J8 turn 2nd L, hotel 2m)

☎ 01577 830241 📠 01577 830665

Popular with golfers this long established hotel offers good value for money. Bistro and restaurant.

£ 15 bedrooms (3 fmly) Pool table Wkly live entertainment No smoking in restaurant 🍷

GLENSHEE (SPITTAL OF)

DALMUNZIE HOUSE ★★🏵

PH10 7QG *(L off A93 to Glenshee, entrance 400 yards on L)*

☎ 01250 885224 📠 01250 885225

(Rosette awarded for dinner only)

Genuine hospitality at this country house peacefully set on a 6,500 acre estate. Enjoyable Scottish cooking.

££ 18 bedrooms Lift Golf 9 Tennis (hard) Fishing Croquet lawn Clay pigeon shooting Deer stalking Mountain bikes No smoking in restaurant Closed end Nov-27 Dec 🍷

KILLIECRANKIE

KILLIECRANKIE ★★🏵🏵

PH16 5LG

(turn off A9 at Killiecrankie, hotel 3m on B8079 on R)

☎ 01796 473220 📠 01796 472451

(Rosettes awarded for dinner only)

Charming small hotel in peaceful gardens. Ground-floor suite available. Innovative Scottish fare.

££££ 10 bedrooms (1 fmly) No smoking in 1 bedroom Croquet lawn Putting green Closed 3 Jan-Feb & 10 days Dec 🍷

DALNASGADH HOUSE ◼◼

PH16 5LN

(turn off A9 N of Pitlochry for Killiecrankie B8079)

☎ 01796 473237

Warm welcome assured at this lovely detached home standing in well tended gardens.

£ 5 bedrooms No smoking TV available No dogs (ex guide dogs) Closed Nov-Mar

KINCLAVEN

BALLATHIE HOUSE ★★★🏵🏵

PH1 4QN

(from A9, 2m N of Perth, B9099 through Stanley & signposted/or off A93 at Beech Hedge follow signs for hotel, 2.5m)

☎ 01250 883268 📠 01250 883396

Splendid mansion in a superb setting beside the banks of the famous River Tay. Innovative modern cooking.

£££ 27 bedrooms (2 fmly) Tennis (hard) Fishing Croquet lawn Putting green Clay pigeon shooting No smoking in restaurant 🍷

KINNESSWOOD

LOMOND COUNTRY INN ★★🏵

KY13 7HN *(on A911)*

☎ 01592 840253 📠 01592 840693

Welcoming atmosphere, loch views and honest fare at this small hotel.

££ 4 bedrooms 8 annexe bedrooms (2 fmly) No smoking in restaurant 🍷

Call the AA Hotel Booking Service on 0990 050505 to book at AA recognised hotels and B&Bs in the UK, or through our internet site: http://www.theaa.co.uk/hotels

GREEN ★★★
2 The Muirs KY13 7AS

(M90 J6 to Kinross. Hotel on A922)

☎ 01577 863467 🖷 01577 863180

Every modern comfort and amenity at this former coaching inn built around a grass courtyard.

£££ 47 bedrooms (4 fmly) Night porter Indoor swimming pool (heated) Golf 36 Fishing Squash Sauna Solarium Gym Pool table Croquet lawn Putting green Curling in season Childrens facilities 🗪

WINDLESTRAE HOTEL BUSINESS & LEISURE CENTRE ★★★
Windlestrae 7AS *(exit M90 J6 into Kinross, L at mini rdbt, hotel 350yds on R)*

☎ 01577 863217 🖷 01577 864733

Friendly family run business and tourist hotel. Split-level bar, spacious foyer lounge and attractive restaurant.

££££ 45 bedrooms (10 fmly) No smoking in 8 bedrooms Night porter Air conditioning Indoor swimming pool (heated) Snooker Sauna Solarium Gym Jacuzzi/spa Beautician Steam room Toning tables 🗪

KIRKLANDS ★★
20 High St KY13 7AN

☎ 01577 863313 🖷 01577 863313

Colourful window boxes adorn this family run, former coaching inn, now a hotel with all modern comforts.

££ 9 bedrooms No dogs (ex guide dogs) 🗪

TRAVELODGE
Kincardine Rd KY13 7NQ

(on A977, off M90 J6)

☎ Central Res 0800 850950
🖷 01577 864108

Modern building offering smart, spacious and well equipped bedrooms, suitable for family use. Nearby family restaurant.

££ 35 family bedrooms

THE MUIRS INN ▯▯▯▯
49 Muirs KY13 7AU

(off M90 J6 follow signs for A922. At T-junct, the Inn is diagonally opp on R)

☎ 01577 862270 🖷 01577 862270

Ever popular cottage-style pub and restaurant, brimming with character. Interesting and varied menus.

££ 5 bedrooms 3 annexe No dogs (ex guide dogs) No children under 11yrs 🗪

Queens Hotel

KINFAUNS CASTLE ★★★❀❀
Kinfauns PH2 7JZ

(2m beyond Perth on A90, Perth/Dundee rd)

☎ 01738 620777 🖷 01738 620778

Very distinctive country house hotel stylishly adorned with many Far Eastern furnishings. Menus feature the finest Scottish ingredients.

££££ 16 bedrooms Fishing Sauna Croquet lawn Putting green No smoking in restaurant 🗪

MURRAYSHALL COUNTRY HOUSE HOTEL & GOLF COURSE ★★★❀❀
New Scone PH2 7PH

(from Perth take A94 towards Coupar Angus, after 1m turn R to hotel just before New Scone)

☎ 01738 551171 🖷 01738 552595

Splendid converted mansion house amid 300 acres of parkland where golf is the main attraction.

£££ 27 bedrooms (3 fmly) No smoking in 1 bedroom Night porter Golf 18 Tennis (hard) Sauna Gym Croquet lawn Putting green Jacuzzi/spa Bowling green Driving range 🗪

HUNTINGTOWER ★★★❀
Crieff Rd, Almondbank PH1 3JT

(3m W off A85)

☎ 01738 583771 🖷 01738 583777

Attractive Edwardian house with conservatory for informal eating and also elegant Oak Restaurant for serious dining.

£££ 15 bedrooms 12 annexe bedrooms (2 fmly) No smoking in 5 bedrooms Night porter Childrens facilities 🗪

PARKLANDS ★★★❀
St Leonards Bank PH2 8EB

(leave M90 J10, after 1m turn L at end of park area at traffic lights, hotel on L)

☎ 01738 622451 🖷 01738 622046

(Rosette awarded for lunch only)

Bright and boldly decorated, enjoying a fine outlook and offering imaginative Taste of Scotland menus, this is a hotel of distinction.

£££ 14 bedrooms No smoking in restaurant 🗪

LOVAT ★★★
90 Glasgow Rd PH2 0LT

(from M90 follow signs for Stirling to rdbt, then R into Glasgow Rd, hotel 1.5m on R)

☎ 01738 636555 🖷 01738 643123

Popular business and tourist hotel offering smart bedrooms. Extensive range of bar and restaurant meals.

£££ 31 bedrooms (1 fmly) No dogs (ex guide dogs) Night porter Pool table No smoking in restaurant 🗪

QUALITY STATION ★★★
Leonard St PH2 8HE

(A9 towards city centre & pass Perth Leisure Pool on R. Turn R & straight on for 300yds)

☎ 01738 624141 🖷 01738 639912

Typical Victorian in style offering well appointed, spacious accommodation. Friendly and cheerful staff.

£££ 70 bedrooms (4 fmly) No smoking in 25 bedrooms Lift Night porter Gym Mini-gym No smoking area in restaurant 🗪

QUEENS HOTEL ★★★
Leonard St PH2 8HB

☎ 01738 442222 🖷 01738 638496

Close to the railway and bus stations this hotel offers all the expected range of amenities.

£££ 51 bedrooms (6 fmly) No dogs (ex guide dogs) Lift Night porter Indoor swimming pool (heated) Sauna Solarium Gym Pool table Jacuzzi/spa Steam room No smoking area in restaurant 🗪

The Muirs Inn

THE ROYAL GEORGE ★★★
Tay St PH1 5LD
(from Edinburgh, through 2 sets of lights, R at 3rd set, L at next set, hotel 200 metres on L)
☎ 01738 624455 📠 01738 630345
Overlooking the River Tay this former traditional Scottish coaching inn offers spacious and comfortable accommodation.
£££ 42 bedrooms No smoking in 14 bedrooms Night porter No smoking in restaurant 🍴

NEWMILN COUNTRY HOUSE HOTEL ★★ ⊛⊛⊛
Newmiln Estate PH2 6AE
(follow signs for Scone Palace, take A93 Blairgowrie rd out of Perth. 3.5m after Scone Palace, Newmilns a tree-lined avenue is signposted on the L)
☎ 01738 552364 & 0831 624 949
📠 01738 553505
Magnificent 17th-century mansion on a 700 acre sporting estate. Fine cuisine, with an emphasis on game.
7 bedrooms No smoking in all bedrooms No dogs (ex guide dogs) Tennis (hard) No smoking in restaurant Closed Feb, 25 & 26 Dec 🍴

ISLE OF SKYE TOBY ★★
Queen's Bridge, 18 Dundee Rd PH2 7AB
☎ 01738 624471 📠 01738 622124
On the north side of the River Tay. Modern and more traditional bedrooms available. Popular Toby Carvery.
47 bedrooms (37 fmly) No smoking in 19 bedrooms Lift Night porter No smoking in restaurant 🍴

WOODLEA ★
23 York Place PH2 8EP
(A9 into Perth city centre, hotel on L, next to church & opposite library)
☎ 01738 621744 📠 01738 621744
Conveniently situated this small, welcoming family run hotel offers good value accommodation.
£ 11 bedrooms (1 fmly) No dogs (ex guide dogs) Night porter No smoking in restaurant

ABERCROMBIE ◲◲◲◲
85 Glasgow Rd PH2 0PQ
☎ 01738 444728
Charming semi-detached Victorian home within a short walk of central amenities.
£ 4 bedrooms No smoking No dogs No children 🍴

ARDFERN HOUSE ◲◲◲◲
15 Pitcullen Crescent PH2 7HT
(on A94 Perth-Forfar rd, 0.25m from Old Perth Bridge)
☎ 01738 637031
Victorian house immaculately maintained. Hearty breakfasts and enjoyable home cooked evening meals.
£ 3 bedrooms (1 fmly) No smoking

Call the AA Hotel Booking Service on 0990 050505 to book at AA recognised hotels and B&Bs in the UK, or through our internet site: http://www.theaa.co.uk/hotels

---

KINNAIRD ◲◲◲◲
5 Marshall Place PH2 8AH
☎ 01738 628021 📠 01738 444056
Part of a Georgian terrace this is a welcoming and immaculate family run guest house.
£ 7 bedrooms No smoking No dogs No children under 12yrs Closed Xmas & New Year 🍴

PARK LANE ◲◲◲◲
17 Marshall Place PH2 8AG
(from M90 enter town on A912. L at 1st set of lights. Park Lane on R opp park)
☎ 01738 637218 📠 01738 643519
Near central amenities this Georgian terraced house offers extensive, imaginative breakfast menu.
£ 6 bedrooms (1 fmly) No smoking in 3 bedrooms No smoking in dining room No smoking in lounges No dogs (ex guide dogs) Squash Solarium Gymnasium Closed 7 Dec-20 Jan 🍴

ADAM ◲◲◲
6 Pitcullen Crescent PH2 7HT
(from town centre, over bridge onto A94, (few minutes drive) guest house on L)
☎ 01738 627179
Just north of the city this house offers spacious bedrooms and enjoyable home cooked evening meals.
5 bedrooms (1 fmly) No smoking in dining room 🍴

ANGLERS INN ◲◲◲
Main Rd, Guildtown PH2 6BS
(4.5m N of Perth on A93)
☎ 01821 640329 📠 01821 640329
Small village inn offers excellent value accommodation. Light and airy bedrooms.
£ 4 bedrooms (1 fmly) Childrens facilities 🍴

THE BRIDGEHOUSE ◲◲◲
86 Main St, Methven PH1 3PS
(5m from Perth on A85. Opposite post office)
☎ 01738 840006
Relaxed welcoming atmosphere prevails. Pretty bedrooms. Guests may use video collection.
£ 3 bedrooms (1 fmly) No smoking in bedrooms No smoking in dining room No dogs (ex guide dogs) Childrens facilities 🍴

CASTLEVIEW ◲◲◲◲
166 Glasgow Rd PH2 0LY
☎ 01738 626415
Welcoming family run guest house, a detached Victorian house south of the city centre.
£ 3 bedrooms (1 fmly) No smoking in 2 bedrooms No smoking in dining room No smoking in lounges No dogs (ex guide dogs) Closed 25th Dec-Feb 🍴

CLARK KIMBERLEY ◲◲◲
57-59 Dunkeld Rd PH1 5RP
(0.5m N on A912)
☎ 01738 637406 📠 01738 643983
Two semi-detached linked houses created to make a comfortable and welcoming guest house.
£ 7 bedrooms (4 fmly) No smoking No dogs 🍴

CLUNIE ◲◲◲
12 Pitcullen Crescent PH2 7HT
(on A94 opposite side of river from town)
☎ 01738 623625
Semi-detached villa with a welcoming atmosphere, modern bedrooms and enjoyable home cooked fare.
£ 7 bedrooms (3 fmly) No smoking in dining room 🍴

IONA ◲◲◲
2 Pitcullen Crescent PH2 7HT *(on A94, approx 300yds from A94/A93 junct)*
☎ 01738 627261 📠 01738 444098
Good value accommodation, hearty breakfasts and home cooked evening meals at this friendly family-run guest house.
£ 5 bedrooms (1 fmly) No smoking in bedrooms No smoking in dining room 🍴

PITCULLEN ◲◲◲
17 Pitcullen Crescent PH2 7HT
(on A94)
☎ 01738 626506 📠 01738 628265
Welcoming guest house offering good value accommodation. Bright bedrooms and first floor lounge.
£ 6 bedrooms (1 fmly) No smoking in 2 bedrooms No smoking in dining room No dogs (ex guide dogs) 🍴

STRATHCONA ◲◲◲
45 Dunkeld Rd PH1 5RP
☎ 01738 626701 & 626185
📠 01738 628773
Convenient for central amenities and good value accommodation in this welcoming guest house.
£ 3 bedrooms (1 fmly) No smoking No dogs (ex guide dogs) No children under 3yrs 🍴

THE GABLES ◲◲
24 Dunkeld Rd PH1 5RW
(A912 towards Perth. Gables approx 1.5m on R just beyond 4th rdbt)
☎ 01738 624717 📠 01738 624717
Well maintained, friendly family run licensed guest house. High teas and hot snacks.
8 bedrooms (2 fmly) No smoking in bedrooms No smoking in dining room Licensed 🍴

THE HEIDL ◲◲
43 York Place PH2 8EH
(town centre end of Glasgow road)
☎ 01738 635031
Convenient to central amenities this family run guest house offers good value accommodation.
£ 8 bedrooms (2 fmly) No smoking in dining room

PITLOCHRY

PINE TREES ★★★⊛
Strathview Ter PH16 5QR
☎ 01796 472121 📠 01796 472460
Delightful Scottish mansion peacefully set amid 14 acres of mature grounds. Daily changing menu of Scottish specialities.
££ 20 bedrooms No dogs (ex guide dogs) Putting green No smoking in restaurant 🍴

GREEN PARK ★★★
Clunie Bridge Rd PH16 5JY
(turn off A9 at Pitlochry, follow signs 0.25m through town, hotel on banks of Loch Fascally)
☎ 01796 473248 🔧 01796 473520
Well established hotel in an idyllic location on the edge of Loch Faskally.
££ 38 bedrooms No smoking in all bedrooms Putting green No smoking in restaurant 🍽

ATHOLL PALACE ★★★
Atholl Rd PH16 5LY
(South-Pitlochry rd off A9, hotel just after rail bridge on R into town. North- straight through town & turn L just before rail bridge)
☎ 01796 472400 🔧 01796 473036
Built in the 'Grand Resort' style, this hotel has magnificent views, and pleasing, unique atmosphere.
££££ 76 bedrooms (4 fmly) No smoking in 30 bedrooms Lift Night porter Outdoor swimming pool (heated) Tennis (hard) Snooker Sauna Solarium Pool table Putting green 9 Hole pitch & putt Games room No smoking in restaurant 🍽

PITLOCHRY HYDRO ★★★
Knockard Rd PH16 5JH
(turn off A9, on to town centre & turn R onto A924. Hotel 0.5m on R)
☎ 01796 472666 🔧 01796 472238
Large resort and conference hotel, dominating the skyline, where professional staff have the light-hearted approach.
£££ 64 bedrooms (6 fmly) Lift Night porter Indoor swimming pool (heated) Snooker Sauna Solarium Gym Croquet lawn Putting green Jacuzzi/spa No smoking in restaurant Closed Jan 🍽

SCOTLAND'S ★★★
40 Bonnethill Rd PH16 5BT
☎ 01796 472292 🔧 01796 473284
Long established tourist hotel in the centre of town.
£ 60 bedrooms (14 fmly) No dogs (ex guide dogs) Lift Night porter Indoor swimming pool (heated) Sauna Solarium Gym Beauty room No smoking in restaurant 🍽

KNOCKENDARROCH HOUSE ★★ ❀
Higher Oakfield PH16 5HT
(from S turn off A9 at Pitlochry sign. After railway bridge, take 1st R then 2nd L)
☎ 01796 473473 🔧 01796 474068
A very personal level of attention is assured. For theatre-going guests, there's dinner from 6pm.
££ 12 bedrooms No smoking in all bedrooms No dogs (ex guide dogs) Leisure facilities at nearby hotel No children under 12yrs No smoking in restaurant Closed Dec-Jan 🍽

ACARSAID ★★
8 Atholl Rd PH16 5BX
(take A9 Perth to Pitlochry, hotel on R on entering town)
☎ 01796 472389 🔧 01796 473952
Bedrooms are bright and airy with practical modern appointments at this comfortable holiday hotel.
££ 18 bedrooms (1 fmly) No dogs (ex guide dogs) No children under 10yrs No smoking in restaurant Closed 6 Jan-5 Mar 🍽

BALROBIN ★★
Higher Oakfield PH16 5HT
(from S (A9), pass distillery on R, take 2nd R, up steep hill & Higher Oakfield second on L, hotel just round corner)
☎ 01796 472901 🔧 01796 474200
Very personal level of service and welcoming hospitality. Views over the town to the hills beyond.
£ 15 bedrooms (2 fmly) No children under 5yrs No smoking in restaurant Closed Dec-Feb (ex New Year) 🍽

BIRCHWOOD ★★
2 East Moulin Rd PH16 5DW
(200 m off Atholl Rd on S side of town)
☎ 01796 472477 🔧 01796 473951
Peacefully set in large grounds, this welcoming hotel attracts guests to return time and again.
£ 12 bedrooms 5 annexe (4 fmly) No smoking in restaurant Closed Dec-Feb 🍽

CLAYMORE ★★
162 Atholl Rd PH16 5AR
(turn off A9 into Pitlochry, hotel last on R after passing through town centre - heading N)
☎ 01796 472888 🔧 01796 474062
Enthusiastic owners look forward to welcoming guests to their delightful hotel in two acre gardens.
£ 7 bedrooms 4 annexe bedrooms (1 fmly) No smoking in 7 bedrooms No smoking in restaurant Closed 3 Jan-14 Feb 🍽

CRAIG URRARD ★★
10 Atholl Rd PH16 5BX
☎ 01796 472346
Friendly informal atmosphere at this small family run hotel in the south of town.
£ 10 bedrooms 2 annexe (2 fmly) No dogs No smoking in restaurant 🍽

CRAIGVRACK ★★
West Moulin Rd PH16 5EQ
(turn off A9 into Pitlochry. Follow sign for Braemar A93, turn R on main street Kirkmichael/Braemar A93 hotel on R after 500 mtrs)
☎ 01796 472399 🔧 01796 473990
Elevated position beside the Braemar road, enjoying views over the surrounding wooded hills.
£ 16 bedrooms (2 fmly) No smoking in restaurant 🍽

DUNDARACH ★★
Perth Rd PH16 5DJ
(S of town centre on main route)
☎ 01796 472862 🔧 01796 473024
Popular mansion house in several acres of grounds where a warm welcome is assured.
££ 23 bedrooms 3 annexe bedrooms (2 fmly) Closed Jan RS Dec-early Feb 🍽

WESTLANDS OF PITLOCHRY ★★
160 Atholl Rd PH16 5AR *(turn off A9 into Pitlochry, hotel at N end of town)*
☎ 01796 472266 🔧 01796 473994
Guests old and new will be warmly welcomed here. Charming garden restaurant with Taste of Scotland dishes.
15 bedrooms (2 fmly) Fishing No smoking in restaurant 🍽

COMAR HOUSE ◫◫◫◫
Strathview Ter PH16 5AT
(turn off A9 to Pitlochry, last street on R going N, signed to Golf Course, R at top of hill 2nd house on L)
☎ 01796 473531 🔧 01796 473811
From its elevated position this detached house enjoys lovely views over the town to the hills beyond.
£ 6 bedrooms No smoking Etr-Oct 🍽

CRAIGROYSTON HOUSE ◫◫◫◫
2 Lower Oakfield PH16 5HQ *(in town centre just above Information Centre car park)*
☎ 01796 472053 🔧 01796 472053
Charming Victorian home, with lovely views, conveniently close to central amenities.
£ 8 bedrooms (1 fmly) No smoking in bedrooms No smoking in dining room No dogs (ex guide dogs)

DUNDARAVE HOUSE ◫◫◫◫
Strathview Ter PH16 5AT
(from Pitlochry main street turn into West Moulin Rd, 2nd L into Strathview Terrace)
☎ 01796 473109 🔧 01796 473109
Warm personal welcome assured at this detached Victorian house above the town.
£ 7 bedrooms (1 fmly) No smoking in dining room Mar-Nov

TORRDARACH HOTEL ◫◫◫◫
Golf Course Rd PH16 5AU
(turn off Athol Road to golf course, last hotel before golf course (red house))
☎ 01796 472136
Victorian house peacefully set in wooded grounds and enjoying views over the Tummel Valley.
£ 7 bedrooms No smoking No dogs (ex guide dogs) Licensed No children under 12yrs Closed Mid Oct-Easter

ARRANDALE HOUSE ◫◫◫
Knockfarrie Rd PH16 5DN
☎/🔧 01796 472987
Welcoming family run guest house enjoying lovely views over the Tummel Valley.
£ 7 bedrooms (2 fmly) No smoking No dogs Nov-Mar

WELL HOUSE PRIVATE HOTEL ◫◫◫
11 Toberargan Rd PH16 5HG
(road running parallel to the main street)
☎ 01796 472239
Near the central amenities, with bright, airy bedrooms and enjoyable home cooking.
£ 6 bedrooms (1 fmly) No smoking in bedrooms No smoking in dining room No dogs (ex guide dogs) Licensed Closed mid Nov - early Mar 🍽

WHINSMUIR COUNTRY INN ★★★ ❀
FK14 7NW *(on A977)*
☎ 01577 840595 🔧 01577 840779
Country inn with spacious bedrooms in a modern wing. Robust bistro cooking and Taste of Scotland dishes.
££ 13 bedrooms (5 fmly) No smoking in 2 bedrooms Pool table 🍽

ST FILLANS

THE FOUR SEASONS HOTEL ★★★⊛⊛
Loch Earn PH6 2NF *(on A85)*
☎ 01764 685333 📠 01764 685333
Genuine hospitality at this honest hotel
overlooking picturesque Loch Earn. Bar
and restaurant menus.
*££ 12 bedrooms (2 fmly) Fishing Private
foreshore & jetty Free launching facilities
for guest's boats No smoking in restaurant
Closed Jan-Feb RS mid Nov-end Dec* 🗡

ACHRAY HOUSE ★★
Loch Earn PH6 2NF
(on A85 12m from Crieff)
☎ 01764 685231 📠 01764 685320
Enjoys a wonderful outlook over Loch
Earn. Informal conservatory eating and
restaurant dining.
*££ 9 bedrooms (1 fmly) No dogs (ex guide
dogs) No smoking in restaurant* 🗡

STANLEY

THE TAYSIDE ★★⊛
Mill St PH1 4NL *(6m N of Perth)*
☎ 01738 828249 📠 01738 827216
(Rosette awarded for dinner only)
Distinctive Edwardian character prevails at
this welcoming fishing and golfing hotel.
Robust country cooking.
££ 16 bedrooms (2 fmly) Fishing 🗡

WHERE TO EAT

RESTAURANTS

AA RECOMMENDED

ABERFELDY

LA MERIDIANA ⊛
The Square, PH15 2DD
☎ 01887 829000 📠 01887 473256
Simply decorated Italian restaurant where
the extensive carte may list tagliatelle
carbonara, rack of lamb with a mint and
berry sauce, and dark chocolate mousse.
Pizzas and pasta at lunchtime.
ALC ££ 🗡

GUINACH HOUSE HOTEL ⊛⊛
'By the Birks', Urlar Road PH15 2ET
☎ 01887 820251 📠 01887 829607
Country house hotel producing regional
inspired dinner menus with Loch Fyne
smoked salmon, Isle of Barra queen
scallops with Noilly Prat, or breast of
Tombuie smoked guinea fowl.
Fixed D ££ 🗡

ALYTH

DRUMNACREE HOUSE ⊛⊛
St Ninians Road, PH11 8AP
☎/📠 01828 632194
Scottish and more exotic ideas abound. A
smooth Arbroath smokie mousse, French
black pudding with caramelised apples,
spiced suprême of pigeon on a bed of
couscous, and sweet poached pears with
cinnamon ice cream.
Fixed D ££ ALC ££ 🗡

AUCHTERARDER

AUCHTERARDER HOUSE ⊛⊛
PH3 1DZ
☎ 01764 663646 📠 01764 662939
The very best Scottish produce is used in a
terrine of wild mushroom and pigeon,
lightly grilled fillet of fresh halibut and a
dark chocolate soufflé with a light, white
chocolate sauce and fresh strawberries.

CAIRN LODGE ⊛
Orchil Road, PH3 1LX
☎ 01764 662634 📠 01764 664866
In the elegant Capercaillie Restaurant enjoy
an innovative menu based on Scotland's

rich larder. Expect roast pheasant stuffed
with pork and apricots, or corn-fed chicken
filled with smoked Tay salmon mousse.
Fixed L £ ALC £££ 🗡

DUCHALLY HOUSE HOTEL ⊛
PH3 1PN
☎ 01764 663071 📠 01764 662464
A set gourmet menu and a 'Taste of
Scotland' carte. A typical meal could take
in cornets of oak-smoked salmon with a
mousse of Arbroath smokie, roast cutlets
of lamb with olives and couscous, and
apple fritter in beer batter.
Fixed L £ ALC ££ 🗡

THE GLENEAGLES HOTEL ⊛⊛⊛
PH3 1NF
☎ 01764 662231 📠 01764 662134
Tip-top Scottish ingredients are given a
modern interpretation. Traditional roast of
the day is still popular plus dishes such as
Ravioli of lobster and saffron bisque, and
toffee cheesecake.
Fixed D £££ ALC £££ 🗡

BLAIRGOWRIE

KINLOCH HOUSE HOTEL ⊛⊛⊛
PH10 6SG
☎ 01250 884237 📠 01250 884333
The carte is imaginative and extensive. Try
perhaps Mallard duck liver pâté, fillet of
hare marinated in port, and delicious
marmalade and whisky soufflé.
Fixed D £££

CLEISH

NIVINGSTON HOUSE HOTEL ⊛
Cleish Hills, KY13 7LS
☎ 01577 850216 📠 01577 850238
Interesting menus that combines Scottish
produce with more exotic fare. Lookout for
medallions of pork with prune, apple and
Calvados sauce, and Scotch salmon with
hollandaise.

COUPAR ANGUS

MOORFIELD HOUSE ⊛⊛
PH13 9HS
☎ 01828 627303 📠 01828 627339
The cooking describes itself as 'rustic' but
is more sophisticated in concept. Maybe a
warm salad or fish soufflé to start then a
steak dish, with a ragout of creamed
mushrooms and bacon. For dessert a tarte
Tatin or chocolate brioche.
Fixed L £ 🗡

DUNKELD

ATHOLL ARMS ⊛
Bridgehead, PH8 0AQ,
☎/📠 01350 727219
The comfortably traditional dining room
boasts open fires and a menu built around
local produce. Expect dishes such as
cullen skink, chicken suprême with haggis,
and steamed ginger pudding.
ALC £ 🗡

KINNAIRD ⊛⊛⊛
Kinnaird, PH8 0LB
☎ 01796 482440 📠 01796 482289
Unashamedly luxurious. Brochette of king
scallops with Parma ham and braised
lentils; risotto of white truffle and cep, loin
of venison in a mousse of herbs and
pastry and a wonderfully wicked dark
chocolate marquise all display sound
technical skills and the use of superb raw
ingredients.
🗡

KILLIECRANKIE

KILLIECRANKIE HOTEL ⊛⊛
Pitlochry, PH16 5LG
☎ 01796 473220 📠 01796 472451
Personal attention and a terrific
atmosphere. Baked Isle of Gigha goat's,
pan-fried fillet of rock turbot in Malaysian
red curry, and white chocolate mousse
cake for dessert are all highly
recommended.
Fixed D £££

KINCLAVEN

BALLATHIE HOUSE HOTEL ✿✿
Stanley, PH1 4QN
☎ 01250 883268 ✆ 01250 883396
Locally caught salmon, king scallops from Skye and Aberdeen Angus beef typically find their way onto the menu. Chilled citrus fruit tart to a steamed marmalade pudding for dessert.
Fixed D £££ ALC £

KINNESSWOOD

LOMOND COUNTRY INN ✿
KY13 7HN
☎ 01592 840253 ✆ 01592 840693
Popular village inn offering strong Scottish flavours and sound modern ideas. Cullen skink, Pittenweem haddock, and deep-fried haggis being just three examples.
Fixed L/D £ ALC £

KINROSS

CROFT BANK ✿✿
KY13 7TG
☎ 01577 863819
Two contrasting dining rooms provide the setting for the best from Scotland's larder. Game terrine, poached Shetland salmon and medallions of Scotch beef followed by raspberry crème brûlée or banana pavlova.
Fixed L £ ALC ££

PERTH

HUNTINGTOWER HOTEL ✿
Crieff Road, Almondbank, PH1 3JT
☎ 01738 583771 ✆ 01738 583777
A Taste of Scotland is assured in both the conservatory and the elegant dining room. Dishes can include Highland game terrine flavoured with malt whisky, and fillet of cod roasted with sesame seeds and garlic.
Fixed L £

KINFAUNS CASTLE ✿✿
Kinfauns, PH2 7JZ
☎ 01738 620777 ✆ 01738 620778
The use of excellent raw ingredients is reflected in the tastes of 'pottage grisons' (a Swiss-style Scotch broth), and medallions of Ceannacroc Blackface lamb. Delicious petits fours with coffee. Booking is essential.
Fixed L ££

LET'S EAT ✿✿
77/79 Kinnoull Street,
☎ 01738 643377 ✆ 01738 621464
Lunch and dinner menus brim over with ideas and ingredients of the moment – tapenade, pancetta, truffle oil, lemon grass. More traditionally a chicken liver terrine or mélange of seared halibut, salmon and squat lobsters.
ALC ££

MURRAYSHALL COUNTRY HOUSE HOTEL ✿✿
New Scone PH2 7PH
☎ 01738 551171 ✆ 01738 552595
Consistently good food at affordable prices. Expect mousseline of Arbroath smokies, main course roasted loin of woodland roe deer and steamed orange sponge pudding.
Fixed D ££ ALC ££

NEWMILN COUNTRY ESTATE ✿✿✿
By Scone Palace PH2 6AE
☎ 01738 552364 ✆ 01738 553505
Honest flavours and commitment to local produce. Dinner could feature a mousseline of scallops with dill, new season's Perthshire lamb and iced Drambuie parfait with seasonal fruits.
Fixed L ££ ALC £££

NUMBER THIRTY THREE SEAFOOD RESTAURANT ✿
33 George Street, PH1 5LA
☎ 01738 633771
Cooking majors on fresh fish and flavours to shine through. Crab terrine with prawns, halibut with yoghurt and orange sauce, and sticky toffee pudding. Lighter meals are served in the Oyster Bar.
ALC ££

PARKLANDS HOTEL ✿
St Leonards Bank PH2 8EB
☎ 01738 622451 ✆ 01738 622046
Pleasant hotel with an attractive conservatory restaurant. Look out for medallions of monkfish, pan-fried Aberdeen Angus sirloin steak, and pot-roast breast of pheasant. Service is very friendly and attentive.
Fixed L £ ALC ££

PITLOCHRY

KNOCKENDARROCH HOUSE HOTEL ✿
Higher Oakfield, PH16 5HT
☎ 01796 473473 ✆ 01796 474068
At this Victorian mansion, choices from the short menu might include baked Tay salmon with mild grain mustard sauce, and roast haunch of venison.
Fixed D ££

PINE TREES HOTEL ✿
Strathview Terrace, PH16 5QR
☎ 01796 472121 ✆ 01796 472460
Elegant mansion in a beautiful setting. Daily changing menu that embraces the likes of pigeon and duck terrine, paupiettes of sole filled with trout mousseline and a creamy herb sauce, and poached pear in red wine with Atholl brose.
Fixed D ££

POWMILL

WHINSMUIR COUNTRY INN ✿
By Dollar, FK14 7NW
☎ 01577 840595 ✆ 01577 840779
Bistro-style restaurant serving 'Taste of Scotland' dishes. These include west coast prawns, prime beef, and roast salmon. Frosted Turkish delight soufflé is among the imaginative puddings.
Fixed L £ ALC £

SPITTAL OF GLENSHEE

DALMUNZIE HOUSE ✿
Blairgowrie, PH10 7QG
☎ 01250 885224 ✆ 01250 885225
Sound hospitality and uncomplicated Scottish fare. Quality local ingredients are used in such successful dishes as smoked trout mousse with dill cream, baked halibut with a herb crust and red caviar cream, and sherry trifle.
Fixed D ££

ST FILLANS

THE FOUR SEASONS HOTEL ✿✿
Crieff, PH6 2NF
☎/✆ 01764 685333
Good choice dinner menu based on fresh local produce. Saddle of venison with juniper and whisky flavourings or fillet of lamb with rosemary and shallots. Desserts might be warm lemon tart, apple and sultana crumble, or iced blackcurrant parfait.

STANLEY

THE TAYSIDE HOTEL ✿
Mill Street, PH1 4NL
☎ 01738 828249 ✆ 01738 827216
The restaurant with tartan wall coverings makes a strong impression. Robust country cooking, based on good quality local ingredients, may include Royal Perth haggis, prime Scottish steak, and venison MacDuff.
Fixed D ££ ALC ££

THE NORTH EAST
ABERDEENSHIRE & MORAY

Thanks to the protective Cairngorm and Grampian Mountains, the spacious, wide open spaces of Moray and Aberdeenshire enjoy a surprisingly mild, dry climate; one reason, among many, why visitors are drawn to this stunning north-east shoulder of Scotland. Here, the largely undiscovered Moray coast offers miles of red sandstone cliffs that spill down to fine sandy beaches split by dramatic rocky headlands, and a chain of small towns, sleepy villages and fishing ports look across the Moray Firth to the shifting mass of the North Sea beyond. The gentle breezes and warm sunshine of lazy summer days gives the place a restful, relaxing air, and the evenings are a magical time too. This part of Scotland is renowned for its superb sunsets.

To the south, a low-lying Scandinavian landscape of lush fields, winding rivers and dense forest rises steadily towards the foothills of the Cairngorm range. Reaching to the heart of this district is the River Spey, Scotland's fastest flowing river and a mecca for salmon anglers and malt whisky tipplers. There are numerous distilleries on this stretch of the Spey, some are open to the public and offer the opportunity to sample a wee dram!

Buchan Ness is the easternmost point of Scotland and from here you can follow the coast south to Peterhead, once an important whaling community. Beyond it is Aberdeen, where the eastern spur of the Grampians gives way to the North Sea, and two famous salmon rivers, the Don and the Dee, reach the end of their spectacular journey. Heading west out of Scotland's granite city, you are soon in a magical world of heather moorland, rolling hills and densely wooded valleys, cut by meandering rivers and picturesque lochs. It is here that you can discover a staggering number of castles and ancient strongholds - more than 150 in all - the most famous being Balmoral, the summer home of the Royal Family.

PRINCIPAL TOWNS

ELGIN

Elgin, the commercial and administrative centre for Moray for over eight centuries, stands on a meadering loop of the River Lossie in a richly fertile agricultural district known as the Garden of Moray. Although the townscape has been reworked and rebuilt over the years, it retains a medieval street plan with narrow alleyways leading off the broad main street, a cobbled market place, and some fine old 18th- and 19th-century buildings.

Elgin has long been a favoured tourist centre for exploring the north-west corner of Grampian and offers a host of attractions for the discerning visitor.

ABERDEEN

Aberdeen, dubbed the 'capital' of the North Sea oil industry, with its new found prosperity, multi-national contracts, mighty oil rig vessels and a vibrant cosmopolitan appearance, is Scotland's third largest settlement and Britain's most northerly city. Built between the mouths of the River Dee and the Don, the true character of this long-established port and busy commercial centre - a royal burgh since 1124 - is revealed, despite the excesses of the oil boom, through gracious terraces, squares and crescents in the beautiful Georgian part of the city, and numerous architectural gems, including the oldest medieval bridge in Scotland, the Brig O'Balgownie over the River Don.

Whether you are attracted here for its granite splendour of the city centre, notably the world's only granite cathedral - St Machar's, for the numerous historic buildings and fascinatinging museums that exist, or for the excellent shopping facilities, the lively nightlife and the 'festival' atmosphere that engulfs the city, there's a wealth of attractions to absorb your time.

EVENTS & FESTIVALS

January

Burning of the Clavie,
Burghead, Moray

February

Scottish International Open Snooker Championship,
Exhibition & Conference Centre, Aberdeen

March

Spring Flower Shows,
Aberdeen,
Aberlour, Moray
Lossiemouth, Moray

North of Scotland Model Railway Show,
Elgin, Moray

European Mogul Challenge,
Glenshee Ski Centre, Braemar, Aberdeenshire

April

Garioch Fiddler's Rally,
Inverurie, Aberdeenshire

Spring Show,
Banff, Aberdeenshire

Royal Lipizanner Stallion Show,
Exhibition & Conference Centre, Aberdeen

May

Beltane Fair,
Aberdeen

Don Raft Race,
Kemnay, Inverurie, Aberdeenshire

Festival of Scottish Music,
Banchory, Aberdeenshire

Royal Deeside Golf Week,
Ballater, Aberdeenshire

Buchan Heritage Festival,
Strichen, Aberdeenshire

Crathes Craft & Design Fair,
Crathes Castle, Banchory, Aberdeenshire

June

Feein' Market,
Stonehaven, Aberdeenshire

Ythan Raft Race,
Ellon, Aberdeenshire

Kaleidoscope, Children's Festival,
Haddo House, Moray

Kildrummy Castle Rally,
Kildrummy, Aberdeenshire

Traditional Festival of Music,
Keith, Aberdeenshire

Scottish Country Dance Weekend,
Fochabers, Moray

Moray Science Festival,
Elgin, Moray

R W Thomson Vintage Vehicle Rally,
Stonehaven, Aberdeenshire

Highland Games,
Aberdeen

Drumtochty Highland Games,
Auchenblae, Aberdeenshire

Oldmeldrum Sports & Highland Games,
Oldmeldrum, Aberdeenshire

Scottish Traditional Boat Festival,
Portsoy, Aberdeenshire

Maggie Fair,
Garmouth, Moray

Steam Engine Rally,
Hazlehead Park, Aberdeen

July

Aboyne & Deeside Festival,
Throughout the region

Gala Month,
Braemar, Aberdeenshire

Folk Festival,
Stonehaven, Aberdeenshire

Echt, Skene & Midmar Agricultural Show,
Echt, Aberdeenshire

Highland Games,
Dufftown, Moray
Elgin, Moray
Forres, Moray
Stonehaven, Aberdeenshire
Tomintoul & Strathavon, Moray

Folk Festival,
Lossiemouth, Aberdeenshire

Alford Calvacade,
Grampian Transport Museum, Alford, Aberdeenshire

Scottish Week,
Peterhead, Aberdeenshire

Agricultural Show,
Banchory, Aberdeenshire

Fish Festival,
Fraserburgh, Aberdeenshire

New Deer Show & Sports,
New Deer, Aberdeenshire

Huntly Gala,
Huntly, Aberdeenshire

International Youth Festival,
Aberdeen

August

Highland Games,
Aberlour & Strathspey, Moray
Aboyne, Aberdeenshire
Ballater, Aberdeenshire

Agricultural Shows,
Keith, Moray
Tarland, Aberdeenshire
Turriff, Aberdeenshire

Ballater Victoria Week,
Ballater, Aberdeenshire

The Clan Fraser Gathering,
Castle Fraser, Sauchen, Inverurie, Aberdeenshire

Harbour Open Day,
Peterhead, Aberdeenshire

Taste of Moray,
Brodie Castle, Forres, Moray

Clydesdale Horse Show,
Duthie Park, Aberdeen

Summer Flower Show,
Aberdeen

Lonach Highland Gathering & Games,
Bellabeg, Strathdon, Aberdeenshire

Lourin' Fair,
Old Rayne, Aberdeenshire

Echt Horticultural Show,
Echt, Aberdeenshire

September

Braemar Royal Highland Gathering,
Braemar, Aberdeenshire

Techfest, Science & Technology Festival,
Aberdeen

Ancient Craft Fair,
Archaeolink, Oyne, Aberdeenshire

Fiddlers' Rally,
Elgin, Moray

October

Aberdeen Alternative Festival,
Aberdeen

Doric Festival,
Throughout Aberdeenshire

International Scotch Whisky Festival,
Throughout Speyside

November

Taste of Royal Deeside.
Ballater, Aberdeenshire

Aberdeen Winter Festival

December

Fireball Festival,
Stonehaven, Aberdeenshire

MAPS

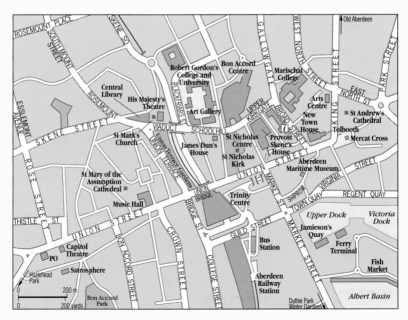

MUST SEE

Fyvie Castle

ABERDEENSHIRE

ABERDEENSHIRE FARMING MUSEUM,
Mintlaw ☎ 01771 622906

Set in the beautiful surroundings of Aden Country Park, this award-winning heritage centre explores two centuries of farming history and innovation through exhibitions housed in unique 19th-century farm buildings. The story of the Aden estate is well illustrated and a visit to Hareshowe, a reconstructed working farmstead, shows farming life in the 1950s.

ABERDEEN MARITIME MUSEUM,
Provost Ross's House, Shiprow, Aberdeen
☎ 01224 585788

Situated on the ancient route from the harbour to the city centre in Aberdeen's oldest building, the 400-year-old former home of a Lord Provost (Mayor), the museum tells the fascinating story of the city's maritime history, and its oil industry, in dramatic fashion. Multi-media displays, computer visual databases, audio-visual theatre and a collection of maritime paintings illustrate the North East's long association with the sea. Shop and café.

CASTLE FRASER,
Kemnay ☎ 01330 833463

The massive Z-plan castle was begun in 1575 by the 6th Laird and completed in 1636. The low wings emphasize the magnificence of the towers, and its architectural embellishments make it one of the grandest of the Castles of Mar. Fine furnishings, paintings and memorabilia are a feature of the interior, which was remodelled in 1838 and evokes the atmosphere of past centuries. A formal garden has been created in the old walled garden. Woodland walks, an adventure playground, regular events and tearoom.

CRATHES CASTLE & GARDENS,
Crathes, By Banchory ☎ 01330 844525

This impressive 16th-century tower house with fairytale-like turrets, magnificent interiors and painted ceilings has royal associations dating from 1323. A prized relic is the ancient Horn of Leys which was given to Alexander Burnett in 1323 by King Robert the Bruce. The eight-linked gardens, each one different, are enclosed within 300-year-old yew hedges and include a 3-acre walled garden, wild gardens, nature trails and woodland walks.

FYVIE CASTLE,
Fyvie, Turriff ☎/🅖 01651 891266

One of the grandest examples of Scottish baronial architecture dating from the 13th century. Five towers, each built in a different century, bear witness to the five families who have owned it. It contains the finest wheel stair in Scotland, and a 17th-century morning room which, along with other rooms, has been decorated and furnished in lavish Edwardian grandeur. There is a superb collection of arms, armour and paintings, including works by Raeburn, Gainsborough and Hoppner.

SCOTLAND'S LIGHTHOUSE MUSEUM,
Fraserburgh ☎ 01346 511022

Discover the skill, the dedication, the science and the romance of Scotland's lighthouses. This purpose-built museum features fascinating displays, including multi-screen technology, that portray the story and traditions of lighthouse service, now ending with automation. A visit incorporates a tour to the top of Kinnaird Lighthouse itself.

MORAY

BRODIE CASTLE,
Forres ☎ 01309 641371

A handsome, gabled castle based on a 16th-century Z-plan with later additions, and home to the Brodie family for hundreds of years until 1980, when it was passed to the National Trust for Scotland. It contains some fine treasures, including French furniture, porcelain, and an impressive collection of paintings. The extensive grounds have a woodland walk, daffodils and a wildlife hide. Adventure playground, special events and restaurant

BUCKIE DRIFTER,
Freuchny Rd, Buckie
☎ 01542 834646

An exciting maritime heritage centre where visitors can discover and experience what life was like in the fishing communities of Moray during the herring boom years between the 1890s and 1930s. Learn how to catch herring, try your hand at packing fish in a barrel and discover the undersea life through 'hands-on' displays. Changing displays, conducted harbour tours and restaurant.

GLENFIDDICH DISTILLERY VISITOR CENTRE,
Dufftown ☎ 01340 820373

Set close to Balvenie Castle, the distillery was founded in 1887 by William Grant and has stayed in the hands of the family ever since. The visitor centre offers one of the best audio-visuals on the history and manufacture of whisky, a Scottish whisky museum and tours, showing all the stages from malting through to bottling. At the end of the tour there is the chance to sample the finished product.

SPEYSIDE COOPERAGE VISITOR CENTRE,
Craigellachie ☎ 01340 871108

An award-winning working cooperage with a unique visitor centre, where skilled coopers practise their ancient craft of coopering. Watch them repairing the oak casks (around 100,000 a year) for the whisky industry, and savour the sights, sounds and smells of the bustling workshops from the viewing gallery. An 'Acorn to Cask' exhibition traces the development of the coopering industry and includes a Victorian cooperage with speaking life-size models.

SPEYSIDE WAY

The 45 mile (72km) Speyside Way, begins at Spey Bay on the coast and then runs through the heart of the district to finish at Tomintoul, in the shadow of the Cairngorms. Apart from the magnificent scenery, it's a wonderful way of discovering the culture and unique character of Moray. It follows part of the 70 mile (112km) Malt Whisky Trail, stumbling upon several distilleries directly on the route of the walk. The trail traverses some of the grandest landscapes in Scotland, and the further south you go, the more impressive the surroundings become.

QUEEN VICTORIA

Queen Victoria loved to explore Scotland and you can follow in her footsteps by taking the Victorian Heritage Trail, discovering the best of Royal Deeside.

There are plenty of opportunities for walking, where you can soak in the beauty of this regal landscape, little changed in centuries. It was Queen Victoria who wrote 'the scenery all around is the finest almost I have seen anywhere...we are certainly in the finest part of the Highlands. You can walk forever..and the wildness, the solitariness of everything is so delightful, so refreshing...' Keen walkers will identify with her sentiments.

ART GALLERIES

ABERDEENSHIRE

ABERDEEN ART GALLERY,
Schoolhill, Aberdeen ☎ 01224 646333
The gallery's 16th to 20th-century Scottish art includes sculpture and decorative arts, and an outstanding collection of modern paintings.

DUFF HOUSE COUNTRY GALLERY,
Banff ☎ 01261 818181
Magnificent Baroque mansion by William Adam displaying Scottish portraiture of the 18th and 19th centuries, as well as fine period furniture.

THE MCEWAN GALLERY,
Glen Gardens, Ballater ☎ 01339 755429
18th-century and modern paintings, pottery and sculpture.

SYLLAVETHY GALLERY,
Montgarrie, Alford ☎ 019755 62273
TOLQUHON GALLERY,
Tolquhon, Tarves ☎ 01651 842343

MORAY

PETER ANSON GALLERY,
Cluny Pl, Buckie ☎ 01309 673701
BARNYARD STUDIOS,
Connagedale, Garmouth ☎ 01343 870599
GREEN HALL GALLERY,
Craigellachie ☎ 01340 871010

MUSEUMS

ABERDEENSHIRE

ARBUTHNOT MUSEUM & ART GALLERY,
St Peter St, Peterhead ☎ 01771 622906
Specialising in local exhibits, particularly those relating to the fishing industry, the museum also displays Arctic and whaling specimens and a British coin collection.

JAMES DUN'S HOUSE,
Schoolhill, Aberdeen ☎ 01224 646333
Restored Georgian house housing special exhibitions, including fine art, photography and local history.

GARLOGIE MILL POWER HOUSE MUSEUM,
Garlogie, Skene, Westhill ☎ 01771 622906
A restored building housing the only beam engine of its type insitu in Scotland.

THE GORDON HIGHLANDERS MUSEUM
Viewfield Rd, Aberdeen ☎ 01224 311200
Interactive displays, audio-visual theatre and life-size reconstructions tell the compelling and dramatic story of one of the British Army's most famous regiments.

GRASSIC GIBBON VISITOR CENTRE,
Arbuthnott, Laurencekirk ☎ 01561 361668
A visitor centre dedicated to Lewis Grassic Gibbon (James Leslie Mitchell), the Scottish writer who vividly portrayed life in this part of North East Scotland in his trilogy Ascots Quair.

HIGHLAND HERITAGE CENTRE,
Mar Rd, Braemar ☎ 013397 41944
Explores the royal connection with the area, as well as featuring Braemar's landscape and the Highland Gathering.

PETERHEAD MARITIME HERITAGE,
South Rd, Peterhead ☎/✆ 01779 473000
Hands-on and interactive displays, and an innovative video presentation recall the maritime heritage of the port.

TOLBOOTH MUSEUM,
Castle St, Aberdeen ☎ 01224 621167
Housed in the 17th-century Tolbooth, Aberdeen's museum of civic history charts the growth and history of the city.

TOLBOOTH MUSEUM,
Old Pier, Stonehaven ☎ 01771 622906
Local history and fishing exhibitions housed in a 16th-century Tolbooth.

UNIVERSITY ZOOLOGY MUSEUM,
Tillydrone Av, Aberdeen ☎ 01224 493288
Large range of zoological specimens, from fish to elephants, bird gallery, whale skeletons and fossils.

MORAY

BAXTERS VISITOR CENTRE,
Fochabers ☎ 01343 820666
Manufacturer of quality Scottish food for the past 125 years. See the original shop, take a guided tour of the factory and watch an audio-visual display.

ELGIN MUSEUM,
1 High St, Elgin ☎/✆ 01343 543675
An award-winning local museum famous for its fossil fish and fossil reptiles, and for its Pictish stones.

FALCONER MUSEUM,
Tolbooth St, Forres ☎ 01309 673701
Displays of fossil mammals collected by Hugh Falconer, a distinguished scientist, and exhibits on local wildlife, geology, archaeology and history.

FOCHABER FOLK MUSEUM,
High St, Fochabers ☎ 01343 821204
A converted church housing collections of horse-drawn carriages, vehicles, costumes, model engines, a village shop and Victorian parlour.

TOMINTOUL MUSEUM,
The Square, Tomintoul ☎ 01309 673701
Rural life, landscape, wildlife, skiing and local history displays, including a reconstructed crofter's kitchen and smiddy.

TUGNET ICE HOUSE,
Tugnet, Spey Bay ☎ 01309 673701
History of the River Spey and salmon fishing in Scotland's largest ice house, built in 1830.

HISTORIC & ANCIENT SITES

ABERDEENSHIRE

DUNNOTAR CASTLE,
Stonehaven *2m/3.2km south*
Former stronghold of the Earls Marischal of Scotland, this impressive 14th-century fortress enjoys a spectacular setting on a rocky headland. Franco Zeffirelli chose it for his film Hamlet in 1990.

FYVIE CHURCH,
Fyvie, By Turriff
A 19th-century church containing a notable modern window of the Archangel Michael, designed by Tiffany.

HUNTLY CASTLE,
Huntly ☎ 01466 793191
An imposing ruin with heraldic adornments on its walls set beside the River Deveron.

KILDRUMMY CASTLE,
Kildrummy, By Alford ☎ 01975 571331
Though far from complete, 13th-century Kildrummy Castle is one of the best preserved medieval fortresses in Scotland.

KING'S COLLEGE CHAPEL,
College Bounds, Old Aberdeen ☎ 01224 273702
Collegiate chapel built around 1500 with a fine crown spire, ornate medieval woodcarving and 16th-century choir stalls.

LOANHEAD OF DAVIOT STONE CIRCLE,
By Inverurie *on B9001, 5m/8km north*
Burial cairn marked by a ring of standing stones, possibly 4000 years old.

MONYMUSK CHURCH,
Monymusk ☎ 01467 651470
A 12th-century church with an exhibition of 7th- 9th-century Pictish stones.

PITSLIGO CASTLE,
Rosehearty
Built by the Frasers in 1424, this large and impressive ruin of a courtyard castle (now part renovated) was once the stronghold of the Forbes family.

ST ANDREW'S CATHEDRAL,
King St, Aberdeen ☎ 01224 640290
Fine sandstone church built in 1817 in Perpendicular Gothic style.

ST MACHAR'S CATHEDRAL,
Old Aberdeen ☎ 01224 485988
Fortified 15th-century granite cathedral with twin spires and an impressive heraldic ceiling dating from 1520.

SLAINS CASTLE,
Built in 1598 by the 9th Earl of Errol, the awe-inspiring ruins of Slains Castle stand high above the sea and, reputedly, inspired Bram Stoker to write Dracula.

STONE CIRCLE TRAIL,
Well signposted tourist route/theme trail highlighting some of the fascinating carved Pictish stones, stone cricles and hilltop forts in the area. Enquire at Tourist Information Centres.

TOLQUHON CASTLE,
Pitmedden, By Ellon ☎ 01651 851286
A 15th-century ruined tower attached to a 16th-century quadrangular mansion.

MORAY

AUCHINDOUN CASTLE,
Dufftown *2m (3km) south-east*
Enclosed by prehistoric earthworks, this massive, three-storey keep was built on a steep hill above the River Fiddich.

BALVENIE CASTLE,
Dufftown ☎ 01340 820121
Former ancient stronghold of the Comyn family, this ruined courtyard castle has a fine Renaissance facade.

ELGIN CATHEDRAL,
North College St, Elgin ☎ 01343 547171
Founded in 1224 and burnt down in 1390, along with most of the town, by the notorious Wolf of Badenoch - Alexander Stewart, Earl of Buchan. The fine west towers and the octagonal chapter house are to be admired among the ruins.

MORTLACH PARISH CHURCH,
Dufftown
Founded in 566 by St Moluag, it is one of the oldest places of Christian worship in Scotland featuring 13th-century windows and Pictish stones and crosses.

SUENOS' STONE,
Findhorn Rd, Forres
Splendid 20ft-high stone, elaborately carved in the 9th or 10 century.

GREAT FOR KIDS

ABERDEENSHIRE

ALFORD VALLEY RAILWAY,
Alford ☎ 019775 62326
Narrow-gauge passenger railway in two 1-mile sections linking Alford and Murray Park. Steam weekends and events.

ARCHAEOLINK PREHISTORY PARK,
Berryhill, Oyne ☎ 01464 851500
A stunning audio-visual show together with a Myths and Legends Gallery and a whole range of interpretation techniques allows visitors to journey back in time to the drama and excitement of 6,000 years ago. Discover the bustling reconstruction of an Iron Age Farm, a prehistoric play corner and landscaped walkways to the top of an ancient fort for views across this fascinating 40 acre park.

CULLERLIE FARM PARK,
Echt, Skene ☎ 01330 860549
Farm museum and heritage centre with animals and demonstration days. Tearoom.

GRAMPIAN TRANSPORT MUSEUM,
Alford ☎ 019775 62292
Exhibitions trace the history of road and rail transport in North East Scotland. Large collection of vintage vehicles, as well as climb-aboard and push-button exhibits.

JONAH'S JOURNEY,
Rosemount Place, Aberdeen
☎ 01224 647614
An award-winning activities-based learning centre which places the emphasis firmly on participation. It gives a practical insight into life 3000 years ago, and in today's Third World.

MACDUFF MARINE AQUARIUM,
High Shore Rd, Macduff ☎ 01261 833369
Enjoy spectacular views of the sea life of the Moray Firth, including wolf-fish, conger eel and octopus, in Britain's deepest tank with its unique kelp forest.

SATROSPHERE,
Justice Mill Lane, Aberdeen
☎ 01224 213232
A fascinating, interactive science and technology discovery centre where everything is 'hands-on'. The emphasis is on doing and finding out, not just looking and standing back.

STORYBOOK GLEN,
Maryculter ☎ 01224 732941
This is a children's fantasy land set in 20 acres of gardens, where nursery rhyme and fairytale characters are brought to life.

MORAY

DARNAWAY FARM VISITOR CENTRE,
Forres ☎ 01309 672213
Houses an exhibition on the work on the extensive Darnaway Estate, and offers the opportunity to see a working dairy farm.

MORAY FIRTH WILDLIFE CENTRE,
Tugnet, Spey Bay ☎ 01343 820339
Dedicated dolphin watch centre and exhibitions.

HOMES & GARDENS

ABERDEENSHIRE

BALMORAL CASTLE GROUNDS & EXHIBITION,
Balmoral ☎ 013397 42334
Balmoral is the focal point of what is now called Royal Deeside, a landscape of woodlands and plantations sweeping up to grouse moors and distant mountains. The wooded grounds and gardens can be visited from May to July. There are beautiful country walks, pony trekking, an exhibition of paintings in the castle ballroom and a Travel and Carriage exhibition.

BRAEMAR CASTLE,
Braemar ☎ 013397 41219
An impressive fortress built in 1628 as a hunting lodge by the Earl of Mar. Set beside the River Dee, it is now a fully furnished residence of great charm, featuring barrel-vaulted ceilings, and some valuable pieces of furniture and paintings.

CRAIGIEVAR CASTLE,
off A980 25m/40km west of Aberdeen
An isolated, romantic L-shaped tower house built in 1626 by William Forbes. Set within the peaceful Don Valley, its rises up 7 storeys to a fairytale skyline of turrets and fancy gables, and remains virtually untouched since its completion.

DELGATIE CASTLE,
Delgatie, Turriff ☎ 01888 653479
Dating back to the 12th century, this impressive tower house houses 16th-century painted ceilings, and the widest turnpike stair in Scotland.

DRUM CASTLE & ROSE GARDEN,
Peterculter ☎ 01330 811204
Situated within the Old Wood of Drum, a natural oak wood, Drum Castle is a combination of 13th-century square tower and a handsome Jacobean mansion with Victorian additions.

FASQUE HOUSE,
Fettercairn ☎ 01561 340569
A castellated mansion, built in 1809 in Georgian Gothic style, that was the home of W.E. Gladstone, four times Prime Minister, from 1830 to 1851.

HADDO HOUSE,
Methlick ☎ 01651 851440
A splendid Palladian-style mansion designed by William Adam in 1731 for William, 2nd Earl of Aberdeen. Refurbished in the 1880s in the 'Adam Revival' style, the interior features sweeping Italianate staircases and an atmospheric library.

LEITH HALL & GARDEN,
Kennethmont, By Huntly ☎ 01464 831216
This 17th-century mansion house was the home of the Leith family for over 400 years. Visitors can be view graciously furnished rooms and a unique collection of military memorabilia. The 286 acre estate has formal and informal gardens.

KILDRUMMY CASTLE GARDENS,
Kildrummy ☎ 019755 71277
With the picturesque ruin of Kildrummy Castle as a backdrop, these gardens are not only beautiful but also noted for their botanical interest.

PITMEDDEN GARDEN,
Pitmedden ☎ 01651 842352
A fine late 17th-century 5-acre walled garden with sundials, pavilions and fountains. There is also a visitor centre, walks and a Museum of Farming Life.

Archaeolink Prehistory Park,

PROVOST SKENE'S HOUSE,
Flourmill Lane, Aberdeen ☎ 01224 641086
A handsome 16th-century town mansion
with notable decorated ceilings and
panelling. Now a museum of local history
and social life, it recreates the atmosphere
of the 17th and 18th centuries with rooms
decorated in period style. Coffee shop.

MORAY

BALLINDALLOCH CASTLE,
Ballindalloch ☎ 01807 500205
Magnificent 16th-century castle with
Victorian additions set in beautiful grounds
beside the Rivers Spey and Avon.
Impressive interior, river walks, rock and
rose gardens, shop, crafts and tearoom.

PLUSCARDEN ABBEY,
Elgin ☎ 01343 890257
Originally a 13th-century foundation, the
abbey was deserted from 1560 to 1948,
when it was taken over by the monks
from Prinknash Abbey near Gloucester.
Visitors can view ancient wall paintings,
stained glass windows and a well-
preserved chapel.

Call the AA Hotel Booking Service on
0990 050505 to book at AA recognised
hotels and B&Bs in the UK,
or through our internet site:
http://www.theaa.co.uk/hotels

BIG OUTDOORS

ABERDEENSHIRE

BULLERS OF BUCHAN,
north of Cruden Bay on A975
A breathtaking, 200ft (60m) rock chasm
eroded by the sea.

FOWLSHEUGH RSPB SEABIRD COLONY,
Crawton, By Stonehaven ☎ 01224 624824
Home to the largest seabird colony in
mainland Britain.

GLEN TANAR,
Aboyne ☎ 013398 86072
Peaceful wooded glen with a wealth of
walks. The Braeloine Visitor Centre has
information on the area.

LINN OF DEE,
Inverey, By Braemar
A picturesque rocky chasm about 150
yards (138m) long on the River Dee.

**LOCH OF STRATHBEG RSPB NATURE
RESERVE,**
Crimmond, Fraserburgh ☎ 01346 532017
Covering 2300 acres including the loch,
this important reserve is haven to a wealth
of birdlife, notably birds of prey, breeding
terns and large numbers of wintering
wildfowl.

MUIR OF DINNET NATURE RESERVE,
Dinnet, By Aboyne ☎ 013398 81022
Incorporating woodland, heather moors
and various glacial landscape features, this
reserve is rich with flora and birdlife.

QUEEN'S VIEW,
Tarland
One of the most spectacular viewpoints in
the North-East. Much loved by Queen
Victoria, the view stretches across the
fertile lands of the Howe of Cromar to
Mount Keen and Lochnagar.

**SANDS OF FORVIE NATIONAL NATURE
RESERVE,**
Collieston ☎ 01358 751330
A wild habitat of dune, cliff and coastal
heath on the northern bank of the Ythan
estuary, renowned for its rich wildlife.

MORAY

GLENLIVET ESTATE,
Information Centre, Main St, Tomintoul
☎ 01807 580283
Huge Highland estate located in the
foothills of the Cairngorms. Excellent
waymarked walks, cycling trails and
downhill and Nordic skiing. Ranger service.

RANDOLPH'S LEAP,
Forres *7m (12km) south on B9007*
A popular beauty spot on the River
Findhorn, where the river narrows
amongst rocks and woodland to form an
impressive gorge.

SPEYSIDE WAY VISITOR CENTRE,
Craigellachie ☎ 01340 881266
Information about the Moray countryside
the Speyside Way.

ESSENTIAL INFORMATION

TOURIST INFORMATION

ABERDEENSHIRE

**ABERDEEN & GRAMPIAN TOURIST
BOARD,**
North Silver St, Aberdeen AB10 1RJ
☎ 01224 848848 ☎ 01224 639836
ABERDEEN,
Broad St, Aberdeen AB10 1DE
☎ 01224 632727 ☎ 01224 620415
ABOYNE SEASONAL,
☎ 013398 86060
ALFORD *seasonal,*
Railway Museum, Alford ☎ 019755 62052
BALLATER *seasonal,*
Albert Hall, Station Square, Ballater
☎ 013397 55306
BANCHORY *seasonal,*
Bridge St, Banchory AB31 3SX
☎ 01330 822000 ☎ 01330 825126
BANFF *seasonal,*
Collie Lodge, Banff ☎ 01261 812419
BRAEMAR *seasonal,*
Mar Rd, Braemar ☎ 013397 41600
CRATHIE *seasonal*
The Car Park, Crathie ☎ 013397 42414
FRASERBURGH *seasonal,*
Saltoun Sq, Fraserburgh ☎ 01346 518315
HUNTLY *seasonal,*
9A The Square, Huntly ☎ 01466 792255
STONEHAVEN *seasonal*
Allardice St, Stonehaven ☎ 01569 762806

MORAY

DUFFTOWN *seasonal,*
The Square, Dufftown ☎ 01340 820501
ELGIN,
17 High St, Elgin IV30 1EG
☎ 01343 543388 ☎ 01343 552982
FORRES *seasonal,*
116 High St, Forres ☎ 01309 672938
TOMINTOUL *seasonal,*
The Square, Tomintoul ☎ 01807 580285

ACCESS

AIR ACCESS

ABERDEEN AIRPORT ☎ 01224 722331
INVERNESS AIRPORT ☎ 01463 232471

SEA ACCESS

P&O SCOTTISH FERRIES *Aberdeen-Lerwick
(Shetland)* ☎ 01224 572615

CRAFTS

*Kiltmaking, pottery, glassmaking,
knitwear, woodcraft and jewellery are
among the crafts to lookout for.*

ABERDEENSHIRE

FOGGIELEY TANNERY,
Craigievar, Alford ☎ 013398 83317

FORDYCE JOINER'S WORKSHOP
Church St, Fordyce ☎ 01771 622906

P & D FORSYTH,
23 Kirk Brae, Fraserburgh ☎ 01346 514919
Wood-turning and pyrograph
demonstrations.

MCCALLS LTD,
Bridge St, Aberdeen ☎ 01224 582291
Kiltmakers.

MCLEAN OF BRAEMAR,
Invercauld Rd, Braemar ☎ 013397 41602
Horncraft and jewellery.

STAINED GLASS WORKSHOP,
Arbuthnott Pl, Stonehaven ☎ 01569 767081

MORAY

A'ANSIDE STUDIO
Main St, Tomintoul ☎ 01807 580430
Stained glass & furniture.

CASHMERE VISITOR CENTRE,
Newmill, Elgin ☎ 01343 554099

LOGIE STEADING,
Logie, Forres ☎ 01309 611378
Gunmaker, sealmaker, engraver.

**PORTSOY MARBLE
WORKSHOP & POTTERY,**
Shorehead, Portsoy ☎ 01261 842404

RON PARKER (WOOD SCULPTURE)
Dunphail, Forres ☎ 01309 611273

TOUCH WOOD TURNERY,
Old Mills Oldmills Rd, Elgin

ENTERTAINMENT

CINEMAS

ABERDEENSHIRE

ABC,
Union St, Aberdeen ☎ 01224 591477
CAPITOL THEATRE & CINEMA,
Union St, Aberdeen ☎ 01224 583141
ODEON CINEMA,
Justice Mill Lane, Aberdeen ☎ 01224 587160
VIRGIN CINEMA COMPLEX,
Queen's Links, Aberdeen ☎ 01541 550502

MORAY

MURRAY PLAYHOUSE,
Elgin ☎ 01343 541625

THEATRE

ABERDEENSHIRE

ABERDEEN ARTS CENTRE,
King St ☎ 01224 641122
**ABERDEEN EXHIBITION
& CONFERENCE CENTRE,**
Bridge of Don ☎ 01224 824824
HADDO HOUSE ARTS TRUST,
Methlick ☎ 01651 851440
Small theatre in the grounds.
HIS MAJESTY'S THEATRE,
Aberdeen ☎ 01224 641122
LEMON TREE,
Aberdeen ☎ 01224 642230
MUSIC HALL,
Union St, Aberdeen ☎ 01224 641122

FOOD & DRINK

ABERDEENSHIRE

Aberdeenshire is rich farming and fishing
country, renowned for producing top
quality Aberdeen Angus beef, the best
salmon and the abundance of fresh fish
landed at its bustling ports.
**UGIE SALMON FISHINGS,
GOLF RD, PETERHEAD ☎ 01779 476209**
Fresh and smoked salmon from Scotland's
oldest fish house built in 1585.

MORAY

WALKERS SHORTBREAD,
Fishertown, Aberlour ☎ 01340 871555
Buttery shortbread made to an original
family recipe.

BAXTERS
Fochabers ☎ 01343 820666
Long-established family business (1868)
producing a wide range of quality Scottish
foods. Factory tours and visitor centre.

WHISKY DISTILLERIES

ABERDEENSHIRE

FETTERCAIRN DISTILLERY,
Fettercairn ☎ 01561 340205
GLENDRONACH DISTILLERY,
Forgue, By Huntly ☎ 01466 730222
ROYAL LOCHNAGAR DISTILLERY
Crathie, Ballater ☎ 013397 42273

MORAY

The unpolluted waters of the River Spey
and its tributaries produce some of the
finest whiskies in Scotland. In fact,
Speyside is home to over half the
distilleries in Scotland. The 'Malt Whisky
Trail' brochure is available from
Information Centres.

CARDHU DISTILLERY,
Knockando, Aberlour ☎/📠 01340 810498
DALLAS DHU DISTILLERY,
Mannachie Rd, Forres ☎ 01309 676548
GLENFARCLAS DISTILLERY,
Ballindalloch ☎ 01807 500245
GLENFIDDICH DISTILLERY,
Dufftown ☎ 01340 820373
GLEN GRANT DISTILLERY,
Elgin Rd, Rothes ☎ 01542 783318
GLENLIVET DISTILLERY,
Glenlivet, Ballindalloch ☎/📠 01542 783220
STRATHISLA DISTILLERY,
Seafield Av, Keith ☎ 01542 783044

TRANSPORT

BOAT TRIPS & CRUISES

ABERDEENSHIRE

FRASERBURGH HARBOUR TOURS,
The Harbour, Fraserburgh ☎ 01346 518315

MORAY

BENBOLA,
Portessie, Buckie ☎ 01542 832289
Seal cruises, dolphin watching and fishing.

CULLEN MARINE SERVICES,
☎ 01542 840323
Trips, charters and angling.

MORAY YACHT CHARTERS, Lossiemouth
☎ 01343 812134
Dolphin watching, charter and fishing.

BUS SERVICES

GRAMPIAN BUSLINE,
Aberdeen area ☎ 01224 633333
BLUEBIRD,
Grampian Highland ☎ 01224 212266

CAR HIRE

ABERDEENSHIRE

ABERDEEN 4X4 SELF DRIVE,
☎ 01224 790858
ARNOLD CLARK HIRE DRIVE,
Aberdeen ☎ 01224 249159
BUDGET RENT A CAR,
Aberdeen ☎ 01224 488770
CHEYNES COACHES,
Daviot, Inverurie ☎ 01467 671400
4X4 4U,
Newmachar ☎ 01651 863247
MITCHELLS SELF DRIVE,
Aberdeen ☎ 01224 642642

COACH TOURS

ABERDEENSHIRE

GRAMPIAN COACHES,
King St, Aberdeen ☎ 01224 650024
KIRKPATRICK OF DEESIDE,
Dee St, Banchory ☎ 01330 823456

MCINTYRE'S COACH TOURS,
High St, Old Aberdeen ☎ 01224 493112
WHYTE'S COACH TOURS,
Newmachar ☎ 01651 862211

MORAY

BEN AIGEN TOURS,
Dufftown ☎ 01340 820718

CYCLE HIRE

ABERDEENSHIRE

HUNTLY NORDIC SKI CENTRE,
Hill of Haugh, Huntly ☎ 01466 794428
MONSTER BIKES,
Banchory ☎ 01330 825313

MORAY

RECYCLES,
Rafford, ☎ 01309 672811

GUIDED TOURS

BON ACCORD TOURS,
Aberdeen ☎ 01224 733704
Themed walks, talks, trips & trails.

GRAMPIAN RAILTOURS LTD,
Newburgh, Ellon ☎ 01358 789513
Chartered rail trips.

SCOTTISH TOURIST GUIDES ASSOCIATION,
317 Broomhill Rd, Aberdeen ☎ 01224 319483

TRAINS

Aberdeen has direct services to and from
London King's Cross, Edinburgh and
Glasgow, and to Inverness, via Elgin, Forres
and Keith in Moray. ☎ 01224 594222.

SPORT & LEISURE

ACTIVITY CENTRES

ABERDEENSHIRE

BIGFOOT ADVENTURES,
Strathdon ☎ 019756 51312
DAVID LATHAM OUTDOOR ACTIVITIES,
Banchory ☎ 01330 850332
GRAMPIAN ACTIVITY HOLIDAYS,
Aberdeen ☎ 01224 741310
HOWIE-IRVINE SPORTING FACTORS,
Lumphanan ☎ 013398 83536
MAKING TREKS,
Ballater ☎ 013397 55865

MORAY

HIGHLAND ACTIVITY HOLIDAYS,
Dufftown ☎ 01340 820892
LOCH PARK ADVENTURE CENTRE,
Drummuir, Keith ☎ 01542 810334

ANGLING

ABERDEENSHIRE

The rivers Dee, Don, Deveron, Ythan and
North Esk provide excellent trout and
salmon fishing. Sea angling oppotunities
are good from many of the ports and
harbours around the coast. For details on
where to fish contact the Tourist
Information Centres.

MORAY

The Spey and Findhorn are famous salmon and trout rivers, but their burn tributaries and the small lochs in the foothills of the Cairngorms also provide some excellent fishing.

CYCLING

ABERDEENSHIRE

An intricate network of rural backroads, ideal for leisurely cycling, criss-cross the gently rolling Aberdeenshire countryside, linking many of the places of interest. Off-road enthusiasts can explore the many waymarked trails created through Forestry Commission woodlands, namely in Kirkhill Forest at Banchory, Bunzeach Forest (family biking) near Strathdon, Pitfichie Forest near Monymusk, and through upland forests at Gartly, near Huntly. Contact Forest Enterprise ☎ 01466 794161.

ROYAL DEESIDE CIRCLE
A circular route of 54 miles/86km from Banchory to Ballater and back, following the River Dee.

MORAY

Waymarked mountain bike trails for all abilities exist on the Glenlivet Estate in the foothills of the Cairngorms. A good network of level country roads near the coast offer peaceful pedalling for families, especially on the arrowed Inverness to Lossiemouth (47m/75km) route.

GLIDING

DEESIDE GLIDING CLUB,
Aboyne Airfield ☎ 013398 85339
HIGHLAND GLIDING CLUB,
Elgin, Moray ☎ 01343 860272

GOLF

For a full list of golf courses in the North East, refer to the AA Guide to Golf Courses or contact the Tourist Information Offices.

ABERDEENSHIRE

CRUDEN BAY ☎ 01779 812285
A seaside links which provides golf of a high order and magnificent views.

ROYAL ABERDEEN,
Bridge of Don t 01224 702571 Championship links course with undulating dunes.

MORAY

ELGIN ☎ 01343 542338
One of the finest inland courses in Scotland, with undulating greens and compact holes.

FORRES ☎ 01309 672250
An all-year parkland course laid on light, well-drained soil in wooded countryside.

MORAY,
Lossiemouth ☎ 01343 812018
Two fine Scottish Championship links courses situated on the Moray Firth.

HORSE RIDING

ABERDEENSHIRE

ANNANDALE EQUESTRIAN CENTRE,
Kinimouth, By Mintlaw ☎ 01771 622598
BRIDESWELL RIDING CENTRE,
Cushnie, Alford ☎ 019755 81266
EDEN EQUESTRIAN CENTRE,
Dunlugas, Turriff ☎ 01261 821214
GLEN TANAR EQUESTRIAN CENTRE,
Glen Tanar, Aboyne ☎ 013398 86448
HAYFIELD RIDING CENTRE,
Hazlehead Park, Aberdeen ☎ 01224 315703
LADYMIRE EQUESTRIAN CENTRE,
Ladymire, Ellon ☎ 01358 721075
LONACH FARM RIDING CENTRE,
Strathdon ☎ 01975 651275
WESTERTON TREKKING CENTRE,
Forgue, By Huntly ☎ 01466 730294

MORAY

ABERLOUR RIDING & TREKKING CENTRE,
☎ 01340 871467
DRUMBAIN RIDING ESTABLISHMENT,
Drumbain, Rothes ☎ 01340 831883
REDMOSS RIDING CENTRE,
Drybridge, Buckie ☎ 01542 833140
SEAFIELD RIDING CENTRE,
Forres ☎ 01309 672253
TOMINTOUL RIDING CENTRE,
☎ 01807 580210

ICE RINKS

ABERDEENSHIRE

DYCE LEISURE CLUB,
Dyce, Aberdeen ☎ 01224 724454
LINK ICE ARENA,
Beach Promenade, Aberdeen
☎ 01224 649930

MORAY

MORAY LEISURE CENTRE,
Borough Briggs Rd, Elgin ☎ 01343 550033

LEISURE CENTRES

ABERDEENSHIRE

There are sports/leisure centres in Aboyne, Banff, Fraserburgh, Inverbervie, Laurencekirk, Stonehaven and Turriff. The following centres are in Aberdeen:

BEACH LEISURE CENTRE,
Beach Promenade ☎ 01224 655401
BON ACCORD BATHS & LEISURE CENTRE,
Justice Mill Lane ☎ 01224 587920
LORD PROVOST ALEXANDER COLLIE SPORTS CENTRE,
Bridge of Don ☎ 01224 826769
TORRY SPORTS CENTRE,
Oscar Road ☎ 01224 871213

SAILING

ABERDEENSHIRE

The ports and small harbours around coastline of Aberdeenshire offer plenty of opportunities for excellent sailing, especially at Inverbervie, Stonehaven, Bridge of Don (Aberdeen), Collieston, Peterhead, Fraserburgh, Pennan and Banff.

NORTH EAST SCOTLAND SAILING TRUST,
Albert St, Aberdeen ☎ 01224 644606

MORAY

Findhorn is a popular watersports centre on the Moray Firth, offering excellent canoeing, sailing, waterskiing and windsurfing facilities. Sailing can also be enjoyed from Lossiemouth, Hopeman, Buckie, Findochty, Portknockie and Cullen.

SCENIC DRIVES

Scenic themed trails through the beautiful Aberdeenshire and Moray countryside link the area's main attractions and offer something of interest for everyone. Availble in detailed leaflets are 'The Coastal Trail', 'The Victorian Heritage Trail' which links the places associated with Queen Victoria; 'The Malt Whisky Trail' 'The Stone Circle Trail', and 'The Castle Trail' which takes in nine of the region's great houses and castles

SKIING

ABERDEENSHIRE

ALFORD SKI CENTRE,
Greystone Rd, Alford ☎ 019755 63024
CAIRNWELL MOUNTAIN SPORTS,
Gulabin Lodge, Glenshee ☎ 01250 885255
GLENSHEE SKI CENTRE,
Cairnwell, Braemar
☎ 013397 41320 & 41325
HUNTLY NORDIC SKI CENTRE,
Hill of Haugh, Huntly ☎ 01466 794428
LECHT SKI CENTRE,
Corgarff, Strathdon ☎ 019756 51440

SWIMMING

BEACHES

The best bathing beaches in Aberdeenshire can be found at Aberdour Bay, Pennan, Peterhead, Whitehill, Banff and Cruden Bay. In Moray, head for Lossiemouth, Roseisle, Culbin Sands, Burghead and Hopeman.

INDOOR POOLS

There are swimming pools at Aberlour, Aboyne, Banchory, Banff, Ellon, Fraserburgh, Huntly, Inverurie, Peterhead, Stonehaven, Turriff and nine in Aberdeen. There is a pool at Buckie in Moray.

WALKING

ABERDEENSHIRE

Among the delightful walks in the county are gentle forest strolls on waymarked paths, invigorating cliff and coastal walks and energetic hillwalking up a 'Munro' in the Cairngorms..

MORAY

SPEYSIDE WAY
A 45 mile (72km) trail that follows the valley of the famous salmon river from Tomintoul in the foothills of the Cairngorms to Spey Bay on the coast.

WHERE TO STAY

ABERDEEN CITY

HOTELS

AA RECOMMENDED

ABERDEEN CITY

ARDOE HOUSE ★★★★❀❀
Blairs, South Deeside Rd AB12 5YP
(4m W of city off B9077)
☎ 01224 867355 ☏ 01224 861283
Turreted baronial mansion in beautiful
grounds retaining many original features.
Tempting carte menu in elegant
restaurant.
*££££ 71 bedrooms (3 fmly) No smoking
in 40 bedrooms or restaurant Lift Night
porter Croquet lawn Putting green Petanque*
🍷

THE COPTHORNE ABERDEEN ★★★★❀
122 Huntly St AB10 1SU
*(W of city centre, off Union St, up Rose St,
hotel 0.25m on R on corner with Huntley St)*
☎ 01224 630404 ☏ 01224 640573
Friendly hotel convenient for shops and
theatre. Lounge bar and restaurant for
menus with Scottish theme.
*££ 89 bedrooms (15 fmly) No smoking in
30 bedrooms Lift Night porter Weekly live
entertainment No smoking area in
restaurant* 🍷

PATIO HOTEL ABERDEEN ★★★★❀
Beach Boulevard AB24 5EF
*(from A90 follow signs for city centre, then
sea/beach. On Beach Boulevard, turn L at
lights. Hotel on R)*
☎ 01224 633339 ☏ 01224 638833
Conveniently located, newly built hotel
radiating from a central atrium. Several
eating options.
*££££ 92 bedrooms (8 fmly) No smoking
in 58 bedrooms Lift Night porter Indoor
swimming pool (heated) Sauna Solarium
Gym Jacuzzi/spa Steam room, Treatment
Room No smoking area in restaurant* 🍷

The Maredrcliffe at Pitfodels

THE ABERDEEN THISTLE ★★★★
Souter Head Rd, Altens AB12 3LF
(3m S off A956, on A90)
☎ 01224 877000 ☏ 01224 896964
Modern, purpose-built with attractive split-
level bar, a choice of formal and informal
eating options.
*££££ 221 bedrooms (70 fmly) No
smoking in 105 bedrooms Lift Night porter
Outdoor swimming pool (heated) Gym No
smoking area in restaurant RS Xmas wk* 🍷

HOLIDAY INN CROWNE PLAZA ★★★★
Malcom Rd Bucksburn AB21 9LN
(3m N off A947)
☎ 01224 409988 ☏ 01224 714020
Popular business hotel with spacious
bedrooms, restaurant, a choice of bars.
*££££ 144 bedrooms (35 fmly) No
smoking in 45 bedrooms Lift Night porter
Indoor swimming pool (heated) Sauna
Solarium Gym Steam room No smoking
area in restaurant* 🍷

THE MAREDRCLIFFE AT PITFODELS
★★★★
North Deeside Rd AB1 9YA
*(A90 onto A93 signposted Braemar. 1m on R
after turn off at traffic lights)*
☎ 01224 861000 ☏ 01224 868860
Distinguished hotel in eight acres of
grounds. Master to standard rooms. Two
restaurants.
*££££ 42 bedrooms (4 fmly) No smoking
in 10 bedrooms No dogs (ex guide dogs) Lift
Night porter Snooker Croquet lawn Putting
green No smoking area in restaurant* 🍷

MARYCULTER HOUSE HOTEL ★★★❀
AB1 6BB *(8m along B9077 off A90 on S
side of Aberdeen)*
☎ 01224 732124 ☏ 01224 733510
Popular hotel in five acres of wooded
grounds beside the River Dee Eat in The
Priory Restaurant or Poachers Bar.
*£££ 23 bedrooms (2 fmly) No smoking in
12 bedrooms Night porter Fishing Clay
pigeon shooting Weekly live entertainment
No smoking in restaurant* 🍷

ATHOLL ★★★
54 Kings Gate AB15 4YN
*(in West End 400yds from Anderson Drive,
the main ring road)*
☎ 01224 323505 ☏ 01224 321555
Many guests return regularly to this
comfortable and popular business hotel.
Bar, coffee lounge and smart restaurant.
*£££ 35 bedrooms (1 fmly) No smoking in
all bedrooms No dogs (ex guide dogs) Night
porter* 🍷

The Copthorne Aberdeen

CALEDONIAN THISTLE ★★★
10 Union Ter AB10 1WE
(follow directions to city centre, Union Terrace is half way along Union St)

☎ 01224 640233 🖷 01224 641627

Genuine hospitality and efficiency at this popular hotel. Elegant cocktail bar, restaurant and lively cafe bar.

£££££ 80 bedrooms (4 fmly) No smoking in 17 bedrooms Lift Night porter Weekly live entertainment No smoking area in restaurant 🛏

The Craighaar

THE CRAIGHAAR ★★★
Waterton Rd, Bankhead AB21 9HS
(NW near airport off A947)

☎ 01224 712275 🖷 01224 716362

Near the airport, this welcoming hotel is popular visiting businessman. Comfortable sitting areas, bar and smart restaurant.

£ 55 bedrooms (11 fmly) Night porter 🛏

PALM COURT ★★★
81 Seafield Rd AB15 7YU
(take A92 to Seafield rndbt, up Seafield Rd. Hotel on L)

☎ 01224 310351 🖷 01224 312707

A welcoming hotel with modern bedrooms, lively, semi-open plan conservatory bar and restaurant.

££ 24 bedrooms (1 fmly) Night porter No smoking area in restaurant 🛏

QUEENS ★★★
51-53 Queens Rd AB15 4YP

☎ 01224 209999 🖷 01224 209009

Popular with businessmen, near the city centre, this personally run hotel has spacious bar and pleasant restaurant.

£££ 26 bedrooms (3 fmly) No dogs (ex guide dogs) Night porter Closed 25-26 Dec & 1-2 Jan 🛏

WESTHILL ★★★
Westhill AB32 6TT
(follow A944 W of city towards Alford. Westhill is 6m out of centre on R)

☎ 01224 740388 🖷 01224 744354

Modern business hotel, near town centre and airport. Well equipped bedrooms. Choice of bars and attractive restaurant.

££ 37 bedrooms 13 annexe bedrooms (2 fmly) No smoking in 8 bedrooms Lift Night porter Weekly live entertainment 🛏

WATERWHEEL ★★
203 North Deeside Rd Bieldside AB1 9EN

☎ 01224 861659 🖷 01224 861515

Six miles west of the city this hotel was built on the site of a grain mill. Conservatory bar and Carvery.

21 bedrooms Night porter Weekly live entertainment 🛏

Palm Court

FORTE POSTHOUSE ABERDEEN
Claymore Dr, Bridge of Don AB23 8BL

☎ 01224 706707

Bright hotel offering modern accommodation, well equipped bedrooms, an informal bar and dining area.

123 bedrooms

TRAVEL INN
Murcar, Bridge of Don AB23 8BP
(on A92, close to Aberdeen Exhibition Centre)

☎ 01224 821217 🖷 01224 706869

Modern building offers smart, spacious and well equipped bedrooms, suitable for family use. Nearby family restaurant.

££ (fmly room) 40 bedrooms

TRAVEL INN (ABERDEEN SOUTH)
Mains of Balquharn, Portlethen AB12 4QS

☎ 01224 783856 🖷 01224 783856

Modern building offers smart, spacious and well equipped bedrooms, suitable for family use. Nearby family restaurant.

££ (fmly room) 40 bedrooms

BED & BREAKFAST ACCOMMODATION
AA RECOMMENDED

EWOOD HOUSE ◻◻◻◻◻
12 Kings Gate AB15 4EJ

☎ 01224 648408 🖷 01224 648408

Victorian home in award-winning gardens, has top-class accommodation for its warmly welcomed visitors. Excellent breakfasts.

££ 6 bedrooms (1 for disabled) No smoking No dogs (ex guide dogs) No children 🛏

THE JAYS ◻◻◻◻
422 King St AB24 3BR
(A90 from south to Main St/Union St. Continue on A92 to King St (North))

☎ 01224 638295 🖷 01224 638295

Warm welcome and meticulous attention to detail at this detached home with quality accommodation.

£ 10 bedrooms No smoking No dogs No children under 12yrs Closed Aug & Jan

MANORVILLE ◻◻◻◻
252 Gt Western Rd AB10 6PJ

☎ 01224 594190 🖷 01224 594190

Look forward to a warm welcome here. Bright, modern cheery bedrooms. Delightful sitting room.

£ 3 bedrooms (2 fmly) No smoking in dining room No dogs (ex guide dogs) 🛏

STRATHISLA ◻◻◻◻
408 Gt Western Rd AB10 6NR *(off A93)*

☎ 01224 321026

High levels of comfort and hospitality. Attractive, bright, airy bedrooms. Continental and traditional breakfasts.

£ 5 bedrooms (1 fmly) No smoking No dogs No children under 8yrs

CORNER HOUSE HOTEL ◻◻◻
385 Great Western Rd AB10 6NY
(on A93)

☎ 01224 313063 🖷 01224 313063

Welcoming atmosphere at this family run establishment. Modern bedrooms.

££ 17 bedrooms (3 fmly) No smoking in dining room Licensed 🛏

FOURWAYS ◻◻◻
435 Great Western Rd AB10 6NJ

☎ 01224 310218 🖷 01224 310218

Family run guest house beside the ring road. Tastefully decorated bedrooms.

£ 7 bedrooms (2 fmly) No dogs (ex guide dogs) 🛏

MANNOFIELD HOTEL ◪◪◪
447 Great Western Rd AB10 6NL
(from S-cross Bridge of Dee and follow signs for Inverness, A96 South Anderson Drive)
☎ 01224 315888 🖷 01224 208971
A welcoming atmosphere prevails. Spacious, comfortable accommodation. Hearty breakfasts.
£ 9 bedrooms (3 fmly) No smoking in 7 bedrooms No smoking in dining room Licensed 🍷

STRATHBOYNE ◪◪◪
26 Abergeldie Ter AB10 6EE
(0.5m N from bridge of Dee rdbt on A92)
☎ 01224 593400
Friendly guest house. TV lounge with board games and magazines.
£ 5 bedrooms (1 fmly) No smoking in bedrooms or dining room No dogs No children under 6yrs

APPLEWOOD ◪◪
154 Bon-Accord St AB1 2TX
☎ 01224 580617
Welcoming guest house close to the city centre. Bedrooms offer smart matching pine furnishings.
8 bedrooms(2 fmly) No smoking in 4 bedrooms No smoking in dining room or lounges No dogs (ex guide dogs)

Call the AA Hotel Booking Service on 0990 050505 to book at AA recognised hotels and B&Bs in the UK, or through our internet site: http://www.theaa.co.uk/hotels

---

BIMINI ◪◪
69 Constitution St AB24 5ET
☎ 01224 646912 🖷 01224 646912
Near the seafront, this friendly guest house offers good value accommodation.
7 bedrooms(1 fmly) No smoking No dogs (ex guide dogs) 🍷

KLIBRECK◪◪
410 Great Western Rd AB10 6NR *(100mtrs from the junct of the A90, A93 & A96)*
☎ 01224 316115
Good value accommodation at this family-run guest house. Hearty breakfasts.
£ 6 bedrooms No smoking No dogs Closed Xmas & New Year

OPEN HEARTH ◪◪
349 Holburn St AB10 7FQ
☎ 01224 596888
South west of the town centre guest house offering modern bedrooms and hearty breakfasts.
£ 12 bedrooms(2 fmly) No smoking in dining room

ABERDEEN AIRPORT THISTLE ★★★★
Argyll Rd AB2 0DU *(adjacent to main airport entrance 1m N of A96)*
☎ 01224 725252 🖷 01224 723745
Busy hotel beside the airport. Built around a grassy courtyard with outdoor swimming pool. Spacious bar and restaurant.
££££ 148 bedrooms (44 fmly) No smoking in 60 bedrooms Night porter Outdoor swimming pool (heated) No smoking area in restaurant 🍷

ABERDEEN MARRIOTT ★★★★
Overton Circle Dyce AB21 7AZ
(follow A96 to Bucksburn, turn R at rdbt onto A947. In 2m hotel at 2nd rndbt)
☎ 01224 770011 🖷 01224 722347
Modern hotel near the airport and city centre offers spacious, well equipped accommodation. Eating options.
£££ 155 bedrooms (68 fmly) No smoking in 88 bedrooms No dogs (ex guide dogs) Night porter Air conditioning Indoor swimming pool (heated) Sauna Solarium Gym Whirlpool Children's facilities No smoking area in restaurant 🍷

DYCE SKEAN DHU ★★★
Farburn Ter Dyce AB21 7DW *(off A947)*
☎ 01224 723101 🖷 01224 722965
Modern, motel style accommodation near the airport. Comfortable traditional feel throughout. Executive and standard rooms.
220 bedrooms No smoking in 40 bedrooms Night porter Squash Sauna Solarium Gym 🍷

TRAVEL INN
Burnside Dr off Riverside Dr Dyce AB2 0HW
☎ 01224 772787 🖷 01224 772968
Modern building offers smart, spacious and well equipped bedrooms, suitable for family use. Nearby family restaurant.
££ (fmly room) 40 bedrooms

ABERDEENSHIRE

Balgonie Country House

BIRSE LODGE ★★
20 Charleston Rd AB34 5EL
(on A93, midway between Banchory/Ballater. Hotel in centre of Aboyne)
☎ 013398 86253 🖷 013398 87796
Relaxed, friendly hotel in grounds near the River Dee. Restaurant specialising in seafood.
££ 12 bedrooms No dogs (ex guide dogs) Weekly live entertainment 🍷

ARBOR LODGE ◪◪◪◪◪
Ballater Rd AB34 5HY
(on A93 0.5m W of village centre)
☎ 01339 886951 🖷 01339 886951 In extensive gardens offering high standards of comfort and quality. Bedrooms have walk-in dressing rooms and luxurious bathrooms.
£ 3 bedrooms No smoking in bedrooms, dining room or in 1 lounge No children under 12yrs Mar-Oct 🍷

DARROCH LEARG ★★★
Braemar Rd AB35 5UX
(on A93 at west end of town)
☎ 013397 55443 🖷 013397 55252
In hillside gardens facing the River Dee and Lochnagar mountain. Country house atmosphere. Naturally friendly staff.
££ 13 bedrooms 5 annexe bedrooms No smoking in 4 bedrooms No smoking in restaurant Closed Xmas & Jan (ex New Year) 🍷

BALGONIE COUNTRY HOUSE ★★ ✿✿
Braemar Place AB35 5NQ
(turn off A93 on western outskirts of Ballater, hotel is signposted)
☎ 013397 55482 🖷 013397 55482
One of Scotland's most charming small country house hotels. Edwardian-style, in extensive gardens with wonderful views.
£££ bedrooms No dogs (ex guide dogs) Croquet lawn No smoking in restaurant Closed 6 Jan-Feb 🍷

Alexandra

ALEXANDRA ★ ★
12 Bridge Square AB35 5QJ
☎ 013397 55376 ☎ 013397 55466
Good value accommodation and welcoming atmosphere at this small hotel near the River Dee.
7 bedrooms (1 fmly)

BANK HOUSE ◙ ◙ ◙ ◙
Station Square AB35 5QB
(centre of town, opp the old station. Adjacent to Albert & Victoria Halls)
☎ 013397 55996
In Ballater's centre, this lovely home is smartly decorated. Relaxing lounge and stylish dining room.
4 bedrooms (2 fmly) No smoking

GLEN LUI HOTEL ◙ ◙ ◙ ◙
Invercauld Rd AB35 5RP
(Invercauld Rd is off A93 in Ballater)
☎ 013397 55402 ☎ 013397 55545
Comfortable small hotel in wooded grounds. Food available in the bar/bistro or dining room.
££ 10 bedrooms 9 annexe bedrooms (2 fmly) No smoking in bedrooms, dining room or in 1 lounge Licensed Children's facilities 16 Mar–14 Jan

GREEN INN ◙ ◙ ◙ ◙
9 Victoria Rd AB35 5QQ
(on A93 in Ballater on the green)
☎ 013397 55701 ☎ 013397 55701
Small inn is a 'restaurant with rooms' beside the village green. Welcoming

hospitality and innovative cooking.
£ (inc dinner) 3 bedrooms No smoking in bedrooms or dining room Licensed Closed Sun Oct–Mar & 2 wks in Oct

MOORSIDE ◙ ◙ ◙ ◙
Braemar Rd AB35 5RL *(on L of main rd when entering Ballater on A93 from SW)*
☎ 013397 55492 ☎ 013397 55492
Welcoming guest house with smart modern furnishing. Comfortable lounge.
£ 9 bedrooms (3 fmly) No smoking in bedrooms or dining room No dogs (ex guide dogs) Children's facilities Closed Nov–Feb

NETHERLEY ◙ ◙ ◙
2 Netherley Place AB35 5QE
☎ 013397 55792
Recognised by its blue and white facade and flowering window boxes. Attractive sitting area. Hearty breakfasts.
££££ 9 bedrooms (3 fmly) No smoking in dining room or in 1 lounge No children under 4yrs Closed Nov–Jan rs Feb

Braemar Lodge

BANCHORY

RAEMOIR HOUSE ★ ★ ★ ◈
Raemoir AB31 4ED
(take A93 to Banchory turn R onto A980 to Torphins. Main drive is 2m ahead at T-junct)
☎ 01330 824884 ☎ 01330 822171
Wonderful country house in part of a 3,500 acre estate. Tapestry covered walls and fine antiques. Elegant dining room.
£££ 17 bedrooms 6 annexe bedrooms (1 fmly) Tennis (hard) Sauna Solarium Gym Croquet lawn Pitch & putt Shooting Stalking Children's facilities No smoking in restaurant

BANCHORY LODGE ★ ★ ★
AB31 5HS *(off A93 13m W of Aberdeen)*
☎ 01330 822625 ☎ 01330 825019
Georgian house in large grounds on the River Dee. Roaring log fires and wonderful fresh flowers. Bedrooms are spacious.
££££ 22 bedrooms (11 fmly) Fishing Sauna Children's facilities

TOR-NA-COILLE ★ ★ ★
AB31 4AB *(on A93, 0.5m W of Banchory, opp golf course)*
☎ 01330 822242 ☎ 01330 824012
Lovely ivy clad house in wooded grounds. Taste of Scotland dishes. Staff are friendly.
££££ 23 bedrooms (4 fmly) Lift Croquet lawn Children's facilities No smoking area in restaurant Closed 25–28 Dec

BURNETT ARMS ★ ★
25 High St AB31 5TD
(town centre on N of A93)
☎ 01330 824944 ☎ 01330 825553
Former coaching inn offering traditional values with modern comforts. Good value high teas and dinners.
££ 16 bedrooms No smoking in restaurant

THE STAG HOTEL ◙ ◙ ◙
40 High St AB31 5SR
(in the centre of village)
☎ 01330 824671 ☎ 01330 824020
Relaxed, informal atmosphere at this friendly hostelry. Restaurant, residents bar/lounge.
££ 9 bedrooms

BANFF

BANFF SPRINGS ★ ★ ★
Golden Knowes Rd AB45 2JE
(western outskirts of town on A98)
☎ 01261 812881 ☎ 01261 815546
Warm welcome can be expected at this hotel overlooking the Moray Firth. Comfortably modern bedrooms.
££ 31 bedrooms Night porter Gym No smoking in restaurant Closed 25 Dec

Green Inn

Tor-na-Coille

BRYVARD ◙ ◙ ◙ ◙
Seafield St AB45 1EB *(on a A98 100mtrs from junct with Castle St nr the war memorial)*
☎ 01261 818090
Pretty fabrics used in period-style bedrooms with thoughtful touches. Inviting, comfortable lounge.
£ 5 bedrooms No smoking in bedrooms or dining room or in 1 lounge No dogs (ex guide dogs)

MORAYHILL ◙ ◙ ◙
Bellevue Rd AB45 1BJ *(A947 onto A97, towards Aberchirder, 2nd R. 3rd house on L)*
☎ 01261 815956 🄵 01261 818717
Elegant Victorian house with comfortable bedrooms. Golf and fishing can be arranged.
£ 3 bedrooms (2 fmly) No smoking in bedrooms

BRAEMAR

INVERCAULD ARMS ★ ★ ★
AB35 5YR *(on the A93)*
☎ 013397 41605 🄵 013397 41428
Traditional Highland hotel amid spectacular scenery. A small team of attentive and friendly staff.
££££ 68 bedrooms (11 fmly) No smoking in 18 bedrooms Lift Night porter Weekly live entertainment No smoking in restaurant 🍴

BRAEMAR LODGE ★ ★
Glenshee Rd AB35 5YQ
(on the A93 south approach to Braemar)
☎ 013397 41627 🄵 013397 41627
Small hotel, a converted Victorian lodge, in well tended grounds. Modern and traditional bedrooms.
£ 7 bedrooms (2 fmly) No smoking in all bedrooms or restaurant 🍴

FIFE ARMS ★ ★
Mar Rd AB35 5YL
☎ 01339 741644 🄵 01339 741545
Formerly a hunting lodge, now a busy hotel with comfortable, traditional feel.
££ 84 bedrooms (10 fmly) Lift Night porter Sauna Weekly live entertainment 🍴

CALLATER LODGE HOTEL ◙ ◙ ◙ ◙
9 Glenshee Rd AB35 5YQ
(adjacent to A93, 300yds S of Braemar centre)
☎ 013397 41275 🄵 013397 41275
In large grounds this detached house offers spacious bedrooms, welcoming fires, and a good choice at breakfast.

£ 6 bedrooms No smoking in 2 bedrooms No smoking in dining room or lounges Licensed No children under 4yrs rs Nov–Dec 🍴

BRIDGE OF MARNOCH

OLD MANSE OF MARNOCH ★ ★ ❀ ❀
AB54 7RS
(on B9117 less than 1m off A97)
☎ 01466 780873 🄵 01466 780873
Stylish riverside country house hotel in large gardens - a haven of peace. One of longest breakfast menus to be found.
£££ 5 bedrooms Fishing No children under 12yrs No smoking in restaurant Closed 2 wks Nov Xmas & New Year 🍴

CRUDEN BAY

RED HOUSE ★ ★
Aulton Rd AB42 0NJ
(turn off A952 at Little Chef onto A975 towards Cruden Bay)
☎ 01779 812215 🄵 01779 812320
Welcoming hotel overlooking the golf course. Modern style bedrooms. Foyer lounge, choice of bars and restaurant.
£ 6 bedrooms (1 fmly) 🍴

HUNTLY

CASTLE ★ ★ ★
AB54 4SH
☎ 01466 792696 🄵 01466 792641
Impressive 18th-century building in extensive grounds. Comfortable traditional accommodation. Scottish fare.
££ 19 bedrooms (4 fmly) Fishing No smoking in restaurant 🍴

DRUMDELGIE HOUSE ◙ ◙ ◙
Cairnie AB54 4TH
(4m NW of Huntly, off A96 (signed))
☎ 01466 760368
Victorian home, peacefully amid gentle rolling countryside. Main house and cottage bedrooms. Enjoyable home cooking.
£ 1 bedrooms 3 annexe bedrooms (4 fmly) No smoking in bedrooms No dogs (ex guide dogs) Licensed 🍴

DUNEDIN ◙ ◙ ◙
17 Bogie St AB54 8DX
(follow signs for The Square from A96. R into Duke St/Bogie St - opp fish and chip shop car park at rear of house)
☎ 01466 794162
Welcoming, conveniently situated family-run guest house.
£ 6 bedrooms (1 fmly) No smoking in bedrooms or dining room No dogs (ex guide dogs)

INVERURIE

THAINSTONE HOUSE HOTEL AND COUNTRY CLUB ★ ★ ★ ★ ❀ ❀ ❀
AB51 5NT *(A96 from Aberdeen, through Kintore, hotel entrance at 1st rdbt)*
☎ 01467 621643 🄵 01467 625084
(Rosettes awarded for dinner only)
Palatial mansion in 40 acre park combining modern comforts with classical elegance.
48 bedrooms (3 fmly) No dogs (ex guide dogs) Lift Night porter Indoor swimming pool (heated) Snooker Gym Jacuzzi/spa Archery Shooting JCB digger driving No smoking in restaurant 🍴

PITTODRIE HOUSE ★ ★ ★
AB51 5HS *(A96, Chapel of Garioch turn off)*
☎ 01467 681444 🄵 01467 681648
Turreted baronial mansion in 2000 acre estate and surrounded by beautiful countryside. Unashamedly opulent reception rooms.
££££ 27 bedrooms (7 fmly) Night porter Squash Snooker Croquet lawn Off road driving Clay pigeon shooting No smoking in restaurant 🍴

Banff Springs

Kildrummy Castle

STRATHBURN ★★★
Burghmuir Dr AB51 4GY
(at Blackhall rbt into Blackhall Rd. 100yds then into Burghmuir Dr)
☎ 01467 624422 ⊕ 01467 625084
Efficiently run, comfortable modern hotel popular with businessmen. Eating options.
££ 25 bedrooms (1 fmly) No smoking in 12 bedrooms No dogs (ex guide dogs) No smoking in restaurant

KILDRUMMY

KILDRUMMY CASTLE ★★★⊛
AB33 8RA
(off A97, Huntly/Ballater road)
☎ 019755 71288 ⊕ 019755 71345
Victorian country mansion in magnificent gardens. High standards and hospitality. Service is natural and friendly.
££££ 16 bedrooms (4 fmly) Fishing Snooker Children's facilities Closed 4–31 Jan

KINTORE

TORRYBURN ★★
School Rd AB51 0XP
(from S on A96, 1st hotel on L in Kintore)
☎ 01467 632269 ⊕ 01467 632271
Popular hotel. Bedrooms have the expected modern amenities. eating options.
££ 9 bedrooms (1 fmly) Tennis (hard) Fishing Snooker Shooting

MACDUFF

THE HIGHLAND HAVEN ★★
Shore St AB44 1UB
(A947 from Aberdeen, R into Macduff at caravan site. Hotel 100 metres on L)
☎ 01261 832408 ⊕ 01261 833652
Family run hotel overlooking the harbour. Bedrooms with modern appointments.
££ 30 bedrooms (8 fmly) Sauna Gym Jacuzzi/spa Weekly live entertainment

NEWBURGH

UDNY ARMS ★★⊛
Main St AB41 6BL *(turn off A92 at sign marked Newburgh. Hotel 2m, in village on R)*
☎ 01358 789444 ⊕ 01358 789012
Traditional values, modern amenities and good food at this popular hotel.
26 bedrooms (1 fmly) No smoking in all bedrooms Fishing Petanque No smoking in restaurant

OLDMELDRUM

MELDRUM ARMS ★
The Square AB51 0DS *(off B947, in village centre)*
☎ 01651 872238 ⊕ 01651 872238
Friendly, family run hotel offering Taste of Scotland dishes, excellent value bar menu and high tea.
££ 7 en suite (shr) 4 annexe bedrooms No dogs (ex guide dogs) No smoking area in restaurant

OLD RAYNE

LODGE ★★
AB52 6RY *(just off A96)*
☎ 01464 851205 ⊕ 01464 851205
Warm welcome at this comfortable small hotel. Spacious bedrooms. Eating options.
3 en suite (shr) 4 annexe bedrooms (1 fmly) Closed 25-26 Dec & 1 Jan

PETERHEAD

WATERSIDE INN ★★★⊛
Fraserburgh Rd AB42 3BN
(A90 1st rndbt - straight on & L for Fraserburgh)
☎ 01779 471121 ⊕ 01779 470670
Modern hotel offering executive rooms, suites and studio rooms. Several eating options.
££££ 69 bedrooms 40 annexe bedrooms (15 fmly) No smoking in 55 bedrooms Night porter Indoor swimming pool (heated) Snooker Sauna Solarium Gym Jacuzzi/spa Steam room, childrens play area Weekly live entertainment Children's facilities No smoking in restaurant

PALACE ★★★
Prince St AB42 1PL
(A90 from Aberdeen to Peterhead. In Peterhead turn into Prince St, then R into main car park)
☎ 01779 474821 ⊕ 01779 476119
Good value for money at this modern commercial hotel. café/diner, cocktail bar and Brasserie.
££ 66 bedrooms (2 fmly) No smoking in 8 bedrooms Lift Night porter Snooker

STONEHAVEN

COUNTY HOTEL & LEISURE CLUB ★★
Arduthie Rd AB39 2EH
(off A90, opp railway station)
☎ 01569 764386 ⊕ 01569 762214
Leisure facilities are a feature of this hotel, near the station and with easy access to A92 southbound.
££ 14 bedrooms (1 fmly) No dogs (ex guide dogs) Squash Sauna Solarium Gym

WHERE TO EAT
RESTAURANTS
AA RECOMMENDED

ABERDEEN

ARDOE HOTEL ⊛⊛
South Deeside Road, Blairs AB1 5YP
☎ 01224 867355 ⊕ 01224 861283
Game, seafood and prime Aberdeen Angus beef are features of the carte. The quality and freshness of ingredients comes through in dishes such as tian of marinated scallops and crab with a chilled gazpacho dressing, and orange and honey brûlée with Drambuie sabayon.
Fixed L £££ ALC £££

MARYCULTER HOUSE ⊛
South Deeside Road AB1 6BB
☎ 01224 732124 ⊕ 01224 733510
The restaurant of this historic hotel produces dishes such as smoked salmon wrapped around smoked mackerel mousse, and chargrilled Aberdeen sirloin with Chinese straw mushrooms on a red wine sauce.
Fixed D £££

PATIO HOTEL ⊛
Beach Boulevard AB24 1EF
☎ 01224 633339 ⊕ 01224 638833
The kitchen has a seafood emphasis and delivers honest-flavoured lobster bisque, lobster and monkfish tails on a bed of squid-ink noodles and a delicate creamy citrus sauce, or the likes of Moroccan lamb casserole, and calves' liver and locally smoked bacon.
ALC ££

Q BRASSERIE ✦✦
9 Alfred Place AB1 1YD
☎ 01224 595001 ℱ 01224 584425

A meal here could open with four slices of breast of pigeon on a reduced red wine sauce followed by pan-fried calves' liver set between puff pastry. One 'wicked' dessert is the dark chocolate samosa and vanilla ice cream.

ALC £,£, 🍴

ABOYNE

WHITE COTTAGE ✦✦
AB34 5BP
☎/ℱ 013398 86265

The menu reflects modern trends, with Scotland's abundant larder providing the likes of Glenberrie beef in Madeira sauce with roast shallots and wild mushrooms, and deep-fried saffron sea-cakes of red haddock and smoked mackerel.

Fixed D £,£,£, ALC £,£, 🍴

BALLATER

BALGONIE HOUSE HOTEL ✦✦
Braemar Place, AB35 5RQ,
☎/ℱ 013397 55482

Examples of Balgonie's menus include croquette of salmon topped with a quail's egg and glazed hollandaise sauce, breast of guinea fowl on a bed of couscous with Mediterranean-style vegetables, and a light lemon mousse served with raspberry coulis.

Fixed D £,£,£, 🍴

DARROCH LEARG HOTEL ✦✦✦
Braemar Road, AB35 5UX
☎ 013397 55443 ℱ 013397 55252

The fixed-price menus might open with ravioli of crotin cheese with artichokes and crispy leeks, followed by superbly tender fillet of Aberdeen Angus beef. Rounding things off in style might be an iced vanilla parfait and roasted rhubarb.

Fixed D £,£, 🍴

GREEN INN ✦✦
9 Victoria Road, AB35 5QQ
☎/ℱ 013397 55701

A thoroughly unpretentious restaurant-with-rooms that dusts off a number of old Scottish dishes such as inky pinky (a kind of beef hash), and whipkull (a variant on zabaglione).The line-up of local and regional cheeses is a credit to the place.

Fixed £,£, ALC £,£, 🍴

BANCHORY

RAEMOIR HOUSE HOTEL ✦
AB31 4ED
☎ 01330 824884 ℱ 01330 822171

The Regency-style restaurant has wonderful antique chandeliers, huge windows and high ceilings. The best local produce is used in dishes such as deep-fried haggis, and poached darne of salmon with lime and cucumber sauce.

Fixed D £,£,£, ALC £,£,£, 🍴

BRIDGE OF MARNOCH

THE OLD MANSE OF MARNOCH ✦✦
By Huntly, AB54 5RS
☎/ℱ 01466 780873

In the dining room, bedecked with paintings and prints of boats and ships, guests are offered a menu might feature richly coloured roasted red pepper soup, baby haggis rolled in breadcrumbs or a chocolate and orange mousse.

Fixed D £,£, 🍴

INVERURIE

THAINSTONE HOUSE ✦✦
AB51 5NT
☎ 01467 621643 ℱ 01467 625084

The kitchen produces clean, honest, wholesome flavours, and keeps a firm eye on what is happening elsewhere. Dinner may open with spinach and ricotta ravioli, followed by a Mediterranean dish of grilled chicken breast with vegetables and couscous, with a warmed chocolate tart to finish.

ALC £,£, 🍴

KILDRUMMY

KILDRUMMY CASTLE ✦
AB33 8RA
☎ 019755 71288 ℱ 019755 71345

In one of Scotland's finest country houses the cooking is based on the best local produce, including game, fish and prime Aberdeen Angus beef.

Fixed L £, ALC £,£,£, 🍴

NEWBURGH

UDNY ARMS HOTEL ✦
Main Street, Ellon, AB41 0BL
☎ 01358 789444 ℱ 01358 789012

The split-level bistro offers a sound choice of dishes prepared from quality ingredients. Expect Shetland salmon, Orkney oysters, chargrilled Grampian chicken breast and Aberdeen Angus steaks.

Fixed D £, ALC £,£, 🍴

PETERHEAD

WATERSIDE INN ✦
Fraserburgh Road AB42 3BN
☎ 01779 471121 ℱ 01779 470670

The Ogilvies Restaurant provides an appropriate setting for some carefully prepared Scottish fare. Dishes include shellfish bisque, fillet of monkfish with saffron and herb beurre blanc, and bread-and-butter pudding.

Fixed D £,£, ALC £,£,£, 🍴

Call the AA Hotel Booking Service on
0990 050505 to book at AA recognised
hotels and B&Bs in the UK,
or through our internet site:
http://www.theaa.co.uk/hotels

Q Brasserie

PUBS, INNS & OTHER PLACES
ABERDEEN CITY

BOND BAR
Broad Street
☎ 01224 623123
Atmospheric city bar with regular live music

CAMERON'S INN
6-8 Little Belmont Street
☎ 01224 644487
One of the oldest hostelries in Aberdeen, open from early to late, this lively pub serves bar meals.

GERARD'S BRASSERIE
50 Chapel Street
Long established, with a reputation for its fine French cuisine and atmosphere, unique decor and extensive menu.

LA BONNE BAGUETTE
Correction Wynd
☎ 01224 644445
French cafe and brasserie close to all the major shopping centres.

LEMON TREE
5 West North
☎ 01224 642230
Popular lunchtime restaurant with a wide vegetarian selection.

O'DONOGHUES
16 Justice Mill Lane
☎ 01224 575040
Lively Irish bar with regular music.

OWLIES BRASSERIE
Littlejohn Street
☎ 01224 649267
Within easy walking distance of the city centre this brasserie has a wide range of food, especially vegetarian, available.

PRINCE OF WALES
St Nicholas AB10 1HF
☎ 01224 640597
Dating from 1850 with the longest bar in the city at 60 feet. Good value and home-cooked food might include steak pie, breaded haddock or macaroni cheese.

WILD BOAR
19 Belmont Street
☎ 01224 625357
Relaxed city centre cafe/bar/restaurant/ patisserie serving food all day.

THE WINDMILL CAFE BAR
23 Wildmill Brae
☎ 01224 210677
City centre cafe bar with an open fire and traditional lively pub atmosphere.

ABERDEENSHIRE

Gordon Arms Hotel

KINCARDINE O'NEIL

GORDON ARMS HOTEL
North Deeside Rd AB34 5AA
☎ 01339 884236
A coaching inn where all meals are prepared on the premises using fresh local ingredient. The traditional high teas are particularly family orientated.
Accommodation

MARYCULTER

OLD MILL INN
South Deeside Rd AB12 5FX
(5m W of Aberdeen on B9077)
☎ 01224 733212
200-year-old mill on the River Dee. Dishes range from steak and kidney pie to grilled halibut, and banana with a mango chutney cream and raspberries.
Accommodation

NETHERLEY

LAIRHILLOCK INN AND RESTAURANT
AB39 3QS *(A90 from Aberdeen then B9077 for Durris then B979)*
☎ 01569 730001
A former farmhouse, then coaching inn, in 50 acres on Royal Deeside. A signature dish is rack of lamb with glazed shallots, bacon julienne, rosemary gravy and hot mint jelly.
Accommodation

OLDMELDRUM

THE REDGARTH
Kirk Brae AB51 0DJ *(On A947)*
☎ 01651 872353
Magnificent views from this friendly establishment. Cask conditioned ales from all over the UK. A varied menu of home-cooked dishes. *Accommodation*

STONEHAVEN

MARINE HOTEL
9/10 Shorehead AB39 2JY
(15m south of Aberdeen on A90)
☎ 01569 762155
100-year-old hotel in a fishing village. Not surprisingly, seafood figures prominently, alongside steak sizzlers, chilli and burgers, and sticky toffee pudding and death by chocolate.
Accommodation

Lairhillock Inn and Restaurant

WHERE TO STAY

MORAY
HOTELS
AA RECOMMENDED

ARCHIESTOWN

ARCHIESTOWN ★★◉◉
AB38 7QL *(on B9102, 5m SW of Craigellachie)*
☎ 01340 810218 📠 01340 810239
Although most of the guests here are fishermen, the relaxed atmosphere is appreciated by all. Pretty bedrooms. Superb food.
££ 9 bedrooms No smoking area in restaurant Closed end Sep – early Feb

BUCKIE

MILL HOUSE ★★
Tynet AB56 5HJ *(on A98 between Buckie and Fochabers)*
☎ 01542 850233 📠 01542 850331
Friendly hotel, formerly a mill, and featuring the original water-driven wheel machinery inside. Modern bedrooms. Dining options.
££ 15 bedrooms (2 fmly) Night porter No smoking in restaurant 🦢

CRAIGELLACHIE

CRAIGELLACHIE ★★★◉◉
AB38 9SR *(on the A95 in Craigellachie, 300 yards from the A95/A941 crossing)*
☎ 01340 881204 📠 01340 881253
Impressive Victorian hotel with delightful bedrooms and lounges. Three dining areas featuring innovative cuisine.
£££ 29 bedrooms Sauna Gym No smoking in restaurant 🦢

CULLEN

CULLEN BAY ★★
Cullen AB56 4XA
(on A98, 0.5m W of Cullen Village)
☎ 01542 840432 📠 01542 840900
Panoramic sea views from this family-run hotel with tasteful bedrooms. The restaurant features local seafood.
14 bedrooms (2 fmly) No smoking in 4 bedrooms Children's facilities No smoking area in restaurant 🦢

ELGIN

MANSEFIELD HOUSE ★★★◉
Mayne Rd IV30 1NY
☎ 01343 540883 📠 01343 552491
(from Inverness side of A96, head for town centre. At rdbt, turn R, at mini rdbt hotel on R)
Elegant former manse, sympathetically converted. Delightful bedrooms. The restaurant has a large and loyal local following.
£££ 21 bedrooms (3 fmly) No smoking in 5 bedrooms or restaurant No dogs (ex guide dogs) Lift 🦢

MANSION HOUSE ★★★◉
The Haugh IV30 1AW *(turn off A96 into Haugh Rd, hotel at end of road by river)*
☎ 01343 548811 📠 01343 547916
Imposing baronial style mansion set in lovely grounds close to river. Comfortable bedrooms, some with four-posters. Good dining options.
£££ 22 bedrooms (3 fmly) No dogs (ex guide dogs) Night porter Indoor swimming pool Snooker Sauna Solarium Gym Jacuzzi/spa Hairdresser Beauty therapist No smoking in restaurant 🦢

LAICHMORAY ★★
Maisondieu Rd IV30 1QR *(opp railway station)*
☎ 01343 540045 📠 01343 540055
Long-established family-run hotel with comfortable bedrooms. Good range of meals in bar or restaurant.
£££ 35 bedrooms (5 fmly) No smoking in 4 bedrooms Darts 🦢

FORRES

KNOCKOMIE ★★★◉◉
Grantown Rd IV36 0SG
(S on A940 towards Grantown)
☎ 01309 673146 📠 01309 673290
(Rosettes awarded for dinner only)
Charming country house in four acres of grounds. Bedrooms range from Grand Master and Master rooms with period furnishings, to the smaller standard rooms.

Public rooms include a bistro and an elegant main restaurant.
££££ 16 bedrooms (1 fmly) No smoking in 3 bedrooms Putting green Children's facilities No smoking in restaurant 🦢

RAMNEE ★★◉
Victoria Rd IV36 0BN
(turn off A96 at roundabout on eastern side of Forres, hotel 200yds on right)
☎ 01309 672410 📠 01309 673392
Built in 1907 as a private residence. The lounge bar is popular and can get very busy. Bedrooms vary in size, the superior rooms being the most spacious.
£££ 20 bedrooms (4 fmly) No smoking in restaurant RS Xmas day 1–3 Jan 🦢

LOSSIEMOUTH

STOTFIELD ★★★
Stotfield Rd IV31 6QS
(from Elgin, take directions to Lossiemouth, follow sign showing West Beach, Golf Club)
☎ 01343 812011 📠 01343 814820
A substantial Victorian hotel situated opposite the golf course. Public areas include a lounge bar and dining room. In addition there is an American-style bar called Bourbon Street.
££ 45 bedrooms (3 fmly) No smoking in 11 bedrooms No dogs Sauna Gym No smoking in restaurant 🦢

ROTHES

ROTHES GLEN ★★★◉◉
AB38 7AQ *(6m S of Elgin, on A941)*
☎ 01340 831254 📠 01340 831566
Set in 10 acres, this mansion has elegant public rooms, an attractive dining room which provides innovative Scottish fare, and well proportioned bedrooms.
£££ 16 bedrooms (2 fmly) No dogs (ex guide dogs) Fishing Croquet lawn Putting green Small trout Loch (for fishing) No smoking in restaurant 🦢

BED & BREAKFAST ACCOMMODATION

CULLEN

TORRACH ◉◉
147 Seatown AB56 4SL
☎ 01542 840724
(enter Cullen on A98 turn 1st L after viaduct at Royal Oak Hotel, then 1st R after 150yds. Next to post box)
A warm welcome awaits at this charming

former fisherman's cottage. Bright and airy rooms. Hearty breakfasts.
£ 2 bedrooms (1 fmly) Easter–Sep

DUFFTOWN

FIFE ARMS HOTEL ◉◉
2 The Square AB55 4AD
☎ 01340 820220 📠 01340 821137

(take A920 at Huntly to Dufftown hotel in village square)
Popular hostelry with comfortable pine-furnished bedrooms in a modern annexe. Interesting bar menu.
£ 6 annexe bedrooms (2 fmly) Children's facilities Parking 🦢

ELGIN

THE CROFT 🛏🛏🛏🛏🛏
10 Institution Rd IV30 1QX *(turn off A96 at Safeway, down Queen St turn R at end)*
☎ 01343 546004
Lovely period mansion set in its own mature grounds. Excellent bedrooms. Wonderful breakfasts.
£ *3 bedrooms (1 fmly) No smoking No dogs*

PINES 🛏🛏🛏🛏🛏
East Rd IV30 1XG ☎ 01343 542766
(on the eastern approach of A96)
Charming home set in lovely gardens near cathedral. Attractive bedrooms, one with a four poster.
£ *4 bedrooms (1 fmly) No smoking*

BELLEVILLE 🛏🛏🛏
14 South College St IV30 1EP *(follow signs to Museum, turn R at end of Glover St. 200 yds on R opp Safeway car park)*
☎ 01343 541515 ☎ 01343 540033
Traditional stone house near town centre with attractive bedrooms. Lots of tourist information plus toys for the children.
£ *2 bedrooms No smoking No dogs (ex guide dogs)*

FORESTERS HOUSE 🛏🛏🛏
Newton IV30 3XW ☎ 01343 552862
(3m W, off A96, situated on R of B9013)
19th-century house is its own garden. Bedrooms each have their own toilet and a general bath is available.
£ *2 bedrooms (2 fmly) No smoking in bedrooms No smoking in area of dining room*

LODGE 🛏🛏🛏
20 Duff Av IV30 1QS *(turn off A9 N of Aviemore onto A95 (signposted Elgin) until Craigellachie where road becomes A941)*
☎ 01343 549981 📠 01343 549981
A large detached Victorian house, not far from the station. Bedrooms are furnished in pine and are en suite.
£ *8 bedrooms (1 fmly) No smoking in bedrooms No smoking in dining room No dogs (ex guide dogs)* 🛏

NON SMOKERS HAVEN 🛏🛏
37 Duff Av IV30 1QS *(follow signs for Railway St or Perth, Duff Avenue is approx 150mtrs east of Railway St)*
☎ 01343 541993 & 07050 371891
Bedrooms are nicely appointed and there is a comfortable sun lounge to the rear of the house.
£ *3 bedrooms No smoking No dogs (ex guide dogs) No children under 14yrs*

FORRES

MAYFIELD 🛏🛏🛏🛏
Victoria Rd IV36 0BN *(opposite Grant Park car park on main road through town)*
☎ 01309 676931
Victorian house situated just off the main road. Lots of useful tourist information is provided and breakfast is served at a communal table in the dining room.
£ *3 bedrooms (1 fmly) No smoking in bedrooms No smoking in dining room No dogs* 🛏

GLENLIVET

ROADSIDE COTTAGE 🛏🛏🛏
Tomnavoulin AB37 9JL *(on B9008 Tomintoul to Dufftown road, 0.75m S of Tomnavoulin)*
☎ 01807 590486
A renovated stone cottage in the heart of whisky distilling country. Bedrooms are pine furnished and a new lounge has been constructed.
£ *3 bedrooms (1 fmly)*

HOPEMAN

ARDENT HOUSE 🛏🛏🛏🛏
43 Forsyth St IV30 2SY *(A9 to Inverness, on to A96 to Elgin, B9012 to Hopeman, Ardent House on main road opposite Bowling Green)*
☎ 01343 830694 📠 01343 830694
Detached house in its own walled garden. Speciality breakfasts include home smoked fish, garden produce and delicious home baking. This is a non smoking establishment.
£ *3 bedrooms No smoking No dogs Closed 13-31 Dec*

KEITH

THE HAUGHS 🛏🛏🛏🛏
AB55 6QN
(1m from Keith off A96, signed Inverness)
☎ 01542 882238
A traditional farmhouse on the outskirts of town. There is an inviting lounge and

The Haughs

farmhouse fare is served at individual tables in the dining room.
£ *4 bedrooms (1 fmly) No smoking in bedrooms No smoking in dining room No dogs (ex guide dogs) 165 acres beef mixed sheep*

LOSSIEMOUTH

CARMANIA 🛏🛏🛏
45 St Gerardines Rd IV31 6JX
(on entering town from Elgin A941, branch left uphill. House on left just over brow)
☎ 01343 812276
Occupying an elevated position, this detached bungalow offers carefully maintained and comfortable modern bedrooms, one of which is en suite.
£ *2 bedrooms No smoking in bedrooms No smoking in dining room No dogs (ex guide dogs) No children under 12yrs Closed Nov-Mar*

LOSSIEMOUTH HOUSE 🛏🛏🛏
33 Clifton Rd IV31 6DP *(entering town from Elgin on A941, house is on right before police station)*
☎ 01343 813397
16th-century dower house close to the beach. There are 2 spacious family rooms sharing 2 bathrooms, plus a single and double with modern en suite shower rooms.
£ *4 bedrooms (2 fmly) No smoking in 2 bedrooms No smoking in dining room No smoking in lounges*

CAMPING & CARAVANNING

ABERLOUR

ABERLOUR GARDENS CARAVAN PARK
AB38 9LD
(Signed off A95 halfway between Aberlour and Craigellachie.)
☎ 01340 871586
Family Park
A quiet walled garden park with very clean modern facilities. 3 acres with 30 touring pitches and 26 statics.
Open Apr-Oct Booking advisable bank hols & Jul-Aug

ALVES

NORTH ALVES CARAVAN PARK
IV30 3XD
From A96 take unclass rd signed Alves.
☎ 01343 85223
Family Park
A quiet rural site in attractive rolling countryside within 3m of a good beach . 10 acres with 45 touring pitches and 12 statics.
Open Apr-Oct Booking advisable peak periods Last arrival 23.00hrs Last departure noon

BURGHEAD

RED CRAIG HOTEL
CARAVAN & CAMPING PARK
Mason Haugh IV30 2XX *(On outskirts of Burghead at junc of B9012 and B9040.)Signposted Nearby town: Elgin*
☎ 01343 835663
Family Park
A slightly sloping site with level pitches, overlooking the Moray Forth. 3 acres with 30 touring pitches and 8 statics.
Open Apr-Oct Booking advisable Jul & Aug Last arrival 22.30hrs Last departure noon 🛏

CRAIGELLACHIE

CAMPING & CARAVANNING CLUB SITE
Elchies AB38 9SD *(From Craigellachie travel N on A941, turn left onto B9102 (signed Archiestown), and site is 2.5m on left.)*
☎ 01340 810414 (in season)
& 01203 694995
Family Park
A rural site with views across meadowland towards Speyside, and the usual high Club standards. 6 acres with 75 touring pitches.
Open all year Booking advisable bank hols & Jul-Aug Last arrival 21.00hrs Last departure noon 🚲

FOCHABERS

BURNSIDE CARAVAN SITE
Keith Rd IV32 7PF
(.5m E of town off the A96.) Signposted Nearby town: Elgin
☎ 01343 820511 & 820362
Family Park
Attractive site in tree-lined sheltered valley with footpath to the village. 5 acres with 110 touring pitches and 60 statics.
Open Apr-Oct Booking advisable Jul-Aug Last departure noon

LOSSIEMOUTH

SILVER SANDS LEISURE PARK
Covesea, West Beach IV31 6SP
(2m W B9040) Signposted
☎ 01343 813262
De-Luxe Park
A holiday park with entertainment for all during the peak season. 7 acres with 140 touring pitches and 180 statics.
Open Jun-Sep (rs Apr, May & Oct shops & entertainment restricted) Booking advisable Jul-Aug Last arrival 23.00hrs Last departure noon Childrens entertainment 🚲

RESTAURANTS
AA RECOMMENDED

ARCHIESTOWN

ARCHIESTOWN HOTEL ❀❀
Aberlour, AB38 7QX
☎ 01340 810218 🖷 01340 810239
Delightful little hotel with an informal bistro whose blackboard menu changes daily. Poached halibut with a white butter sauce, baked salmon with samphire, cod with parsley sauce, or steak and chips, might be on the menu.
ALC ££ 🚲

CRAIGELLACHIE

CRAIGELLACHIE HOTEL ❀❀
AB38 9SR
☎ 01340 881204 🖷 01340 881253
The Rib Room restaurant provides an elegant setting in which to enjoy a daily changing menu. Options might be langoustine bisque with garlic and parsley crostini, pan-fried calves' liver with creamed leeks and lime jus.
ALC ££ 🚲

DRYBRIDGE

THE OLD MONASTERY RESTAURANT ❀❀❀
Buckie, AB56 2JB
☎/🖷 01542 832660
Lunch in the informal Cloisters Bar may consist of French onion soup and local seafood in a herb sauce, followed by chilled Monastery Mist (a dessert of crushed meringues, flaked chocolate and nuts laced with a touch of Benedictine).
ALC £££ 🚲

DUFFTOWN

A TASTE OF SPEYSIDE ❀
10 Balvenie Street, AB5 4AB
☎/🖷 01340 820860
Value-for-money menus featuring local ingredients, are served at this simple, pine furnished restaurant. Dishes may include cullen skink, Lossiemouth scampi with birch wine and cream, and hot fruit dumpling with Drambuie cream.
Fixed D £ ALC ££ 🚲

ELGIN

MANSEFIELD HOUSE HOTEL ❀
Mayne Road, IV30 1NY
☎ 01343 540883 🖷 01343 552491
Converted Georgian manse - the restaurant is housed within the former stable block. Fish ranges from grilled fillets of lemon sole with parsley butter to seafood provençale and lobster.
ALC ££ 🚲

MANSION HOUSE HOTEL ❀
The Haugh, IV30 1AW
☎ 01343 548811 🖷 01343 547916
Contemporary dishes featured on the set-price menus and carte may include medallions of pork with plum and pear sauce, and scampi and monkfish tails topped with crispy aubergine.
Fixed L £ ALC ££ 🚲

FORRES

KNOCKOMIE HOTEL ❀❀
Grantown Road, IV36 0SG
☎ 01309 673146 🖷 01309 673290
Scottish villa with a choice of dining rooms. Oak-smoked salmon canapés, might precede a soufflé made with smoked haddock and a hint of fennel, and Angus beef steaks, not surprisingly, are a regular fixture.
Fixed L ££ ALC ££ 🚲

RAMNEE HOTEL ❀
Victoria Road, IV36 0BN
☎ 01309 672410 🖷 01309 673392
Honest cooking with dinner taking in lattice of haddock and salmon on a chive cream sauce, peach sorbet, breast of roast chicken with rosemary and onion, with a tomato and provençale sauce.
Fixed L £ ALC ££ 🚲

ROTHES

THE ROTHES GLEN HOTEL ❀❀
AB38 7AQ
☎ 01340 831254 🖷 01340 831566
A daily changing menu offering Macallan smoked salmon parcels and medallions of venison with a red cabbage marmalade and a piquant sauce.
Fixed L £ 🚲

PUBS, INNS & OTHER PLACES

ABERLOUR

THE OLD PANTRY
The Square
☎ 01340 871617
The Old Pantry offers meals to suit all tastes in a warm and friendly atmosphere. Morning coffee, lunch, afternoon and high tea.

BUCKIE

NEMAT
52 West Church Street
☎ 01542 834440/835194
Tandoori restaurant with eat in and take away indian cuisine. Table booking advisable. Special 'Eat as much as you like' buffet on Monday nights.

THE PUB IN THE SQUARE
7 Cluny Square
☎ 01542 831294
Traditional fishing memorabilia decorate this village pub where you'll find traditional pub food. Live music. Satellite TV.

GREAT GLEN & WESTERN HIGHLANDS

ARGYLL, with its standing stones, cairns, and fortified strongholds, is a sea-fringed mountain wilderness, where the first 'Scots' settled from Ireland in the 6th century. Oban, on the coast, is the main tourist centre, with coastal walks and forest trails, as well as quiet roads and tracks for cyclists.

South-east lies Loch Awe, set in magnificent peaks, including Ben Cruachan,(over 3,500ft). In the far south is the Kintyre peninsula, which has the air of an island even though part of the mainland.

HIGHLANDS (SOUTH) Highlights of the dramatic scenery of this area are Glencoe's wild peaks where Campbells massacred Macdonalds in 1692, and mysterious Loch Ness, with its elusive monster.

Fort William is the tourist centre, sheltered by Scotland's highest mountain, Ben Nevis (4,418ft, 1343m). The Caledonian Canal, linking a chain of lochs from the Irish to the North Seas, is perfect for cruising to Inverness and the Moray Firth.

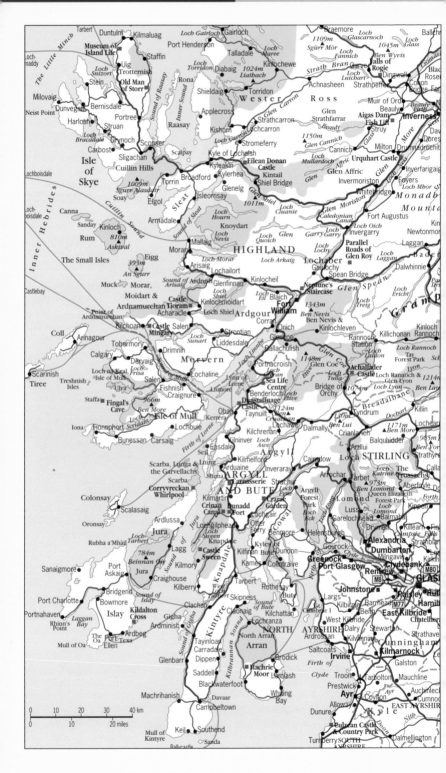

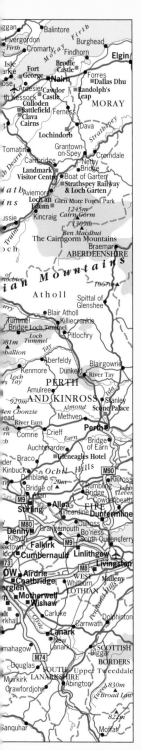

EVENTS & FESTIVALS

February

Traditional Music Festival,
Dornie, Highland

March

Cairngorm Snow Festival,
Aviemore, Highland

Badenoch & Strathspey Music Festival,
Kingussie, Highland

April

Fiddlers' Rally,
Oban, Argyll

Folk Festival,
Inverness, Highland

May

Highlands & Islands Music & Dance Festival,
Oban, Argyll

Highland Festival,
venues throughout the Highlands end May-early June

June

Kilmore & Kilbride Highland Games,
Oban, Argyll

Highland Games,
Campbeltown, Argyll, Grantown-on-Spey, Highland

Horse Trials,
Inveraray, Argyll

July

Highland Games,
Inveraray & Taynuilt, Argyll
Strachur Carnival,
Argyll

Loch Fyne Fair,
Tarbert, Argyll

Kilchoan Show,
Highland

Morven Games,
Knock Park, Lochaline, Highland

Morven Gala Week,
Lochaline area, Highland

Lochaber Highland Games,
Fort William, Highland

Highland Games,
Inverness, Highland

Inverness Tattoo,
Highland

Rothiemurchus International Highland Games,
Aviemore, Highland

August

Cowal Highland Gathering,
Dunoon, Argyll

Argyllshire Highland Gathering,
Oban, Argyll

Mull of Kintyre Music Festival,
Campbeltown, Argyll

Classic Boat Festival,
Inveraray, Argyll

Agricultural Shows,
Campbeltown, Argyll, Grantown-on-Spey, Highland

Lorn Show,
Oban, Argyll

Sunart & District Agricultural Show,
Strontian, Highland

Glenfinnan Gathering & Games,
Highland

Lochaber Agricultural Show,
Torlundy, By Fort William, Highland

Glenurquhart Highland Gathering & Games,
Drumnadrochit, Highland

Clan MacPherson Rally & Highland Games,
Newtonmore, Highland

Glen Nevis River Race,
Fort William, Highland

September

Highland Dancing Festival,
Dunoon, Argyll

Music Festival,
Tarbert, Argyll

Seafood Festival,
Oban, Argyll

Festival of Music,
Carrbridge, Highland

October

Jazz Festival,
Dunoon, Argyll

Highland Trade Fair,
Aviemore, Highland

Scottish Balloon Festival,
Aviemore, Highland

PRINCIPAL TOWNS

OBAN

Visitors should climb to the top of Pulpit Hill, crowned with a curious amphitheatre-like folly built in 1890, to appreciate the true splendour of Oban. Here, especially at sunset, you can marvel at the stunning view across the Firth of Lorn and the mountains of Morvern and Mull. At its foot, sheltered by the long island of Kerrara and built round a curving bay dotted with colourful craft, is the bustling town, a favoured summer resort with good sea angling, sandy beaches and ferry connections to most of the Inner Hebrides.

CAMPBELTOWN

Campbeltown is the major centre on the Kintyre Peninsula, an unexplored and unique peninsula characterised by lush gardens, heather-clad hills, sandy coves, rocky headlands and charming fishing villages. Once a thriving town, busy with whisky, creameries and fishing, it is now a sleepy little town close to the Mull of Kintrye, a windswept place immortalised by Paul McCartney's song. Clustering around its sheltered sea-loch, Campbeltown makes a peaceful base from which to explore this gentle corner of the Highlands.

MUST SEE

AUCHINDRAIN OLD HIGHLAND TOWNSHIP,

Auchindrain, Inveraray ☎ 01499 500235

This original West Highland township, or communal tenancy farming village, is a fascinating survivor from an earlier age, providing a glimpse of Highland rural life over the past 1000 years. Its buildings have been restored and preserved, and furnished and equipped in the style of various periods. Excellent on-site museum.

CRARAE GARDENS,

Minard, Inveraray ☎ 01546 886614

Set in a spectacular rocky gorge beside Loch Fyne, these gardens are among the loveliest on the west coast. Rare trees and exotic shrubs from around the world, notably rhododendrons, azaleas, conifers and a variety of Himalayan species, thrive in this magnificent setting. Resplendant in spring and autumn, this 50-acre garden affords wonderful views.

CRUACHAN POWER STATION,

Lochawe ☎ 01866 822673

A vast cavern inside Ben Cruachan contains a 400,000-kilowatt hydro-electric power station which is driven by water drawn from a high-level reservoir up the mountain. Mini-buses takes visitors 1km into the mountain to view the impressive turbine hall, 300ft (91.4m) long and 120ft (36.6m) high. Fascinating displays in the Visitor Centre.

INVERARAY JAIL,

Church Sq, Inveraray ☎ 01499 302381

A superb exhibition that re-creates life in an early 19th-century county prison and courtroom through a clever use of models, recordings and a variety of 'hands-on' exhibits. Experience prison sounds and smells, hear trials in progress in the courtroom, try out canvas hammocks, turn the handle of an original crank machine and speak to live warders and prisoners.

LOCH AWE & KILCHURN CASTLE,

At 25 miles (41km) in length, Loch Awe is Scotland's longest loch and dominated by the peak of Ben Cruachan at its northern end. Steamboats from the village of Lochawe explore the loch, including the impressive ruins of Kilchurn Castle. Built by Sir Colin Campbell in the 15th century, it commands outstanding views of the loch and surrounding mountains.

SEA LIFE CENTRE,

Barcaldine *10m/16km N of Oban on A828* ☎ 01631 720386

Set in one of Scotland's most picturesque locations, on the shore of beautiful Loch Creran, the Sea Life Centre provides dramatic views of native undersea life from stingrays and seals to octopus and catfish. Informative talks and feeding demonstrations throughout the day.

ART GALLERIES

WAVEWHISPER GALLERY,

Innellan ☎ 01369 830141

MUSEUMS

AN TAIRBEART HERITAGE CENTRE,

Tarbert, Loch Fyne ☎ 01880 820190

A celebration of Argyll life - its people and wildlife through various displays and demonstrations, woodland crafts, exhibitions and traditional farm animals.

CAMPBELTOWN HERITAGE CENTRE,

Campbeltown ☎ 01586 551400

Displays and artefacts depicting the cultural and economic history and development of Kintyre.

CASTLE HOUSE MUSEUM,

Castle Gardens, Dunoon ☎ 01369 701422

Historic buildings housing a local museum.

KILMARTIN HOUSE,

Kilmartin ☎ 01546 510278

Explores Argyll's ancient past through audio-visual displays.

HISTORIC & ANCIENT SITES

BARCALDINE CASTLE,

Benderloch, Oban ☎ 01631 720598

An early 16th-century tower house associated with the Massacre of Glencoe.

CASTLE SWEEN,

Knapdale

Ruins of one of the oldest fortresses in Scotland, overlooking Loch Sween.

DUNADD FORT,

Kilmartin *1m W of Kilmichael Glassary*

Situated on a rocky hillock overlooking a meandering river, Dunadd Fort dates from around AD 500.

DUNSTAFFNAGE CASTLE,

Oban *N* ☎ 01631 562465

Now ruined, this four-sided, 13th-century stronghold has a gatehouse, two round towers and walls 10ft thick. It enjoys spectacular views and was once the prison of Flora MacDonald.

KILMARTIN CHURCH,

Kilmartin *5m/8km N of Lochgilphead*

The graveyard has a fine collection of preaching crosses and medieval grave slabs from the 9th to the 16th centuries. The area around Kilmartin is the most comprehensive site of prehistoric monuments in Scotland.

MCCAIG'S TOWER,

Oban

A coliseum-style monument or folly built in 1897, affording outstanding views across Oban Bay to Mull.

GREAT FOR KIDS

ARCTIC PENGUIN MARITIME HERITAGE CENTRE,

The Pier, Inveraray ☎ 01499 302213

On this three-masted old 'cutter' you can take a turn at steering, visit the engine room and watch archive film of old sailing and steam ships in the on-board cinema.

ARGYLL WILDLIFE PARK,

Inveraray ☎ 01499 302264

A 60-acre site featuring Scottish wildlife, including wildcats, Highland foxes and soay sheep, European wildfowl, a large owl collection, nature walks, picnic area and tearoom.

COWAL BIRD GARDEN,

Sandbank Rd, Dunoon ☎ 01369 707999

Ancient woodlands with nature trails and hides, exotic birds and a farmyard pet area.

OBAN RARE BREEDS FARM PARK,

New Barran, Oban ☎ 01631 770608

Collection of unusual breeds of sheep, cattle, goats, pigs, poultry and other farm animals. Also a pet's corner, woodland walks and conservation centre.

HOMES & GARDENS

ARDANAISEIG GARDENS,

Kilchrenan ☎ 01866 833333

Impressive gardens, full of rhododendrons, azaleas, specimen trees and rare shrubs, on the eastern shore of Loch Awe.

ARDCHATTAN GARDEN,

Ardchattan Priory, Loch Etive

Extensive garden on the shore of Loch Etive displaying herbaceous borders, roses and shrubs in an attractive setting around the 13th-century priory and chapel ruins.

ARDUAINE GARDEN,

KIMELFORD ☎ 01852 200233

An outstanding 18-acre garden on a promontory by Loch Melfort and the Sound of Jura. Noted for rhododendrons, azaleas and other rare trees and shrubs.

GLENBARR ABBEY VISITOR CENTRE

Glenbarr, Tarbert ☎ 01583 421247

A glimpse of family living in a beautiful 18th-century house, home of the Lairds of Glenbarr. Walks, shop and tearoom.

INVERARAY CASTLE,

Inveraray ☎ 01499 302203

The seat of the Duke of Argyll since the early 15th century. The present classical building dates from 1743 and is noted for its beautiful interior decoration.

KILMORY CASTLE GARDEN,

Lochgilphead ☎ 01546 602127

Historic gardens within the attractive grounds of Kilmory Castle (not open), featuring rare trees and shrubs, herbaceous borders and collections of hardy ferns and alpines.

YOUNGER BOTANIC GARDEN,

Benmore *7m/11.2km N of Dunoon* ☎ 01369 706261

This is a woodland garden on a grand scale, with some of the largest trees in Scotland and a world famous rhododendron collection.

BIG OUTDOORS

ARGYLL FOREST PARK,
Kilmun ☎ 01369 840666
Established in 1935, the Forest Park covers 100 sq miles of pine-clad mountains, deep valleys and narrow lochs on the Cowal Peninsula between Lochs Fyne and Long. Numerous forest walks, cycling trails, horse riding routes and picnic sites allow the forest to be explored in detail.

CRINAN CANAL,
Crinan
Opened in 1801 so that ships could avoid the long journey around the Mull of Kintyre, the 14km canal links the Sound of Jura with Loch Fyne. It is now popular with leisure craft.

Call the AA Hotel Booking Service on **0990 050505** to book at AA recognised hotels and B&Bs in the UK, or through our internet site: **http://www.theaa.co.uk/hotels**

ESSENTIAL INFORMATION

TOURIST INFORMATION

INFORMATION CENTRES

ARDGARTAN *seasonal,*
Glen Croe, Ardgartan ☎ 01301 702432
CAMPBELTOWN,
MacKinnon House, The Pier,
Campbeltown ☎ 01586 552056
DUNOON,
7 Alexandra Parade, Dunoon
☎ 01369 703785
INVERARAY,
Front St, Inveraray ☎ 01499 302063
LOCHGILPHEAD *seasonal,*
Lochnell St, Lochgilphead ☎ 01546 602344
OBAN,
Boswell House, Argyll Sq, Oban
☎ 01631 563122
TARBERT (LOCH FYNE) *seasonal*
Harbour St, Tarbert ☎ 01880 820429

ACCESS

AIR ACCESS

GLASGOW AIRPORT
☎ 0141 887 1111
BRITISH AIRWAYS EXPRESS
☎ 0345 222111

SEA ACCESS

CALEDONIAN MACBRAYNE,
☎ 01475 650100
Services to the islands and the Cowal & Kintyre peninsulas.
WESTERN FERRIES (CLYDE) LTD,
☎ 01369 704452
Service between Dunoon and Gourock

CRAFTS

Local crafts include pottery and ceramics, glassmaking, ironwork, jewellery, knitwear, woodturning, tanning and distilling.

ARGYLL POTTERY,
Barcaldine, Oban ☎ 01631 720503
CAITHNESS GLASS VISITOR CENTRE,
Railway Pier, Oban ☎ 01631 563386
CAMPBELTOWN POTTERY
Unit 2, Hazelburn Business Park, Mill Knowe,
Campbeltown ☎ 01586 553550
DUNOON CERAMICS,
Hamilton St, Dunoon ☎ 01369 704360
EARRA GAEL CRAFT SHOP,
Tarbert ☎ 01880 820428

GROGPORT RUGS
Carradale ☎ 01583 431255
Organic tannery..
KILMARTIN CRAFTS,
Kilmartin ☎ 01546 510270
**STRACHUR SMIDDY
(MUSEUM & CRAFT SHOP)**
Between Dunoon and Inveraray on Loch Fyne
WALLIS HUNTER,
Carradale ☎ 01583 431683
Jewellery workshop.

FOOD & DRINK

CHEESES

The Campbeltown Creamery produces 'Mull of Kintyre', a mature cheddar coated in black wax with a nutty aroma and rounded taste (also a smoked version); 'Highland', a mature cheese with a unique, soft texture and smooth flavour, and the traditional Scottish Cheddar.

SMOKERIES

INVERAWE SMOKERY,
Bridge of Awe, Taynuilt ☎ 01866 822446
LOCH FYNE OYSTERS LTD,
Clachan, Cairndow ☎ 01499 600264
Restaurant, shop and smokehouse.
OTTER FERRY SALMON LTD,
Lephinmore, Strathlachlan, By Strachur
☎ 01369 860400
Loch Fyne smokehouse - smoked salmon, patés and chutneys.

WHISKY DISTILLERY TOURS

OBAN DISTILLERY VISITOR CENTRE,
Stafford St, Oban ☎ 01631 572004
SPRINGBANK DISTILLERY,
Campbeltown ☎ 01586 552985

ENTERTAINMENT

CINEMAS

THE PICTURE HOUSE LTD,
Hall St, Campbeltown ☎ 01586 553657
STUDIO CINEMA,
John St, Dunoon ☎ 01369 704545

THEATRES

OBAN HIGHLAND THEATRE,
George St, t 01631 562444

TRANSPORT

BOAT TRIPS & CRUISES

BORRO BOATS,
Oban ☎ 01631 563292
Sailing cruises on a skippered yacht.
CLYDE MARINE CRUISES,
☎ 01475 721281
Cruises to scenic lochs from Dunoon.
FARSAIN CRUISES,
Lochgilphead ☎ 01852 500664
Cruises to the Islands.
GEMINI CRUISES,
Crinan ☎ 01546 830238
Boat trips from Crinan Harbour.
GORDON GRANT TOURS,
Oban ☎ 01631 562842
Excursions to Mull, Iona and Staffa.
LOCH ETIVE CRUISES,
☎ 01866 822430
PORPOISE CHARTERS,
Easdale, By Oban ☎ 01852 300203
Whale-watching and diving day charters.

CAR HIRE

CAMPBELTOWN MOTOR COMPANY,
☎ 01586 552030
COUNTRY GARAGE,
Dunoon ☎ 01369 703199
HAZELBANK MOTORS,
Oban ☎ 01631 566476

COACH TOURS

GOLD LINE TOURS,
Dunoon ☎ 01369 705663
OBAN & DISTRICT BUSES LTD,
☎ 01631 562856

CYCLE HIRE

ARDFERN CYCLE HIRE,
Ardfern, Lochgilphead ☎ 01852 500662
BARMOLLOCK FARM,
Ford ☎ 01546 810209
CRINAN CYCLES,
Ardrishaig ☎ 01546 603511
DM AUTO MARINE,
Lochgilphead ☎ 01301 703432

TRAINS

West Coast Line services link Glasgow and Oban ☎ **Scotrail 0345 212282,**

SPORT & LEISURE

ACTIVITY CENTRES

ARDENTINNY OUTDOOR CENTRE,
By Dunoon ☎ 01369 870249
ARGYLL RIDING & ACTIVITIES,
Inveraray ☎ 01499 302611
EXTREME LEISURE PAINTBALL GAMES,
Oban ☎ 01631 562104
WEST HIGHLAND KARTING,
Kilninver, By Oban ☎ 01852 314256

ACTIVITY HOLIDAYS

LOCH FYNE ART COURSES,
☎ 01369 860379

ANGLING

There are ample opportunities for angling of all kinds in the area. The Loch and River Awe, and the rivers of Kintyre are noted for salmon and sea trout fishing. Excellent coarse fishing (pike and perch) can be found on Lochs Awe and Lomond, and the spectacular coastline provides fine shore fishing. Sheltered sea lochs and the Clyde estuary have good boat hire facilities. Enquire at Tourist Information Offices.

CYCLING

Traffic-free cycling is provided on waymarked forest routes through the Argyll Forest Park ☎ 01369 840666, and the Lauder Forest on the Glenbranter Estate near Strachur. Level off-road cycling can be enjoyed on the Crinan Canal towpath between Ardrishaig and Crinan. On-road cycling varies from level lochside roads to challenging mountain or coast roads.

GOLF COURSES

GLENCRUITTEN,
Oban ☎ 01631 562868
A scenic downland course.
MACHRIHANISH ☎ 01586 810213
Magnificent seaside links.
BLAIRMORE & STRONE,
Strone, By Dunoon ☎ 01369 860307
CARRADALE ☎ 01583 431643
COWAL,
Dunoon ☎ 01369 705673

DALMALLY ☎ 01838 200370
DUNAVERTY,
Campbeltown ☎ 01586 830677
INNELLAN ☎ 01369 830242
INVERARAY ☎ 01499 302508
KYLES OF BUTE,
Tighnabruaich ☎ 01700 811603
LOCHGILPHEAD ☎ 01546 602340
TARBERT ☎ 01880 820536

LEISURE CENTRES

ATLANTIS LEISURE
Dalriach Rd, Oban ☎ 01631 566800
DRIMSYNIE LEISURE CENTRE,
Drimsynie House Hotel, Lochgoilhead
☎ 01301 703247
KINTYRE COMMUNITY EDUCATION CENTRE,
Stewart Rd, Campbeltown
☎ 01586 552732

RIDING

APPALOOSA RIDING CENTRE,
Lochgilphead ☎ 01852 500632
ARDNADAM RIDING CENTRE,
Sandbank, Dunoon ☎ 01369 706400
CASTLE RIDING CENTRE
Brenfield, Ardrishaig ☎ 01546 603274
COILESSAN TREKKING & RIDING CENTRE,
Arrochar ☎ 01301 702523
LETTERSHUNA RIDING CENTRE,
Appin ☎ 01631 730227
MELFORT RIDING CENTRE,
Kilmelford, By Oban ☎ 01852 200322
MULL OF KINTYRE EQUESTRIAN CENTRE,
Campbeltown ☎ 01586 552437
TIGHNABRUAICH RIDING CENTRE,
Tighnabruaich ☎ 01700 811449

SAILING

ALBA YACHT SERVICES LTD,
Oban ☎ 01631 565630
ARGYLL ISLES CRUISING TUITION,
Lochgilphead ☎ 01546 602670

OBAN SEA SCHOOL,
Oban ☎ 01631 562013
TIGHNABRUAICH SAILING SCHOOL,
Tighnabruaich ☎ 01700 811396

SCENIC DRIVES

Argyll is blessed with a stunning landscape. The unspoilt indented coastline, its magnificent lochs and forested glens, and the spectacular, heather-clad mountains are criss-crossed by a simple, yet very scenic network of lanes and main roads. Routes to savour include the road round the Kintyre Peninsula, the steep road north from Tighnabruaich to the splendid viewpoint above the romantic Kyles of Bute, and the lochside roads around Lochs Awe, Eck and Fyne.

SWIMMING

See also Leisure Centres
CAMPBELTOWN ☎ 01586 553037
DUNOON ☎ 01369 702800
HAFTON HOLIDAY CENTRE,
Hafton, Dunoon ☎ 01369 706205
MID-ARGYLL SWIMMING POOL,
Lochgilphead ☎ 01546 606676

WALKING

From gentle shoreline strolls and well waymarked forest trails to adventurous hill walking, Argyll offers a wealth of walking opportunities.

ARGYLL FOREST PARK
Open to the public with many waymarked walks created by the Forestry Commission, the best known being up Puck's Glen at the foot of Loch Eck ☎ 01369 840666.

WATERSPORTS

CARRADALE CANOE CENTRE,
☎ 01583 431610
CRAOBH HAVEN WATERSPORTS,
Lochgilphead ☎ 01852 500664
LINNHE MARINE,
Appin ☎ 01631 730401
MARLIN WATERSPORTS & DIVE CENTRE,
Dunoon ☎ 01369 705552
PUFFIN DIVE CENTRE,
Oban ☎ 01631 566088

THE GREAT GLEN AND WEST HIGHLANDS

The Great Glen, one of Scotland's most famous landmarks, through which flows the Caledonian Canal, cuts across the country between Loch Linnhe in the south-west and Inverness on the Moray Firth, acting as a symbolic borderline between the grandeur of the Grampian Mountains and the spectacular rocky landscape of the North Highland. Geologically, the Great Glen is a fissure, dividing Scotland into two separate land masses

For dramatic beauty and majestic scenery on a grand scale, the Western Highlands are hard to beat. With numerous attractions, plenty of superb coastal scenery and mountains soaring in every direction, you are really spoilt for choice in this beautiful corner of Scotland. Fort William and bustling Oban are popular bases for exploration and adventure, though they do get busy in season.

Castle Tioram

PRINCIPAL TOWNS

INVERNESS

Set on the banks of the River Ness at the northern head of the Great Glen, Inverness, the 'Capital of the Highlands', is steeped in history. The town has seen its fair share of historical happenings since St Columba visited here in 565AD, notably the murder of King Duncan by Macbeth in 1040, numerous invasions by clan chiefs, and the bloody Jacobite rebellions during the 1700s. Few remnants of this past survive, as most of the present town dates from the 19th century, including Inverness Castle, an impressive red sandstone structure built as a Sherrif Court and Jail during Victoria's reign.

If you're here to shop, then Inverness will not disappoint. From modern malls, and bustling markets to antique shops and top department stores, Inverness can service all your needs. If it's peace and quiet you desire, then a short riverside stroll will bring you to the wooded Ness Islands, reached via footbridges.

FORT WILLIAM

A popular tourist centre situated at the southern entrance to the Great Glen beside Loch Linnhe and famed for its close proximity to Ben Nevis, Britain's highest mountain. Fort William is not just a base for climbers and car-bound visitors exploring the Great Glen and the Highland's west coast, for among the town has numerous attractions such as the fascinating West Highland Museum and the steam trains that run to Mallaig, past many historic sites, through glorious scenery

MUST SEE

CAWDOR CASTLE,
Cawdor ☎ 01667 404615
The romantic home of the Thanes of
Cawdor since the 14th century, the castle
has a drawbridge and an ancient central
tower with 15th-century fortifications.
Generations of the family have
accumulated a variety of artefacts, namely
Flemish tapestries, paintings, weapons,
Venetian bed hangings and household
equipment, all of which can be viewed,
with the help of amusing historical notes,
in the comfortable, 17th-century wings
that make up the present family home.
Gardens, restaurant and shop.

CULLODEN BATTLEFIELD,
Culloden Moor, Inverness *5m/8km E*
☎ 01463 790607
Scene of the last major battle to be fought
on mainland Britain. On 16th April 1746
'Bonnie' Prince Charles Edward Stuart's
army was bloodily routed by the Duke of
Cumberland's forces.The battlefield has
been restored to its state on the day of
the battle, and the excellent visitor centre
presents a historical display, with weapons
and objects associated with the Rising,
and an audio-visual show..

FORT GEORGE & QUEEN'S OWN HIGHLANDERS REGIMENTAL MUSEUM,
Fort George 11m/17.6km NE of Inverness
☎ 01667 462777
Built following the Battle of Culloden as a
Highland fortress for the army of George
II, it is considered to be the finest example
of late artillery fortification in Europe. It
occupies 12 acres of headland jutting out
into the Moray Firth and comprises the
oldest barracks in the world still occupied
by British soldiers. The attractive
sandstone garrison buildings house a
visitors centre, period rooms of soldiers'
quarters and the regimental museum of
the Queen's Own Highlanders, the latter
featuring uniforms, medals and pictures.

GLEN AFFRIC,
SW of Cannich off A831
One of the most beautiful glens in all of
Scotland. Magnificent scenery
accompanies the road as it winds through
one of the largest remnants of the ancient
Caledonian Pine Forest, via the popular
Dog Falls and Loch Benevean, to the
wilder upper reaches of the valley and fine
walks to the isolated expanse of Loch
Affric, surrounded by superb hills, birch
and pine forest.

HIGHLAND FOLK MUSEUM,
Duke St, Kingussie ☎ 01540 661307
A fascinating and comprehensive highland
collection of social history material,
displayed in realistic settings and
reconstructed buildings. The museum
comes alive with the sights and sounds of:
delightful baking smells from the
Blackhouse, the farrier shoeing a horse,
the spinner at her wheel, and the clarsach
player. Displays in the main house include
traditional farming, country crafts,
costume, furniture and a Highland kitchen.
Outside, you will find a Victorian
smokehouse and a Hebridean mill.

LANDMARK HIGHLAND HERITAGE & ADVENTURE PARK,
Carrbridge ☎ 01479 841613
The innovative centre portrays many
aspects of the Highlands, from the
landscape and history to wildlife, by

means of audio-visuals and displays.
Outdoor attractions, set amidst a 30-acre
pine wood, include a 70ft forest viewing
tower, a working steam-powered sawmill
and demonstration of timber sawing and
log hauling by a Clydesdale horse. Nature
trails, adventure playgrounds and a fun
maze will keep children amused.
Restaurant and craft shop.

LOCH GARTEN NATURE RESERVE,
Forest Lodge, Boat Of Garten
☎ 01479 810363
Home of the Loch Garten Osprey site, this
extensive reserve features forest bogs,
moorland, mountain tops, lochs and
crofting land. It is a haven to the Scottish
crossbill, black grouse, red squirrel, pine
marten, wildcat and red deer, as well as
winter visiting geese and goosanders. The
Osprey Centre/Viewing Hide has
telescopes and binoculars, and a live TV
link to the nest in the breeding season.

STRATHSPEY STEAM RAILWAY,
Aviemore Speyside Station, Dalfaber Rd,
Aviemore ☎ 01479 810725
Take a nostalgic five mile (8km) trip
through dramatic mountain scenery on
board a steam train between Aviemore
and Boat of Garten. Allow an hour for the
round trip and take time to view the small
museum of railwayana at Boat of Garten
station. .

Loch Garten Nature Reserve,

ART GALLERIES

LIME TREE STUDIO,
Achintore Rd, Fort William ☎ 01397 701806
MILLBANK GALLERY,
9 Millbank St, Nairn ☎ 01667 453493
PICCOLO GALLERY & OLD PRINT SHOP,
Harbour St, Nairn ☎ 01667 454508
Scottish art and ceramics. Victorian print
shop with working printing presses.
RIVERSIDE GALLERY,
Bank St, Inverness ☎ 01463 224781

MUSEUMS

BALNAIN HOUSE,
Huntly St, Inverness ☎ 01463 715757
Discover for yourself the richness of
Highland music in the audio-visual

exhibition. Play the Highland bagpipe,
fiddle or harp and join in a traditional
music session in the café/bar.
GLENCOE & LORN FOLK MUSEUM,
Glencoe
Two heather-thatched cottages containing
Jacobite and historic exhibits, domestic
and farming implements.
GLENCOE VISITOR CENTRE,
Glencoe ☎ 01855 811307
Set close to the scene of the Glencoe
Massacre in 1692, it tells the story of the
slaughter of 38 members of the
MacDonald clan, and houses a display on
the history of mountaineering in the glen.
GLENFINNAN MONUMENT & VISITOR CENTRE,
Glenfinnan ☎ 01397 722250

The monument commemorates
Highlanders who fought and died for
Bonnie Prince Charlie in 1745. Built in
1815 it commands an awe-inspiring
setting at the head of Loch Shiel.
HIGHLAND FOLK MUSEUM (TURUS TIM)
Aultlarie, Newtonmore ☎ 01540 661307
Go on a 'journey through time' and
experience the working croft of 1900 and
view a reconstructed farm settlement of
1700.
INVERNESS MUSEUM & ART GALLERY
Castle Wynd, Inverness ☎ 01463 237114
Displays of social and natural history of
the Highlands, archaeology, and examples
of Highland and Jacobite artefacts.
IONAD NIBHEIS VISITOR CENTRE,
Glen Nevis, Fort William ☎ 01397 700774

Enjoying a stunning Highland setting, the visitor centre houses an exhibition and audio-visual display about the history, wildlife and social history of Glen Nevis.

MALLAIG HERITAGE CENTRE,
Station Rd, Mallaig ☎/✆ 01687 462085
Provides a fascinating insight into the history and culture of the wild and lonely area west of Fort William.

NAIRN FISHERTOWN MUSEUM,
King St, Fishertown ☎ 01667 456798
Local museum illustrating the growth and decline of the herring fishing industry around the Moray Firth.

ORIGINAL LOCH NESS VISITOR CENTRE,
Drumnadrochit ☎ 01456 450342
Large-screen cinema show on Loch Ness and the monster.

WEST HIGHLAND MUSEUM,
Cameron Sq, Fort William ☎ 01397 702167
Founded in 1922, this is one of the oldest museums in the Highlands and is famous for its Jacobite collections.

HISTORIC & ANCIENT SITES

BEAULY PRIORY,
Beauly
Romantic 13th-century ruin linked with Mary Queen of Scots.

CASTLE TIORAM
Acharacle *4m/6.4km N*
One of the most romantic and beautifully situated ruins in the Western Highlands, this 13th-century castle stands on a rocky promontory in Loch Moidart .

CLAVA CAIRNS,
6m/10km E of Inverness
A group of circular burial cairns dating from around 1600BC One of Scotland's finest prehistoric monuments.

LOCHINDORB CASTLE,
10m/16km N of Carrbridge off A939
Set on a small island in a loch of the same name, high up in the middle of bleak Dava Moor, this lonely ruined castle was once a Comyn stronghold, before being occupied by Edward I in 1303.

MINGARRY CASTLE,
Kilchoan
Impressive 13th-century ruin built on a sheer cliff to guard the entrance to Loch Sunart and the Sound of Mull.

PARALLEL ROADS,
Glen Roy
Glen Roy and its side valleys are etched by curious parallel lines, a geological phenomenon which is unique to Britain. Known as the 'Parallel Roads' they mark the shoreline of an ancient glacial loch.

RUTHVEN BARRACKS,
Kingussie
Despite being blown up by 'Bonnie' Prince Charlie's Highlanders, the ruins of these infantry barracks, remnants of a building completed in 1716, are still the best preserved of the four built after the Jacobite uprising.

ST ANDREW'S CATHEDRAL,
Inverness
An imposing building built on the banks of the River Ness between 1866 and 1874,

with a richly decorated interior and an interesting collection of Russian icons.

URQUHART CASTLE,
Commanding fine views across Loch Ness from from its lonely rocky promontory, Urquhart Castle dates from the 14th century and is one of the largest castles in Scotland. The extensive ruins are a favoured spot for sightings of the Loch Ness Monster.

GREAT FOR KIDS

ARDNAMURCHAN NATURAL HISTORY CENTRE,
Glenmore, Acharacle ☎ 01972 500209
An informative and highly entertaining introduction to Ardnamurchan's wildlife.

CAIRNGORM REINDEER CENTRE,
Glenmore, Aviemore ☎/✆ 01479 861228
Britain's only herd of reindeer, living in their natural surroundings on the northern slopes of the Cairngorms. They are very tame and friendly, and visitors can learn about, stroke and feed them.

CASTLE GARRISON EXPERIENCE,
Ardconnel St, Inverness ☎ 01463 243563
Enlist in the garrison and meet some of the characters who volunteered to fight Prince Charlie. A live historical show explains what it was like to be a soldier in Inverness at the time of the Jacobite rising.

CHILDHOOD MEMORIES, THE TOY MUSEUM FOR THE OLD & YOUNG,
Coylumbridge, ☎ 01479 812022
Toys from the 1800's to Superman, holograms and collectable limited edition teddies and dolls.

CLUANIE PARK,
Teanassie, By Beauly ☎ 01463 782415
Bird of prey centre, daily flying demonstrations with eagles, hawks, kites, falcons and owls.

HIGHLAND GATEWAY CENTRE,
By Newtonmore ☎/✆ 01540 673650
Information centre with touch screen computers to help visitors discover more about the landscapes, wildlife, heritage and ancient forests of the Highlands.

HIGHLAND MYSTERYWORLD,
Glencoe, Fort William ☎ 01855 811660
Discover the myths, learn the legends and sense the superstitions of the Highlands in a magical world brought to life by actors and the latest animatronic effects. Lochside trails and adventure playground.

HIGHLAND WILDLIFE PARK,
Kincraig ☎ 01540 651270
In this magnificent natural setting get eye-to-eye with Scottish wildlife - past and present! Discover European bison, red deer, ibex, wild horses and Highland cattle in the fascinating drive-through reserve.

OFFICIAL LOCH NESS MONSTER EXHIBITION,
Loch Ness Centre ☎ 01456 450573
A fascinating computer-controlled, multi-media presentation lasting 40 minutes. Ten themed areas cover the story from the pre-history of Scotland, through the cultural roots of the legend of the monster in Highland folklore, and into the fifty-year controversy which surrounds it.

SANTA CLAUS LAND & CRAFT VILLAGE,
Aviemore ☎ 01479 810624
Popular children's theme park.

HOMES & GARDENS

CASTLE STUART,
Petty Parish, Inverness *5m/8km E*
☎ 01463 790745
Ancient home of the Earls of Moray and the Stuart family, constructed in 1621, located close to High Culloden Moor.

FORT AUGUSTUS ABBEY,
Fort Augustus ☎ 01320 366233
A working Benedictine Abbey on the shores of Loch Ness. Comprehensive heritage centre, cruises, Clansman centre, shop and restaurant.

REVACK GARDENS & WOODLAND WALKS,
Grantown-on-Spey ☎ 01479 872234
Beautiful gardens, ornamental lochans, orchid houses and an extensive network of walks and nature trails.

BIG OUTDOORS

CAIRNGORMS,
Britain's largest continuous stretch of high ground, an arctic tundra plateau, containing four of the five highest mountains in Britain, some fine hill passes and, arguably, the best skiing, walking, rock and ice climbing in Scotland, The less adventurous can scale the heights by way of the Cairngorm Chairlift ☎ 01479 861261.

CALEDONIAN CANAL,
West Coast to Moray Firth
Constructed by Thomas Telford between 1803 and 1822 along the Great Glen, this 107km long canal links the east and west coasts, incorporating Lochs Lochy, Oich and Ness, It has a total of 28 locks, including the famous 'Neptune's Staircase', a series of eight locks at Banavie near Fort William.

FALLS OF FOYER,
Foyer, Whitebridge, Loch Ness
Spectacular waterfall and woodland walks.

FORESTS OF LOCHABER,
Torlundy, Fort William ☎ 01397 702184
Forestry Commission woodlands managed by Forest Enterprise, with waymarked walks, picnic areas, viewpoints and, in selected forests, mountain bike trails.

GLENCOE,
17m south of Fort William
☎ 01855 811307 Visitor Centre
Probably the most famous glen in Scotland, noted for its stunning scenery and some of the best climbing and walking in the Highlands. The visitor centre explains the Glencoe Massacre of 1692 and has information on local walks.

INSH MARSHES RESERVE (RSPB)
Kingussie
Scotland's largest freshwater marsh is important for wintering wildfowl.

LOCH AN EILEAN,
Aviemore
The beautiful 'Loch of the Island' has a famous ruined castle on an island, a former stronghold of the Comyn family, a visitor centre, and a splendid nature trail round this inspiring loch.

ESSENTIAL INFORMATION

TOURIST INFORMATION

INFORMATION CENTRES

AVIEMORE,
Grampian Rd, Aviemore PH22 1PP
ⓘ/ⓕ 01479 810363
BALLACHULISH,
Albert Rd, Ballachulish PA39 4JR
☎ 01855 811296 ☎ 01855 811720
CARRBRIDGE *(seasonal)*
Village Car Park, Carrbridge PH23 3AS
☎ 01479 841630
DAVIOT *(seasonal)*
Picnic Area (A9), Daviot Wood, By Inverness
IV1 2ER
☎ 01463 772203
FORT AUGUSTUS *(seasonal)*
The Car Park, Fort Augustus PH22 4DD
☎ 01320 366367
FORT WILLIAM,
Cameron Centre, Cameron Square, Fort
William PH33 6AJ
☎ 01397 703781 ☎ 01397 705184
GRANTOWN-ON-SPEY, *(seasonal)*,
54 High St, Grantown-on-Spey PH26 3EH
☎ 01479 872773
INVERNESS,
Castle Wynd, Inverness IV2 3BJ
☎ 01463 234353 ☎ 01463 710609
KILCHOAN ,
Pier Rd, Kilchoan, Acharacle PH36 4LH
☎ 01972 510222
KINGUSSIE *(seasonal)*,
King St, Kingussie PH21 1HP
☎ 01540 661297
MALLAIG *(seasonal)*,
The Harbour, Mallaig PH41 4SQ
☎ 01687 462170
NAIRN,
62 King St, Nairn IV2 4DN
☎ 01667 452753
RALIA *(seasonal)*,
A9 North, By Newtonmore PH20 1BD
☎ 01540 673263
SPEAN BRIDGE *(seasonal)*,
Spean Bridge PH34 4EP
☎ 01397 712576 ☎ 01397 712675
STRONTIAN *(seasonal)*
Strontian, Acharacle PH36 4HZ
☎ 01967 402131

ACCESS

AIR ACCESS

INVERNESS AIRPORT ☎ 01463 232471
BRITISH AIRWAYS ☎ 01667 462280

FERRIES

CALEDONIAN MACBRAYNE
☎ 01475 650100
Connect Fort William & Lochaber with
Mull, the Small Isles and Skye.

CRAFTS

*Lookout for tartan weaving, kiltmaking,
jewellery, leather goods, woodturning &
carving, pottery, candlemaking.*

ARCHES CRAFT SHOP,
East Laroch, Ballachulish ☎ 01855 811866
BEN NEVIS WOOLLEN MILL,
Belford Rd, Fort William ☎ 01397 704244
CLOG & CRAFT SHOP,
Invermoriston ☎ 01320 351318
COTTAGE WOODCRAFT,
Drumnadrochit ⓘ/ⓕ 01456 450423
CRAFTS & THINGS,
Glencoe ☎ 01855 811325
CULLODEN POTTERY,
Gollanfield, Inverness
☎ 01667 462340
HECTOR RUSSELL KILTMAKER,
Huntly St, Inverness ☎ 01463 222781
ICEBERG GLASSBLOWING STUDIO,
Drumnadrochit ☎ 01456
450601
JAMES PRINGLE WEAVERS,
Dores Rd, Inverness ☎ 01463 223311
J.F. LINDSAY (TARGEMAKER)
North Kessock, Inverness ☎ 01463 731577
Reproductions of Highland shields.
MADE IN SCOTLAND LTD,
The Craft Centre, Station Rd, Beauly
☎ 01463 782578
SPEAN BRIDGE WOOLLEN MILL,
Spean Bridge ☎ 01397 712260
STEPHEN HAYWARD (WOODCARVING)
Tigh Bea, Kiltarlity ☎ 01463 741425

ENTERTAINMENT

CINEMA/THEATRE

AVIEMORE MOUNTAIN RESORT,
☎ 01479 810624
EDEN COURT THEATRE,
Bishops Rd, Inverness ☎ 01463 234234

FOOD & DRINK

HIGHLAND WINERY,
Moniack Castle, Kirkhill, Inverness
☎ 01463 831283
Traditional 'country wines' - elderflower,
silver birch, mead, sloe gin - and preserves
(Moniack marmalade, chutneys & jellies)
STRATHAIRD SALMON,
Speyside Valley Smokehouse, Achnagonalin,
Grantown-on-Spey ☎ 01479 873078
**CONFECTIONERY FACTORY VISITOR
CENTRE,**
North Ballachulish, Fort William
ⓘ/ⓕ 01855 821277
Hand-made traditional sweetmaking.

WHISKY DISTILLERY TOURS

DALWHINNIE DISTILLERY,
Dalwhinnie ☎ 01528 522208
TOMATIN DISTILLERY,
Tomatin ☎ 01808 511444
CAIRNGORM WHISKY CENTRE,
Inverdruie, Aviemore ☎ 01479 810574

TRANSPORT

BOAT TRIPS & CRUISES

ARDNAMURCHAN CHARTERS,
☎ 01972 500208
Wildlife tours on Loch Sunart and trips to
the Islands.
ARISAIG MARINE LTD,
☎ 01687 450224
Hebridean wildlife cruises.
BRUCE WATT CRUISES,
☎ 01687 462233
Loch Ness, the Small Isles and Skye.
CRUISE LOCH NESS,
☎ 01320 366277
**JLOCH NESS & GREAT GLEN CRUISE
COMPANY,**
ⓘ/ⓕ 01463 711913
Barge cruising the Great Glen.

BUS SERVICES

HIGHLAND COUNTRY BUS LTD,
ⓘ/ⓕ 01479 811211 & ⓘ 01397 702373
Strathspey and Lochaber services.

CAR HIRE

ARNOLD CLARK HIRE DRIVE,
Inverness ☎ 01463 713322
BUDGET CAR HIRE,
Fort William ☎ 01397 702500
HERTZ RENT-A-CAR,
Inverness ☎ 01463 711479
MACDONALD'S SELF DRIVE,
Aviemore ⓘ/ⓕ 01497 811444
NEVIS GARAGE LTD,
Fort William ☎ 01397 702432

CYCLE HIRE

GLENCOE MOUNTAIN BIKE CENTRE,
☎ 01855 811252
GREAT GLEN CYCLE HIRE,
Inverness ☎ 01468 627414
GREAT GLEN SCHOOL OF ADVENTURE,
South Laggan ☎ 01809 501381
OFF BEAT BIKES,
Fort William ⓘ/ⓕ 01397 704008
INVERDRUIE MOUNTAIN BIKES,
Rothiemurchus Visitor Centre, Inverdruie
☎ 01479 810787
WILDERNESS CYCLES,
Drumnadrochit ☎ 01456 450223

TRAINS

The West Highland Line links Glasgow
with Fort William and Mallaig. Inverness is
on the line linking Edinburgh with
Caithness and Kyle of Lochalsh
☎ 01463 238924 (ScotRail Inverness)

SPORT & LEISURE

ACTIVITY CENTRES

ALFRESCO ADVENTURE,
Onich, Fort William ☎/☎ **01855 821248**
AVIEMORE MOUNTAIN BIKES & ACTIVITIES,
☎ **01479 811007**
DULNAIN BRIDGE OUTDOOR CENTRE,
☎/☎ **01479 851246**
LANDWISE OFF ROAD,
Boat of Garten ☎ **01479 831609**
MOUNTAIN CRAFT,
Fort William ☎ **01397 722213**
TALISMAN MOUNTAINEERING ACTIVITIES,
Carrbridge ☎/☎ **01479 841576**

ACTIVITY HOLIDAYS

BOBSPORT LTD,
☎/☎ **0131 447 3500**
Salmon and fishing holidays in Speyside.
CALEDONIAN DISCOVERY LTD,
☎ **01397 772167**
Barge cruising the Great Glen & Loch Ness.

ANGLING

Excellent salmon and trout fishing can be enjoyed throughout the Great Glen lochs and rivers. Enquire at local Tourist Information Offices.

CYCLING

Mountain bikers are spoilt for choice, with miles of challenging moorland tracks for the adventurous, and easy waymarked forest trails (Rothiemurchus Estate, Inchnacardoch Forest, Forestry Commission woodland) for the less experienced to explore. Good family biking can be found through the scenic glens, especially Glen Strathfarrar (off A831 near Struy) via a private road.
THE GREAT GLEN CYCLE ROUTE
Over 50 miles of forest tracks and small back roads linking Inverness to Fort William

CYCLE TOURS

BESPOKE HIGHLAND TOURS,
☎ **01687 450272**
CALEDONIAN ACTIVITY BREAKS,
☎ **01397 772373**

GLIDING

CAIRNGORM GLIDING CLUB,
☎ **01631 740316**

GOLF

FORT WILLIAM ☎ **01397 704464**
Spectacular moorland course.
NAIRN ☎ **01667 453208**
Seaside links created from a wilderness of heather and whin
ABERNETHY,
Nethy Bridge ☎ **01479 821305**
BOAT OF GARTEN ☎ **01479 831282**
CARRBRIDGE ☎ **01479 841623**
CRAGGAN,
Grantown-on-Spey ☎ **01479 873283**
FORT AUGUSTUS ☎ **01320 366660**

GRANTOWN-ON-SPEY ☎ **01479 872079**
INVERNESS ☎ **01463 239882**
NAIRN DUNBAR ☎ **01667 452741**
NEWTONMORE ☎ **01540 673328**
TORVEAN,
Inverness ☎ **01463 711434**

ICE RINKS

AVIEMORE MOUNTAIN RESORT,
☎ **01479 810624**
INVERNESS ICE RINK,

LEISURE CENTRES

INVERNESS SPORTS CENTRE,
Bught Park ☎ **01463 713585**
LOCHABER LEISURE CENTRE & SWIMMING POOL
Fort William ☎ **01397 704359**
NAIRN LEISURE PARK
☎ **01667 453061**

RIDING

BRAESIDE TREKKING & RIDING CENTRE,
Kiltarlity, Beauly ☎ **01463 741525**
CARRBRIDGE TREKKING CENTRE,
☎ **01479 841602**
FORT AUGUSTUS RIDING CENTRE,
☎ **01320 366418**
HIGHLAND ICELANDIC HORSE TREKKING,
Spean Bridge ☎ **01397 712427**
HIGHLAND RIDING CENTRE,
Drumnadrochit ☎ **01456 450220**
JLOCH NESS RIDING,
Dores, Inverness ☎ **01463 751251**
MOIDART PONY TREKKING,
Acharacle ☎ **01967 431229**
STRATHSPEY HIGHLAND PONY CENTRE,
Grantown-on-Spey ☎ **01479 873073**

SCENIC DRIVES

Outstanding mountain scenery makes driving a pleasure, although some roads can be narrow and twisting, and the main roads through the Great Glen are likely to be very busy in high season. Notable explorations include the west coast drive from Fort William to Mallaig, a tour of the Ardnamurchan peninsula, and scenic journeys to the head of two beautiful glens - Glen Affric and Glen Cannich.

SKIING

AVIEMORE SKI SCHOOL,
☎/☎ **01479 810296**
CARRBRIDGE SKI SCHOOL,
☎ **01479 841246**
GLENCOE SKI CENTRE,
☎ **01855 851226**
INSH HALL SKI SCHOOL & SKI LODGE,
Kincraig ☎ **01540 651272**
THE MOUNTAIN SKI SCHOOL & ARTIFICIAL SKI SLOPE,
Aviemore ☎ **01479 811707**
NETHYBRIDGE SKI SCHOOL,
☎/☎ **01479 821333**
SCOTTISH NORWEGIAN SKI SCHOOL,
Aviemore ☎ **01479 810656**

SWIMMING

See also Leisure Centres

BEACHES

Good sandy beaches can be found at Nairn, in the secluded bays on the Ardnamurchan peninsula, and the Silver Sands of Morar, near Mallaig, is a famous sandy beach.
AQUADOME,
Bught Park, Inverness ☎ **01463 667500**
AVIEMORE MOUNTAIN RESORT,
☎ **01479 810624**

WALKING

The Spey Valley, unspoilt wooded glens, lochs and forests offer gentle walking on well waymarked trails for the less energetic. Adventurous walkers can head for the hills and bag a few peaks in the Cairngorms, Glencoe and in the Nevis Range, with Ben Nevis (4409ft/1343m), Britain's highest mountain, the ultimate challenge for keen hill walkers. Make sure you are well equipped for all weathers.
WEST HIGHLAND WAY
A long-distance trail linking Milngavie (north of Glasgow) with Fort William.
GREAT WALKS LEAFLETS
Series of five walking leaflets highlighting various trails from easy to difficult grades
☎ **01631 566155 (Forest Enterprise)**

WALKING TOURS/GUIDES

DROVERS GUIDED WALKS,
☎ **01463 242095**
HIGHLAND GUIDES,
☎ **01479 810729**
LOCHABER WALKS,
☎ **01397 703828**
NEVIS GUIDES,
☎ **01397 712356**
TRAVEL LITE,
☎ **0141 956 7890**
Rucksack-carrying van service for those walking the West Highland Way.

WATERSPORTS

GREAT GLEN SCHOOL OF ADVENTURE,
South Laggan ☎ **01809 501223**
HIGHLAND DRASCOMBE SAILING SCHOOL,
North Kessock, Inverness ☎ **01463 731493**
LOCH INSH WATERSPORTS CENTRE,
Kincraig ☎ **01540 651272**
LOCH MORLICH WATERSPORTS,
Glenmore Forest Park ☎ **01497 861221**
NAIRN WATERSPORTS,
☎/☎ **01667 155416**
THE UNDERWATER CENTRE,
Fort William ☎ **01397 703786**

TOURS

EXECUTIVE TRAVEL,
☎ **01667 462209**
Car tours of the Highlands.
GLENGARRY MINIBUS TOURS & GUIDE SERVICES,
☎ **01809 501297**
Tours of the glens. Walkers taxi bus for West Highland Way.
GUIDE FRIDAY,
☎ **01463 224000**
Open-topped bus tours of Inverness.

WHERE TO STAY
ARGYLL

AA RECOMMENDED

Rockhill

ARDBRECKNISH

ROCKHILL ◙◙◙
PA33 1BH *(from Inverary take A819 then
B840 at Cladich for 3 m to Rockhill)*
☎ 01866 833218
Quiet position with lovely views over the
loch this farmhouse offers traditionally
styled bedrooms. Good home-cooking.
Hanovarian horses bred on the farm.
*£ 5 bedrooms (3 fmly) No smoking in
dining room or lounges Licensed No children
under 8yrs Fishing 200 acres horses sheep
May–Sep*

ARDENTINNY

ARDENTINNY ★★◉
PA23 8TR *(M8 to Gourock, ferry to Dunoon
(every 30mins, duration 20mins) 12m N on
A880 off A815, alternative route by Erskine
Bridge & Loch Lomond)*
☎ 01369 810209 ☎ 01369 810241
With a backdrop of wooded hills beside
Loch Long. Bright, modern
accommodation. Facilities for watersports.
Several dining options.
*11 bedrooms (1 fmly) Boating Children's
facilities No smoking in restaurant Closed
Nov–Feb* ▰

ARDUAINE

LOCH MELFORT ★★★◉◉
PA34 4XG
*(on A816, midway between Oban and
Lochgilphead)*
☎ 01852 200233 ☎ 01852 200214
Genuine hospitality, good food and
glorious views in relaxed and convivial
atmosphere are the appeal here. Cocktail
bar, library, and a restaurant specialising in
seafood.
*7 bedrooms 20 annexe bedrooms (2 fmly) No
smoking in restaurant Closed 4 Jan–Feb* ▰

ARROCHAR

BEMERSYDE ◙◙◙
Tarbet, Loch Lomond G83 7DE *(on A82)*
☎ 01301 702230
Good value accommodation at this
extended detached bungalow. One ground
floor bedroom. Cosy sitting room with CTV.
*££ 3 bedrooms (1 fmly) No smoking
Mar–Oct*

CAMPBELTOWN

SEAFIELD ★★
Kilkerran Rd PA28 6JL
☎ 01586 554385 ☎ 01586 552741
Small hotel overlooking the bay.
Bedrooms, in the main and garden
houses, are well equipped and pleasantly
furnished. Good sea food.
££ 3 bedrooms 6 annexe bedrooms (1 fmly)
▰

WESTBANK ◙◙◙
Dell Rd PA28 6JG *(A83 to Campbeltown, R
at T-junct follow signs for Southend, B842,
through S bend Heritage Centre on L, first R)*
☎ 01586 553660 ☎ 01586 553660
Family run, detached Victorian house

offering good value accommodation.
Bedrooms offer modern appointments.
*£ 8 bedrooms No smoking in dining room
No dogs (ex guide dogs) Licensed No
children under 3yrs Feb–Oct* ▰

CARDROSS

KIRKTON HOUSE ◙◙◙◙◙
Darleith Rd G82 5EZ *(0.5m N of village -
turn N off A814 into Darleith Road at W
end of village. Kirkton House is half mile on
right) (Logis)*
☎ 01389 841951 ☎ 01389 841868
Spacious, traditional farmhouse with
panoramic views. Rustic atmosphere
within. Splendid home cooking ensures
that many guests return regularly.
*££ 6 bedrooms(4 fmly) No smoking in
dining room Licensed Children's facilities
Riding Closed Dec 6–Jan 25* ▰

CARRADALE

DUNVALANREE ◙◙◙
Portrigh Bay PA28 6SE *(from village centre turn
L at sign for Portrigh Bay, follow road to end)*
☎ 01583 431226 ☎ 01583 431339
Peacefully situated beside a small bay with
glorious views over the water to the hills.
Bedrooms are bright and fresh. Enjoyable
home cooking a feature.
*14 bedrooms (3 fmly) No smoking in dining
room Licensed Golf 9 Fishing Squash* ★★

CLACHAN-SEIL

WILLOWBURN ★★◉
PA34 4TJ *(0.5m from Atlantic Bridge)*
☎ 01852 300276 ☎ 01852 300597
Tranquility and good food at this small
white painted cottage hotel in idyllic
position by the water's edge.
*££ (inc bkfst & dinner) 7 bedrooms No
smoking in all bedrooms No smoking in
restaurant Closed Jan–Mar* ▰

Loch Melfort

Ards House

CONNEL

FALLS OF LORA ★ ★
PA37 1PB *(off A85, overlooking Loch Etive, 5m from Oban)*
☎ 01631 710483 ⊕ 01631 710694
Friendly personally run hotel enjoying views of Loch Etive. Informal food all day plus more formal dining. Bedrooms with styles and tariffs to suit most tastes and pockets.
£ 30 bedrooms (4 fmly) No smoking area in restaurant Closed 25 Dec & Jan 🔌

ARDS HOUSE ⬚ ⬚ ⬚ ⬚ ⬚
PA37 1PT *(on A85, 4m N of Oban)*
☎ 01631 710255
Spectacular views over the bay from this lovely detached house. Individually decorated bedrooms many thoughtful personal touches.
£££ 6 bedrooms No smoking No dogs Licensed No children under 12yrs Closed Dec-Jan 🔌

LOCH ETIVE HOUSE HOTEL ⬚ ⬚ ⬚ ⬚ ⬚
Main St PA37 1PH *(200yds from A85)*
☎ 01631 710400 ⊕ 01631 710680
Genuine warm welcome together with good food are the appeal of this hotel. Comfortable bedrooms in both modern and traditional furnishings.
£ 6 bedrooms (2 fmly) No smoking in 3 bedrooms No smoking in dining room or lounges Licensed 🔌

RONEBHAL ⬚ ⬚ ⬚ ⬚
PA37 1PJ *(on A85. 4th house past turn for Fort William overlooking the bay)*
☎ 01631 710310
An attractive detached Victorian house standing in its well-tended gardens with lovely outlook over Loch Etive offering high standards of comfort and appointment throughout.
£ 6 bedrooms (1 fmly) No smoking No dogs No children under 5yrs Apr-Oct 🔌

KILCHURN ⬚ ⬚ ⬚
PA37 1PG *(on A85)* ☎ 01631 710581
Victorian villa with views across Loch Etive. Comfortable, attractive bedrooms with nice personal touches.
£ 3 bedrooms No smoking in bedrooms or dining room No dogs No children under 12yrs Etr-Oct

DUNOON

ENMORE ★ ★ ⬚
Marine Pde, Kirn PA23 8HH *(on coastal route between two ferries, 1m N of Dunoon)*
☎ 01369 702230 ⊕ 01369 702148
(Rosette awarded for dinner only)
Hospitable welcome and caring attention at this comfortable hotel overlooking the Firth of Clyde. Bedrooms are traditional in style, but some have water beds or four-poster beds.
££ 10 bedrooms (2 fmly) Squash No smoking in restaurant Meeting room Closed 2-12 Jan Res Nov-Feb 🔌

ROYAL MARINE ★ ★
Hunters Quay PA23 8HJ *(located on A815 opposite Western Ferries terminal)*
☎ 01369 705810 ⊕ 01369 702329
Friendly hotel standing in its own well tended garden. Lovely views over the Firth of Clyde. Tasty bar meals available. Bright modern dining room to watch the ferries from.
£ 25 bedrooms 10 annexe bedrooms (3 fmly) No dogs (ex guide dogs) Snooker Wkly live entertainment No smoking in restaurant 🔌

LYALL CLIFF ★
141 Alexandra Pde, East Bay PA23 8AW *(on A815 between Kirn and Dunoon)*
☎ 01369 702041 ⊕ 01369 702041
Excellent value for money is offered at this friendly hotel on the seafront overlooking the Firth of Clyde. Brightly decorated bedrooms.
£ 10 en suite (2 fmly) No children under 3yrs No smoking in restaurant Closed 20 Dec-7 Jan Res Nov-Mar 🔌

THE ANCHORAGE ⬚ ⬚ ⬚ ⬚ ⬚
Lazaretto Point, Shore Rd, Ardnadam, Holy Loch PA23 8QG *(3m N on A815)*
☎ 01369 705108 ⊕ 01369 705108
On the scenic route from the Clyde to the Argyll coast, this pleasant house, is near the ferry terminals. Conservatory Restaurant is popular locally. True Scottish breakfasts.

Falls of Lora

££ 5 bedrooms (1 fmly) No smoking No dogs (ex guide dogs) Licensed Closed Nov Discount on membership of country club 🔌

THE CEDARS ⬚ ⬚ ⬚
51 Alexandra Pde, East Bay PA23 8AF *(on the seafront)*
☎ 01369 702425 ⊕ 01369 706964
Standing on the esplanade overlooking the Firth of Clyde. Smartly decorated bedrooms. Hearty breakfasts in the dining room that overlooks the sea.
£ 11 bedrooms (1 fmly) No smoking in 8 bedrooms No smoking in dining room or lounges No dogs Licensed 🔌

Enmore

ERISKA

ISLE OF ERISKA ★ ★ ★ ❀ ❀ ❀
PA37 1SD
☎ 01631 720371 ⓕ 01631 720531
Cross a bridge (or land by helicopter) to reach this baronial mansion on its own picturesque island. Wildlife abounds. Keen and professional staff. Innovative menus.
17 bedrooms Night porter Indoor swimming pool (heated) Tennis (hard) Sauna Solarium Gym Pool table Croquet lawn Jacuzzi/spa 6 hole executive golf Closed Jan 🗨

Royal Marine

INVERARAY

FERNPOINT ★
PA32 8UX
(A83 through Inveraray, hotel on pierhead)
☎ 01499 302170 ⓕ 01499 302366
Friendly and relaxed service at this hotel beside Loch Fyne close to the Town Jail, a popular tourist attraction! Bedrooms vary in size. Extensive range of food available.
£ 8 bedrooms (3 fmly) Night porter Affiliated to golf course Local riding stables Children's facilities Closed 5 Jan-5 Feb 🗨

KILFINAN

KILFINAN ★ ★ ❀ ❀
PA21 2EP *(on B8000 east coast of Loch Fyne, between Otter Ferry and Tignabruaich)*
☎ 01700 821201 ⓕ 01700 821205
Set in thousands of acres of unspoilt countryside, once a coaching inn, its a haven for country pursuits and relaxation. A certain rustic character yet very comfortable and hospitable.

Kilfinan

££ 11 en suite (bth) (1 fmly) No dogs (ex guide dogs) Fishing Private beach No children under 12yrs No smoking in restaurant Closed Feb 🗨

> **Call the AA Hotel Booking Service on 0990 050505 to book at AA recognised hotels and B&Bs in the UK, or through our internet site: http://www.theaa.co.uk/hotels**

KILCHRENAN

ARDANAISEIG ★ ★ ★ ❀ ❀
PA35 1HE *(from A85 take B845, follow signs for Kilchrennan, turn L then follow signs for Ardanaiseig)*
☎ 01866 833333 ⓕ 01866 833222
Peacefully set amid spectacular gardens and breathtaking scenery. Charming day rooms, bedrooms from master suites to standard. Table d'hote and carte menus.
££ 15 bedrooms No smoking in 2 bedrooms Tennis (hard) Fishing Snooker Croquet lawn Putting green Boating Clay pigeon shooting No smoking in restaurant Closed 3 Jan-13 Feb 🗨

TAYCHREGGAN ★ ★ ★ ❀ ❀
PA35 1HQ *(W from Glasgow A82 to Crianlarich, onto A85 to Taynuilt, then S for 7m on B845 to Kilchrenan)*
☎ 01866 833211 & 833366
ⓕ 01866 833244
Relaxation is all at this home from home, once a drover's inn and standing in a beautiful, peaceful location. The bedrooms are delightful.
££££ (inc bkfst & dinner) 20 bedrooms Fishing Snooker No children under 14yrs No smoking in restaurant 🗨

LOCHGILPHEAD

THE STAG ★ ★
Argyll St PA31 8NE *(A82 then A38, follow rd to Inveraray, turn R at mini rdbt into main street)*
☎ 01546 602496 ⓕ 01546 603549
Long established, family-run hotel offering good-value accommodation. Bedrooms have a wide range of amenities though they do tend to be compact.
££ 17 bedrooms Pool table 🗨

OBAN

COLUMBA ★ ★ ★
North Pier PA34 5QD
(A82, A85 to Oban, onto George St, on approach to mini rdbt turn R, hotel on L)
☎ 01631 562183 ⓕ 01631 564683
Standing beside the North Pier enjoying views over the bay to Kerrera and Mull beyond. Many of the comfortable modern bedrooms overlook the bay .
££ 48 bedrooms (6 fmly) No smoking in 14 bedrooms Lift Night porter Wkly live entertainment No smoking in restaurant Closed 1 Dec-Feb 11 🗨

CALEDONIAN ★ ★ ★
Station Square PA34 5RT
(opp Railway station at edge of Oban Bay)
☎ 01631 563133 ⓕ 01631 562998
Popular hotel from the Victorian era. Conveniently situated beside the railway station and ferry terminal, it enjoys lovely views over the bay.
70 bedrooms (10 fmly) Lift Night porter No smoking in restaurant 🗨

Taychreggan

MANOR HOUSE ★★ ⊛⊛
Gallanach Rd PA34 4LS
(Follow signs MacBrayne Ferries and pass ferry entrance for hotel on right)
☎ 01631 562087 🖷 01631 563053
Comfortable hotel, with much original character and superb views of nearby islands. The public rooms are a delight. Daily-changing dinner menu and extensive carte.
£££ (inc bkfst & dinner) 1 bedroom No children under 12yrs No smoking in restaurant Res 1 Nov-28 Feb 🛏

FOXHOLES ★★
Cologin, Lerags PA34 4SE
(3m S of Oban)
☎ 01631 564982
Charming small country hotel set amid peaceful countryside within spacious and well tended gardens. Bedrooms decorated to a high standard, some having patio doors to the garden.
££ 7 bedrooms No dogs No smoking in restaurant Closed 31 Oct-Mar 🛏

ARGYLL ★★
Corran Esplanade PA34 5PZ
(A85 to town centre, hotel 500 yards from main rail, taxi and bus terminal)
☎ 01631 562353 🖷 01631 565472
Friendly atmosphere prevails at this hotel by the North Pier and overlooking Oban Bay. Bedrooms are fresh and bright, although they vary in size.
££ 27 bedrooms (5 fmly) No smoking in 9 bedrooms Night porter Wkly live entertainment No smoking in restaurant 🛏

DUNGALLAN HOUSE HOTEL ★★⊛
Gallanach Rd PA34 4PD
(at Argyll Sq (town centre) follow signs for Gallanch, hotel 0.5m)
☎ 01631 563799 🖷 01631 566711
(Rosette awarded for dinner only)
Delightful small hotel standing in elevated and well tended grounds overlooking the bay. Cosy lounge and spacious bar.
££ 13 bedrooms No smoking in restaurant Closed Nov & Feb 🛏

LANCASTER ★★
Corran Esplanade PA34 5AD
(on seafront near St Columba's Cathedral)
☎ 01631 562587 🖷 01631 562587
Superb views over the bay to the islands from this friendly family hotel on the waterfront. Bedrooms neatly furnished to make the best use of space.
£ 27 bedrooms (3 fmly) Indoor swimming pool (heated) Sauna Solarium Pool table Jacuzzi/spa 🛏

ARD STRUAN GUEST HOUSE ◫◫◫◫
Croft Rd PA34 5JN
(down hill into Oban L into Croft Rd, Ard Struan on L at end)
☎ 01631 563689
Immaculately maintained detached modern home, in a quiet residential area. Attractive bedrooms, one with four-poster bed, are decorated to a high standard.
£ 4 bedrooms No smoking in dining room

Foxholes

BRIARBANK ◫◫◫◫
Glencruitten Rd PA34 4DN
☎ 01631 566549
Detached house on a hillside site just a short walk from the town centre. Access by steep flight of external steps from street car park.
3 bedrooms No smoking No dogs (ex guide dogs) No children under 12yrs

DRUMRIGGEND ◫◫◫◫
Drummore Rd PA34 4JL
(from Oban follow Campbelltown Rd signs (A816), 1st on L after BP filling station)
☎ 01631 563330 🖷 01631 563330
Smart, detached house with bedrooms tastefully decorated and comfortably furnished in the modern style.
£ 3 bedrooms (1 fmly) No smoking in dining room

GLENBERVIE HOUSE ◫◫◫◫
Dalriach Rd PA34 5NL
☎ 01631 564770 🖷 01631 566723
Welcoming Victorian house overlooking the bowling green and bay. Bedrooms are brightly decorated and comfortably furnished. Enjoyable home cooked evening meals.
£ 8 bedrooms (2 fmly) No smoking in dining room No dogs (ex guide dogs) Licensed

GLENBURNIE PRIVATE HOTEL ◫◫◫◫
The Esplanade PA34 5AQ
(On seafront, follow signs for Ganavan)
☎ 01631 562089
Situated on the sea front with beautiful views over the bay to the Isle of Mull. Bedrooms include a superior four-poster suite, while others are generously proportioned.
£ 16 bedrooms 1 annexe bedroom No smoking No dogs (ex guide dogs) No children under 12yrs Apr-Oct 🛏

OLD MANSE ◫◫◫◫
Dalriach Rd PA34 5JE *(from A85 follow signs for swimming pool & bowling green)*
☎ 01631 564886 Mar-Nov
Charming atmosphere at this substantial house in elevated position with lovely views of the bay. Decor throughout is very fresh and comfortable.
£ 4 bedrooms (1 fmly) No smoking in bedrooms or dining room or in 1 lounge No dogs (ex guide dogs)

RHUMOR ◫◫◫◫
Drummore Rd PA34 4JL
☎ 01631 563544
Visitors are warmly welcomed to this comfortable detached bungalow. Bedrooms have tasteful décor and attractive co-ordinated fabrics.
£ 3 bedrooms (1 fmly) No smoking Closed Dec

ARDBLAIR ◫◫◫
Dalriach Rd PA34 5JB
☎ 01631 562668 🖷 01631 562668
Friendly guest house enjoys delightful views over the bay. Bedrooms, all well equipped, are a mix of modern and more traditional styles.
£ 14 bedrooms (2 fmly) No smoking in bedrooms or dining room No dogs Closed Oct-Apr Res Easter

GLENRIGH ◫◫◫
Esplanade PA34 5AQ
(on main Esplanade 5 blocks from Cathedral)
☎ 01631 562991 🖷 01631 562991
Enjoying a fine position on the Esplanade overlooking the bay, this family run guest house within its own well tended garden offers good value accommodation.
£ 14 bedrooms (6 fmly) No smoking in dining room Closed Nov-Feb 🛏

ROSENEATH ◫◫◫
Dalriach Rd PA34 5EQ
(turn L off A85 beyond Kings Knoll Hotel & follow signs for swimming pool, then straight on for 300metres)
☎ 01631 562929
Comfortable terraced house on the hill above the town that combines a welcoming atmosphere with good value accommodation. Smartly decorated bedrooms. Lounge with bay views.
£ 8 bedrooms No smoking No dogs (ex guide dogs) Feb-Oct

SGEIR MHAOL ◫◫◫
Soroba Rd PA34 4JF
(on A816 - opposite Oban High School)
☎ 01631 562650 🖷 01631 562650
Friendly welcome is assured at this comfortable detached bungalow. Well maintained bedrooms designed to make the best use of available space.
£ 7 bedrooms (3 fmly) No smoking in dining room No dogs (ex guide dogs)

THORNLOE 🞐🞐🞐
Albert Rd PA34 5JD

(from A85, turn L at King's Knoll Hotel and pass swimming pool, last house on R)

☎ 01631 562879

Situated on the hill above the town, enjoying views over the bay. Bedrooms, two of which have four-poster beds, are comfortably appointed.

£ 8 bedrooms (2 fmly) No smoking in 4 bedrooms No smoking in dining room or lounges No dogs (ex guide dogs) Closed Nov

WELLPARK HOTEL🞐🞐🞐
Esplanade PA34 5AQ *(A55 to Oban sea front, turn R, 200 yards to hotel)*

☎ 01631 562948 🅵 01631 565808

From its position on the Esplanade this semi-detached Victorian house enjoys fine views over the bay and offers good value accommodation.

£ 17 bedrooms No smoking in 8 bedrooms No smoking in dining room or lounges Closed Nov-end May Res Easter

GLENROY 🞐🞐
Rockfield Rd PA34 5DQ

(at the S end of Gorge Street, turn into Stevenson Street, keep left of Rockfield School, go behind school onto Rockfield Road)

☎ 01631 562585

A warm welcome awaits at this comfortable semi-detached Victorian home, on the hill overlooking the bay. Offering good value accommodation.

£ 7 bedrooms No smoking in dining room No dogs (ex guide dogs)

AIRDS ★★★🞑🞑🞑
PA38 4DF *(16m S of Ballachulish Bridge turn off A828, then 2m)*

☎ 01631 730236 🅵 01631 730535

Former Ferry Inn now a stylish and peaceful haven amid spectacular scenery with stunning views. Enjoy delightful cuisine in attractive dining room.

££££ (inc bkfst) 12 bedrooms No dogs (ex guide dogs) No smoking in restaurant

THISTLE HOUSE 🞐🞐🞐🞐
PA25 8AZ *(A83 onto A815 (Dunoon) at Cairndow, 5m to St.Catherines. Thistle House is on left beyond the village)*

☎ 01499 302209 🅵 01499 302531

Hospitality is first class at this house overlooking Loch Fyne offering spacious and comfortable bedrooms furnished along traditional lines.

£ 4 bedrooms (1 fmly) No smoking in dining room Closed Nov-Mar

CREGGANS INN ★★★🞑
PA27 8BX *(take A815 to Stachur)*

☎ 01369 860279 🅵 01369 860637

Lady MacLean and her staff welcome visitors to this charming Highland inn with superb views. Bar meals and imaginative short table d'hôte menu available.

££ 19 bedrooms No smoking in restaurant

STONEFIELD CASTLE ★★★
PA29 6YJ *(off A83, 2m N)*

☎ 01880 820836 🅵 01880 820929

Impressive baronial mansion peacefully set in 60 acres of wooded gardens. Delightful day rooms and spacious restaurant loroverlooking Loch Fyne.

33 bedrooms (1 fmly) Lift Outdoor swimming pool (heated) Fishing Snooker Sauna Solarium No smoking in restaurant

BRANDER LODGE ★★
Bridge of Awe PA35 1HT

(set back from A85, 2.5m E of Taynuilt, 7m W of Lochawe)

☎ 01866 822243 🅵 01866 822273

A family-owned and run hotel, with friendly and attentive service. Modern and spacious bedrooms with satellite TV.

££ 20 bedrooms (4 fmly) Pool table No smoking in restaurant

POLFEARN ★★
PA35 1JQ

(turn N off A85, then 1.5m through village down to Loch Shaw)

☎ 01866 822251 🅵 01866 822251

Friendly and informal service at this family-owned hotel close to Loch Etive, enjoying delightful all round views. Good range of food available in bar or dining room.

£ 16 bedrooms (2 fmly) No smoking in restaurant Res end of January

WHERE TO EAT

RESTAURANTS
AA RECOMMENDED

ARDMORY HOUSE HOTEL 🞑
Ardmory Road, Isle of Bute PA20 0EG

☎ 01700 502346 🅵 01700 505596

Fresh and interesting cooking at this welcoming small hotel. Haggis flavoured with whisky in a filo parcel with plum sauce, cream of broccoli soup, steamed suprême of Loch Fad trout drizzled with citrus herb butter, and Ardmory style mango cheesecake with Cointreau might be a typical four-course dinner.

Fixed D ££

ARDENTINNY HOTEL 🞑
Loch Long, Nr Dunoon PA23 8TR

☎ 01369 810209 🅵 01369 810241

Fresh Scottish produce is used in dishes such as braised venison with pastry fleurons and wild rice, and grilled scallops with pickled ginger and tarragon beurre blanc.

Fixed D ££

Assapool House Hotel

LOCH MELFORT HOTEL 🞑
Oban PA34 4XG

☎ 01852 200233 🅵 01852 200214

The hotel overlooks Loch Asknish Bay, so not surprisingly the restaurant specialises in seafood, though other tastes are well catered for. Dishes include shellfish bisque, halibut with asparagus sauce, and pears in red wine with vanilla cream terrine.

Fixed D £££

ASSAPOOL HOUSE HOTEL 🞑
PA67 6DW

☎ 01681 700258 🅵 01681 700445

This charming small country house hotel has a welcoming atmosphere. Watercress and almond soup, salmon with dill hollandaise, and hay-baked chocolate cheesecake are typical choices on the short set menu.

Fixed D £

CLACHAN-SEIL, ISLE OF SEIL

WILLOWBURN HOTEL ⊛
PA34 4TJ

☏ 01852 300276

The dining room overlooks the Atlantic and is more formal than the Waterside Bistro. Menus include Willowburn pâté, with chicken liver, smoky bacon, oatmeal and whisky, pan-roasted salmon fillet with orange and Drambuie, and butterscotch tart.

Fixed D ££ ALC ££ 🍴

DERVAIG, ISLE OF MULL

DRUIMARD HOTEL ⊛⊛
PA75 6QW

☏ ⊕ 01688 400345

There is plenty of local and Scottish produce on show here. Potted wild salmon served with chive sauce and oatcakes, saddle of wild venison on a bed of braised red cabbage with game sauce. Desserts such as rich chocolate torte or trifle laced with Bailey's liqueur are both adventurous and decadent.

Fixed D ££ ALC ££ 🍴

DUNOON

BEVERLEY'S RESTAURANT ⊛
West Bay, PA23 7QJ

☏ 01369 702267 ⊕ 01369 702501

A meal in the elegant restaurant could start with Loch Fyne smoked salmon, or chicken liver, garlic and brandy pâté. Main courses include honey-roast duck cooked with cherries and ginger, and haunch of wild boar with a burgundy and spice sauce.

Fixed D ££ 🍴

ENMORE HOTEL ⊛
Marine Parade Kirn, PA23 8HH

☏ 01369 702233 ⊕ 01369 702148

Sample imaginative modern dishes such as roast monkfish with saffron and red pepper dressing, and oven-baked trout with a fresh chive and cream sauce.

Fixed D ££ ALC ££ 🍴

ERISKA

ISLE OF ERISKA ⊛⊛⊛
Ledaig by Oban, PA37 1SD

☏ 01631 720371 ⊕ 01631 720531

If you don't have a helicopter, then you have to cross a metal bridge to reach this baronial mansion situated on its own picturesque island. Dinner always features a daily roast such as rib of Scottish beef. The focus, otherwise, is on fish and seafood - tian of scallop mousse, in a thinly sliced courgette with champagne and chive butter sauce, followed by a selection of fish - turbot, seatrout, hake and monkfish. Game is also much used, and there are ornate desserts, such as chunks of honey marinated pear in a brandy snap, with a smooth crème de cacao sorbet and pistachio cream.

Fixed D £££ 🍴

Beverley's Restaurant

KILCHRENAN

ARDANSAISEIG HOTEL ⊛⊛
Taynuilt, PA35 1HE

☏ 01866 833333 ⊕ 01866 833222

The set dinner menu offers a choice of three dishes at each course. A typical menu features leek and potato soup, confit of pheasant legs with mustard vinaigrette and tartare of scallops with marinated aubergine, followed by tournedos of pork with glazed sweet potatoes, pan-fried salmon with fennel and mushroom ragout and lasagne of chargrilled vegetables.

ALC ££ 🍴

TAYCHREGGAN HOTEL ⊛⊛
Taynuilt, PA35 1HQ

☏ 01866 833211/366 ⊕ 01866 833244

Choose between roasted loin of hare sliced around braised leeks and toasted pine nuts with a rich red wine sauce, or a timbale of chicken, celery and scallops, bound in crème fraîche laced with herbs and set on a citrus dressing - and that's only the starters. Dinner offers a choice at each course, in which local ingredients feature strongly - Loch Etive scallops, Spean Bridge hare, Coulter's black pudding and Grampian pork, for example.

Fixed L £ ALC £ 🍴

KILFINAN

KILFINAN HOTEL ⊛⊛
Tighnabruaich, PA21 2EP

☏ 01700 821201 ⊕ 01700 821205

The Kilfinan serves a daily fixed-price menu of four courses based on local produce. King scallops in hazelnut oil, langoustines with garlic butter or a trio of rainbow trout, salmon and hake in tarragon sauce, are some examples. Aberdeen Angus steaks might be paired with green peppercorns and Italian mostarda di frutta.

Fixed D £££ 🍴

KILLIECHRONAN, ISLE OF MULL

KILLIECHRONAN HOUSE ⊛⊛
PA72 6JU

☏ 01680 300403 ⊕ 01680 300463

Dinner may open with thinly sliced oak-smoked venison and a Waldorf salad, went on to cream of asparagus soup, then a blackberry sorbet, before medallions of pork with wild mushrooms and gnocchi, served with cabbage, aubergine provençale and fondant potatoes, and finished with a first-class chocolate marquise and Grand Marnier sauce.

Fixed D ££ 🍴

KILMARTIN

CAIRN RESTAURANT ⊛
Longilphead, PA31 8RQ

☏ 01546 510254

The menu features a mix of new and old ideas - expect dishes such as fillet of pork with apple and prune stuffing, Highland venison with port and redcurrant sauce, and duck breast coated in poppy seeds with a gooseberry sauce.

Fixed L £ ALC ££ 🍴

OBAN

DUNGALLAN HOUSE ⊛
Gallanach Road, PA34 4PD

☏ 01631 563799 ⊕ 01631 566711

Fresh local produce prevails on the daily-changing menu at this Victorian mansion, which overlooks the bay to the Isle of Mull. Choices may include baked sole with lobster sauce or roast Highland beef, with blueberry crème brûlée for pudding.

Fixed L £ 🍴

MANOR HOUSE HOTEL ⊛
Gallanach Road, PA34 4LS

☏ 01631 562087 ⊕ 01631 563053

Excellent ingredients and classic ideas are used to good effect. Look out for terrine of west coast scallops, seasonal leaves and truffle-oil dressing, roasted saddle of Isle of Mull lamb with ratatouille in a port and rosemary jus, and whisky and toasted oatmeal parfait.

Fixed D ££ ALC ££ 🍴

PORT APPIN

AIRDS HOTEL ⊛⊛⊛
PA38 4DF

☏ 01631 730236

A winter dinner opened with roast loin of rabbit, served with tagliatelle, and interspersed with wild mushrooms. Cream of red pepper and fennel soup followed, then fillet of monkfish with scallops, and squat lobster. Apple and cinnamon flan with cinnamon ice cream came with a light sauce anglaise.

Fixed D £££ 🍴

SCALASAIG

COLONSAY HOTEL ❀
Isle of Colonsay PA61 7YP
☎ 01951 200316 📠 01951 200353
Colonsay is a remote Hebridean island with a ferry service every second day. The hotel's daily changing, fixed-price menu offers no choice, but features the likes of grilled Colonsay mackerel with gooseberry sauce, smoked Argyll venison, gratin of Colonsay crab, and fillet of salmon with hollandaise sauce.
Fixed D ££ 🦐

STRACHUR

CREGGANS INN ❀
PA27 8BX
☎ 01369 860279 📠 01369 860637
Good use is made of Scottish produce such as game, prime beef and seafood. A typical meal might be seafood and scallop terrine, baked sea bass with red wine butter, followed by a tangy lemon tart.
Fixed D ££ 🦐

Call the AA Hotel Booking Service on 0990 050505 to book at AA recognised hotels and B&Bs in the UK, or through our internet site:
http://www.theaa.co.uk/hotels

PUBS, INNS & OTHER PLACES

The Galley of Lorne Inn

ARDENTINNY

ARDENTINNY HOTEL
Loch Long PA23 8TR
☎ 01369 810209
1720 droving inn beside Loch Long. Bar and restaurant meals include beef olives, skippers macaroni, Barbary duck breast, leek and potato crumble, and local salmon.

ARDFERN

THE GALLEY OF LORNE INN
PA31 8QH
(25 S of Oban. A816 then B8002)
☎ 01852 500284
Former droving inn besideLoch Craignish, where seals can often be seen. Two restaurants, offering local seafood, game and char-grilled steaks.

ARDLUI

THE STAGGER INN
Inverarnan, Glen Fllach, G83 7ZZ
☎ 01301 704274
A taste of the Glens - salmon, venison, pigeon. Light meals, afternoon teas served all day. Families welcome.

ARROCHAR

RENDEZVOUS COFFEE SHOP
G83 7AA
☎ 01301 702223
A wide selection of freshly prepared food to take away or to eat in.

CAIRNBAAN

CAIRNBAAN HOTEL & RESTAURANT
PA31 8SJ
(From Glasgow Airport take A82/A83 to Lochilphead, then A816 to Cairnbaan)
☎ 01546 603668
Originally a coaching inn, main dishes include casserole of West Highland lamb cooked, smoked haddock and salmon Boulangére, and mushroom Stroganoff.

CLACHAN-SEIL

TIGH AN TRUISH INN
PA34 4QZ
(14m S of Oban, take A816, 12m turn off B844 towards Atlantic Bridge)
☎ 01852 300242
Originally a drover's inn this is a small, homely pub. Enjoy home made fare with a wealth of fresh seafood in season.

DUNOON

COYLET INN
Loch Eck PA23 8SG
☎ 01369 840426
18th-century coaching inn on the shore of Loch Eck, used for a BBC ghost story. Bar snacks, seafood starters and Scottish beef steaks are regulars. Daily blackboard menus too.

HELENSBURGH

CRAIGARD TEAROOM II
51 Sinclair Street
☎ 01436 677787
Well established and old-fashioned, family run tearoom. Light lunches, high teas, take-away. Extensive selection of 'homemade' cakes on offer.

HUMBLES CAFE BAR
19 Colquhoun Square, G84 8AD
Cafe bar/restaurant serving fine Italian coffee, freshly baked French bread, light meals, salads, pasta and vegetarian choices. Evening licensed restaurant menu.

LE JARDIN
Ardencaple Garden Centre, Rhu Road Higher, G84 8JZ
☎ 01436 672245
Family restaurant. Lunches, teas and coffees daily in comfortable, friendly atmosphere. Waitress service, licensed and ample free parking.

MIRA MARE
82 West Clyde Street, G84 8BB
☎ 01436 673766
Italian continental cuisine in warm, friendly atmosphere. Extensive a la carte menu, wine list, special lunchtime menu and traditional Sunday family lunch.

THE UPPER CRUST RESTAURANT
88a West Clyde Street, G84 8BB
☎ 01436 678035
Licensed restaurant specialising in seafood and game dishes using the best of Scottish produce. Vegetarian choices. Courtyard garden.

KILBERRY

KILBERRY INN
PA29 6YD *(From Lochgilphead take A83 south, then B8024)*
☎ 01880 770223
Converted post office croft with white stone walls and red tin roof. Home-made meals posted on the blackboard. Try rump steak and kidney pie, and local salmon fish pie salad, or Scotch beef in red wine topped with Stilton.

KILNINVER

SCOTTISH SALMON CENTRE
PA34 4QS *(6m S of Oban on A816)*
☎ 01852 316202
Bar and restaurant in an exhibition centre dedicated to the life of the salmon. Obviously, salmon features on the menu but also steamed Scottish mussels, butterfly chicken breast, Langoustine prawns, and sirloin steak in whisky and mustard sauce.

LUSS

FARM MILK BAR
Car Park, G83 8NY ☎ 01436 860621
Milk bar run by farming family serving tea, ground coffee, hot and cold snacks, soft ice cream and confectionery.

MULL, ISLE OF

DERVAIG

THE OLD BYRE HERITAGE CENTRE
PA75 6QR *(on B8073 from Tobermory)*
☎ 01688 400229
Previously a cowshed and a chocolate factory, this licensed tearoom is part of a museum that explores the history, flora and wildlife of Mull. Typical menu includes vegetable quiche, vegetable and lentil soup, a selection of filled rolls, and the Mull speciality - Clootie Dumpling.

OBAN

THE BARN
Cologin, Lerags PA34 4SE
☎ 01631 564618
Good-value home-cooked food including snacks, seafood (Friday night's speciality), game casserole and mushroom moussaka. Cranachan and apple pie.

RHU

ARDENCAPLE HOTEL
Shore Road, by Helensburgh, G84 8LA
☎ 01436 820200
Delightful setting on the shores of the Gareloch. Food served throughout the day.

TARBET

THE BLACK SHEEP RESTAURANT
by Arrochar, G83 7DA
☎ 01301 702393
Unique setting to enjoy lunches, a la carte evening menu, creative vegetarian meals.

TARBET TEAROOM
by Arrochar, G83 7DD
☎ 01301 702200
A selection of hot and cold snacks and home-style baking in a warm and friendly atmosphere. Take away also available.

WEAVER'S COFFEE SHOP
Inverhoullin, G83 7DN
☎ 01301 702685
Situated beside the loch, serving freshly prepared mels and snacks all day, using local produce.

TAYNUILT

POLFEARN HOTEL
PA35 1JT
☎ 01866 822251
Once the home of Colonel Campbell-Preston, a celebrated former Colditz POW. The extensive bar menu contains many seafood dishes, including moules ó Loch Etive- mussels cooked in wine, onions and parsley. Game and vegetarian dishes are also available.

TAYVALLICH

TAYVALLICH INN
PA31 8PL
(From Lochgilphead take A816 then B841/B8025)
☎ 01546 870282
Situated on the shores of Loch Sween in a superb natural anchorage, this small inn features the freshest of local scallops, mussels, oysters, crab and lobster.

WHERE TO STAY

HIGHLAND (SOUTH)
AA RECOMMENDED

ARISAIG

ARISAIG HOUSE ★★★ ❀❀❀
Beasdale PH39 4NR *(3m E A830)*
☎ 01687 450622 ☎ 01687 450626
Beautifully situated in extensive grounds close to the sea. Unobtrusive luxury abounds.
14 bedrooms No dogs (ex guide dogs) Snooker Croquet lawn No children under 10yrs No smoking in restaurant Closed Nov-Mar ☜

ARISAIG ★★
PH39 4NH *(on A830 opposite harbour)*
☎ 01687 450210 ☎ 01687 450310
Comfortable Highland hotel in an enviable position with fine views towards the islands of Rhum, Eigg, Muck and Skye.
££££ 13 bedrooms (2 fmly) Children's facilities No smoking in restaurant ☜

AVIEMORE

AVIEMORE HIGHLANDS ★★★
Aviemore Mountain Resort PH22 1PJ
(off A9 to Aviemore B9152, turn L opp rail station via ring road hotel 2nd on L)
☎ 01479 810771 ☎ 01479 811473
Popular hotel in the Aviemore Centre with a wide range of amenities and panoramic views.
£££ 103 bedrooms (37 fmly) Lift Night porter Games room Weekly live entertainment Children's facilities No smoking in restaurant ☜

THE MERCURY ★★★
Avimore Centre PH22 1PF
(from A9 to Aviemore, hotel in Leisure Centre)
☎ 01479 810781 ☎ 01479 811167
Busy, popular hotel in the Aviemore Centre, Bedrooms feature small kitchenette areas.
££ 94 bedrooms (85 fmly) No smoking in 6 bedrooms Lift Night porter Weekly live entertainment Children's facilities ☜

RAVENSCRAIG ◘◘◘
Grampian Rd PH22 1RP
☎ 01479 810278 ☎ 01479 811800
A warm welcome awaits at this guest house beside the main road.
£ 8 bedrooms 6 annexe bedrooms (2 fmly) No smoking in dining room ☜

BALLACHULISH

BALLACHULISH ★★★
PA39 4JY *(on A828, 3m N of Glencoe)*
☎ 01855 811606 ☎ 01855 821463
Long established hotel with a smart wing where all rooms enjoy glorious views of Loch Linnhe.
££ 54 bedrooms (4 fmly) Night porter Complimentary Membership of Leisure Club at nearby Sister Hotel Weekly live entertainment Children's facilities No smoking in restaurant ☜

THE ISLES OF GLENCOE HOTEL & LEISURE CENTRE
PA39 4HL *(off A82, 1m W of Glencoe)*
☎ 01855 811602 🅖 01855 811770
Located beside Loch Leven under the shadow of the spectacular Glencoe mountains. All day food in The Brasserie.
££ 39 bedrooms (6 fmly) Night porter Indoor swimming pool (heated) Fishing Sauna Solarium Gym Jacuzzi/spa Turbo pool Steam room Childern's Adventure play area Weekly live entertainment Children's facilities No smoking in restaurant 🍽

FERN VILLA ◙◙◙◙
East Laroch PA39 4JE *(turn L on entering Glencoe village, house 150yds on L)*
☎ 01855 811393 🅖 01855 811727
Comfortable granite-built Victorian villa where dining on home cooked food is quite special.
£ 5 bedrooms No smoking No dogs (ex guide dogs) Licensed No children under 10yrs

LYN-LEVEN ◙◙◙◙
White St PA39 4JP *(off A82)*
☎ 01855 811392 🅖 01855 811600
Genuine Highland hospitality at this modern guesthouse, with lovely views over Loch Leven.
£ 8 bedrooms (1 fmly) No smoking in 1 bedrooms Licensed 🍽

BEAULY

PRIORY ★★★
The Square IV4 7BX *(signposted from A832)*
☎ 01463 782309 🅖 01463 782531
In a prime position this hotel has a split-level restaurant with a range of menus throughout the day.
££ 22 bedrooms (2 fmly) Lift Night porter Snooker Children's facilities 🍽

CHRIALDON HOTEL ◙◙◙◙
Station Rd IV4 7EH *(in main street)*
☎ 01463 782336
Comfortable and well appointed Victorian home beside the main road. Traditional Scottish fare.
£ 9 bedrooms (2 fmly) No smoking in bedrooms or dining room Licensed Closed 25 Dec 🍽

HEATHMOUNT ◙◙◙
Station Rd IV4 7EQ *(20mtrs from post office)*
☎ 01463 782411
Good value at this detached Victorian house with brightly decorated, spacious, well maintained bedrooms.
£ 5 bedrooms (2 fmly) No smoking in bedrooms or dining room Closed Xmas & New Year

BOAT OF GARTEN

BOAT ★★★
PH24 3BH *(leave A9 N of Aviemore onto A95 to Boat of Garten)*
☎ 01479 831258 🅖 01479 831414
Family-run golfing and holiday hotel. Contemporary bedrooms with splendid Cairngorm Mountain views.
£ 32 bedrooms (1 fmly) No smoking in restaurant 🍽

Priory

HEATHBANK◙◙◙◙◙
The Victorian House PH24 3BD
(in middle of village near Boat Hotel)
☎ 01479 831234
Welcoming Victorian house restored to its former splendour. Bedrooms furnished with taste and flair.
£ 7 bedrooms (1 fmly) No smoking No dogs (ex guide dogs) Licensed No children under 10yrs Closed 1 Nov-25 Dec

MOORFIELD HOUSE HOTEL ◙◙◙
Deshar Rd PH24 3BN *(in centre of village)*
☎ 01479 831646
Friendly and comfortable Victorian house with bright and cheerful bedrooms, and elegant lounge.
£ 4 bedrooms (1 fmly) No smoking Licensed No children under 14yrs

CANNICH

MULLARDOCH HOUSE ★★🌑
Glen Cannich IV4 7LX
(8m W on unclass Glen Cannich rd)
☎ 01456 415460 🅖 01456 415460
In a dramatic location that takes your breath away. Former hunting lodge with high standards of comfort.
6 bedrooms (1 fmly) Fishing Deer stalking No smoking in restaurant 🍽

CARRBRIDGE

DALRACHNEY LODGE ★★★
PH23 3AT *(off A938)*
☎ 01479 841252 🅖 01479 841383
Victorian hunting lodge, in mature grounds near the golf course where smart staff provide courteous service.
£ 11 bedrooms (3 fmly) No smoking in 3 bedrooms Fishing No smoking in restaurant 🍽

FAIRWINDS ★★
PH23 3AA
(leave A9 1m N of Aviemore. Follow A95 signed Carrbridge for 3m then B9153, hotel on L)
☎ 01479 841240 🅖 01479 841240
Former Victorian manse in mature gardens with large conservatory lounge/dining room. Wide range of good-value meals.
£ 5 bedrooms No dogs (ex guide dogs) Croquet lawn No children under 12yrs No smoking in restaurant Closed 2 Nov-20 Dec 🍽

CARRMOOR ◙◙◙◙
Carr Rd PH23 3AD *(1sr R after bistro)*
☎ 01479 841244 🅖 01479 841244
Charming village home provides a comfortable base for holidaymakers. Brightly decorated bedrooms.
£ 6 bedrooms (1 fmly) No smoking in bedrooms or dining room Licensed 🍽

FEITH MHOR COUNTRY HOUSE ◙◙◙
Station Rd PH23 3AP
(off A9 to Carrbridge. Station Rd is opp grocers shop. 1.25m and house on R)
☎ 01479 841621
Amidst quiet open countryside this substantial detached house offers a peaceful and relaxing atmosphere.
£ 6 bedrooms (1 fmly) No smoking in dining room or lounges Licensed No children under 12yrs Closed 16 Nov-26 Dec

CULLODEN MOOR

CULDOICH ◙◙
Culloden Moor IV1 2EP
☎ 01463 790268
In pleasant countryside overlooking the famous battlefield, this traditional farmhouse has a homely atmosphere.
£ 2 bedrooms (1 fmly) No smoking in dining room No dogs Parking 200 acres mixed May-Oct

DALCROSS

EASTER DALZIEL FARMHOUSE◙◙◙
Easter Dalziel Farm, Dalcross IV1 2JL
(between A96 and B9039, 6m E of Inverness)
☎ 01667 462213 🅖 01667 462213
Welcoming atmosphere at this comfortable early Victorian farmhouse in wooded countryside.
£ 3 bedrooms 210 acres arable/beef/sheep Closed 20 Dec-6 Jan Res 1-20 Dec & 6 Jan-28 Feb 🍽

DAVIOT

CHALNA ◙◙◙
IV1 2XQ
☎ 01463 772239
Comfortable, quiet detached house that offers excellent value accommodation. Ground flour bedrooms.
3 bedrooms (1 fmly) No smoking 1 Mar-Nov

DRUMNADROCHIT

POLMAILY HOUSE★★★
IV3 6XT *(in village take A831 signed to Cannich, hotel 2m on R)*
☎ 01456 450343 🖷 01456 450813
Refreshingly unpretentious atmosphere at this country house hotel in large grounds. Children specially catered for.
££ 10 bedrooms (4 fmly) Indoor swimming pool (heated) Tennis (hard) Fishing Gym Croquet lawn Indoor/outdoor childrens play area Boating Pony rides Beauty/massage Children's facilities No smoking in restaurant 🗨

KILMORE FARM HOUSE ◻◻◻◻
IV3 6UH *(from Inverness on A82 take 1st road on L after leaving Drumnadrochit village - signposted)*
☎ 01456 450524
Attractive modern house in a quiet location close to Loch Ness with comfortable modern ground floor bedrooms.
£ 3 bedrooms (1 fmly) No smoking Sauna 🗨

WOODLANDS ◻◻◻◻
East Lewiston IV3 6UL
☎ 01456 450356
Modern villa with attractive, spacious bedrooms. Enjoyable home cooking and baking a real treat.
£ 3 bedrooms No smoking in bedrooms or dining room No dogs (ex guide dogs) Closed Christmas & Boxing Day 🗨

ENRICK COTTAGE ◻◻◻
IV3 6TZ *(on A831 immediately before West End garage)*
☎ 01456 450423 🖷 01456 450423
Excellent value and tremendously welcoming atmosphere at this cottage. En suite bedrooms.
£ 2 bedrooms No smoking No children under 15yrs Chair making course Wood turning Mar-Oct 🗨

GLEN ROWAN ◻◻◻
West Lewiston IV3 6UW
☎ 01456 450235 🖷 01456 450817
Beside a river, a welcoming atmosphere prevails at this comfortable detached house.
£ 3 bedrooms No smoking No dogs (ex guide dogs) Closed 24-26 Dec 🗨

Borlum Farmhouse

BORLUM FARMHOUSE ◻◻◻◻
IV3 6XN *(0.5m S of Lemiston on A82)*
☎ 01456 450358 🖷 01456 450358
From its elevated position this charming farmhouse enjoys panoramic views over Loch Ness.
6 bedrooms (2 bth) No smoking No dogs Fishing Riding 300 acres Sheep/horses 🗨

DULNAIN BRIDGE

MUCKRACH LODGE ★★★❀
PH26 3LY
☎ 01479 851257 🖷 01479 851325
Former shooting lodge overlooking fields, woodlands and mountains with informal ambience and attentive service.
10 bedrooms 4 annexe bedrooms (2 fmly) No dogs (ex guide dogs) Fishing Children's facilities 🗨

BYDAND ◻◻
PH26 3LU
(10m N of Aviemore, take A938 house 200 metres on R)
☎ 01479 851278
Conveniently situated house. Good access for disabled travellers. Sunny dining room.
£ 2 bedrooms No smoking in bedrooms or dining room 🗨

DUROR

STEWART ★★❀❀
PA38 4BW *(on A828)*
☎ 01631 740268 🖷 01631 740328
This friendly hotel is in gloriously colourful gardens with outstanding loch views.
££ 20 bedrooms (2 fmly) No smoking in restaurant Closed 16 Oct-31 Mar 🗨

FORT AUGUSTUS

THE BRAE ★★❀
PH32 4DG
(turn L off A82 just before leaving Fort Augustus towards Inverness.)
☎ 01320 366289 🖷 01320 366702
Many guests regularly return to this comfortable small hotel with splendid views.
£££ (inc dinner) 7 bedrooms No smoking in 5 bedrooms No children under 7yrs No smoking in restaurant Closed Nov-Feb 🗨

LOVAT ARMS ★★★
PH32 4DU *(on A82 nr village centre)*
☎ 01320 366206 & 366204
🖷 01320 366677
Close to the Abbey and canal this hotel has mostly spacious bedrooms some with fine traditional furnishings.
££ 23 bedrooms (4 fmly) Gym Putting green No smoking in restaurant 🗨

FORT WILLIAM

INVERLOCHY CASTLE ★★★★❀❀❀
Torlundy PH33 6SN *(3m NE A82)*
☎ 01397 702177 🖷 01397 702953
In 500 acre grounds in the foothills of Ben Nevis, this imposing Victorian building shows suitably polished and welcoming service.
££££ 17 bedrooms No dogs Night porter Tennis (hard) Fishing Snooker Weekly live entertainment No smoking in restaurant Closed 5 Jan-1 Mar 🗨

MOORINGS ★★★❀
Banavie PH33 7LY
(3m N of Fort William off A830)
☎ 01397 772797 🖷 01397 772441
With views of Ben Nevis this modern hotel offers guests high levels of care and attention by smart staff .
21 bedrooms 3 annexe bedrooms (1 fmly) No dogs (ex guide dogs) No smoking in restaurant Closed 22-26 Dec 🗨

ALEXANDRA ★★★
The Parade PH33 6AZ *(N end of town centre)*
☎ 01397 702241 🖷 01397 705554
Long established welcoming Victorian hotel remains popular. All day meals in coffee shop.
££ 97 bedrooms (14 fmly) Lift Night porter Weekly live entertainment No smoking in restaurant 🗨

Moorings

Nevis Bank

MERCURY ★ ★ ★
Achintore Rd PH33 6RW
(on A 82, just S of Fort William centre)
☎ 01397 703117 📠 01397 700550
Popular, modern purpose built hotel
enjoying lovely views over Loch Linnhe.
*£££ 86 bedrooms (12 fmly) No smoking in
2 bedrooms Lift Night porter Sauna Weekly
live entertainment No smoking in restaurant*

NEVIS BANK ★ ★
Belford Rd PH33 6BY
(on A82, at junct to Glen Nevis)
☎ 01397 705721 📠 01397 706275
Privately owned hotel offering traditional
Highland hospitality. Welcoming staff are
attentive and friendly.
*££ 31 bedrooms 8 annexe bedrooms (2
fmly) Sauna Solarium Gym Beauty salon
Hairdressers*

GRAND ★ ★
Gordon Square PH33 6DX
(on A82 at W end of High St)
☎ 01397 702928 📠 01397 702928
Friendly family run tourist hotel with a
choice of inviting non smoking lounges, a
bar and dining room.
*£ 33 bedrooms (4 fmly) Night porter No
smoking in restaurant Closed Jan*

IMPERIAL ★ ★
Fraser's Square PH33 6DW
☎ 01397 702040 & 703921
📠 01397 706277
Long-established family-run hotel in the
town centre. Staff are friendly and willing
to please.
*££ 32 bedrooms (3 fmly) No smoking in
restaurant*

MILTON ★ ★
North Rd PH33 6TG *(N of town, on A82)*
☎ 01397 702331 📠 01397 700132
Popular base for visiting tour groups and
families. Bedrooms range from executive
to smaller rooms.
*££ 52 bedrooms 67 annexe bedrooms (14
fmly) Night porter Indoor swimming pool
(heated) Sauna Solarium Gym Jacuzzi/spa
Weekly live entertainment No smoking in
restaurant*

TRAVEL INN
Loch Eli, An Aird PH33 6AN
☎ 01397 703707
Modern building offering smart, spacious
and well equipped bedrooms, suitable for
family use. Nearby family restaurant.
££ (fmly room) 40 bedrooms

ASHBURN HOUSE ◙ ◙ ◙ ◙ ◙
8 Achintore Rd PH33 6RQ
*(junc A82 & Ashburn Ln. 500yds from rbt at
S end of High St)*
☎ 01397 706000 📠 01397 706000
Lovingly restored Victorian home
overlooking Loch Linnhe. High standards
of quality and comfort. Noteworthy
breakfasts.
*£ 7 bedrooms No smoking No dogs (ex
guide dogs) Feb–Nov*

THE GRANGE ◙ ◙ ◙ ◙ ◙
Grange Rd PH33 6JF
☎ 01397 705516
An extremely high standard of care and
comfort is offered to guests. Beautiful
views over Loch Linnhe.
*££ 3 bedrooms No smoking No dogs (ex
guide dogs) No children under 13yrs Closed
Nov–Mar*

TORBEAG HOUSE ◙ ◙ ◙ ◙ ◙
Muirshearlich, Banavie PH33 7PB
*(5m N, from A830 take B8004 going N from
Banavie - follow for 2.5m)*
☎ 01397 772412 📠 01397 772412
An inviting modern country house in
natural woodland. Home-cooked
breakfasts and dinners.
*3 bedrooms No smoking No children under
10yrs Tennis (grass)*

CLINTWOOD ◙ ◙ ◙ ◙
23 Hillview Dr Corpach PH33 7LS
*(500 mtrs past village sign on L, "Clintwood"
sign at entrance to Hillview Dr, house 400
mtrs on L)*
☎ 01397 772680
A happy visit is assured to this very
individual and well presented villa, full of
objects of interest.
*£ 3 bedrooms No smoking No dogs
Easter –Oct*

DISTILLERY HOUSE ◙ ◙ ◙ ◙
Nevis Bridge, North Rd PH33 6LH
*(from S A82 3rd rdbt, on L/from N A82 just
prior to Glen Nevis rdbt, on R)*
☎ 01397 700103 📠 01397 702980
In the grounds of the former Glenlochy
Distillery, this friendly guest house offers
comfort and hearty breakfasts.
*£ 7 bedrooms (1 fmly) No smoking in
bedrooms or dining room Fishing*

BENVIEW ◙ ◙ ◙
Belford Rd PH33 6ER
(A82, near town centre)
☎ 01397 702966
Good value accommodation and fine
outlooks are offered at this friendly
personally-run guest house.
*£ 12 bedrooms No smoking in bedrooms or
dining room No dogs (ex guide dogs) Apr–
Oct*

GLENLOCHY ◙ ◙ ◙
Nevis Bridge PH33 6PF *(0.5m N on A82)*
☎ 01397 702909
Friendly guest house with spotlessly clean
accommodation. Attractive first floor
lounge.
*£ 10 bedrooms (2 fmly) No smoking in
bedrooms or dining room No dogs (ex guide
dogs)*

GUISACHAN HOUSE ◙ ◙ ◙
Alma Rd PH33 6HA
(off A82, 100yds past St Marys Church)
☎ 01397 703797 📠 01397 703797
Friendly guest house in an elevated
position. High standards of cleanliness and
maintenance.
*£ 13 bedrooms (2 fmly) No smoking in
bedrooms or dining room No dogs (ex guide
dogs) Licensed*

Grand

LOCHVIEW ◘◘◘
Heathercroft, Argyll Rd PH33 6RE
*(up hill at rdbt at West End Hotel on A82. L
into Argyll Ter & 1st R into private rd to end)*
☎ 01397 703149 ☏ 01397 703149
Hillside position above the town this
modern house enjoys fine views over Loch
Linnhe.
*£ 8 bedrooms No smoking No dogs May-
Sept* 🛏

MANSEFIELD HOUSE ◘◘◘
Corpach PH33 7LT
*(A82 onto A830 , House 2m from junct on L
on corner of Hill View Drive)*
☎ 01397 772262 ☏ 01397 772262
Former Victorian manse restored to reflect
its traditional character. Enjoyable home
cooking.
*£ 6 bedrooms (2 fmly) No smoking in
bedrooms or dining room No dogs (ex guide
dogs) Closed 24-28 Dec*

RHU MHOR ◘
Alma Rd PH33 6BP
(N on A82, after hospital 1st R then 1st L)
☎ 01397 702213
Edwardian house overlooking Loch Linnhe.
Genuine hospitality. Enjoyable home
cooking.
*£ 7 bedrooms (1 fmly) No smoking in
dining room or1 lounge Fishing Riding 1
acre of wild gardens Closed Nov-Easter*

FOYERS

FOYERS BAY HOUSE ◘◘◘◘
Lochness IV1 2YB
☎ 01456 486624 ☏ 01456 486337
This restored Victorian house proves
popular for its hospitality and high
standards. Glorious views of Loch Ness.
*£ 3 bedrooms No smoking in bedrooms No
dogs (ex guide dogs)* 🛏

GLENCOE

GLENCOE ★★
PA39 4HW *(on A82 in Glencoe village, 15m
S of Fort William)*
☎ 01855 811245 ☏ 01855 811687
Welcoming atmosphere at this long established Highland hotel. Popular bar food.
*££ 15 bedrooms (4 fmly) Games room No
smoking in restaurant* 🛏

SCORRYBREAC ◘◘◘
PA39 4HT *(off A82 just outside village, 500
metres from Bridge of Coe)*
☎ 01855 811354 ☏ 01855 811354
Relaxed, friendly comfortable guest house
on a wooded hillside above the village
with loch views.
£ 6 bedrooms No smoking Closed Nov

GLENFINNAN

THE PRINCES HOUSE ★★
Glenfinnan, By Fort William PH37 4LT
*(15m W of Fort William on A830, 0.5m on
R past monument)*
☎ 01397 722246 ☏ 01397 722307
Genuine hospitality and good food at this
charming hotel. Taste of Scotland dishes in
Flora's Restaurant.

The Princes House

*£££ 8 bedrooms (1 fmly) No smoking in
all bedrooms Fishing Mountain bike hire
No children under 4yrs No smoking in
restaurant Closed 4 Jan-Feb & 10-25 Dec
Res Mar & Nov* 🛏

GRANTOWN-ON-SPEY

GARTH ★★★⌖
Castle Rd PH26 3HN
*(take A9 N to Aviemore. A95 to Grantown-
on-Spey, hotel on square on L)*
☎ 01479 872836 & 872162 ☏ 01479
872116
A welcoming atmosphere at this holiday
and sporting hotel with fine, carefully
prepared Scottish cuisine.
*££ 17 bedrooms No smoking in restaurant
Closed 9-31 Nov* 🛏

CULDEARN HOUSE ★★⌖
Woodlands Ter PH26 3JU
☎ 01479 872106
Lovingly restored, charming Victorian
house where many guests return for the
hospitality and good home cooking.
£££ (inc dinner) 9 bedrooms

ARDCONNEL HOUSE ◘◘◘◘◘
Woodlands Ter PH26 3JU *(from SW approach
to town off A95, on L nr Craislynne Hotel)*
☎ 01479 872104 ☏ 01479 872104
Fine Victorian house, in attractive grounds,
continues to provide high standards of
comfort.
*£ 6 bedrooms (2 fmly) No smoking No dogs
Licensed No children under 10yrs Closed
Nov-Feb* 🛏

ARDLARIG ◘◘◘◘
Woodlands Ter PH26 3JU *(just off A95)*
☎ 01479 873245
A warm welcome at this attractive
Victorian house. Cordon Bleu style
cooking. Vegetarian and special diets
catered for.
*£ 7 bedrooms (2 fmly) No smoking No dogs
Licensed Golf shooting & fishing can be
arranged Closed 22 Dec-2 Jan*

GARDEN PARK ◘◘◘◘
Woodside Av PH26 3JN
*(turn off High St at Forest Rd, Garden Park
at junc of Forest Rd & Woodside Av)*
☎ 01479 873235
Described as a home from home this
comfortable Victorian house is near the
golf course.

*£ 5 bedrooms No smoking in dining room
No dogs (ex guide dogs) Licensed No
children under 12yrs Mar-Oct*

PINES ◘◘◘
Woodside Av PH26 3JR *(at traffic lights follow
Elgin signs then take 1st R)*
☎ 01479 872092 ☏ 01479 872092
In a wooded area near the River Spey this
is a comfortable Victorian house. Garden
play amenities for children.
*£ 9 bedrooms (3 fmly) No smoking in
dining room Licensed No children under
6yrs Jan-Oct*

ROSSMOR ◘◘◘
Woodlands Ter PH26 3JU *(take A95 from
Aviemore. L fork at rdbt on approach to town
through pine woods, on L opp park)*
☎ 01479 872201 ☏ 01479 872201
An enthusiastic welcome awaits at this
sturdy Victorian house set in its own pretty
garden.
*£ 6 bedrooms No smoking No dogs No
children under* 🛏

INVERGARRY

GLENGARRY CASTLE ★★★
PH35 4HW
(on A82, 0.5m from A82/A87 junction)
☎ 01809 501254 ☏ 01809 501207
Impressive baronial mansion in parkland
by the shores of Loch Oich, with a choice
of smart standard or superior rooms.
*££ 26 bedrooms (4 fmly) No smoking in 2
bedrooms Tennis (hard) Fishing No smoking
in restaurant Closed 3 Nov-2 Apr* 🛏

CRAIGARD ◘◘◘
PH35 4HG
(exit A82 onto A87, house 1m on R)
☎ 01809 501258 21
A welcoming atmosphere prevails at this
guesthouse backed by a wooded hillside.
*£ 7 bedrooms No smoking No dogs (ex
guide dogs) Licensed No children Mar-Oct*

FOREST LODGE ◘◘◘
South Laggan PH34 4EA
(3m SW off Invergarry on N side of A82)
☎ 01809 501219
Purpose-built, modern guesthouse in well
tended gardens. Bright and individually
decorated bedrooms.
*£ 7 bedrooms (2 fmly) No smoking in
bedrooms or dining room No smoking in
lounges*

Craigmonie

INVERMORISTON

GLENMORISTON ARMS ★★
IV3 6YA *(at the junct of A82/A877)*
☎ 01320 351206 ☎ 01320 351308
Friendly family-run Highland hotel close to
Loch Ness. Popular Tavern and Bistro in
the grounds.
*££ 8 bedrooms Fishing Stalking Shooting
No smoking in restaurant* 🍴

INVERNESS

KINGSMILLS ★★★★⊛
Culcabock Rd IV2 3LP
*(from S on A9, exit at Culduthell/Kingsmills
sign. 5th exit at rdbt, follow rd 0.5m, over
mini rdbt pass golf club, hotel on L after lights)*
☎ 01463 237166 ☎ 01463 225208
In four acres of carefully tended gardens
this tastefully appointed hotel looks
forward to welcoming you.
*££££ 78 bedrooms 6 annexe bedrooms (11
fmly) No smoking in 23 bedrooms Lift
Night porter Indoor swimming pool (heated)
Sauna Solarium Gym Putting green
Jacuzzi/spa Hair & beauty salon Steam
room Weekly live entertainment No smoking
in restaurant* 🍴

CULLODEN HOUSE ★★★★⊛
Culloden IV1 2NZ
*(take A96 from town & turn R for Culloden.
After 1m L at White Church after 2nd lights)*
☎ 01463 790461 ☎ 01463 792181
A fine, sympathetically restored Adam-style
Georgian mansion in wooded grounds.
Bedrooms range from opulent suites and
master rooms.
*££££ 23 bedrooms 5 annexe bedrooms (1
fmly) No smoking in 5 bedrooms Night
porter Tennis (hard) Sauna Solarium Croquet
lawn Boules Badminton No children under
10yrs No smoking in restaurant* 🍴

CRAIGMONIE ★★★
9 Annfield Rd IV2 3HX
*(off A9/A96 follow signs Hilton, Culcabock.
Pass golf course 2nd on R)*
☎ 01463 231649 ☎ 01463 233720
A welcoming hotel offering attractive
poolside suites and balcony to the
variable-sized standard rooms.
*£££ 35 bedrooms (3 fmly) No smoking in
10 bedrooms Lift Night porter Indoor
swimming pool (heated) Sauna Solarium
Gym Jacuzzi/spa No smoking in restaurant* 🍴

BUNCHREW HOUSE ★★★⊛
Bunchrew IV3 6TA *(3m W off A862)*
☎ 01463 234917 ☎ 01463 710620
Carefully restored 17th-century mansion in
20 acres of wooded grounds on the
shores of the Beauly Firth.
*11 bedrooms (1 fmly) Fishing Croquet lawn
No smoking in restaurant* 🍴

INVERNESS THISTLE ★★★⊛
Millburn Rd IV2 3TR *(on A9 head N, exit at
A96, follow signs to town centre (B865))*
☎ 01463 239666 ☎ 01463 711145
This modern hotel offers well equipped
accommodation. Good range of carefully
prepared dishes in the restaurant.
*££££ 118 bedrooms (11 fmly) No
smoking in 24 bedrooms Lift Night porter
Res 1 Jan* 🍴

LOCHARDIL HOUSE ★★★
Stratherrick Rd IV2 4LF *(follow Island Bank
Rd for 1m, fork L into Drummond Cres, into
Stratherrick Rd, 0.5m hotel on L)*
☎ 01463 235995 ☎ 01463 713394
A welcoming atmosphere at this
castellated Victorian house in attractive
gardens. Popular conservatory restaurant.
£££ 12 bedrooms No dogs (ex guide dogs) 🍴

LOCH NESS HOUSE ★★★
Glenurquhart Rd IV3 6JL
(1.5m from town centre)
☎ 01463 231248 ☎ 01463 239327
Popular family run hotel with comfortable
lounge and restaurant. Scottish fare and
fresh seafood.
*£££ 22 bedrooms (3 fmly) No smoking in
6 bedrooms Weekly live entertainment No
smoking area in restaurant* 🍴

PALACE ★★★
Ness Walk IV3 5NE
(town centre on banks of River Ness)
☎ 01463 223243 ☎ 01463 236865
Beside the river with views of the castle
this hotel remains a popular base for
visiting tour groups.
*42 bedrooms 41 annexe bedrooms (12 fmly)
Lift Night porter No smoking in restaurant* 🍴

DUNAIN PARK ★★⊛
IV3 6JN *(on A82, 1m from Inverness)*
☎ 01463 230512 ☎ 01463 224532
Set in 6 acres of grounds, this delightful

part Italianate Georgian villa is superbly
situated.
*£££ 12 bedrooms (6 fmly) Indoor
swimming pool (heated) Sauna Croquet
lawn Badminton No smoking in restaurant
Closed 10 Jan-20 Feb* 🍴

BEAUFORT ★★
11 Culduthel Rd IV2 4AG
*(1st L off dual carriageway, past Kingsmills
Hotel 1st R, L at lights into Southside Rd, R
into Culduthel Rd)*
☎ 01463 222897 ☎ 01463 711413
Popular, relaxed and friendly hotel where
a variety of bedroom styles is available.
36 bedrooms (6 fmly) Air conditioning 🍴

WINDSOR ★★
22 Ness Bank IV2 4SF *(follow signs Dores/
Holm Mills rd B862, hotel below castle)*
☎ 01463 715535 ☎ 01463 713262
Close to the castle, this friendly town
house hotel sits beside River Ness.
*££ 18 bedrooms (1 fmly) No smoking in 16
bedrooms No dogs (ex guide dogs) No
smoking in restaurant Closed 23 Dec-4 Jan
Res 1 Nov-30 Apr* 🍴

SMITHTON ★★
Smithton IV1 2NL
(A96, 2m turn 1st R, 2m to Smithton Hotel)
☎ 01463 791999 ☎ 01463 794559
Purpose-built hotel in the centre of a
small village. Bedrooms are attractively
furnished in pine and offer good
amenities.
*£ 10 bedrooms No dogs (ex guide dogs)
Weekly live entertainment* 🍴

TRAVEL INN
Millburn Rd IV2 3QX
☎ 01463 712010 ☎ 01463 717826
Modern building offerings smart, spacious
and well equipped bedrooms, suitable for
family use. Nearby family restaurant.
££ (fmly room) 40 bedrooms

TRAVEL INN (INVERNESS EAST)
Beechwood Business Park IV2 3BW
(on A9, 2m E of Inverness)
☎ 01463 232727 ☎ 01463 231553
Modern building offerings smart, spacious
and well equipped bedrooms, suitable for
family use. Nearby family restaurant.
££ (fmly room) 40 bedrooms

BALLIFEARY HOUSE HOTEL ▢▢▢▢▢
10 Ballifeary Rd IV3 5PJ
*(off A82, 0.5m from town centre, L into
Bishops Rd and sharp R into Ballifeary Rd)*
☎ 01463 235572 ☎ 01463 717583
Throughout a comfortable and welcoming
atmosphere. Bedrooms assure a peaceful
nights' sleep.
*££ 5 bedrooms No smoking No dogs (ex
guide dogs) Licensed No children under
12yrs Closed mid Oct - Easter* 🍴

Millwood House

CULDUTHEL LODGE ⬛⬛⬛⬛⬛
14 Culduthel Rd IV2 4AG
(follow B861 Castle St from town centre)
☎ 01463 240089 🅕 01463 240089
Lovingly restored Georgian residence, with views of River Ness provides superior standards of accommodation.
££ 12 bedrooms (1 fmly) No smoking in 11 bedrooms or dining room Licensed No children under 10yrs 🍴

MILLWOOD HOUSE ⬛⬛⬛⬛⬛
36 Old Mill Rd IV2 3HR
(from A9 towards town centre through rdbt & lights to mini-rdbt. L fork pass golf course through lights. house 2nd turning on R)
☎ 01463 237254 🅕 01463 719400
Many personal effects and touches make this a "home from home".
£ 3 bedrooms No smoking No dogs No children April–31 Oct 🍴

MOYNESS HOUSE ⬛⬛⬛⬛⬛
6 Bruce Gardens IV3 5EN
(off A82, almost opp Highland Regional Council HQ)
☎ 01463 233836 🅕 01463 233836
Comfortable small hotel with cosy bedrooms. Imaginative short choice menu available.
7 bedrooms No smoking in 2 bedrooms or dining room Licensed Closed 24 Dec–3 Jan 🍴

ARDMUIR HOUSE ⬛⬛⬛⬛
16 Ness Bank IV2 4SF
(on E bank of river, opposite the cathedral)
☎ 01463 231151 🅕 01463 231151
Genuine hospitality at this small private hotel standing by River Ness.
£ 11 bedrooms (2 fmly) No smoking in dining room No dogs (ex guide dogs) Licensed 🍴

ARDROSS HOUSE ⬛⬛⬛⬛
18 Ardross St IV3 5NS
(first turning on R at St Andrews Cathedral)
☎ 01463 241740
Good-value accommodation at this detached Victorian house. Bright and airy bedrooms.
££ 8 bedrooms (2 fmly) No smoking in 1 bedroom, dining room or lounges

BRAE NESS HOTEL ⬛⬛⬛⬛
17 Ness Bank IV2 4SF
(from town centre towards Dores (B562) 0.25m on river bank below Inverness Castle)
☎ 01463 712266 🅕 01463 231732
Pleasantly situated by the river Brae Ness is this friendly establishment.
£ 10 bedrooms (2 fmly) No smoking in 7 bedrooms or dining room No dogs (ex guide dogs) Licensed Closed Dec–Mar 🍴

CLACH MHUILINN ⬛⬛⬛⬛
7 Harris Rd IV2 3LS
(off A9 onto B9006 signed Hilton/Culcabock. At rdbt follow town centre signs then over mini-rdbt & 2nd L after lights)
☎ 01463 237059 🅕 01463 242092
In a quiet residential area this attractive detached house is maintained to a high standard.
3 bedrooms No smoking No dogs No children under 10yrs Closed Dec–Jan 🍴

DIONARD ⬛⬛⬛⬛
39 Old Edinburgh Rd IV2 3HJ
☎ 01463 233557 🅕 01463 710526
Immaculately maintained detached Victorian house standing in its own attractive garden.
£ 3 bedrooms No smoking in 1 bedrooms, dining room or lounges No children under 6yrs

EDEN HOUSE HOTEL ⬛⬛⬛⬛
8 Ballifeary Rd IV3 5PJ
(cross Ness Bridge from High St. 1st L & 1st L again, 2nd L. 200mtrs from Eden Court Theatre)
☎ 01463 230278 🅕 01463 230278
Charming semi detached Victorian villa with conservatory lounge, elegant dining room and pretty bedrooms.
£ 5 bedrooms (2 fmly) No smoking No dogs (ex guide dogs) Licensed No children under 5yrs 🍴

KERRISDALE ⬛⬛⬛⬛
4 Muirfield Rd IV2 4AY
☎ 01463 235489 🅕 01463 235489
Immaculately maintained semi-detached Victorian home offering excellent value accommodation.
3 bedrooms (2 fmly) No smoking No dogs Closed Xmas/New Year

LAGGAN VIEW ⬛⬛⬛⬛
Ness Castle Fishings, Dores Rd IV1 2DH
(3m from town centre on B862)
☎ 01463 235996 🅕 01463 711552
Comfortable bungalow in attractive garden with outstanding views of River Ness and Caledonian Canal.
£ 2 bedrooms (1 fmly) No smoking in bedrooms or dining room Squash 🍴

THE OLD RECTORY ⬛⬛⬛⬛
9 Southside Rd IV2 3BG
☎ 01463 220969
A welcoming atmosphere at this comfortable detached home offering excellent value accommodation.
£ 4 bedrooms No smoking No dogs (ex guide dogs) No children under 7yrs Closed 21 Dec–5 Jan

TRAFFORD BANK ⬛⬛⬛⬛
96 Fairfield Rd IV3 5LL
☎ 01463 241414
Large detached Victorian house in its own gardens close to the canal. Bedrooms with many thoughtful extras.
5 bedrooms No smoking 🍴

ABERFELDY LODGE ⬛⬛⬛
11 Southside Rd IV2 3BG
☎ 01463 231120 🅕 01463 231120
A welcoming atmosphere. Two bedrooms have disabled access. Championship Siamese cats also in residence!
£ 9 bedrooms (4 fmly) No smoking in 3 bedrooms, dining room or lounges No dogs

BORVE ⬛⬛⬛
9 Old Edinburgh Rd IV2 3HF
(past Castle, up Castle St, 200yds on L. 1st house on L)
☎ 01463 234728
Good value accommodation at this friendly personally-run guest house. Brightly decorated bedrooms.
£ 4 bedrooms (2 fmly) No smoking

CRAIGSIDE ⬛⬛⬛
4 Gordon Ter IV2 3HD
(from town centre take Castle St, then 1st L (Old Edinburgh Rd) then three 1st L turns)
☎ 01463 231576 🅕 01463 713409
Welcoming, centrally situated Georgian lodge with super views over the castle, the Firth and beyond.
£ 6 bedrooms No smoking in bedrooms or dining room No dogs (ex guide dogs) 🍴

EDINBANE ⬛⬛⬛
14 Ballifeary Rd IV3 5PJ
(off A82 into Bishops Rd then 1st R)
☎ 01463 236411
Situated in a residential area this homely semi-detached house offers good value accommodation.
3 bedrooms No smoking No dogs (ex guide dogs) Apr–Sep

ESKDALE HOUSE ◙◙◙
41 Greig St IV3 5PX
(from A9 to A82, through ind. estate, over R.Ness into Kenneth St, L at yellow box junction)
☎ 01463 240933
A warm welcome assured, especially to children, at this comfortable end terraced home.
£ 5 bedrooms (2 fmly) No smoking

HEATHFIELD ◙◙◙
2 Kenneth St IV3 5NR
☎ 01463 230547 ℉ 01463 230547
In a terraced row close to the city centre, this homely guesthouse retains many of its original Victorian features.
£ 3 bedrooms No smoking No dogs (ex guide dogs)

INCHBERRY HOUSE ◙◙◙
Lentran IV3 6RJ
☎ 01463 831342 ℉ 01463 831342
Spacious, hillside farmhouse with fine views across the Firth and mountains beyond. Pedigree Limousin cattle raised here.
6 bedrooms No smoking in bedrooms or dining room No dogs (ex guide dogs) No children under 12yrs May-Oct Res Xmas week

INVERGLEN ◙◙◙
7 Abertarff Rd IV2 3NW
(in town centre follow signs for Crown)
☎ 01463 237610
Exemplary standards at this comfortable detached home near the town centre. Bright airy bedrooms.
£ 5 bedrooms (2 fmly) No smoking No dogs (ex guide dogs)

MACRAE HOUSE ◙◙◙
24 Ness Bank IV2 4SF
(Opp Eden Court Theatre. 5 mins from Castle/town centre)
☎ 01463 243658
Looking out across the river, this attractive home provides comfortable accommodation.
£ 4 bedrooms (1 fmly) No smoking No dogs (ex guide dogs)

MALVERN ◙◙◙
54 Kenneth St IV3 5PZ
(at junct with A82 to Fort William, from A9 L at signs for Inverness/ Ind Estate, over bridge, 2nd L)
☎ 01463 242251
Good value accommodation at this comfortable detached home.
£ 4 bedrooms (2 fmly) No smoking No dogs (ex guide dogs) No children under 7yrs

NESS BANK HOUSE ◙◙◙
7 Ness Bank IV2 4SF
☎ 01463 232939 ℉ 01463 232939
Listed Victorian terraced house overlooking the river and handy for the town centre.
£ 5 bedrooms (1 fmly) No smoking No dogs (ex guide dogs) Feb-Mid Dec

RIVERSIDE HOUSE HOTEL ◙◙◙
8 Ness Bank IV2 4SF
(town side of river, past castle)
☎ 01463 231052
Beside the River Ness this welcoming personally-run guest house, provides good value accommodation.
11 bedrooms (3 fmly) No smoking in dining room or 1 lounge No dogs Licensed No children under 8yrs P

RYEFORD ◙◙◙
21 Ardconnel Ter IV2 3AE
☎ 01463 242871 ℉ 01463 242871
In a quiet terrace close to town centre with splendid views. Hearty breakfasts.
£ 6 bedrooms (2 fmly) No smoking in bedrooms or dining room

ST ANN'S HOUSE ◙◙◙
37 Harrowden Rd IV3 5QN *(at rdbt junct A82 & A862 at W side of Friars Shott Bridge)*
☎ 01463 236157 ℉ 01463 236157
Comfortable homely atmosphere. Attractive conservatory dining room overlooking the garden.
£ 6 bedrooms (3 fmly) No smoking in 3 bedrooms or dining room No dogs Licensed Closed Nov-Jan Res Jun-Aug

SUNNYHOLM ◙◙◙
12 Mayfield Rd IV2 4AE
☎ 01463 231336
Friendly and comfortable detached bungalow with compact ground floor bedrooms. Hearty breakfasts.
£ 4 bedrooms No smoking No dogs (ex guide dogs)

WHITE LODGE ◙◙◙
15 Bishops Rd IV3 5SB *(Off A82)*
☎ 01463 230693
Sympathetically extended Victorian house only a short walk from the theatre.
7 bedrooms (3 fmly) No smoking in dining room or lounges ◄

LEINSTER LODGE ◙◙
27 Southside Rd IV2 4XA
(10 minutes walk to town centre)
☎ 01463 233311
Victorian corner guest house that's friendly and personally-run offering good value accommodation.
£ 6 bedrooms (2 fmly) Closed Xmas & New Year

PARK ◙◙
51 Glenurquhart Rd IV3 5PB
(on A82 leaving town centre, on W side of river)
☎ 01463 231858
Victorian villa with distinctive ivy clad frontage. Bedrooms have attractive decor and good facilities.
£ 6 bedrooms (3 fmly) No smoking No dogs (ex guide dogs) ◄

TARANSAY ◙◙◙◙
Lower Muckovie IV1 2BB
(off A9 onto B9177 past Drumossie Hotel)
☎ 01463 231880 ℉ 01463 231880
Adjacent to the family farm this comfortable and smart home has splendid views to the Black Isle and hills beyond.
£ 2 bedrooms (1 fmly) No smoking No dogs (ex guide dogs) No children under 5yrs 170 acres dairy Mar-Nov

HEATHMOUNT ◙◙◙
Kingsmills Rd IV2 3JU
☎ 01463 235877 ℉ 01463 715749
Friendly family-run hotel dating back to 1868. Well proportioned and comfortable modern bedrooms.
££ 7 bedrooms (2 fmly) No smoking in area of dining room Closed 31 Dec-2 Jan Res 25 Dec ◄

KENTALLEN

HOLLY TREE ★ ★
Kentallen Pier PA38 4BY
(3m S of Ballachulish on A828)
☎ 01631 740292 ℉ 01631 740345
Wonderful views over Loch Linnhe and mountains from this welcoming hotel. Two ground floor bedrooms suitable for disabled guests.
££ 10 bedrooms (2 fmly) Fishing Closed 1 Nov-31 Jan ◄

Call the AA Hotel Booking Service on
0990 050505 to book at AA recognised
hotels and B&Bs in the UK,
or through our internet site:
http://www.theaa.co.uk/hotels

Culduthel Lodge

Ardsheal House Hotel

ARDSHEAL HOUSE HOTEL ◙ ◙ ◙ ◙ ◙
PA38 4BX *(4m S of Ballachulish Bridge on A828. 1m private road from A828)*
☎ 01631 740227 🄵 01631 740342
Splendid house on its own estate by Loch Linnhe where the owners take great pleasure in welcoming guests to their home.
££ 6 bedrooms No smoking in dining room or1 lounge Licensed Children's facilities Snooker Closed 21-27 December Res November–February 🗸

ARDSHEAL HOME FARM◙ ◙ ◙
PA38 4BZ
(off A828, 3m S of Ballachulish Bridge)
☎ 01631 740229 🄵 01631 740 229
A warm welcome assured at this comfortable cottage-style farmhouse close to Loch Linnhe.
££ 3 bedrooms (1 fmly) No smoking No dogs (ex guide dogs) 1000 acres beef sheep Apr-Oct

THE CROSS ★ ❀ ❀ ❀
Tweed Mill Brae, Ardbroilach Rd PH21 1TC
(from lights in Kingussie, along Ardbroilach Rd for 300mtrs, turn L into Tweed Mill Brae)
☎ 01540 661166 🄵 01540 661080
Beside a lively stream this converted tweed mill offers superbly comfortable beds and many thoughtful touches.
££££ (inc dinner) 9 bedrooms No smoking in bedrooms or restaurant No dogs (ex guide dogs) No children under 8yrs Closed 1-26 Dec & 8 Jan-28 Feb Res Tuesdays 🗸

THE SCOT HOUSE ★ ★ ❀
Newtonmore Rd PH21 1HE
(from A9 take Kingussie exit, hotel approx 0.50m at S end of main street)
☎ 01540 661351 🄵 01540 661111
(Rosette awarded for dinner only)
Small charming hotel offering attractive and comfortable accommodation, a genuinely warm welcome and good food.
££ 9 bedrooms (2 fmly) Children's facilities No smoking in restaurant Closed 6-31 Jan 🗸

COLUMBA HOUSE ★ ★
Manse Rd PH21 1JF
(at N end of village, off A9)
☎ 01540 661402 🄵 01540 661652

Genuine hospitality, honest home cooking and exemplary standards at this small hotel, a converted 19th-century manse.
££ 7 bedrooms (2 fmly) No smoking in 1 bedroom or restaurant Croquet lawn Putting green Children's facilities 🗸

OSPREY ★ ❀
Ruthven Rd PH21 1EN
(S end of Kingussie High St)
☎ 01540 661510 🄵 01540 661510
Small family-run hotel with bedrooms comfortably furnished in traditional styles with many thoughtful touches.
££ (inc dinner) 8 bedrooms No smoking in 6 bedrooms No smoking in restaurant 🗸

AVONDALE HOUSE ◙ ◙ ◙ ◙
Newtonmore Rd PH21 1HF
☎ 01540 661731 🄵 01540 661731
Welcoming detached Victorian house with bedrooms in pastel colour schemes. Enjoyable home cooking.
£ 7 bedrooms (1 fmly) No smoking No children under 5yrs

SONNHALDE ◙ ◙
East Ter PH21 1JS
(exit A9 & turn L into village. R at lights then 1st R. 3rd house on L)
☎ 01540 661266 🄵 01540 661266
Hillside house where special activity packages for wildlife, climbing, walking, photography and fly fishing enthusiasts are run.
£ 7 bedrooms (2 fmly) No smoking in bedrooms or dining room Closed Nov-27 Dec

BOGROY INN ★ ★
IV5 7PX *(at junct A862/B9164)*
☎ 01463 831296 🄵 01463 831296
With 16th-century origins and historical associations with whisky smuggling this house is now a comfortably modernised hotel.
£ 10 bedrooms (3 fmly) No smoking area in restaurant 🗸

LETTERFINLAY LODGE ★ ★
PH34 4DZ *(7m N of Spean Bridge, on A82)*
☎ 01397 712622
Long established, welcoming hotel which enjoys a spectacular outlook over Loch Lochy.
£ 13 bedrooms (5 fmly) Fishing No smoking in restaurant Closed Nov-Feb 🗸

MARINE ★ ★
PH41 4PY
(adjacent to railway terminal, 1st hotel on R off A830)
☎ 01687 462217 🄵 01687 462821
Friendly family-run centrally located hotel with a tastefully appointed restaurant. Fresh local seafood.
£ 19 bedrooms (2 fmly) No smoking in restaurant Closed Xmas & New Year Res Nov-Mar 🗸

WEST HIGHLAND ★ ★
PH41 4QZ
(from Fort William turn R at rdbt then 1st R up hill/from ferry L at rdbt then 1st R up hill)
☎01687 462210 🄵01687 462130
From its hillside position this popular family-run hotel enjoys fine views over the sea to Skye.
££ 34 bedrooms (6 fmly) Weekly live entertainment No smoking in restaurant Closed 15 Nov-15 Mar Res 15 Mar, 1 Nov, 15 Nov 🗸

MORAR ★ ★
PH40 4PA *(on A830)*
☎ 01687 462346 🄵 01687 462130
Friendly family-run hotel, beside the scenic West Highland Railway, enjoys superb

Allt-Nan-Ros

views over the bay to the islands beyond. £ 27 bedrooms (3 fmly) Fishing Weekly live entertainment No smoking in restaurant Closed 22 Oct–Mar

NAIRN

GOLF VIEW ★★★★
Seabank Rd IV12 4HD
(off A96, next to Nairn Golf Course)
☎ 01667 452301 🖨 01667 455267
Close to the golf course and beach, this hotel enjoys lovely views of the Moray Firth.
££££ 47 bedrooms (3 fmly) No smoking in 8 bedrooms Lift Night porter Indoor swimming pool (heated) Tennis (hard) Sauna Solarium Gym Putting green Jacuzzi/spa No smoking in restaurant 🍴

NEWTON ★★★★✿
Inverness Rd IV12 4RX
(15m from Inverness on A96, turn L into tree lined driveway)
☎ 01667 453144 🖨 01667 454026
In 21 acres of mature grounds, this hotel boasts impressive baronial architecture. Access to leisure facilities at sister hotel.
29 bedrooms 14 annexe bedrooms (3 fmly) Lift Night porter Fishing Croquet lawn Putting green Jacuzzi/spa No smoking in restaurant 🍴

CLAYMORE HOUSE ★★★
45 Seabank Rd IV12 4EY
(from A96 turn into Seabank Rd at the parish church)
☎ 01667 453731 & 453705
🖨 01667 455290
Within easy reach of the beach and golf courses, the house has a relaxed friendly atmosphere.
££ 16 bedrooms (2 fmly) No smoking in 4 bedrooms Night porter Weekly live entertainment No smoking in restaurant 🍴

ALTON BURN ★★
Alton Burn Rd IV12 5ND
☎ 01667 452051
Turn of the century, traditional resort hotel with views across the Moray Firth.
££ 19 bedrooms 7 annexe bedrooms (6 fmly) Outdoor swimming pool (heated) Tennis (hard) Putting green Games room Children's facilities Res Nov–Mar 🍴

Columba House

GREENLAWNS ◙◙◙◙
13 Seafield St IV12 4HG *(from A96, turn L into Albert St just before lights. 300 yds on L)*
☎ 01667 452738 🖨 01667 452738
Comfortable Victorian house includes many personalised touches.
£ 8 bedrooms (2 fmly) No smoking in dining room Licensed 🍴

COVENANTERS ◙◙◙
High St, Auldearn IV12 5TG
(1m E of Nairn off A96 in Auldearn)
☎ 01667 452456 🖨 01667 453583
Charming country inn with restaurant and Kiln Bar. All ground floor bedrooms.
8 bedrooms (2 fmly) No smoking in 1 lounge Children's facilities 🍴

NETHY BRIDGE

AULTMORE HOUSE ◙◙◙◙
PH25 3ED *(turn R 0.5m N of Nethybridge, off B970 & then 1st L)*
☎ 01479 821473 🖨 01479 821709
Impressive manor house, in secluded grounds, more akin to family country house than a hotel. Fine views of the Cairngorms.
£ 3 bth No smoking in bedrooms or dining room No smoking in 1 lounge No children under 12yrs Fishing Snooker Croquet Easter –1 Nov Res 26 Dec–5 Jan

NORTH BALLACHULISH

LOCH LEVEN ★★
Onich PH33 6SA *(off A82)*
☎ 01855 821236
17th-century former coaching inn on the northern shore of Loch Leven. Popular menu in the bar/dining area.
£ 10 bedrooms (1 fmly) No smoking area in restaurant 🍴

ONICH

ALLT-NAN-ROS ★★★✿✿
PH33 6RY
(1.5m N of Ballachulish Bridge on A82)
☎ 01855 821210 🖨 01855 821462
Superb views over Loch Linnhe, tastefully decorated bedrooms and an imaginative menu.
££££ (inc dinner) 21 bedrooms (2 fmly) No smoking in restaurant m 🍴

ONICH ★★★✿
PH33 6RY
(beside A82, 2m N of Ballachulish Bridge)
☎ 01855 821214 🖨 01855 821484
In landscaped gardens sweeping down to picturesque Loch Linnhe, this friendly hotel is for those seeking comfort and relaxation.
££ 27 bedrooms (6 fmly) Solarium Jacuzzi/spa Games room Children's facilities No smoking in restaurant 🍴

LODGE ON THE LOCH ★★★
PH33 6RY
(beside A82 - 5m N of Glencoe, 10m S of Fort William)
☎ 01855 821237 🖨 01855 821238
In attractive grounds that include palm trees this comfortable hotel enjoys a panoramic outlook over Loch Linnhe.
£££ (inc dinner) 20 bedrooms (2 fmly) Leisure facilities at sister hotel Weekly live entertainment Children's facilities No smoking in restaurant Closed Jan–Feb 🍴

CREAG MHOR ★★
PH33 6RY *(beside A82)*
☎ 01855 821379 🖨 01855 821579
Overlooking Loch Linnhe this hotel's owner looks forward to welcoming guests old and new.
££ 14 bedrooms (3 fmly) Fishing No smoking in restaurant Res Late Nov–17 Jan (open Xmas & New Year) 🍴

ROY BRIDGE

GLENSPEAN LODGE HOTEL ★★★
PH31 4AW *(2m E on A86)*
☎ 01397 712223 🖨 01397 712660
A memorable stay is assured at this attractive hotel with lovely views of the Glen and mountains.
££ 17 bedrooms (2 fmly) No smoking in 2 bedrooms No smoking in restaurant 🍴

Onich

Lodge on the Loch

STRONLOSSIT ★ ★
PH31 4AG
☎ 01397 712253
Delightful mountain views from this friendly hotel that caters for tourists and outdoor enthusiasts.
9 bedrooms (2 fmly) Closed 10 Nov–10 Dec & Jan 🛥

SPEAN BRIDGE

DISTANT HILLS 🔲 🔲 🔲 🔲
PH34 4EU *(on A86)*
☎ 01397 712452
A warm personal welcome at this attractive detached modern home. Enjoyable home-cooking.
£ 7 bedrooms No smoking in 2 bedrooms or dining room

THE SMIDDY HOUSE 🔲 🔲 🔲 🔲
PH34 4EU
☎ 01397 712335 ☎ 01397 712043
This fine detached house is a tribute to its dedicated owners. Food available all day in the Bistro.
£ 4 bedrooms (1 fmly) No smoking in dining room Licensed Closed Nov 🛥

INVEROUR 🔲 🔲 🔲
PH34 4EU
(10m NE of Fort William turn onto A86, 1st turning on R, 10yds from junct)
☎ 01397 712218
High standards of cleanliness and maintenance at this friendly family-run house.
£ 7 bedrooms No smoking in bedrooms or dining room No dogs Licensed No children under 3yrs Res Jan

COIRE GLAS 🔲 🔲
Roy Bridge Rd PH34 4EU
(on A86, 0.5m from junct of A82)
☎ 01397 712272
Friendly family-run guest house with panoramic views of the surrounding mountains.
£ 11 bedrooms (2 fmly) No smoking in bedrooms or dining room No dogs (ex guide dogs) Licensed Children's facilities All above facilities available within 10miles Jan–Oct 🛥

Loch Sunart

Call the AA Hotel Booking Service on 0990 050505 to book at AA recognised hotels and B&Bs in the UK, or through our internet site: http://www.theaa.co.uk/hotels

STRONTIAN

KILCAMB LODGE ★ ★ ❀ ❀
PH36 4HY *(off A861)*
☎ 01967 402257 ☎ 01967 402041
(Rosettes awarded for dinner only)
Uninterrupted loch views from this immaculately restored former hunting lodge.
£££ 11 bedrooms (1 fmly) No smoking in all bedrooms Mountain bike hire No smoking in restaurant Closed Dec–Feb (ex New Year) 🛥

LOCH SUNART ★ ★
PH36 4HZ
(turn off A82 at Corran Ferry, cross ferry, turn L onto A861 to Strontian)
☎ 01967 402471
Family hotel in splendid Loch side location. Friendly, tranquil atmosphere. Reliable home-cooking.
££ 11 bedrooms (1 fmly) No children under 8yrs No smoking in restaurant Closed Nov–Mar

WHITEBRIDGE

KNOCKIE LODGE ★ ★ ❀ ❀
IV1 2UP *(signposted from B862)*
☎ 01456 486276 ☎ 01456 486389
Former shooting lodge amid peaceful yet dramatic scenery, makes an elegant and comfortable retreat.
£££ 10 bedrooms Fishing Snooker Sailing No children under 10yrs No smoking in restaurant Closed Nov–Apr 🛥

WHITEBRIDGE ★ ★
IV1 2UN
(leave A9 onto B851, follow signs to Fort Augustus, hotel in 24m)
☎ 01456 486226 & 486272
☎ 01456 486413
South of Loch Ness, this long established family-run hotel has a relaxed and welcoming atmosphere.
£ 12 bedrooms (3 fmly) Fishing Closed 21 Dec–Feb 🛥

Stronlossit

WHERE TO EAT

RESTAURANTS

AA RECOMMENDED

ARISAIG

ARISAIG HOUSE ❀❀❀
Beasdale PH39 4NR
☎ 01687 450622 📠 01687 450626
High quality ingredients are treated with care, tarte Tatin of scallops with red pepper and chive oils or grilled fillet of hare with rabbit and mushroom steamed pudding, for instance. Classic saucing also sets off whole grilled Eigg lobster with sauce choron.
Fixed L £ Fixed D £££ 🍷

CANNICH

MULLARDOCH HOUSE ❀
Glen Cannich Beauly IV4 7LX
☎/📠 01456 415460
Dinner - a fixed four-course affair - could follow the lines of cauliflower and Stilton soup, sirloin steak with a well-balanced pepper sauce, and a smooth lemon posset.
Fixed D ££ 🍷

DULNAIN BRIDGE

MUCKRACH LODGE HOTEL ❀
PH26 3LY
☎ 01479 851257 📠 01479 851325
Daily five–course dinners are served in the conservatory, and the kitchen delivers dishes such as Thai fish cakes, carrot and celeriac soup and roast pork fillet, stir–fried vegetables and soy sauce.
Fixed D ££ 🍷

DUROR

STEWART HOTEL ❀❀
Appin PA38 4BW
☎ 01631 740268 📠 01631 740328,
The dinner menu changes daily in order to make the best use of local ingredients, such as sautéed scallops, steamed salmon and sole with lime beurre blanc sauce. Loin of lamb is enlivened with a honey and ginger sauce, pheasant well paired with cranberry and gooseberry sauce.
Fixed D ££ 🍷

FORT AUGUSTUS

BRAE HOTEL ❀
PH32 4DG
☎ 01320 366289 📠 01320 366702
House party-style cooking is based on quality raw ingredients. Expect warm bacon and scallop salad, carrot, apple and cashew soup, and pan-fried fillet steak with malt whisky and cream.
Fixed D ££ 🍷

FORT WILLIAM

INVERLOCHY CASTLE ❀❀❀
Torlundy, PH33 6SN
☎ 01397 702177 📠 01397 702953
The cooking is founded on a bedrock of classical technique and training although current trends are taken on board. Try perhaps duck galantine studded with pistachios to start, then a succulent, browned tranche of halibut with an orange sauce.
Fixed L £££ ALC £££ 🍷

MOORINGS HOTEL ❀❀
Banavie PH33 7LY
☎ 01397 772797 📠 01397 772441
Local produce features strongly on the carte where you might find Highland venison sausage, soused Mallaig herrings, fillets of West Coast sole with saffron cream sauce, and saddle of Mamore lamb served with a compote of shallots, garlic and pine kernels.
Fixed D £££ ALC £££ 🍷

GRANTOWN-ON-SPEY

GARTH HOTEL ❀
Castle Road PH26 3HN
☎ 01479 872836 📠 01479 872116
The daily-changing set-price menu offers dishes based on prime Scottish produce and cooked with a French accent. Typical main courses include pan-fried Buchan steak with whisky sauce, and poached fillet of Spey salmon with a white wine sauce.
Fixed D £££ ALC ££ 🍷

CULDEARN HOUSE ❀
Woodlands Terrace PH26 3JU
☎ 01479 872106 📠 01479 873641
Uncomplicated yet honest style of cooking that wins much praise. A typical menu might include home made chicken pate enhanced with brandy, breast of pheasant with a cream sauce and a fresh fruit Pavlova.

INVERNESS

BUNCHREW HOUSE HOTEL ❀
Bunchrew IV3 6TA
☎ 1463 234917 📠 01463 710620
The evening carte features local produce in dishes such as aromatic salmon with beetroot and crème fraîche, haunch of venison with braised chestnuts, and a caramelised lemon tart.
Fixed L ££ ALC ££ 🍷

CAFÉ 1 ❀
75 Castle Street IV2 3EA
☎ 01463 226200 📠 01463 716363
Trendy venue for modern Scottish cooking. A winter meal might include smooth chicken liver parfait and Cumberland sauce, West Coast salmon fillet, roasted with pine kernels and basil and finally a rich, tangy lemon torte.
Fixed L ALC ££ 🍷

CULLODEN HOUSE HOTEL ❀
Culloden IV1 2NZ
☎ 01463 790461 📠 01463 792181
An imaginative fixed-price menu, served in the elegant Adam dining room, reflects use of quality ingredients in such dishes as quail filled with orange and pork mousse with a wild mushroom and red wine sauce.
Fixed D £££ ALC ££ 🍷

DUNAIN PARK HOTEL ❀
IV3 6JN
☎ 01463 230512 📠 01463 224532
The restaurant is divided into three smaller areas, allowing guests to enjoy a more intimate atmosphere. Beef Wellington contrasted well with a mille-feuille of asparagus at a May meal. Whisky fans will be impressed by the 200 or more malts on offer.

INVERNESS THISTLE ❀
Millburn Road IV2 3TR
☎ 01463 239666 📠 01463 711145
A genuine effort is made to create interesting food. Fixed-price menus are backed up by themed cartes of Eastern and Scottish influence - dim sum and char sui duck breast, matched by Orkney cheese mousse and saddle of Scotch lamb, for example.
Fixed D ££ ALC ££ 🍷

KINGSMILLS HOTEL ❀
Culcabock Roa IV2 3LP
☎ 01463 237166 📠 01463 225208
Serious eating is done in the comfort of the Inglis Restaurant. Dishes such as scallops with fennel and lightly roasted best end of lamb with rosemary sauce are typical of the care with which fine Scottish produce is handled.
Fixed L £££ ALC ££ 🍷

KINGUSSIE

THE CROSS 🌸🌸🌸
Tweed Mill Brae, Ardbroilach Road PH21 1TC
📞 01540 661166 📠 01540 661080
A five-course dinners might kick off with
salmon tartare with quail's egg before, say,
a delicate scallop mousse alongside a
prawn and basil sauce. New season's
lamb or Ayrshire guinea fowl for the main
course and to finish expect a choice of
three desserts.
Fixed D £££ 🍷

OSPREY HOTEL 🌸
Ruthven Road, PH21 1EN
📞/📠 01540 661510
The best of Scotland's larder with up-to-
date ideas in dishes such as pan-fried
chicken fillet with fennel and tarragon, and
guinea fowl with lime and ginger sauce.
For dessert don't resist the temptation of
raspberry shortcake with whisky custard.

THE SCOT HOUSE HOTEL 🌸
Newtonmore Road PH21 1HE
📞 01540 661351 📠 01540 661111
The cooking features the best of local
produce. This might be roast noisettes of
lamb with heather honey and ginger
sauce, and pan-fried escalope of pork in a
whisky and mustard sauce.
Fixed D ££ ALC ££ 🍷

NAIRN

NEWTON HOTEL 🌸
Inverness Road IV12 4RX
📞 01667 453144 📠 01667 454026
The short set-dinner menu offers an
choice of well-prepared, modern Scottish
dishes at realistic prices. Expect pigeon
with black pudding fritter and onion
marmalade, Cajun-style beef with red
wine and balsamic vinegar essence, and
crème caramel.
Fixed D ££ 🍷

ONICH

ALLT-NAN-ROS HOTEL 🌸🌸
PH33 6RY
📞 01855 821210 📠 01855 821462
An imaginative menu of French-based
dishes with a strong modern west
Highland accent. For instance a May meal
featured lightly roasted scallops with
pesto, mushroom soup with chopped
chives, roast breast of guinea fowl with
grain mustard, and brandied date pudding
with hot caramel sauce.
Fixed D ££ 🍷

STRONTIAN

KILCAMB LODGE 🌸🌸
Acharacle PH36 4HY
📞 01967 402257 📠 01967 402041
Organic vegetables and local produce
figure strongly on the menu. Typically
offered are pot–roast quail with apricot
stuffing, main course fillets of lemon sole
with couscous and pimento fondue and
bringing up the rear Scottish cheeses, and
desserts.
Fixed D ££ 🍷

WHITEBRIDGE

KNOCKIE LODGE HOTEL 🌸🌸
IV1 2UP
📞 01456 486276 📠 01456486389
'Very fine' set dinners are served at 8pm,
with no choice except for pudding. This
could be an amuse-gueulle of oyster with
scrambled egg and chopped chives, ravioli
of foie gras with truffle sauce, rosette of
Loch Fyne scallops with a creamy sauce , a
'hearty portion' of fillet of Aberdeen Angus
beef with a morel butter sauce.
Fixed D £££ 🍷

NORTH
HIGHLANDS

The far north of Scotland is characterized by some of the wildest and most beautiful scenery in Europe. A sparsely populated land of majestic mountains, fertile straths, forests and sparkling lochs, there is much to do and see here, it is hard to know where to begin. Pentland Firth, Sutherland, Caithness, Ross and Cromarty are names that have long been etched into the Highlands map, but there are also numerous lesser-known gems and hidden places to seek out and explore. Travelling between Inverness, in the south of the region, and Cape Wrath, the most northerly outpost of mainland Britain, offers a constant, unfolding backdrop of ever-changing landscape. It is this sheer diversity of scenery and wealth of attractions that make the North Highlands such a popular destination.

However, no visit to this corner of Scotland is complete without a tour along its breathtaking coastline, where you will find Britain's highest sea cliffs and loneliest beaches – the exclusive domain of some of the world's rarest mammals. The deeply indented west coast, distinguished by its long sea lochs, sandy coves and red-sandstone hills, is the perfect base for fishing and hill-walking.

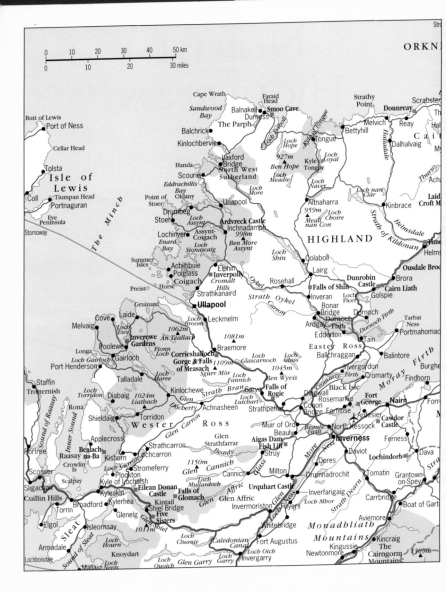

ULLAPOOL

Freshly painted houses and hotels overlook a jumble of quays and slipways, crowded with colourful fishing boats, nets and spars, along the charming seafront in this bustling little port and thriving tourist centre. Neatly laid out on a spit of land curving into the waters of Loch Broom, Ullapool is a model fishing village, developed by the British Fishery Society in 1788 for its deep-water anchorage and for the herring that were abundant in Loch Broom. Despite the subsequent decline in herring fishing, the town still has a busy working harbour, maintaining its strong fishing connection with the presence of huge foreign factory ships, or 'Klondykers' - vessels buying fish for on-board processing, from eastern Europe.

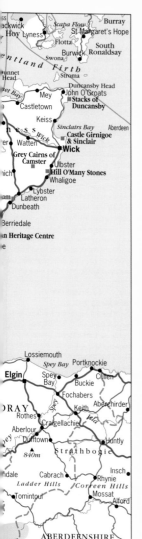

EVENTS & FESTIVALS

February

Traditional Music Festival,
Dornie, Ross-shire

May

Brora Golf Week
Sutherland

Highland Festival
(throughout The Highlands end May-early June)

June

Fyrish Hill Race,
Evanton, Ross-shire

Gala Day,
Contin & Evanton, Ross-shire

Gala Week,
Tain, Ross-shire

Highland Traditional Music Festival,
Dingwall, Ross-shire

Victorian Market Day,
Strathpeffer, Ross-shire

July

Agricultural Shows,
Latheron & Scrabster, Caithness, Dornoch, Sutherland

Caithness Highland Gathering,
Wick, Caithness

Gala Week,
Wick, Caithness

Highland Games,
Applecross & Lochcarron, Ross-shire, Halkirk, Caithness

Highland Gatherings,
Dingwall, Ross-shire, Durness, Caithness

August

Ardgay Fair
Ardgay, Sutherland

Assynt Highland Gathering,
Lochinver, Sutherland

Black Isle Show,
Muir of Ord, Ross-shire

Crofters Show,
Lairg, Sutherland

Dunrobin Vintage Car Rally,
Dunrobin Castle, Sutherland

Festival Week,
Dornoch, Sutherland

Gairloch Show,
Ross-shire

Golspie Gala Week,
Sutherland

Highland Gatherings,
Dornoch & Helmsdale Sutherland, Dunbeath, Caithness, Invergordon, Strathconon, Strathpeffer & Tain in Ross-shire

Royal British Legion Games,
Mey, Caithness

St Boniface Fair,
Fortrose, Ross-shire

September

Invercharron Highland Gathering,
Bonar Bridge, Sutherland

Northlands Festival,
Thurso & Wick, Caithness

DORNOCH

A dignified little town and resort offering miles of golden sandy beaches, a famous golf course and charming views over the Dornoch Firth. A royal burgh, formerly the seat of the Bishop of Caithness, Dornoch remains unspoilt and full of character, with streets of mellow sandstone buildings surrounding its tiny, restored 13th-century cathedral, delightfully situated in the spacious main square.

MUST SEE

Dunrobin Castle

CORRIESHALLOCH GORGE AND THE FALLS OF MEASACH,

11 miles south of Ullapool.

At the Falls of Measach the River Broom plunges over 60m into the spectacular Corrieshalloch Gorge, a mile-long chasm of sheer rock created by meltwaters from a glacier at the end of the Ice Age. The tumult of water is almost deafening as the river rushes along the gorge. The whole dramatic scene can be viewed from a spindly, vertigo-inducing suspension bridge, reached by footpaths from the main road.

DUNROBIN CASTLE,

Golspie ☎ 01408 633177

Looking more like a fairytale chateau with its splendid, gleaming turrets and its

MUSEUMS

CROMARTY COURTHOUSE,

Church St, Cromarty ☎ 01381 600418

Award-winning visitor centre and museum featuring animatronic displays and a reconstructed trial in the courtroom.

HIGHLAND MUSEUM OF CHILDHOOD,

The Old Station, Strathpeffer

☎ 01997 421031

Housed in a renovated Victorian railway station, this fascinating museum tells the story of childhood in the Highlands.

HUGH MILLER'S COTTAGE,

Church St, Cromarty ☎ 01381 600245

Birthplace of Hugh Miller, local geologist and fossil collector, in the 19th century, now housing an exhibition of his life and work.

LAIDHAY CROFT MUSEUM,

Dunbeath ☎ 01593 731244

A thatched, 200-year-old longhouse, with the dwelling quarters, byre and stable under one roof, is the main building here.

TAIN THROUGH TIME,

Tower St, Tain ☎/✉ 01862 894089

Discover 1000 years of Highland history at this unique visitor centre built around the Collegiate Church of St. Duthac. It combines original artefacts, live action and the very latest interactive technology.

THURSO HERITAGE MUSEUM,

Thurso ☎ 01847 892692

An absorbing little museum containing

beautiful setting overlooking the sea, Dunrobin is the ancient seat of the Earls and Dukes of Sutherland, who have had their power base here since the 13th century. The present 19th-century building has 189 furnished rooms of which 17 are open to the public, many of them set out with fine antique funishings, paintings and objet d'art. There's an excellent museum housing outstanding Victorian memorabilia, and the grand gardens were inspired by Versailles.

GAIRLOCH HERITAGE MUSEUM,

Auchtercairn ☎ 01445 712287

Situated in a complex of converted farm buildings, this award-winning museum illustrates the way of life in this typical West Highland parish from the Stone-Age

displays of Pictish stones and a complete Victorian living room.

TORRIDON COUNTRYSIDE CENTRE,

The Mains, Torridon ☎ 01445 791221

Set amid some of Scotland's finest mountain scenery the centre offers audio-visual presentations on the local wildlife, and helps put the scenery in context. Deer Park & Museum; estate walks.

ULLAPOOL MUSEUM

West Argyll St, Ullapool ☎/✉ 01854 612987

Housed in a former Telford Parliamentary church, this award-winning museum tells the story of the people of Loch Broom.

WICK HERITAGE CENTRE,

Bank Row, Wick ☎ 01955 605393

A museum carved out of harbourside houses, yards and outbuildings. It illustrates local history from Neolithic times to the herring fishing industry.

HISTORIC & ANCIENT SITES

ARDVRECK CASTLE,

Loch Assynt, Lochinver

Ruined MacLeod stronghold romantically situated on the shores of Loch Assynt.

CASTLES SINCLAIR & GIRNIGOE

Wick

Dramatically set on a peninsula overlooking Sinclair's Bay are the jagged ruins of these adjacent castles, the latter

to the 20th century. Exhibits include a reconstructed croft house, two 1930s fishing boats and some original machinery from nearby Rubha Reidh Lighthouse, plus hands-on activities and quizzes for children, and live demonstrations of spinning, butter-making and net making.

INVEREWE GARDEN,

Poolewe ☎ 01445 781200

The winter warming effect of the Gulf Stream enables this remarkable sub-tropical garden to flourish on this barren windswept peninsula. Planted and beautifully laid out by Osgood Mackenzie in 1860, this exotic collection of over 2,500 tender and hardy flowers, shrubs and trees is at its best in early June, but full of beauty from March to October. Twisting paths through this 64 acre site afford ever-changing views of garden, sea and the magnificent mountain backdrop.

TIMESPAN HERITAGE CENTRE,

Helmsdale ☎ 01431 821327

The North's most exciting heritage centre features the dramatic story of the Highlands, from Picts and Vikings, to the last burning of a witch and the Highland Clearances through to crofting, fishing and the present day oil fields. The whole story is told in devastating detail through life-size sets, sound effects, and an audio-visual programme. Café, riverside garden.

was built in the late 15th century.

EILEAN DONAN CASTLE

5m east of Kyle of Lochalsh

☎ 01599 534276

Built in the 13th century and restored in the 19th, this much photographed castle enjoys an idyllic setting on an islet at the meeting of three lochs.

FEARN'S ABBEY,

Fearn

Much of the original 13th-century structure remains, but only the choir and the nave are still in use.

GLENELG BROCHS

on minor rd from Glen Shiel

The best preserved circular walled defensive structures on the Scotland mainland, built against sea-borne raiders around 1st century BC to 3rd century AD. Nearby stand the ruins of Bernera Barracks.

GREAT FOR KIDS

BLACK ISLE COUNTRY PARK,

Drumsmittal, North Kessock

☎ 01463 731656

Collection of ornamental waterfowl, wallabys, deer, goats and other farmyard animals in a quiet rural setting. Tearoom and forest walk.

CHORAIDH CROFT FARM PARK,

94 Laid Loch Eriboliside, by Altnaharra

☎ 01971 511235

Crofting museum, illustrating crofting life over the past 150 years, and farm park with over 40 breeds of animals to view at close quarters. Tearoom.

CRAIG HIGHLAND FARM,
Craig, Plockton ☎/☎ 01599 544205
Open rare breeds farm and animal sanctuary on the shores of Lochcarron with spectacular views.

HIGHLAND RARE BREEDS FARM,
Elphin ☎ 01854 666204
There are over 36 breeds, both ancient and modern, some of which you may stroke or feed; also a pets corner, riverside walk and a shop.

HOMES & GARDENS

ACHILTIBUIE HYDROPONICUM,
Achiltibuie, Ullapool ☎ 01854 622202
A unique and beautiful indoor garden overlooking the Summer Isles.

ATTADALE GARDEN & WOODLAND WALKS,
Attadale, Strathcarron ☎ 01520 722217
A twelve acre garden planted from 1900 with rhododendrons, azaleas and rare southern hemisphere plants.

BALMACARA (LOCHALSH WOODLAND GARDEN)
Kyle of Lochalsh ☎ 01599 566325

This 5600 acre crofting estate comprises seven villages (including Plockton), forest walks and Lochalsh Woodland Garden, where a variety of exotic and native trees flourish close to the shores of Loch Alsh.

BIG OUTDOORS

BEACHES AND LOCHS
Wildlife boat trips explore the fjord-like sea lochs that penetrate deep inland on the west coast. Beyond lofty headlands are remote and peaceful bays and beaches, notably Gruinard Bay and Sandwood Bay, near Cape Wrath.

BEINN EIGHE NATURE RESERVE,
Kinlochewe ☎ 01445 760254
Surrounded by the giant sandstone monoliths of Torridon and set beside beautiful Loch Maree, Britain's first National Nature Reserve protects the best remaining areas of the Caledonian pine forest and its wealth of wildlife. Nature trails, ranger-led walks and visitor centre.

DUNCANSBY HEAD AND DUNNET HEAD
near John O'Groats
Wild, cliff-edged promontories jutting out into the Pentland Firth, echoing with the screams of seabirds.

FLOW COUNTRY,
around Forsinard
Visitor Centre ☎ 01641 571225
An awe-inspiring landscape of austere beauty covering 2,500 sq km around the Caithness/Sutherland border. The seemingly endless upland peat bog moor is haven to a range of wildfowl and wading birds found nowhere else.

HANDA ISLAND NATURE RESERVE
accessible by boat from Tarbet
As well as towering cliffs, this small island has one of the most important seabird breeding sites in Britain.

INVERPOLLY NATURE RESERVE,
near Ullapool
From wide, flat expanses of moor and unusual shaped mountains to woodland and loch, this varied landscape is home to a rich variety of fauna and flora.

SHIN FALLS,
Achany, Lairg ☎ 01549 402231
One of Scotland's most spectacular waterfalls, especially when the salmon are leaping (May-October), in their bid to reach their spawning grounds.

SMOO CAVE
east of Durness
Huge, impressive limestone cave at the head of a narrow inlet.

ESSENTIAL INFORMATION

TOURIST INFORMATION

INFORMATION CENTRES

BETTYHILL *seasonal,*
Clachan, Bettyhill, By Thurso KW14 7SS
☎ 01641 521342

DORNOCH,
The Square, Dornoch IV25 3SD
☎ 01862 810400 ☎ 01862 810644

DURNESS *seasonal,*
Durine, Durness, By Lairg IV27 4PN
☎ 01971 511259 ☎ 01971 511368

GAIRLOCH
Achtercairn, Gairloch IV21 2DN
☎ 01445 712130 ☎ 01445 712071

HELMSDALE *seasonal,*
Coupar Park, Helmsdale KW8 6HH
☎ 01431 821640

JOHN O'GROATS *seasonal,*
Country Rd, John O'Groats KW1 4YR
☎ 01955 611373

KYLE OF LOCHALSH *seasonal,*
Kyle of Lochalsh IV40 8AQ
☎ 01599 534276 ☎ 01599 534808

LAIRG *seasonal,*
Ferrycroft Countryside Centre, Lairg IV27 4AZ
☎ 01549 402160

LOCHCARRON *seasonal,*
Main St, Lochcarron IV54 8YD
☎ 01520 722357 ☎ 01520 722324

LOCHINVER *seasonal,*
Kirk Lane, Lochniver, By Lairg IV27 4LT
☎ 01571 844330

NORTH KESSOCK *seasonal,*
Picnic Site, North Kessock IV1 1XB
☎ 01463 731505 ☎ 01463 731701

STRATHPEFFER *seasonal,*
The Square, Strathpeffer IV14 9DW
☎ 01997 421415 ☎ 01997 421460

THURSO *seasonal,*
Riverside, Thurso KW14 8BU
☎ 01847 892371

ULLAPOOL *seasonal,*
Argyll St, Ullapool IV26 2UB
☎ 01854 612135 ☎ 01854 613031

WICK,
Whitechapel Rd, Wick KW1 4EA
☎ 01955 602596 ☎ 01955 604940

ACCESS

AIR ACCESS

INVERNESS AIRPORT ☎ 01463 232471
BRITISH AIRWAYS ☎ 01667 462280
LOGANAIR ☎ 01667 462332

SEA ACCESS

ARNISDALE FERRY SERVICE *passenger,*
Arnisdale, Kyle ☎ 01599 522352

CALEDONIAN MACBRAYNE
Ullapool-Stornaway
☎ 01475 650100

CAPE WRATH FERRY SERVICE *passenger,*
Durness ☎ 01971 511376

P&O SCOTTISH FERRIES *Scrabster-Orkney*
☎ 01224 572615

SEABOARD MARINE LTD *Cromarty-Nigg car ferry,*
☎ 01862 871254

CRAFTS

Look out for spinning and weaving, especially tweeds and tartans, glassware, woodcraft, pottery, and basket-weaving.

AULTBEA WOODCRAFT,
Drumchork, Aultbea ☎ 01445 731422

BALNAKEIL CRAFT VILLAGE,
Durness ☎ 01971 511277

CAITHNESS GLASS VISITOR CENTRE,
Wick ☎ 01955 602286

DORNOCH CRAFT CENTRE,
Town Jail, Dornoch ☎/☎ 01862 810555

GAIRLOCH CRAFT STUDIO,
Auchtercairn ☎ 01445 712456

HIGHLAND LINE CRAFT CENTRE,
Achnasheen ☎ 01445 720227

KNOCKAN STUDIO,
Elphin ☎/☎ 01854 666261

NORTHSHORE CERAMICS,
Wick ☎ 01955 605899

SUTHERLAND POTTERY,
Shinness, Lairg ☎ 01549 402223

ENTERTAINMENT

CINEMA

THOR LEISURE LTD,
The Viking Bowl, Thurso ☎ 01847 895050

THEATRE

INVERGORDON ARTS CENTRE,
☎ 01349 854414

LYTH ARTS CENTRE,
Wick ☎ 01955 641270

FOOD & DRINK

CHEESES

CABOC - a traditional cream cheese rolled in oatmeal from .
CROWDIE - a soft fresh cheese originally made using milk left after the cream had separated naturally.
HIGHLAND FINE CHEESES,
Blairliath, Tain ☎ 01862 892034
Conducted tours and tastings
WEST HIGHLAND DAIRY,
Achmore, Stromeferry ☎ 01599 577203
Produces 15 different cheeses,

SMOKERY

ACHILTIBUIE SMOKEHOUSE,
Achiltibuie, Ullapool ☎ 01854 622353
Specialist curers and smokers of fish and cheese.

WHISKY DISTILLERY TOURS

CLYNELISH DISTILLERY,
Brora ☎ 01408 621444
GLENMORANGIE DISTILLERY,
Tain ☎ 01862 892477
GLEN ORD DISTILLERY,
Muir of Ord ☎ 01463 870421

TRANSPORT

BOAT TRIPS & CRUISES

DOLPHIN ECOSSE,
Cromarty ☎/☎ 01381 600323
Dolphin and wildlife trips.
ISLANDER CRUISES,
Ullapool ☎ 01854 612385
3-hour wildlife cruises to Bird Island.
JOHN O'GROATS FERRIES,
John O'Groats ☎ 01955 611353
Day trips to Orkney and wildlife cruises.
LAXFORD CRUISES,
Scourie, Lairg ☎ 01971 502251
Wildlife cruises around Loch Laxford.
LEISURE MARINE,
Plockton ☎ 01599 544308
Seal Trips
'SMOO' INNER CAVE TOURS,
38 Sangomor, Durness, IV27 4PZ
Geological and natural history tours.
STATESMAN CRUISES,
Lochinver ☎ 01571 844446
Trip to 'Eas à Chual Aullin' waterfall.
SUMMER QUEEN CRUISES,
Ullapool ☎ 01854 612472
Cruises to the Summer Isles and Bird Island of Loch Broom.

BUS SERVICES

Local bus services are reliable although not always frequent. Contact local Tourist Information Centres for timetable details.

CAPE WRATH MINI-BUS SERVICE,
☎ 01971 511287

CAR HIRE

HOLIDAY CAR & CYCLE HIRE,
'Kyle of Lochalsh ☎ 01599 534707
ROSS RENTALS,
Strathcarron ☎ 01520 722205

COACH TOURS

HIGHLAND SAFARIS (MINI-BUS),
Strathpeffer ☎ 01997 421618
Birdwatching and natural history tours.
SPA COACHES,
Strathpeffer ☎ 01997 421311

CYCLE HIRE

DORNOCH LINKS CAMPING & CARAVANNING SITE,
Dornoch ☎ 01862 810423
MILECROFT HOTEL,
Gairloch ☎ 01445 712376

TRAINS

Inverness to Kyle of Lochalsh (Scotrail)
☎ 0345 484950.

SPORT & LEISURE

ACTIVITY CENTRES

FAIRBURN ACTIVITY CENTRE,
Urray, Muir of Ord ☎ 01997 433397

ANGLING

Opportunites to fish abound throughout the northern Highlands, from sea fishing from hundreds of harbours to serious game fishing - salmon, sea trout, brown trout, gillaroo and char - on the many sea lochs, inland lochs and streams that cover the area. For more information contact the local Tourist Information Centres

CYCLING

The area is great cycling country. There are long, quiet roads meandering through glens, over rolling moorland, through forests, past lochs and rivers, as well as winding coastal roads round sea lochs and over headlands. The road network is simple, but the few roads that do exists can be busy in the high season. Be prepared for some steep hills. Traffic-free routes have been created by Forest Enterprise. Information ☎ 01862 810359.

GOLF COURSES

ROYAL DORNOCH ☎ 01862 810219
Very challenging championship links course ranked 13th in the world.
THE CARNEGIE CLUB,
Dornoch ☎ 01862 894600
Set within the grounds of an enchanting castle, with the sea and hills all around.
ALNESS ☎ 01349 883877
BONAR BRIDGE-ARDGAY
Bonar Bridge ☎ 01863 766375
BRORA ☎ 01408 621417
DURNESS ☎ 01971 511364
FORTROSE & ROSEMARKIE
Fortrose ☎ 01381 620529
GAIRLOCH ☎ 01445 712407
GOLSPIE ☎ 01408 633266
HELMSDALE ☎ 01431 821650
INVERGORDON ☎ 01349 852715
LOCHCARRON ☎ 01520 722257
MUIR OF ORD ☎/☎ 01463 870825
REAY ☎ 01847 811288

STRATHPEFFER SPA ☎ 01997 421219
TAIN ☎ 01862 892314
TARBAT,
Portmahomack ☎ 01862 871236
THURSO ☎ 01847 893807
WICK ☎ 01955 602726

LEISURE CENTRES

AVERON,
Alness ☎ 01349 882287
BLACK ISLE,
Fortrose ☎ 01381 621252
DINGWALL ☎ 01349 864224
GAIRLOCH ☎ 01445 712345
INVERGORDON ☎ 01349 853689
LOCH BROOM,
Ullapool ☎ 01854 612884

RIDING

ACHALONE ACTIVITIES,
North Achalone, Halkirk ☎ 01847 831326
LYTH STABLES,
Lyth, Wick ☎ 01955 641318
MORNESS TREKKING & RIDING CENTRE,
Rhiandoggie, Rogart ☎ 01408 641337
NORTH COAST ADVENTURE HOLIDAYS,
Lundies, Tongue-by-Lairg ☎ 01847 55256
NORTHWILDS RIDING CENTRE,
Fendom, By-Tain ☎ 01862 892468

SAILING

LEISURE MARINE,
Plockton ☎ 01599 544308

SCENIC DRIVES

The scenic splendour of the west coast is best experienced between Ullapool and Kyle of Lochalsh, via the breathtaking road across the Applecross Peninsula. In the far north, a tour of the awe-inspiring Flow Country from Wick is to be recommended, returning along the north coast via Thurso, Dunnet Bay, John O'Groats and the giddily steep cliffs at Duncansby Head.

SWIMMING

ALNESS ☎ 01349 882456
LOCHALSH & SKYE,
Kyle of Lochalsh ☎/☎ 01599 534838
SWIMMING POOL COMPLEX,
Golspie ☎ 01408 633437
THURSO ☎ 01847 893260
WICK ☎ 01955 603711

WALKING

The Northern Highlands offers a wealth of walking opportunities, from strenuous hill climbing, like 'bagging' Munro's (peaks above 3,000ft/914m), and lonely walks across dramatic upland landscapes, to bracing hikes around exposed headlands and peninsulas and gentle strolls on well waymarked forest trails (leaflets from Forest Enterprise ☎ 01862 810359).

WATERSPORTS

HIGHLAND WATERSPORTS,
Lairg, ☎/☎ 01549 402103

WHERE TO STAY

AA RECOMMENDED

Aultbea

ACHNASHEEN

LEDGOWAN LODGE ★ ★ ★
IV22 2EJ *(0.25m on A890 to Kyle of Lochalsh - from Achnasheen)*
☎ 01445 720252 🖷 01445 720240
Popular, friendly Highland hotel ideally situated to explore Wester Ross. Meals and snacks all day.
££ 12 bedrooms (2 fmly) No dogs No smoking in restaurant Res Jan–Mar & Nov–Dec 🛱

ARDELVE

CONCHRA HOUSE ★ ★
Sallachy Rd IV40 8DZ
(turn N off A87 1m W of Eilean Donan Castle (Dornie) signpost Sallachy/Killilan)
☎ 01599 555233 🖷 01599 555433
Lovingly restored Georgian house with views over Loch Long. A haven of peace.
££ 6 bedrooms No smoking in all bedrooms Fishing Pool table Croquet lawn Putting green Recreation room Table tennis No smoking in restaurant Closed 24 Dec–3 Jan 🛱

LOCH DUICH ★ ⊛
IV40 8DY *(A82 towards Fort William, R at Invermoriston onto A887 then A87 to Ardelve)*
☎ 01599 555213 🖷 01599 555214
Former drovers' inn beside the Road to the Isles with views of Eilean Donan Castle. Good food.
£ 18 bedrooms (1 fmly)
Fishing, Shooting, Sailing Weekly live entertainment Children's facilities No smoking in restaurant Closed 4 Jan–1 Mar & 19–28 Dec Res Nov–18 Dec 🛱

AULTBEA

AULTBEA ★ ★
IV22 2HX *(turn off A832 at Aultbea signs, hotel seen in 400yds)*
☎ 01445 731201 🖷 01445 731214
Many guests return year after year to this charming hotel on the shore of Loch Ewe.
££ 8 bedrooms 3 annexe bedrooms (1 fmly) Pool table 🛱

BONAR BRIDGE

KYLE HOUSE ⊙⊙
Dornoch Rd IV24 3EB *(on A949, 4th house on L after newsagents going N out of village)*
☎ 01863 766360
Spacious roadside house with splendid views over the Kyle of Sutherland towards the Ross-shire hills.
£ 6 bedrooms (2 fmly) No smoking in bedrooms or dining room No dogs (ex guide dogs) Licensed No children under 5yrs Feb–Nov

BRORA

ROYAL MARINE ★ ★ ★ ⊛
Golf Rd KW9 6QS *(turn off A9 in village towards beach and golf course)*
☎ 01408 621252 🖷 01408 621181
Many traditional features retained. Restaurant and bar enjoy busy trade.
££ 16 bedrooms (1 fmly) Indoor swimming pool (heated) Tennis (hard) Fishing Snooker Sauna Solarium Gym Pool table Croquet lawn Putting green Jacuzzi/spa Ice curling rink in season Table Tennis No smoking in restaurant 🛱

THE LINKS ★ ★ ★
Golf Rd KW9 6QS *(turn off A9 in Brora towards beach and golf course)*
☎ 01408 621225 🖷 01408 621383
Occupies an enviable position overlooking the golf course to the sea beyond.
££ 23 bedrooms (2 fmly) Indoor swimming pool (heated) Fishing Snooker Sauna Solarium Gym Pool table Croquet lawn Putting green Jacuzzi/spa No smoking in restaurant Closed 31 Oct–Mar Res 1 Apr–30 Apr, 1 Oct–30 Oct 🛱

LYNWOOD ⊙⊙⊙⊙
Golf Rd KW9 6QS
(turn off A9 by river bridge into Golf Rd)
☎ 01408 621226 🖷 01408 621226
Welcoming family home near the golf course. Enjoyable home cooking and hearty breakfasts.
£ 3 bedrooms 1 annexe bedrooms (1 fmly) No smoking in bedrooms No smoking in 1 lounge Closed Jan & Feb 🛱

CONTIN

COUL HOUSE ★ ★ ★ ⊛
IV14 9EY *(from S -through Inverness on A9 over Moray Firth bridge. After 5m 2nd exit at rndbt onto A835 to Contin)*
☎ 01997 421487 🖷 01997 421945
Genuine warm welcome and good food at this lovely Victorian country house. Tempting Taste of Scotland specialities.
£££ 20 bedrooms (3 fmly) Pool table Putting green Pitch & putt Children's facilities No smoking in restaurant 🛱

ACHILITY ★ ★
IV14 9EG
(on A835, at the northern edge of Contin)
☎ 01997 421355 🖷 01997 421923
Renovated 18th-century former coaching inn with an attractive restaurant.
£ 12 bedrooms (3 fmly) No smoking in 6 bedrooms Pool table No smoking in restaurant 🛱

DINGWALL

KINKELL HOUSE ★ ★ ⊛
Easter Kinkell by Conon Bridge IV7 8HY *(10m N of Inverness turn off A9 onto B9169 for 1m)*
☎ 01349 861270 🖷 01349 865902
Lovingly restored 19th-century farmhouse now a comfortable small country house hotel. Splendid views.
££ 7 bedrooms (1 fmly) No smoking in all bedrooms Croquet lawn No smoking in restaurant 🛱

MILLCRAIG ⊙⊙
18 Millcraig Rd IV15 9PS ☎ 01349 862194
Well maintained semi detached home close to the town and sports centre.
3 bedrooms

DORNIE

DORNIE ★ ★
Francis St IV40 8DT
(follow A87, turn into Dornie, hotel on R)
☎ 01599 555205 🖷 01599 555429
Warm welcome assured at this small hotel beside Loch Duich close to Eilean Donan Castle. Well earned reputation for good food.
£ 12 bedrooms (2 fmly) Pool table Weekly live entertainment Closed 25 Dec Res Jan (ex New Year) & Feb 🛱

DORNOCH

ROYAL GOLF HOTEL ★ ★ ★
The First Tee Grange Rd IV25 3LG
☎ 01862 810283 🖷 01862 810923
Beside the Royal Dornoch Golf Club attracts golfers from all around the world. Near beach and Dornoch Firth.
££ 25 bedrooms 8 annexe bedrooms (2 fmly) Night porter Tennis (grass) Fishing Riding No smoking in restaurant Closed Jan–Feb Res Nov, Dec & Mar 🛱

Highfield

DORNOCH CASTLE ★★
Castle St IV25 3SD *(2m N, on A949)*

☎ 01862 810216 ☎ 01862 810981

Once a Bishop's Palace now a family run
hotel popular with visiting holidaymakers
and golfers.

*££ 4 bedrooms 13 annexe bedrooms (2 fmly)
Lift No smoking in restaurant Closed Nov–
Mar*

BURGHFIELD HOUSE ★★
IV25 3HN

☎ 01862 810212 ☎ 01862 810404

Victorian mansion in six acres of
immaculately kept gardens. Traditional
menus.

*£ 14 bedrooms 20 annexe bedrooms (8 fmly)
Night porter Sauna Solarium Putting green
Closed Nov–Mar (ex Xmas & New Year)*

FOURPENNY COTTAGE ◙◙◙◙◙
Skelbo IV25 3QF

☎ 01862 810727 ☎ 01862 810727

Glorious views of Dornoch Firth are
enjoyed from this welcoming and
comfortable guest house.

*£ 2 bedrooms 2 annexe bedrooms No
smoking in bedrooms, dining room or 1
lounge No dogs (ex guide dogs) Children's
facilities bird watching Closed 20 Dec–20 Feb*

HIGHFIELD ◙◙◙◙◙
Evelix Rd IV25 3HR

*(take A9 N over Dornoch Bridge. After 2m
turn R onto A949. Then 1.5m, past schools
on L, Highfield 500yds on left)*

☎ 01862 810909 ☎ 01862 810909

This modern house overlooks Dornoch
Firth. A wide choice at breakfast.

*3 bedrooms No smoking No children under
12yrs*

DRUMBEG

DRUMBEG ★★
IV27 4NW *(on B896)*

☎ 01571 833236 ☎ 01571 833333

Small hotel surrounded by dramatic
countryside - ideal for a walking or fishing
holiday.

*££ 6 bedrooms No smoking in all bedrooms
No dogs Pool table No children No smoking
in restaurant Closed Nov–Mar*

DUNDONNELL

DUNDONNELL ★★★◈
IV23 2QS

(turn off A835 at Braemore junct onto A832)

☎ 01854 633204 ☎ 01854 633366

Genuine Highland hospitality at this
comfortable hotel at the head of Little
Loch Broom. Tempting Taste of Scotland
specialities.

*£ 28 bedrooms (2 fmly) Pool table No
smoking in restaurant Closed 22 Nov–Feb
(ex Xmas/New Year)*

DUNNET

NORTHERN SANDS ★★
KW14 8DX

☎ 01847 851270 ☎ 01847 851626

Family-run hotel close to glorious sandy
beach. Meals with Italian overtones or
popular Taste of Scotland specialities.

9 bedrooms (3 fmly) No dogs (ex guide dogs)

GAIRLOCH

CREAG MOR ★★★
Charleston IV21 2AH

*(A9 to Inverness, then A832. Follow signs to
Ullapool, through Garve & follow signs for
Gairloch, 1st hotel on R)*

☎ 01445 712068 ☎ 01445 712044

Warm welcome at this comfortable hotel,
with harbour views. Local produce
features strongly on menus.

*££ 17 bedrooms 2 annexe bedrooms (1 fmly)
Night porter Fishing Pool table No smoking
in restaurant Closed 16 Nov–Feb*

MYRTLE BANK ★★
Low Rd IV21 2BS

(off B8012 Melvaig road)

☎ 01445 712004 ☎ 01445 712214

Comfortable and welcoming hotel beside
the picturesque shore of Loch Gairloch.
Enjoyable Scottish fare.

*12 bedrooms (3 fmly) No smoking in
restaurant*

THE OLD INN ★★
Flowerdale IV21 2BD

(on A832 - at S end of village nr harbour)

☎ 01445 712006 ☎ 01445 712445

Former coaching inn attractively sited by a
small river across the road from the
harbour. All day food.

*£ 14 bedrooms (4 fmly) No smoking area in
restaurant*

BIRCHWOOD ◙◙◙◙
IV21 2AH

☎ 01445 712011

Lovely views over the old harbour from
this welcoming guest house in well
tended gardens.

*6 bedrooms (1 fmly) No smoking in
bedrooms or dining room Apr–mid Oct*

BAINS ◙◙
Strath IV21 2BZ

*(A332 to Gairloch. Onto B8021. Strath
0.25m past car park on R)*

☎ 01445 712472

Pleasant roadside house. Bedrooms have
radios, TV's and tea making facilities.

*£ 6 bedrooms (3 fmly) No smoking in
dining room or in lounges*

GARVE

INCHBAE LODGE ★★◈
Inchbae IV23 2PH

(on the A835, 6m W of Garve)

☎ 01997 455269 ☎ 01997 455207

Relaxing hotel. Bedrooms have no
televisions or telephones to detract from
the peace and quiet. Good food.

*££ 6 bedrooms 6 annexe bedrooms (3 fmly)
No smoking in all bedrooms Fishing
Walking-routes are available Clay pigeon
shooting No smoking in restaurant Closed
25–29 Dec*

Dundonnell

Kinlochberviea

OLD MANSE ⊞⊞⊞
IV23 2PX *(turn off A835 by AA telephone 0.5m W of village)*
☎ 01997 414201
Former manse that provides comfortable accommodation for touring holidaymakers.
£ 3 bedrooms No smoking No dogs (ex guide dogs) Closed 24 Dec-1 Jan

GOLF LINKS ★★
KW10 6TT
(off A9, hotel 300 yards along coast rd)
☎ 01408 633408 ☎ 01408 634184
Small family-run hotel,near the beach and next to golf course with fine views over the Dornoch Firth.
£ 9 bedrooms (1 fmly) Putting green 🍴

ULBSTER A BEDROOMS ★★
Bridge St KW12 6XY
(A9 to Latheron from Perth left onto A895)
☎ 01847 831206 & 831641
☎ 01847 831206
Adjacent to the River Thurso, this long-established Highland hotel is popular with sporting clientele.
10 bedrooms 16 annexe bedrooms Fishing Pool table 🍴

BENCORRAGH HOUSE ⊞⊞⊞
Upper Gills, Canisbay KW1 4YB
(to Canisbay from A9 - 3m S of John O'Groats - continue for 3.5m. Take 2nd on L, 2nd house on L)
☎ 01955 611449 ☎ 01955 611449
Working croft of ten acres, with panoramic views. Spacious guest accommodation.
£ 4 bedrooms (1 fmly) No smoking in bedrooms, dining room or in 1 lounge Apr-5 Oct 🍴

POST OFFICE HOUSE ⊞⊞⊞
Canisbay KW1 4YH
(3m from town on A836)
☎ 01955 611213 ☎ 01955 611213
100-year-old house with fine views is the home of an AA Landlady of the Year so a genuine welcome is assured. Breakfast menu is notably extensive.
£ 3 bedrooms No smoking in bedrooms or dining room No dogs No children under 12yrs Easter-October

KINLOCHBERVIE ★★★
IV27 4RP
(turn off A838 onto B801, through village, turn R at junct above harbour, hotel 250metres on L)
☎ 01971 521275 ☎ 01971 521438
From its Hillside position this comfortable modern hotel enjoys a lovely outlook over the harbour.
£££ 14 bedrooms (5 fmly) Fishing Pool table No smoking in restaurant Closed 23 Dec-4 Jan Res Nov-Mar 🍴

OLD SCHOOL RESTAURANT & GUEST HOUSE ⊞⊞⊞
Inshegra IV27 4RH *(from A838 at Rhiconich take B801 to Kinlochbervie, 2m on L)*
☎ 01971 521383 ☎ 01971 521383
Former schoolhouse retains quite a bit of its original character. Lovely views.
6 annexe bedrooms (1 fmly) No smoking in dining room or 1 lounge Licensed Closed 25 Dec & 1 Jan 🍴

LOCHALSH ★★★
Ferry Rd IV40 8AF *(turn off A82 onto A87)*
☎ 01599 534202 ☎ 01599 534881
Views over the Kyles to Skye from this friendly hotel. Seafood specialities.
£££ 38 bedrooms (8 fmly) Lift Night porter No smoking in restaurant 🍴

Call the AA Hotel Booking Service on 0990 050505 to book at AA recognised hotels and B&Bs in the UK, or through our internet site: http://www.theaa.co.uk/hotels

KYLE ★★
Main St IV40 8AB *(A87 just before Skye bridge, turn R into main street in village)*
☎ 01599 534204 ☎ 01599 534932
Personally run holiday hotel. Compact accommodation is bright and cheerful.
££ 31 bedrooms No smoking in 2 bedrooms No smoking in restaurant Res Nov-Mar 🍴

KYLESKU ★★⊛
IV27 4HW *(In village hotel at end of rd at Old Ferry Pier)*
☎ 01971 502231 & 502200
☎ 01971 502313
In a waterside position this pleasant small hotel has a good reputation for seafood.
£ 7 bedrooms 1 annexe bedrooms (1 fmly) Fishing Pool table No smoking in restaurant Closed Nov-Feb 🍴

NEWTON LODGE ⊞⊞⊞⊞
IV27 4HW *(1.5m S on A894)*
☎ 01971 502070
Guests regularly return to this hotel enjoying spectacular views over Loch Glencoul to the mountains.
£ 7 bedrooms No smoking in bedrooms No smoking in dining room Licensed No children 13yrs Easter-mid Oct 🍴

OVERSCAIG ★★
Loch Shin IV27 4NY *(on A838)*
☎ 01549 431203
For pure isolation it is hard to beat this welcoming hotel, beside picturesque Loch Shin.
9 bedrooms (2 fmly) No dogs (ex guide dogs) Fishing No smoking in restaurant

UPPER LATHERON ⊞⊞⊞
KW5 6DT *(2m N of Dunbeath off A9, and 2m S of Latheron)*
☎ 01593 741224
Pretty farmhouse enjoying panoramic views over the North Sea. A working farm where ponies are bred.
£ 3 bedrooms (1 fmly) No smoking No dogs (ex guide dogs) 200 acres Cattle Ponies Sheep Closed Oct-Apr

Kylesku

LOCHCARRON

LOCHCARRON ★★
Main St IV54 8YS
*(take A9 N, then A835 at Tore rdbt for
Ullapool, then A890 Kyle of Lochalsh, hotel
in E end of village on Lochcarron)*
☎ 01520 722226 🅕 01520 722612
A touch of Irish hospitality at this
welcoming hotel overlooking the loch.
Local seafood.
*££ 10 bedrooms (2 fmly) No smoking in 2
bedrooms Pool table Hunting Shooting
Fishing No smoking in restaurant* 🍴

LOCHINVER

INVER LODGE ★★★❀
IV27 4LU
*(A835 to Lochinver, through village & L. after
village hall, follow private rd for 0.5m)*
☎ 01571 844496 🅕 01571 844395
Well appointed modern hotel with enjoys
superb views across the river mouth and
harbour.
*££££ 20 bedrooms Fishing Snooker
Sauna Solarium No smoking in restaurant
Closed 1 Nov-9 Apr* 🍴

LYBSTER

PORTLAND A BEDROOMS ★★
KW3 6BS
*(beside A9. From Inverness Hotel is on L,
200yds from the Lybster sign)*
☎ 01593 721208 🅕 01593 721446
Popular roadside hotel. Four-poster, half
tester and family rooms available.
*££ 19 bedrooms (3 fmly) Night porter
Fishing* 🍴

MELVICH

TIGH-NA-CLASH ❑❑❑
Tigh-na-Clash KW14 7YJ
(on A836 opposite the Croft Inn)
☎ 01641 531262 🅕 01641 531262
Welcoming atmosphere at this
comfortable detached modern house in
well tended gardens.
*£ 8 bedrooms No smoking in bedrooms No
smoking in dining room No dogs (ex guide
dogs) No children 8yrs Mar-Oct* 🍴

Lochcarron

MEY

CASTLE ARMS ★★
KW14 8XH *(on A836)*
☎ 01847 851244 🅕 01847 851244
Genuine hospitality at this modernised
coaching inn with uninterrupted views to
Orkney.
*££ 3 bedrooms 5 annexe bedrooms (1 fmly)
Fishing Pool table Children's facilities Res
Oct-Mar* 🍴

MUIR OF ORD

ORD HOUSE ★★
Muir of Ord IV6 7UH *(off A832)*
☎ 01463 870492 🅕 01463 870492
Former Laird's house now a comfortable
country house hotel in 60 acre grounds.
Enjoyable country cooking.
*££ 11 bedrooms Croquet lawn Putting
green Clay pigeon shooting Children's
facilities No smoking area in restaurant
May-Oct* 🍴

THE DOWER HOUSE ★❀❀
Highfield IV6 7XN
(on Dingwall rd A862, 1m from town on L)
☎ 01463 870090 🅕 01463 870090
Charming hotel, in secluded grounds, ideal
for those touring the Highlands. Skilful
cooking.
*5 bedrooms 2 annexe bedrooms No dogs
Croquet lawn Children's facilities No
smoking in restaurant Closed Xmas day &
1wk Mar* 🍴

PLOCKTON

HAVEN ★★❀
Innes St IV52 8TW *(turn off A87 before Kyle
of Lochalsh, after Balmacana to Plockton)*
☎ 01599 544334/544223
🅕 01599 544467
(Rosette awarded for dinner only)
Charming hotel in a village now famous
for the TV series Hamish Macbeth. Dinner
here retains a sense of occasion.
*££ 15 bedrooms No children under 7yrs
No smoking in restaurant Closed 20
Dec-1 Feb* 🍴

PORTMAHOMACK

CALEDONIAN ★★
Main St IV20 1YS
☎ 01862 871345 🅕 01862 871757
Overlooks an attractive sandy beach across
the Firth towards the Sutherland hills.
Popular range of food.
*£ 16 bedrooms (1 fmly) Pool table No
smoking in restaurant* 🍴

PORTNANCON

PORT-NA-CON HOUSE ❑❑❑
Loch Eriboll IV27 4UN
*(0.25m off A838, on loch shore , 6 m SE of
Durness)*
☎ 01971 511367 🅕 01971 511367
Comfortable house peacefully set beside
picturesque Loch Eriboll. Emphasis on
local seafood.
*£ 3 bedrooms (1 fmly) No smoking Licensed
Air available for divers Mar-Oct* 🍴

ROGART

ROVIE ❑❑❑❑
IV28 3TZ *(A838 into village. 1st L over rail
crossing & follow sign to guest house)*
☎ 01408 641209 🅕 01408 641259
Home of the first AA Landlady of the Year.
Highest standards of accommodation and
food. Home baking legendary.
*6 bedrooms (1 fmly) No smoking in 4
bedrooms No smoking in dining room or in
lounges Children's facilities Golf 9 Fishing
Rough shooting Trout fishing 120 acres beef
sheep Closed Dec-mid Mar*

Ben Loyal

ROSEHALL

ACHNESS ★★
IV27 4BD *(just off A837 Bonar Bridge to Lochinver Road)*
☎ 01549 441239 🌐 01549 441324
Many guests return regularly to this small comfortable fishing hotel. Hot buffet table.
5 bedrooms 7 annexe bedrooms Fishing Closed Oct–Feb 🍴

SCOURIE

EDDRACHILLES ★★
Badcall Bay IV27 4TH
(2m S on A894, 7m N of Kylesku Bridge)
☎ 01971 502080 🌐 01971 502477
££ 11 bedrooms (1 fmly) No dogs (ex guide dogs) Fishing Boats for hire No children under 3yrs Closed Nov–Feb 🍴

SCOURIE ★★
IV27 4SX *(on A894 in Scourie)*
☎ 01971 502396 🌐 01971 502423
Extensive fishing rights on a 25,000 acre estate - an anglers' paradise. Relaxed friendly atmosphere.
18 bedrooms 2 annexe bedrooms (2 fmly) Fishing Pool table Closed mid Oct –end Mar 🍴

SHIELDAIG

TIGH AN EILEAN ★★⊛
IV54 8XN
☎ 01520 755251 🌐 01520 755321
On the sea-shore amidst whitewashed crofts and fishermen's cottages, sheltered by pines. Skilful cooking.
££ 11 bedrooms (1 fmly) No smoking in restaurant Closed Nov–Easter 🍴

STRATHPEFFER

BRUNSTANE LODGE ★★
Golf Rd IV14 9AT
☎ 01997 421261
Elevated position, warm welcome and high standards at this Victorian lodge.
££ 7 bedrooms (2 fmly) No dogs Children's facilities No smoking in restaurant Closed 1 & 2 Jan 🍴

CRAIGVAR ◫◫◫◫◫
The Square IV14 9DL
☎ 01997 421622 🌐 01997 421796
Lovingly restored Georgian house overlooking The Square of this highland spa town.
£ 3 bedrooms No smoking in dining room or lounges Direct dial from bedrooms No dogs (ex guide dogs) Closed Xmas & New Year 🍴

INVER LODGE ◫◫◫
IV14 9DL *(from A834 through town centre, turn by Spa Pavilion signposted Bowling Green, Inver Lodge on R)*
☎ 01997 421392
Sound standards of accommodation with a welcoming atmosphere and delicious food.
£ 2 bedrooms (1 fmly) No dogs Children's facilities Fishing and riding can be arranged Mar–mid Dec 🍴

STRATHY

CATALINA ◫◫◫◫
Aultivullin KW14 7RY
(turn off A836 at Strathy into Strathy Point Rd, 1.5m turn L and 1m to end)
☎ 01641 541279 🌐 01641 541314
Unique and relaxing experience at this comfortable former croft house. Meals taken at times to suit guests.
£ 1 bedroom No smoking No children Walking

TAIN

MORANGIE HOUSE ★★★
Morangie Rd IV19 1PY *(from S turn R off A9)*
☎ 01862 892281 🌐 01862 892872
Welcoming family-run hotel with fine views of Dornoch Firth. Eating options.
££ 26 bedrooms (1 fmly) No smoking in 4 bedrooms Night porter 🍴

MANSFIELD HOUSE ★★★
Scotsburn Rd IV19 1PR
(A9 from S, ignore 1st exit signed Tain & take 2nd exit signed police station)
☎ 01862 892052 🌐 01862 892260
Impressive extended mansion house which in own grounds opposite the Royal Academy. Friendly staff.
££ 8 bedrooms 10 annexe bedrooms (6 fmly) No smoking in 4 bedrooms Night porter Croquet lawn Beauty Salon offering beauty therapies, aromatheray, reflexology No smoking in restaurant 🍴

GOLF VIEW HOUSE◫◫◫◫
13 Knockbreck Rd IV19 1BN
(1st R off A9 at Tain (B9174), follow for 0.5m, house signposted on R)
☎ 01862 892856 🌐 01862 892856
Warm welcome assured this former manse in two acres of secluded gardens. Splendid views to the Firth.
£ 5 bedrooms (1 fmly) No smoking in bedrooms No dogs (ex guide dogs) Closed 16 Dec–15 Jan 🍴

THURSO

PARK HOTEL ★★
KW14 8RE
(on approach to Thurso on R of A882)
☎ 01847 893251 🌐 01847 893252
Modern styled, family operated hotel offers bright well equipped bedrooms - most being suitable for families.
£ 11 bedrooms (8 fmly) No smoking in restaurant Closed 1-3 Jan 🍴

TONGUE

BEN LOYAL ★★⊛
IV27 4XE *(village centre. Tongue on intersection of A838/A836)*
☎ 01847 611216 🌐 01847 611212
Comfortable holiday and sporting hotel with splendid outlook. Tempting range of Taste of Scotland specialities.
£ 12 bedrooms Fishing Pool table Fly fishing tuition No smoking in restaurant Closed Nov-Feb Res late Oct–Mar & early Apr 🍴

TONGUE

TONGUE ★★
IV27 4XD *(from A9 turn L after Bonar Bridge onto A836. In Tongue, 1st hotel on R)*
☎ 01847 611206 🌐 01847 611345
Former Victorian hunting lodge now a long established sporting and holiday hotel.
££ 9 bedrooms (2 fmly) No smoking in 14 bedrooms Fishing Pool table Pony trekking No smoking in restaurant Closed Oct–Mar 🍴

TORRIDON

LOCH TORRIDON ★★★⊛⊛
IV22 2EY
(from A832 at Kinochewe take A896 towards Torridon. Do not turn into village, continue for 1m, hotel on R)
☎ 01445 791242 🌐 01445 791296
Former shooting lodge with wooded mountain backdrop and Highland cattle grazing in the fields around.
££££ 21 bedrooms (4 fmly) No smoking in all bedrooms No dogs (ex guide dogs) Lift Fishing Pool table Croquet lawn No smoking in restaurant 🍴

ULLAPOOL

CEILIDH PLACE ★★
West Argyle St IV26 2TY
(along Shore St, pass pier and take 1st R, hotel at top of hill)
☎ 01854 612103 🌐 01854 612886
Refreshingly different. Regular and varied music festivals, drama and exhibitions. Genuine hospitality.
13 bedrooms Children's facilities No smoking in restaurant 🍴

ARDVRECK ◫◫◫◫◫
Morefield Brae IV26 2TH
(N out of Ullapool on A835, 1.5m to top of hill turn L at sign to Ardvreck)
☎ 01854 612028 🌐 01854 613000
Spectacular views over Loch Broom towards Ullapool from this friendly family-run guesthouse.
£ 10 bedrooms (2 fmly) No smoking No dogs (ex guide dogs) Children's facilities Closed 1 Dec–28 Feb 🍴

DROMNAN ◫◫◫◫
Garve Rd IV26 2SX *(turn L at 30mph sign as you enter town from A835)*
☎ 01854 6123333 🌐 01854 6123333
Comfortable family home overlooking Loch Broom provides comfortable tourist accommodation.
£ 7 bedrooms (2 fmly) No smoking No dogs (ex guide dogs) 🍴

THE SHEILING ◫◫◫◫
Garve Rd IV26 2SX
(on A835, at S end of village)
☎ 01854 612947 🌐 01854 612947
Overlooking Loch Broom this house has been extended to provide comfortable accommodation.
7 bedrooms No smoking No dogs (ex guide dogs) Fishing Sauna Closed Xmas & New Year

LADYSMITH HOUSE & SCOTTISH LARDER ◫◫
24 Pulteney St IV26 2UP
(from E, continue on North Rd which turns R after Royal Hotel, take 2nd on L)
☎ 01854 612185
Near the waterfront this is both a bed and breakfast house and a restaurant.
£ 6 bedrooms (1 fmly) No smoking in dining room Licensed Res New Year–Easter (restaurant closed)

WICK

MACKAY'S ★★
Union St KW1 5ED
(opposite Caithness General Hospital)
☎ 01955 602323 ☏ 01955 605930
Long established commercial hotel on the south shore of the River Wick near the town centre.
26 bedrooms (4 fmly) Lift Night porter Closed 1–2 Jan 🐟

MERCURY ★★
Riverside KW1 4NL
☎ 01955 603344 ☏ 01955 605456
In the town close to the river, this purpose built hotel offers a split-level bar and spacious restaurant.
££ 48 bedrooms (5 fmly) Night porter Closed 26 Dec–7 Jan 🐟

THE CLACHAN ◫◫◫◫
South Rd KW1 5NH
(on A9 1st house on R. S side of Wick)
☎ 01955 605384
Enthusiastic owner maintains high standards at this welcoming and comfortable detached home. Hearty breakfasts.
£ 3 bedrooms No smoking No dogs No children under 7yrs

> **Call the AA Hotel Booking Service on 0990 050505 to book at AA recognised hotels and B&Bs in the UK, or through our internet site: http://www.theaa.co.uk/hotels**

WHERE TO EAT

RESTAURANTS

AA RECOMMENDED

BRORA

ROYAL MARINE HOTEL ❀
Golf Road KW9 6QS
☎ 01408 621252 ☏ 01408 621181
The carte is supported by a range of house specialities and visitors enjoy ample choice. Good use of quality produce is seen in a pan-fried seafood terrine, and local lobster with a thermidor sauce.
ALC ££ 🐟

CONTIN

COUL HOUSE ❀
By Strathpeffer IV14 9EY
☎ 01997 421487 ☏ 01997 421945
'Taste of Scotland' dishes feature prominently on a something for everyone menu. Roast crown of Highland lamb stuffed with smoked ham and mushrooms in a red wine sauce. Look out for Ecclefechan butter tart.
Fixed D £££ ALC ££ 🐟

DINGWELL

KINKELL HOUSE ❀
Easter Kinkell IV7 8HY
☎ 01349 861270 ☏ 01349 865902
Typical main courses include seared scallops with fettucine, and pan-fried fillet of venison with sloe gin sauce. A star dessert is the delicious Kinkell brioche bread and butter pudding.
Fixed L £ ALC ££ 🐟

DUNDONNELL

DUNDONNELL HOTEL ❀
IV23 2QS
☎ 01854 633204 ☏ 01854 633366
A dinner here could feature a delicious parcel of smoked salmon filled with trout mousse, courgette and ginger soup, and medley of seafood served with vermouth and dill sauce.
Fixed D ££ 🐟

FORT WILLIAM

CRANNOG RESTAURANT ❀
PH33 7NG
☎ 01397 705589 ☏ 01397 705026
The building is a converted fishermen's bait shed, with white walls, blue carpet and natural wood furniture. There's a patio section with spectacular views of Loch Linnhe, where you can see the boats off-loading the day's catch. Scottish seafood is the speciality of the house, particularly local langoustine.
ALC ££ 🐟

GARVE

INCHBAE LODGE HOTEL ❀
Inchbae IV23 2PH
☎ 01997 455269 ☏ 01997 455207
Freshly prepared, good local produce such as pot-roasted whole wood pigeon braised with red wine, mushrooms, bacon and celery. Other dishes might include chicken liver, garlic and herb pâté, mint, pea and lettuce soup and sticky toffee pudding. Booking for non-residents is essential.
Fixed D ££ 🐟

KYLESKU

KYLESKU HOTEL ❀
Lairg IV27 4HW
☎ 01971 502231 ☏ 01971 502313
With a good reputation for seafood that guests can often see landed minutes before it appears on their dinner table. Expect local salmon with lobster sauce, pan-fried haddock, and grilled jumbo langoustine with garlic mayonnaise.
Fixed L £ ALC £ 🐟

LOCHINVER

LOCHINVER LARDER ❀
Main Street IV27 4JY
☎ 01571 844356 ☏ 01571 844688
This restaurant-cum-coffee shop serves a home-cooked mix of local seafood, prime sirloin steaks and other dishes such as chicken in white wine, roghan josh lamb curry and nut roast. Childrens meals available.
ALC ££ 🐟

MUIR OF ORD

THE DOWER HOUSE ❀❀
Highfield IV6 7XN
☎/☏ 01463 870090
The no-choice menu (apart from dessert) could begin with spinach tagliatelle, sliced scallops and cockles or excellent roasted pepper soup. On to fillet of beef with rösti, and shallot marmalade. Orange crème brûlée, decorated with caramelised orange peel, finishes a meal nicely.
Fixed D £££ 🐟

Altnaharrie Inn

PLOCKTON

HAVEN HOTEL ❀
IV52 8TW
☎ 01599 544223 📠 01599 544467
The kitchen combines up-to-date thinking
with the best quality ingredients to
produce dishes such as Plockton prawns
with lime and coriander dip and honey-
roasted gammon with a plum and sherry
sauce.
Fixed D £ £ 🍽

SHIELDAIG

TIGH AN EILEAN HOTEL ❀
Strathcarron IV54 8XN
☎ 01520 755251 📠 01520 755321
The 'house of the island' produces a short
menu of popular dishes, which includes
local fish, beef and lamb, and is
sympathetically cooked to retain full
flavours.
Fixed D £ £ 🍽

SPEAN BRIDGE

OLD STATION RESTAURANT ❀
Station Road PH34 4EP
☎ 01397 712535
Trainspotting is an added attraction at this
popular little restaurant carved out of the
ticket office of a still working station. From
the short menu try baked goat's cheese,
grilled duck breast with apricot and lemon
sauce, and white chocolate cheesecake.
ALC £ £ 🍽

TONGUE

BEN LOYAL HOTEL ❀
Sutherland IV27 4XE
☎ 01847 611216 📠 01847 611212
A short, well balanced menu features
quality Scottish produce. Expect leek and
potato soup, Scrabster cod with Orkney
cheese sauce, and Atholl brose for
pudding.
Fixed D £ £ 🍽

TORRIDON

LOCH TORRIDON ❀❀
Achnasheen IV22 2EY
☎ 01445 791242 📠 01445 791296
The wood-panelled dining room provides
a formal setting for creative cooking such
as langoustine, scallop and potato terrine,
halibut with a mushroom crust and
tomato, basil and black olive compote. For
dessert, a lemon tart and a bitter sweet
chocolate sorbet.
Fixed D £ £ £ 🍽

ULLAPOOL

ALTNAHARRIE INN ❀❀❀❀❀
IV26 2SS
☎ 01854 633230
Wow! This is a truly magical place. Gunn
Ericksen's cooking is simply outstanding -
words can hardly describe it. Guests never
eat the same dish twice - meticulous
records are kept. On one occasion
canapés were whole prawns served warm
with a parsley and garlic dressing, and a
small light pastry case filled with creamed
salmon and prawn roe topped with caviar.
Dinner opened with the lightest of
seafood mousses, next came lobster soup
with mayonnaise and crème fraîche
crammed with the freshest lobster, topped
with truffle. Main course was squab
pigeon served with chanterelle
mushrooms and a sweet rowan jelly.
Then cheese, a wide selection of Scottish,
French, English and Irish, all perfectly
presented. Pineapple pudding proved to
be a warm tart of sweet, tender pineapple,
a slightly sharper pineapple sauce and a
small amount of caramel. (Incidently you
don't get away with just one pudding!).
Fixed D £ £ £ 🍽

THE ISLANDS

Glancing at a map of Scotland reveals a liberal sprinkling of islands anchored off its north and west coasts. It is the savage beauty of these islands that has helped to shape Scotland's character over the years, forging its reputation as one of the wildest, most spectacular regions of Europe. Its is easy to spend much of your time here island hopping, and there is so much to see and do that you'll want to return again and again. Once you leave the Scottish mainland, you are filled with an immediate sense of adventure. This is where seascape and landscape meet to create a magical world steeped in history and legend and unique in character and culture. Here, scattered islands and outlying archipelagoes are blessed with long hours of summertime daylight, jagged mountain ridges offer wonderful views to distant horizons and craggy cliffs spill down to white sandy beaches.

The two most northerly island groups are Orkney and Shetland, which are closer to the Arctic Circle that London. In fact, Shetland is more than 100 miles from the Scottish coast, so remote from the rest of the country that it might just as well belong in a distant quarter of the world. The communities of Lewis, Harris, Uist and Barra in the Outer Hebrides also have an isolated feel to them; lonely outposts in one of Scotland's loneliest locations. But it is the remoteness of these islands that adds to their appeal.

Closer to the mainland and, on the whole, more accessible for the visitor are the islands of the Inner Hebrides – Mull, Iona, Coll, Tiree, Jura and Islay among them. Wherever you venture in these islands, there is always something new and unexpected to see; perhaps a hidden mountain path to climb or a secret bay to explore. It is the relaxing air of tranquility, wealth of attractions and immense variety of scenery that make Scotland's islands such a favourite holiday destination. When people fall in love with this enchanting corner of Britain, the affair usually lasts a lifetime.

EVENTS & FESTIVALS

January

Fire Festival,
Scalloway, Shetland

Up Helly Aa,
Lerwick, Shetland

Feburary

Traditional Music Festival,
Dornie, Isle of Skye

Scottish Drama Festival,
Portree, Isle of Skye

Up Helly Aa,
Bressay, Cullivoe,
Nesting & Girlsta, Northmavin and,
Uyeasound, Shetland

April

Mull Music Festival

Jazz Festival,
Stromness, Orkney

Shetland Folk Festival,
venues throughout Shetland

May

Isle of Bute Jazz Festival

Arran Dramafest

Arran Festival of Music
Islay Festival (late May-end June)
The Highland Festival
various locations, Skye & The Western Isles

Country & Irish Music Festival,
venues across Orkney

Orkney Folk Festival,
Stromness

Classic Motor Show,
Clickimin Centre, Lerwick

June

Arran Festival of Folk

Cumbrae Week
Isle of Cumbrae

Loch Maddy Boat Festival,
Isle of North Uist

St Magnus Festival,
Kirkwall & Stromness Orkney

St Andrews Gala
Orkney

Finstown Gala Day
Orkney

Regattas
Burra & Sandwick, Shetland

Whiteness & Weisdale
Gala & Regatta
Shetland

Grand Gala and Mid Summer
Festival,
Lerwick, Shetland

RSPB Open Day,
Fetlar

Lerwick Lifeboat Gala Day
Shetland

July

Isle of Bute Folk Festival
Tiree Festival

Tobermory Highland Games,
Isle of Mull

Isle of Barra Festival

Hebridean Celtic Music Festival,
Stornaway, Isle of Lewis

Highland Games,
Tong, Isle of Lewis, Borve, Isle of Barra,
Hosta, Isle of North Uist, Askernish, Isle of
South Uist

Isle of Harris Gala

Berneray Week,
Berneray, Isle of North Uist

Feisean (Music & Drama Festivals)
Stornoway, Isle of Lewis, Paible, North Uist,
Harris & Barra

Skye Folk Festival,
Portree, Isle of Skye

Dunvegan Castle Music Festival,
Isle of Skye

Skye & Lochalsh Festival

Regattas
Longhope, Stronsay, Stromness and Westray,
Orkney

Hoy Gala Day,
Orkney

Sanday Show,
Orkney

Regattas, *Brae, Airth Uyeasound (Unst),*
Buravoe (Yell), Walls and Skeld, Shetland

Scalloway Gala
Shetland

August

Isle of Bute Country Music Festival

Bute Highland Games

Corrie Capers,
Corrie, Isle of Arran

Highland Games,
Brodick, Isle of Arran

Millport Country & Western Festival,
Isle of Cumbrae

Isle of Cumbrae Gala Day,
Islay Agricultural Show

Salen Show & Dance,
Isle of Mull

Islay Raft Race

Fish Festival,
Stornoway, Isle of Lewis

Lewis Carnival,
Stornoway, Isle of Lewis

Harris Arts Featival,
Tarbert, Isle of Harris

Isle of Skye Highland Gathering,
Portree, Isle of Skye

Isle of Skye Show,
Portree, Isle of Skye

Kirkwall Regatta,
Orkney

East Mainland Show.
St Andrews Showpark, Orkney

Shapinsay Show
Orkney

Hope Show
Orkney

West Mainland Show,
Dounby, Orkney

Orkney County Show,
Bignold Park, Kirkwal, Orkneyl

Orkney Vintage Rally,
Kirkwall, Orkney

St Magnus Fair,
Kirkwall, Orkney

Holm Regatta
Orkney

Festival of the Horse & Boys
Ploughing Match,
South Ronaldsay, Oekney

Regattas,
Mid Yell, Scalloway, Bastavoe (Yell) and
Lerwick, Shetland

Agricultural Shows
Voe, Cunningsburgh, Walls and Unst,
Shetland

September

Fiddlers' Rally,
Isle of Mull

Fishing Co-ops (UK) Exhibition,
Stornoway, Isle of Lewis

New Music Festival,
venues throughout Skye & Lochalsh
Orkney Science Festival,
venues across Orkney

October

Tiree Wave Classic

Tour of Mull Car Rally,
Isle of Mull

Shetland Accordian
& Fiddle Festival

December

Christmas Day Ba'
Kirkwall

THE CLYDE ISLANDS
(ARRAN, BUTE & CUMBRAE)

The Isle of Arran, located at the gateway to the Firth of Clyde, is only a 30-minute ferry ride from Kintyre and the access points of the Scottish mainland. With few roads and miles of unpopulated open country, Arran has a real island feel about it – many have described it as Scotland in miniature. To the south lies a gentle fertile plain while in the north the scene is made up of dramatic hills and granite peaks – many of them rising to over 2,000ft in an area of 12 square miles. It is this changing character that adds to Arran's appeal and makes it one of Scotland's most alluring island haunts.

Bute is just a stone's throw from the Cowal Peninsula and the island's close proximity to the Scottish mainland makes it an obvious destination for many day visitors and holidaymakers. It is here you can discover some of the finest golden beaches anywhere on the west coast. But there is much more to Bute than its spectacular coastline and gently curving bays dotted with sails. It may not boast the wild mountain grandeur of some of Scotland's other islands, but Bute is blessed with swathes of heathery moorland and a range of low, fertile hills – perfect for walking and studying the local wildlife

Next door to Bute and a 30-minute ferry journey from Largs on the Ayrshire coast, the Cumbrae Islands feature firmly on Scotland's list of lesser-known treasures. Nicknamed Big and Wee Cumbrae, the two islands couldn't be more different in character and scenery. Little Cumbrae is the playground of divers, yachtsmen and fishermen, while Great Cumbrae Island, to the north, has more general appeal, with plenty to attract the holidaymaker, as well as the short stay visitor.

PRINCIPAL TOWNS

BRODICK, ISLE OF ARRAN

Overlooking Brodick Bay with the magnificent peak of Goatfell as a backdrop, the bustling village of Brodick, with its sandy beach, numerous hotels and guesthouses is the island's main resort and the port of call for the ferry from Ardrossan in Ayrshire.

ROTHESAY, ISLE OF BUTE

Centred around a 13th-century ruined fortress and commanding a delightful position overlooking Rothesay Bay, the old traditional resort of Rothesay maintains a distinct Victorian and Edwardian feel about it. Until the 1950s it was probably the most popular of the Clyde resorts, with paddle steamers ferrying hundreds of people from Glasgow for their holidays. Thanks to serious local investment the Winter Garden, a unique, iron and glass structure built in the 1920's on the esplanade, has been beautifully restored. The town offers visitors a comprehensive range of leisure activities and accommodation, making it the obvious base from which to explore the island.

MUST SEE

BRODICK CASTLE, GARDEN & COUNTRY PARK.
Brodick, Arran ☎ 01770 302202

Visit Arran's most famous attraction, a tall, stately castle of red sandstone, surrounded by lovely gardens and fronted by a magnificent bay, with views of majestic mountains dominated by Goatfell. Built in the 13th century on the site of a Viking fortress, it was extended in 1652 and 1844 and has been the stronghold of the Earls of Arran since 1503. Splendid silver, fine porcelain and paintings acquired over the centuries can be seen, including many sporting pictures and trophies. Enjoy wandering around the restored 18th-century formal gardens and through one of Europe's finest woodland gardens, famous for its rhododendrons and azaleas. There is also an adventure playgound, a shop and a restaurant.

Call the AA Hotel Booking Service on 0990 050505 to book at AA recognised hotels and B&Bs in the UK, or through our internet site: http://www.theaa.co.uk/hotels

Brodick Castle, Garden & Country Park

MACHRIE MOOR STANDING STONES,
Near Blackwaterfoot, Arran

Arran is rich with prehistoric monuments but the most impressive lie on the desolate and quite beautiful Machrie Moor. Here you will see a remarkable collection of Bronze age (around 4,000 years old) standing stones, chambered cairns and hut circles. The five mystical, yet fragmentary, stone cirles, feature some individual stones at over 15-ft in height.

MOUNT STUART HOUSE & GARDENS
Rothesay, Bute ☎ 01700 503877

View the ancestral home of the Marquesses of Bute, a majestic Victorian Gothic palace with plenty to admire within its splendid interior, from the amazing Marble Hall with galleries, stained glass and astronomical painted vault, to outstanding furniture, paintings and tapestries. Outside, there are 300 acres of designed landscape and gardens to explore. Picnic area and tearoom.

ART GALLERIES

MICHAEL MAIN GALLERY,
Auchrannie Rd, Brodick, Arran
☎ 01770 302007

Paintings and sculpture by Scottish contemporary artists.

LOCHRANZA STUDIO GALLERY,
Lochranza, Arran ☎ 01770 830651

MUSEUMS

BUTE MUSEUM,
Stuart St, Rothesay, Bute ☎ 01700 502033

Displays and exhibits, housed in two small galleries, explain all you need to know about Bute, from its natural and ancient history and geology, to models of old Clyde steamers.

ARRAN HERITAGE CENTRE,
Rosaburn, Arran ☎ 01770 302636

Learn about island life over the centuries at this 18th-century croft farm, complete with blacksmith's shop, milk house, and a cottage restored to its pre-1920 state.

MUSEUM OF THE CUMBRAES,
Millport, Cumbrae ☎ 01475 530741

Illustrates the history of Millport, the island and its people over the centuries.

HISTORIC & ANCIENT SITES

KING'S CAVE,
Drumadoon, Blackwaterfoot, Arran

Reached by a coastal footpath or a track from the Machrie to Torbeg road, this cave is where Robert the Bruce was supposedly inspired by a spider refusing to admit defeat while attempting to spin a web, True or not, there are rock carvings of typical Pictish hunting scenes inside.

LOCHRANZA CASTLE,
Lochranza, Arran

Former hunting lodge established by the Stewart Kings of Scotland in the 14th century on the shores of Loch Ranza.

ROTHESAY CASTLE,
Rothesay, Bute ☎ 01700 502691

Partly ruined 13th-century fortress, one of the best preserved early castles in Scotland.

ST BLANE'S CHAPEL,
Southern end of Bute

A 6th-century religious foundation with a 12th-century ruined chapel, enjoying a peaceful location amid hushed trees..

GREAT FOR KIDS

NORTH SANNOX FARM PARK,
Sannox, Arran ☎ 01770 810222

Children will love Ollie the llama and enjoy the company of small and pet animals, including chipmunks and pigs.

SOUTH BANK FARM PARK,
East Bennan Arran ☎ 01770 820221

Enjoy a day out at this working farm which exhibits rare and minority breeds of farm animals and poultry.

HOMES & GARDENS

ARDENCRAIG GARDENS,
Rothesay, Bute PA20 9HA
☎ 01700 504225

A splendid show garden with fuschia greenhouses and rare plants. Tearoom.

BIG OUTDOORS

GLENASHADALE FALLS & GIANT'S GRAVES,
south of Whiting Bay, Arran

Cascading waterfall situated up a steep, wooded glen. Also signposted is the nearby stone circle (Giant's Graves) that is associated with Fionn MacCumhail.

GLEN SANNOX,
near Sannox Bay, north of Brodick, Arran

One of Arran's wildest glens, a delightful secret place with a dramatic moorland landscape surrounded by lofty peaks.

ESSENTIAL INFORMATION

TOURIST INFORMATION

INFORMATION CENTRES

AYRSHIRE & ARRAN TOURIST BOARD,
Burns House, Burns Statue Square, Ayr,
South Ayrshire
☎ 01292 262555 📠 01292 269555
ARRAN,
The Pier, Brodick, Arran
☎ 01770 302140 📠 01770 302395
BUTE,
15 Victoria St, Rothesay, Bute
☎ 01700 502151
CUMBRAE seasonal,
28 Stuart St, Millport, Cumbrae
☎ 01475 530753

TRANSPORT

AIR ACCESS

GLASGOW INTERNATIONAL AIRPORT
☎ 0141 887 1111
PRESTWICK AIRPORT ☎ 01292 479822

SEA ACCESS

CALEDONIAN MACBRAYNE FERRIES,
☎ 01475 650100
Operates all the ferries serving Arran, Bute
and Cumbrae with the mainland.

BOAT TRIPS & CRUISES

PS WAVERLEY,
☎ 0141 221 8152
Paddle steamer cruises in summer from
Rothesay Pier, Bute.

BUS SERVICES

STAGECOACH ARRAN,
Brodick, Arran ☎ 01770 302000
Open-top, vintage or coach tours of Arran.

STAGECOACH WESTERN BUSES LTD,
☎ 01700 502076
Open-top bus or coach tours of Bute.

CAR HIRE

A C HENDRY,
Brodick, Arran ☎ 01770 302274

CYCLE HIRE

BRODICK CYCLES,
Brodick, Arran ☎ 01770 302460
F V G MAPES & SON,
Millport, Cumbrae ☎ 01475 530444
MOUNTAIN BIKE CENTRE,
Rothesay, Bute ☎ 01700 502333

CRAFTS

*Crafts to look out for include pottery,
ceramics, woodcraft, knitwear and
jewellery making. The Isle of Bute has
few craft shops*

ARRAN POTTERY,
Thunderguy, Arran ☎ 01770 850238

ISLAND PORCELAIN,
Kilmory, Arran ☎ 01770 870360
OLD PIER CRAFT CENTRE,
Whiting Bay, Arran ☎ 01770 700484
PINE CRAFT SHOP,
Rothesay, Bute ☎ 01700 502891
TRAREOCH CRAFT & WOOL SHOP,
Whiting Bay, Arran ☎ 01770 700226
THE WHINS CRAFT WORKSHOP,
Lochranza, Arran ☎ 01770 830650

ENTERTAINMENT

CINEMA

WINTER GARDEN VISITOR CENTRE,
Rothesay, Bute ☎ 01700 502487
Restored 1920s seaside theatre with
entertainment and cinema facilities,

FOOD & DRINK

*On Arran & Bute try the specialist
cheeses and the excellent range of fresh
fish and seafood, and, from Arran, take
home a bottle of whisky distilled at
Scotland's newest malt whisky distillery*

CHEESES

'Arran' cheddar - a mellow medium to
mature cheddar with a creamy soft
texture. Dunlop - soft textured cheese
resembling Scottish cheddar. Brodick Blue
- ewes milk blue cheese; the Arran Blue is
made from cows milk. On Bute, lookout
for 'Drumleish', a mild cheese, and the
hard Bute cheddar.

ISLAND CHEESE CO LTD,
Brodick, Arran ☎ 01770 302788
ROTHESAY CREAMERY,
Rothesay, Bute ☎ 01700 503186

WHISKY DISTILLERY TOURS

ARRAN DISTILLERS,
Lochranza, Arran ☎ 01770 830264
Visitor centre and distillery tours.

SPORT & LEISURE

ACTIVITY CENTRES

ARRAN OUTDOOR CENTRE,
Shiskine, Arran ☎ 01770 860333
BUTE OUTDOOR ACTIVITIES,
Rothesay, Bute ☎ 01700 504250

ANGLING

Arran is noted for its freshwater fishing,
especially on the rivers Machrie and Iorsa,
and popular places to fish for trout are
Loch Garbad (brown trout) and Port-na-
Lochan Fishery (rainbow trout), near
Blackwaterfoot. Bute is unique in offering
game, coarse and sea fishing

CYCLING

Great Cumbrae, at only four miles (6.4km)
long and two miles (3.2km) wide, has few
hills and virtually traffic-free roads making

it the perfect destination for family cycling.
Equally appealing, although requiring
more stamina, are the larger Isles Bute
and Arran, the latter offering an undulating
route right around the island.

GOLF COURSES

For a full list contact the Tourist Offices.

LAMLASH,
Arran ☎ 01770 600296
Undulating heathland course with
magnificent views of mountains and sea.

ROTHESAY,
Bute ☎ 01700 502244
A scenic, fairly hilly course with views of
Rothesay Bay and the Kyles of Bute.

LEISURE CENTRES

AUCHRANNIE LEISURE CENTRE,
Brodick, Arran ☎ 01770 302234

KINLOCH HOTEL LEISURE CENTRE,
Blackwaterfoot, Arran ☎ 01770 860444

PARAGLIDING

FLYING FEVER,
Kildonan, Arran ☎ 01770 820292

RIDING

CLOYBURN EQUESTRIAN CENTRE,
Brodick, Arran ☎ 01770 302800

NORTH SANNOX TREKKING CENTRE,
Arran ☎ 01770 810222

ROTHESAY RIDING CENTRE,
Bute ☎ 01700 504971

SAILING

Pontoons for boats are available at
Lochranza, Brodick and Lamlash on Arran,
at Millport on Cumbrae, and at Rothesay
and Port Bannatyne on Bute.

SWIMMING

BEACHES

You will find peaceful sheltered bays with
good sandy beaches on all the islands

ROTHESAY LEISURE POOL,
Bute ☎ 01700 504300 ext 217

WALKING

Arran offers strenuous hill walks, including
a challenging ascent of Goatfell, Arran's
highest peak at 2,866ft (874m), and
gentle, low-level woodland strolls. The less
dramatic, but equally memorable,
landscape of Bute offers walkers
undemanding moorland walks and coastal
strolls. Tiny Cumbrae is the perfect size for
a day's exploration on foot.

WATERSPORTS

BUTE SUB-AQUA CENTRE,
Ascog, Bute ☎ 01700 505271

INNER HEBRIDES
(COLL & TIREE, COLONSAY, GIGHA, ISLAY, JURA, MULL & IONA)

Jura, one of the wildest and most mysterious of the Hebridean islands, is a geological masterpiece. Most of the island consists of a fascinating mixture of moorland, rock and peat bog. This is Britain at its most primitive – an empty, uncultivated landscape largely inhabited by deer and their stalkers. For some the island may be something of an acquired taste, perhaps too quiet and remote, but whatever your preference, Jura is undeniably a beautiful place – timeless and unspoilt.

Islay, pronounced I'la, is synonymous with whisky distilling. The most southerly of those islands that form the Inner Hebrides, Islay's scenery is very varied and includes everything from boggy lowlands to dramatic cliffs. To the north of Islay and to the west of Jura lie Colonsay and Oronsay, which join forces every day when low tide reveals a sandy beach linking the two neighbouring islands.

Mull is a magical place. Early summer is a good time to visit this unspoilt island, but then so is autumn, when the hills and mountains are often dusted with snow and the colours are glorious. But whatever time you choose to go to the island, there is always plenty to see and do. Mull's wild and breathtaking 300-mile (480km) coastline is home to all manner of wildlife. You may even catch sight of a golden eagle swooping across the island, a stunning image that will linger long in the memory. If you enjoy historic castles and beautiful gardens, then you will find much on the island to keep you entertained.

Coll is deceptively rugged when viewed from the sea. In fact, much of its interior is made up of heather moorland, while the coast is distinguished by bands of shell-sand and long, deep dunes. Visit Tiree in early summer and you will certainly benefit from its long hours of sunshine. In fact, the island is known as the sunniest place in Britain.

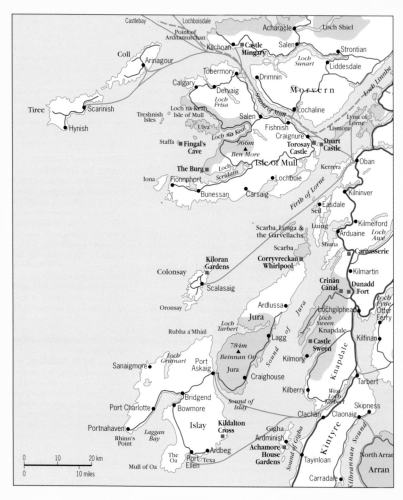

PRINCIPAL TOWNS

TOBERMORY, ISLE OF MULL

Visitors arriving by boat from Oban quickly make for Tobermory, the island's capital, enjoying a relaxing stroll along the picturesque waterfront, with its colour-washed houses rising steeply up a wooded bank and views across the harbour and Tobermory Bay. The harbour bustles, especially in season, with yachts and yachtsmen, giving this popular base for exploring Mull a lively atmosphere.

BOWMORE, ISLE OF ISLAY

Tiny Bowmore, a planned 18th-century village overlooking Loch Indaal, is well known among whisky enthusiasts, as it gives its name to the excellent malt whisky distilled at the island's oldest legal distillery, established in 1779 on the shores of the loch. Dominating the village and definately worth closer inspection is the unique, circular parish church. Visitors will find Bowmore's central position on the island a convenient place from which to tour the island.

MUST SEE

ACHAMORE HOUSE GARDENS,
Gigha PA41 7AD
☎ 01583 505267
Lying just 3 miles (4.8km) off the Kintyre coast and well worth the ferry journey from Tayinloan, tiny Gigha, at just 5 miles (8km) in length, has one of the region's unsung treasures in the remarkable woodland gardens at Achamore. Developed by Sir James Horlick, who bought the island in 1944, it is a paradise of rhododendrons, azaleas, camelias and other sub tropical plants and shrubs, thanks to the mild climate created by the warm air of the Gulf Stream.

CARSAIG ARCHES,
Carsaig, Mull
Take the footpath (west of Carsaig) at low tide along the coast to reach the impressive Carsaig Arches, two of the most spectacular natural rock formations on Mull. Giant tunnels in the black basalt, one some 140ft in length, have been created from former sea caves by waves.

FINGAL'S CAVE,
Staffa
During the season you can travel by boat from Iona and Mull to the uninhabited island of Staffa, famous for Fingal's Cave. The awesome, Cathedral-like cavern, 227ft long and 66ft high, is defenceless against the constant pounding of the Atlantic waves which inspired Mendelssohn's 'Hebridean Overture'. A visit to Staffa can be rough at any time of the year and it is not always possible to go ashore, but to take a boat trip to this isolated lump of rock, characterised by its distinctive basalt columns, a relic of volcanic actions, is always an unforgettable experience.

IONA,
accessible by ferry from Fionnphort on Mull
Iona hasn't changed in centuries and it was here, in 563 AD, that St Columba, Celtic poet, prophet and sage, landed from Ireland, dispatching his missionaries to convert Scotland to Christianity and founding the island's world famous abbey. Most visitors make straight for the abbey,

now the home of the Iona Community, founded in 1938, which welcomes pilgrims, but you should find time to explore the remains of the 13th-century priory, built for Augustinian nuns, and the oldest Christian cemetery in Scotland - the burial place of many Scottish kings - including, Duncan, murdered by Macbeth in 1040. John Smith, the late Labour Party leader, is also buried on the island.

TOROSAY CASTLE & GARDENS,
Craignure, Mull ☎ 01680 812421
Completed in the Scottish baronial-style, this beautiful and welcoming Victorian family home, with its 12 acres of superb gardens, is full of interest and character. Inside, you can view furniture, portraits and wildlife pictures, and browse through fascinating Edwardian family albums and scrapbooks. Take a stroll through the statue walk, lined with 19 lifesize limestone figures acquired from a deserted Italian villa, the water garden and the formal terraced gardens, all offset by dramatic views over the Sound of Mull.

ART GALLERIES

AN TOBAR - THE TOBERMORY CENTRE,
Argyll Ter, Tobermory, Mull
☎ 01688 302211
Venue for music, exhibitions, workshops and events.

MUSEUMS

FINLAGGAN VISITOR CENTRE,
Ballygrant, Islay ☎ 01496 840644
Ruins of the medieval centre of the Macdonalds, the Lords of the Isles. Learn about their story in the small visitor centre overlooking Loch Finlaggan, with its little island on which their headquarters stood.

MULL MUSEUM,
Main St, Tobermory, Mull
Learn all about the history of Mull, in particular, the fascinating story about the Spanish galleon, supposedly laden with treasure, which sank in Tobermory Bay in 1588, following the defeat of the Armada.

MUSEUM OF ISLAY LIFE,
Port Charlotte, Islay ☎ 01496 850358
Housed in a converted church, this award-winning museum covers all aspects of Islay life through the ages.

OLD BYRE HERITAGE CENTRE,
Dervaig, Mull ☎ 01688 400229
Discover Mull's past and crofting life through a fascinating tableaux of historical models.

HISTORIC & ANCIENT SITES

AROS CASTLE,
Salen, Mull
Situated on cliffs close to the Tobermory road north of Salen, this ruined 13th-century castle was the seat of government until the end of the 18th century.

DUNIVAIG CASTLE,
Lagavulin, Islay
Dating from the early 16th century, this impressive ruined stronghold was once the home of the Lords of the Isles, the Macdonalds.

KILDALTON CROSS,
Ardmore Point, Port Ellen, Islay
An impressively large 8th-century cross carved from epidiorite rock and decorated with Celtic motifs and figures.

KILNINIAN CHURCH,
Kilninian, Mull
The fine medieval gravestones, especially the one featuring Maclean, Chief of Torloisk, with helmet, sword and kilt, are worth stopping to see.

MACQUARIE MAUSOLEUM,
Gruline Home Farm, near Knock, Mull
An unusual monument to Lachlan Macquarie (1762-1824), soldier, administrator and Governor of New South Wales, known as the 'Father of Australia', who was born on the island of Ulva.

ORONSAY PRIORY,
Oronsay
Ruins of a 14th-century priory and a collection of ancient carved gravestones housed within the old Prior's House. The island is accessible by foot at low tide.

GREAT FOR KIDS

MULL ANGORA RABBIT FARM,
Bunessan, Mull ☎ 01681 700507
Stroke fluffy bunnies and watch clipping and spinning demonstrations. Also nature trails and a children's playground.

MULL & WEST HIGHLAND NARROW GAUGE RAILWAY,
Craignure, Mull ☎ 01680 812494
Enjoy a scenic journey on Scotland's first island passenger railway (260mm gauge), which runs for 1.5 miles (2.4km) between Craignure and Torosay Castle. Pulled by both steam and diesel locomotives, the carriages afford extensive and dramatic woodland and mountain views. Shop.

HOMES & GARDENS

DUART CASTLE,
Craignure, Mull ☎ 01680 812309
Perched at the end of a craggy point with wonderful views along the Sound of Mull, this fine castle is the ancient seat of the Maclean chiefs. You can visit the dungeons and view the state rooms in the keep, then climb to the top for spectacular views.

KILORAN GARDENS,
Colonsay
The grounds of Colonsay House, a rambling pink mansion owned by Lord Strathcona, feature tender rhododendrons, thickets of rampant escallonia and many much rarer species.

BIG OUTDOORS

Whether you desire deserted sandy beaches, bracing coastal walks, peaceful, traffic-free cycling, or extensive tidal sandflats, impressive sea cliffs and isolated moorland for some of the best wildlife watching in Scotland, then the Inner Hebrides, in particular Coll, Tiree, The Treshnish Isles and Islay, will more than satisfy those of you who love nature, wild open spaces and all the activities associated with the great outdoors.

ESSENTIAL INFORMATION

TOURIST INFORMATION

INFORMATION CENTRES

BOWMORE INFORMATION CENTRE,
The Square, Bowmore, Islay
☎ 01496 810254

CRAIGNURE INFORMATION CENTRE,
The Pier, Mull ☎ 01680 812377

TOBERMORY INFORMATION CENTRE
The Pier, Tobermory, Mull *seasonal,*
☎ 01688 302182

ACCESS

AIR ACCESS

Tiree, Colonsay and Islay are accessible by plane from Glasgow.

LOGANAIR ☎ 0141 889 3181

SEA ACCESS

CALEDONIAN MACBRAYNE FERRIES,
☎ 01475 650100
Operator of all the vehicle ferries throughout the Inner Hebridean Islands.

CRAFTS

Crafts to look out for include pottery, knitwear, jewellery, woodcraft, basketry and paintings by local artists.

THE CARTHOUSE GALLERY,
By Dervaig, Mull ☎ 01688 400256

CELTIC HOUSE,
Bowmore, Islay ☎/☎ 01496 810304

FARM COTTAGE CRAFTS,
Craignure, Mull ☎ 01680 812321

IONA POTTERY,
Iona ☎ 01681 700439

ISLAY WOOLLEN MILL COMPAY LTD,
Bridgend, Islay ☎ 01496 810563
The oldest working mill in Britain.

ISLE OF MULL WEAVERS,
Torosay Castle, Craignure, Mull
☎ 01680 812381

PORT ELLEN POTTERY,
Islay ☎ 01496 302345

ENTERTAINMENT

THEATRES

MULL LITTLE THEATRE,
Dervaig, Mull ☎ 01688 400245
The smallest professional theatre in Britain with only 43 seats.

FOOD & DRINK

The Inner Hebrides, notably Mull and Islay, are renowned for their whisky distilleries, the production of farmhouse cheeses and excellent fish and seafood.

CHEESES

'Dunlop', a soft textured cheese resembling Scottish cheddar, is made on Islay; ' Mull', an unpasteurised farmhouse cheddar is produced at Tobermory on Mull; 'Inverloch', a pasteurised goat's cheese is made on Gigha.

MULL CHEESES,
Sgriob-Ruadh Farm, Tobermory, Mull
☎ 01688 302235

WHISKY DISTILLERY TOURS

On Islay, there are 8 distilleries producing the world famous and distinctively peaty and strong malt whiskies. Mull and Jura have only one distillery.

BOWMORE DISTILLERY,
Bowmore, Islay ☎ 01496 810441

BUNNAHABHAIN DISTILLERY,
Port Askaig, Islay ☎ 01496 840646

CAOL ILA DISTILLERY,
Port Askaig, Islay ☎ 01496 840207
(appointment only)

LAGAVULIN DISTILLERY,
Port Ellen, Islay ☎ 01496 302400
(appointment only)

LAPHROAIG DISTILLERY,
Port Ellen, Islay ☎ 01496 302400
(appointment only)

TOBERMORY DISTILLERY,
Tobermory, Mull ☎ 01688 302645

TRANSPORT

BOAT TRIPS & CRUISES

CRAIGNURE CHARTERS,
Gorsten, Loch Don, Mull ☎ 01680 812332
Fishing & wildlife cruises.

GORDON GRANT MARINE,
Achavaich, Iona ☎ 01681 700338
Cruises to Staffa and the Treshnish Isles.

ISLAY MARINE CRUISES,
Gruinart, Bridgend, Islay ☎ 01496 850436
Sea angling and cruises.

CAR HIRE

BAYVIEW GARAGE,
Craignure, Mull ☎ 01680 812444

BOWMORE ENGINEERING,
Bowmore, Islay ☎ 01496 810206

CYCLE HIRE

GIGHA HOTEL,
Gigha ☎ 01583 505254

MACAULAY & TORRIE,
Port Ellen, Islay ☎ 01496 302053

VICKI & NEIL MACLEAN,
Tiree ☎ 018792 220482

PEDAL POWER,
Tobermory, Mull ☎ 01688 302480

WILDLIFE TOURS

MULL WILDLIFE EXPEDITIONS,
☎ 01688 302044

WILDLIFE WALKS & TALKS,
☎ 01951 200326
Walks and talks on Colonsay.

SPORT & LEISURE

ANGLING

On Islay, the rivers Duich and Sorn, and lochs Gorm, Torrabus and Ballygrant are excellent for salmon and trout. On Jura, the rivers Inver, Corran and Lussa are also noted for their salmon, although fishing is restricted due to much of it being on private estates. Mull has numerous spate rivers for good salmon and sea trout fishing, and several lochs (Mishnish, Tor, Frisa) for wet- or dry-fly fishing.

CYCLING

Cycling is the best (and cheapest) way to explore the islands, especially the smaller islands of Gigha, Coll, Tiree and Colonsay which make ideal day or weekend excursions. The larger islands of Mull and Islay may be more hilly, but they have better roads (can be busy in summer).

GOLF COURSES

COLONSAY ☎ 01951 200316

CRAIGNURE,
Mull ☎ 01680 812487

GIGHA ☎ 01583 505287

MACHRIE HOTEL,
Port Ellen, Islay ☎ 01496 302310

TOBERMORY,
Mull ☎ 01688 302338

RIDING

BALLIVICAR FARM,
Port Ellen, Islay ☎ 01496 302251

LOCHSIDE PONIES,
Crannich, Aros, Mull ☎ 01688 500206

WALKING

Mull is excellent for walking and exploring on foot. Parts of the island are surprisingly mountainous and if you feel particularly adventurous you could climb to the 3,169ft (966m) summit of Ben More - Mull's highest peak. In fact, all the islands in the Inner Hebrides, especially Islay, Jura and the smaller islands of Coll and Tirees, are best explored on foot.

WATERSPORTS

ISLAY DIVING CENTRE ☎ 01496 302441

MULL DIVING CENTRE,
Salen, Mull ☎ 01680 300411

SKYE & THE WESTERN ISLES

Fifty miles (80km) long and never more than 6 miles (10km) from the sea, Skye is infused with a tangible air of the past. With tracts of heather moorland, plenty of rugged mountain scenery and hundreds of years of history and legend running through it, the island is one of the most popular holiday destinations in Scotland. The jagged peaks and high ridges of the Cuillin Hills conspire to offer the visitor a wonderful outdoor playground for walking and climbing, though much of it is reserved only for the most experienced and hardened enthusiast. However, there are many parts of Skye which reveal a softer face, places where you can escape the tourists and be completely alone.

Characterised by their own language and culture and blessed with miles of glorious scenery, the Western Isles are more commonly known as the Outer Hebrides. Facing the Atlantic and stretching from the Butt of Lewis in the north to Barra Head in the south, this 130 mile (208km) chain of islands acts as a vital storm defence for the Western Highlands and the Inner Hebrides. The Western Isles are rich in historical and archaeological detail; everywhere you look there is something new to see, as well as a wealth of glorious vistas to admire. Lewis and Harris join together to form one island, with a population of over 20,000. By exploring on foot or by car you quickly appreciate the immense diversity of landscape to be found here. Harris, famous for its tweed, has the highest hills and is generally more mountainous, while Lewis consists of rolling moorland, low-lying hills and white sandy beaches. Further south lies a necklace of beautiful islands – the Uists and Benbecula – linked by various bridges and causeways.

The Isles of Muck, Eigg, Rhum and Canna are collectively known as the Small Isles and lie off the south coast of Skye, beyond the Cuillin Sound.

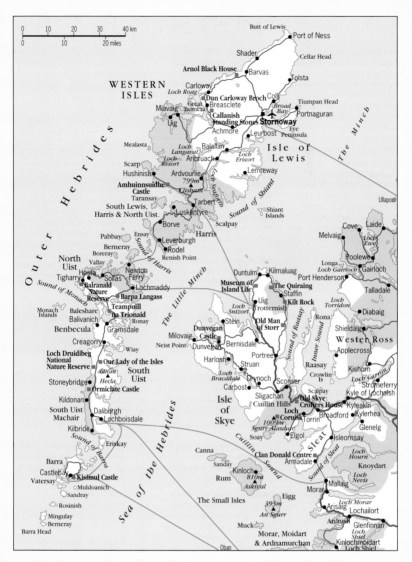

PRINCIPAL TOWNS
PORTREE, ISLE OF SKYE

Named after a royal visit in 1540 by James V – port righ means king's harbour – Portree is the island's capital and a busy little tourist resort. Set around a charming bay sheltered by two headlands, it has a pretty harbour lined with neat and brightly-painted houses.

STORNOWAY, ISLE OF LEWIS

Stornoway, established from the 17th century by the Clan MacKenzie, is the only town in the Western Isles – hence it is the main administrative and shopping centre. A good excursion centre for visiting the attractions on Lewis and Harris, it is also an important centre for the fishing industry and boasts a picturesque, boat-filled harbour.

MUST SEE

THE AROS HERITAGE CENTRE,
Viewfield Rd, Portree, Skye ☎ 01478 613649
A must for all visitors wishing to understand the history of Skye, particularly the struggles of the crofters. Enjoy the fascinating audio tour that portrays life on Skye from the 18th century to the present day, then take a lesiurely walk in Portree Forest, relax in the restaurant, or browse around the excellent shop. Gaelic concerts.

BLACK HOUSE MUSEUM,
Arnol, Lewis ☎ 01851 710395
Visit a traditional thatched Hebridean dwelling, complete with original furnishings, a central peat fire in the kitchen and adjacent barn, byre and stockyard. Once indigenous to rural Lewis, this crofting way of life only declined after the 1st World War.

ART GALLERIES

AN LANNTAIR GALLERY,
Town Hall, Stornoway, Lewis
☎/📠 01851 703307
Local, national and international exhibitions.

AN TUIREANN ARTS CENTRE,
Struan Rd, Portree, Skye ☎ 01478 613306
Arts and crafts venue.

MUSEUMS

CLAN DONALD VISITOR CENTRE,
Armadale, Skye ☎ 01471 844305
Discover thrilling tales about the Clan Donald, the Lords of the Isles, whose history stretches back some 1300 years, at the partly restored Armadale Castle. 40 acres of woodland gardens.

COLBOST FOLK MUSEUM,
Dunvegan, Skye ☎ 01470 521296
Crofting museum with a reconstructed straw-roofed cottage.

GEARRANNAN 'BLACK HOUSE' VILLAGE,
No 3 Garenin, Lewis ☎ 01851 643416
The remains of a traditional crofting village abandoned in 1973. The black houses are gradually being restored.

KILDONAN MUSEUM,
Kildonan, South Uist ☎ 01878 710343
Local history exhibitions and museum.

LOCHCROISTEAN CENTRE,
Uig, Lewis ☎ 01851 672238
Visitor centre with photographic exhibitions and small museum. Tearoom.

MACCRIMMON PIPING HERITAGE CENTRE,
Boreraig, Dunvegan, Skye ☎ 01470 511316
History of the MacCrimmon family, pipers to Clan MacLeod, the bagpipe and the piobreachaid, the great pipe music.

CALLANISH STANDING STONES,
Callanish, Lewis ☎ 01851 621422
Often referred to as Scotland's Stonehenge, this avenue of of 19 monoliths and a circle of 19 stones is the most famous of prehistoric sites, possibly dating from 3,000 BC. Learn about how the stones were built and used, and what they have meant to the people through the centuries, by means of graphic panels, models and audio-visual displays in the excellent visitor centre. Shop, café

DUNVEGAN CASTLE.
Dunvegan, Skye ☎ 01470 521206
Visit Skye's major attraction and learn about the powerful Skye clan, the Macleod's, who have occupied this austere battlemented castle, dramatically sited on a rock overlooking Loch Dunvegan, since the 13th century. Thought to be Scotland's oldest inhabited castle, it is worth exploring, not only for its richly furnished rooms and treasured relics of the clan, but

MUSEUM NAN EILEAN,
Francis St, Stornoway, Lewis
☎ 01851 703773
Island exhibits and displays.

OLD SKYE CROFTER'S HOUSE,
Luib, Skye ☎ 01470 521296
This thatched, traditional period-piece shows the kind of dwelling that the crofters of Skye once lived in.

SHAWBOST CROFTING MUSEUM,
Shawbost, Lewis
Housed in an old church beside the Community School, it features a fascinating collection of artefacts from all walks of Hebridean life.

SHAWBOST NORSE MILL & KILN,
Shawbost, Lewis ☎ 01851 643416
See how barley grain was processed into meal at this reconstructed traditional thatched water-powered grain mill and corn-drying kiln barn.

TAIGH CHEARSABHAGH VISITOR CENTRE,
Lochmaddy, North Uist ☎/📠 01876 500293
Museum and arts centre with exhibitions of local history and activity workshops.

HISTORIC & ANCIENT SITES

BARPA LANGASS,
North Uist *S of A867, on NW side of Ben Langass*
The best preserved Neolithic chambered cairn in the Western Isles.

CLACH AN TRUISEIL,
Ballantrushal, Lewis
The tallest standing stone in Scotland, nearly 6m high.

for the fine gardens and grounds, craft shops and boat trips to the nearby seal colony. Restaurant and shop.

MUSEUM OF ISLAND LIFE,
Hungladder, Kilmuir, Skye
☎ 01470 511279
Learn about the rural life of crofters during the mid 19th century at this facinating collection of restored thatched cottages and buildings, complete with furniture, farming and domestic implements.

QUIRANG
Trotternish Peninsula, Skye
Take a leisurely drive around the Trotternish Penisula, famous for its amazing rock scenery, and don't miss this impressive collection of bizarrely-shaped basalt rocks, with rock towers, jagged peaks and pinnacles, located at the top of the peninsula. Best appreciated on foot, they are easily reached from the minor road between Uig and Staffin.

DUN CARLOWAY BROCH,
Carloway, Lewis *1.5m/2.4km S of Carloway*
One of the best examples of a late-prehistoric circular stone tower, standing 30ft (9m) high.

DUNTULM CASTLE,
Trotternish Peninsula, Skye
Precariously-perched ruined castle that was once a Macdonald stronghold.

FLORA MACDONALD'S BIRTHPLACE,
Milton, South Uist
Ruined dwelling of the most famous of Bonnie Prince Charlie's helpers. It was Flora who took the Prince, dressed in women's clothing, 'over the sea to Skye'.

KILMUIR CHURCH
Kilmuir, Syke
The Hebridean heroine Flora MacDonald is buried in the churchyard.

OLD CHAPELS & BURIAL GROUNDS,
Howmore, South Uist
Remains of five churches and chapels dating from the 12th and 13th centuries.

ORMACLETE CASTLE,
Ormaclete, South Uist
Attached to a later farmhouse, the two-storey castle was built in 1704 for Allan Macdonald of Clan Ranald.

ST BARR'S CHAPEL,
Barra
A restored medieval church dating from the 12th century, containing the replica of a unique grave slab which features Norse runic markings and a Celtic cross. The author Sir Compton MacKenzie, who wrote Whisky Galore, is buried here.

ST CLEMENT'S CHURCH,
Rodel, Harris
An outstanding cruciform church built around 1500 by the 8th chief of the Macleods (Alexander Macleod), featuring his magnificent sculptured tomb.

GREAT FOR KIDS

KYLERHEA OTTER SANCTUARY,
Broadford, Skye ☎ 01471 822487
Visit the Otter Survival Fund headquarters in Broadford and see live video links to the otter pens at Kylerhea, as well as a display on otter natural history. Children's corner, shop and guided walks.

SKYE SERPENTARIUM,
Harrapool, Broadford, Skye
☎ 01471 822209
Children will enjoy watching the snakes, lizards, frogs and tortoises in their natural surroundings at this unique award-winning exhibition and breeding centre.

TOY MUSEUM,
Glendale, Skye ☎ 01470 511240
A delight for children of all ages. Exhibits include trains, books, meccano, jigsaws, dolls and puppets from a bygone era.

HOMES & GARDENS

KISIMUL CASTLE,
Castlebay, Barra ☎ 01871 810336
Restored medieval tower-house standing on a rock in the middle of the harbour. Access by boat.

BIG OUTDOORS

BALRANALD RSPB NATURE RESERVE,
Hougharry, North Uist ☎ 0131 556 5624
Bring your binoculars and see the large numbers of waders, duck and sea birds that breed on this important nature reserve. If you are lucky you may see an otter and the rare red-necked phalarope.

CUILLIN HILLS,
Skye
Dominating every view you will enjoy on Skye are the high peaks of the Cuillin Hills. Formed from gabbro, a volcanic rock, and granite, they prove an irresistable challenge for climbers but with over 20 peaks above 3,000ft (900m), they are the domain of experienced hillwalkers and mountaineers only.

KILT ROCK,
Trotternish Peninsula, Skye
Worth seeking out for, as its name suggests, it resembles a tartan garment in its basaltic columns and colours.

LOCH CORUISK,
Elgol, Skye
Walk or take a boat from Elgol to view the most dramatic loch in Scotland, painted by Turner among many others.

LOCH DRUIDIBEG NATURE RESERVE,
South Uist ☎ 01870 620206
Covering a wide area on either side of the A865 at Loch Druidibeg, this reserve is an important breeding site for greylag geese and the elusive corncrake.

OLD MAN OF STORR,
Trotternish Peninsula, Skye
This curious rock pinnacle stands 165ft (50m) above the cliffs and is shaped like a huge, elongated pear.

ISLE OF RAASAY,
Vehicle ferry from Sconser on Skye
Ideal for a day trip, especially for those interested in exhilarating walks, birdlife and total peace and quiet.

ST KILDA NATURE RESERVE,
St Kilda 40m (64km) from the Western Isles
☎ 01870 620238
Scotland's only World Heritage Site, St Kilda, is a remote group of rocky islands, the largest being inhabited until 1930. The old village houses are gradually being restored, but is it really the domain of thousands of sea birds - including puffins, gannets and razorbills - which breed on the huge cliffs. Accessible via organised boat tours.

ESSENTIAL INFORMATION

TOURIST INFORMATION

INFORMATION CENTRES

WESTERN ISLES TOURIST BOARD,
26 Cromwell St, Stornoway, Lewis HS1 2DD
☎ 01851 703088 📠 01851 705244

BARRA *seasonal,*
Main St, Castlebay, Barra ☎ 01871 810336

BROADFORD *seasonal,*
Broadford, Skye ☎ 01471 822361

HARRIS *seasonal*
Pier Rd, Tarbert, Harris ☎ 01859 502011

NORTH UIST *seasonal,*
Pier Rd, Lochmaddy, North Uist
☎ 01876 500321

PORTREE *seasonal,*
Meall House, Portree, Skye ☎ 01478 612137

SOUTH UIST *seasonal,*
Pier Rd, Loch Boisdale, South Uist
☎ 01878 700286

ACCESS

AIR ACCESS

British Regional Airlines fly direct to Stornoway from both Glasgow and Inverness. They also fly, as do Loganair, from Glasgow to Barra and Benbecula. British Airways Reservations ☎ 0345 222111

SEA ACCESS

CALEDONIAN MACBRAYNE FERRIES,
☎ 01475 650100
For the Hebrides via the Firth of Clyde, or the west coast ports; also inter island services.

BERNARAY CAR FERRY,
North Uist to Bernaray ☎ 01876 500337
ERISKAY CAR FERRY,
South Uist to Eriskay ☎ 01878 720261
SKYE CAR FERRY,
Glenelg to Kylerhea ☎/📠 01599 511302
SKYE TO WESTERN ISLES FERRY
Uig to Tarbert (Lewis) & Lochmaddy (North Uist) ☎ 01470 542219
SOUND OF BARRA FERRY,
South Uist to Barra ☎ 01878 720238

CRAFTS

Look out for pottery, batik work, hand spinning and weaving, in particular Harris tweeds, knitwear, Celtic jewellery, woodturning and local paintings at the numerous small galleries. For a detailed brochure on arts and crafts in the area contact the local Tourist Information Centres.

BORGH POTTERY,
Fivepenny House, Borve Lewis
☎ 01851 850345
COLL POTTERY,
Back, Lewis ☎ 01851 820219

CROFT CRAFTS,
4 Plockropool, Drinishader, Harris
☎ 01859 511217
DUNHALLIN CRAFTS,
Waternish, Skye ☎ 01470 592271
EDINBANE POTTERY,
Edinbane, Skye ☎ 01470 582234
GISLA WOODCRAFT,
Gisla, Uig, Lewis ☎ 01851 672371
HARRIS TWEED SHOP,
Tarbert, Harris ☎ 01859 502493
MACGILLIVRAYS,
Balivanich, Benbecula ☎ 01870 602525
Harris tweeds and hand-knitted sweaters.
JOAN MACLENNAN TWEEDS,
1a Drinishader, Harris ☎ 01859 511266
MACLEOD HARRIS TWEED MILL,
9 North Shawbost, Lewis ☎ 01851 710251
MORVEN GALLERY,
Barvas, Lewis ☎ 01851 840216
Original paintings, ceramics and textiles.

NORTH SKYE CRAFT & COFFEE SHOP,
Culnacnoc, Staffin, Skye ☎ 01470 562708
SOAY STUDIO,
West Tarbert, Harris ☎ 01859 502361
SKYE BATIKS,
Armadale, Sleat, Skye ☎ 01478 640254
SKYE JEWELLERY,
Broadford, Skye ☎ 01471 822100
SKYESKYNS TANNERY,
Waternish, Skye ☎ 01470 592237
SCALPAY LINEN,
Scalpay ☎ 01859 540298
UIG POTTERY & GALLERY,
Uig, Skye ☎ 01470 542421

ENTERTAINMENT

THEATRE

AN TUIREANN ARTS CENTRE,
Struan Rd, Portree, Skye ☎ 01478 613306

FOOD & DRINK

*Expect to find the freshest of fish and
shellfish - including salmon and lobster
- on your travels, as fishing is an
important element in the economy of the
islands. Benbecula is particulary noted
for its cockles.*

COLIN MACDONALD & SONS,
Shell St, Stornoway, Lewis ☎ 01851 702723
Traditionally smoked salmon and kippers.

SALAR SMOKEHOUSE
The Pier, Lochcarnon, South Uist
☎ 01870 610324
Specialist for flaky smoked salmon.

WHISKY DISTILLERY TOURS

TALISKER DISTILLERY VISITOR CENTRE,
Carbost, Skye ☎ 01478 640314
Peaty Talisker whisky has been produced
here since 1831 and it is now the only
distillery on the island.

TRANSPORT

BOAT TRIPS & CRUISES

BARRA BOAT TRIPS,
☎ 01878 720238 & 720265
Day trips to Mingulay and Eriskay.

BELLA JANE BOAT TRIPS,
Skye ☎ 01471 866244
See Loch Coruisk and seals.

ROSA HEBRIDEAN CRUISES,
Stornoway, Lewis ☎ 01851 702901
Cruises to St Kilda and Hebridean Isles.

BUS SERVICES

GALSON MOTORS,
Lewis ☎ 01851 840269
HARRIS COACHES,
Tarbert, Harris ☎ 01859 502441
Bus service operators and coach tours.

HIGHLAND BUSES,
Portree, Skye ☎ 01478 612622
MACDONALD'S COACHES,
Stornoway, Lewis ☎ 01851 706267
Connecting bus services, coach tours.

CAR HIRE

ARNOL MOTORS,
Arnol, Lewis ☎ 01851 710548
ASK CAR HIRE,
Liniclate, Benbecula ☎ 01870 602818
PETER BROWN CAR HIRE,
Castlebay, Barram ☎ 01871 810243
JACKIES HIRE-DRIVE,
Barvas, Lewis ☎/ℱ 01851 840343
LAING MOTORS,
Lochboisdale, South Uist
☎/ℱ 01878 700267
LEWIS CAR RENTALS,
Stornoway, Lewis ☎ 01851 703760

MACLENNAN MOTORS,
Balivanich, Benbecula ☎ 01870 602191
MACRAES CAR HIRE,
Portree, Skye ☎ 01478 612554
SKYE CAR RENTAL,
Broadford, Skye ☎ 01471 822225

COACH/MINIBUS TOURS

CAMERON TOURS,
Portree, Skye ☎ 01478 844361
1 Dalbeg, Lewis ☎/ℱ 01851 710265
PORTREE MINIBUS TOURS,
Skye ☎ 01478 613641
RED DEER TRAVEL,
Portree, Skye ☎ 01478 612142
SKYETRAK SAFARI,
Edinbane, Skye ☎ 01470 582224
Landrover tours.

CYCLE HIRE

BARRA CYCLE HIRE,
29 St Brendan's Rd, Isle of Barra
☎ 01871 810284
ALEX DAN'S CYCLE CENTRE,
67 Kenneth St, Stornoway, Lewis
☎ 01851 704025
FAIRWINDS CYCLE HIRE,
Broadford, Skye ☎ 01471 822270
ISLAND CYCLES,
The Green, Portree, Skye ☎ 01478 613121
D. M. MACKENZIE,
Pier Rd, Tarbert, Harris ☎ 01859 502271
ROTHAN CYCLES,
9 Howmore, South Uist ☎ 01870 620283

SPECIAL TOURS

HEBRIDEAN EXPLORATION,
Stornoway, Lewis ☎ 01851 870716
HEBRIDEAN HORSE-DRAWN HOLIDAYS,
Bayhead, North Uist ☎/ℱ 01876 510706
OUT & ABOUT TOURS,
Great Bernera, Lewis ☎ 01851 612288
Guided day tours of Lewis and Harris.

SCOTSELL LTD,
☎ 0141 772 5928
Imaginative car tours.

SPORT & LEISURE

ACTIVITY CENTRES

UIST OUTDOOR CENTRE,
Lochmaddy, North Uist ☎ 01876 500480

ANGLING

From excellent sea angling and prime sea
trout and salmon fishing around the sea
lochs to inland loch and estate river
fishing for brown trout, both Skye and the
Western Isles offer an unsurpassed variety
of sport for the angler. Enquire at local
Tourist Information Offices for more
details.

CYCLING

Cycling on Skye is good, but the hilly,
sometimes mountainous, terrain is more
suitable for the fit cyclist. The excellent
main roads are less taxing than the often
single-track side roads, but are best

avoided in high summer as they can be
very busy. Generally, more gentler cycling
can be enjoyed in the Western Isles, in
particular on the Isles of Lewis, Harris,
North & South Uist and Barra.

GOLF

ISLE OF SKYE
Sconser ☎ 01478 650351
Windy seaside course, splendid views.

STORNOWAY
Lewis ☎ 01851 702240
Undulating parkland course with a few
testing par 3's.

ASKERNISH
South Uist No telephone
BARRA
Isle of Barra ☎ 01871 810451

SKEABOST
Skye ☎ 01470 532202

LEISURE CENTRES

CASTLEBAY COMMUNITY SCHOOL,
Barra ☎ 01871 810471
COLL SPORTS CENTRE,
Coll, Lewis
SGOIL LIONACLEIT
Balivanich, Benbecula
SHAWBOST COMMUNITY SCHOOL,
Shawbost, Lewis
STORNOWAY SPORTS CENTRE,
Lewis ☎ 01851 702603

RIDING

SKYE RIDING CENTRE,
Portree, Skye ☎ 01470 532233
U I G PONY TREKKING,
Uig Hotel, Uig, Skye ☎ 01470 542205

SCENIC DRIVES

Awe-inspiring moorland, mountain and
coastal views greets you at every turn
along the scenic roads on Skye and in the
Western Isles. On Skye, don't miss touring
round the Trotternish and Duirnish
peninsula's, and savour the drive from
Broadford to Elgol which affords
wonderful views to Rhum.

SWIMMING

PORTREE SWIMMING POOL,
Skye

WALKING

From bracing coastal walks, incorporating
magnificent beaches and spectacular cliff
scenery, and challenging moor and
mountain walks, to fascinating strolls
around nature reserves or one of the
many prehistoric sites, walking possibilities
abound on the Western Isles. On Skye, the
Cuillin Hills are the preserve of the rock
climber or experienced hillwalker, but less
demanding, although often equally
remote, walks can be found around the
coast. A series of walking leaflets for both
Skye and the Western Isles are available
from Tourist Information Offices

ORKNEY & SHETLAND

Are there really 70 islands in Orkney? The answer, incredibly, is yes, though today less than 20 are actually inhabited. Orkney, blessed with some of the finest cliff and coastal scenery anywhere in Britain, was occupied continuously for more than 6,000 years and there was never a moment when these islands were not vulnerable to enemy attack. The islands may be calm and tranquil now but they can still evoke vivid memories of bitter naval battles and torpedo bombardment, especially at the natural harbour of Scapa Flow. Orkney is an eerily beautiful part of Scotland, a place of colourful legends, stone circles, standing stones and curious fortified dwellings known as 'brochs'. Explore these islands and you will discover its fascinating and archaeological heritage for yourself.

104 miles (166.4km) north-east of John O'Groats, Shetland consists of a group of windswept islands whose names are more Norse than Scottish. Characterized by bare, peat-covered landscapes and a convoluted maze of sea lochs, bays and inlets – or 'voes' as they are known here, Shetland has a distinctive character and spirit that separates it from the rest of Scotland. On the largest island, Mainland there are numerous opportunities to explore on foot, breathe in all that bracing Shetland air and savour the timeless appeal of these wonderful islands. At Mavis Grind, near the oil terminal at Sulham Voe, you can walk from the North Sea to the Atlantic and back, marvelling as you go at mysterious prehistoric ruins and spectacular cliff scenery.

North of Mainland lie the smaller islands of Fetlar, famous for its bird population, Yell, the second largest island in Shetland, and Unst – Britain's most northerly outpost.

PRINCIPAL TOWNS

KIRKWALL, ORKNEY

An early Christian settlement, taking its name from the Old Norse *kirkjuvagr*, 'church bay,' it appears under the date 1046 in the great Norse saga The Orkneyinga Saga. Built by a natural harbour, Kirkwall never became a great sea port, but gained prominence after the completion of its fine sandstone cathedral in the 15th century. Historic character remains in the form of narrow winding streets and lanes, lined with compact old houses, which cluster around the cathedral and the outstanding ruins of the Bishop's and Earl's Palaces, the latter featuring fine French Renaissance architecture. Kirkwall is the ideal touring centre with easy access to all parts of the Mainland.

LERWICK, SHETLAND

Having started as a fishing season trading post, Lerwick only became a permanent town as late as the mid- 17th century at the time of the Anglo-Dutch wars. Now the main town and capital of Shetland, and the centre of the fishing industry, it is full of character, especially along the waterfront, with its older buildings hard against the sea, and in the southern, older part of the town with its narrow, winding lanes s behind houses. Lerwick has a good range of shops, especially those selling Shetland knitwear and crafts.

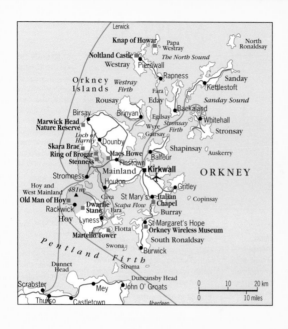

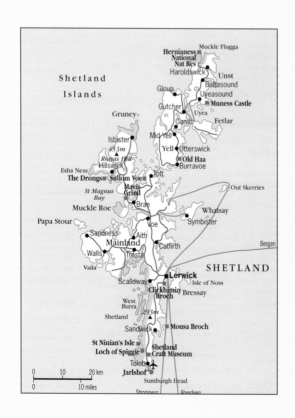

MUST SEE

Ring of Brogar & The Stenness Standing Stones,

MAES HOWE CHAMBERED CAIRN,
Finstown, Mainland ☎ 01856 761606
Standing in a field at the south end of Loch Harray is this huge chambered tomb, the largest and best preserved in Western Europe, and unmissable for its awesome interior and for the magnificent Viking runic inscriptions on the walls. Built around 2700 BC (at least a century before Stonehenge in Wiltshire), it was already 3500 years old when Vikings broke in to the inner chamber, which is 15ft (4.5m) square and reached by a 47ft (14.5m) long passage, to loot the burial cells and leave stone carvings and runes.

NORTH HOY NATURE RESERVE,
Hoy *accessible by ferry from Stromness*
Taking in the famous Old Man of Hoy, a huge, red sandstone stack rearing 450ft (135m) out of the sea, and some of the finest cliff scenery in the islands, this part of Hoy, easily reached from Randwick, is exhilarating walking country. Administered by the RSPB, the reserve is noted for its seabird colonies, in particular for the great skua, of which 1,500 pairs breed here.

RING OF BROGAR & THE STENNESS STANDING STONES,
Stenness, Mainland ☎ 0131 668 8800
Erected by neolithic man and originally consisting of 60 stones, the Ring of Brogar is Orkney's best-known stone circle, the remaining 36 stones still having a dramatic effect, especially when silhouetted against the hills of Hoy. Close by are the Standing Stones of Stenness, a small circle erected in 3,000 BC, consisting originally of 12 stones. Adjacent to the stones is Barnhouse, a partly reconstructed Stone Age village, thought to be the home of the builders of Maeshowe and the Standing Stones.

ST MAGNUS' CATHEDRAL,
Kirkwall, Mainland
Magnificent St Magnus' Cathedral, one of only two intact pre-Reformation cathedrals in Scotland, dominates tiny Kirkwall. Step inside this architectural masterpiece and admire the Romanesque, Transitional and Gothic styles that feature in the spacious and tranquil interior. Founded in 1137 by Earl Rognvald Kolsson it took three centuries to complete.

SKARA BRAE,
Sandwick, Mainland ☎ 01856 841815
Explore one of the most fascinating ancient sites in Western Europe. Engulfed in drift sand for 4,000 years before a storm revealed its treasures in 1850, this complete neolithic settlement, comprising ten one-roomed houses, gives a remarkable glimpse of domestic life in earlier centuries. Wander through the excavations and marvel at the beauty and ingenuity of the buildings, each furnished with 5,000 year old stone dressers, beds and cupboards, and linked by a web of passages. The visitor centre details the history of the site, with two replica houses allowing you walk through and experience what life would have been like.

TANKERNESS HOUSE MUSEUM,
Kirkwall, Mainland ☎ 01856 873191
Discover more about Orkney's history, including the island's rich archaeology, at this fascinating museum of Orkney life, housed within one of the finest vernacular town houses in Scotland, a 16th-century merchant-laird's mansion. Shop.

ART GALLERIES

PIER ARTS CENTRE,
Stromness, Mainland ☎ 01856 850209
Housed in 18th-century restored warehouse standing on its own stone pier, this art gallery features the best collection of modern British art in the north of Scotland.

MUSEUMS

ORKNEY FARM & FOLK MUSEUM,
Harray & Birsay, Mainland ☎ 01856 771411
At Harray, a late-19th-century restored farmstead with circular grain kiln, weaver's loom and horse-powered implements illustrates Orkney life a century ago. At Kirkbuster, an early 19th-century farmhouse features an unaltered example of an old Orkney kitchen, complete with central hearth and stone bed.

ORKNEY FOSSIL VINTAGE CENTRE,
Burray ☎ 01856 731255
Fascinating for kids and adults, this small museum displays fossil fish over 300 million years old and vintage farm machinery.

ORKNEY MARITIME & NATURAL HISTORY MUSEUM,
52 Alfred St ☎ 01856 850025
Learn about Orkney's birds, butterflies, shells and fossils, as well as Arctic whaling and the German fleet in Scapa Flow.

SCAPA FLOW VISITOR CENTRE,
Lyness Naval Base, Hoy ☎ 01856 791300
Discover everything you need to know about wartime Orkney, including the scuttling of the German High Seas Fleet in Scapa Flow in 1919.

TRUMLAND ORIENTATION CENTRE,
Rousay
Explains the history of the island from prehistoric times to the present day.

WESTRAY HERITAGE CENTRE,
Pierowall, Westray
Innovative displays, including collages of tapestry and knitting, illustrate Westray's natural history and way of life.

HISTORIC & ANCIENT SITES

BISHOP'S & EARL'S PALACES,
Kirkwall, Mainland ☎ 01856 875461
The Bishop's Palace is a hall-house dating from the mid-12th century. Earl Patrick's Palace was built in 1600 for Patrick Stewart, ruler of the islands, in a splendid Renaissance style.

BROCH OF GURNESS,
Evie, Mainland
Situated on the shore overlooking the island of Rousay, this is the best broch in Orkney, occupied and added to by a succession of Iron Age people, Picts and Vikings from 100 BC.

BROUGH OF BIRSAY,
Birsay, Mainland
This ruined Romanesque church stands next to the remains of a Norse village on a tidal island, only accessible at low tide.

IBSTER CHAMBERED CAIRN,
Liddel, St Margaret's Hope, Mainland
☎ 01856 831339
Visit the 4,000 year old burial chamber and then enjoy the 'hands on' approach to

ancient artefacts at Liddel Farm where you can handle a prehistoric stone axe and skulls, among other relics.

ITALIAN CHAPEL,
Lamb Holm *halfway along Churchill Causeway*
Italian prisoners-of-war transformed two corrugated iron Nissen huts into an ornately decorated Catholic chapel, with beautiful trompe l'oeil paintings, in their spare time while constructing the Churchill Barriers in 1943.

KNAP OF HOWAR,
Papa Westray ☎ 0131 668 8800
Having yielded whalebone artefacts and stone grinders, these two 5,000 year old dwellings are believed to be the oldest houses in Europe.

MIDHOWE BROCH AND CHAMBERED CAIRN,
Rousay ☎ 0131 668 8800
Overlooking Eynhallow Sound, the fine broch, occupied between 200 BC and 200 AD, stands 13ft high, while the magnificent cairn, at 76ft (23m) in length, is one of the best examples ever discovered.

NOLTLAND CASTLE,
Westray ☎ 0131 668 8800
Started in the 16th century, this ruined 'Z-plan' castle was never completed. You will see a fine hall, a vaulted kitchen and a notable winding staircase.

ORPHIR ROUND KIRK & ORKNEYINGA SAGA EXPERIENCE,
Orphir, Mainland
See the remains of Scotland's only circular medieval church and Earl's Bu, a Viking drinking hall mentioned in the Orkneyinga Saga. Learn about the tales of heroic events in the adjacent interpretation centre through a video show and fascinating information panels.

HOMES & GARDENS

BALFOUR CASTLE,
Shapinsay ☎ 01856 711282
The world's most northerly castle dating back to 1840, now a charming small hotel with original Victorian furnishings and a Victorian walled garden.

CARRICK HOUSE,
Eday ☎ 01857 622260
A fine 17th-century Laird's house overlooking the shore. Beautiful garden.

SKAILL HOUSE,
Sandwick, Mainland ☎ 01856 841501
View Orkney's best preserved Laird's mansion, built in the 17th century and displaying the dinner service from Captain Cook's ship 'The Discovery'.

Call the AA Hotel Booking Service on 0990 050505 to book at AA recognised hotels and B&Bs in the UK, or through our internet site: http://www.theaa.co.uk/hotels

---

BIG OUTDOORS

HOY
In contrast to Orkney's prevailing low-lying greenness, the island of Hoy, especially its north and west, has an almost Highland character, with heather moorland, a high and craggy landscape, including glacial corries and U-shaped valleys, and a spectacular coastline.

ISLAND WILDLIFE,
Orkney is a naturalists paradise. With such a varied landscape, including cliffs, maritime heath, moorland, freshwater loch, beaches and the sea, the islands are haven to a wide range fauna and flora. A million seabirds - razorbills, puffins, shags, guillemots - crowd the cliffs and, a little way inland, 20,000 Arctic terns and 1,000 pairs of Arctic skua nest on the maritime heath, which is also home to a rich flora. On Papa Westray you can still hear, if not see, the elusive corncrake and throughout the islands you may be lucky to see otters, as well as common and grey seals.

MARWICK HEAD NATURE RESERVE,
near Birsay, Mainland
See around 35,000 guillemots on these easily reached great red cliffs.

SANDAY,
Appropriately named, this big, low-lying island is for beach lovers, with its indented coastline hiding beautiful sandy bays and miles of rolling dunes. The island is also the place to see birds, especially terns, and some of the best prehistoric sites.

ESSENTIAL INFORMATION

TOURIST INFORMATION

INFORMATION CENTRES

KIRKWALL,
6 Broad St, Kirkwall, Mainland KW15 1NX
☎ 01856 872856 🖷 01856 875056

ROUSAY TOURIST ASSOCIATION,
c/o Bellona, Rousay ☎/🖷 01856 821234

STROMNESS,
Terminal Building, Pier Head, Stromness, Mainland KW16 3AA ☎ 01856 860716

WESTRAY & PAPA WESTRAY TOURIST ASSOCIATION,
c/o Furrigarth, Dykeside, Westray KW17 2DW
☎ 01857 677404 🖷 01857 677403

ACCESS

AIR ACCESS

BRITISH AIRWAYS EXPRESS (LOGANAIR)
☎ 0345 222111
Services from Aberdeen, Glasgow, Edinburgh & Inverness to Kirkwall and Wick to Kirkwall.

KIRKWALL AIRPORT ☎ 01856 872494
For details on Inter-island flights to Eday,

Stronsay, Sanday, Westray, Papa Westray and North Ronaldsay, all operated by British Airways Express.

FERRIES

ORKNEY FERRIES ☎ 01856 872044
Orkney mainland and 13 smaller islands.

P & O SCOTTISH FERRIES,
☎ 01856 850655
Aberdeen and Scrabster on the Scottish mainland to Stromness.

JOHN O'GROATS FERRIES,
☎ 01955 611353
John O'Groats to Burwick, South Ronaldsay (summer only).

CRAFTS

Among the many fine crafts produced in Orkney, lookout for silverwork, jewellery, knitwear, tapestry weaving, pottery and ceramics. woodcraft and hand-made felt. For a detailed list of craftworkers obtain the free Craft Trail Brochure from the Tourist Information offices.

ORKNEYINGA SILVER,
Marwick, Birsay, Mainland
☎ 01856 721359

FURSBRECK POTTERY,
Harray ☎ 01856 771419

TRADITIONAL ORKNEY CRAFTS,
Kirkwall, Mainland ☎ 01856 875110
Orkney chairs

THE WORKSHOP,
St Margaret's Hope, South Ronaldsay
☎ 01856 831587
HOXA TAPESTRY GALLERY,
Hoxa, South Ronaldsay ☎ 01875 831395
Tapestry weaving

SHEILA FLEET JEWELLERY,
Tankerness, Mainland ☎ 01856 861203

TAIT & STYLE,
Stromness, Mainland ☎ 01856 851186
Felt, woollen fabrics, jewellery.

HROSSEY SILVER,
Orphir, Mainland ☎ 01856 811347

JUDITH GLUE KNITWEAR,
Kirkwall, Mainland ☎ 01856 874225

ELLI PEARSON POTTERY,
Windwick, South Ronaldsay
☎ 01856 831355

THE SMITHY,
Hand-made knitwear

Balfour Village, Shapinsay ☎ 01856 711258
Knitwear, woodturning, jewellery and
paintings.

ENTERTAINMENT

THEATRE

ORKNEY ARTS THEATRE,
Mill St, Kirkwall, Mainland

FOOD & DRINK

*On Orkney you will find the freshest
fish and seafood, the finest beef, delicious
farmhouse cheeses, very moreish fudge,
oatcakes and pastries, excellent real ale
from the Orkney Brewery, and the most
northerly whisky distillery in the world.*

CHEESE

Lookout for Shapinsay goat's cheese,
Swanney, Grimbister and How farm-
produced cheeses, and the distinctive
cheddar made in two creameries.

WHISKY DISTILLERYS

HIGHLAND PARK DISTILLERY,
Kirkwall, Mainland ☎ 01856 874619
Visitor centre and conducted tours.

SCAPA DISTILLERY,
Kirkwall, Mainland
Limited access but open to visitors by
arrangement.

TRANSPORT

BOAT TRIPS & CRUISES

ROVING EYE ENTERPRISES,
Orphir, Mainland ☎ 01856 811360
Explore the wrecks of the German fleet in
Scapa Flow on board a boat with an
underwater camera.

BUS/COACH SERVICES

CAUSEWAY COACHES,
St Margaret's Hope, Mainland
☎ 01856 831444

JAMES D PEACE & CO,
Kirkwall, Mainland ☎ 01856 872866

ROSIE COACHES,
Evie, Mainland ☎ 01856 751232

SHALDER COACHES LTD,
Stromness, Mainland ☎ 01856 850809

CAR HIRE

SCARTH HIRE,
Kirkwall, Mainland ☎ 01856 872125

JOHN SHEARER & SONS,
Kirkwall, Mainland ☎ 01856 872950

STROMNESS SELF DRIVE CARS & TAXIS,
Stromness, Mainland ☎ 01856 850973

CYCLE HIRE

ORKNEY CYCLE HIRE,
Stromness, Mainland ☎ 01856 850255

TOURS

D A STUDY TOURS ☎ 01383 882200
Discover Orkney's rich heritage.

GO ORKNEY ☎ 01856 871871
Tours, walks and boat trips.

ISLAND EXPLORER ☎ 01856 677355
Guided tours and short walks of Westray.

NORTH RONALDSAY TOURS,
☎ 01857 633217
Off-rd vehicle tours of Orkney's most
remote island.

ORCADIAN REFLECTIONS,
☎ 01856 781327
Guided car tours.

ORKNEY ISLAND WILDLIFE,
☎ 01856 711373
Guided holidays by minibus and boat.

ROUSAY TRAVELLER GUIDE,
☎/📠 01856 821234
Natural history, archaeology and history
tours of Rousay.

A & R M STEWART,
☎ 01857 622206
Minibus tours of Eday.

WILDABOUT,
☎ 01856 851011
Imaginative tours of Orkney.

SPORT & LEISURE

ANGLING

Some of the best trout fishing in Scotland
can be found at Loch Harray, the largest
Orkney water, as well as Lochs Stennes,
Swanney, Boardhouse and Hundland. For
sea trout head for Loch Stennes and
Kirbister, and in the bays and shorelines
around the coast. There are also excellent
opportunities for sea angling. Enquire at
Tourist Information Offices for more
details.

CYCLING

Due to the small size of some of the
islands, cycling is often, and in some
cases, the best (and cheapest) way of
exploring the sights and beautiful scenery
on offer, many of the smaller islands can
easily be cycled round on a day trip.
Mainland is criss-crossed by a good
network of quiet lane; hilly Hoy and
Rousay are for the fit cyclist, whereas the
gentle landscape of Sanday, Shapinsay
and Westray is ideally suited to leisurely
cycling.

GOLF COURSES

ORKNEY,
Kirkwall, Mainland ☎ 01856 872457

STROMNESS,
Mainland ☎ 01856 850772

WESTRAY ☎ 01857 677373

LEISURE CENTRES

KIRKWALL GRAMMAR SCHOOL
Kirkwall, Mainland

RIDING

GARSON FARM,
Stromness, Mainland ☎ 01856 850304

HROSSLAND TREKKING CENTRE,
Hilltoft, Littlequoy Rd, Burray

SAILING

ORKNEY SAILING CLUB,
Kirkwall, Mainland ☎ 01856 872331

SWIMMING

see Leisure Centres

BEACHES

The best beaches can be found on Sanday
(Bay of Lopness), Stronsay, Westray and
around the eastern coast of Mainland.

STROMNESS SWIMMING POOL,
Mainland ☎ 01856 850552

WATERSPORTS

Diving is a very popular activity, especially
around the wrecks in Scapa Flow, and
exhilarating activities like windsurfing and
sea kayaking are also available.

THE DIVING CELLAR,
Stromness, Mainland ☎ 01856 850055

DOLPHIN SCUBA SERVICES,
Garisle, Burray ☎ 01856 731269

SCAPA SCUBA,
Stromness, Mainland ☎ 01856 851218

MUST SEE

ESHA NESS (THE DRONGS)
Mainland *15m/24km north-west of Brae*
Magnificent precipitous cliffs afford breathtaking views of weird and awesome rock features created by the force of the sea, all with equally strange names - the Holes of Scraada, the Heads of Grocken, the Grind of the Navir. South of the B9078, The Drongs, sea stacks in the bay, resemble a Norse galley under sail. The Tangwick Haa Museum ☎ **01806 503389** illustrates the history of the area.

HERMANESS NATIONAL NATURE RESERVE,
Burrafirth, Unstn ☎ **01957 711662**
Visit the northernmost part of the British Isles and see some of the 100,000 breeding seabirds that inhabit the dramatic cliffs, rising up to 558ft (170m), and surrounding moorland. Take the rough moorland path to the top of Hermaness Hill for a fine view of Muckle Flugga and its lighthouse, then explore the puffin-hollowed cliffs (taking great care), in search of gannets and the dive-bombing great and arctic skuas. Stout footwear essential. Back at the former lighthouse shore station, the visitors centre houses excellent interpretative displays and information about the reserve.

ISLE OF NOSS NATURE RESERVE,
accessible by boat from Lerwick and Bressay
☎ **01595 693345**
Take the waymarked walking route around the island, which consists of heather covered moorland and plunging cliffs, to view the amazing nesting colonies of gannets, kittiwakes, fulmars, puffins and guillemots, among other breeding birds,

and lookout for porpoises and seals in Noss Sound and, if you're lucky an otter. You will also find a rich variety of flora on the island, including heath spotted orchids among the 150 species recorded.

JARLSHOF PREHISTORIC SITE,
Sumburgh, Mainland ☎ **01950 460112**
Explore one of the most remarkable archaeological sites in Europe and view remains of Bronze Age houses built around courtyards, Iron Age wheel-houses and Viking longhouses, as well as a medieval farmstead and the 16th- and 17th-century houses of Stewart earls all excavated on one site. As a record of human habitation in Shetland through the ages, Jarlshof is a supreme example.

> **Call the AA Hotel Booking Service on 0990 050505 to book at AA recognised hotels and B&Bs in the UK, or through our internet site: http://www.theaa.co.uk/hotels**

MOUSA BROCH,
Mousa Island
accessible by boat from Sandwick
☎ **0131 668 8800**
Mousa Island is well worth the boat trip for its superb wildlife, let alone this magnificent broch, the best-preserved example of an Iron Age drystone tower in Scotland. Nearly complete, it rises to a height of 36ft (12m), and both the outer and inner walls contain staircases that may be climbed to the parapet.

SHETLAND CROFT HOUSE MUSEUM,
Dunrossness, Mainland ☎ **01595 695057**
Learn about rural life in Shetland over the years at this fascinating museum housed within a restored, 19th-century thatched building, typical of the style of croft house found throughout the islands. It is furnished with furniture and utensils used last century, and you can also see a corn-drying kiln and an operational mill of the horizontal Norse type.

Jarlshof Prehistoric Site

ART GALLERIES

BONHOGA GALLERY,
Weisdale Mill, Weisdale, Mainland
☎ **01595 830400**

MUSEUMS

BOD OF GREMISTA MUSEUM,
Gremista, Lerwick, Mainland
☎ **01595 695057**
A restored 18th-century fishing booth. One room is devoted to Arthur Anderson, the co-founder of the Peninsular and Oriental Steam Navigation Company, now P & O, who was born in the building.

OLD HAA OF BURRAVOE VISITOR CENTRE,
Burravoe, Yell ☎ **01957 722339**
Restored 17th-century house, the oldest on Yell, housing an exhibition of local flora, fauna, arts and social history.

SCALLOWAY MUSEUM,
Scalloway, Mainland ☎ **01595 880256**
Tells the story, among other maritime matters, of the Shetland Bus, the name given to Norwegian fishing vessels which

sailed overnight from German-occupied Norway to Shetland with refugees, returning with arms during World War II.

SHETLAND MUSEUM,
Lerwick, Mainland ☎ **01595 695057**
Covers all the main Shetland themes of folk life, shipping, art and archaeology.

TINGWALL AGRICULTURAL MUSEUM,
Tingwall, Mainland ☎ **01595 840344**
Fascinating collection of old crofting, fishing and household implements.

UNST BOAT HAVEN,
Haroldswick, Unst ☎ **01957 711324**
At the Boat Haven you can view a collection of traditional Shetland boats.

UNST HERITAGE CENTRE,
Haroldswick, Unst ☎ **01957 711662**
Houses various displays and exhibitions about the island.

HISTORIC & ANCIENT SITES

BREMEN BOD,
Symbister, Whalsay
A curious little building, a restored Hanseatic storage and trading booth, possibly dating from the 17th century.

CLICKHIMIN BROCH,
Lerwick, Mainland
The remains of a prehistoric settlement that was fortified at the beginning of the Iron Age with a stone-built fort.

FORT CHARLOTTE,
Lerwick, Mainland
An artillery fort built in the 17th century to protect the Sound of Bressay.

ST NINIAN'S ISLE,
4m/6.8km south-west of Sandwick
Connected to the mainland by a tongue of white sand, or tombolo, this small, uninhabited island was where St Ninian, the first Christian missionary to travel to Shetland, made his base. You will find the ruins of a medieval church, built in the 12th and 13th centuries.

SCALLOWAY CASTLE,
Scalloway, Mainland
The ruins of a castle designed on the medieval two-step plan and built in 1600.

BIG OUTDOORS

FAIR ISLE,
accessible by ferry from Grutness (Sumburgh) and Lerwick, and by air from Tingwall Airport.
☎ 01595 760244.
Rising out of the sea midway between Orkney and Shetland, Fair Isle is one of Britain's loveliest and remotest inhabited islands. Visit for the prehistoric remains near Funniquoy Hill and Vaasetter, for the most spectacular scenery and, as most visitors do, for the world-famous Bird

Observatory with its excellent research facilities for monitoring the thousands of migrant birds that find the island a welcome staging post to and from Iceland, Scandinavia and Central Europe. The George Waterston Memorial Centre, with its various displays is a good way of discovering the varied history of the island.

FETLAR,
accessible by ferry from Unst & Yell
☎ 01957 733206
A fertile island with a good crofting community, numerous archaeological remains, notably a Neolithic chambered cairn at Vord Hill and a Norse burial site (Giant's Grave) at Aith, and a remarkable RSPB reserve which attracts most of the

visitors to the island. Avid birdwatchers may see a snowy owl.

FOULA,
accessible by ferry from Walls, Mainland
The most westerly of the Shetland Islands (27m/43km west of Scalloway), Foula, a Norse word for bird island, offers spectacular coastal scenery, including the second highest cliff in Britain, and the opportunity to view thousands of seabirds.

SUMBURGH HEAD,
Sumburgh, Mainland
A must for all puffin-lovers! The colony of the cliffs (not far from the lighthouse) is convenient to view at close quarters.

ESSENTIAL INFORMATION

TOURIST INFORMATION

INFORMATION CENTRES

SHETLAND ISLANDS,
Market Cross, Lerwick, Mainland ZE1 0LU
☎ 01595 693434 ☎ 01595 695807

ACCESS

AIR ACCESS

SUMBURGH AIRPORT
25 miles/40km south of Lerwick
☎ 01590 460654

BRITISH AIRWAYS 01595 460345
TINGWALL AIRPORT
5 miles/8km north of Lerwick
☎ 01595 840246 (Loganair)

SEA ACCESS

P & O SCOTTISH FERRIES
☎ 01224 572615
Daily service from Aberdeen to Lerwick
For all details regarding inter-island air, road and sea travel contact Shetland Island Tourism ☎ 01595 693434

CRAFTS

Crafts to lookout for include the world famous Shetland knitwear, tweed and sheepskin rugs, silverwork, soapstone carvings, glassware, woodcraft, pottery, leathercraft, marquetry, and local paintings.

BETH ABBA STUDIO,
Setter, Hamnavoe, Mainland
☎ 01595 859688
Hand-spinning and dyeing tuition and craft goods.

LESLEY BURR CERAMIC TILES,
Melby, Sandwick ☎ 01595 870248

MARGARET HAMILTON KNITWEAR,
Westerhouse, Sellafirth, Yell
☎ 01957 744203

BARBARA IBISTER KNITWEAR,
Meadows, Cunningsburgh, Mainland
☎ 01950 477241

NORNOVA KNITWEAR WORKSHOP,
Muness, Unst ☎ 01957 755373

SHETLAND GLASS,
East Voe, Scalloway, Mainland
☎ 01595 880432

SHETLAND JEWELLERY,
Weisdale, Mainland ☎ 01595 830275

SHETLAND WOOLLEN COMPANY,
Scalloway, Mainland ☎ 01595 880243

SHETLAND WORKSHOP GALLERY,
Lerwick, Mainland ☎ 01595 693343

ROSS SMITH STAINED GLASS,
Fair Isle ☎ 01595 760208

EWAN THOMSON VIOLIN MAKER,
1 Aesterhoull, Fair Isle ☎ 01595 760276

VALLEYFIELD CRAFTS,
Brae, Mainland ☎ 01806 522563

ENTERTAINMENT

THEATRE

ISLESBURGH COMMUNITY CENTRE,
Lerwick, Mainland ☎ 01595 692114

FOOD & DRINK

Shetland is reknowned for the fresh fish and seafood caught off its shores and, in particular, for high quality fresh or smoked salmon, farmed in the sheltered voes arounds the island's shores. Also found on menus throughout the island, and well worth sampling, is the succulent Shetland lamb, as is he local speciality 'Reestit Mutton', mutton salted and dried over a peat fire.

TRANSPORT

BOAT TRIPS & CRUISES

BRESSABOATS,
Sundside, Bressay ☎ 01595 693434
Trips to the seabird colony on Noss.

DIM RIVER,
Lerwick, Mainland ☎ 01595 693434
Trips in a Viking longship.

TOM JAMIESON,
Sandwick, Mainland ☎ 01950 431367
Trips to Mousa.

SELKIE CHARTERS,
Fograbreck, Voe, Mainland ☎ 01806 588297

SHETLAND SEA CHARTERS,
Lerwick, Mainland ☎ 01595 693434
Trips around Bressay and Noss.

VIKING SEA TAXIS,
Blimister, Burra Isle ☎ 01595 859431

BUS/COACH SERVICES

R G JAMIESON & SON,
Moarfield, Cullivoe, Yell ☎ 01957 744214

JOHN LEASK & SON,
Lerwick, Mainland ☎ 01595 693162
Services and organised tours.

ROBINSON & MORRISON,
Wesidale, Mainland ☎ 01595 830263

CAR HIRE

BOLTS CAR HIRE,
Lerwick, Mainland ☎ 01595 693636

GRANTFIELD GARAGE,
Lerwick, Mainland ☎ 01595 692709

CYCLE HIRE

GARDIESFAULD HOSTEL,
Uyeasound, Unst ☎ 01967 755298

GRANTFIELD GARAGE,
Lerwick, Mainland ☎ 01595 692709

TAXIS

R G JAMIESON & SON,
Moarfield, Cullivoe, Yell ☎ 01957 744212

ROBINSON & MORRISON,
Weisdale, Mainland ☎ 01595 830263

SHETLAND TAXI TOURS,
Lerwick, Mainland ☎/🖷 01595 692080

TOURS

SHETLAND TOURIST GUIDES ASSOCIATION,
☎ 01595 696671
Special interest tours, guided walks of Lerwick and general tours.

SHETLAND WILDLIFE TOURS,
☎ 01950 460254

SPORT & LEISURE

ANGLING

Good brown trout fishing can be found in the hundreds of lochs, including Tingwall, Benston and Girla, and sea trout can be caught in the Voes. The outer islands also have excellent fishing; Whalsay has three good lochs; Unst has sea trout fishing at Burra Firth and Dales Voe, and Loch Papil is a favoured spot for both sea and brown trout on Yell. Some of the best sea angling in Scotland can be enjoyed in Shetland; boat hire/charters available. Enquire at Tourist Information Offices for a booklet on where to fish in Shetland

CYCLING

With over 500 miles (800km) of good and generally quiet roads, cycling is, if you have the time and energy, one of the best ways to explore these beautiful islands.

GOLF COURSES

SHETLAND,
Lerwick, Mainland ☎ 01595 84369
Challenging moorland course with hard walking.

WHALSAY ☎ 01806 566450
The most northerly golf course in Britain, with a splendid coastline setting and spectacular holes .

LEISURE CENTRES

CLICKIMIN LEISURE COMPLEX,
Lerwick, Mainland ☎ 01595 741000

FRASER PETERSON CENTRE,
Firth, Mossbank, Mainland

UNST LEISURE CENTRE,
Baltasound, Unst

WHALSAY LEISURE CENTRE,
Symbister, Whalsay

YELL LEISURE CENTRE,
Mid Yell, Yell

RIDING

BROOTHOM PONIES,
Dunrossness, Mainland ☎ 01950 460556

SAILING

Lerwick, Scalloway, Brae and Whalsay Boating Clubs offers temporary membership and use of facilities to visiting yachtsmen.
LERWICK BOATING CLUB,
Mainland ☎ 01595 692407

SWIMMING

In addition to the Leisure Centres (see above), there are swimming pools on Mainland at Scalloway, Walls, Aith, Brae and Sandwick.

WALKING

Good waymarked walks can be enjoyed around most of the reserves in Shetland, notably on the Isle of Noss, on the RSPB Reserves at Lumbister and Black Park on Yell, and Fetlar and Hermaness Reserves on Unst. Guidebooks on walking around the island's coastline and other walks are available from the Tourist Office.

WATERSPORTS

Opportunities abound for sailing, windsurfing and waterskiing, and sub aqua enthusiasts will find the clear water, marine life and numerous wrecks around the coast most inviting.

DIVING & SIGHTSEEING TRIPS,
Voe, Mainland ☎/🖷 01806 588297

SKOLLA DIVING CENTRE,
Gulberwick, Mainland

WHERE TO STAY

CLYDE ISLANDS

Ardmory House

ARRAN, ISLE OF

North Ayrshire

BRODICK

AUCHRANNIE COUNTRY HOUSE
★★★⚜⚜

KA27 8BZ *(R from Brodick Ferry terminal, through Brodick, 2nd L after Brodick Golf Course clubhouse, then 300yds)*

☎ 01770 302234 🖷 01770 302812

Genuine hospitality, good food at this Victorian mansion, in six acres of grounds.
£££ 28 bedrooms (3 fmly) No dogs (ex guide dogs) Night porter Indoor swimming pool (heated) Snooker Sauna Solarium Gym Jacuzzi/spa Hair & beauty salon Aromatherapy Shiatsu No smoking area in restaurant 🍴

KILMICHAEL COUNTRY HOUSE ★⚜⚜
Glen Cloy KA27 8BY

(from Brodwick Ferry Terminal N on Lochranza rd for 1m. At golf course turn inland past sports field & church, follow signs)

☎ 01770 302219 🖷 01770 302068

Attractive historical house in a peaceful glen. Friendly staff will make your stay a memorable one.
£££ 6 bedrooms 3 annexe bedrooms No smoking in all bedrooms Jacuzzi/spa No children 12yrs No smoking in restaurant Closed Xmas 🍴

DUNVEGAN HOUSE ◙◙◙◙
Dunvegan Shore Rd KA27 8AJ *(R from ferry terminal, 500yds along Shore Rd)*

☎ 01770 302811

Lovely detached home overlooking the bay towards the castle and mountains. Taste of Scotland dishes.
9 bedrooms (1 fmly) No smoking in bedrooms No dogs (ex guide dogs) Licensed

ALLANDALE ◙◙◙
KA27 8BJ

☎ 01770 302278

Detached house in own gardens just outside the village. Bright cheery bedrooms.
£ 4 bedrooms 2 annexe bedrooms (4 fmly) No smoking in dining room or 1 lounge Licensed Jan-Oct

LAMLASH

LILYBANK HOTEL ◙◙◙◙
Shore Rd KA27 8LS

(4m S of Brodick Ferry Terminal)

☎ 01770 600230 🖷 01770 600230

This 18th-century home, overlooks the bay and is a welcoming small hotel.
6 bedrooms (1 fmly) No smoking in bedrooms or dining room Licensed Mar-Oct

LOCHRANZA

KINCARDINE LODGE ◙◙
KA27 8HL

☎ 01770 830267

Victorian lodge with a picture postcard outlook over the bay and castle.
6 bedrooms (2 fmly) No smoking in bedrooms, dining room No smoking in 1 lounge Apr-Oct

WHITING BAY

GRANGE HOUSE HOTEL ◙◙◙◙
KA27 8QH

(from Ferry Terminal turn L for Whiting Bay. In village, house 0.25m on R)

☎ 01770 700263 🖷 01770 700263

Fine Victorian house in attractive gardens looking out across the bay.
£ 7 bedrooms (1 fmly) No smoking No dogs Licensed 8 hole putting lawn Sauna Easter-Oct 🍴

INVERMAY HOTEL ◙◙◙
Shore Rd KA27 8PZ

☎ 01770 700431

Relaxed, friendly atmosphere at this comfortble house overlooking the Firth of Clyde.
£ 7 bedrooms No smoking in bedrooms No smoking in dining room No dogs (ex guide dogs) Licensed Apr-Oct

BUTE, ISLE OF

Argyll & Bute

ARDBEG

ARDMORY HOUSE HOTEL & RESTAURANT ★★⚜
Ardmory Rd PA20 0PG *(N from Rothesay on A844, 1m L into Ardmory Rd, 300mtrs on L)*

☎ 01700 502346 🖷 01700 505596

High levels of care at this most welcoming of small hotels, in own grounds overlooking the bay.
££ 5 bedrooms No smoking in all bedrooms or restaurant 🍴

INNER HEBRIDES

COLONSAY, ISLE OF

Argyll & Bute

SCALASAIG

COLONSAY ★⚜
PA61 7YP *(400mtrs W of Ferry Pier)*

☎ 01951 200316 🖷 01951 200353

Well worth the journey to sample the genuine hospitality and good food.
£££ (inc dinner) 10 bedrooms 1 annexe bedroom (1 fmly) Golf 18 ent No smoking in restaurant Closed 6 Nov-27 Dec & 12 Jan-Feb 🍴

ISLAY, ISLE OF

Argyll & Bute

BOWMORE

LOCHSIDE ★★
19 Shore St PA43 7LB

(on A846, 100yds from main village square)

☎ 01496 810244 🖷 01496 810390

The unassuming frontage gives no clue to the stunning outlook over Loch Indaal from this hotel. Seafood a speciality.
8 bedrooms (1 fmly) Pool table 🍴

BRIDGEND

BRIDGEND ★★
PA44 7PQ

☎ 01496 810212 🖷 01496 810960

In the middle of the island, this Victorian hotel, has a delightfully relaxed and friendly atmosphere.
££ 10 bedrooms (3 fmly) Fishing Bowls 🍴

Fairways Lodge

PORT ASKAIG ★★
PA46 7RD *(at Ferry Terminal)*
☎ **01496 840245** 🖷 **01496 840295**
Overlooking the Sound of Islay this welcoming hotel combines solid traditional hospitality and modern amenities.
8 bedrooms (1 fmly) No children 5yrs No smoking in restaurant

Argyll & Bute

ASSAPOL HOUSE ★◈
PA67 6DW *(turn off A849 just after school. Follow sign. 1m on minor rd)*
☎ **01681 700258** 🖷 **01681 700445**
(Rosette awarded for dinner only)
A small, relaxing country house enjoying a peaceful setting beside Loch Assapol.
££ (inc dinner) 5 bedrooms No dogs Fishing No children 10yrs No smoking in restaurant Closed Nov-Mar 🛥

DRUIMARD COUNTRY HOUSE ★★◈◈
PA75 6QW *(from Craignure ferry terminal turn R towards Tobermory, go through Salen Village, after 1.5m turn L to Dervaig, hotel on R)*
☎ **01688 400345** 🖷 **01688 400345**
Attractively restored Victorian country house where the cooking is very much an attraction.
£££ (inc dinner) 6 bedrooms (1 fmly) No smoking in restaurant Closed Nov-Mar Res Sunday Evenings 🛥

Bridgend

◙◙
PA75 6QJ *(through village past pink house, large house on ring)*
☎ **01688 400254** 🖷 **01688 400254**
Large white country house in own grounds. Two bedrooms have four poster beds.
£ 7 bedrooms (1 fmly) No smoking in 1 bedrooms or dining room Licensed Fishing 🛥

Western Isles

KILLIECHRONAN HOUSE ★★◈◈
Killiechronan Estate PA72 6JU
(from ferry R to Tobermory A849, in Salen turn L onto B8035. 2m turn R to Ulva ferry B8073, hotel on R)
☎ **01680 300403** 🖷 **01680 300463**
Small country house hotel with very high levels of service from enthusiastic staff.
£££ (inc dinner) 6 en suite (bth) TV available Fishing Riding No children 12yrs No smoking in restaurant Closed 1 Nov-28 Feb 🛥

PENNYGHAEL ★★
PA70 6HB
☎ **01681 704288**
This friendly family run hotel on the road to Iona enjoys superb views over Loch Scridain.
£££ (inc dinner) 6 en suite (bth) 🛥

WESTERN ISLES ★★★
PA75 6PR
☎ **01688 302012** 🖷 **01688 302297**
Commanding picture-postcard views of the bay with conservatory bar and restaurant specialising in eastern cuisine.
££ 26 bedrooms (2 fmly) No smoking in restaurant Closed 17-28 Dec 🛥

ULVA HOUSE ★
PA75 6PR
☎ **01688 302044**
Personal and friendly attention assured at this charming small hotel on the hill above the town.
£££ 6 bedrooms (1 fmly) No smoking in all bedrooms Landrover wildlife expeditions No smoking in restaurant Closed Nov-Mar

FAIRWAYS LODGE ◙◙◙◙◙
PA75 6PS
(in Tobermory follow signs for golf course)
☎ **01688 302238** 🖷 **01688 302238**
High levels of hospitality and views over golf course and the Sound of Mull.
5 bedrooms (1 fmly) No smoking in bedrooms or dining room Golf 9

SKYE & THE WESTERN ISLES

BARRA, ISLE OF

Western Isles

TANGUSDALE

ISLE OF BARRA ★ ★
Tangusdale Beach PA80 5XW
*(L after leaving ferry terminal onto A888,
hotel 2m on L)*
☎ 01871 810383 🕿 01871 810385
In a stunning position overlooking the
white sands of Halaman Bay and of the
Atlantic beyond.
*££ 30 bedrooms Pool table Wkly live
entertainment No smoking in restaurant
Closed 18 Oct–20 Mar* 🍴

HARRIS, ISLE OF

Western Isles

TARBERT

HARRIS ★ ★
HS3 3DL
(on A859, 500 yards from ferry terminal)
☎ 01859 502154 🕿 01859 502281
Traditional values of service, hospitality
and comfort are the hallmarks of this
holiday hotel.
*££ (inc dinner) 25 bedrooms (2 fmly) Pool
table Children's facilities No smoking area
in restaurant* 🍴

LEWIS, ISLE OF

Western Isles

BREASCLETE

ESHCOL ◙ ◙ ◙ ◙
HS2 9ED
*(from Stornoway take A859 to Tarbert, at
Luerbost turn R onto A858. 10m on look for
Eshcol sign)*
☎ 01851 621357 🕿 01851 621357
In a small croft this comfortable family
home has lovely views over Loch Roag to
the Harris hills beyond.
*££ 3 bedrooms No smoking in bedrooms,
dining room or lounges No children 8yrs
mid Mar–mid Oct*

Roskhill

SOUTH GALSON

GALSON FARM ◙ ◙ ◙ ◙
HS2 0SH *(off A857)*
☎ 01851 850492 🕿 01851 850492
Restored croft house with glorious views
of the Atlantic provides high standards of
comfort.
*3 bedrooms No smoking Licensed Clay
Pigeon Shooting* 🍴

STORNOWAY

CABARFEIDH ★ ★ ★
HS1 2EV *(1m from town centre on rd to
Tarbert, turn L at rndbt & then 1st R)*
☎ 01851 702604 🕿 01851 705572
Welcoming and comfortable modern hotel
with friendly staff willing to please.
*£££ 46 bedrooms (36 fmly) Lift Night
porter Air conditioning* 🍴

NORTH UIST, ISLE OF

Western Isles

HOUGHARRY

SGEIR RUADH ◙ ◙ ◙
HS6 5DL
☎ 01876 510312
Quietly located in a traditional crofting
community this detached modern home
overlooks Hougharry Bay and the Atlantic.
3 bedrooms

LOCHMADDY

LOCHMADDY ★ ★
HS6 5AA *(100yds from ferry terminal)*
☎ 01876 500331 🕿 01876 500210
This long established welcoming hotel is
especially popular with visiting anglers.
*££ 15 bedrooms (1 fmly) Fishing Pool table
No smoking in restaurant* 🍴

SKYE, ISLE OF

ARDVASAR

ARDVASAR ★ ★ ☸
IV45 8RS *(leave ferry, 50yds & turn L)*
☎ 01471 844223
Genuine warmth, good food and a
wonderfully relaxed atmosphere continues
to entice guests back.
*££ 9 bedrooms (3 fmly) No dogs (ex guide
dogs) Pool table No smoking in restaurant
Closed 24-25 Dec & 1-3 Jan Res Nov–Mar*
🍴

DUNVEGAN

ATHOLL HOUSE ★ ★ ☸
IV55 8WA
☎ 01470 521219 🕿 01470 521481
Personally run, warmly welcoming and
comfortable hotel at the southern end of
village.
*££ 9 bedrooms (1 fmly) No smoking in
restaurant Closed end Dec–end Feb* 🍴

ROSKHILL ◙ ◙ ◙ ◙
Roskhill IV55 8ZD *(2m S A863)*
☎ 01470 521317 🕿 01470 521761
Cottage-style former croft beside the
burbling River Rosgill, upgraded to provide
comfortable accommodation
*£ 5 bedrooms (1 fmly) No smoking Licensed
No children 10yrs* 🍴

HARLOSH

HARLOSH HOUSE ★ ☸ ☸ ☸
IV55 8ZG *(A863 between Roag & Caroy,
follow sign for Harlosh)*
☎ 01470 521367 🕿 01470 521367
Wonderfully tranquil setting on Loch
Bracadale, this house looks to the distant
Cuillins. Seafood well worth trying.
*££ 6 bedrooms (2 fmly) No smoking in
bedrooms or restaurant No dogs (ex guide
dogs) Closed mid Oct– Easter* 🍴

Ardvasar

ISLE ORNSAY

KINLOCH LODGE ★★ ⊛ ⊛
IV43 8QY *(on A851 6m S of Broadford/10m N of Armadale)*
☎ 01471 833214/833333 🖷 01471 833277
At the end of long forest track. Former lodge where guests are made to feel like friends. Renowned cuisine.
££ 10 bedrooms No smoking in all bedrooms Fishing Stalking No smoking in restaurant Closed Dec–14 Mar 🗫

HOTEL EILEAN IARMAIN ★ ⊛
IV43 8QR *(A851, A852, R to Isle Ornsay harbour front)*
☎ 01471 833332 🖷 01471 833275
Traditional hospitality and comfort at this 19th-century inn of old world charm. Innovative Scottish fare.
£££ 6 bedrooms 6 annexe en suite (bth) (2 fmly) No smoking in 6 bedrooms or restaurant Fishing Shooting Fishing Walking Children's facilities 🗫

> **Call the AA Hotel Booking Service on 0990 050505 to book at AA recognised hotels and B&Bs in the UK, or through our internet site: http://www.theaa.co.uk/hotels**

PORTREE

CUILLIN HILLS ★★★ ⊛
IV51 9LU *turn R 0.25m N of Portree on A855. Follow hotel signs)*
☎ 01478 612003 🖷 01478 613092
(Rosette awarded for dinner only)
Enjoys superb views over Portree Bay to the Cuillins beyond. Modern cuisine and Highland specialities.
£££ 16 bedrooms 9 annexe bedrooms (2 fmly) No smoking in restaurant 🗫

ROSEDALE ★★ ⊛
IV51 9DF *(hotel on the waterfront)*
☎ 01478 613131 🖷 01478 612531
(Rosette awarded for dinner only)
Ingeniously converted from three 19th-century harbour-front buildings. Interesting, praiseworthy menus.
££ 20 bedrooms 3 annexe bedrooms (1 fmly) No smoking in restaurant Closed Oct–mid May 🗫

BOSVILLE ★★ ⊛
Bosville Ter IV51 9DG
☎ 01478 612846 🖷 01478 613434
Well established family hotel providing good standards of accommodation. Interesting seafood dishes.
15 bedrooms (2 fmly) No smoking in 10 bedrooms No dogs (ex guide dogs) Night porter 🗫

Hotel Eilean Iarmain

ROYAL ★★
IV51 9BU *(A850 onto A855, hotel on corner overlooking harbour)*
☎ 01478 612525 🖷 01478 613198
Long established hotel with bistro, lounge and bars. Live entertainment in high season.
21 bedrooms (5 fmly) No smoking in 4 bedrooms Sauna Solarium Gym Pool table Jacuzzi/spa Wkly live entertainment No smoking area in restaurant 🗫

QUIRAING ◨◨◨◨
Viewfield Rd IV51 9ES *(on A850 - from S pass BP station & guest house is 400m on R)*
☎ 01478 612870 🖷 01478 612870
Comfortable family run bungalow just a four minute walk from town.
£ 6 bedrooms (2 fmly) No smoking in bedrooms No smoking in 1 lounge No dogs (ex guide dogs)

CRAIGLOCKHART ◨◨◨
Beaumont Crescent IV51 9DF
☎ 01478 612233
A warm Island welcome assured at this friendly family run guest house overlooking the bay and harbour.
10 bedrooms No dogs Closed Dec

UIG

UIG ★★
IV51 9YE
☎ 01470 542205 🖷 01470 542308
Well established hotel overlooking the bay. Many Scottish dishes on the menus.
££ 10 bedrooms 7 annexe bedrooms (2 fmly) Riding Sauna No smoking in restaurant 🗫

FERRY INN ★
IV51 9XP
(Pantree to Ung road, near ferry terminal)
☎ 01470 542242
Comfortable small Island inn with views over the bay. Gourmet and wholesome fare.
£ 6 bedrooms No smoking in 3 bedrooms No smoking area in restaurant Closed 25 Dec & 1 Jan Res Nov– Easter 🗫

ORKNEY

KIRKWALL

AYRE ★★★
Ayre Rd KW15 1QX
(follow A9 N to Scrabster. Car ferry to Stromness, A965 to Kirkwall)
☎ 01856 873001 🖷 01856 876289
Friendly family run hotel beside Kirkwall Bay. Bedrooms are tastefully decorated.
33 bedrooms (7 fmly) Night porter Pool table Wkly live entertainment 🗫

ALBERT ★★
Mounthoolie Ln KW15 1JZ
(from harbour into Junction Rd, 1st L into P&D car park. Hotel adjacent to opticians)
☎ 01856 876000 🖷 01856 875397
Close to the harbour and town centre, this comfortable hotel stands in a conservation area.
££ 19 bedrooms (2 fmly) Wkly live entertainment 🗫

SANDERLAY ◨◨◨
2 Viewfield Dr KW15 1RB
☎ 01856 872343 🖷 01856 876350
Modern house near the town centre. Three family rooms have small kitchen units.
£ 6 bedrooms (2 fmly) No smoking in 3 bedrooms, dining room or lounges No dogs (ex guide dogs) 🗫

ORPHIR

WESTROW LODGE ◨◨◨◨
KW17 2RD *(on A964)*
☎ 01856 811360 🖷 01856 811360
Peaceful, modern Norwegian-style timber house enjoying glorious views over Scappa Flow.
£ 2 bedrooms (1 fmly) No smoking No dogs

SHETLAND

BRAE

BUSTA HOUSE ★★★
ZE2 9QN
(from Brae follow road N, bearing L around Busta Voe. In 1m hotel signposted)
☎ 01806 522506 ⓕ 01806 522588
Charming 16th-century former laird's home peacefully set in its own grounds overlooking Busta Voe.
£££ 20 en suite bedrooms (bedrooms) (2 fmly) Sea fishing Water sports No smoking in restaurant Closed 23 Dec-2 Jan

LERWICK

SHETLAND ★★★⚙
Holmsgarth Rd ZE1 0PW *(opp P&O ferry terminal, on main rd N from town centre)*
☎ 01595 695515 ⓕ 01595 695828
Modern purpose-built hotel in ideal setting. Refined and more relaxed dining options.
£££ 64 bedrooms (4 fmly) No smoking in 14 bedrooms No dogs (ex guide dogs) Lift Night porter No smoking in restaurant

LERWICK ★★★
15 South Rd ZE1 0RB
(near town centre, on main rd)
☎ 01595 692166 ⓕ 01595 694419
Popular hotel just a ten minute walk of central amenities. Views over Breiwick Bay.
£££ 35 bedrooms (3 fmly) No dogs (ex guide dogs) Night porter No smoking area in restaurant

GLEN ORCHY HOUSE ◗◗◗◗
20 Knab Rd ZE1 0AX
(adjct to coastguard station)
☎ 01595 692031 ⓕ 01595 692031
Former convent now a welcoming small hotel near the golf course. Enjoyable home-cooking.
14 bedrooms (3 fmly) No smoking in dining room Licensed Golf 9

UNST

THE BALTASOUND ★★
ZE2 9DS
☎ 01957 711334 ⓕ 01957 711358
Friendly and informal family-run hotel, the most northerly in the British Isles.
££ 10 bedrooms 17 annexe bedrooms (17 fmly) No dogs (ex guide dogs) Fishing Pool table

Busta House

WHERE TO EAT

RESTAURANTS

AA RECOMMENDED

ARRAN, ISLE OF

BRODICK

AUCHRANNIE HOTEL ⚙⚙
KA27 8BZ
☎ 01770 302234 ⓕ 01770 302812
The fixed-price menu changes daily and might include wild rabbit saddle stuffed with Agen prunes in a puff pastry net or crisp breast of Gressingham duck paired with a rillette, black pudding and apple stack and a warm apple charlotte made with brioche.
Fixed D ££

KILMICHAEL COUNTRY HOUSE HOTEL ⚙⚙
Glen Cloy KA27 8BY
☎ 01770 302219 ⓕ 01770 302068
To begin there may be an unusual ravioli, beetroot filled with four cheeses or hare and rosemary packed into rich chocolate pasta. Main courses could be seared king scallops with a rich orange and wasabi beurre blanc and to finish, a feuillantine with berries and a Chartreuse sabayon.
Fixed D £££ ALC ££

BUTE, ISLE OF

ARDBEG

ARDMORY HOUSE HOTEL ⚙
Ardmory Road PA20 0EG
☎ 01700 502346 ⓕ 01700 505596
Haggis flavoured with whisky in a filo parcel with plum sauce, cream of broccoli soup, steamed suprême of Loch Fad trout drizzled with citrus herb butter, and Ardmory style mango cheesecake with Cointreau might be a typical four-course dinner, but there's plenty of choice.
Fixed D ££

COLONSAY, ISLE OF

SCALASAIG

COLONSAY HOTEL ⚙
PA61 7YP
☎ 01951 200316 ⓕ 01951 200353
Colonsay is a remote Hebridean island with a ferry service every second day. To make the most of fresh produce, the hotel's daily changing, fixed-price menu offers no choice, but features the likes of grilled Colonsay mackerel with gooseberry sauce, smoked Argyll venison and gratin of Colonsay crab.
Fixed D ££

MULL, ISLE OF

BUNESSAN

ASSAPOOL HOUSE HOTEL ⚙
PA67 6DW
☎ 01681 700258 ⓕ 01681 700445
Peacefully set beside Loch Assapool, this charming small country house hotel offers a welcoming atmosphere and home-cooked food. Watercress and almond soup, salmon with dill hollandaise, and hay-baked chocolate cheesecake are typical choices on the short set menu.
Fixed D £

DERVAIG

DRUIMARD HOTEL ⚙⚙
PA75 6QW
☎/ⓕ 01688 400345
There is plenty of local and Scottish produce on show here. Potted wild salmon is served with chive sauce and oatcakes, saddle of wild venison appears on a bed of braised red cabbage with game sauce and desserts such as rich chocolate torte or trifle laced with Bailey's liqueur are both unusual and decadent.
Fixed D ££ ALC ££

Creel Restaurant

KILLIECHRONAN

KILLIECHRONAN HOUSE ❀❀
PA72 6JU
☎ 01680 300403 ☎ 01680 300463
Opening with thinly sliced oak-smoked venison and a Waldorf salad, on to cream of asparagus soup, then a blackberry sorbet, before medallions of pork with wild mushrooms and gnocchi, and finishing with a chocolate marquise and Grand Marnier sauce.
Fixed D ££ 🍷

ORKNEY

ST MARAGRET'S HOPE

CREEL RESTAURANT ❀
Front Road KW17 2SL
☎ 01856 831311
Has a sound reputation with visitors and islanders alike. The focus is on fresh Orkney produce. Specialities include seafood, prime Scottish beef and 'bere bannocks' - a traditional Orkney scone. Advance booking is advisable.
ALC ££ 🍷

SHETLAND

LERWICK

SHETLAND HOTEL ❀
Holmsgarth Road ZE1 0PW
☎ 01595 695515 ☎ 01595 695828
In the Ninian Restaurant expect to find dishes as local Herring fillets marinated in dill and white wine, grouse with oatmeal and orange skirlie and apple and sultana pie with strong Drambuie ice cream.
Fixed D ££ 🍷

SKYE, ISLE OF

ARDVASAR

ARDVASAR HOTEL ❀
Isle of Skye IV45 8RS
☎ 01471 844223
Quality island produce is used to good effect in dishes such as fresh Skye salmon mousse, potted crab, roast chicken leg with Skye honey-mustard glaze, and braised local lamb chops with rosemary, tomato and potato crust.
ALC ££ 🍷

COLBOST

THREE CHIMNEYS RESTAURANT ❀❀
Dunvegan IV55 8ZT
☎ 01470 511258 ☎ 01470 511358
Fresh seafood is the star attraction. Partan bree (a traditional crab soup) is a favourite way to start followed by hot lobster and langoustines flamed in brandy. For red meat lovers there's a trio of red deer, pigeon and hare.
ALC £££ 🍷

DUNVEGAN

ATHOLL HOUSE HOTEL ❀
IV55 8WA
☎ 01470 521219 ☎ 01470 521481
From the short carte you can expect to find dishes such as local mussel and prawn chowder, a full flavoured rib eye steak Forestierre and strawberries with brandy and caramel with pancakes.
ALC ££ 🍷

HARLOSH

HARLOSH HOUSE ❀❀❀
Dunvegan IV55 8ZG
☎/☎ 01470 521367
So that returning guests always taste something new, a record is kept of every dish and meal eaten. The sheer freshness of the fish is impressive as in tip–top monkfish arranged atop a construction of spinach and onion marmalade and also Loch Bracadale crab with a salad of chargrilled asparagus.
Fixed D £££ 🍷

ISLE ORNSAY

HOTEL EILEAN IARMAIN ❀
IV43 8QR
☎ 01471 833332 ☎ 01471 833275
What a waterside position! The kitchen is ambitious and offers innovative cooking of local seafood and game. A typical meal could take in pheasant soup, gently steamed scallops with a saffron sauce, and hot chocolate and almond pudding.
Fixed L ££ 🍷

KINLOCH LODGE ❀❀
IV43 8QY
☎ 01471 833214 ☎ 01471 833277
Lord and Lady Macdonald's converted 300–year–old lodge where dishes are based resolutely on what the local region can provide. On one occasion there was a full flavoured scallop terrine, a clear mushroom soup tinged with fresh mint, then roast breast and leg of duck accompanied by Calvados and apple purée.
Fixed D £££ 🍷

PORTREE

BOSVILLE HOTEL ❀
Bosville Terrace IV51 9DG
☎ 01478 612846 ☎ 01478 613434
Two restaurants, one offers an all day menu, while Chandlery's (evenings only) specialises in seafood dishes. Expect seafood and avocado baked with Pernod cream, panaché of seafood with dill and lemon butter, and white and dark chocolate terrine.
Fixed L £ ALC ££ 🍷

CUILLIN HILLS HOTEL ❀
IV51 9LU
☎ 01478 612003 ☎ 01478 613092
Expect a modern style of cooking highlighting quality local ingredients. Specialities may include venison steak with juniper berry, gin and garlic jus, and oven-roasted pheasant with green peppercorn whisky sauce.
Fixed D ££ 🍷

ROSEDALE HOTEL ❀
IV51 9DB
☎ 01478 613131 ☎ 01478 612531
Innovative modern cooking using prime local ingredients produces dishes such as lentil and apricot soup, pot roast beef with prunes and Guinness, and rhubarb tarte Tatin.
Fixed D £££ 🍷

EDINBURGH

Where to Eat page 35

36 at the Howard, Edinburgh

EDINBURGH

Must See pages 18 & 19

City of Edinburgh Museums

CENTRAL

Hotel Accommodation page 135

Lovat Hotel, Perth

ARGYLL & BUTE

Hotel Accommodation pages 173 & 178

Willowburn Hotel, Isle of Seil

NORTH EAST

Where to Eat page 160

Old Monastery Restaurant, Drybridge

NORTH EAST

Ramnee Hotel, Forres

Hotel Accommodation & Restaurant
pages 158 & 160

HIGHLANDS

Hotel Accommodation & Restaurant
pages 203 & 205

Loch Torridon Hotel, Torridon

HIGHLANDS

Hotel Accommodation & Restaurant
pages 158 & 160

Mansion House Hotel, Moray

THE ISLANDS

Hotel Accommodation page 231

Pennyghael Hotel, Isle of Mull

Port Askaig, Islay

THE ISLANDS

Hotel Accommodation page 231

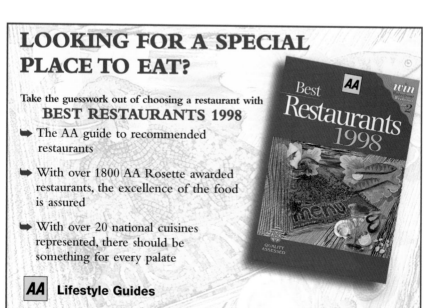

LOOKING FOR A SPECIAL PLACE TO EAT?

Take the guesswork out of choosing a restaurant with
BEST RESTAURANTS 1998

➡ The AA guide to recommended restaurants

➡ With over 1800 AA Rosette awarded restaurants, the excellence of the food is assured

➡ With over 20 national cuisines represented, there should be something for every palate

AA **Lifestyle Guides**

Best **AA** *win*
Restaurants *1998*
menu
QUALITY
ASSESSED

A

A & R M Stewart, Eday 226
A'Anside Studio, Tomintoul, Moray 147
Aaron Glen, Loanhead, Midlothian 39
Abbotsford Arms, Galashiels, Borders 47
Abbotsford House, Melrose, Borders 43
Abbotsford Lodge, Callander, Central 125
Abcorn, Edinburgh 30
Abercrn, Edinburgh 30
Abercrombie, Perth, Central 136
Aberdeen 141
Aberdeen Airport 147
Aberdeen Airport Thistle, Aberdeen 152
Aberdeen Art Gallery, Aberdeen 145
Aberdeen Maritime Museum, Aberdeen 144
Aberdeen Marriott, Aberdeen 152
The Aberdeen Thistle, Aberdeen 150
Aberdeenshire 140
    access 147
    accommodation 150-5
    beaches 149
    crafts 147
    entertainment 148
    food and drink 148
    pubs, inns and other eating places 157
    restaurants 155-6
    scenic drives 149
    sightseeing 144, 145, 146-7
    sport and leisure 148-9
    tourist information 147
    tours 148
    transport 148
Aberdeenshire Farming Museum, Mintlaw,
    Aberdeenshire 144
Aberdour Castle, Aberdour, Fife 104
Aberdour Golf Course, Fife 106
The Aberdour Hotel, Aberdour, Fife 114
Aberfeldy Distillery, Aberfeldy, Central 131
Aberfeldy Golf Course, Central 131
Aberfeldy Lodge, Inverness, Highlands 186
Aberfeldy Recreation Centre, Central 131
Aberfeldy Water Mill, Aberfeldy, Central 129
Aberfoyle Golf Course, Stirling 122
Aberlemno Sculptured Stones, Brechin,
    Angus 103
Aberlour Gardens Caravan Park, Aberlour,
    Moray 159
Aberlour Riding & Trekking Centre, Moray 149
Abernethy Golf Course, Nethy Bridge,
    Highlands 172
About Argyll Walking Holidays, Central 123
Acarsaid, Pitlochry, Central 137
Achalone Activities, Halkirk, Highlands 198
Achamore House Gardens, Gigha 214
Achiltibuie Hydroponicum, Ullapool,
    Highlands 197
Achiltibuie Smokehouse, Ullapool, Highlands 198
Achilty, Contin, Highlands 199
Achness, Rosehall, Highlands 203
Achray House, St Fillans, Central 138
Acorn Lodge, Edinburgh 29
Adam Hotel, Edinburgh 29
Adam, Perth, Central 136
The Adria Hotel, Edinburgh 32
Aikwood Tower, Selkirk, Borders 43
Ainslie Park, Edinburgh 24
Aird Donald Caravan Park, Dumf/Gal 64
Airds Hotel, Port Appin, Argyll 177, 178
Aisla Craig, Ayrshire 67
Alan Lees - Woodcarver, Kirkmichael,
    Dumf/Gal 55
Alba Yacht Services Ltd, Oban, Argyll 167
Albert, Kirkwall, Orkney 233
Alexandra, Ballater, Aberdeenshire 153
Alexandra, Fort William, Highlands 182
Alexandra Golf Course, Glasgow 81
Alexandra Wolffe Studio Gallery, Gatehouse of
    Fleet, Dumf/Gal 55
Alford Ski Centre, Alford, Aberdeenshire 149
Alford Valley Railway, Alford, Aberdeenshire 146
Alfresco Adventure, Fort William, Highlands 172
All Saints Leisure Centre, Glasgow 81
Allandale, Brodick, Arran 230
Allison House, Edinburgh 27
Alloa Gallery & Museum, Alloa, Central 120
Alloa Golf Course, Alloa, Central 122
Alloa Leisure Bowl, Alloa, Central 122

Alloa Tower, Alloa, Central 121
Allt-Nan-Ros Hotel, Onich, Highlands 189, 192
Almardon, Callander, Central 125
Almond Valley Heritage Centre, Livingston Village,
    West Lothian 21
Alness Golf Course, Highlands 198
Aloft - Largs Yacht Haven Gallery, Largs,
    Ayrshire 67
Alp Restaurant, Edinburgh 36
Altnaharrie Inn, Ullapool, Highlands 205
Alton Burn, Nairn, Highlands 189
Alva Golf Course, Central 122
Alyth Golf Course, Central 131
Amaryllis, Edinburgh 30
Amberside, St Andrews, Fife 115
An Fuaran, Edinburgh 30
An Lanntair Gallery, Stornoway, Lewis 218
An Tairbeart Heritage Centre, Loch Fyne,
    Argyll 165
An Tobar - The Tobermory Centre, Tobermory,
    Mull 214
An Tuireann Arts Centre, Portree, Skye 218
Anchor Hotel, Dalbeattie, Dumf/Gal 60
The Anchorage, Dunoon, Argyll 174
Ancrum Centre for the Environment, Dundee 106
Ancrum Craig, Ancrum, Borders 47
Andrew Carnegie Birthplace Museum,
    Dunfermline, Fife 103
Andrew Elliot Ltd, Selkirk, Borders 45
Anglers Inn, Perth, Central 136
Angus 100
    access 105
    accommodation 108-10
    beaches 107
    crafts 105
    entertainment 105
    food and drink 105
    pubs, inns and other eating places 110
    restaurants 110
    scenic drives 107
    sightseeing 102, 103-4
    sport and leisure 106-7
    tourist information 105
    tours 105
    transport 105
Angus, Blairgowrie, Central 133
Angus Folk Museum, Glamis, Angus 103
Angus Glens, Angus 102
Angus Gliding Club, Forfar, Angus 106
Angus Hotel, Glasgow 84
Ann Hughes Pottery, Balmaclellan, Dumf/Gal 55
The Annan Gallery, Glasgow 79
Annandale Arms Hotel, Moffat, Dumf/Gal 59
Annandale Equestrian Centre, Mintlaw,
    Aberdeenshire 149
Annfield, Callander, Central 125
Anstruther Golf Course, Fife 106
Anstruther Pleasure Trips, Fife 105
Antonine Wall, Falkirk 20
Anvilla, Edinburgh 32
Anwoth Caravan Site, Gatehouse of Fleet,
    Dumf/Gal 63
Apex International, Edinburgh 26
Appaloosa Riding Centre, Lochgilphead,
    Argyll 167
Appin Equestrian Centre, North Berwick,
    East Lothian 24
Applewood, Aberdeen 152
Aquadome, Inverness, Highlands 172
Arbigland Gardens, Kirkbean, Dumf/Gal 54
Arbor Lodge, Aboyne, Aberdeenshire 152
Arbor Lodge, Balloch, Central 124
Arbroath Abbey, Arbroath, Angus 103
Arbroath Cliff Nature Trail, Arbroath, Angus 104
Arbroath Golf Course, Arbroath, Angus 106
Arbroath Signal Tower Museum, Arbroath,
    Angus 103
Arbroath Sports Centre, Angus 106
Arbuthnot Museum & Art Gallery, Peterhead,
    Aberdeenshire 145
Archaeolink Prehistory Park, Oyne,
    Aberdeenshire 146
Arches Craft Shop, Ballachulish, Highlands 171
Archiestown Hotel, Archiestown, Moray 158, 160
Arctic Penguin Maritime Heritage Centre,
    Inveraray, Argyll 165
Ard Struan Guest House, Oban, Argyll 176

Ardanaiseig Gardens, Kilchrenan, Argyll 165
Ardansaiseig Hotel, Kilchrenan, Argyll 175, 178
Ardbeg House, Dervaig, Mull 231
Ardblair, Oban, Argyll 176
Ardchattan Garden, Loch Etive, Argyll 165
Ardchoille, Auchtermuchty, Fife 114
Ardconnel House, Grantown-on-Spey,
    Highlands 184
Arden, Edinburgh 30
Arden House, Callander, Central 125
Arden House, Edinburgh 30
Ardencaple Hotel, Rhu, Argyll 180
Ardencraig Gardens, Rothesay, Bute 210
Ardent House, Hopeman, Moray 159
Ardentinny Hotel, Ardentinny, Argyll 173, 177, 179
Ardentinny Outdoor Centre, Dunoon, Argyll 167
Ardestie & Carlungie Earth-Houses, Angus 103
Ardfern House, Perth, Central 136
Ardgowan, St Andrews, Fife 113
Ardlarig, Grantown-on-Spey, Highlands 184
Ardmory House Hotel & Restaurant, Ardbeg,
    Bute 177, 230, 234
Ardmuir House, Inverness, Highlands 186
Ardnadam Riding Centre, Dunoon, Argyll 167
Ardnamurchan Natural History Centre, Acharacle,
    Highlands 170
Ardoch Cottage, Gartocharn, Central 126
Ardoe House Hotel, Aberdeen 150, 155
Ardross House, Inverness, Highlands 186
Ardrossan Castle, Ardrossan, Ayrshire 66
Ards House, Connel, Argyll 174
Ardsheal Home Farm, Kentallen, Highlands 188
Ardsheal House Hotel, Kentallen, Highlands 188
Arduaine Garden, Kilmelford, Argyll 165
Arduli Hotel, Marina & Holiday Park, Loch
    Lomond, Central 123
Ardvasar Hotel, Ardvasar, Skye 232, 235
Ardveck, Ullapool, Highlands 203
Ardvreck Castle, Lochinver, Highlands 196
Ardwell House Gardens, Ardwell, Dumf/Gal 54
Argyll 161, 164-7, 173-9
    access 166
    accommodation 173-7
    crafts 166
    entertainment 166
    food and drink 166
    pubs, inns and other eating places 179-80
    restaurants 177-9
    scenic drives 167
    sightseeing 165-6
    sport and leisure 167
    tourist information 166
    transport 166
Argyll Forest Park 167
Argyll Forest Park, Kilmun, Argyll 166
Argyll Isles Cruising Tuition, Lochgilphead,
    Argyll 167
Argyll Pottery, Oban, Argyll 166
Argyll Riding & Activities, Inveraray, Argyll 167
Argyll Wildlife Park, Inveraray, Argyll 165
Arisaig, Arisaig, Highlands 180
Arisaig House, Arisaig, Highlands 180, 191
Arniston House, Gorebridge, Midlothian 21
Aros Castle, Salen, Mull 214
The Aros Heritage Centre, Portree, Skye 218
Arran 208, 209, 210, 211
Arran Distillers, Lochranza, Arran 211
Arran Heritage Centre, Rosaburn, Arran 210
Arran House, St Andrews, Fife 115
Arran Lodge, Callander, Central 125
Arran Outdoor Centre, Shiskine, Arran 211
Arran Pottery, Thunderguy, Arran 211
Arrandale House, Pitlochry, Central 137
Ashburn, Kilbarchan, Renfrewshire 94
Ashburn House, Fort William, Highlands 183
Ashcroft Farmhouse, East Calder, West Lothian 38
Ashdene House, Edinburgh 30
Ashgrove House, Edinburgh 30
Ashlyn, Galashiels, Borders 47
Askernish Golf Course, South Uist 220
Assapool House Hotel, Bunessan,
    Mull 177, 231, 234
A.S.W. Fishing Charters, Dalry, Ayrshire 68
Atholl, Aberdeen 150
Atholl Arms, Blair Atholl, Central 132
Atholl Arms, Dunkeld, Angus 109, 138

Atholl Country Collection, Blair Atholl, Central 129
Atholl Curling Rink, Pitlochry, Central 131
Atholl House Hotel, Dunvegan, Skye 232, 235
Atholl Palace, Pitlochry, Central 137
Atlantis Leisure, Oban, Argyll 167
Atrium, Edinburgh 34
Attadale Garden & Woodland Walks, Strathcarron, Highlands 197
Aubigny Sports Centre, Haddington, East Lothian 24
Auchen Castle, Beattock, Dumf/Gal 57
Auchencloigh, Galston, Ayrshire 70
Auchenlarie Holiday Farm, Gatehouse of Fleet, Dumf/Gal 63
Auchenlea, Coatbridge, N. Lanarkshire 94
Auchenskeoch Lodge, Dalbeattie, Dumf/Gal 60
Auchindoun Castle, Dufftown, Moray 145
Auchindrain Old Highland Township, Inveraray, Argyll 165
Auchingarrich Wildlife Centre, Comrie, Central 129
Auchrannie Country House, Brodick, Arran 230
Auchrannie Hotel, Brodick, Arran 234
Auchrannie Leisure Centre, Brodick, Arran 211
Auchterarder Golf Course, Central 131
Auchterarder House, Auchterarder, Central 132, 138
Auchterarder Motors, Central 131
Auchterhouse Country Sports, Dundee 106
Auld Reekie (bed and breakfast), Edinburgh 31
Auld Reekie Tours, Borders 45
Auld Reekie Tours, Edinburgh 24
Aultbea, Aultbea, Highlands 199
Aultmore House, Nethy Bridge, Highlands 189
Aulton Farm, Kilmarnock, Ayrshire 70
Avalon Trekking Scotland, Central 131
Averon, Edinburgh 33
Averon Leisure Centre, Alness, Highlands 198
Aviemore Highlands, Aviemore, Highlands 180
Aviemore Mountain Bikes & Activities, Highlands 172
Aviemore Mountain Resort, Highlands 171, 172
Aviemore Ski School, Highlands 172
Avondale House, Kingussie, Highlands 188
Avonlea, Strathaven, S. Lanarkshire 94
Ayr 52
Ayr Ice Rink, Ayrshire 68
Ayr Racecourse, Ayrshire 68
Ayr Sea Angling Centre, Ayr, Ayrshire 68
Ayre, Kirkwall, Orkney 233
Ayrshire 51, 66-73
    access 67
    accommodation 69-72
    beaches 68
    crafts 67
    entertainment 67
    food and drink 68
    restaurants 72-3
    scenic drives 68
    sightseeing 66-7
    sport and leisure 68
    tourist information 67
    tours 68
    transport 68
Ayrshire Equitation Centre, Ayrshire 68
Ayton Castle, Eyemouth, Borders 44

B

Bachelors' Club, Tarbolton, Ayrshire 66
Backcountry Adventure, Innerleithen, Borders 45
Bailey Mill Trekking Centre, Newcastleton, Borders 46
Bains, Gairloch, Highlands 200
Balbirnie Craft Centre, Markinch, Fife 105
Balbirnie House, Markinch, Fife 112, 117
Balbirnie Park Golf Course, Markinch, Fife 106
Balcary Bay, Auchencairn, Dumf/Gal 57
Balcaskie House, Pittenweem, Fife 104
Balcomie Golf Course, Fife 106
Balcomie Links, Crail, Fife 111
Balmerino Abbey, Balmerino, Fife 104
Balfour Castle, Shapinsay 225
Balgeddie House, Glenrothes, Fife 111
Balgonie House Hotel, Ballater, Aberdeenshire 152, 156

Balhall Riding Stables, Menmuir, Angus 106
Balkissock Lodge, Ballantrae, Ayrshire 69
Ballachulish, Ballachulish, Highlands 180
Ballathie House Hotel, Kinclaven, Central 134, 139
Ballifeary House Hotel, Inverness, Highlands 185
Ballindalloch Castle, Ballindalloch, Moray 147
Ballivicar Farm, Port Ellen, Islay 215
Balmacara (Lochalsh Woodland Garden), Kyle of Lochalsh, Highlands 197
Balmoral, Edinburgh 25
Balmoral Castle Grounds, & Exhibition, Balmoral, Aberdeenshire 146
Balmoral Mill Shop, Galston, Ayrshire 67
Balnain House, Inverness, Highlands 169
Balnakeil Craft Village, Durness, Highlands 197
Balnakilly Riding Centre, Kirkmichael, Central 131
Balranald RSPB Nature Reserve, Hougharry, North Uist 219
Balrobin, Pitlochry, Central 137
The Baltasound, Unst, Shetland 234
Balvenie Castle, Dufftown, Moray 146
Banchory Lodge, Banchory, Aberdeenshire 153
Banff Springs, Banff, Aberdeenshire 153
Bank House, Ballater, Aberdeenshire 153
Bankell Farm Stables, Milngavie, E. Dunbartonshire 91
Bankfoot Riding School, Inverkip, Inverclyde 91
Bannockburn Heritage Centre, Stirling 120
Barbara Davidson Pottery, Larbert, Falkirk 22
Barbara Ibister Knitwear, Cunningsburgh, Mainland 228
Barbarafield Riding School, Cupar, Fife 107
Barcaldine Castle, Oban, Argyll 165
Barend Riding Centre, Dalbeattie, Dumf/Gal 56
Barholm Mains Open Farm, Creetown, Dumf/Gal 54
Barlochan Caravan Park, Palnackie, Dumf/Gal 64
The Barn, Oban, Argyll 180
Barnhill Springs, Moffat, Dumf/Gal 61
Barnsoul Farm, Irongray, Dumf/Gal 63
Barnton Thistle, Edinburgh 26
Barnyard Studios, Garmouth, Moray 145
Barpa Langass, North Uist 218
Barra 218, 219, 220
Barra Boat Trips 220
Barra Golf Course 220
Barrack Street Natural History Museum, Dundee 103
The Barras Market, Glasgow 80
Barrie's Birthplace, Kirriemuir, Angus 103
Barrington House, Castle Douglas, Dumf/Gal 60
Barry Mill, Barry, Angus 103
Bass Rock 21
Bathgate Sports Centre, West Lothian 24
Baxters Visitor Centre, Fochabers, Moray 145, 148
Bayswell, Dunbar, East Lothian 37
Baytree House, St Andrews, Fife 115
Beach House Hotel, Dundee 109
Beach Leisure Centre, Aberdeen 149
Beachway House, St Andrews, Fife 115
Beacon Leisure Centre, Burntisland, Fife 106
Beardmore, Glasgow 82
Beardmore Hotel, Clydebank, W. Dunbartonshire 92, 95
Beattock House, Beattock, Dumf/Gal 57
Beattock House Hotel Caravan Park, Beattock, Dumf/Gal 62
Beaufort, Inverness, Highlands 185
Beauly Priory, Beauly, Highlands 170
Beaumont Lodge, Anstruther, Fife 114
The Beeches, Gretna, Dumf/Gal 60
Beechgrove Sports Centre, Moffat, Dumf/Gal 56
Beechwood Country House Hotel, Moffat, Dumf/Gal 59, 65
Beeswing Caravan Park, Beeswing, Dumf/Gal 62
Beinn Eighe Nature Reserve, Kinlochewe, Highlands 197
Belgrave, Glasgow 83
The Belhaven, Glasgow 84
Bell Craig, St Andrews, Fife 115
Bella Jane Boat Trips, Skye 220
Bellahouston Leisure Centre, Glasgow 81
Bellahouston Park, Glasgow 80
Belleville, Elgin, Moray 159
The Belmonte Fish and Chip Shop, Carnoustie, Angus 110
Belsyde House, Linlithgow, West Lothian 38

The Belvedere, Kirkcaldy, Fife 112
Bemersyde, Arrochar, Argyll 173
Ben Doran, Edinburgh 32
Ben Loyal Hotel, Tongue, Highlands 203, 205
Ben Nevis Woollen Mill, Fort William, Highlands 171
Benbecula 216, 219, 220
Bencorragh House, John O'Groats, Highlands 201
Benmore Lodge, Crianlarich, Central 125
Bennybeg Craft Centre, Crieff, Central 130
Benvenuto Pizzeria Trattoria, Dumfries, Dumf/Gal 65
Benview, Fort William, Highlands 183
Bernaray Car Ferry 219
Bespoke Highland Tours, Highlands 172
Beth Abba Studio, Hamnavoe, Mainland 228
Beverley Hotel, Edinburgh 31
Beverley's Restaurant, Dunoon, Argyll 178
Bigfoot Adventures, Strathdon, Aberdeenshire 148
Biggar Gasworks Museum, Biggar, S. Lanarkshire 88
Biggar Puppet Theatre, Biggar, S. Lanarkshire 89
Bimini, Aberdeen 152
Binniemyre, Galashiels, Borders 47
Birchwood, Gairloch, Highlands 200
Birchwood, Pitlochry, Central 137
Birkhill Clay Mine, Birkhill, Falkirk 20
Birnam House, Birnam, Central 132
Birse Lodge, Aboyne, Aberdeenshire 152
Bishop's & Earl's Palaces, Kirkwall, Mainland 224
Black Bull, Killearn, Central 126, 128
Black Bull Inn, Moffat, Dumf/Gal 65
Black Bull Thistle, Milngavie, E. Dunbartonshire 93
Black House Museum, Arnol, Lewis 218
Black Isle Country Park, North Kessock, Highlands 196
Black Isle Leisure Centre, Fortrose, Highlands 198
The Black Sheep Restaurant, Tarbet, Argyll 180
Black Watch Regimental Museum, Perth, Central 129
Blackaddie House, Sanquhar, Dumf/Gal 60
Blackhill, S. Lanarkshire 89
Blackness Castle, Linlithgow, West Lothian 20
Blackshaw Farm Park, West Kilbride, Ayrshire 67
Bladnoch Distillery Visitor Centre, Bladnoch Wigtown, Dumf/Gal 56
Blair Athol Distillery, Pitlochry, Central 131
Blair Atholl Golf Course, Central 131
Blair Castle, Blair Atholl, Central 129
Blair Castle Riding Centre, Blair Atholl, Central 131
Blair Drummond Safari & Leisure Park, Blair Drummond, Stirling 120
Blairgowrie Golf Course, Central 131
Blairgowrie Recreation Centre, Central 131
Blairmore & Strone Golf Course, Dunoon, Argyll 167
Blantyre Sports Centre, S. Lanarkshire 91
Blawearie House, Turnberry, Ayrshire 72
Blinkbonnie, Portpatrick, Dumf/Gal 61
Boat, Boat of Garten, Highlands 181
Boat of Garten Golf Course, Highlands 172
Bobbin, Gatehouse of Fleet, Dumf/Gal 60
Bobsport Ltd, Highlands 172
Bod of Gremista Museum, Lerwick, Mainland 227
Bogroy Inn, Kirkhill, Highlands 188
Boisdale Hotel, Edinburgh 33
Boleskine, Moffat, Dumf/Gal 61
Bon Accord, Melrose, Borders 48
Bon Accord Baths & Leisure Centre, Aberdeen 149
Bon Accord Tours, Aberdeen 148
Bonar Bridge-Ardgay Golf Course, Highlands 198
Bonars Restaurant, Gifford, East Lothian 40
Bond Bar, Aberdeen 157
Bo'ness & Kinneil Railway, Bo'ness, Falkirk 18
Bonhoga Gallery, Weisdale, Mainland 227
Bonnington, Edinburgh 29
Bonnyrigg Leisure Centre, Midlothian 24
Bonnyton Golf Club, Eaglesham, Renfrewshire 91
The Border Country Route, Borders 46
Borders 41-50
    access 45
    accommodation 47-9
    beaches 46

crafts 45
entertainment 45
food and drink 45
restaurants 50
scenic drives 46
sightseeing 43-4
sport and leisure 45-6
tourist information 45
tours 45, 46
transport 45
Boreland Riding Centre, Aberfeldy, Central 131
Borgh Pottery, Borve, Lewis 219
Borlum Farmhouse, Drumnadrochit,
Highlands 182
Borve, Inverness, Highlands 186
Bosville Hotel, Portree, Skye 233, 235
Botanic Gardens, Glasgow 80
Botanic Hotel, Glasgow 84
Bothwell Bridge, Bothwell, S. Lanarkshire 92
Bothwell Castle, Bothwell, S. Lanarkshire 88
Bourbon Street, Glasgow 87
Bowfield Hotel & Country Club, Howwood,
Renfrewshire 93
Bowhill House & Country Park, Selkirk,
Borders 43
Bowmore, Islay 213
Bowmore Distillery, Bowmore, Islay 215
Bracklinn Falls, Callander, Stirling 121
Braden Crafts, Coldstream, Borders 45
Bradfords, Glasgow 87
The Brae Hotel, Fort Augustus, Highlands 182, 191
Brae Ness Hotel, Inverness, Highlands 186
Braemar Castle, Braemar, Aberdeenshire 146
Braemar Lodge, Braemar, Aberdeenshire 154
Braeside Trekking & Riding Centre, Beauly,
Highlands 172
Braeval, Aberfoyle, Central 128
Braid Hills, Edinburgh 26
Braidenhill, Glenmavis, N. Lanarkshire 94
Braids Caravan Park, Gretna, Dumf/Gal 63
Braidwood Sporting Clays, Selkirk, Borders 45
Braidwoods, Dalry, Ayrshire 93
Brander Lodge, Taynuilt, Argyll 177
Branklyn Garden, Perth, Central 130
Breadalbane Folklore Centre, Killin, Stirling 120
Brechin Cathedral & Round Tower, Brechin,
Angus 103
Brechin Golf Course, Angus 106
Bremen Bod, Symbister, Whalsay 227
Brenalder Lodge, Ayr, Ayrshire 69
Bressary 228
Briarbank, Oban, Argyll 176
Brideswell Riding Centre, Alford,
Aberdeenshire 149
Bridge of Allan Golf Course, Stirling 122
Bridge of Cally, Bridge of Cally, Central 133
The Bridge Inn, Ratho, Edinburgh 36
The Bridgehouse, Perth, Central 136
Bridgend, Islay 230
Bridgend House, Callander, Central 124
Bridgend Sporting Agency, Stranraer,
Dumf/Gal 56
Brighouse Bay Holiday Park, Brighouse Bay,
Dumf/Gal 62
Brisbane House, Largs, Ayrshire 71, 73
British Airways 197
British Golf Museum, St Andrews, Fife 103
Broch of Gurness, Evie, Mainland 224
Brodick, Arran 209
Brodick Castle, Garden & Country Park, Brodick,
Arran 210
Brodie Castle, Forres, Moray 144
Brodie's Close, Edinburgh 19
Brook Linn Country House, Callander,
Central 125
Broom Farm Riding School, Stevenston,
Ayrshire 68
Broothom Ponies, Dunrossness, Mainland 229
Broughton Gallery, Broughton, Borders 43
Broughton House & Garden, Kirkcudbright,
Dumf/Gal 54
Broughty Castle Museum, Dundee 103
Bruce, Newton Stewart, Dumf/Gal 59
Bruce Hotel, East Kilbride, S. Lanarkshire 92
Brunstane Lodge, Strathpeffer, Highlands 203

Brunswick Hotel, Edinburgh 29
Bruntsfield, Edinburgh 26
Bryvard, Banff, Aberdeenshire 154
Bubbles Leisure Centre, Livingston,
West Lothian 24
Buccleuch Arms, St Boswells, Borders 49
Buccleuch Country Ride, Borders 46
Buchan Hotel, Edinburgh 31
Buchanan, Edinburgh 33
Buchanan Arms, Drymen, Central 125
Buchanan Castle Golf Course, Drymen,
Stirling 122
Buchlyvie Pottery Shop, Buchlyvie, Stirling 121
Buckie Drifter, Buckie, Moray 144
Bullers of Buchan, Aberdeenshire 147
Bunchrew House Hotel, Inverness,
Highlands 185, 191
Bunnahabhain Distillery, Port Askaig, Islay 215
Burghfield House, Dornoch, Highlands 200
Burleigh Castle, Kinross, Central 129
Burnbrae, Bearsden, E. Lanarkshire 92
Burness House, St Andrews, Fife 115
Burnett Arms, Banchory, Aberdeenshire 153
Burns Heritage Park, Alloway, Ayrshire 66
Burns House, Dumfries, Dumf/Gal 53
Burns House Museum, Mauchline, Ayrshire 66
Burns Mausoleum, Dumfries, Dumf/Gal 54
Burns Memorial Tower, Mauchline, Ayrshire 66
Burnside Caravan Site, Fochabers, Moray 160
Burnside Hotel, Kilmarnock, Ayrshire 70
Burntisland Watersports Centre, Fife 107
Burra 228
Burray 224, 226
Burrell Collection, Glasgow 78
Burrowhead Holiday Village, Isle of Whithorn,
Dumf/Gal 63
Burts Hotel, Melrose, Borders 48, 50
Busta House, Brae, Shetland 234
Bute 208, 209, 210, 211
Bute Museum, Rothesay, Bute 210
Bute Outdoor Activities, Rothesay, Bute 211
Bute Sub-Aqua Centre, Ascog, Bute 211
But'N Ben, Auchmithie, Angus 110
Butterchurn Craft Centre, Kelty, Fife 105
Buttery Restaurant, Glasgow 85, 87
Bydand, Dulnain Bridge, Highlands 182
Bygones Museum & Balquhidder Visitor Centre,
Lochearnhead, Stirling 120
Bysantium, Edinburgh 22

C

C-N-Do Scotland Ltd, Central 123
Cabarfeidh, Stornoway, Lewis 232
Caerlaverock Castle, Caerlaverock, Dumf/Gal 53
Caerlaverock National Nature Reserve,
Caerlaverock, Dumf/Gal 53
Café Gandolfi, Glasgow 87
Café 1, Inverness, Highlands 191
Caiplie, Crail, Fife 114
Caird Park Golf Course, Dundee 106
Cairn Lodge, Auchterarder, Central 132, 138
Cairn Restaurant, Kilmartin, Argyll 178
Cairnbaan Hotel & Restaurant, Cairnbaan,
Argyll 179
Cairndale Hotel & Leisure Club, Dumfries,
Dumf/Gal 58
Cairngorm Gliding Club, Highlands 172
Cairngorm Reindeer Centre, Aviemore,
Highlands 170
Cairngorm Whisky Centre, Aviemore,
Highlands 171
Cairngorms, Highlands 170
Cairnpapple Hill, Torphichen, West Lothian 20
Cairnryan Caravan & Chalet Park, Cairnryan,
Dumf/Gal 62
Cairns, Glasgow 87
Cairnwell Mountain Sports, Glenshee,
Aberdeenshire 149
Caithness Glass Visitor Centre, Oban, Argyll 166
Caithness Glass Visitor Centre, Perth, Central 130
Caithness Glass Visitor Centre, Wick,
Highlands 197
Calderglen Country Park, East Kilbride, S.
Lanarkshire 89
Caldons Campsite, Glen Trool, Dumf/Gal 63
Caledonian, Leven, Fife 112
Caledonian, Oban, Argyll 175

Caledonian, Portmahomack, Highlands 202
Caledonian Activity Breaks, Highlands 172
Caledonian Canal, Highlands 170
Caledonian crafts Marketing Ltd, Paisley,
Renfrewshire 90
Caledonian Discovery Ltd, Highlands 172
Caledonian Equestrian Centre, Perth, Central 131
Caledonian Hotel, Edinburgh 25, 34
Caledonian MacBrayne, Ayrshire 67
Caledonian MacBrayne, Argyll 166
Caledonian MacBrayne, Fort William,
Highlands 171
Caledonian MacBrayne Ferries,
Inner Hebrides 215
Caledonian MacBrayne Ferries, Clyde Islands 211
Caledonian MacBrayne Ferries, Western Isles 219
Caledonian MacBrayne, Ullapool, Highlands 197
Caledonian Thistle, Aberdeen 151
Callander 119
Callander Crags, Callander, Stirling 121
Callander Golf Course, Stirling 122
Callanish Standing Stones, Callanish, Lewis 218
Callater Lodge Hotel, Braemar,
Aberdeenshire 154
Callendar House, Callendar Park, Falkirk 21
Cally Palace, Gatehouse of Fleet, Dumf/Gal 58
Calton Hill, Edinburgh 18
Cambo Gardens, St Andrews, Fife 104
Cambuskenneth Abbey, Stirling 121
Camera Obscura and Outlook Tower,
Edinburgh 19-20
Cameron House Hotel, Balloch, Central 95, 124
Cameron's Inn, Aberdeen 157
Campbeltown, Argyll 164
Campbeltown Heritage Centre, Argyll 165
Campbeltown Pottery, Campbeltown, Argyll 166
Camperdown Country Park, Dundee 104
Camperdown Golf Course, Dundee 106
Camperdown Stables, Dundee 107
Camping & Caravanning Club Site, Moffat,
Dumf/Gal 64
Camping and Caravanning Club Site,
Craigellachie, Moray 160
Canal Museum, Linlithgow, West Lothian 20
Canmore Golf Course, Dunfermline, Fife 106
Canna 216
Canongate Kirk, Edinburgh 19
Cantina Del Rey, Glasgow 87
Canto Ila Distillery, Port Askaig, Islay 215
Cape Wrath Ferry Service, Durness,
Highlands 197
Cape Wrath Mini-Bus Service, Highlands 198
Cardhu Distillery, Aberlour, Moray 148
Cardoness Castle, Gatehouse of Fleet,
Dumf/Gal 54
Cardross Golf Course, Central 122
Carlogie House, Carnoustie, Angus 108
Carlton Highland Hotel, Edinburgh 25, 34
Carlton Toby, Prestwick, Ayrshire 71
Carmania, Lossiemouth, Moray 159
The Carnegie Club, Dornoch, Highlands 198
Carnegie Leisure Centre, Fife 106
Carnoustie Golf Course, Angus 106
Carradale Canoe Centre, Argyll 167
Carradale Golf Course, Argyll 167
Carrbridge Golf Course, Highlands 172
Carrbridge Ski School, Highlands 172
Carrbridge Trekking Centre, Highlands 172
Carrick, Glasgow 83
Carrick Forest, Ayrshire 67
Carrick House, Eday 225
Carrick Lodge, Ayr, Ayrshire 69
Carrmoor, Carrbridge, Highlands 181
Carsaig Arches, Carsaig, Mull 214
Carseview, Stirling 127
The Carthouse Gallery, Dervaig, Mull 215
Cartland Bridge, Lanark, S. Lanarkshire 93
Cashmere Visitor Centre, Elgin, Moray 147
The Cask & Still, Glasgow 87
Castle, Dirleton, East Lothian 37
Castle Arms, Mey, Highlands 202
Castle Campbell, Dollar, Stirling 120
Castle Cary Holiday Park, Creetown, Dumf/Gal 62
Castle Douglas Art Gallery, Castle Douglas,
Dumf/Gal 53
Castle Douglas Golf Course, Dumf/Gal 56
Castle Fraser, Kemnay, Aberdeenshire 144

Castle Garrison Experience, Inverness, Highlands 170
Castle Girnigoe, Wick, Highlands 196
Castle House Museum, Dunoon, Argyll 165
Castle, Huntly, Aberdeenshire 154
Castle Kennedy Gardens, Stranraer, Dumf/Gal 53
Castle Menzies, Aberfeldy, Central 130
Castle Point Caravan Park, Rockcliffe, Dumf/Gal 64
Castle Riding Centre, Ardrishaig, Argyll 167
Castle of St John, Stranraer, Dumf/Gal 54
Castle Semple Country Park, Lochwinnoch, Renfrewshire 91
Castle Sinclair, Wick, Highlands 196
Castle Stuart, Inverness, Highlands 170
Castle Sween, Knapdale, Argyll 165
Castle Tioram, Acharacle, Highlands 170
Castle Venlaw Hotel, Peebles, Borders 49
Castlebay Community School, Barra 220
Castlecroft, Stirling 127
Castlemilk Sports Centre, Glasgow 81
Castleton House Hotel, Glamis, Angus 110
Castleview, Perth, Central 136
Catalina, Strathy, Highlands 203
The Caterthuns, Brechin, Angus 104
The Cathedral Museum, Dunblane, Stirling 120
Cavens House, Kirkbean, Dumf/Gal 61
Cawdor Castle, Cawdor, Highlands 169
The Cedars, Dunoon, Argyll 174
Ceilidh Place, Ullapool, Highlands 203
Cellar Restaurant, Anstruther, Fife 116
Celtic Art & Travel Centre, Edinburgh 22
Celtic House, Bowmore, Islay 215
Central Scotland 97-139
    Angus, Dundee and Fife 100-17
    events and festivals 98-9
    map 98-9
    Stirling & Loch Lomond, Perth & Kinross 118-39
Central Scotland Shooting School, Cumbernauld, N. Lanarkshire 91
Centre for Contemporary Arts, Glasgow 79
Chalna, Daviot, Highlands 181
Chalumna, Edinburgh 33
Champany Inn, Linlithgow, West Lothian 40
Channings, Edinburgh 26, 34
Chapeltoun House, Stewarton, Ayrshire 72, 73
Charelton Golf Course, Colinsburgh, Fife 106
Charing Cross, Glasgow 84
Charlotte Square, Edinburgh 19
Chatelherault, Hamilton, S. Lanarkshire 88
Childhood Memories, The Toy Museum for the Old & Young, Coylumbridge, Highlands 170
Chirnside Hall Country House Hotel, Chirnside, Borders 47, 50
Choraidh Croft Farm Park, Altnaharra, Highlands 196-7
Chrialdon Hotel, Beauly, Highlands 181
Citadel Leisure Centre, Ayr, Ayrshire 68
City Art Gallery, Edinburgh 19
City Chambers, Glasgow 79
Clach An Truiseil, Ballantrushal, Lewis 218
Clach Mhuilinn, Inverness, Highlands 186
The Clachan, Wick, Highlands 204
Claish Farm Pony Trekking, Callander, Stirling 122
Clan Donald Visitor Centre, Armadale, Skye 218
Clan Donnachaidh (Robertson) Museum, Bruar, Central 129
Clark Kimberley, Perth, Central 136
Clarke Cottage, Dunfermline, Fife 114
Classic House, Edinburgh 31
Clatteringshaws Forest Wildlife Centre, Dumf/Gal 54
Clatteringshaws Red Deer Range and Wild Goat Park, Dumf/Gal 54
Clatto Country Park, Dundee 107
Clava Cairns, Highlands 170
Claymore, Pitlochry, Central 137
Claymore House, Nairn, Highlands 189
Cleveden House, St Andrews, Fife 115
Clickhimin Broch, Lerwick, Mainland 227
Clickhimin Leisure Complex, Lerwick, Mainland 229
Clifton Private Hotel, Edinburgh 33
Clintwood, Fort William, Highlands 183
Clog & Craft Shop, Invermoriston, Highlands 171

The Clog & Shoe Workshop, Castle Douglas, Dumf/Gal 55
Clonyard House, Colvend, Dumf/Gal 57
Cloyburn Equestrian Centre, Brodick, Arran 211
Cluanie Park, Beauly, Highlands 170
Clunie, Perth, Central 136
Cluny House, Aberfeldy, Central 130
Clyde Coast Cycle Routes 81
Clyde Islands 208-11, 230
Clyde Valley 75, 88-95
    access 90
    accommodation 92-4
    camping and caravanning 94-5
    crafts 90
    entertainment 90
    events and festivals 77
    food and drink 90
    map 76-7
    restaurants 95
    scenic drives 91
    sightseeing 88-90
    sport and leisure 91
    tourist information 90
    tours 90
    transport 90-1
Clyde Valley Caravan Park, Kirkfieldbank 94
Clyde Valley Farm Park, Garrion Bridge, S. Lanarkshire 91
Clyde Valley Hawks, Crossford, S. Lanarkshire 89
Clyde Walkway, Glasgow 81
Clynelish Distillery, Brora, Highlands 198
Coats Observatory, Paisley, Renfrewshire 88
Cock Inn Caravan Park, Auchenmalg, Dumf/Gal 62
The Coffee Shop, Edzell, Angus 110
Cogrie's, Beattock, Dumf/Gal 60
Coilessan Trekking & Riding Centre, Arrochar, Argyll 167
Coire Glas, Spean Bridge, Highlands 190
Colbost Folk Museum, Dunvegan, Skye 218
Colgrain Equestrian Centre, Cardross, Central 123
Coll 212
Coll Pottery, Back, Lewis 219
Coll Sports Centre, Coll, Lewis 220
Colliston Inn, Arbroath, Angus 110
Colonsay 212, 214, 215
Colonsay Golf Course, Colonsay 215
Colonsay Hotel, Scalasaig, Colonsay 179, 230, 234
Columba, Oban, Argyll 175
Columba House, Kingussie, Highlands 188
Colvend Golf Course, Dumf/Gal 56
Colzie Hill Recreation, Auchtermuchty, Fife 106
Colzium House & Estate, Kilsyth, N. Lanarkshire 89
Comar House, Pitlochry, Central 137
Comeley Bank, Crieff, Central 134
Comfort Friendly Inn, Falkirk, Falkirk 38
Comlongon Castle, Clarencefield, Dumf/Gal 54
Commodore Toby, Helensburgh, Central 126
Compass Gallery, Glasgow 79
Comrie Golf Course, Central 131
Conchra House, Ardelve, Highlands 199
The Copthorne Aberdeen, Aberdeen 150
The Copthorne Glasgow, Glasgow 82
Corbiewood Stadium Ltd, Bannockburn, Stirling 122
Corner House Hotel, Aberdeen 151
Corrieshalloch Gorge, Highlands 196
Corsemalzie House, Port William, Dumf/Gal 59
Corsock Crafts, Castle Douglas, Dumf/Gal 55
Corstorphine, Edinburgh 31
Cosses Country House, Ballantrae, Ayrshire 69
Cottage Woodcraft, Drumnadrochit, Highlands 171
Coul House, Contin, Highlands 199, 204
County Hotel & Leisure Club, Stonehaven, Aberdeenshire 155
The Courtyard Gallery, Crail, Fife 103
Cove Conservation Park, Helensburgh, Central 121
Covenanters, Nairn, Highlands 189
Cow Glen Golf Course, Glasgow 81
Cowal Bird Garden, Dunoon, Argyll 165
Cowal Golf Course, Dunoon, Argyll 167
Cowans Law Shooting School, Moscow, Ayrshire 68
Cowdenbeath Golf Course, Fife 106

Cowdenbeath Leisure Centre, Fife 106
Cowdenknowes Equicentre, Earlston, Borders 46
Coylet Inn, Dunoon, Argyll 179
Crafts & Things, Glencoe, Highlands 171
Craggallan, Ayr, Ayrshire 69
Craggan Golf Course, Grantown-on-Spey, Highlands 172
Craig Highland Farm, Plockton, Highlands 197
Craig Urrard, Pitlochry, Clyde 137
Craigard, Invergarry, Highlands 184
Craigard Tearoom II, Helensburgh, Argyll 179
Craigellachie Hotel, Craigellachie, Moray 158, 160
The Craighaar, Aberdeen 151
Craighall, Forgandenny, Central 134
Craigie Hill Golf Course, Central 131
Craigievar Castle, Aberdeenshire 146
Craiglea, Troon, Ayrshire 72
Craiglockhart, Portree, Skye 233
Craiglockhart Sports Centre, Edinburgh 24
Craigmillar Castle, Edinburgh 20
Craigmonie, Inverness, Highlands 185
Craigmore, St Andrews, Fife 115
Craignethan Castle, Lanark, S. Lanarkshire 89
Craignure Golf Course, Mull 215
Craigroyston House, Pitlochry, Central 137
Craigside, Inverness, Highlands 186
Craigtoun Country Park, St Andrews, Fife 104
Craigtoun Meadows Holiday Park, St Andrews, Fife 116
Craigvar, Strathpeffer, Highlands 203
Craigview, North Berwick, East Lothian 39
Craigvrack, Pitlochry, Central 137
Crail Museum & Heritage Centre, Crail, Fife 103
Crail Pottery, Crail, Fife 105
Crannog Restaurant, Fort William, Highlands 204
Craobh Haven Watersports, Lochgilphead, Argyll 167
Crarae Gardens, Inveraray, Argyll 165
Crathes Castle & Gardens, Banchory, Aberdeenshire 144
Crawford Arts Centre, St Andrews, Fife 103
Creag Mhor, Onich, Highlands 189
Creag Mor, Gairloch, Highlands 200
Creagan House, Strathyre, Central 127, 128
Creebridge Caravan Park, Newton Stewart, Dumf/Gal 64
Creebridge House Hotel, Newton Stewart, Dumf/Gal 59, 65
Creebridge Mohair & Woollens, Newton Stewart, Dumf/Gal 55
Creel Restaurant, St Margaret's Hope, Orkney 235
Creelers Seafood Bar, Edinburgh 36
Creetown Caravan Park, Creetown, Dumf/Gal 62
Creetown Gem Rock Museum, Creetown, Dumf/Gal 53
Creetown Gold & Silversmithing Workshop, Creetown, Dumf/Gal 55
Creggans Inn, Strachur, Argyll 177, 179
The Crescent, Ayr, Ayrshire 69
Cressfield Caravan Park, Ecclefechan, Dumf/Gal 62-3
Crichton Castle, Crichton, Midlothian 20
Crichton Royal Museum, Dumfries, Dumf/Gal 53
Crieff, Crieff, Central 134
Crieff Golf Course, Crieff, Central 131
Crieff Hydro, Crieff, Central 133
Crieff Visitor Centre, Crieff, Central 130
Criffel Inn, New Abbey, Dumf/Gal 65
Crinan Canal, Crinan, Argyll 166
Cringletie House, Peebles, Borders 48, 50
Crion, Edinburgh 31
Croft Bank, Kinross, Central 139
Croft Crafts, Drinishader, Harris 219
The Croft, Elgin, Moray 159
Croft-na-Caber Watersports Centre, Kenmore, Central 131
Croftburn Cottage, Drymen, Central 125
Croma, Crail, Fife 111
Cromarty Courthouse, Cromarty, Highlands 196
Cromlix House, Dunblane, Central 126
Cromlix House Hotel, Dunblane, Central 128
Crookston Castle, Glasgow 79
Cross Keys, Kelso, Borders 48
The Cross, Kingussie, Highlands 188, 192
Crossmyloof Ice Rink, Glasgow 81
Crossraguel Abbey, Maybole, Ayrshire 66
Croy Brae, Ayrshire 67

245

Cruachan Power Station, Lochawe, Argyll 165
Cruden Bay Golf Course, Aberdeenshire 149
Crumstane Farm Park, Duns, Borders 44
Cuillin Hills, Skye 219
Cuillin Hills Hotel, Portree, Skye 233, 235
Cul de Sac Westend, Glasgow 87
Culcreuch Castle & Country Park, Fintry,
  Stirling 121
Culdearn House, Grantown-on-Spey,
  Highlands 184, 191
Culdoich, Culloden Moor, Highlands 181
Culduthel Lodge, Inverness, Highlands 186
Cullen Bay, Cullen, Moray 158
Cullerlie Farm Park, Skene, Aberdeenshire 146
Culloden Battlefield, Culloden Moor,
  Highlands 169
Culloden House Hotel, Inverness,
  Highlands 185, 191
Culloden Pottery, Inverness, Highlands 171
Culloden Riding School, Stanley, Central 131
Culross - Palace, Town House & The Study,
  Culross, Fife 102
Cultoquhey House, Crieff, Central 134
Culzean Castle & Country Park, Culzean Castle,
  Ayrshire 66
Cumbraes 208, 210, 211
Cupar Golf Course, Fife 106
Cupar Sports Centre, Fife 106
Cyril Gerber Fine Art, Glasgow 79

D

D A Study Tours, Orkney 226
Dalgair House, Callander, Central 124
Dalgreine, Blair Atholl, Central 133
Dalhousie Castle Hotel, Bonnyrigg, Midlothian 37
Dalkeith Country Park, Dalkeith, Midlothian 21
Dall Lodge Country House, Killin, Central 126
Dallas Dhu Distillery, Forres, Moray 148
Dalmally Golf Course, Argyll 167
Dalmeny House, Edinburgh 20
Dalmeny Park Country House, Barrhead,
  Renfrewshire 92
Dalmeny Park Country House, Glasgow 84
Dalmore House Hotel, Blairgowrie, Central 133
Dalmunzie House, Glenshee, Central 134, 139
Dalnasgadh House, Killiecrankie, Central 134
Dalrachney Lodge, Carrbridge, Highlands 181
Dalvennan Country Sports Ground, Kirkmichael,
  Ayrshire 68
Dalwhinnie Distillery, Dalwhinnie, Highlands 171
Dalzell Country Park, Motherwell,
  N. Lanarkshire 89
D'Arcys Wine Bar and Restaurant, Glasgow 87
Dargill, Ayr, Ayrshire 69
Darnaway Farm Visitor Centre, Forres, Moray 146
Darroch Learg Hotel, Ballater,
  Aberdeenshire 152, 156
David Latham Outdoor Activities, Banchory,
  Aberdeenshire 148
David Livingstone Centre, Blantyre,
  S. Lanarkshire 89
Dawyck Botanic Gardens, Stobo, Borders 44
Dean Castle Country Park Riding Centre,
  Kilmarnock, Ayrshire 68
Dean Castle, Kilmarnock, Ayrshire 67
Dean Park, Glasgow 85
Dean Park, Kirkcaldy, Fife 112
Deauvilles, Glasgow 84
Deep-Sea World, North Queensferry, Fife 102
Deepwater Equitation Centre, Dumfries,
  Dumf/Gal 56
Deeside Gliding Club, Aboyne Airfield,
  Aberdeenshire 149
Delgatie Castle, Turriff, Aberdeenshire 146
Denmill Stables, Kirriemuir, Angus 107
Deugh Studio, Carsphairn, Dumf/Gal 55
Devon River Riding Centre, Alloa, Central 123
The Devonshire Hotel of Glasgow,
  Glasgow 83, 85
Dewars Rinks, Perth, Central 131
Di Maggio's Pizzeria, Glasgow 87
Dick Institute, Kilmarnock, Ayrshire 66
Dingwall Leisure Centre, Highlands 198
Dionard, Inverness, Highlands 186
Dirleton Castle, Dirleton, East Lothian 20
Discover Carmichael Visitor Centre, Carmichael,
  S. Lanarkshire 89

Discovery Point, Dundee 102
Distant Hills, Spean Bridge, Highlands 190
Distillery House, Fort William, Highlands 183
Diving & Sightseeing Trips, Voe, Mainland 229
The Diving Cellar, Stromness, Mainland 226
Dollar Golf Course, Central 122
Dolphin Scuba Services, Burray 226
Doniford, Brechin, Angus 108
Doonhamer Restaurant, Dumfries, Dumf/Gal 65
Dornie, Dornie, Highlands 199
Dornoch 195
Dornoch Castle, Dornoch, Highlands 200
Dornoch Craft Centre, Dornoch, Highlands 197
Dornoch Links Camping & Caravanning Site,
  Dornoch, Highlands 198
Dorstan Private Hotel, Edinburgh 29
Douglas Arms, Castle Douglas, Dumf/Gal 57
Doune Castle, Doune, Stirling 120
Doune Motor Museum, Doune, Stirling 120
The Dower House, Muir of Ord,
  Highlands 202, 204
Dragon Way, Edinburgh 36
The Dreel Tavern, Anstruther, Fife 117
Drimsynie Leisure Centre, Lochgoilhead,
  Argyll 167
Dromnan, Ullapool, Highlands 203
Drovers Guided Walks, Highlands 172
Druimard Hotel, Dervaig, Mull 178, 231, 234
Drum Castle & Rose Garden, Peterculter,
  Aberdeenshire 146
Drumbain Riding Establishment, Rothes,
  Moray 149
Drumbeg, Drumbeg, Highlands 200
Drumdelgie House, Huntly, Aberdeenshire 154
Drumlanrig Castle, Thornhill, Dumf/Gal 53
Drumlanrig Tower, Hawick, Borders 44
Drumlochart Caravan Park, Lochnaw,
  Dumf/Gal 63
The Drummond Arms, Crieff, Central 134
Drummond Castle Gardens, Muthill, Central 130
Drummond House, Edinburgh 29
Drumnacree House, Alyth, Central 132, 138
Drumpellier Country Park, Coatbridge,
  N. Lanarkshire 89
Drumriggend, Oban, Argyll 176
Drumyat Leisure Centre, Menstrie, Falkirk 24
Dryburgh Abbey, Dryburgh, Borders 43
Dryburgh Abbey (hotel), St Boswells, Borders 49
Dryfesdale Hotel, Lockerbie, Dumf/Gal 59, 65
Duart Castle, Craignure, Mull 214
Dubh Prais Restaurant, Edinburgh 36
Duchally House Hotel, Auchterarder, Central 138
Duck's at Le March_ Noir, Edinburgh 34
Duff House Country Gallery, Banff,
  Aberdeenshire 145
Dulnain Bridge Outdoor Centre, Highlands 172
Dumbarton Castle, Dumbarton, Central 121
Dumbarton Golf Course, Central 122
Dumbreck Riding School, Glasgow 81
Dumbuck, Dumbarton, Central 126
Dumfries 52
Dumfries & County Golf Club, Dumf/Gal 56
Dumfries & Galloway 51-65
  access 55
  accommodation 57-61
  camping and caravanning 62-4
  crafts 55
  entertainment 55
  food and drink 55-6
  pubs, inns and other eating places 65
  restaurants 65
  scenic drives 54
  sightseeing 53-5
  sport and leisure 56
  tourist information 55
  tours 56
  transport 56
Dumfries & Galloway Activity Line, Dumf/Gal 56
Dumfries & Galloway Aviation Museum,
  Dumfries, Dumf/Gal 53
Dumfries & Galloway Golf Course, Dumf/Gal 56
Dumfries Ice Bowl, Dumfries, Dumf/Gal 56
Dumfries Museum & Camera Obscura, Dumfries,
  Dumf/Gal 53
Dun Carloway Broch, Carloway, Lewis 218
Dunadd Fort, Kilmartin, Argyll 165

Dunaskin Heritage Centre, Patna, Ayrshire 67
Dunaverty Golf Course, Campbeltown, Argyll 167
Dunbar Golf Course, East Lothian 23
Dunbar Leisure Centre, East Lothian 24
Dunblane Cathedral, Central 121
Dunblane Golf Course, Stirling 122
Duncansby Head, Highlands 197
Duncraggan, Blairgowrie, Central 133
Duncryne Trekking Centre, Loch Lomond,
  Central 123
Dundarach, Pitlochry, Central 137
Dundarave House, Pitlochry, Central 137
Dundee 101
  accommodation 109
  entertainment 105
  food and drink 105
  sightseeing 102, 103, 104
  sport and leisure 106-7
  tourist information 105
  transport 105
Dundee Airport 105
Dundonnell Hotel, Dundonnell,
  Highlands 200, 204
Dundrennan Abbey, Dundrennan, Dumf/Gal 54
Dunduff, Dunure, Ayrshire 70
Dunedin, Huntly, Aberdeenshire 154
Dunfermline Abbey, Pittencrieff Park, Fife 104
Dunfermline Golf Course, Fife 106
Dunfermline Heritage Trust, Dunfermline, Fife 103
Dunfermline House, Melrose, Borders 48
Dungallan House Hotel, Oban, Argyll 176, 178
Dunhallin Crafts, Waternish, Skye 219
Dunivaig Castle, Lagavulin, Islay 214
Dunkeld & Birnam Golf Course, Central 131
Dunkeld Cathedral, Dunkeld, Central 129
Dunlaverock House, Coldingham Bay, Borders 47
Dunnet Head, Highlands 197
Dunnikier Caravan Park, Kirkcaldy, Fife 116
Dunnikier Park, Kirkcaldy, Fife 106
Dunning Golf Course, Central 131
Dunnottar Castle, Stonehaven, Aberdeenshire 145
Dunoon Ceramics, Dunoon, Argyll 166
Dunrobin Castle, Golspie, Highlands 196
Duns Castle Nature Reserve, Borders 44
Duns Golf Course, Borders 46
Duns Sports Complex, Duns, Borders 45
Dunstaffnage Castle, Oban, Argyll 165
Dunstane House, Edinburgh 31
Duntulm Castle, Skye 218
Dunvalanree, Carradale, Argyll 173
Dunvegan Castle, Dunvegan, Skye 218
Dunvegan Equestrian Training, Newburgh,
  Fife 107
Dunvegan House, Brodick, Arran 230
Durness Golf Course, Highlands 198
Dyce Leisure Club, Aberdeen 149
Dyce Skean Dhu, Aberdeen 152
Dykecroft, Kirkmuirhill, S. Lanarkshire 94

E

Earlshall Castle & Gardens, Leuchars, Fife 104
Earra Gael Craft Shop, Tarbert, Argyll 166
East Kilbride Ice Rink, S. Lanarkshire 91
East Lochhead, Lochwinnoch, Renfrewshire 94
East Neuk Outdoors, Anstruther, Fife 106
East Sands Leisure Centre, St Andrews, Fife 106
Easter Dalziel Farmhouse, Dalcross,
  Highlands 181
Easterhill Farm Trekking Centre, Aberfoyle,
  Stirling 123
Easterhouse Sports Centre, Glasgow 81
Eastern Dawn Boat Charter, Methilhill, Fife 105
Eastwood Butterfly Kingdom, Giffnock,
  Renfrewshire 89
Ecosse International, Edinburgh 31
Eday 225, 226
Eddrachilles, Scourie, Highlands 203
Eden Equestrian Centre, Turriff,
  Aberdeenshire 149
Eden House Hotel, Cupar, Fife 111, 116
Eden House Hotel, Inverness, Highlands 186
Eden Park Leisure Centre, Cupar, Fife 106
Edenside House, St Andrews, Fife 115
Edenside Riding Stables, Garbridge, Fife 107
Edinbane, Inverness, Highlands 186
Edinbane Pottery, Edinbane, Skye 219
Edinburgh 16, 19-20

access 22
accommodation 25-34
car hire 23
caravanning and camping 34
crafts 22
entertainment 22
food and drink 22
pubs, inns and other eating places 36
restaurants 34-5
shopping 21
sightseeing 18-21
sport and leisure 23-4
tourist information 22
transport 22-3
walking tours 24
dinburgh & Lasswade Riding Centre, Lasswade, Midlothian 24
dinburgh Butterfly & Insect World, Lasswade, Midlothian 21
dinburgh Canal Centre, Edinburgh 22
dinburgh Capital Moat House, Edinburgh 26
dinburgh Castle, Edinburgh 18
dinburgh Crystal Visitor Centre, Penicuik, Midlothian 22
dinburgh Festival Theatre, Edinburgh 22
dinburgh Festival Voluntary Guides, Edinburgh 24
dinburgh Zoo, Edinburgh 21
din's Hall Broch, Duns, Borders 44
dmore, Dunoon, Argyll 174
dnam House, Kelso, Borders 48
dradour Distillery, Pitlochry, Central 129
duardo Alessandro Studios, Dundee 103
dzell Castle, Edzell, Angus 102
dzell Golf Course, Angus 106
dzell Tweed Warehouse, Edzell, Angus 105
glinton Castle & Country Park, Kilwinning, Ayrshire 66
glinton, Eaglesham, Renfrewshire 92
igg 216
ilean Donan Castle, Highlands 196
lcho Castle, Perth, Central 129
lder York, Edinburgh 31
1 Park Avenue, Carnoustie, Angus 110
lgin 141
lgin Cathedral, Elgin, Moray 146
lgin, Dunfermline, Fife 111
lgin Golf Course, Moray 149
lgin Museum, Elgin, Moray 145
lie Golf Course, Fife 106
lie Watersports, Fife 107
llesmere House, Edinburgh 29
lli Pearson Pottery, Windwick, South Ronaldsay 225
lm House, Galashiels, Borders 47
lms Court, Ayr, Ayrshire 69
lmview, Edinburgh 29
nmore Hotel, Dunoon, Argyll 178
nrick Cottage, Drumnadrochit, Highlands 182
riskay Car Ferry 219
riskay, Kilmarnock, Ayrshire 70
rrol Bank, Dundee 109
shcol, Breasclete, Lewis 232
shna Ness (The Drongs), Mainland 227
skbank Motor, Dalkeith, Midlothian 37
skdale House, Inverness, Highlands 187
skdale, Langholm, Dumf/Gal 58
ttrick Valley Stables, Thornhill, Dumf/Gal 56
wan Thomson Violin Maker, Fair Isle 228
wington, Glasgow 83
wood House, Aberdeen 151
xtreme Leisure Paintball Games, Oban, Argyll 167
yemouth Golf Course, Borders 46
yemouth Leisure Centre, Eyemouth, Borders 45

F

Fair Isle 228
airburn Activity Centre, Muir of Ord, Highlands 198
airfield House Hotel, Ayr, Ayrshire 69, 72
airways Hotel, Prestwick, Ayrshire 71
airways Lodge, Tobermory, Mull 215
airwinds, Carrbridge, Highlands 181
alconer Museum, Forres, Moray 145
alkirk & the Lothians 16-40
   accommodation 37-9

beaches 24
crafts 22
entertainment 22
food and drink 22
restaurants 40
sightseeing 18, 20, 21
sport and leisure 23, 24
tourist information 22
tours 24
transport 23
Falkirk Riding Centre, Woodend Farm, Falkirk 24
Falkland Golf Course, Fife 106
Falkland Palace & Garden, Falkland, Fife 102
Falls of Bruar, Blair Atholl, Central 130
Falls of Clyde, New Lanark, S. Lanarkshire 88
Falls of Foyer, Loch Ness, Highlands 170
Falls of Leny, Callander, Stirling 121
Falls of Lora, Connel, Argyll 174
Falls of Measach, Highlands 196
Farm Cottage Crafts, Craignure, Mull 215
Farm Milk Bar, Luss, Argyll 180
Farmhouse Kitchen, Arbroath, Angus 108
Faskally, Pitlochry, Central 130
Fasque House, Fettercairn, Aberdeenshire 146
Faussetthill House, Gullane, East Lothian 38
Fearn's Abbey, Fearn, Highlands 196
Feith Mhor Country House, Carrbridge, Highlands 181
Fenwick, Fenwick, Ayrshire 70
Fergusson Gallery, Perth, Central 129
Fern Villa, Ballachulish, Highlands 181
Fernbank House, Aberfeldy, Central 132
Fernbank, Prestwick, Ayrshire 71
Fernhill, Portpatrick, Dumf/Gal 59
Fernie Castle Hotel, Letham, Fife 112, 117
Ferniehurst Mill Lodge, Jedburgh, Borders 46, 48
Fernpoint, Inveraray, Argyll 175
Ferry Inn, Uig, Skye 233
Fetlar 221, 228
Fettercairn Distillery, Edzell, Angus 105
Fettercairn Distillery, Fettercairn, Aberdeenshire 148
Field End, Crawford, S. Lanarkshire 94
Fife 100
   access 105
   accommodation 111-15
   beaches 107
   camping and caravanning 116
   children's entertainment 104
   crafts 105
   entertainment 105
   food and drink 105
   pubs, inns and other eating places 117
   restaurants 116-17
   scenic drives 107
   sightseeing 102-3, 104
   sport and leisure 106-7
   tourist information 105
   tours 105
   transport 105
Fife Arms, Braemar, Aberdeenshire 154
Fife Arms Hotel, Dufftown, Moray 158
Fife Folk Museum, Ceres, Fife 103
Finavon Farmhouse, Forfar, Angus 109
Fingal's Cave, Staffa 214
Finlaggan Visitor Centre, Ballygrant, Islay 214
Finlay, Edinburgh 31
Finlaystone Country Estate, Langbank, Renfrewshire 94
Fintry Sports & Recreation Centre, Fintry, Stirling 122
The Fire Station Restaurant, Glasgow 87
Firpark Ski Centre, Tillicoultry, Central 123
Flamingo Yacht Charter, Largs, Ayrshire 68
Flemings Laces, Kilmarnock, Ayrshire 67
Floors Castle, Kelso, Borders 43
Flora Macdonald's Birthplace, Milton, South Uist 218
Flow Country, Forsinard, Highlands 197
'Flying Eagle' Charters, Saltcoats, Ayrshire 68
Flying Fever, Kildonan, Arran 211
Fochaber Folk Museum, Fochabers, Moray 145
Foggieley Tannery, Alford, Aberdeenshire 147
Fordbank Riding & Livery Stables, Johnstone, Renfrewshire 91
Fordyce Joiner's Workshop, Fordyce, Aberdeenshire 147

Forest Hills Hotel, Auchtermuchty, Fife 114
Forest Lodge, Invergarry, Highlands 184
Foresters House, Elgin, Moray 159
Forests of Lochaber, Fort William, Highlands 170
Forfar Golf Course, Angus 106
Forres Golf Course, Moray 149
Fort Augustus Abbey, Fort Augustus, Highlands 170
Fort Augustus Golf Course, Highlands 172
Fort Augustus Riding Centre, Highlands 172
Fort Charlotte, Lerwick, Mainland 227
Fort George & Queen's Own Highlanders Regimental Museum, Fort George, Highlands 169
Fort William, Highlands 168
Fort William Golf Course, Highlands 172
Forte Posthouse Aberdeen, Aberdeen 151
Forte Posthouse Edinburgh, Edinburgh 28
Forte Posthouse Glasgow Airport, Glasgow 85
Forte Posthouse Glasgow City, Glasgow 84
Forte Posthouse Glasgow/Erskine, Glasgow 85, 93
Forth & Clyde Canal 81
Forth Bridges (hotel), South Queensferry 34
Forth Craig Private Hotel, Inverkeithing, Fife 114
Forth Helicopters, Edinburgh Airport 23
Fortingall, Fortingall, Central 134
Fortrose & Rosemarkie Golf Course, Fortrose, Highlands 198
Fossil House, St Andrews, Fife 115
Foula 228
Four Abbeys Cycle Route, Borders 46
The Four Seasons Hotel, St Fillans, Central 138, 139
Fourpenny Cottage, Dornoch, Highlands 200
Fourways, Aberdeen 151
Fouters Bistro, Ayr, Ayrshire 72-3
Fowlis Church, Easter by Liff, Angus 104
Fowlsheugh RSPB Seabird Colony, Stonehaven, Aberdeenshire 147
Foxholes, Oban, Highlands 176
Foyers Bay House, Foyers, Highlands 184
Fraser Peterson Centre, Mossbank, Mainland 229
Fraserburgh Harbour Tours, Fraserburgh, Aberdeenshire 148
Fresh Fields, Twynholm, Dumf/Gal 61
Froggies Restaurant & New Orleans Bar, Glasgow 87
Froylehurst, Jedburgh, Borders 47
Fruitmarket Gallery, Edinburgh 19
Fursbreck Pottery, Harray 225
Fyvie Castle, Turriff, Aberdeenshire 144
Fyvie Church, Turriff, Aberdeenshire 145

G

The Gables, Perth, Central 136
Gairloch Craft Studio, Auchtercairn, Highlands 197
Gairloch Golf Course, Highlands 198
Gairloch Heritage Museum, Auchtercairn, Highlands 196
Gairloch Leisure Centre, Highlands 198
Galabank Caravan Park, Annan, Dumf/Gal 62
Galashiels Golf Course, Borders 46
Galleon Centre, Kilmarnock, Ayrshire 68
Gallery of Modern Art, Glasgow 78
The Galley of Lorne Inn, Ardfern, Argyll 179
Galloway, Edinburgh 31
Galloway Country Sports, Wigtown, Dumf/Gal 56
Galloway Forest Park, Dumf/Gal 55
Galloway Point Holiday Park, Portpatrick, Dumf/Gal 64
Galloway Sailing Centre, Loch Ken, Dumf/Gal 56
Galson Farm, South Galson, Lewis 232
Garden House, Gretna, Dumf/Gal 58
Garden Park, Grantown-on-Spey, Highlands 184
Garlogie Mill Power House Museum, Westhill, Aberdeenshire 145
Garnock Lodge, Beith, Ayrshire 69
Garson Farm, Stromness, Mainland 226
Garth Hotel, Grantown-on-Spey, Highlands 184, 191
Garth House, Bridge of Weir, Renfrewshire 94
Gatehouse of Fleet Golf Course, Dumf/Gal 56
The Gatehouse Pottery, Edinburgh 22
G.C.G. Crafts, Castle Douglas, Dumf/Gal 55
Gean House, Alloa, Central 124

Gearrannan 'Black House' Village, Garenin, Lewis 218
General Register House, Edinburgh 19
Geoffrey (Tailor) Highland Crafts, Edinburgh 22
Geoffrey (Tailor) Highland Crafts, Glasgow 80
George & Abbotsford, Melrose, Borders 48
The Georgian House, Edinburgh 19
Gerard's Brasserie, Aberdeen 157
Giant's Graves, Arran 210
Gigha 214, 215
Gigha Golf Course, Gigha 215
Gilbert House, Moffat, Dumf/Gal 61
Gilmore House, Blairgowrie, Central 133
Gisla Woodcraft, Uig, Lewis 219
Giuliano's, Edinburgh 36
Gladstone Court Museum, Biggar, S. Lanarkshire 88
Gladstone House, Kirkcudbright, Dumf/Gal 61
Gladstone's Land, Edinburgh 19
Gladyer Inn, Rosyth, Fife 113
Glamis Castle, Glamis, Angus 102
Glasgow 75, 78-87
    access 80
    accommodation 82-5
    crafts 80
    entertainment 80
    pubs, inns and other eating places 87
    restaurants 85-6
    shopping 80
    sightseeing 78-80
    sport and leisure 81
    tourist information 80
    tours 81
    transport 80-1
Glasgow - Loch Lomond Cycleway 81, 91
Glasgow Airport 55
Glasgow Art Gallery & Museum, Glasgow 78
Glasgow Cathedral, Glasgow 78
Glasgow Golf Course, Irvine, Ayrshire 68
Glasgow Green, Glasgow 80
Glasgow Hilton, Glasgow 82, 85
Glasgow International Airport 90
Glasgow Marriott, Glasgow 82
Glasgow Moat House, Glasgow 82, 85
Glasgow School of Art, Glasgow 79
Glasgow Thistle, Glasgow 82
Glasgow to Edinburgh Trail 81
Glasgow Tourist Information Orientation Centre, Glasgow 79
Glasgow Vennel Museum & Burns Heckling Shop, Irvine, Ayrshire 66
Glasgow Zoopark, Uddingston, S. Lanarkshire 89
Gleddoch House Hotel, Langbank, Renfrewshire 93, 95
Gleddoch Riding School, Langbank, Renfrewshire 91
Glen Affric, Highlands 169
Glen Grant Distillery, Rothes, Moray 148
Glen Isle Inn, Castle Douglas, Dumf/Gal 65
Glen Lui Hotel, Ballater, Aberdeenshire 153
Glen Orchy House, Lerwick, Shetland 234
Glen Ord Distillery, Muir of Ord, Highlands 198
Glen Rowan, Drumnadrochit, Highlands 182
Glen Sannox, Arran 210
Glen Tanar, Aboyne, Aberdeenshire 147
Glen Tanar Equestrian Centre, Aboyne, Aberdeenshire 149
Glen Trool, Dumf/Gal 55
Glen Trool Holiday Park, Dumf/Gal 63
Glenalmond, Edinburgh 31
Glenardran Guest House, Crianlarich, Central 125
Glenbarr Abbey Visitor Centre, Tarbert, Argyll 165
Glenbervie House, Oban, Argyll 176
Glenburnie Private Hotel, Oban, Argyll 176
Glencoe & Lorn Folk Museum, Glencoe, Highlands 169
Glencoe, Carnoustie, Angus 108
Glencoe, Highlands 170
Glencoe (hotel), Glencoe, Highlands 184
Glencoe Ski Centre, Highlands 172
Glencoe Visitor Centre, Glencoe, Highlands 169
Glencruitten Golf Course, Oban, Argyll 167
Glendashadale Falls, Arran 210
Glenderran, St Andrews, Fife 115
Glendronach Distillery, Huntly, Aberdeenshire 148

Gleneagles of Edinburgh, Broxburn, West Lothian 22
Gleneagles Hotel, Auchterarder, Central 131, 132, 138
The Gleneagles Mark Phillips Equestrian Centre, Auchterarder, Central 131
Glenelg Brochs, Highlands 196
Glenesk, Edzell, Angus 109
Glenfarclas Distillery, Ballindalloch, Moray 148
Glenfarg, Glenfarg, Central 134
Glenfiddich Distillery Visitor Centre, Dufftown, Moray 144, 148
Glenfinnan Monument & Visitor Centre, Glenfinnan, Highlands 169
Glengarry Castle, Invergarry, Highlands 184
Glengarry Minibus Tours & Guide Services, Highlands 172
Glengoulandie Deer Park, Aberfeldy, Central 130
Glengoyne Distillery, Killearn, Stirling 122
Glenisla Hotel, Edinburgh 33
The Glenisla Hotel, Glenisla, Angus 110
Glenkinchie Distillery Visitor Centre, Pencaitland, East Lothian 22
Glenlivet Distillery, Ballindalloch, Moray 148
Glenlivet Estate, Tomintoul, Moray 147
Glenlochy, Fort William, Highlands 183
Glenluce Abbey, Glenluce, Dumf/Gal 54
Glenluce Caravan & Camping Park, Glenluce, Dumf/Gal 63
Glenluce Motor Museum, Glenluce, Dumf/Gal 53
Glenmarkie Farm Riding Centre, Blairgowrie, Central 131
Glenmorangie Distillery, Tain, Highlands 198
Glenmore, Ayr, Ayrshire 69
Glenmoriston Arms, Invermoriston, Highlands 185
Glenorchy Hotel, Edinburgh 33
Glenrigh, Oban, Argyll 176
Glenrothes Golf Course, Fife 106
Glenrothes Riding Centre, Fife 107
Glenroy, Oban, Argyll 177
Glenshee Ski Centre, Glenshee, Angus 107, 131, 149
Glenspean Lodge Hotel, Roy Bridge, Highlands 189
Glentairie Riding Centre, Glen Prosen, Angus 107
Glentarkie Off-Rd, Strathmiglo, Fife 106
Glenturret Distillery, Crieff, Central 131
Globe Inn, Dumfries, Dumf/Gal 65
Glynhill Hotel & Leisure Club, Glasgow 84
Go Blue Banana, Edinburgh 23
Go Orkney, Orkney 226
Golf Hotel, Crail, Fife 114
Golf Hotel, Powfoot, Dumf/Gal 60
Golf Links Hotel, Golspie, Highlands 201
Golf View Hotel, Prestwick, Ayrshire 71
Golf View House, Tain, Highlands 203
Golf View, Nairn, Highlands 189
Golspie Golf Course, Highlands 198
Gordon Arms Hotel, Kincardine O'Neil, Aberdeenshire 157
The Gordon Highlanders Museum, Aberdeen 145
Gordon's Restaurant, Inverkeilor, Angus 110
Gorgie City Farm, Edinburgh 21
Goven Old Parish Church, Glasgow 79
Gracefield Arts Centre, Dumfries, Dumf/Gal 53
Gracemount Leisure Centre, Edinburgh 24
Graham Stewart Gold & Silversmith, Dunblane, Stirling 122
Grainstore, Edinburgh 36
Grampian Activity Holidays, Aberdeen 148
Grampian Busline, Aberdeen 148
Grampian Rail tours Ltd, Ellon, Aberdeenshire 148
Grampian Transport Museum, Alford, Aberdeenshire 146
The Granary, Glasgow 87
Grand, Fort William, Highlands 183
The Grange, North Berwick, East Lothian 40
The Grange, Lauder, Borders 48
Grange, Ayr, Ayrshire 69
The Grange, Fort William, Highlands 183
Grange House Hotel, Whiting Bay, Arran 230
Grange Manor Hotel, Grangemouth, Falkirk 38, 40
Grange Riding Centre, West Calder, West Lothian 24

Grangemouth Sports Complex, Falkirk 24
Grantown-on-Spey Golf Course, Highlands 172
Grassic Gibbon Visitor Centre, Laurencekirk, Aberdeenshire 145
Great Glen 167
Great Glen Cycle Route, Highlands 172
Great Glen and Western Highlands 161-92
    events and festivals 163
    map 162-3
Green, Kinross, Central 135
The Green Gallery, Aberfoyle, Stirling 120
Green Hall Gallery, Craigellachie, Moray 145
Green Inn, Ballater, Aberdeenshire 153, 156
Green Park, Pitlochry, Central 137
Greenan Castle, Ayr, Ayrshire 67
Greenbank House & Gardens, Clarkston, Renfrewshire 89
Greenhill Covenanters' House, Biggar, S. Lanarkshire 88
Greenlaw, Gretna, Dumf/Gal 61
Greenlawns, Nairn, Highlands 189
Greenock Custom House Museum, Greenock, Inverclyde 88
Greens Hotel, Edinburgh 26
Greenside Hotel, Edinburgh 31
Gretna Chase, Gretna, Dumf/Gal 58
Gretna Golf Course, Dumf/Gal 56
Grey Mare's Tail, Dumf/Gal 55
Greyfriars Kirkyard, Edinburgh 19
Greystonelees, Burnmouth, Borders 47
Greywalls Hotel, Gullane, East Lothian 38, 40
Griselda Hill Pottery, Ceres, Fife 105
Grogport Rugs, Carradale, Argyll 166
Grosvenor Gardens Hotel, Edinburgh 29
Guide Friday Bus Tours, Perth, Central 131
Guide Friday, Edinburgh 23
Guide Friday, Glasgow 81
Guide Friday, Inverness 172
Guinach House, Aberfeldy, Central 132
Guinach House Hotel, Aberfeldy, Central 138
Guisachan House, Fort William, Highlands 183
Gwydir House Hotel, Crieff, Central 134
Gytes Leisure Centre, Peebles, Borders 45

H

Haddington, East Lothian 17
Haddo House, Methlick, Aberdeenshire 146
Hafton Holiday Centre, Dunoon, Argyll 167
Haggs Castle Golf Course, Glasgow 81
Haggs Castle Museum, Glasgow 78
Hailes Castle, East Linton, East Lothian 20
Halcyon Hotel, Edinburgh 34
Halleaths Caravan Site, Lochmaben, Dumf/Gal 63
Halliwells House Museum, Selkirk, Borders 43
Hamilton Mausoleum, S. Lanarkshire 89
Hamilton Old Parish Church, Hamilton, S. Lanarkshire 89
Hamilton Park Racecourse, S. Lanarkshire 91
Hamilton Toy Collection, Callander, Stirling 121
Handa Island Nature Reserve, Highlands 197
Handloom Weavers, Tarbet, Central 122
Harlosh House, Harlosh, Skye 232, 235
Harp Toby, Edinburgh 27
Harris 216, 218, 219, 220
Harris (hotel), Tarbert, Harris 232
Harris Tweed Shop, Tarbert, Harris 219
Harry Ramsdens, Edinburgh 36
Harry Ramsdens, Glasgow 87
Hartfell House, Moffat, Dumf/Gal 61
Harvest, Edinburgh 33
Harvies Leisure Centre, Stevenston, Ayrshire 68
Harviestoun Country Inn, Tillicoultry, Central 127
The Haughs, Keith, Moray 159
The Haven, Ballantrae, Ayrshire 69
A Haven, Edinburgh 29
Haven Hotel, Plockton, Highlands 202, 205
Hawes Inn, South Queensferry, Edinburgh 36
Hawick Golf Course, Borders 46
Hawick Museum & Scott Art Gallery, Hawick, Borders 43
Hawkcraig House, Aberdour, Fife 114
Hayfield Riding Centre, Aberdeen 149
Hazelbank Private Hotel, St Andrews, Fife 115
Hazeldean Riding Centre, Hawick, Borders 46
Hazelden Saddlery, Newton Mearns, Renfrewshire 91
Heads of Ayr Farm Park, Ayr, Ayrshire 67

Heathbank, Boat of Garten, Highlands 181
Heathfield, Inverness, Highlands 187
Heathmount, Beauly, Highlands 181
Heathmount, Inverness, Highlands 187
Heathpark Lodge, Blairgowrie, Central 133
Hebridean Exploration, Stornoway, Lewis 220
Hebridean Horse-Drawn Holidays, North Uist 220
Hector Russell Kiltmaker, Glasgow 80
Hector Russell Kiltmaker, Inverness,
    Highlands 171
The Heidl, Perth, Central 136
Helensburgh Golf Course, Central 122
Helios Fountain, Edinburgh 36
Helmsdale Golf Course, Highlands 198
Heriott Park, Edinburgh 33
Hermaness National Nature Reserve, Unst 227
Hermitage, Anstruther, Fife 114
The Hermitage, Dunkeld, Central 130
Hermitage Castle, Hermitage, Borders 44
Heroncraft Scotland, Ghriothaich, Stirling 122
Hetland Hall, Carrutherstown, Dumf/Gal 57
High Belltrees, Lochwinnoch, Renfrewshire 94
Highfield, Dornoch, Highlands 200
Highgrove House, Troon, Ayrshire 72, 73
Highland Activity Holidays, Dufftown, Moray 148
Highland Adventure Outdoor Pursuits Centre,
    Glenisla by Alyth, Angus 106
Highland Country Bus Ltd, Highlands 171
Highland Drascombe Sailing School, Inverness,
    Highlands 172
Highland Folk Museum, Kingussie, Highlands 169
Highland Folk Museum (Turus Tim),
    Newtonmore, Highlands 169
Highland Gateway Centre, Newtonmore,
    Highlands 170
Highland Gliding Club, Elgin, Moray 149
Highland Guides, Highlands 172
The Highland Haven, Macduff, Aberdeenshire 155
Highland Heritage Centre, Braemar,
    Aberdeenshire 145
Highland House, Callander, Central 125
Highland Icelandic Horse Trekking, Spean Bridge,
    Highlands 172
Highland Line Craft Centre, Achnasheen,
    Highlands 197
Highland Museum of Childhood, Strathpeffer,
    Highlands 196
Highland Mysteryworld, Fort William,
    Highlands 170
Highland Park Distillery, Kirkwall, Mainland 226
Highland Rare Breeds Farm, Elphin,
    Highlands 197
Highland Riding Centre, Drumnadrochit,
    Highlands 172
Highland Safaris, Strathpeffer, Highlands 198
Highland Watersports, Lairg, Highlands 198
Highland Wildlife Park, Kincraig, Highlands 170
Highlands 168-72, 193-205
    access 171, 197
    accommodation 180-90, 199-204
    beaches 172, 197
    crafts 171, 197
    entertainment 171, 197
    events and festivals 195
    ferries 171, 197
    food and drink 171, 198
Highlands (north) 193-205
Highlands (south) 161, 168-72, 180-92
    restaurants 191-2, 204-5
    scenic drives 172, 198
    sightseeing 169-70, 196-7
    sport and leisure 172, 198
    tourist information 171, 197
    tours 172, 198
    transport 171, 198
The Hilcroft, Whitburn, West Lothian 39
Hill House, Helensburgh, Central 120
Hill of Tarvit Mansionhouse & Garden, Cupar,
    Fife 102
Hillhead Equestrian Centre, Carluke,
    S. Lanarkshire 91
Hillholm, Selkirk, Borders 49
Hillpark House, Leuchars, Fife 114
Hillview Leisure Centre, Kirkconnel, Dumf/Gal 56
Hilton National Edinburgh, Edinburgh 28
Hilton National Livingston, Livingston, West
    Lothian 39

The Hirsel, Coldstream, Borders 44, 45
Hirsel Golf Course, Borders 46
HM Frigate Unicorn, Dundee 104
Hoddom Castle Caravan Park, Ecclefechan,
    Dumf/Gal 62
Holiday Inn, Glasgow 83
Holiday Inn Crowne Plaza, Aberdeen 150
Holiday Inn Express, Hamilton, S. Lanarkshire 93
Holiday Inn Garden Court, Edinburgh 26
Holiday Inn Garden Court, Glasgow 85
Holly Tree, Kentallen, Highlands 187
Holyrood Park, Edinburgh 20
Hopetoun, Edinburgh 33
Hopetoun House, South Queensferry, West
    Lothian 18
Hopetoun Lodge, Dunfermline, Fife 114
Horn & Country Crafts, Hawick, Borders 45
Hospitality Inn, Irvine, Ayrshire 70
Hotel Eilean Iarmain, Isle Ornsay, Skye 233, 235
Hotel Enterprise, Glasgow 84
Hotel Seaforth, Arbroath, Angus 108
House for an Art Lover, Glasgow 79
House of Binns, Linlithgow, West Lothian 18
House of Dun, Montrose, Angus 102
House O'Hill, Edinburgh 31
Houston Farm Riding School, Broxburn, West
    Lothian 24
Houston House Hotel, Uphall,
    West Lothian 39, 40
The Howard, Edinburgh 27
Howie Irvine Loch Lomond, Arden, Central 122
Howie-Irvine Sporting Factors, Lumphanan,
    Aberdeenshire 148
Hoxa Tapestry Gallery, South Ronaldsay 225
Hoy 224, 225
Hrossey Silver, Orphir, Mainland 225
Hrossland Trekking Centre, Burray 226
Hugh Miller's Cottage, Cromarty, Highlands 196
Humbles Cafe Bar, Helensburgh, Argyll 179
Hunter House, East Kilbride, S. Lanarkshire 88
Hunterian Museum & Art Gallery, Glasgow 78
Hunterston Power Station, Hunterston,
    Ayrshire 66
Huntingtower Castle, Perth, Central 130
Huntingtower Hotel, Perth, Central 135, 139
Huntly Castle, Huntly, Aberdeenshire 145
Huntly House Museum, Edinburgh 18
Huntly Nordic Ski Centre, Huntly,
    Aberdeenshire 148, 149
Hutchesons' Hall, Glasgow 79
Hydro-Electric Visitor Centre, Dam & Fish Pass,
    Pitlochry, Central 130

I

Ibster Chambered Cairn, St Margaret's Hope,
    Mainland 224-5
Ice World Ice Rink, Forfar, Angus 106
Iceberg Glassblowing Studio, Drumnadrochit,
    Highlands 171
Idvies House, Forfar, Angus 109
Iggs, Edinburgh 35
Il Pavone Italian Restaurant, Glasgow 87
Imperial, Castle Douglas, Dumf/Gal 57
Imperial, Fort William, Highlands 183
Incharvie Equestrian Centre, Leven, Fife 107
Inchbae Lodge Hotel, Garve, Highlands 200, 204
Inchberry House, Inverness, Highlands 187
Inchholm Island & Abbey, Fife 104
Inchmahome Priory, Port of Monteith, Stirling 121
Inchview Hotel, Burntisland, Fife 111
Inchyra Grange, Polmont, Falkirk 39
Innellan Golf Course, Argyll 167
Innerleithen Golf Course, Borders 46
Insh Hall Ski School & Ski Lodge, Kincraig,
    Highlands 172
Insh Marshes Reserve (RSPB), Kingussie,
    Highlands 170
International, Edinburgh 29
Inver Lodge, Lochinver, Highlands 202
Inver Lodge, Strathpeffer, Highlands 203
Inveraray Castle, Inveraray, Argyll 165
Inveraray Golf Course, Argyll 167
Inveraray Jail, Inveraray, Argyll 165
Inverbeg Galleries, Inverbeg, Central 120
Inverbeg Inn, Luss, Central 127
Invercarse, Dundee 109

Invercauld Arms, Braemar, Aberdeenshire 154
Inveresk House, Edinburgh 31
Inveresk Lodge Garden, Musselburgh,
    East Lothian 21
Inverewe Garden, Poolewe, Highlands 196
Inverglen, Inverness, Highlands 187
Invergordon Golf Course, Highlands 198
Invergordon Leisure Centre, Highlands 198
Inverlochy Castle, Fort William,
    Highlands 182, 191
Invermark Hotel, Dundee 109
Invermay Hotel, Whiting Bay, Arran 230
Inverness, Highlands 168
Inverness Airport 147
Inverness Golf Course, Highlands 172
Inverness Ice Rink, Highlands 172
Inverness Museum & Art Gallery, Inverness,
    Highlands 169
Inverness Sports Centre, Highlands 172
Inverness Thistle, Inverness, Highlands 185, 191
Inverour, Spean Bridge, Highlands 190
Inverpolly Nature Reserve, Ullapool,
    Highlands 197
Iona 214, 215
Iona, Edinburgh 28
Iona, Perth, Central 136
Iona Pottery, Iona 215
Ionad Nibheis Visitor Centre, Fort William,
    Highlands 169-70
Island Explorer, Westray 226
Island House, Galashiels, Borders 47
Island Porcelain, Kilmory, Arran 211
The Islands 206-35
    events and festivals 207
    see also individual groups eg Orkney
Islay 212, 213, 214, 215
Islay Diving Centre, Islay 215
Islay Marine Cruises, Bridgend, Islay 215
Islay Woollen Mill Company Ltd, Bridgend,
    Islay 215
Isle of Barra, Tangusdale, Barra 232
Isle Crafts, Isle of Whithorn, Dumf/Gal 55
Isle of Eriska, Eriska, Argyll 175, 178
Isle of May, Fife 104
Isle of Mull Weavers, Craignure, Mull 215
Isle of Noss Nature Reserve 227
Isle of Raasay 219
Isle of Skye Golf Course, Sconser, Skye 220
Isle of Skye Toby, Perth, Central 136
Islescroft Caravan & Camping Site, Dalbeattie,
    Dumf/Gal 62
The Isles of Glencoe Hotel & Leisure Centre,
    Ballachulish, Highlands 181
Italian Chapel, Lamb Holm 225
Ivy House, Edinburgh 31

J

Jack Kane Centre, Edinburgh 24
Jacksons, Edinburgh 35
Jacobs Ladder, Wigtown, Dumf/Gal 61
James Dun's House, Aberdeen 145
James Hamilton Heritage Park, East Kilbride,
    S. Lanarkshire 90, 91
James Paterson Museum, Moniaive, Dumf/Gal 53
James Pringle Weavers, Inverness, Highlands 171
Jane Welsh Carlyle Museum, Haddington, East
    Lothian 20
Jarlshof Prehistoric Site, Mainland 227
The Jays, Aberdeen 151
Jedburgh Abbey, Jedburgh, Borders 43
Jedburgh Castle Jail & Museum, Jedburgh,
    Borders 44
Jedburgh Golf Course, Borders 46
Jedburgh Sports Centre, Jedburgh, Borders 45
Jedforest Deer & Farm Park, Jedburgh,
    Borders 44
The Jenny, Glasgow 87
J.F. Lindsay (Targemaker), Inverness,
    Highlands 171
Jim Clark Room, Duns, Borders 43
Joan Maclennan Tweeds, Harris 219
Jock Tamson's, Glasgow 87
Jock Tamson's (city centre), Glasgow 87
John Buchan Centre, Broughton, Borders 43
John Cockburn Off Road, Cambusbarron,
    Stirling 122
John Knox House, Edinburgh 19

John Muir Country Park, Dunbar, East Lothian 21
John O'Groats Ferries, John O'Groats,
    Highlands 198
John Paul Jones Birthplace Museum, Kirkbean,
    Dumf/Gal 53
Johnstounburn House, Humbie, East Lothian 38
Jonah's Journey, Aberdeen, Aberdeenshire 146
Joppa Rocks, Edinburgh 31
Judith Glue Knitwear, Kirkwall, Mainland 225
June Dunn Jewellery, Scone, Central 130
Junkanoo Tapas Bar/Caf_, Glasgow 87
Jura 212
Jurys Glasgow, Glasgow 83

K

Kailzie Gardens, Peebles, Borders 44
Kariba, Edinburgh 33
Kathryn Ade Jewellery, Newton Stewart,
    Dumf/Gal 55
Keavil House Hotel, Dunfermline, Fife 111, 117
Kelburn Country Centre, Largs, Ayrshire 66
Kellie Castle & Garden, Pittenweem, Fife 102
Kelly's, Edinburgh 35
Kelso Abbey, Kelso, Borders 44
Kelso Golf Course, Borders 46
Kelso Museum & The Turret Gallery, Kelso,
    Borders 43
Kelso Pottery, Kelso, Borders 45
Kelso Racecourse, Wooler, Borders 46
Kelton Mains Open Farm, Castle Douglas,
    Dumf/Gal 54
Kelvin Hall Sports Arena, Glasgow 81
Kelvin Park Lorne, Glasgow 83
Kelvin Private Hotel, Glasgow 84
Kelvin Walkway, Glasgow 81
Kelvingrove Park, Glasgow 80
Ken-Dee Marshes Nature Reserve, Castle
    Douglas, Dumf/Gal 55
Ken Lochhead Gallery, East Linton,
    East Lothian 22
Kenmore Bank Hotel, Jedburgh, Borders 48
Kenmore Golf Course, Central 131
Kerrisdale, Inverness, Highlands 186
Kerrs Miniature Railway, Arbroath, Angus 104
Kew, Edinburgh 30
Kilberry Bagpipes, Edinburgh 22
Kilberry Inn, Kilberry, Argyll 179
Kilcamb Lodge, Strontian, Highlands 190, 192
Kilchurn, Connel, Argyll 174
Kilchurn Castle, Argyll 165
Kildalton Cross, Port Ellen, Islay 214
Kildonan Lodge Hotel, Edinburgh 30
Kildonan Museum, Kildonan, South Uist 218
Kildrummy Castle, Kildrummy,
    Aberdeenshire 145
Kildrummy Castle Gardens, Kildrummy,
    Aberdeenshire 146
Kildrummy Castle (hotel), Kildrummy,
    Aberdeenshire 155, 156
Kilfinan Hotel, Kilfinan, Argyll 175, 178
Killermont Polo Club, Glasgow 85
Killiechronan House, Killiechronan,
    Mull 178, 231, 235
Killiecrankie, Pitlochry, Central 129
Killiecrankie Hotel, Killiecrankie, Central 134, 138
Killin Golf Course, Killin, Stirling 122, 131
Kilmarnock Golf Course, Ayrshire 68
Kilmartin Church, Kilmartin, Argyll 165
Kilmartin Crafts, Kilmartin, Argyll 166
Kilmartin House, Kilmartin, Argyll 165
Kilmaurs, Edinburgh 30
Kilmichael Country House Hotel, Brodick,
    Arran 230, 234
Kilmore Farm House, Drumnadrochit,
    Highlands 182
Kilmory Castle Garden, Lochgilphead, Argyll 165
Kilmuir Church, Kilmuir, Skye 218
Kilninian Church, Kilninian, Mull 214
Kiloran Gardens, Colonsay 214
Kilspindie House, Aberlady, East Lothian 37
Kilt Rock, Skye 219
Kilwinning Abbey, Kilwinning, Ayrshire 67
Kincaid House Hotel, Glasgow 87
Kincardine Lodge, Lochranza, Arran 230
Kincraig Private Hotel, Prestwick, Ayrshire 72
Kind Kyttock's Kitchen, Falkland, Fife 117
Kinfauns Castle, Perth, Central 135, 139

King James Thistle, Edinburgh 26
King James VI Golf Course, Perth, Central 131
King Malcolm Thistle, Dunfermline, Fife 111
King Robert the Bruce's Cave, Kirkpatrick
    Fleming, Dumf/Gal 54
Kinghorn Golf Course, Fife 106
Kinglass, Bo'ness, Falkirk 37
King's, Galashiels, Borders 47
King's Arms, Castle Douglas, Dumf/Gal 57
Kings Arms Hotel, Lockerbie, Dumf/Gal 59
King's Cave, Blackwaterfoot, Arran 210
King's College Chapel, Aberdeen 145
Kings Manor, Edinburgh 26
Kings Park, Glasgow 83
Kings Park Golf Course, Glasgow 81
Kingsknowes, Galashiels, Borders 47
Kingsley, Arbroath, Angus 108
Kingsley, Edinburgh 33
Kingsmills Hotel, Inverness, Highlands 185, 191
Kingsmuir, Peebles, Borders 49
Kinkell Braes Caravan Site, St Andrews, Fife 116
Kinkell House, Dingwall, Highlands 199, 204
Kinloch Anderson, Edinburgh 22
Kinloch Hotel Leisure Centre, Blackwaterfoot,
    Arran 211
Kinloch House Hotel, Blairgowrie,
    Central 133, 138
Kinloch Lodge, Isle Ornsay, Skye 233, 235
Kinlochbervie, Kinlochbervie, Highlands 201
Kinnaird, Dunkeld, Angus 109, 138
Kinnaird, Perth, Central 136
Kinneil Museum & Roman Fortlet, Bo'ness,
    Falkirk 20
Kinnoull Hill Woodland Park, Perth, Central 130
Kinross 118
Kinshaldy Riding Stables, Leuchars, Fife 107
Kinsman Blake Ceramics, Kelso, Borders 45
Kintyre Community Education Centre,
    Campbeltown, Argyll 167
Kippford Caravan Park, Kippford, Dumf/Gal 63
Kirkcaldy Golf Course, Fife 106
Kirkcaldy Ice Rink, Angus 106
Kirkcaldy Museum & Art Gallery, Fife 103
Kirkcudbright Golf Course, Dumf/Gal 56
Kirkcudbright Marina, Kirkcudbright,
    Dumf/Gal 56
Kirkhill Golf Course, Glasgow 81
Kirkhouse Inn, Strathblane, Central 127
Kirklands, Galashiels, Borders 47
Kirklands, Kinross, Central 135
Kirklea, Edinburgh 33
Kirkliston Leisure Centre, West Lothian 24
Kirkloch Brae Caravan Site, Lochmaben,
    Dumf/Gal 63
Kirkton House, Cardross, Argyll 173
Kirkwall, Orkney 222
Kirkwall Airport, Mainland 225
Kirkwall Grammar School, Mainland 226
Kirriemuir Golf Course, Angus 106
Kirroughtree House, Newton Stewart,
    Dumf/Gal 59, 65
Kisimul Castle, Castlebay, Barra 219
Klibreck, Aberdeen 152
Knap of Howar, Papa Westray 225
Knightswood Golf Course, Glasgow 81
Knockan Studio, Elphin, Highlands 197
Knockendarroch House Hotel, Pitlochry,
    Central 137, 139
Knockie Lodge Hotel, Whitebridge,
    Highlands 190, 192
Knockinaam Lodge, Portpatrick, Dumf/Gal 59, 65
Knockomie Hotel, Forres, Moray 158, 160
Koh I Noor Restaurant, Glasgow 87
Kyle, Kyle of Lochalsh, Highlands 201
Kyle House, Bonar Bridge, Highlands 199
Kylerhea Otter Sanctuary, Broadford, Skye 219
Kyles of Bute Golf Course, Tighnabruaich,
    Argyll 167
Kylesku Hotel, Kylesku, Highlands 201, 204

L

La Bonne Baguette, Aberdeen 157
La Meridiana, Aberfeldy, Central 138
La Parmigiana, Glasgow 86
La Potiniere, Gullane, East Lothian 40
Ladybank Golf Course, Fife 106

Ladymire Equestrian Centre, Ellon,
    Aberdeenshire 149
Ladysmith House & Scottish Larder, Ullapool,
    Highlands 204
Lagavulin Distillery, Port Ellen, Islay 215
Laggan View, Inverness, Highlands 186
Laichmoray, Elgin, Moray 158
Laidhay Croft Museum, Dunbeath, Highlands 196
Laing Museum, Newburgh, Fife 103
The Lairg, Edinburgh 31
Lairhillock Inn and Restaurant, Netherley,
    Aberdeenshire 157
Lake Hotel, Port of Menteith, Central 127, 128
Lamlash Golf Course, Arran 211
Lanark Museum, Lanark, S. Lanarkshire 88
Lanark, S. Lanarkshire 77
Lanarkshire Riding Centre, Lanark,
    S. Lanarkshire 91
Lancaster, Oban, Argyll 176
Landmark Highland Heritage & Adventure Park,
    Carrbridge, Highlands 169
Landwise Off Road, Boat of Garten,
    Highlands 172
Langholm Golf Course, Dumf/Gal 56
Laphroaig Distillery, Port Ellen, Islay 215
L'Aristo Ristorante, Glasgow 87
Larkhall Leisure Centre, S. Lanarkshire 91
L'Auberge Restaurant, Edinburgh 34
Lauder Golf Course, Borders 46
Lauderdale, Lauder, Borders 48
The Laurels, Blairgowrie, Central 133
Lauriston Castle, Edinburgh 20
Le Jardin, Helensburgh, Argyll 179
Le Sept Restaurant, Edinburgh 36
Lea-Mar, Largs, Ayrshire 71
Leamington, Edinburgh 31
Lecht Ski Centre, Strathdon, Aberdeenshire 149
Ledgowan Lodge, Achnasheen, Highlands 199
Leinster Lodge, Inverness, Highlands 187
The Leith Gallery, Edinburgh 19
Leith Hall & Garden, Huntly, Aberdeenshire 146
Lemon Tree, Aberdeen 157
Lennoxlove House & Gardens, Haddington,
    East Lothian 21
Lerwick, Shetland 222
Lerwick Boating Club, Mainland 229
Lerwick (hotel), Lerwick, Shetland 234
Lesley Burr Ceramic Tiles, Sandwick,
    Mainland 228
Leslie Golf Course, Fife 106
Letham Grange, Arbroath, Angus 108
Letham Grange Resort, Arbroath, Angus 106
Lethamhill Golf Course, Glasgow 81
Let's Eat, Perth, Central 139
Letterfinlay Lodge, Letterfinlay, Highlands 188
Lettershuna Riding Centre, Appin, Argyll 167
Leven Links, Fife 106
Lewis 216, 217, 218, 219, 220
Lilybank Hotel, Lamlash, Arran 230
Lime Tree Studio, Fort William, Highlands 169
Lindean Mill Glass, Galashiels, Borders 45
Lindsay, Edinburgh 33
Link Ice Arena, Aberdeen 149
The Links, Brora, Highlands 199
Links Hotel, Montrose, Angus 110
Linlithgow, West Lothian 17
Linlithgow Leisure Centre, West Lothian 24
Linlithgow Loch, Linlithgow, West Lothian 21
Linlithgow Palace, Linlithgow, West Lothian 20
The Linlithgow Story, Linlithgow, West Lothian 21
Linlithgow Union Canal Society, Linlithgow,
    West Lothian 23
Linn of Dee, Inverey, Aberdeenshire 147
The Linn Gardens, Helensburgh, Central 121
Linn Park Golf Course, Glasgow 81
Linnhe Marine, Appin, Argyll 167
Linwood Sports Centre, Renfrewshire 91
Lionsgate Stables, Ayr, Ayrshire 68
Livingston's Restaurant, Linlithgow,
    West Lothian 40
Loanhead of Daviot Stone Circle, Inverurie,
    Aberdeenshire 145
Loanhead Leisure Centre, Midlothian 24
Loch an Eilean, Aviemore, Highlands 170
Loch Awe, Argyll 165
Loch Broom Leisure Centre, Ullapool,
    Highlands 198

Loch Coruisk, Elgol, Skye 219
Loch Doon, Ayrshire 67
Loch Druidibeg Nature Reserve, South Uist 219
Loch Duich, Ardelve, Highlands 199
Loch Etive House Hotel, Connel, Argyll 174
Loch Fyne Art Courses, Argyll 167
Loch Garten Nature Reserve, Boat of Garten,
    Highlands 169
Loch Insh Watersports Centre, Kincraig,
    Highlands 172
Loch Leven Castle, Kinross, Central 129
Loch Leven (hotel), North Ballachulish,
    Highlands 189
Loch Leven Leisure, Kinross, Central 131
Loch Lomond 118
Loch Lomond Golf Course, Luss, Central 122
Loch Lomond Park Centre, Balloch, Central 121
Loch Lomond Water Ski Club, Central 123
Loch of the Lowes Nature Reserve, Dunkeld,
    Central 130
Loch Melfort Hotel, Arduaine, Argyll 173, 177
Loch Morlich Watersports, Glenmore Forest Park,
    Highlands 172
Loch Ness & Great Glen Cruise Company,
    Highlands 171
Loch Ness House, Inverness, Highlands 185
Loch Ness Riding, Inverness, Highlands 172
Loch Park Adventure Centre, Keith, Moray 148
Loch of Strathbeg RSPB Nature Reserve,
    Fraserburgh, Aberdeenshire 147
Loch Sunart, Strontian, Highlands 190
Loch Tay Boating Centre, Kenmore, Central 131
Loch Tay Highland Equestrian Centre, Killin,
    Central 131
Loch Torridon, Torridon, Highlands 203, 205
Lochaber Leisure Centre & Swimming Pool, Fort
    William, Highlands 172
Lochaber Walks, Highlands 172
Lochalsh, Kyle of Lochalsh, Highlands 201 ,
Lochardil House, Inverness, Highlands 185
Lochcarron Cashmere & Wool Centre, Galashiels,
    Borders 45
Lochcarron Golf Course, Highlands 198
Lochcarron (hotel), Lochcarron, Highlands 202
Lochcroistean Centre, Uig, Lewis 218
Lochearnhead, Lochearnhead, Central 126
Lochearnhead Watersports Ltd, Lochearnhead,
    Stirling 123, 131
Lochee Swimming & Leisure Centre, Dundee 106
Lochgelly Golf Course, Fife 106
Lochgilphead Golf Course, Argyll 167
Lochgreen House, Troon, Ayrshire 72, 73
Lochindorb Castle, Highlands 170
Lochinver Larder, Lochinver, Highlands 204
Lochmaben Castle, Lochmaben, Dumf/Gal 54
Lochmaben Centre, Dumf/Gal 56
Lochmaben Golf Course, Dumf/Gal 56
Lochmaddy, Lochmaddy, North Uist 232
Lochnagar Craft Shop, Bridge of Weir,
    Renfrewshire 90
Lochnaw Castle Equestrian Centre, Stranraer,
    Dumf/Gal 56
Lochore Meadows Country Park, Lochgelly,
    Fife 106
Lochore Meadows Riding Centre, Lochgelly,
    Fife 107
Lochranza Castle, Lochranza, Arran 210
Lochranza Studio Gallery, Lochranza, Arran 210
Lochside, Bowmore, Islay 230
Lochside Caravan & Camping Site, Castle
    Douglas, Dumf/Gal 62
Lochside Ponies, Aros, Mull 215
Lochview, Fort William, Highlands 184
Lochview Motel, Crocketford, Dumf/Gal 58
Lochwinnoch RSPB Nature Reserve,
    Lochwinnoch, Renfrewshire 90
Lock Ken Holiday Park, Parton, Dumf/Gal 64
Lockerbie Golf Course, Dumf/Gal 56
Locke's Acre, Crieff, Central 134
Lodge, Old Rayne, Aberdeenshire 155
Lodge, Elgin, Moray 159
The Lodge Hotel, Edinburgh 30
The Lodge House, Crianlarich, Central 125
The Lodge on Loch Lomond, Luss, Central 127
Lodge on the Loch, Onich, Highlands 189
Logan Botanic Garden, Port Logan, Dumf/Gal 53
Loganair 197

Logie Steading, Forres, Moray 147
Lomond Centre, Glenrothes, Fife 106
Lomond Country Inn, Kinnesswood,
    Central 134, 139
Lomond Hills, Fife 104
Lomond Hills (hotel), Freuchie, Fife 111
Lomond Hotel, Glasgow 84
Lomond Walking Holidays, Central 123
Lomondside Equestrian Centre, Drymen,
    Stirling 123
Lonach Farm Riding Centre, Strathdon,
    Aberdeenshire 149
Lord Provost Alexander Collie Sports Centre,
    Aberdeen 149
Lorimer House, St Andrews, Fife 115
Losset, Alyth, Central 132
Lossiemouth House, Lossiemouth, Moray 159
Lothian Regional Transport Service, Edinburgh 23
Lothianburn Golf Course, Edinburgh 23
The Lothians see Falkirk & the Lothians
Loudon Castle Theme Park, Galston, Ayrshire 67
Lovat Arms, Fort Augustus, Highlands 182
Lovat, Perth, Central 135
Low Parks, Hamilton, S. Lanarkshire 88
Lower City Mills, Perth, Central 129
Lowland Buses, Dalkeith, Midlothian 23
Lubnaig Hotel, Callander, Central 125, 128
Lundin Golf Course, Fife 106
Lyall Cliff, Dunoon, Argyll 174
Lyn-Leven, Ballachulish, Highlands 181
Lynedoch, Stirling 127
Lynnhurst, Glasgow 84
Lynwood, Brora, Highlands 199
Lyth Stables, Wick, Highlands 198

M

M & D's Theme Park, Motherwell,
    N. Lanarkshire 89
MacBackpackers Holidays, Edinburgh 23
The 'Macbeth' Experience, Perth, Central 130
Maccrimmon Piping Heritage Centre, Dunvegan,
    Skye 218
Macdonald Thistle, Giffnock, Renfrewshire 93
Macduff Castle, East Wemyss, Fife 104
Macduff Marine Aquarium, Macduff,
    Aberdeenshire 146
Macgillivrays, Benbecula 219
Machrie Hotel, Port Ellen, Islay 215
Machrie Moor Standing Stones, Arran 210
Machrihanish Golf Course, Argyll 167
Mackay's, Wick, Highlands 204
Mackinnon Mills, Coatbridge, N. Lanarkshire 90
Maclaurin Art Gallery & Rozelle House, Ayr,
    Ayrshire 66
Macleod Harris Tweed Mill, Lewis 219
Macquarie Mausoleum, Knock, Mull 214
Macrae House, Inverness, Highlands 187
Maddy Moss Ltd, Alva, Central 122
Made In Scotland Ltd, Beauly, Highlands 171
Maes Howe Chambered Cairn, Finstown,
    Mainland 224
Magnum Leisure Centre, Irvine, Ayrshire 67, 68
'Maid of the Forth' Cruises, Edinburgh 22
Maid of the Forth, North Queensferry, Fife 105
Mainland 221, 224-5, 226, 227, 228, 229
Mainsriddle Pottery, Kirkbean, Dumf/Gal 55
Maitland Hotel, Edinburgh 30
Making Treks, Ballater, Aberdeenshire 148
Malin Court, Turnberry, Ayrshire 72, 73
Mallaig Heritage Centre, Mallaig, Highlands 170
Malleny Garden, Edinburgh 20
Malmaison, Edinburgh 26, 35
Malmaison Hotel, Glasgow 83, 85
Malvern, Inverness, Highlands 187
Manderston, Duns, Borders 44
Mannofield Hotel, Aberdeen 152
Manor House Hotel, Oban, Argyll 178
Manor House Hotel, Oban, Highlands 176
Manor Park, Largs, Ayrshire 71
Manorville, Aberdeen 151
Mansefield House, Fort William, Highlands 184
Mansefield House Hotel, Elgin, Moray 158, 160
Mansewood Country House, Lochearnhead,
    Central 126
Mansfield House, Tain, Highlands 203
Mansion House Hotel, Elgin, Moray 158, 160
Maple Leaf Quarter Horses, Clynder, Central 123

Maplehurst, Galashiels, Borders 47
Marchhall Hotel, Edinburgh 33
Mardale, Edinburgh 31
Mardella, Gartocharn, Central 126
The Maredrcliffe at Pitfodels, Aberdeen 150
Margaret Hamilton Knitwear, Sellafirth, Yell 228
Mari Donald Knitwear, Comrie, Central 130
The Marine, North Berwick, East Lothian 39
Marine, Mallaig, Highlands 188
Marine Highland Hotel, Troon, Ayrshire 72, 73
Marine Hotel, Stonehaven, Aberdeenshire 157
Marlin Watersports & Dive Centre, Dunoon,
    Argyll 167
Marriott Dalmahoy Hotel Golf & Country Club,
    Edinburgh 23, 25, 35
Mars Wark, Stirling 121
Marthrown of Mabie Education Centre, Dumfries,
    Dumf/Gal 56
Martin's Restaurant, Edinburgh 35
Marwick Head Nature Reserve, Birsay,
    Mainland 225
Mary Queen of Scots House, Jedburgh,
    Borders 43
Maryculter House Hotel, Aberdeen 150, 155
The Matthew Architecture Gallery, Edinburgh 19
Mavis Hall Park, Humbie, East Lothian 23
Maxwelton House, Moniaive, Dumf/Gal 54
Mayfield, Forres, Moray 159
McCaig's Tower, Oban, Argyll 165
McCalls Ltd, Aberdeen 147
McClays, Glasgow 84
McClean of Braemar, Braemar,
    Aberdeenshire 147
McClean Museum & Art Gallery, Greenock,
    Inverclyde 88
McClellan Galleries, Glasgow 79
The McEwan Gallery, Ballater, Aberdeenshire 145
McManus Galleries, Dundee 103
Meadhon House, Jedburgh, Borders 48
Meadow Sports Centre, Dumbarton, Central 122
Meadowbank Inn, Arbroath, Angus 110
Meadowbank Sports Centre, Edinburgh 24
Meadowmill Sports Centre, Tranent,
    East Lothian 24
Meadows, Edinburgh 31
Mearns Craft, Kirriemuir, Angus 105
Meffan Gallery & Museum, Forfar, Angus 103
Meikleour Beech Hedge, Meikleour, Central 129
Meldrum Arms, Oldmeldrum, Aberdeenshire 155
Melfort Riding Centre, Oban, Argyll 167
Mellerstain House, Gordon, Borders 44
Melrose, Borders 42
Melrose Abbey & Abbey Museum, Borders 43
Melrose Golf Course, Borders 46
Menstrie Castle, Menstrie, Central 120
Menzies, Edinburgh 34
Merchants' House, Glasgow 79
The Mercury, Aviemore, Highlands 180
Mercury, Fort William, Highlands 183
Mercury, Wick, Highlands 204
Mersehead Nature Reserve, Southwick,
    Dumf/Gal 55
Michael Gill Jewellery, Kirkcudbright,
    Dumf/Gal 55
Michael Main Gallery, Brodick, Arran 210
Mid Drumloch Farm Riding & Livery, Hamilton,
    S. Lanarkshire 91
Midhowe Broch and Chambered Cairn,
    Rousay 225
Midlothian Ski Centre, Hillend, Midlothian 24
Milecroft Hotel, Gairloch, Highlands 198
The Mill, Gretna, Dumf/Gal 61
Mill on the Fleet, Gatehouse of Fleet,
    Dumf/Gal 53
Mill House, Buckie, Moray 158
Millbank Gallery, Nairn, Highlands 169
Millcraig, Dingwall, Highlands 199
Mills Observatory, Dundee 103
Millwood House, Inverness, Highlands 186
Milnathort Golf Course, Central 131
Milton, Fort William, Highlands 183
Mingarry Castle, Kilchoan, Highlands 170
Minto Golf Course, Borders 46
Mira Mare, Helensburgh, Argyll 179
Mitchell Library, Glasgow 79
Moat Park Heritage Centre, Biggar,
    S. Lanarkshire 88

Moffat Golf Course, Dumf/Gal 56
Moffat House, Moffat, Dumf/Gal 59
Moffat Pottery, Moffat, Dumf/Gal 55
Moidart Pony Trekking, Acharacle, Highlands 172
Molly Malones, Glasgow 87
Monachyle Mhor, Balquhidder, Central 124, 128
Moniack, Balmaha, Central 124
Monifieth Golf Course, Angus 106
Monikie Country Park, Dundee 104, 107
Monreith Animal World, Shore Centre & Museum, Low Knock Farm, Dumf/Gal 54
Monteviot House Gardens, Jedburgh, Borders 44
Montgreenan Mansion House, Kilwinning, Ayrshire 70-1, 73
Montrose Basin Wildlife Centre, Montrose, Angus 104
Montrose Golf Course, Angus 106
Montrose Museum & Art Gallery, Panmure Place, Angus 103
Monymusk Church, Monymusk, Aberdeenshire 145
Moonweave Mill Shop, Newmilns, Ayrshire 67
Moorfield House, Coupar Angus, Central 133, 138
Moorfield House Hotel, Boat of Garten, Highlands 181
Moorings Hotel, Fort William, Highlands 182, 191
Moorside, Ballater, Aberdeenshire 153
Morangie House, Tain, Highlands 203
Morar, Morar, Highlands 188-9
Moray 140
    access 147
    accommodation 158-9
    beaches 149
    camping and caravanning 159-60
    crafts 147
    entertainment 148
    food and drink 148
    pubs, inns and other eating places 160
    restaurants 160
    scenic drives 149
    sightseeing 144-6, 147
    sport and leisure 148-9
    tourist information 147
    tours 148
    transport 148
Moray Firth Wildlife Centre, Spey Bay, Moray 146
Moray Golf Course, Lossiemouth, Moray 149
Moray Leisure Centre, Elgin, Moray 149
Moray Place, Edinburgh 19
Moray Yacht Charters, Lossiemouth, Moray 148
Morayhill, Banff, Aberdeenshire 154
Morness Trekking & Riding Centre, Rogart, Highlands 198
Mortlach Parish Church, Dufftown, Moray 146
Mortonhall Caravan Park, Edinburgh 34
Morven Gallery, Barvas, Lewis 219
Morven Hotel, Aucheterarder, Central 132
Mossgiel, Comrie, Central 133
Mossyard Caravan & Camping Park, Gatehouse of Fleet, Dumf/Gal 63
Motherwell Heritage Centre, Motherwell, N. Lanarkshire 89
Motte of Urr, Dumf/Gal 54
Mount Stuart House & Gardens, Rothesay, Bute 210
Mountain Craft, Fort William, Highlands 172
The Mountain Ski School & Artificial Ski Slope, Aviemore, Highlands 172
Mousa Broch, Mousa Island 227
Mousa Island 227
Moyness House, Inverness, Highlands 186
Muck 216
Muckhart Golf Course, Central 122, 131
Muckrach Lodge Hotel, Dulnain Bridge, Highlands 182, 191
Muir of Dinnet Nature Reserve, Aboyne, Aberdeenshire 147
Muir of Ord Golf Course, Highlands 198
Muiravonside Country Park, Linlithgow, West Lothian 21
Muirdyke Stud Farm, Cumnock, Ayrshire 68
Muirfield Golf Club, Gullane, East Lothian 23
Muirhead Riding School & Stables, Angus 107
The Muirs Inn, Kinross, Central 135
Mull 212, 213, 214, 215
Mull & West Highland Narrow Gauge Railway, Craignure, Mull 214

Mull Angora Rabbit Farm, Bunessan, Mull 214
Mull Diving Centre, Mull 215
Mull of Kintyre Equestrian Centre, Campbeltown, Argyll 167
Mull Little Theatre, Dervaig, Mull 215
Mull Museum, Tobermory, Mull 214
Mull Wildlife Expeditions, Mull 215
Mullardoch House, Cannich, Highlands 181, 191
Mungo Jerry's, Glasgow 87
Murray Arms Hotel, Gatehouse of Fleet, Dumf/Gal 58, 65
Murray Lodge, Montrose, Angus 110
Murrayfield (hotel), Edinburgh 28
Murrayfield Ice Rink, Edinburgh 23
Murrayfield Park (bed and breakfast), Edinburgh 32
Murrayfield Scottish Rugby Union Ground, Edinburgh 24
Murraypark, Crieff, Central 134
Murrayshall Country House Hotel & Golf Course, Perth, Central 135, 139
Museum of the 602 Squadron, Glasgow 79
Museum of the Argyll & Sutherland Highlanders, Stirling 120
Museum of Childhood, Edinburgh 18
Museum of the Cumbraes, Millport, Cumbrae 210
Museum of Flight, East Fortune, East Lothian 20
Museum of Island Life, Kilmuir, Skye 218
Museum of Islay Life, Port Charlotte, Islay 214
Museum of Lead Mining, Wanlockhead, Dumf/Gal 54
Museum Nan Eilean, Stornoway, Lewis 218
Museum of Transport, Glasgow 79
Musselburgh Racecourse, East Lothian 23
Musselburgh Sports Centre, East Lothian 24
Musselburgh Water Ski Club, East Lothian 24
Muthill Golf Course, Central 131
Myfarrclan, Glasgow 85
Myothill House Equestrian Centre, Denny, Stirling 123
Myreton Motor Museum, Aberlady, East Lothian 20
Myrtle Bank, Gairloch, Highlands 200

N

Nairn Dunbar Golf Course, Highlands 172
Nairn Fishertown Museum, Fishertown, Highlands 170
Nairn Golf Course, Highlands 172
Nairn Leisure Park, Highlands 172
Nairn Watersports, Highlands 172
National Gallery of Scotland, Edinburgh 18
National Trust for Scotland, Glasgow 80
National Wallace Monument, Causewayhead, Stirling 120
Neidpath Castle, Peebles, Borders 44
Neilston Leisure Centre, Renfrewshire 91
Nelson Monument, Edinburgh 20
Nemat, Buckie, Moray 160
Nenthorn Riding Stables, Kelso, Borders 46
Neocropolis, Glasgow 79
Ness Bank House, Inverness, Highlands 187
Nestlers, Newbigging, S. Lanarkshire 94
Nether Abbey, North Berwick, East Lothian 39
Netherley, Ballater, Aberdeenshire 153
Nethybridge Ski School, Highlands 172
Nevis Bank, Fort William, Highlands 183
Nevis Guides, Highlands 172
New Borland, Eaglesham, S. Lanarkshire 94
New Galloway Golf Course, Dumf/Gal 56
New Lanark Visitor Centre, Lanark, S. Lanarkshire 88
New Town Conservation Centre, Edinburgh 19
Newark Castle, Port Glasgow, Inverclyde 89
Newcastleton Golf Course, Borders 46
Newhouse Caravan & Camping Park, Lanark 95
The Newington, Edinburgh 32
Newmiln Country House Hotel, Perth, Central 136, 139
Newton Hill Country Sports, St Andrews, Fife 106
Newton Hotel, Nairn, Highlands 189, 192
Newton Lodge, Kylesku, Highlands 201
Newton Stewart Golf Course, Dumf/Gal 56
Newtonmore Golf Course, Highlands 172
Nivingston House Hotel, Cleish, Central 133, 138
Noltland Castle, Westray 225
Non Smokers Haven, Elgin, Moray 159

Nornova Knitwear Workshop, Muness, Unst 228
North Alves Caravan Park, Alves, Moray 159
North Ayrshire Museum, Saltcoats, Ayrshire 66
North Berwick, East Lothian 16
North Berwick Golf Club, East Lothian 23
North Berwick Leisure Centre, East Lothian 24
North Coast Adventure Holidays, Tongue-by-Lairg, Highlands 198
the North East 140-60
    events and festivals 142
    map 143
North East Scotland Sailing Trust, Aberdeen 149
North Highlands 193-205
North Hoy Nature Reserve, Hoy 224
North Ronaldsay 226
North Ronaldsay Tours 226
North Sannox Trekking Centre, Arran 211
North Skye Craft & Coffee Shop, Staffin, Skye 219
North West Castle, Stranraer, Dumf/Gal 60
North Woodside Leisure Centre, Glasgow 81
Northern, Brechin, Angus 108
Northern Sands, Dunnet, Highlands 200
Northshore Ceramics, Wick, Highlands 197
Northwilds Riding Centre, Fendom, Highlands 198
Norton House, Edinburgh 27, 35
Norwood House, Blairgowrie, Central 133
Number Thirty Three Seafood Restaurant, Perth, Central 139

O

Oakbank, Newton Stewart, Dumf/Gal 61
Oaklands, Montrose, Angus 110
Oban, Argyll 164
Oban & District Buses Ltd, Argyll 166
Oban Distillery Visitor Centre, Oban, Argyll 166
Oban Rare Breeds Farm Park, Oban, Argyll 165
Oban Sea School, Oban, Argyll 167
Ochil Craft Association, Alva, Central 122
Ochil Hills Woodland Park, Alva, Central 121
O'Donoghues, Aberdeen 157
Official Loch Ness Monster Exhibition, Loch Ness Centre, Highlands 170
The Old Brew House, Arbroath, Angus 110
Old Bridge House Museum, Dumfries, Dumf/Gal 53
Old Byre Heritage Centre, Dervaig, Mull 180, 214
Old Chapels & Burial Grounds, Howmore, South Uist 218
The Old Course Hotel, St Andrews, Fife 113, 117
Old Haa of Burravoe Visitor Centre, Yell 227
The Old Inn, Gairloch, Highlands 200
Old Man of Storr, Skye 219
Old Manor Hotel, Lundin Links, Fife 112, 117
Old Manse, Oban, Argyll 176
Old Manse, Garve, Highlands 201
The Old Manse of Marnoch, Bridge of Marnoch, Aberdeenshire 154, 156
Old Mansion House, Auchterhouse, Angus 108
Old McDonald's Farm Park, Garrion Bridge, S. Lanarkshire 89
Old Mill Inn, Maryculter, Aberdeenshire 157
The Old Monastery Restaurant, Drybridge, Moray 160
The Old Pantry, Aberlour, Moray 160
Old Pier Craft Centre, Whiting Bay, Arran 211
The Old Rectory, Inverness, Highlands 186
Old School Restaurant & Guest House, Kinlochbervie, Highlands 201
Old Skye Crofter's House, Luib, Skye 218
Old Smiddy, Blair Atholl, Central 130
Old Station Restaurant, Spean Bridge, Highlands 205
Old Town Jail, Stirling 121
Old Waverley, Edinburgh 27
Olde Original Rosslyn, Roslin, Midlothian 39
Olympia Leisure Centre, Dundee 106
One Devonshire Gardens, Glasgow 82, 86
Onich, Onich, Highlands 189
Open Arms Hotel, Dirleton, East Lothian 37, 40
Open Hearth, Aberdeen 157
Orcadian Reflections, Orkney 226
Orchard House, Dumfries, Dumf/Gal 60
Orchardton Tower, Palnackie, Dumf/Gal 54
Ord House, Muir of Ord, Highlands 202
Original Loch Ness Visitor Centre, Drumnadrochit, Highlands 170
Orkney 221-6, 233, 235

Orkney Farm & Folk Museum, Harray & Birsay, Mainland 224
Orkney Ferries 225
Orkney Fossil Vintage Centre, Burray 224
Orkney Golf Course, Kirkwall, Mainland 226
Orkney Island Wildlife, Orkney 226
Orkney Maritime & Natural History Museum, Mainland 224
Orkney Sailing Club, Kirkwall, Mainland 226
Orkneyinga Silver, Birsay, Mainland 225
Ormaclete Castle, Ormaclete, South Uist 218
Oronsay 212, 214
Oronsay Priory, Oronsay 214
Orphir Round Kirk & Orkneyinga Saga Experience, Orphir, Mainland 225
Orwell Lodge, Edinburgh 28
Osprey Hotel, Kingussie, Highlands 188, 192
Ostlers Close Restaurant, Cupar, Fife 116
Ostrich Kingdom Visitor Centre, Collessie, Fife 104
Out & About Tours, Great Bernera, Lewis 220
Outer Hebrides see Western Isles
Overcliffe, Dunbar, East Lothian 38
Overscaig, Lairg, Highlands 201
Overshiel Farm, East Calder, West Lothian 38
Owlies Brasserie, Aberdeen 157

P

P & D Forsyth, Fraserburgh, Aberdeenshire 147
P & O European Services, Cairnryan, Dumf/Gal 55
P & O Scottish Ferries 147
Paisley, Renfrewshire 77
Paisley - Greenock Cycle Route 91
Paisley Abbey, Paisley, Renfrewshire 88
Paisley Museum & Art Galleries, Paisley, Renfrewshire 88
Palace, Peterhead, Aberdeenshire 155
Palace, Inverness, Highlands 185
Palace of Holyroodhouse, Edinburgh 18
Palacerigg Country Park, Cumbernauld, N. Lanarkshire 89
Palm Court, Aberdeen 151
Pancho Villas Restaurant, Edinburgh 36
Panmure Golf Course, Barry, Angus 106
Papa Westray 225
Papingo Restaurant, Glasgow 86
Parallel Roads, Glen Roy, Highlands 170
Park, Peebles, Borders 49
Park, Montrose, Angus 110
Park, Inverness, Highlands 187
Park of Brandedleys, Crocketford, Dumf/Gal 62
Park Hotel, Thurso, Highlands 203
Park House, Carnoustie, Angus 108
Park Lane, Perth, Central 136
Parkland Hotel, St Andrews, Fife 117
Parklands, Edinburgh 32
Parklands Hotel, Perth, Central 135, 139
Parklands Hotel & Restaurant, St Andrews, Fife 113
Parkstone, Prestwick, Ayrshire 71
Parliament House, Edinburgh 19
Patio, Clydebank, W. Dunbartonshire 92
Patio Hotel, Aberdeen 150, 155
Paxton House, Berwick-upon-Tweed, Borders 44
The Peat Inn, Peat Inn, Fife 112, 117
Peebles, Borders 42
Peebles Craft Centre, Peebles, Borders 45
Peebles Golf Course, Borders 46
Peebles Hydro, Peebles, Borders 49
Peebles Hydro Stables, Peebles, Borders 46
Peel Farm Crafts, Kirriemuir, Angus 105
Pennyghael, Pennyghael, Mull 231
Penpont Caravan and Camping Park, Penpont, Dumf/Gal 64
Pentland Hills, Edinburgh 21
Pentland Hills Icelandics, Carlops, Midlothian 24
People's Palace, Glasgow 78
The People's Story, Edinburgh 20
Perth 118, 119
Perth & Kinross 129-39
  access 130
  accommodation 132-8
  crafts 130
  entertainment 130
  food and drink 130-1
  restaurants 138-9
  scenic drives 131
  sightseeing 129-30
  sport and leisure 131
  tourist information 130
  tours 131
  transport 131
Perth Hunt Racecourse, Perth, Central 131
Perth Leisure Pool, Perth, Central 131
Perth Museum & Art Gallery, Perth, Central 129
Perthshire Activity Line, Central 131
Peter Anson Gallery, Buckie, Moray 145
Peter Scott & Co Ltd, Hawick, Borders 45
Peterhead Maritime Heritage, Peterhead, Aberdeenshire 145
Pheasant Hotel, Dalbeattie, Dumf/Gal 60
Piccolo Gallery & Old Print Shop, Nairn, Highlands 169
Pier Art Centre, Stromness, Mainland 224
Piersland House Hotel, Troon, Ayrshire 72, 73
The Pilgrim Way, Dumf/Gal 56
Pine Craft Shop, Rothesay, Bute 211
Pine Trees Hotel, Pitlochry, Central 136, 139
Pines, Elgin, Moray 159
Pines, Grantown-on-Spey, Highlands 184
Pitbauchlie House, Dunfermline, Fife 111
Pitcullen, Perth, Central 136
Pitfirrane Arms, Dunfermline, Fife 111
Pitlochry 119
Pitlochry Golf Course, Pitlochry, Central 131
Pitlochry Hydro, Pitlochry, Central 137
Pitmedden Garden, Pitmedden, Aberdeenshire 146
Pitmuies Gardens, Guthrie, Angus 104
Pitreavie, Dunfermline, Fife 114
Pitsligo Castle, Rosehearty, Aberdeenshire 145
Pittencrieff House Museum, Dunfermline, Fife 103
Pittodrie House, Inverurie, Aberdeenshire 154
Pluscarden Abbey, Elgin, Moray 147
Polfearn Hotel, Taynuilt, Argyll 177, 180
Police Museum, Glasgow 79
Pollockshaws Sport Centre, Glasgow 81
Pollok Country Park, Glasgow 80
Pollok Golf Course, Glasgow 81
Pollok House, Glasgow 79
Polmaily House, Drumnadrochit, Highlands 182
Polmonthill Ski Centre, Polmont, Falkirk 24
Popinjay, Rosebank, S. Lanarkshire 93
Port Askaig, Port Askaig, Islay 231
Port Edgar Sailing School, South Queensferry, Edinburgh 24
Port Ellen Pottery, Islay 215
Port-Na-Con House, Portnancon, Highlands 202
Portland A Bedrooms, Lybster, Highlands 202
Portobello Leisure Centre, Edinburgh 24
Portpatrick Golf Course, Dumf/Gal 56
Portpatrick (hotel), Portpatrick, Dumf/Gal 59
Portree, Skye 217
Portsoy Marble Workshop & Pottery, Portsoy, Moray 147
Post Office House, John O'Groats, Highlands 201
Pots of Pitlochry, Pitlochry, Central 130
The Pottery, Girvan, Ayrshire 67
Powfoot Golf Club, Cummertrees, Dumf/Gal 56
Preston Mill & Phantassie Doocot, East Linton, East Lothian 20
Prestonfield House, Edinburgh 27
Prestwick Airport 55
Prince of Wales, Aberdeen 157
The Princes View, Glenfinnan, Highlands 184
Princes St Gardens, Edinburgh 20
Priory, Beauly, Highlands 181
Priory House, Largs, Ayrshire 71
Priory Lodge, South Queensferry 30, 34
Provan Hall, Glasgow 79
Provand's Lordship, Glasgow 79
Provost Skene's House, Aberdeen 147
PS Waverley, Clyde Islands 211
The Pub in the Square, Buckie, Moray 160
Puffin Dive Centre, Oban, Argyll 167

Q

Q Brasserie, Aberdeen 156
Quality Central Hotel, Glasgow 83
Quality Commodore, Edinburgh 27
Quality Friendly Hotel, Ayr, Ayrshire 69
Quality Station, Perth, Central 135
Quarriers Village, Bridge of Weir, Renfrewshire 89
Queen Elizabeth Forest Park, Central 120
Queens, Dundee 109
Queens, Aberdeen 151
Queens Cross Church, Glasgow 79
Queens Hotel, Perth, Central 135
Queens Park, Glasgow 80
Queen's View, Tarland, Aberdeenshire 147
Queen's View Visitor Centre, Pitlochry, Central 129
Queensberry Arms, Annan, Dumf/Gal 57
Queensberry Bay Caravan Park, Powfoot, Dumf/Gal 64
Queensferry Lodge, Inverkeithing, Fife 112
Quiraing (hotel), Portree, Skye 233
Quirang, Skye 218

R

Rab Ha's, Glasgow 87
Rabbie's Trail Burners, Edinburgh 23
Raemoir House Hotel, Banchory, Aberdeenshire 153, 156
Rainbow Slides Leisure Centre, Stirling 122
Ramnee Hotel, Forres, Moray 158, 160
Randolph's Leap, Forres, Moray 147
Rathcluan, Cupar, Fife 114
Ravenscraig, Aviemore, Highlands 180
Ravensdown, Edinburgh 32
Ravenshill House, Lockerbie, Dumf/Gal 59
Ravensnuek, Edinburgh 32
Reay Golf Course, Highlands 198
Red Castle, Lunan Bay, Angus 104
Red Craig Hotel Caravan & Camping Park, Burghead, Moray 159
Red House, Cruden Bay, Aberdeenshire 154
The Redgarth, Oldmeldrum, Aberdeenshire 157
Redheugh, Dunbar, East Lothian 37
The Redhurst, Giffnock, Renfrewshire 93
Redmoss Riding Centre, Buckie, Moray 149
Redstones, Uddingston, S. Lanarkshire 93
Reediehill Deer Farm, Auchtermuchty, Fife 105
Reekie Linn Falls, Angus 104
Reivers Rest, Langholm, Dumf/Gal 61
Rendezvous Coffee Shop, Arrochar, Argyll 179
Rescobie Hotel, Glenrothes, Fife 112, 117
Restenneth Priory, Angus 104
The Retreat, Folk Museum, Brechin, Angus 103
Revack Gardens & Woodland Walks, Grantown-on-Spey, Highlands 170
Rhu Mhor, Fort William, Highlands 184
Rhum 216
Rhumor, Oban, Argyll 176
Ring of Brogar, Stenness, Mainland 224
Riverside Gallery, Inverness, Highlands 169
Riverside House Hotel, Inverness, Highlands 187
Roadchef Motorway Lodge, Hamilton Motorway Service Area, S. Lanarkshire 93
Roadside Cottage, Glenlivet, Moray 159
Rob Roy & Trossachs Visitor Centre, Callander, Stirling 120
Rob Roy Tryst Craft Centre, Balquhidder, Stirling 122
Rob Roy's Grave, Balquhidder, Stirling 121
Robert Burns Centre, Dumfries, Dumf/Gal 53
Robert Smail's Printing Works, Innerleithen, Borders 43
Rockhill, Ardbrecknish, Argyll 173
Rogano, Glasgow 86
Roman Camp Hotel, Callander, Central 124, 128
Ron Parker (Wood Sculpture), Forres, Moray 147
Ronebhal, Connel, Argyll 174
The Roods, Inverkeithing, Fife 114
Rosa Hebridean Cruises, Stornoway, Lewis 220
Rose Cottage, Castle Douglas, Dumf/Gal 60
Rosedale Hotel, Portree, Skye 233, 235
Rosehill, Lockerbie, Dumf/Gal 61
Roselea, Edinburgh 30
Roseneath, Oban, Argyll 176
Roskhill, Dunvegan, Skye 232
Roslin Glen, Roslin, Midlothian 39
Ross Smith Stained Glass, Fair Isle 228
Rosslea Hall Country House, Rhu, Central 127
Rosslee, Airdrie, N. Lanarkshire 94
Rosslyn Chapel, Roslin, Midlothian 18
Rossmor, Grantown-on-Spey, Highlands 184
The Rothes Glen Hotel, Rothes, Moray 158, 160
Rothesay, Edinburgh 28

Rothesay, Bute 209
Rothesay Castle, Rothesay, Bute 210
Rothesay Golf Course, Bute 211
Rothesay Leisure Pool, Bute 211
Rothesay Riding Centre, Bute 211
Roundknowe Farm, Uddingston, S. Lanarkshire 91
Rousay 224, 225, 226
Rousay Traveller Guide 226
Routes to Roots, Livingston, West Lothian 24
Rovie, Rogart, Highlands 202
Roving Eye Enterprises, Orphir, Mainland 226
Rowan, Edinburgh 32
Rowanlea Riding School Ltd, Carnoustie, Angus 107
Roxburghe, Edinburgh 27
Roxburghe Golf Course, Kelso, Borders 46
Royal, Cumnock, Ayrshire 70
Royal, Bridge of Allan, Central 124
Royal, Comrie, Central 133
Royal, Portree, Skye 233
Royal Aberdeen Golf Course, Bridge of Don, Aberdeenshire 149
The Royal Bank of Scotland, Edinburgh 19
Royal Botanic Garden, Edinburgh 20
Royal Burgess Golf Course, Edinburgh 23
Royal Burgh of Stirling Visitor Centre, Stirling 120
Royal Deeside Circle, Aberdeenshire 149
Royal Dornoch Golf Course, Dornoch, Highlands 198
Royal Ettrick, Edinburgh 28
Royal George, Perth, Central 136
Royal Golf Hotel, Dornoch, Highlands 199
The Royal Highland Fusiliers Museum, Glasgow 79
The Royal Hotel, Kirkcudbright, Dumf/Gal 58, 65
Royal Lochnagar Distillery, Ballater, Aberdeenshire 148
Royal Marine, Dunoon, Argyll 174
Royal Marine Hotel, Brora, Highlands 199, 204
The Royal Mile, Edinburgh 18
The Royal Mile Living Craft Centre, Edinburgh 22
Royal Museum of Scotland, Edinburgh 18
Royal Observatory Centre, Edinburgh 21
Royal Terrace, Edinburgh 25
Royal Troon, Ayrshire 68
RSPB Loch of Kinnordy Reserve, Angus 104
RSPB Nature Reserve Vane Farm, Kinross, Central 130
Ruchill Golf Course, Glasgow 81
Rufflets Country House, St Andrews, Fife 113, 117
Rumbling Bridge Gorge, Kinross, Central 130
Rusacks, St Andrews, Fife 113
Russell Hotel, St Andrews, Fife 113
Ruthven Barracks, Kingussie, Highlands 170
Ruthwell Cross, Ruthwell, Dumf/Gal 54
The Ryan Leisure Centre, Stranraer, Dumf/Gal 56
Ryeford, Inverness, Highlands 187

S

St Abbs Boat Charter, St Abbs, Borders 45
St Abbs Head, Borders 43
St Andrews, Fife 101
St Andrew's & St George's Church, Edinburgh 19
St Andrews Botanic Garden, St Andrews, Fife 104
St Andrews Castle & Visitor Centre, St Andrews, Fife 102-3
St Andrew's Cathedral, Aberdeen 145
St Andrew's Cathedral, Inverness, Highlands 170
St Andrews Cathedral & Museum, St Andrews, Fife 104
St Andrews Golf Course, St Andrews, Fife 106
St Andrews Golf Hotel, St Andrews, Fife 113, 117
St Andrews Museum, St Andrews, Fife 103
St Andrews Preservation Trust Museum, St Andrews, Fife 103
St Andrews Sea Life Centre, St Andrews, Fife 104
St Ann's House, Inverness, Highlands 187
St Barr's Chapel, Barra 218
St Beys, Dunbar, East Lothian 38
St Blane's Chapel, Bute 210
St Boswells Golf Course, Borders 46
St Clement's Church, Rodel, Harris 218
St Cuthbert's Way, Borders 46
St Cyrus Nature Reserve, Angus 104
St Fillans Golf Course, Central 131
St George's Tron Church, Glasgow 79

St Giles' Cathedral, Edinburgh 19
St Kilda Nature Reserve, St Kilda 219
St Machar's Cathedral, Aberdeen 145
St Magnus' Cathedral, Kirkwall, Mainland 224
St Margaret's, Edinburgh 32
St Mary's Cathedral, Glasgow 79
St Mary's Loch, Borders 44
St Michael's Church, Linlithgow, West Lothian 20
St Michael's Golf Course, Leuchars, Fife 106
St Monans Caravan Park, St Monans, Fife 116
St Mungo Museum of Religious Life & Art, Glasgow 79
St Nicholas, Prestwick, Ayrshire 71
St Ninian's Cave, Dumf/Gal 67
St Ninian's Isle 227
St Olaf, Moffat, Dumf/Gal 61
St Vigeans Museum, St Vigeans, Angus 103
Saline Golf Course, Fife 106
Salisbury Hotel, Edinburgh 32
Salisbury View Hotel, Edinburgh 32
Sanday 225
Sanderlay, Kirkwall, Orkney 233
Sandilands House, Edinburgh 32
Sands of Forvie National Nature Reserve, Collieston, Aberdeenshire 147
Sands of Luce Caravan Park, Sandhead, Dumf/Gal 64
Sandyhills Bay Leisure Park, Sandyhills, Dumf/Gal 64
Sanquhar Golf Course, Dumf/Gal 56
Sanquhar Post Office, Sanquhar, Dumf/Gal 53
Sanquhar Tolbooth Museum, Sanquhar, Dumf/Gal 53
Santa Claus Land & Craft Village, Aviemore, Highlands 170
Satrosphere, Aberdeen 146
Savings Bank Museum, Ruthwell, Dumf/Gal 54
Savoy Park, Ayr, Ayrshire 69
Scalloway Castle, Scalloway, Mainland 228
Scalloway Museum, Scalloway, Mainland 227
Scalpay Linen, Scalpay 219
Scapa Distillery, Kirkwall, Mainland 226
Scapa Flow Visitor Centre, Hoy 224
Scapa Scuba, Stromness, Mainland 226
Scone Palace, Perth, Central 129
Scores, St Andrews, Fife 113
Scoretulloch House, Darvel, Ayrshire 70, 73
Scorrybreac, Glencoe, Highlands 184
The Scot House Hotel, Kingussie, Highlands 188, 192
Scotch on the Rocks, Glasgow 80
Scotch Whisky Heritage Centre, Edinburgh 20
Scotkin Scottish Country Workshop, Moffat, Dumf/Gal 55
Scotland's, Pitlochry, Central 137
Scotland's Larder, Upper Largo, Fife 105
Scotland's Lighthouse Museum, Fraserburgh, Aberdeenshire 144
Scotland's Secret Bunker, St Andrews, Fife 104
Scotsell Ltd 220
Scotsgraig Golf Course, Tayport, Fife 106
Scotstarvit Tower, Ceres, Fife 104
Scott, Sir Walter 44
Scott Monument, Edinburgh 19
Scotteries Fisheries Museum, Anstruther, Fife 103
Scottish Academy of Falconry, Hawick, Borders 45
Scottish Agricultural Museum, Edinburgh 20
Scottish Archery Centre, North Berwick, East Lothian 23
The Scottish Craft Centre, Glasgow 80
Scottish Crannog Centre, Loch Tay, Central 129
Scottish Cycling Holidays, Angus 106
Scottish Cycling Holidays, Central 131
Scottish Deer Centre, Cupar, Fife 104
Scottish Equitation Centre, Dunblane, Central 131
Scottish Exhibition & Conference Centre, Glasgow 80
Scottish Gliding Union, Kinross, Central 131
Scottish Historic Tours, Edinburgh 23
Scottish Industrial Railway Centre, Dalmellington, Ayrshire 67
Scottish Maritime Museum, Dumbarton, Central 120
Scottish Maritime Museum, Irvine, Ayrshire 66
Scottish Mask & Puppet Centre, Glasgow 80

Scottish Mining Museum, Newtongrange, Midlothian 18
Scottish Mining Museum, Prestonpans, East Lothian 20
Scottish National Gallery of Modern Art, Edinburgh 19
Scottish National Portrait Gallery, Edinburgh 19
Scottish National Waterski Centre, Dunfermline, Fife 107
Scottish Norwegian Ski School, Aviemore, Highlands 172
Scottish Salmon Centre, Kilninver, Argyll 180
Scottish Tourist Guides Association, Aberdeen 148
Scottish Tourist Guides Association, Glasgow 81
Scottish Vintage Bus Museum, Dunfermline, Fife 103
Scottish Wool Centre, Aberfoyle, Stirling 121
Scott's View, Borders 44
Scourie, Scourie, Highlands 203
Sea Life Centre, Barcaldine, Argyll 165
Seacat, Stranraer, Dumf/Gal 55
Seafield, Campbeltown, Argyll 173
Seafield Riding Centre, Forres, Moray 149
Seaward Caravan Park, Kirkcudbright, Dumf/Gal 63
Selcraig House, Crail, Fife 114
Selkirk, Borders 42
Selkirk Arms, Kirkcudbright, Dumf/Gal 58, 65
Selkirk Glass, Selkirk, Borders 45
Selkirk Golf Course, Borders 46
78 St Vincent, Glasgow 87
Sgeir Mhaol, Oban, Argyll 176
Sgeir Ruadh, Hougharry, North Uist 232
Sgoil Lionacleit, Benbecula 220
The Shaftesbury, Dundee 109
Shambellie House Museum of Costume, New Abbey, Dumf/Gal 54
Shandon Country Pursuits Ltd, Helensburgh, Central 122
Shanter Riding Centre, Girvan, Ayrshire 68
Shape Scape Ceramics, North Berwick, East Lothian 22
Shapinsay 225, 226
Sharmanka Kinetic Gallery & Theatre, Glasgow 79
Shawbost Community School, Shawbost, Lewis 220
Shawbost Crofting Museum, Shawbost, Lewis 218
Shawbost Norse Mill and Kiln, Shawbost, Lewis 218
Shaws Dundee Sweet Factory, Dundee 104
Sheila Fleet Jewellery, Tankerness, Mainland 225
The Sheiling, Ullapool, Highlands 203
Shell Bay Caravan Park, Elie, Fife 116
Sheraton Grand Hotel, Edinburgh 25, 35
Sherwood, Edinburgh 32
Shetland 221, 227-9, 234, 235
Shetland (hotel), Lerwick, Shetland 234
Shetland Croft House Museum, Dunrossness, Mainland 227
Shetland Glass, Scalloway, Mainland 228
Shetland Golf Course, Lerwick, Mainland 229
Shetland Hotel, Lerwick, Shetland 235
Shetland Jewellery, Weisdale, Mainland 228
Shetland Museum, Lerwick, Mainland 227
Shetland Sea Charters, Lerwick, Mainland 228
Shetland Tourist Guides Association, Mainland 229
Shetland Wildlife Tours 229
Shetland Woollen Company, Scalloway, Mainland 228
Shetland Workshop Gallery, Lerwick, Mainland 228
Shieldbank Riding Centre Ltd, Saline, Fife 107
Shieldhill Hotel, Biggar, S. Lanarkshire 92, 95
Shin Falls, Lairg, Highlands 197
The Ship Inn, Elie, Fife 117
Shotts Farm, Beith, Ayrshire 70
Shotts Heritage Centre, Shotts, N. Lanarkshire 89
Sibbet House, Edinburgh 29
Silver Sands Leisure Park, Lossiemouth, Moray 160
Silvercraigs Caravan & Camping Site, Kirkcudbright, Dumf/Gal 63
Silvertrees, Bothwell, S. Lanarkshire 92
Sir Matt Busby Sports Complex, Bellshill, N. Lanarkshire 91
Sir Walter Scott's Courtroom, Selkirk, Borders 43

Six Mary's Place, Edinburgh 32
Skaill House, Sandwick, Mainland 225
Skara Brae, Sandwick, Mainland 224
Skeabost Golf Course, Skye 220
Skelmorlie Aisle, Largs, Ayrshire 67
Skolla Diving Centre, Gulberwick, Mainland 229
Skye 216, 217, 218, 219, 220, 232-3
Skye Batiks, Sleat, Skye 219
Skye Car Ferry 219
Skye Jewellery, Broadford, Skye 219
Skye Riding Centre, Portree, Skye 220
Skye Serpentarium, Broadford, Skye 219
Skye to Western Isles Ferry 219
Skyeskyns Tannery, Waternish, Skye 219
Slains Castle, Aberdeenshire 145
Sma' Shot Cottages, Paisley, Renfrewshire 89
Smailholm Tower, Smailholm, Borders 44
Small Isles 216
The Smiddy House, Spean Bridge, Highlands 190
Smith Art Gallery & Museum, Stirling 120
Smithton, Inverness, Highlands 185
The Smithy, Shapinsay 226
Smoo Cave, Durness, Highlands 197
'Smoo' Inner Cave Tours, Durness, Highlands 198
SMT Eastern Scottish Buses, Edinburgh 23
Smugglers Inn, Anstruther, Fife 111
Soay Studio, West Tarbert, Harris 219
Solway Lodge, Gretna, Dumf/Gal 58
Somerton House, Lockerbie Dumf/Gal 59
Sonas, Edinburgh 32
Sonnhalde, Kingussie, Highlands 188
Sophies Puppenstube & Dolls House Museum,
    Newton Stewart, Dumf/Gal 54
Sorn Castle, Mauchline, Ayrshire 67
Sound of Barra Ferry 219
Souter Johnnie's Cottage, Kirkoswald, Ayrshire 66
the South 13-73
    Borders 41-50
    Dumfries & Galloway and Ayrshire 51-73
    Edinburgh, Falkirk and the Lothians 16-40
    events and festivals 14-15
    map 14-15
South Bank Farm Park, East Bennan, Arran 210
South Ronaldsay 225
South Whittlieburn, Largs, Ayrshire 71
Southern Upland Way, Borders 46
Southern Upland Way, Dumf/Gal 56
Southerness Golf Course, Dumf/Gal 56
Southerness Holiday Village, Southerness,
    Dumf/Gal 64
Spean Bridge Woollen Mill, Spean Bridge,
    Highlands 171
Speyside Cooperage Visitor Centre, Craigellachie,
    Moray 144
Speyside Way, Moray 149
Speyside Way Visitor Centre, Craigellachie,
    Moray 147
The Spindrift, Anstruther, Fife 114
Spinkstown Farmhouse, St Andrews, Fife 115
The Spinney, Jedburgh, Borders 47
Springbank Distillery, Campbeltown, Argyll 166
Springburn Leisure Centre, Glasgow 81
Springfield, Dunbar, East Lothian 38
Springfield, Largs, Ayrshire 71
Springvale Hotel, Strathaven, S. Lanarkshire 94
SS Sir Walter Scott, Callander, Stirling 122
The Stag Hotel, Banchory, Aberdeenshire 153
The Stag, Lochgilphead, Argyll 175
Stagecoach, Perth, Central 131
The Stagger Inn, Ardlui, Argyll 179
Stained Glass Workshop, Stonehaven,
    Aberdeenshire 147
Stakis Dundee Earl Grey, Dundee 109
The Star, Moffat, Dumf/Gal 59
Station (hotel), Dumfries, Dumf/Gal 58
The Steam Packet Inn, Isle of Whithorn,
    Dumf/Gal 65
Stena Line Ltd, Stranraer, Dumf/Gal 55
Stenness Standing Stones, Mainland 224
Stephen Hayward (Woodcarving), Kiltarlity,
    Highlands 171
Stewart Hotel, Duror, Highlands 182, 191
The Stewartry Museum, Kirkcudbright,
    Dumf/Gal 54
Stills Gallery, Edinburgh 19
Stirling 118, 119
Stirling Arms, Dunblane, Central 126

Stirling Castle, Stirling 120
Stirling Golf Course, Stirling 122
Stirling Highland Hotel, Stirling 127, 128
Stirling Ice Rink, Williamfield, Stirling 122
Stirling, Loch Lomond & The Trossachs
    access 121
    accommodation 124-7
    crafts 121-2
    entertainment 122
    food and drink 122
    restaurants 128
    scenic drives 123
    sightseeing 120-1
    sport and leisure 122-3
    tourist information 121
    tours 122, 123
    transport 122
Stock Exchange, Glasgow 79
Stone Circle Trail, Aberdeenshire 145
Stonefield Castle, Tarbert Loch Fyne, Argyll 177
Stornoway, Lewis 217
Stornoway Golf Course, Lewis 220
Stornoway Sports Centre, Lewis 220
Storybook Glen, Maryculter, Aberdeenshire 146
Stotfield, Lossiemouth, Moray 158
Strachur Smiddy (Museum & Craft Shop),
    Loch Fyne, Argyll 166
Stranraer Golf Course, Dumf/Gal 56
Stranraer Museum, Stranraer, Dumf/Gal 54
Strathaven Hotel, Strathaven,
    S. Lanarkshire 93, 95
Strathboyne, Aberdeen 152
Strathburn, Inverurie, Aberdeenshire 155
Strathclyde Buses, Glasgow 81
Strathclyde Country Park, Motherwell,
    N. Lanarkshire 90, 91
Strathclyde Country Park Caravan Site,
    Motherwell, N. Lanarkshire 95
Strathcona, Perth, Central 136
Strathearn Gallery & Pottery, Crieff, Central 129
Strathisla, Aberdeen 151
Strathisla Distillery, Keith, Moray 148
Strathmohr, Edinburgh 32
Strathpeffer Spa Golf Course, Highlands 198
Strathspey Highland Pony Centre,
    Grantown-on-Spey, Highlands 172
Strathspey Steam Railway, Aviemore,
    Highlands 169
Strathtay Golf Course, Central 131
Stravaigin, Glasgow 86
Stra'ven, Edinburgh 32
Stromness Golf Course, Mainland 226
Stronlossit, Roy Bridge, Highlands 190
Stronvar House, Balquhidder, Central 124
Struan Bank Hotel, Cowdenbeath, Fife 114
Struther Farmhouse, Dunlop, Ayrshire 70
Stuart Crystal, Crieff, Central 130
Stuart, East Kilbride, S. Lanarkshire 92
Stuart House, Edinburgh 30
Suenos' Stone, Forres, Moray 146
Sumburgh Airport 228
Sumburgh Head, Mainland 228
Summer Queen Cruises, Ullapool, Highlands 198
Summerlee Heritage Trust, Coatbridge,
    N. Lanarkshire 88
Sunlaws House Hotel & Golf Course, Kelso,
    Borders 48, 50
Sunnyholm, Inverness, Highlands 187
Sunnymeade Caravan Park, Portpatrick,
    Dumf/Gal 64
Surrone House, Gretna, Dumf/Gal 61
Suruchi Restaurant, Edinburgh 36
Sutherland Pottery, Lairg, Highlands 197
Swallow, Dundee 109
Swallow, Glasgow 83
Swallow Royal Scot, Edinburgh 25
Sweetheart Abbey, New Abbey, Dumf/Gal 54
Syllavethy Gallery, Alford, Aberdeenshire 145
Sylvern, Edinburgh 33

T

Taigh Chearsabhagh Visitor Centre, Lochmaddy,
    North Uist 218
Tain Golf Course, Highlands 198
Tain Through Time, Tain, Highlands 196
Tait & Style, Stromness, Mainland 225

Talisker Distillery Visitor Centre, Carbost,
    Skye 220
Talisman Mountaineering Activities, Carrbridge,
    Highlands 172
Talnotry Campsite, Newton Stewart, Dumf/Gal 64
Tankerness House Museum, Kirkwall,
    Mainland 224
Tantallon Castle, North Berwick, East Lothian 18
Taransay, Inverness, Highlands 187
Tarbat Golf Course, Portmahomack,
    Highlands 198
Tarbert Golf Course, Argyll 167
Tarbert Tearoom, Tarbert, Argyll 180
A Taste of Speyside, Dufftown, Moray 160
The Tattler, Edinburgh 36
Taychreggan Hotel, Kilchrenan, Argyll 175, 178
Taymouth Castle Golf Course, Central 131
The Tayside Hotel, Stanley, Central 138, 139
Tayside Tours, Angus 107
Tayvallich Inn, Tayvallich, Argyll 180
Teddy Melrose Teddy Bear Museum, Melrose,
    Borders 44
Templeton's Carpet Factory, Glasgow 79
The Tenement House, Glasgow 78
Tentsmuir Point & Forest, Leuchars, Fife 104
Terrace Hotel, Edinburgh 32
Terraces, Stirling 127
Teviotdale Leisure Centre, Hawick, Borders 45
Thainstone House Hotel and Country Club,
    Inverurie, Aberdeenshire 154, 156
Thirlestane Castle, Lauder, Borders 44
36 at the Howard, Edinburgh 35
Thistle Bagpipe Works, Luss, Central 122
Thistle House, St Catherine's, Argyll 177
Thornhill Golf Course, Dumf/Gal 56
Thornloe, Oban, Argyll 177
Thornton Golf Course, Fife 106
Threave Castle & Estate, Castle Douglas,
    Dumf/Gal 54, 55
Three Chimneys Restaurant, Colbost, Skye 235
Three Lochs Holiday Park, Balminnoch,
    Dumf/Gal 62
Thrums Private Hotel, Edinburgh 28
Thurso Golf Course, Highlands 198
Thurso Heritage Museum, Thurso, Highlands 196
Tibbie Shiels, St Mary's Loch, Borders 49
Tigh An Eilean Hotel, Shieldaig,
    Highlands 203, 205
Tigh An Truish Inn, Clachan-Seil, Argyll 179
Tigh-Na-Clash, Melvich, Highlands 202
Tigh-Na-Lag, Largs, Ayrshire 71
Tighnabruaich Riding Centre, Tighnabruaich,
    Argyll 167
Tighnabruaich Sailing School, Tighnabruaich,
    Argyll 167
Tiki-Bu Pottery, Kingoldrum, Angus 105
Tillicoultry Golf Course, Central 122
Tilt, Blair Atholl, Central 133
The Time Capsule, Coatbridge, N. Lanarkshire 89
Timespan Heritage Centre, Helmsdale,
    Highlands 196
Tingwall Agricultural Museum, Tingwall,
    Mainland 227
Tingwall Airport 228
Tinto, Biggar, S. Lanarkshire 92
Tinto Firs Thistle, Glasgow 83
Tinto Hill, Clyde Valley 89
Tiree 212, 215
Tiree, Edinburgh 33
Tobermory, Mull 213
Tobermory Distillery, Tobermory, Mull 215
Tobermory Golf Course, Mull 215
Todhall House, Cupar, Fife 114
Tolbooth Arts Centre, Kirkcudbright, Dumf/Gal 53
Tolbooth Museum, Aberdeen 145
Tolbooth Museum, Stonehaven,
    Aberdeenshire 145
Tolbooth Steeple, Glasgow 79
Tollcross Park, Glasgow 80
Tollcross Park Leisure Centre, Glasgow 81
Tolquhon Castle, Ellon, Aberdeenshire 145
Tolquhon Gallery, Tarves, Aberdeenshire 145
Tomatin Distillery, Tomatin, Highlands 171
Tomintoul Museum, Tomintoul, Moray 145
Tomintoul Riding Centre, Moray 149
Tongue, Tongue, Highlands 203
The Topps, Denny, Falkirk 37

INDEX

Tor-Na-Coille, Banchory, Aberdeenshire 153
Torbeag House, Fort William, Highlands 183
Torosay Castle & Gardens, Craignure, Mull 214
Torrach, Cullen, Moray 158
Torrdarach Hotel, Pitlochry, Central 137
Torridon Countryside Centre, Torridon, Highlands 196
Torry Sports Centre, Aberdeen 149
Torryburn, Kintore, Aberdeenshire 155
Torvean Golf Course, Highlands 172
Torwoodlee Golf Course, Borders 46
Touch Wood Turnery, Elgin, Moray 147
Tower Farm Riding Stables, Edinburgh 24
The Town House, Edinburgh 30
Town House Hotel, Markinch, Fife 115
Toy Museum, Glendale, Skye 219
Trades Hall, Glasgow 79
Traditional Orkney Crafts, Kirkwall, Mainland 225
Trafford Bank, Inverness, Highlands 186
Traprain Trails, Gullane, East Lothian 24
Traquair Arms Hotel, Innerleithen, Borders 47
Traquair House, Innerleithen, Borders 43, 45
Trareoch Craft & Wool Shop, Whiting Bay, Arran 211
Travel Inn, Aberdeen 151, 152
Travel Inn (Aberdeen South), Aberdeen 151
Travel Inn, Ayr, Ayrshire 69
Travel Inn, Cumbernauld, N. Lanarkshire 92
Travel Inn (Discovery Quay), Dundee 109
Travel Inn, East Kilbride, S. Lanarkshire 92
Travel Inn, Edinburgh 28
Travel Inn (Edinburgh City Centre), Edinburgh 28
Travel Inn, Fort William, Highlands 183
Travel Inn, Glasgow 84
Travel Inn, Glenrothes, Fife 112
Travel Inn (Inveresk), Edinburgh 28
Travel Inn, Inverness, Highlands 185
Travel Inn (Inverness East), Inverness, Highlands 185
Travel Inn, Kilmarnock, Ayrshire 70
Travel Inn (Kingsway West), Dundee 109
Travel Inn, Livingston, West Lothian 39
Travel Inn, Motherwell, N. Lanarkshire 93
Travel Inn, Stirling 127
Travelodge, Dumbarton, Central 126
Travelodge, Dumfries, Dumf/Gal 58
Travelodge, Glasgow 84
Travelodge, Kilmarnock, Ayrshire 70
Travelodge, Kinross, Central 135
Travelodge, Stirling 127
Trignony House, Thornhill, Dumf/Gal 60
Trimontium Exhibition, Melrose, Borders 43
Tropic House, Newton Stewart, Dumf/Gal 54
The Trossachs 121
Trumland Orientation Centre, Rousay 224
Tryst Sports Centre, Cumbernauld, N. Lanarkshire 91
Tugnet Ice House, Spey Bay, Moray 145
Tulliallan Golf Course, Kincardine, Fife 106
Tullibardine Chapel, Auchterarder, Central 129
Tulliechewan Caravan Park, Balloch 94
Turnberry Hotel, Golf Courses & Spa, Ayrshire 68, 72, 73
Tweed Cycleway, Borders 46
Tweed Valley Hotel & Restaurant, Walkersburn, Borders 49
Tweeddale Arms, Gifford, East Lothian 38
Tweeddale Museum & Picture Gallery, Peebles, Borders 43

U

U I G Pony Trekking, Uig, Skye 220
Ubiquitous Chip, Glasgow 86, 87
Udny Arms Hotel, Newburgh, Aberdeenshire 155, 156
Uig, Uig, Skye 233
Uig Pottery & Gallery, Uig, Skye 219
Uist Outdoor Centre, North Uist 220
Uists 216, 218, 219, 220
Ulbster A Bedrooms, Halkirk, Highlands 201
Ullapool, Highlands 194
Ullapool Museum, Ullapool, Highlands 196

Ulva House, Tobermory, Mull 231
The Underwater Centre, Fort William, Highlands 173
Unicorn Inn, Kincardine-on-Forth, Fife 117
University Botanic Garden, Dundee 104
University Zoology Museum, Aberdeen 145
Unst 221, 227, 228, 229
Unst Boat Haven, Haroldswick, Unst 227
Unst Heritage Centre, Haroldswick, Unst 227
Unst Leisure Centre, Unst 229
The Upper Crust Restaurant, Helensburgh, Argyll 179
Upper Latheron, Latheron, Highlands 201
Urquhart Castle, Highlands 170
Urr Valley Country House, Castle Douglas, Dumf/Gal 57

V

Valleyfield Crafts, Brae, Mainland 228
Venlaw Farm, Peebles, Borders 49
Verdant Works, Dundee 102
'Veronica' Charters, Ardrossan, Ayrshire 68
Victoria Park & Fossil Grove, Glasgow 80
Vikingar!, Largs, Ayrshire 66
Villa Nina, Edinburgh 33
Village Glass, Bridge of Allan, Stirling 122
The Vintners Room, Edinburgh 35

W

Wallis Hunter, Carradale, Argyll 166
Warmanbie Hotel & Restaurant, Annan, Dumf/Gal 57
Waterfront Leisure Complex, Greenock, Inverclyde 91
Waterloo Gallery, Stranraer, Dumf/Gal 53
Waterside Inn, Peterhead, Aberdeenshire 155, 156
Waterwheel, Aberdeen 151
Wavewhisper Gallery, Innellan, Argyll 165
Weaver's Coffee Shop, Tarbet, Argyll 180
Weaver's Cottage, Kilbarchan, Renfrewshire 89
Weavers' Cottages Museum, Airdrie, N. Lanarkshire 89
Webster Sports Centre, Kirriemuir, Angus 106
The Weem, Aberfeldy, Central 132
Welcome Break, Gretna, Dumf/Gal 58
Welcome Lodge, Abington, S. Lanarkshire 92
Well House Private Hotel, Pitlochry, Central 137
Well View Hotel, Moffat, Dumf/Gal 59, 65
Wellington Church of Scotland, Glasgow 79
Wellpark Hotel, Oban, Argyll 177
West Drumrae Farm, Whithorn, Dumf/Gal 56
West Highland Karting, Oban, Argyll 167
West Highland, Mallaig, Highlands 188
West Highland Museum, Fort William, Highlands 170
West Highland Way 123, 172
West Linton Golf Course, Borders 46
West Park House, St Andrews, Fife 115
West Register House, Edinburgh 19
Westbank, Campbeltown, Argyll 173
Wester Cash Farmhouse, Strathmiglo, Fife 115
Western Ferries (Clyde) Ltd, Argyll 166
Western Isles 216-20, 232-3
Western Isles (hotel), Tobermory, Mull 231
Westerton Trekking Centre, Huntly, Aberdeenshire 149
Westerwood Hotel Golf & Country Club, Cumbernauld, N. Lanarkshire 91, 92, 95
Westhill, Aberdeen 151
Westlands of Pitlochry, Pitlochry, Central 137
Westmuir Riding Centre Ltd, Winchburgh, West Lothian 24
Westray 224, 225, 226
Westray Golf Course 226
Westray Heritage Centre, Pierowall, Westray 224
Westrow Lodge, Orphir, Orkney 233
Westwood, Dunblane, Central 126
Westwood House, Houndwood, Borders 47
Whalsay 227, 229
Whalsay Golf Course, Whalsay 229
Whalsay Leisure Centre, Whalsay 229

Wheatsheaf Hotel, Swinton, Borders 49, 50
Whin Park, Largs, Ayrshire 71
The Whins Craft Workshop, Lochranza, Arran 211
Whinsmuir Country Inn, Powmill, Central 137, 139
Whisky distillery tours
    Aberdeenshire 148
    Angus 105
    Argyll 166
    Arran 211
    Dumfries & Galloway 56
    Highlands 171, 198
    Inner Hebrides 215
    the Lothians 22
    Moray 148
    Orkney 226
    Stirling 122
    Western Isles 220
White Cottage, Aboyne, Aberdeenshire 156
White Gables, Stirling 127
White Lodge, Inverness, Highlands 187
Whitebridge, Whitebridge, Highlands 190
Whitecairn Farm Caravan Park, Glenluce, Dumf/Gal 63
Whitecroft, Livingston, West Lothian 39
Whitestone House, Peebles, Borders 49
Whithorn - Cradle of Christianity, Whithorn, Dumf/Gal 54
Whithorn Priory & Museum, Whithorn, Dumf/Gal 54
Wick Golf Course, Highlands 198
Wick Heritage Centre, Wick, Highlands 196
Wig Bay Sailing School, Stranraer, Dumf/Gal 56
Wigtown & Bladnoch Golf Course, Dumf/Gal 56
Wigtownshire County Golf Course, Dumf/Gal 56
Wild Boar, Aberdeen 157
Wild Country Expeditions, Central 123
Wildabout, Orkney 226
Wildings, Girvan, Ayrshire 73
Wildlife Park, Kirkcudbright, Dumf/Gal 54
Wildlife Walks & Talks, Colonsay 215
Williamwood Golf Course, Glasgow 81
Willow Court, Jedburgh, Borders 48
Willow Tea Rooms, Glasgow 79
Willowbank, Largs, Ayrshire 71
Willowburn Hotel, Clachan-Seil, Argyll 173, 178
Wilson Lochhead Pottery, Kirkcudbright, Dumf/Gal 55
Windlestrae Hotel Business & Leisure Centre, Kinross, Central 135
The Windmill Cafe Bar, Aberdeen 157
Windsor, Inverness, Highlands 185
Windsor Hotel, Ayr, Ayrshire 69
Windyridge Villa, Stranraer, Dumf/Gal 61
Winkston, Peebles, Borders 49
Winnock, Drymen, Central 125
Winter Garden Visitor Centre, Rothesay, Bute 211
Wishaw Sports Centre, N. Lanarkshire 91
The Witchery by the Castle, Edinburgh 35
Wonderwest World, Ayr, Ayrshire 67, 68
Wood of Cree Nature Reserve, Dumf/Gal 55
Woodland Gardens Caravan & Camping Site, Lundin Links, Fife 116
Woodlands, Drumnadrochit, Highlands 182
Woodlands House Hotel & Restaurants, Galashiels, Borders 47
Woodlands, Lochwinnoch, Renfrewshire 94
Woodlea, Perth, Central 136
Woodlea Hotel, Moniave, Dumf/Gal 64
Woodside, Aberdour, Fife 111
The Workshop, South Ronaldsay 225
Writers' Museum, Edinburgh 19

Y

Yarrow House, Blackford, Central 132
Yell 221, 227, 228, 229
Yell Leisure Centre, Yell 229
Yellow Rose (Buidhe Rus), Edinburgh 32
Yes, Glasgow 86
Yorkston House, St Andrews, Fife 115
Younger Botanic Garden, Benmore, Argyll 165